The Search for Order

Landmarks of
World Civilizations *Volume Two*
from 1500 to the Present

Marc Anthony Meyer
Berry College

Dushkin/McGraw·Hill
A Division of The McGraw·Hill Companies

This book is dedicated with love to
Anne, Walter, Allegra, and Evelynn

Cover Credit

The Meeting of the Theologians, dated to the reign of Abu'l Ghazi'Abd al-'Aziz Bahadur Khan (1540–1549), by 'Abd Allah Musawwir, Central Asia, Bukhara, Uzbek Shaybanid Dynasty. Colors on paper, Nelson-Atkins Museum of Art

The style of "The Meeting of the Theologians" was derived from Persian Timurid painting, characterized by particular attention to detail. The architecture is presented two-dimensionally. 'Abd Allah Musawwir, the artist, depicts a scene in which a young man is seated in a religious school with a teacher and seven other learned men. At the door a theologian is approached by two beggars soliciting alms. The inscription above the doorway at the top of the picture attributes this piece to the reign of Abu'l Ghazi'Abd al-'Aziz Bahadur Khan.

Cover Design

By Charles Vitelli; Photo, The Nelson-Atkins Museum of Art, Kansas City, Missouri (Purchase: Nelson Trust).

Illustration Credits

21 Metropolitan Museum of Art; 39 The Nelson-Atkins Museum of Art, Kansas City, Missouri (Purchase: Nelson Trust) 46–51/2; 134 Biblioteca Medicea-Laurenziana; 148 Metropolitan Museum of Art; 235 Librairie Hachette; 249 By permission of the British Library; 329 Hoover Institute on War, Peace, and Revolution; 367 © 1993 ARS, New York/SPADEM, Paris; 377 © Akademische Verlagsanstalt, distributed in North America by Friendship Press, New York. Used with permission.

Printed in the United States of America
Library of Congress Catalog Card Number
93–073095
International Standard Book Number
(ISBN) 1-56134-231-9

The Dushkin Publishing Group, Inc., Sluice Dock, Guilford, Connecticut 06437

Preface

In the last few decades, historians and humanities professors have displayed an increased awareness of the importance of a world perspective. The trend toward globalization has been unmistakable throughout the twentieth century as more than ever before the vital interests of all peoples are linked. As individuals we have to admit that an incident or series of events occurring thousands of miles away do actually affect us personally. It is hoped that this collection of primary texts, which focus on order in history, will stimulate dialogues about the condition of the global community and the individual's place within it.

Educators are recommending that courses in world civilizations be included in general education programs, and interest as well as enrollments have increased dramatically over the last few years. *The Search for Order: Landmarks of World Civilizations* is a partial response to this academic turn of events. These volumes also arose directly out of the stimulating and challenging task of teaching the history of world civilizations and from discussions with students and colleagues over the years. It has come as no surprise that there are many viable approaches instructors take in teaching world history. Yet it seems to me that to instill in students an appreciation of the vast cultural diversity of humanity commands the greatest efficacy. Understanding distinctive political, economic, social, and religious traditions, and their evolution over the centuries, indeed provides instructors with at least a place to begin. It was one of my initial aims, as an interpreter of history and editor of texts, to furnish students with a body of stimulating and relevant materials, whereby they might form valuable, insightful conclusions about the history of humanity and their own global community. It sometimes comes as a gleeful surprise to students that the issues raised in historical studies are as relevant to their own lives as to this field of study.

In featuring the broad theme of the search for order, it was not so much my intention to provide a solitary, general framework for comprehending world history, and then afterwards to find out whether my fellow historians teaching the subject agreed with it. But its pervasiveness cannot be denied. At the beginning of his multivolume *Order and History*, a stimulating attempt at philosophical inquiry relative to the order of human existence in society, Eric Voegelin astutely suggests that "every society is burdened with the task, under its concrete conditions, of creating an order that will endow the fact of its existence with meaning in terms of ends divine and human." However successful one may judge Voegelin's monumental efforts, the questions he and many other scholars have raised about the history and concept of order are interesting and significant.

If I have succeeded in providing a tolerably secure foundation for further, deeper reflection on crucial issues that are not necessarily confined to these texts and their central theme, *The Search for Order* has achieved what it set out to accomplish. The 156 written and visual sources found in these two volumes reveal much about the collective experience of our race. Topics such as individualism, communal obligation, tradition and change, and humanity's relationship with the divine and nature figure prominently in these books. They also raise profound questions that persist to the present day. The study of world history thus assumes an urgency extending far beyond its place in academic curricula.

In organizing the material, I have tried to provide a degree of continuity to what otherwise might be just a historical smorgasbord of sorts. A measure of selectivity was, of course, necessary:

- These readings are drawn exclusively from historical sources. The musings of contemporary historians and social scientists are more accessible to college and university undergraduates via their libraries.
- The selections in each volume are grouped into three broad historical periods to allow for greater flexibility.
- Each Part is preceded by an interpretative overview of the era and brief chronologies are scattered throughout each Part. These are not intended, however, to supplant material presented in core textbooks or comprehensive lectures by instructors.
- Individual readings and illustrations are accompanied by brief introductory comments focusing on historical context and authorship.
- I have included complete documents whenever possible, and have opted for longer rather than more abbreviated selections. This gives students an opportunity to delve more deeply into them.
- The historical texts themselves are followed in each case by four study questions. These are meant to serve only as a beginning. Readers need to consider further the scope and relevance of the issues presented in texts. The questions also embody themes around which instructors might center classroom discussions and presentations.
- I have included an introductory essay, "An Approach to the Analysis of Primary Historical Sources," to demonstrate some of the problems and issues involved in the creation of history. This offers some methods that may be applied in attempting to analyze the documents.
- In order to tie in these documents to their historical context I have provided a "Reference Guide to Standard World History Textbooks." It relates each reading to relevant chapters in narrative textbooks, and thereby serves as a ready reference table.

Compiling a sourcebook for world civilizations for use in the classroom was more time-consuming and difficult than originally envisioned (as is usually the case with academic projects). Over the years my colleagues in history and religion departments around the country and overseas have offered insightful comments and suggestions. Among many others are C. Warren Hollister and Hal Drake, both of the University of California, Santa Barbara; Joe Leedom, Hollins College; and Frank Moretti, The Dalton School of New York City. Yet the most important contingent of contributors to *The Search for Order: Landmarks of World Civilizations* is my students, especially those who have been enrolled in my World Civilizations courses at Berry College. Their valuable feedback on earlier unpublished test editions helped to shape the design and content of *The Search for Order*. Their queries have in fact served as the basis for the study questions contained herein.

This work was made more manageable with the help of my research assistants, Rachel Clark, Joanna E. Grant, and Cassandra Heine, who was especially helpful in preparing the "Quick Reference Guide to Standard World History Textbooks." My appreciation is also extended to Lance Foldes, Associate Director of Berry College's Memorial Library, for his invaluable assistance. I should also thank a few members of the Berry College faculty and administration, including Drs. Doyle Mathis, Daniel Casey, and Wilson Mixon for their support and encouragement. Also helping to make this book better were, of course, Irving Rockwood, John Holland, Ava Suntoke, Wendy Connal, Elizabeth Hansen, and many others of The Dushkin Publishing Group. Professors Loyd S. Swenson, Jr. of the University of Houston, George E. Snow of Shippensburg University, and Beverly Blois of Northern Virginia Community College graciously consented to review the manuscript and contributed significantly to my own efforts by offering insightful comments and criticisms. All errors, of course, are my own.

Finally, and as always, my loving appreciation goes to my wife Anne Giaever Meyer for her infinite patience and understanding, and her invaluable editorial suggestions.

Marc Anthony Meyer

Table of Contents

Part 1

The Early Modern World
An Age of Philosophers and Reformers   1

Africa and Southwest Eurasia

South and Southeast Eurasia

East Eurasia

West Eurasia

The Americas

Part 2

The Modern World

An Age of Revolutionaries and Reactionaries   138

Africa and Southwest Eurasia

South and Southeast Eurasia

East Eurasia

West Eurasia

The Americas

Part 3

The Contemporary World
An Age of Politicians and Masses   268

Africa and Southwest Eurasia

South and Southeast Eurasia

East Eurasia

West Eurasia

The Americas

Introduction: The Search for Order in History

THE SEARCH FOR ORDER The binding necessity of order is an especially powerful force behind the development and preservation of world cultures and civilizations. In fact, the search for order is as long and complex as the history of humankind itself. At the outset it is imperative to understand what the term implies. In the humanities, arts, and sciences, order is generally defined as a specific arrangement of things. It is a category of understanding applicable to every branch of human knowledge and activity. Indeed, it appears that the concept of order is the essence of reality, a universal quality meaningful to and known implicitly by humanity. For the historian, the idea of order comprises relationships between humanity and the mysterious universe, human beings and their societies, and within members of a single community. That individuals cannot feel comfortable with their own identities in a chaotic world is reflected in the thoughts of the Roman emperor Marcus Aurelius (121–180). He wrote in the *Meditations*:

> He who does not know what the world is, does not know where he is. And
> he who does not know for what purpose the world exists, does not know who
> he is, nor what the world is.

Regardless of whether religious, philosophical, or scientific principles sustain a coherent, consistent structure, humanity must plant a firm foot in an orderly world.

THE DESIRE FOR ORDER Peoples of the ancient world authenticated cosmic order through myths and rituals, a practice still embraced by some primitive societies. Many extant creation myths illustrate a desire to comprehend the order of the universe. The Book of Genesis, for example, records that at the beginning of creation the earth was "without form and void." The ancient Hebrews identified their god Yahweh as the creative principle that negated primeval chaos. With few exceptions historical religions intimate a divine or universal scheme of significant dimensions that protects individuals and their communities from ambiguity, dissonance, and chaos. It may be known variously as ma'at, the Tao, karma and dharma, God's grace, and so forth. Even the musings of an anonymous Chinese poet regarding the fall of the Chou dynasty in the eighth century B.C.E., that "the people desire disorder," is suggestive of the fact that the people desired to secure order within the chaotic political environment of early China. Beneath the random disorder of events the poet yearned to establish some semblance of order.

Viennese psychoanalyst Sigmund Freud (1856–1939) postulated that the world of Genesis was only a "tiny speck in a world-system of a magnitude hardly conceivable." Yet like some inhabitants of the world's earliest societies, twentieth-century men and women are equally dwarfed by the universe, which requires that some principle of order retain its potency in human life. The urgency to operate within an orderly world is no less real for those whose trust is placed in the sciences than in religion or philosophy. The chaos theory of modern science suggests that there is manifest order beneath the gross, random disorder of various physical phenomena. Physicist and Nobel laureate Ivar Giaever (b. 1929) recently remarked, "There is an order to the perceived disorder and chaos inherent in natural phenomena." Descriptions of and explanations for order advanced by the Hebrew of the fourth century B.C.E., who embraces the teachings found in Book of Genesis, and a research scientist of the 1990s are markedly different. Still, some sort of universal order may be construed as a necessity for both.

ORDER AND SOCIETY   Every human society is an enterprise in world-building and world-maintenance. People create the world in which they live so that they may establish and maintain their identities within it. In his multivolume *Order and History*, Eric Voegelin (1901–1985) suggests that "every society is burdened with the task . . . of creating an order that will endow the fact of its existence with meaning in terms of ends divine and human." Societies maintain purposeful standards that reflect what ought to be and what actually is. In the processes of building and maintaining society, the cultural need for stability struggles against discordant elements of flux. Reconciling continuity and change, ideal and actual, are fundamental problems, and failure to harmonize these factors has been the cause of collapse in powerful civilizations as well as isolated tribal communities. The breakdown of Roman civilization in Britain occasioned an eighth-century Anglo-Saxon bard to write:

> How wondrous this wall-stone, shattered by Fate;
> Burg-places broken, the work of giants crumbled.
> Ruined are the roofs, tumbled the towers,
> Broken the barred gate; frost in the plaster,
> Ceilings a-gaping, torn away, fallen,
> Eaten by age, . . .
>
> Bright were the halls, lofty-gabled,
> Many the bath-house; cheerful the clamor
> In many a mead-hall, revelry rampant—
> Until mighty Fate put paid to all that. . . .

As every field archaeologist knows, the image of an extinct society is compelling, and has inspired many poets down through the ages.

ORDER AND CHAOS   The parameters of order are defined by its antithesis, chaos. As an essential element in any worldview, the boundary between order and chaos is established and modified so that human beings might live and function in a world of their own description. A worldview is often molded by beliefs concerning the hierarchy of cosmos, nature, and society, and people either adhere to, offer alternatives to, or reject it. Ancient Hindu tradition asserts that creation broke into countless imperfect fragments of what already existed. *Sat* (order) became *asat* (chaos). This idea is a reversal of the Judeo-Christian perspective of Genesis. Early Greek thinkers articulated their ideas about the *cosmos* (the orderly universe) and *chaos* (the disorderly universe). For them, order could not possibly have existed without chaos. Hellenic tradition poetically asserts that there was not one act of creation that manifestly produced cosmic order, but innumerable acts of procreation by the gods. The established order of things is what saves humans from drowning in a cloudy sea of chaos and helps them to create a more accurate image of themselves. What people collectively view as chaotic and disruptive actually helps to maintain order by protecting humanity from ambiguity and dissonance.

ORDER AND HISTORY   Any writer analyzing historical patterns has assimilated many influences. These include a sense of the past, contemporary social and cultural values, and a vision of the future. Herodotus (484–425 B.C.E.), arguably the world's first historian, states at the beginning of his *Historia* (a word translated as "research" or "inquiry" that gave the discipline of history its specialized meaning) that he intends to preserve the memory of the past by recording astonishing achievements of his fellow Greeks and other peoples. Attempting to understand human behavior and discern the order of existence and experience through the deeds of men and women, Herodotus thought that the notion of order was naturally reflected in historical records. His contemporary, the philosopher Anaxagoras (500–428 B.C.E.) once remarked, "It is mind that produces order and is the cause of everything." Both men conceded that the human mind is the active ingredient in any recipe for order.

This brief essay elaborates diverse aspects of the concept of order. For the historian, they find common ground in religious cosmologies, theological discourses, law codes, political and economic treatises, constitutions, and other historical artifacts. The British philosopher David Hume (1711–1776) thought the task set before students of history was to trace "the history of the human mind." This reason alone may be sufficient justification to examine a collection of primary sources like *The Search for Order: Landmarks of World Civilizations*.

An Approach to the Analysis of Primary Historical Sources

Faced with a collection of primary texts that is used as evidence for things said in discussions or written in academic essays, many people develop an attitude uncannily like that assumed by Dante at the beginning of his *Divine Comedy*. Above the entrance to Hell, into which the poet is about to descend, is a weathered stone engraved with a warning:

> Through me to the city of desolation,
> Through me to daily sorrows,
> Through me to the road among lost creations.
> Abandon hope, you that go in by me!

This excerpt discloses Dante's extreme anxiety as he begins his descent into the mouth of Hell. There is little doubt that analyzing primary sources is difficult. Like Dante, students must, however, press forward with great forbearance if history is to reveal its secrets.

History is created from written documents and other pieces of evidence that are coincident with or nearly contemporary to the time during which they were purportedly composed or constructed. Grasping the historical context for any source is crucial for its proper interpretation. (I have tried to facilitate the process of placing documents in their correct contexts by providing readers with a "Quick Reference Guide to Standard World History Textbooks" table.) The evidence allows historians to establish *fact*, that which the scholarly community commonly accepts as truth. Although not barren of interpretation, the narrative textbooks assigned in history courses relate and display information that can generally be understood as factual. Facts are foundation stones, the building blocks of history. From facts scholars and students draw *inferences*, or logical conclusions. (*Please see Exercise One.*) That Franklin Delano Roosevelt was inaugurated as the 32nd president of the United States in 1933 is accepted; yet the general conditions and specific circumstances

---

EXERCISE ONE: What's in a Name?

This exercise is designed to enhance your understanding of historical evidence, specifically to reinforce the distinction between fact and inference. First, examine the contents of someone's wallet or purse—with, of course, the prior approval of your subject— making a list of the contents, such as a driver's license, library card, lipstick, comb, and other such incidentals. You will undoubtedly discover many facts among the items beyond the physical remains themselves. For example, note the person's age on the driver's license, and record other facts that you uncover. Next, write a brief descriptive biography of the person whose wallet or purse you have examined. The essential question you are attempting to answer is "What kind of person possesses such stuff, and why is it in the wallet or purse?" Attempt to be as objective as possible.

---

relevant to his election are a matter of interpretation. Indeed, authors of textbooks and scholarly monographs attempt to do a number of things, but their main task is to *create* history by ordering the facts and explaining their significance by defining relationships among them. A historian offers explanations about the how and the why of the facts by demonstrating the meaning of the evidence. With this in view, historical facts are not ends in themselves, but a means to an end!

The historian's primary task is to reach conclusions or judgments concerning the relationship between and among the facts. It must be borne in mind, however, that a historical inference differs from an opinion or belief. The latter are personal conclusions conditioned by one's preconceptions and biases and are only similar in kind to an inference. Beliefs and opinions are thus only tangential to the facts. (*Please see Exercise Two.*) At bottom, the evidence provided by primary historical

---

EXERCISE TWO: Say What?

Go to any newspaper or popular weekly newsmagazine, turn to the editorial section, and critically examine any editorial dealing with a national or international political or social issue. Determine what is reputed to be fact by the person writing the article as distinct from his or her opinion on the facts. Then, ascertain and describe in a brief paragraph or two the author's biases and values. You will want to consider as well whether the author's conclusions are based on inferential reasoning or if they have been subjectively conditioned by what you have determined as her or his biases. The main purpose of this exercise is for you to grasp more clearly the differences between opinion and inference, and how a writer's values might affect the presentation of the facts and even what facts are displayed.

---

sources allows historians to establish facts through a rigorous process of critical analysis, from which, in turn, valid inferences are drawn. Understanding what happened in the past is derived from this process of seeing connections between and among facts. (This relationship between *fact* and *inference* is also referred to by some historians as *cause* and *effect*.) Unfortunately, historical documents do not always speak clearly to historians and their students: human history is more complex and ambiguous than most textbooks, monographs, and lectures make it out to be! But primary sources do provide those voices so that students and scholars can thereby draw their own inferences.

Studying primary sources permits a better understanding of history and the process of "doing" history. Furthermore, such activity enhances the ability to think effectively, critically, and creatively. Yet, to gain a solid understanding of the primary historical sources, it is initially important to determine what happened during the time when the document was supposedly produced. The major events that occurred and the people involved in bringing them about ought to be considered. Coordinating lecture and narrative textbook materials helps substantially in this process of situating the documents into their historical context. Then try to determine why such circumstances evolved and how significant historical figures affected or did not affect their outcome. For example, without acknowledging that World War I took place between 1914 and 1918, the poems of W. B. Yeats lose a great deal of their significance. Having come to terms with the general historical context, fit the primary documents into their chronological framework. (*Please see Exercise Three.*)

EXERCISE THREE: **That's All Folks!**

You may recall fond memories from your childhood, particularly those early Saturday mornings you spent glued to the television set watching hours of cartoons. Little did you realize that those cartoons were historical documents! Consider especially those animated short subjects produced during the late 1930s and 1940s. In conjunction with the U.S. war office, film moguls working for Warner Brothers, MGM, and other studios had Bugs Bunny, Daffy Duck, and their cartoon pals fighting Nazis and generally upholding all-American values. After viewing one of these cartoons and determining the year in which it was produced (and thereby establishing the primary aim in making the cartoon), ascertain how the enemy is portrayed by the animators, and what biases or prejudices are revealed in their artistic characters. Furthermore, consider the social and political message conveyed by the cartoon and its characters. Try to react to the cartoon as an audience member would have in wartime, and then determine your own personal reaction to the cartoon.

There are, of course, many different kinds of historical sources, each of which need some special consideration. Unwritten sources include paintings, architecture, archaeological findings, photographs, and many other forms of sensory expression. Just as bits of historical evidence can be culled from written texts, the likes of which are reproduced in this volume, unwritten sources are replete with images that have great symbolic meaning as well. (*Please see Exercise Four.*)

EXERCISE FOUR: **By the Flip of a Coin!**

Historians often use numismatic evidence—that derived from the study of currency and coins—to help recreate the past. Pretending to know virtually nothing about the culture that produced it, take a quarter (or any minted coin) and critically examine it so you can make certain determinations about the society in which it was used. Indeed, it may be that the object is not immediately recognizable as money at all. And don't forget to take a close look at the iconography: the head on the obverse, the bird or foliage on the reverse, or what may pass for writing. Examine the document as a physical as well as a cultural artifact. In the process you may learn something about the country's economy and its level of technology and cultural sophistication.

Like words on a page, visual and auditory images have the power to motivate people to think and act in particular ways. As the universally recognized symbol for infinity, ∞, suggests images of an endless series of numbers to mathematicians and boundless, unconditioned reality to some philosophers, so too does the circular form of the Taoist yin and yang symbol inspire Taoists and similarly the cross inspires Christians, by creating moods and motivations relevant to an entire complex set of beliefs. Such symbols and more complex images constitute invaluable pieces of historical evidence.

Written sources encompass a wide range of documents of either an *immediate* or *designed* provenance. Keep in mind, however, that some of these that you consider as belonging in one class might just cross over into another category. (*Please see Exercise Five.*) Documents of an immediate nature can reflect societal values and other intangibles of culture and can provide the

---

EXERCISE FIVE: Let Your Fingers Do the Walking!

For this exercise you need to find a telephone book and take a close look at the yellow pages. First, assume you know nothing about the geographic area covered in this commercial section of the phone book. Then, compile a list of 25 observations based on your examination of the contents. You may find, for example, a large number of air conditioning specialists, indicating perhaps a hot rather than a temperate climate. A limited variety of churches and a preponderance of one religious denomination may suggest, among other things, a rural as opposed to an urban environment. Indeed, the actual size of the yellow pages itself will be suggestive of a number of things. Once you have completed your observations, write a description of the area based on what you have found out from your careful reading and analysis of the yellow pages.

---

reader with a wealth of historical information. This is often implicit in the words and phrases the author has used. The true meaning of the text thus belies its superficial purpose, intent, and content. Included in this class of documents are private journals and letters, public records, diplomatic agreements, public speeches, court decisions, and law codes. Keeping in mind that public records are primarily concerned with humanity's continual struggle for wealth, power, and order, consider how the piece reflects the functioning of various political, religious, social, and economic institutions. The document may reveal, as well, the methods by which people secured power and wealth and thereby maintained sociopolitical order. Hence, the aims and policies of the authors are exhibited, as are various underlying assumptions and values. This line of analysis often unveils the social, political, or philosophical theory behind the text. However, the historical context again becomes crucial for a proper understanding of a source. One must inquire whether the theory and values are typical for the period during which the document was written or if they radically diverge from the mainstream.

Documents of a designed nature reflect an explicit purpose on the part of the author, who seeks to develop and clarify a fundamental set of values that he or she considers an accurate reflection of reality. Included among this group are formal religious and philosophical treatises, public letters and pamphlets intended for wide circulation, sundry works of literature, films, and eye-witness historical accounts as well as nearly contemporary formal histories and chronicles. If the source is a record of historical events, it is crucial to determine the extent to which the author was in a position to observe firsthand or chronicle accurately the events he or she relates by comparing it with other historical sources. For example, Las Casas's *Brief Description on the Destruction of the Indies* offers its reader not only information based on firsthand accounts, but details the author's perception of the events. The factual accuracy of a narrative and the validity of the interpretations offered by an author will reflect how good a historian she or he is and the value of the text as a whole.

Having determined what kind of document is under consideration, historians must decide whether a document is spurious or authentic. (*Please see Exercise Six.*) The notorious late nine-

---

EXERCISE SIX: A Day in the Life!

In this exercise you are being asked to write a brief description of a 24-hour day in the life of a friend or relative. Keep in mind, however, that even those incidents that you witness require evidence as proof. You need to collect physical evidence to demonstrate that so-and-so actually did what he or she seems to have done. It may take the form of a written statement from someone (an instructor, boss, or friend) who actually saw the person do what was supposedly done, a movie ticket stub, a receipt of purchase, and so on. First compile a chronological description of someone's day, making sure you have physical evidence to substantiate the person's activities. Then write a brief narrative account of that particular day, citing and incorporating the evidence you have gathered and evaluated in terms of its validity and trustworthiness. This is essentially the same process that historians go through when they recreate the past.

---

teenth-century "Protocols of the Learned Elders of Zion," purporting to be a transcript of a secret meeting at which leading Jews conspired to bring the world under Jewish control, is a case in point. In 1921 a non-Jewish British journalist demonstrated the tract to be a fabrication of Czarist anti-Semites in Russia. In fact, it was proved to have been based on a plagiarized mid-nineteenth-century French satire against Napoleon III that had nothing to do with the Jews. For historians not to recognize that the "Protocols" is actually a forgery would have drastic consequences for the interpretation of historical events. (Indeed, despite its exposure as a crude, anti-Semitic forgery, the "Protocols" was—and sometimes still is—circulated by anti-Jewish propagandists.) Analogous situations may be found in every age: the infamous eighth-century "Donation of Constantine," the falsified lists of American communists touted by Senator Joseph McCarthy in the early 1950s, and the "dirty tricks" propaganda produced by the Committee to Re-elect the President that operated during the 1972 presidential campaign may be counted among such pieces of evidence. This is not to suggest that these documents have no value: they simply need to be recognized for what they really are.

The problem of forgery and authenticity leads to further questions concerning authorship itself. The biases, prejudices, and the worldview of the person or group responsible for the composition of a document can be revealed after careful consideration of its contents. Yet, in order to determine this, the implicit and explicit intentions of the author must be recognized. Any words or phrases beyond standard formula that seem to be more emotionally charged or more significant than others will indicate much about the worldview of the writer as well as reveal the work's implicit and explicit purpose. And, if the document is a work of literature (a novel, poem, short story, or play), the extent to which it serves as a vehicle for the author's worldview or as a means of presenting popular ideas and feelings must also be considered. (*Please see Exercise Seven.*)

EXERCISE SEVEN: Name That Tune!

The analysis of historical documents must be approached with rigor and creativity to be successful. Just like poetry, the novel, or any other form of literature, song lyrics have always been good indicators of historical trends, developments, and attitudes when they are placed in historical context. Select one of your favorite songs—rap, country, and rock and roll are all permissible—from any era. Then write out the lyrics and examine them critically. You will want to attempt to understand the poetic imagery of the song and the various themes and subjects the songwriter has addressed. You must also place the lyricist and his or her words in a historical context to appreciate fully the song's meaning and implications. In other words, although the Beatles' *Lucy in the Sky with Diamonds* has intrinsic artistic value, to understand the song it must be seen as a product of the late 1960s. Song lyrics really are terrific historical documents!

Students of history are thus presented with a challenge when confronted by primary sources; and their analysis must be approached with creativity, intelligence, and sensitivity to the human condition. Indeed, it would be well to recall the words of American educator and scientist George Washington Carver, "Anything will give up its secrets if you love it enough." To these mental dispositions one ought to add a healthy dose of inquisitiveness mixed with intellectual assertiveness. Professor C. Warren Hollister, an accomplished historian of the European Middle Ages, is fond of using the analogy that people would be like ants if they never wondered about the "why" of things. Ants, of course, have a good excuse in that they are primarily governed by instinct, and not by complex culture and high intelligence, as human beings are. Even if an ant of extraordinary aptitude and one with an interest in ant hill history were to appear among its droll fellow-ants, the results of its inquiries would be very disappointing. Ant hills come and go; but they are all essentially the same, and beyond their physical characteristics do not change over time. Conversely, human beings are products not only of genetics and instinct, but they produce and are produced by complex culture. Hence, to live fully in this puzzling and perplexing world we must maintain our innate curiosity and care about where we have been and where we might be heading.

Readers of history ought to engage in an authentic inquiry into the nature of the world, its past and its present. Indeed, this position is assumed by peoples of all cultures from the beginning of human history itself and reinforces the idea that there is power in what we *do not know* as well as in what we *do know*. To read effectively the primary historical sources—and to evaluate critically any information or situation, for that matter—requires curiosity, creativity, and assertiveness. By developing these mental dispositions we will participate in the great tradition established by our ancestors. By summoning their courage and defying the certainty and orthodoxy of tradition, people such as Confucius, Plato, Augustine, Chu Hsi, Rousseau, Einstein, and de Beauvoir inquired into the mystery of things by posing new and probing questions.

To live in the spirit of the intellectual tradition established by our ancestors requires perseverance, common sense, and empathy. No one is a *tabula rasa*, a "blank slate." It is virtually impossible to be completely objective, and there may indeed be grave dangers in attempting to be so. If we want to gain a proper understanding of the mytho-poetic worldview of ancient peoples, the rise of slavery in the Americas, or the closed-door policy of the seventeenth-century Tokugawa

Shogunate in Japan, it is necessary to enter into the feelings and beliefs of such people in history. (*Please see Exercise Eight.*) We might evoke in ourselves the sense of power and glory emanating

---

EXERCISE EIGHT: Step Into My Shoes!

Many of the world's great civilizations and cultures have produced myths for a wide variety of reasons, not the least of which is to explain some event or phenomenon that defies explanation in rational terms. Ancient peoples living in the prescientific age accepted their mythologies as true, as accurate and powerful representations of the real state of things. For this exercise, which is designed to reinforce the discipline of empathy, consider some natural phenomenon you have experienced in your life and explain it first by creating a myth. This means you will provide an explanation for the appearance of a violent thunderstorm, the birth of a child, or some similar event in mythic terms. Second, explain the same natural occurrence in scientific terms. Your myth should be a few good paragraphs in length and written in prose or poetry. The scientific explanation should be about equal in length.

---

from the Nuremberg rallies in Hitler's Third Reich as thousands of patriotic Germans chanted *"Sieg Heil."* But this does not mean that we approve of the values postulated by that regime. Yet it is imperative that an attempt be made to experience historical phenomena as objectively as is humanly possible by bracketing our own feelings and thoughts, setting them aside so that a clearer, more empathetic understanding may emerge. This is the real challenge posed by the reading and studying of primary historical sources.

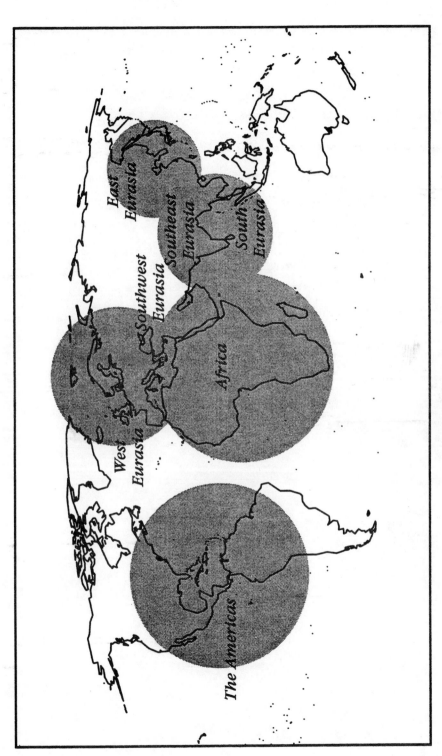

The World

Part 1

The Early Modern World

An Age of Philosophers and Reformers

THE WINDS OF CHANGE   The later Middle Ages was a period of brutality and disorder perhaps to a greater extent than other eras of history. From the Wicklow Mountains of Ireland, to the Hindu Kush Range of India, to the Great Khingan Range of China, the fourteenth and fifteenth centuries were marked by an accelerating decline of confidence in social and cultural values. Powerful creative forces were at work. But they were less conspicuous to most people than the constraints of disintegration and decay. Nonetheless, during the late fifteenth and early sixteenth centuries, the peoples of east and west Eurasia, Africa, the Americas, and the Pacific Basin entered into a continuous and direct—not to mention difficult—cultural dialogue. The interregional empires established by the Mongols, Muslims, and Chinese encouraged intermittent communication and commerce, so that contact among the civilized peoples of Eurasia and Africa was not uncommon prior to the late fifteenth century. A cultural and economic equilibrium had been established in the great Eurasian civilizations by the mid-sixteenth century. But portentous events of the Early Modern period provoked various crises that heralded change. The presence of European explorers, traders, and missionaries, for example, brought about some upheaval in non-Western countries. Stimulated by the significant transformations they experienced, many people in this Age of Philosophers and Reformers reflected deeply about themselves, their place in the world, and the nature of the communities in which they lived. The activities of Italian and northern European Renaissance humanists, religious reformers, and revolutionaries freed millions of people from habitual forms of religious and intellectual authority. The bonds of the hierarchical order of society that reigned supreme in the West throughout Late Antiquity and the Middle Ages were finally being dissolved (Reading 17). Anachronistic values and patterns of behavior, vestiges of medieval Christendom that were unresponsive to fluctuating contemporary conditions, gave way to more viable and flexible expressions of order and stability.

THE NEW WORLD   In the wake of oceanic voyages, exploration of newly discovered continents, and concomitant exploitation of non-European peoples, attempts were made to extend the Western perception of order to all corners of the world (Reading 22). The knowledge of peoples in the Americas who had no prior contact with the Christian religion itself stirred considerable consternation and debate among Europeans. At the same time there was growing discontent with ecclesiastical and secular institutions during this era of geographic expansion, religious fervor, and scientific and philosophical advancement. The works of religious activists (Readings 12, 13) and secular humanists (Reading 10) reflected their authors' disillusionment with the European heritage. Significantly, two major English literary works, Thomas More's *Utopia* and William Shakespeare's *The Tempest,* reflect the fictitious notion that Europeans were going to be revitalized and changed for the better by the settlement of the New World (Reading 11). Many people began to look to the New World for an opportunity to express their passionate desire to restore Christianity to its original state. They hoped to establish truly just and moral societies in the wilderness of "uncivilized" America (Reading 23). Others, though, rejected this as nothing more than quixotic, utopian thinking (Reading 14).

THE "NEW SCIENCE" AND INTELLECTUAL CHANGES   The discovery of the New World and direct contact with non-Western civilizations caused Europeans to reassess conventional points of view, and traditional parameters of knowledge were extended immeasurably. The remarkable scientific and philosophical progress during the European Middle Ages reached its culmination in the Early Modern Age, with men and women celebrating the grandeur of their God's creation. Over the course of a few centuries, the development of scientific methodologies based on empiricism and rationalism and advancement in fields such as astronomy, anatomy, optics, and physics radically transformed the way people viewed the world and themselves. Although scientific theories such as Copernicus's heliocentricism initially lacked formal mathematical and empirical demonstration, it was unavoidable that the archaic cosmology of medieval Christendom (based as it was on Aristotelian natural philosophy and the authority of Holy Writ) would be discredited and replaced by new, more accurate representations of the physical world. Scientific progress also gave birth to controversial new ideas on the relationship between secular learning and theology (Reading 15). It is worth noting that Galileo reintroduced into Western thought an element of skepticism that had subsided during the time when the Catholic church held sway in the Middle Ages. For this great Italian scientist it was not disgraceful to admit ignorance, to confess that one did not know something. This stance of recognizing the inherent power in what one does not know, in fact, became quite fashionable among his followers.

Practitioners of the new science gradually revealed a more secular universe to the European intellectual community, one that operated according to different laws and principles. In the process of being incorporated and adapted by philosophers and metaphysicians, the discoveries and principles of the sciences also produced a surge of philosophical doubt (Reading 16). The initial intellectual uncertainty felt by many prominent thinkers eventually yielded novel, yet more tenable, interpretations of the natural and sociopolitical order (Reading 19). By the late seventeenth and early eighteenth centuries, the pervasive influence of the new science on Western thinking would be manifested in philosophy, art, and poetry (Readings 18, 20, 21). Although the German philosopher Immanuel Kant definitively separated science and philosophy, attributing to each distinct functions and techniques, he was still greatly influenced by contemporary scientific developments. He remained fascinated by the problems of art and aesthetics and in his *Critique of Judgment* established the realm of artistic aesthetics as a legitimate domain of human experience. Writings such as Sir Isaac Newton's magisterial *Mathematical Principles*, published in 1687, directly influenced the study of human nature. Indeed, analogies were drawn between the conclusions of philosophy and the emerging social sciences and the Newtonian premise that the universe operates with mathematical regularity and according to established laws. By the end of the eighteenth century, Europeans in west Eurasia and the Americas were confident in their ability to understand the vast complexities of the world in which they lived.

THE NON-WESTERN WORLD   Newton's scientific conquest of nature was relatively unimportant to the unfolding of history in other parts of the globe. Established non-European societies remained untouched—at least for a time—by the scientific and technological developments taking place in the West, and many states continued to expand geographically. Yet, magnificent cultural and intellectual achievements are attributable to the Chinese, Indians, Africans, and others during the sixteenth through eighteenth centuries. In fact, southwestern and eastern Eurasia and Africa supported many highly developed and wealthy civilizations. For example, the Mughal Empire in the Indian subcontinent extended the limits of its political power and authority throughout the late 1500s. Akbar the Great excelled as an administrator of conquered provinces, introduced many bureaucratic reforms, and was extremely tolerant toward the many religious faiths of India (Reading 2). The emperor's final years were troubled by internal rebellion, and his successors increasingly found it difficult to maintain their imperial hegemony. They abandoned his policy of religious toleration, and Hindus and Muslims resumed their persistent conflict. Yet the Mughal dynasty continually patronized the arts until its demise in the eighteenth century. Many scholars flourished and wrote interesting and important works under Akbar's patronage. One of his contemporaries, the Bengali poet Mahavarcharya, bestowed high praise on his king as a patron of arts and letters. Akbar's rebellious son Jahangir possessed excellent literary tastes and also extended his imperial patronage to scholars. In the imperial prince Dara Shikoh, the Mughals possessed one of the greatest Indian scholars. Well versed in Arabic, Sanskrit, and Persian, he immersed himself in Hindu and Sufi mysticism and was responsible for many prominent works, including Persian translations of the Upanishads and the Bhagavad Gita. Unfortunately, Dara Shikoh's intellectual curiosity and humanitarianism were offset by his militant brother Aurangzeb's Islamic fanaticism. In some ways the conflict between Hindu, Muslim, and Sikh spawned extraordinary cultural achievements in vernacular literature, architecture, and art.

In eastern Eurasia, the Manchus successfully built on China's ancient imperial tradition after they consolidated their power in the late seventeenth century. Rulers of the Celestial Empire made territorial expansions, fostered the arts, and provided their subjects with widespread prosperity, which was only occasionally interrupted by internal dissent and rebellion. Although virtually isolated from the rest of the world, Japan remained a sophisticated, prosperous society where the arts and scholarship flourished. A period of civil unrest prompted the Japanese to create the most effective government in their history. Owing to domestic political turmoil, the Japanese were initially receptive to Western influences and commercial goods when traders and missionaries first arrived in the islands in the mid-sixteenth century. Official isolationist policies later initiated by the Tokugawa shoguns show that the Japanese, like the Chinese, had no desire to treat the "western barbarians" as equals; indeed, the shoguns of Tokugawa Japan believed Western merchantmen and Christian missionaries, as well as Chinese nationals, might subvert the will and loyalty of the Japanese people (Readings 7, 8, 9).

The high level of cultural sophistication found in late Ming and Manchu times left many Chinese rulers and Confucian literati justifiably proud of their ancient traditions and customs (Readings 3, 4, 5, 6). Both the Chinese and Japanese, perhaps too hastily, dismissed the threat posed by the persistent interference of Westerners in their affairs. In spite of their strengths, these states seemed to lack the Faustian motivation of many Europeans and white colonists in North America, which by the middle of the nineteenth century brought Westerners the dubious bounties of their vast empires.

The civilized peoples of south-central and eastern Eurasia did not escape the influence of the Europeans and somewhat later the Americans. Nor did Africans, whose first direct encounter with western Europeans was more cataclysmic than that of the highly advanced societies of eastern Eurasia. Following the lead of the Portuguese and Dutch, the British and French expanded the African slave trade along the western coast of the continent (Reading 1). It was not ancient bureaucratic traditions and elaborate imperial structures, as in China and Japan (although Songhay, the Ashanti, and Oyo could boast of sophisticated, brilliant civilizations), that helped to keep sub-Saharan Africa from being entirely overrun by Muslim and Christian slave traders. Rather, it was tropical diseases that made the penetration of the continent by outsiders virtually impossible during the Early Modern period.

END OF THE EARLY MODERN AGE   By the time of the American and French Revolutions of the late eighteenth century, the world was very different from what it had been in 1500. The Age of Philosophers and Reformers saw both the birth of radically new institutions from the rubble of the past, as well as the evolutionary growth of existing systems. Those countries that kept apace with the enormous changes, those that more readily adapted to the new world order of the late eighteenth and early nineteenth centuries, would emerge seemingly assured of their continued prosperity and good fortune.

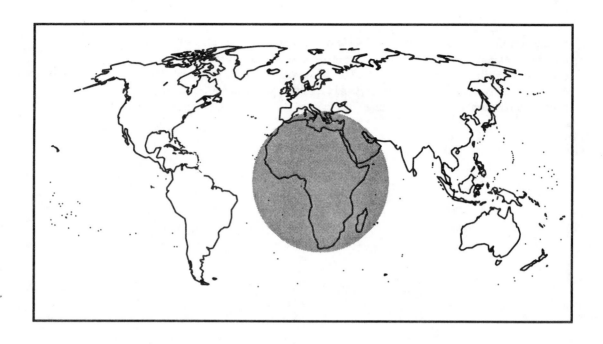

Brief Chronology for the Early Modern World
Southwest Eurasia and Africa

1450–1591	Songhai Empire in West Africa (Askia Muhammad, 1493–1535)
1453	Fall of Constantinople to the Turks
1453–1918	Ottoman Empire (Sultan Suleiman, 1520-1566)
1488	Bartholomew Dias rounds Cape of Good Hope
1500–1722	Safavid Shi'ite rule in Iran (Shah 'Abbas, 1586–1628)
1501	First African slaves imported into Hispaniola
1506	Portuguese domination of east coast of Africa
1517	Ottoman domination of Egypt begins
1591	Collapse of the Songhai Empire
1619	First African slaves arrive in North America in Virginia
1652	Dutch East India Company founds first Cape Colony

1660–1856	Dominance of Omani state in east Africa
1672–1750	British Royal Africa Company, bankrupt in 1683 and reformed
1700	Transatlantic slave trade at its height
1741–1856	United Sultanate of Oman and Zanzibar in East Africa
1769	Ali Bey (1728–1773) declares Egyptian independence from Ottoman Empire
1774	Ottomans lose the Crimea to Russian czar
1795	British dominate Cape Colony, replacing the Dutch

All dates are C.E. and approximate unless otherwise indicated. It should be noted as well that chronologies are constantly being revised. Hence, there may be discrepancies between the dates listed above and those found in other textbooks and scholarly monographs. Throughout the text and in the Glossary, all dates are given in B.C.E. (Before the Common Era) and C.E. (the Common Era). Where there is no era designation C.E. may be assumed.

Francis Moore's *Travels into the Inland Parts of Africa*

With Prince Henry the Navigator (1394–1460) as their inspiration, sailors and adventurers from Portugal began to make their way down the west coast of Africa, ultimately rounding the Cape of Good Hope by the end of the fifteenth century. The Portuguese monopoly did not last long, however; other Europeans soon joined them in establishing trading stations and factories along the coast of the Dark Continent. After enduring a three-month voyage from his home in England to the mouth of the River Gambia, Francis Moore (d. 1750?) remained in Africa from November 1730 to April 1735. He served first as a minor official at James Fort, a trading center run by the British Royal Africa Company located on James Island in the River Gambia. Moore eventually obtained a more substantial position at Joar, where he ran the trading post with William Roberts. The two men did not get along well, and when Roberts was eventually fired for various improprieties, Moore had greater freedom of action, including the possibility of traveling some five hundred miles inland along the Gambia. When Moore left Africa, he was immediately commissioned as storekeeper for the colony of Georgia in North America, where he worked for **James Oglethorpe** until July 1736. Moore made a second trip to Georgia in 1738 and remained there until 1743, having the previous year witnessed the Spanish invasion of the colony. Moore's *Travels* was published in London in 1738, and he subsequently produced many other travelogues characteristic of this early age of colonization.

I left England in July 1730, on my being appointed a writer in the service of the Royal Africa Company, and on the 9th of November came to an anchor in the mouth of the Gambia. . . .

On the second day of February [1731], one of the kings of Fonia came to the fort, and on his landing, was saluted with five guns. He came to see the governor, or rather to ask him for some powder and ball, in order to enable him to defend himself against some people with whom he was at war; he was a young man, very black, tall, and well set, was dressed in a pair of short, yellow cotton-

S. G. Johnson, *The World Displayed; Or A Curious Collection of Voyages and Travels* (Philadelphia: Dobelbower, Key, & Simpson, 1796), vol. 6: 299–337, passim.

cloth breeches, and wore on his back a garment of the same cloth, made like a surplice. He had on his head a very large cap, to which was fastened part of a goat's tail, which is a customary ornament with the great men of this river, but he had no shoes nor stockings. He and his retinue came in a large canoe holding about sixteen people, all armed with guns and cutlasses. With him came two or three women, and the same number of Mundingo drums, which are about a yard long, and a foot, or twenty inches diameter at the top, but less at the bottom; made out of a solid piece of wood, and covered only at the widest end with the skin of a kid. They beat upon them with their left hand, using only one drum stick; and the women will dance very briefly to the sound. They stayed at the fort all night, and then returned home; having nine guns fired at their going off.

It may be here proper to observe, that there are many different kingdoms on the bank of the Gambia, inhabited by several races of people, as Mundingoes, Julloiffs, Pholeys, Sloops, Portuguese. The most numerous are called Mundingoes, as is likewise the country they inhabit; they are generally of a black color, and well set. When this country was conquered by the Portuguese about the year 1420 [sic], some of that nation settled in it, who have cohabited with these Mundingoes, till they are now very near as black as they. But, as they still retain a sort of bastard Portuguese language called Creole and as they christen and marry by the help of a priest annually sent thither from St. Jago, one of the Cape de Verde islands, they still esteem themselves Portuguese Christians, as much as if they were actually natives of Portugal, and nothing angers them more than to call them Negroes, that being a term they use only for slaves.

On the north side of the river Gambia, and from thence inland, are a people called Jolloiffs, whose country extends even to the river Senegal. These people are much blacker, and handsomer than the Mundingoes; for they have not the broad noses and thick lips peculiar to the Mundingoes and Sloops.

In every kingdom and country on each side of the river are people of a tawny color, called Pholeys, who resemble the Arabs, whose language most of them speak; for it is taught in their schools, and the koran, which is also their law, is in that language. They are more generally learned in Arabic, than the people of Europe are in Latin; for they can most of them speak it, though they have a vulgar tongue called Pholey. They live in hoards or clans, build towns, and are not subject to any of the kings of the country, though they live in their territories; for if they are used ill in one nation, they break up their towns, and remove to another. They have chiefs of their own, who rule with such moderation, that every act of government seems rather an act of the people than of one man. This form of government is easily administered, because the people are of a good and quiet disposition, and so well instructed in what is just and right, that a man who does ill, is the abomination of all.

In these countries the natives are not avaricious of lands: they desire no more than what they use; and as they do not plough with horses or cattle, they can use but very little. Hence the kings are willing to allow the Pholeys to cultivate the land, and live in their dominions. They plant tobacco near their houses, and all around their towns they plant cotton; beyond that are their corn fields, of which they raise the four kinds usually produced all over this country; that is maize, or Indian corn, rice and, the larger, and lesser Guinea corn. In Gambia is no wheat, barley, rye, oats, nor any other European grain; but they have a kind of cross between the kidney-bean and pea, and also potatoes and yams. . . .

The natives make no bread, but thicken liquids with the flour of the different grains. The maize they mostly use when green, parching it in the ear, when it eats like green peas. Their rice they boil in the same matter as is practiced by the Turks; and make flour of the Guinea corn and mansaroke, as they also sometimes do of the two former species, by beating it in wooden mortars. The natives never bake cakes or bread for themselves, but those of their women who live among the Europeans learn to do both.

The Pholeys are the greatest planters in the country, though they are strangers in it. They are very industrious and frugal, and raise much more corn and cotton than they consume, which they sell at reasonable rates, and are so remarkable for their hospitality, that the natives esteem it a blessing to have a Pholey town in their neighborhood: besides their behavior has gained them such reputation, that it is esteemed infamous for anyone to treat them in an inhospitable manner. Though their humanity extends to all, they are doubly kind to people of their own race; and if they know of anyone of their body being made a slave, all the Pholeys will unite to redeem him. As they have plenty of food, they never suffer any of their own people to want, but support the old, the blind and the lame, equally with the others. They are seldom angry, and I never heard them abuse each other; yet this mildness does not proceed from want of courage; for they are as brave as any people of Africa, and are very expert in the use of their arms, which are the assagay, short cutlasses, bows and arrows, and even guns upon occasion. They commonly settle near some Mundingo town; there being scarce anyone of note, especially up the river, that has not a Pholey town near it. They are strict Mahometans; and scarcely any of them will drink brandy, or anything stronger than sugar and water.

They breed cattle, and are very dexterous at managing them, so that the Mundingoes leave theirs to their care. The whole herd belonging to a town feed all the day in the savannahs, and after the crop is off, in the rice grounds. They have a place without each town for cattle, in the middle of which they raise a stage about eight feet high from the ground, and eight or ten feet wide; to this is a ladder, and over it a roof thatch, with the sides all open. Round this stage they fix a number of stakes, every night the cattle are brought up, and each beast tied to a separate stake, with a strong rope made of the barks of trees. The cows are then milked, and four or five men stay upon the stage all night with their arms, to guard them from the lions and other wild beasts. Their houses are built in a very regular manner, and placed at a distance from each other, to avoid fire.

They are likewise great huntsmen, and not only kill lions, tigers, and other wild beasts; but often go twenty or thirty in a company to hunt elephants, whose teeth they sell, and whose flesh they smoke-dry and eat, keeping it several months together. The elephants, they say, generally go one or two hundred in a drove, and do great mischief by pulling up the trees by the roots, and trampling down the

9

corn; to prevent which, the natives when they have any suspicion of their coming, make fires all round their corn to keep them out. . . .

On the south side of the river, opposite James' fort, in the empire of Fonia, and but a little way inland, are a fort of people called Sloops, who are in a manner wild. They border on the Mundingoes, who are bitter enemies to them. Their country is of vast extent, but they have no king. Each of their towns is fortified with a double row of stakes drove all round them filled up with clay. But though they are independent of each other, and under the government of no one chief; they unite so firmly, that all of the force of the Mundingoes cannot get the better of them. . . .

On the 11th [of the month], came down the river a vessel commanded by Captain Pyke, a separate trader, from Joar, loaded with slaves, among whom was a person of an elegant figure, named Job Ben Solomon, who was of the Pholey race, and son to the high priest of Bundo, in Soota, a place about ten days journey from Gillyfree. This person was travelling on the south side of the Gambia, with a servant, and about twenty or thirty head of cattle, which induced the king of a country a little way within the land to seize not only the cattle, but Job and his man, both of whom he sold as slaves to Captain Pyke. The Pholeys, his human countrymen, would have redeemed him; but they had the mortification to find that he was carried out of the river before they had notice of his being a slave, and Captain Pyke sailed with him to Maryland. Job, who was a person of extraordinary abilities, and distinguished merit, was not so unhappy as he had reason to expect; but his adventures will be hereafter related, when I shall have occasion to mention his return to this country. . . .

On the 20th of November in the evening was a total eclipse of the moon, and the Mundingoes told me, the darkness was occasioned by the cat putting her paw between the moon and the earth. The Mahometans in this country were singing and dancing the whole time, because they expect their prophet to come in an eclipse. . . .

I was employed in the company's service in different parts of the river till the 13th of July [1734], when I was desired to come down to James Fort, where I was on the 8th of August, when the Dolphin Snow arrived, with four writers, and Job Ben Solomon, on board. We have already mentioned his being robbed and carried to Joar, where he was sold to Captain Pyke, by whom he was carried to Maryland. Job was there sold to a planter, with whom he had lived about a twelve month, in all which time he had the happiness of not being struck by his master, and then had the good fortune to have a letter of his own writing in the Arabic tongue, conveyed to England. This letter coming to the hand of Mr. Oglethorpe, he sent it to Oxford to be translated; which being done, it gave him such satisfaction, and inspired him with so good an opinion of the author, that he immediately sent orders to have him bought of his master. This happened a little before that gentleman's setting out for Georgia, and before his return from thence, Job arrived in England, where being brought to the acquaintance of Sir Hans Sloane, he was found to be a perfect master of the Arabic tongue, by his translating several manuscripts and inscriptions on medals. That learned antiquary recommended him to the duke of Montague, who being pleased with his genius and capacity, the agreeableness of his behavior, and the sweetness of his temper, introduced him to court, where he was graciously received by the royal family and most of the nobility, who honored him with many marks of favor. The African company and the chief merchants of the city strove who should oftenest invite him to their tables. His good sense engaged their esteem, he freely discoursed on every subject, and attended the churches of the most celebrated divines. When he had been in England about fourteen months, his ardent desire to see his native country made him press for his departure. He had wrote from England to the high priest his father, and earnestly longed to see him. Upon his setting out from England, he received many noble presents from Queen Caroline, Prince William, the duke of Montague, and the earl of Pembroke, several ladies of quality, Mr. Holden, and the Royal African Company, and the latter ordered all their agents to show him the greatest respect.

On the arrival at James Fort, Job desired that I should send a messenger to his country to let his friends know where he was. I spoke to one of the blacks whom we usually employed, to procure me a messenger, and he brought me a Pholey, who not only knew the high priest his father, but Job himself, and expressed great joy at seeing him safely returned from slavery, he being the only man, except one, ever known to come back to his country, after being once carried a slave out of it by white men. . . .

In the evening [some time later] as my friend Job and I were sitting under a great tree at Damasensa, there came six or seven of the very people who three years before, had robbed and made a slave out of him, at about thirty miles distance from that place. Job though naturally possessed of a very even temper, could not contain himself on seeing them; he was filled with rage and indignation, and was for attacking them with his broad sword and pistols, which he always took care to have about him. I had much ado to dissuade him from rushing upon them; but at length representing the ill consequences that would infallibly attend so rash an action, and the impossibility that either of us should escape alive. I made him lay aside the attempt, and persuaded him to sit down, and pretending not to know them, to ask them questions about himself; which he accordingly did, and they told him the truth. At last he inquired how the king their master did; they replied that he was dead, and by further inquiry we found that amongst the goods for which he sold Job to Captain Pyke there was a pistol which the king used commonly to wear slung by a string about his neck; and as they never carry arms without their being loaded, the pistol one day accidently went off, and the balls lodging in his throat, he presently died. Job was so transported at the close of this story, that he immediately fell on his knees, and returned thanks to Mahomet for making him die by the very goods for which he sold him into slavery. . . .

The people here, as in all other hot countries, marry their daughters very young; even some are contracted as soon as they are born, and the parents can never after break the match; but it is in the power of the man never to come to claim his wife, and yet without his consent she cannot marry another. Before a man takes his wife, he is obliged to pay her parents two cows, two iron bars, and

200 cola, a fruit that grows a great way within land; it is an exceeding good bitter, and much resembles a horse-chestnut with the skin off.

When a man takes home his wife he makes a feast at his own house, to which all come without the form of an invitation. The bride is brought thither upon the men's shoulders, with a veil over her face, which she keeps on till she has been in bed with her husband, during which the people dance and sing, beat drums, and fire muskets.

After the wife is brought to bed, she is not to lie with her husband for three years, if the child lives so long; for during that term the child sucks, and they are firmly persuaded that lying with their husbands would spoil their milk, and render the child liable to many diseases. The women alone are subject to all the mortifications attending so long an abstinence; for every man is allowed to take as many wives as he pleases; but if the wife is found false to her husband, she is liable to be sold as a slave. Upon any dislike, a man may turn off his wife, and make her take all her children with her; but if he has a mind to take any of them himself, he generally chooses such as are big enough to assist him in providing for his family. He even has the liberty of coming several years after they have parted, and taking from her any of the children he had by her. But if a man is disposed to part with a wife who is pregnant, he cannot oblige her to go till she is delivered.

The women are kept in the greatest subjection; and the men, to render their power as complete as possible, influence their wives to give them unlimited obedience, by all the force of fear and terror. For this purpose the Mundingoes have a kind of image eight or nine feet high, made of the bark of trees, dressed in long coat, and crowned with a wisp of straw. This is called a mumbo jumbo; and whenever the men have any dispute with the women, this is sent for to determine the contest, which is almost always done in favor of the men. One who is in the secret, conceals himself under the coat, and bringing in the image, is the oracle on these occasions. No one is allowed to come armed into his presence. Then the women hear him coming they run away and hide themselves; but if you are acquainted with the person concealed in the mumbo jumbo, he will send for them all to come, make them sit down, and afterwards either sing or dance, as he pleases; and if nay refuse to come, he will send for, and whip them. Whenever anyone enters into this society, they swear in the most solemn manner never to divulge the secret to any woman, or to any person that is not entered into it; and to preserve the secret inviolable, no boys are allowed under sixteen years of age. The people also swear by the mumbo jumbo, and the oath is esteemed irrevocable. There are very few towns of any note that have not one of these objects of terror, to frighten the poor women into obedience. . . .

About a month after the birth of a child they name the child, which is done by shaving its head, and rubbing it over with oil, and a short time before the rainy season begins, they circumcise a great number of boys, of about twelve or fourteen years of age, after which the boys put on a particular habit; the dress of each kingdom being different. From the time of circumcision to that of the rains, they are allowed to commit what outrages they please, without being called to an account for them; and when the first rain falls, the term of this licentiousness being expired, they put on their proper habit. . . .

The behavior of the natives to strangers is really not so disagreeable as people are apt to imagine; for when I went through any of their towns, they almost all come to shake hands with me, except some of the women, who have never before seen a white man, ran away from me as fast as they could, and would not by any means be persuaded to come near me. Some of the men invited me to their houses, and brought their wives and daughters to see me, who then sat down by me, and always found something to wonder at and admire, as my boots, spurs, clothes, or wig. . . .

Besides the slaves brought down by the Negro merchants, there are many bought along the river, who are either taken in war like the former, or condemned for crimes, or stolen by the people: but the company's servants never buy any which they suspect to be of the last sort, till they have sent for the alcalde, and consulted with him. Since this slave trade has been used, all punishments are changed into slavery; and the natives reaping advantage from such condemnations, they strain hard from crimes, in order to obtain the benefit of selling the criminal; hence not only murder, adultery and theft are here punished by selling the male-factor; but every trifling crime is also punished in the same manner. Thus at Cantore, a man seeing a tiger eating a deer, which he himself has killed and hung up near his house, fired at the tiger, but unhappily shot a man. Then the king had not only the cruelty to condemn him for this accident, but had the injustice and inhumanity to order also his mother, his three brothers, and his three sisters to be sold. They were brought down to me at Yamyamacunda, when it made my heart ache to see them; but on my refusing to make this cruel purchase, they were sent farther down the river, and sold to some separate traders at Joar, and the vile avaricious king had the benefit of the goods for which they were sold. . . .

Study Questions

1. What may be learned from Moore's account concerning European and African relations during the eighteenth century?
2. Was Job's experience typical or atypical for native Africans during the Early Modern Age?
3. What were the status and position of women in the African society and culture as described by Moore?
4. How and in what respects were the worldviews of Europeans and Africans different?

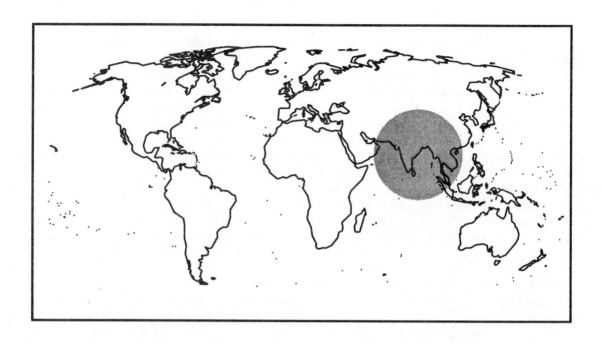

Brief Chronology for the Early Modern World
South and Southeast Eurasia

1206–1526	Delhi Sultanate (Ala-ud-din Khalji, 1296–1316)
1320–1398	Turkic Tughluq dynasty in North India
1469–1538	Nanak, founder of Sikhism
1526–1707	Mughal dynasty in India (Babur, 1526–1530; Akbar, 1556–1605; Aurangzeb, 1658–1707)
1580	Burmese Empire at height of cultural and commercial activity
1601	First English voyage to India
1605–1657	Era of religious toleration in India
1648	Delhi becomes capital of Mughal Empire
1641	Dutch conquest of Malacca, Indonesia
1690	Calcutta founded by English East India Company
1756–1763	Seven Years' War in Europe, North America, and the Indian subcontinent
1757	Robert Clive's (1725–1774) victory at Plassey gives English control of Bengal
1769	Captain James Cook reaches New Zealand
1784	Prime Minister Pitt's "India Act" placing British East India Company under government Board of Control; Asiatick Society founded in Calcutta by Sir William Jones
1788	Sydney Cove, Australia, and Port Jackson, New Zealand, established as British penal colonies

All dates are C.E. and approximate unless otherwise indicated. It should be noted as well that chronologies are constantly being revised. Hence, there may be discrepancies between the dates listed above and those found in other textbooks and scholarly monographs. Throughout the text and in the Glossary, all dates are given in B.C.E. (Before the Common Era) and C.E. (the Common Era). Where there is no era designation C.E. may be assumed.

14

Abu'l Fazl's Accounts of the Reign of Akbar

Claiming descent from **Genghis Khan** and **Tamerlane, Babur** founded the great Mughal Empire in northwestern India in the early sixteenth century. With the accession of his grandson Akbar (1542–1605) in 1556 the Mughal Empire reached the height of its power and glory. Akbar's administration was relatively stable despite continued efforts of territorial expansion and the development of a policy of religious tolerance and universalism. Akbar established a new, official court religion, *Din-i-Ilahi*, a synthesis of all religions practiced in fifteenth-century India, as described in the following excerpt. The new creed, however, did not survive this great Mughal ruler. In fact, Akbar's religious policy was to have a detrimental effect on the state of affairs after his death. As shahinshah, or emperor, Akbar was a generous and discriminating patron of art, literature, and intellectual pursuit. Among those whom he supported was Abu'l Fazl ibn Mubarak (d. 1602), the author of the *Akbarnama,* an official history of the reign, and editor of the so-called Institutes of Akbar.

Akbarnama

So long as the spiritual supremacy over the recluse which is called Holiness and the sway over laymen which is called Sovereignty, were distinct, there was strife and confusion among the children of Noah. Now that in virtue of his exaltation, foresight, comprehensive wisdom, universal benevolence, pervading discernment and perfect knowledge of God, these two great offices . . . which are the guiding thread of the spiritual and temporal worlds, have been conferred on the opener of the hoards of wisdom and claviger of Divine treasuries, a small portion at least—if his holy nature grant the necessary faculty—may be brought from the ambush of concealment to the asylum of publicity. Know you at all who is this world-girdling luminary and radiant spirit? Or whose august advent has bestowed this grace? It is he who by virtue of his enlightenment and truth, is the world-protecting sovereign of our age, . . .

Abul-I-Fazl ibn Mubarak, *Akbarnama,* trans. H. Beveridge (Calcutta, India: The Asiatic Society, 1905–1939), passim.

One of the glorious boons of His Majesty the Shahinshah [Akbar] which shone forth in this auspicious year was the abolition of enslavement. The victorious troops which came into the wide territories of India used in their tyranny to make prisoners of the wives and children and other relatives of the people of India, and used to enjoy them or sell them. His Majesty the Shahinshah, out of his thorough recognition of and worship of God, and from his abundant foresight and right thinking gave orders that no soldier of the victorious armies should in any part of his dominions act in this manner. Although a number of savage natures who were ignorant of the world should make their fastness a subject of pride and come forth to do battle, and then be defeated by virtue of the emperor's daily increasing empire, still their families must be protected from the onset of the world-conquering armies. No soldier, high or low, was to enslave them, but was to permit them to go freely to their homes and relations. It was for excellent reasons that His Majesty gave his attention to this subject, for although the binding, killing or striking the haughty and the chastising of the stiff-necked are part of the struggle for empire—and this is a point about which both sound jurists and innovators are agreed—yet it is outside of the canons of justice to regard the chastisement of women and innocent children as the chastisement of the contumacious. If the husbands have taken the path of insolence, how is it the fault of the wives, and if the fathers have chosen the road of opposition what fault have the children committed? Moreover the wives and innocent children of such factions are not munitions of war! In addition to these sound reasons there was the fact that many covetous and blind-hearted persons from vain imaginings or unjust thoughts, or merely out of cupidity attached villages and estates and plundered them, and when questioned about it said a thousand things and behaved with neglect and indifference. But when final orders were passed for the abolition of this practice, no tribe was afterwards oppressed by wicked persons on suspicion of sedition. As the purposes of the Shah-inshah were entirely right and just, the blissful result ensued that the wild and rebellious inhabitants of portions of India placed the ring of devotion in the ear of obedience, and became the materials of world-empire. Both was religion set in order, for its essence is the distribution of justice, and things temporal were regulated, for their perfection lies in the obedience of mankind. . . .

At this time [1575] when the capital was illuminated by his glorious advent, [Akbar] ordered that a house of worship . . . should be built to the adornment of the spiritual kingdom, and that it should have four verandas. . . . Though the Divine bounty always has an open door and searches for the fit person, and the inquirer, yet as the lord of the universe, from his general benevolence, conducts his measures according to the rules of the superficial, he chose the eve of Friday, which bears on its face coloring . . . of the announcement of auspiciousness, for the out-pouring. . . . A general proclamation was issued that, on that night of illumination, all orders and sects of mankind—those who searched after spiritual and physical truth, and those of the common public who sought for an awakening, and the inquirers of every sect—should assemble in the precincts of the holy edifice, and bring forward their spiritual experiences, and their degrees of knowledge of the truth in various and contradictory forms in the bridal chamber of manifestation.

Wisdom and deeds would be tested, and the essence of manhood would be exhibited. Those who were founded on truth entered the hall of acceptance, while those who were only veneered with gold went hastily to the pit of base metal. There was a feast of theology and worship. The vogue of creature-worship was reduced. The dust-stained ones of the pit of contempt became adorners of dominion, and the smooth-tongued, empty-headed rhetoricians lost their rank. To the delightful precincts of that mansion founded upon Truth, thousands upon thousands of inquirers from the seven climes came with heart-felt respect and waited for the advent of the Shahinshah. The world-lord would, with open brow, a cheerful countenance, a capacious heart and an understanding soul, pour the limpid waters of graciousness on those thirsty-lipped ones of expectation's desert, and act as a refiner. He put them into currency, sect by sect, and tested them company by company. He got hold of every one of the miserable and dust-stained ones, and made them successful in their desires,—to say nothing of the becloaked and the be-turbaned. From this general assemblage [Akbar] selected by his far-reaching eye a chosen band from each class, and established a feast of truth. Occasionally he, in order to instruct the courtiers, sent perspicuous servants who could discriminate among men, and these reflective and keen-sighted men brought every description of person to perform the kornish. Then that cambist and tester of worth examined them anew and invited some of them. . . .

His sole and sublime idea was that, as in the external administration of the dominion, which is conjoined with eternity, the merits of the knowers of the things of this world had by profundity of vision, and observance of justice, been made conspicuous, and there had ceased to be a brisk market for pretence and favoritism, so might the masters of science and ethics, and the devotees of piety and contemplation, be tested, the principles of faiths and creeds be examined, religions be investigated, the proofs and evidences for each be considered, and the pure gold and the alloy be separated from evil commixture. In a short space of time a beautiful, detached building was erected, and the fraudulent vendors of impostures put to sleep in the privy chamber of contempt. A noble palace was provided for the spiritual world and the pillars of Divine knowledge rose high.

At this time, when the center of the Caliphate . . . was glorified by [Akbar's] advent, the former institutions were renewed, and the temple of Divine knowledge was on Thursday nights illuminated by the light of the holy mind. On [3 October 1578], and in that house of worship, the lamp of the privy chamber of detachment was kindled in the banqueting hall of social life. The coin of the hivers of wisdom in colleges and cells was brought to the test. The clear wine was separated from the lees, and good coin from the adulterated. The wide capacity and the toleration of the Shadow of God were unveiled. **Sufi**, philosopher, orator, jurist, **Sunni, Shi'a, Brahmin, Jati, Siura Carbak, Nazarene**, Jew, **Sabi, Zoroastrian**, and others enjoyed exquisite pleasure by beholding the calmness of the assembly, the sitting of the world-lord in the lofty pulpit, . . . and the adornment of the pleasant abode of impartiality. The treasures of secrets were opened up without fear of hostile seekers after battle. The just and truth-perceiving ones of each sect emerged from haughtiness and conceit, and began their search anew. They displayed profundity and meditation, and gathered eternal bliss on the divan of greatness. The conceited and quarrelsome from evilness of disposition and shortness of thought descended into the mire of presumption and sought their profit in loss. Being guided by ignorant companions, and from the predominance of a somnolent fortune, they went into disgrace. The conferences were excellently arranged by the acuteness and keen quest of truth of the world's **Khedive**. Every time, eye and heart gained fresh lustre, and the lamp of vigils acquired new glory. The candle of investigation was lighted for those who loved darkness and sequacity. The families of the colleges and monasteries were tested. The handle of wealth and the material of sufficiency came into the grasp of the needy occupants of the summit of expectation. The fame of this faith-adorning method of world-bestowing made home bitter to inquirers and caused them to love exile. The Shahinshah's court became the home of the inquirers of the seven climes, and the assemblage of the wise of every religion and sect. The veneer and the counterfeitness of all those who by feline tricks and stratagems had come forth in the garb of wisdom were revealed. A few irreverent and crafty spirits continued their old tactics after the appearance of Truth and its concomitant convictions, and indulged in brawling. Their idea was that as in the great assemblies of former rulers the purpose of science and the designs of wisdom had been but little explored owing to the crowd of men, the inattention of the governor of the feast, the briskness of the market of praters, etc., so perhaps in this august assemblage they might succeed by the length of their tongues, and a veil might be hung over the occiput . . . of truth. The Khedive of wisdom by the glory of mind carried out the work to a conclusion deliberately and impartially, and in this praiseworthy fashion, which is seldom found in the saints of asceticism,—how then is it to be found in world-rulers?—tested the various coins of mortals. Many men became stained with shame and chose loss of fame, while some acquired wisdom and emerged from the hollow of obscurity to eminence. Reason was exalted, and the star of fortune shone for the acquirers of knowledge.

The Institutes of Akbar

No dignity is higher in the eyes of God than royalty, and those who are wise drink from its auspicious fountain. A sufficient proof of this, for those who require one, is the fact that royalty is a remedy for the spirit of rebellion, and the reason why subjects obey. Even the meaning of the word *Padshah* shows this; for *pad* signifies stability and possession. If royalty did not exist, the storm of strife would never subside, nor selfish ambition disappear. Mankind, being under the burden of lawlessness and lust, would sink into the pit of destruction; this world, this great market place, would lose its prosperity, and the whole world become a barren

W. T. de Bary, ed., *Sources of Indian Tradition,* comp. A. L. Basham et al. (New York: Columbia University Press, 1958), vol. 1: 497–99. Copyright © 1958 Columbia University Press. Reprinted with permission of the publisher.

waste. But by the light of imperial justice, some follow with cheerfulness the road of obedience, while others abstain from violence through fear of punishment; and out of necessity make choice of the path of rectitude. *Shah* is also a name given to one who surpasses his fellows, as you may see from words like *shah-wuwar, shah-rah;* it is also a term applied to a bridegroom—the world, as the bride, betroths herself to the king, and becomes his worshiper.

Silly and shortsighted men cannot distinguish a true king from a selfish ruler. Nor is this remarkable, as both have in common a large treasury, a numerous army, clever servants, obedient subjects, an abundance of wise men, a multitude of skillful workmen, and a superfluity of means of enjoyment. But men of deeper insight remark a difference. In the case of the former, these things just now enumerated are lasting, but in that of the latter, of short duration. The former does not attach himself to these things, as his object is to remove oppression and provide for everything which is good. Security, health, chastity, justice, polite manners, faithfulness, truth, and increase of sincerity, and so forth, are the result. The latter is kept in bonds by the external forms of royal power, by vanity, the slavishness of men, and the desire of enjoyment; hence everywhere there is insecurity, unsettledness, strife, oppression, faithlessness, robbery.

Royalty is a light emanating from God, and a ray from the sun, the illuminator of the universe, the argument of the book of perfection, the receptacle of all virtues. Modern language calls this light the divine light, and the tongue of antiquity called it the sublime halo. It is communicated by God to kings without the intermediate assistance of anyone, and men, in the presence of it, bend the forehead of praise toward the ground of submission.

Again, many excellent qualities flow from the possession of this light:

1. A paternal love toward the subjects. Thousands find rest in the love of the king, and sectarian differences do not raise the dust of strife. In his wisdom, the king will understand the spirit of the age, and shape his plans accordingly.

2. A large heart. The sight of anything disagreeable does not unsettle him, nor is want of discrimination for him a source of disappointment. His courage steps in. His divine firmness gives him the power of requital, nor does the high position of an offender interfere with it. The wishes of great and small are attended to, and their claims meet with no delay at his hands.

3. A daily increasing trust in God. When he performs an action, he considers God as the real doer of it [and himself as the medium] so that a conflict of motives can produce no disturbance.

4. Prayer and devotion. The success of his plans will not lead him to neglect, nor will adversity cause him to forget God and madly trust in man. He puts the reins of desire into the hands of reason; in the wide field of his desires he does not permit himself to be trodden down by restlessness; nor will he waste his precious time in seeking after that which is improper. He makes wrath, the tyrant, pay homage to wisdom, so that blind rage may not get the upper hand, and inconsiderateness overstep the proper limits. He sits on the eminence of propriety, so that those who have gone astray have a way left to return, without exposing their bad deeds to the public gaze. When he sits in judgment, the petitioner seems

19

to be the judge, and he himself, on account of his mildness, the suitor for justice. He does not permit petitioners to be delayed on the path of hope; he endeavors to promote the happiness of the creatures in obedience to the will of the Creator, and never seeks to please the people in contradiction to reason. He is forever searching after those who speak the truth and is not displeased with words that seem bitter, but are in reality sweet. He considers the nature of the words and the rank of the speaker. He is not content with committing violence, but he must see that no injustice is done within his realm.

Study Questions

1. How does religion function as the foundation for political and social order in Akbar's empire?
2. What effect did Akbar's new religion have on the stability and efficacy of his political regime, and why did he feel it was necessary to create such a system of belief for his Indian subjects?
3. What is the nature of humanity as revealed in Akbar's Institutes?
4. What is the status of the emperor in the universal political order of the Mughal civilization?

Mirza 'Ali's The Ship of Shi'ism

Political unity in the Islamic community did not long survive the death of the Prophet Muhammad (570–632). By the mid-seventh century, the Muslim world was embroiled in controversy over succession to the caliphate, resulting in the division of Islam into the Shi'a and Sunni sects. The tremendous appeal of Shi'a Islam is still readily apparent today in Iran, parts of Iraq, Afghanistan, and western India. Indeed, one of the main factors in the survival of Persian (Iranian) cultural and political identity was the adoption of Shi'ism as a kind of national creed. When the Safavid dynasty established its empire in old Persia in the sixteenth century, Shi'ism became the official religion of the state. The "Ship of Shi'ism" is a Persian manuscript illumination of Mirza 'Ali incorporated into the well-known *A King's Book of Kings* written by Firdawsi for Shah Tahmasp (d. 1576). In it, Iran's identification with Shi'ism is seen in allegorical terms. Many ships in which all the world's religions (Mirza counts 70 of them) are placed set sail across the ocean of eternity. Only the ship carrying Shi'ism reaches the shores of paradise. This ship carries Muhammad, his son-in-law 'Ali, and 'Ali's martyred sons, Hasan and Husayn. All are shown with fiery halos and indistinguishable faces: representing their facial features is sacrilegious according to Muslim tradition.

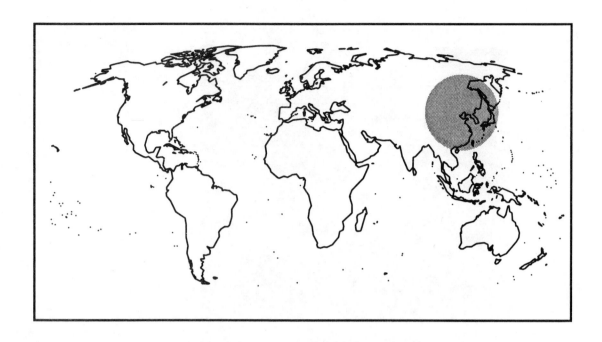

Brief Chronology for the Early Modern World
East Eurasia

1368–1644	Ming dynasty in China (Hung-wu, 1368–1398; Yung-lo, 1403–1424)
1387	Ming reconquest of China completed
1421	Construction of "Forbidden City" in Peking begins
1405–1433	Great maritime expeditions under Cheng Ho—seven voyages to southeast Eurasia
1467–1477	Onin War in Japan
1520	Portuguese embassy to Peking
1542–1616	Tokugawa Ieyasu, Japanese soldier and statesman
1543	Portuguese arrive in Japan
1549	Ming China under continuous attacks by Mongols
1582–1590	Toyotomi Hideyoshi dominates Japan
1592	Japanese invasions of Korea
1598	Japanese forced to abandon Korea
1603–1867	Tokugawa Shogunate in Japan (Ieysau, 1603–1605; Iyemitsu, 1623–1651; Tsunayoshi, 1680–1709)
1644–1911	Ch'ing (Manchu) dynasty in China (Shun-chih, 1644–1662; Ch'ien-lung, 1736–1796)
1650–1750	Foundation of many Japanese schools for Samurai youth
1715	Manchu conquest of Mongolia
1720	Manchu conquest of Tibet
1742	Christianity banned in China
1784	U.S. traders arrive in China
1798	White Lotus Rebellion in China

All dates are C.E. and approximate unless otherwise indicated. It should be noted as well that chronologies are constantly being revised. Hence, there may be discrepancies between the dates listed above and those found in other textbooks and scholarly monographs. Throughout the text and in the Glossary, all dates are given in B.C.E. (Before the Common Era) and C.E. (the Common Era). Where there is no era designation C.E. may be assumed.

Matteo Ricci's *Chinese Journals*

Portuguese traders reached southern China in 1513, establishing a permanent trading post in Macao by 1557. This commercial activity was followed by missionary work some thirty years later. Known for their great learning and erudition, Catholic Jesuit missionaries focused their spiritual efforts of conversion on the intellectual elite. Arriving in China in 1583, Matteo Ricci (1552–1610), whose extensive experiences in China form the basis of his private journals, became well known to Chinese intellectuals. He was appreciated as an expert in physics, mathematics, and geography, as well as for his gifts as a philosopher, Christian theologian, and commentator on the great sage **Confucius**. Ricci so impressed the native intelligentsia that they gave him the title of "Doctor of the Great Western Ocean." The autobiographical material in his diary is preceded by a detailed account of many Chinese customs and traditions. The following excerpt from his journals, which the author never intended to publish, discusses the elaborate educational system of imperial China that had its beginnings during the classical Han period in the second century B.C.E. After nearly two decades in south China, Ricci made his way northward in 1600, and spent several months in a Tientsin jail before the Ming emperor sent for him. Thereafter, Father Ricci lived in the northern capital of Beijing until his death.

It is evident to everyone here that no one will labor to attain proficiency in mathematics or in medicine who has any hope of becoming prominent in the field of philosophy. The result is that scarcely anyone devotes himself to these studies, unless he is deterred from the pursuit of what are considered to be the higher studies, either by reason of family affairs or by mediocrity of talent. The study of mathematics and that of medicine are held in low esteem, because they are not fostered by honors as is the study of philosophy, to which students are attracted by the hope of the glory and the rewards attached to it. This may be readily seen in the interest taken in the study of moral philosophy. The man who is promoted

Matthew Ricci, *China in the Sixteenth Century: Journals of Matthew Ricci,* trans. Louis J. Gallagher, S. J. (New York: Random House, 1953), 32–41, passim. Copyright © 1942 and renewed 1970 Louis J. Gallagher, S. J. Copyright © 1953 Louis J. Gallagher, S. J. Reprinted with permission of Random House, Inc.

to the higher degrees in this field, prides himself on the fact that he has in truth attained to the pinnacle of Chinese happiness.

I think it will be as interesting as it is new to the reader to treat somewhat more fully of this phase of their studies. Confucius, called the Prince of Chinese Philosophers, compiled four volumes of the works of more ancient philosophers and wrote five books of his own. These five he entitled "**The Doctrines**," and they contain the ethical principles of right living, precepts governing the conduct of political life, customs, and examples of the ancient, their rites and sacrifices, and even samples of their poetry and other subjects of this nature. Besides these five books there is another one composed of the precepts of the great philosopher and of his disciples and compiled without particular arrangement. These are chiefly directions for proper moral proceedings, in the light of human reason, with a view to virtuous conduct on the part of the individual, of the family and of the kingdom in general. This volume, being a summary in excerpts from the four books mentioned, is called the *Tetrabiblion*. The nine books of Confucius, making up the most ancient of Chinese libraries, of which all others are a development, are written mostly in hieroglyphic characters, and present a collection of moral precepts for the future good and development of the kingdom.

There is a law in the land, handed down from ancient kings and confirmed by the custom of centuries, stating that he who wishes to be learned, and to be known as such, must draw his fundamental doctrine from these same books. In addition to this it is not sufficient for him to follow the general sense of the text, but what is far more difficult, he must be able to write aptly and exactly of every particular doctrine contained in these books. To this end he must commit the entire *Tetrabiblion* to memory, so as to be a recognized authority thereon. Contrary to what has been stated by some of our writers, there are no schools or public academies in which these books are taught or explained by masters. Each student selects his own master by whom he is instructed in his own home and at his personal expense.

The number of such private teachers, of course, is great, partly because it would be hard for one master to teach many at a time, owing to the difficulty of handling the Chinese characters, and partly because it is an old custom here for each home to have a private school for its own children. At times it happens that tutors, other than the one regularly employed, may be called in, as it would seem, to prevent the custom of bidding for the position from interfering with the interest of their profession.

In the field of philosophy there are three degrees, conferred upon those who pass the written examinations assigned for each degree. The first degree is awarded in the larger cities and in a public academy, by some prominent scholar, appointed by the emperor for that purpose. In virtue of his office this dignitary is known as *Tihio,* and the first degree, corresponding to our baccalaureate, is called *Lieucai.* The *Tihio* visits the various cities of his province in which the degree is to be conferred and for which a triple examination is required. Upon the arrival of this chancellor, as we would call him, the candidates assemble for the examinations. The preliminary examination is conducted by the local teachers who have attained to the baccalaureate and are preparing for a higher degree, and they are paid from the royal treasury for these particular examinations. Anyone may be admitted to the preliminary examinations, and sometimes four or five thousand from a single district will take them. Those who pass the first test are recommended by the teachers to the four city prefects, who are themselves learned men, otherwise they would not be in office. The prefects then select the candidates who are to be presented to the chancellor. Not more than two hundred may be thus presented, and these are chosen for the excellence of their written composition.

The third examination is conducted by the chancellor himself, and is far more rigid than those preceding it. Of the two hundred admitted to this examination, the twenty or thirty obtaining the highest grades are granted the degree, depending upon the size of the district from which the candidates are drawn. They are then known as academic bachelors, a distinguished class representing the advanced citizenry of their particular town, and their company is cultivated by all who hope to attain to the same dignity. Their particular insignia is an ankle-long gown, a cap, and leggings, which no class other than theirs is permitted to wear. They are given honored seats at the conventions of the magistrates, and with them they may employ the more intimate rites of address which the common people are never permitted to use. In their home cities they enjoy a great many civil privileges and are looked upon as inferior to none, save the chancellor and the four city prefects, nor is it easy for other magistrates to pass judgment upon the cases they present or on charges made against them. . . .

The second degree of the Chinese literati is called *Kiugin* and may be compared to our licentiate. This degree is conferred with considerable solemnity in each metropolitan province but only every third year and at the eighth moon. This degree is not open to all who may aspire to it. Only those of the highest ranking are selected for it and their number depends upon the dignity or celebrity of the province. . . .

The degree of licentiate is far superior to that of bachelor and carries with it more dignity and more notable privileges. He who holds a licentiate degree is supposed to continue his studies and to go on to the doctorate, and if he declines to do so he is ineligible for even an inferior public office. When the examinations are over and the ceremonies described at an end, the royal examiners publish a book which is distributed throughout the whole empire, containing the results of the examinations, the names of the new licentiates, and the outstanding manuscripts on the various subjects treated in the examinations. The place of honor in this publication is assigned to the one who received the highest ranking, and he is honored with the title Quiayuen. This book is published as a de luxe edition, and several copies of it are presented to the Emperor and to the palatines.

Ordinarily, bachelors from outside are not admitted to the licentiate examinations. Some few, however, are accepted by special privilege in the capital districts of Peking and Nankin. If they were admitted to study in the district, they became associated to it, and after obtaining the bachelor's degree, they could be received into the college of that district upon payment of a certain sum of gold to the district treasury.

The third literary degree among the Chinese is called *Cin-su* and is equivalent to our doctorate. This degree is also conferred every third year but only in the province of Peking. The year for doctorate is always the one next following that for licentiate. No more than three hundred degrees are conferred at a time, for the entire country. Those holding licentiate degrees from any province are free to take this examination as often as they wish. It is held on the days mentioned, during the second phase of the moon, and in exactly the same manner as described for the former degree save, perhaps because of the great dignity of this degree, with more precaution against fraud or favoritism. The presiding examiners in this instance are chosen from among the strictest of the royal magistrates, called the *Colai*, . . .

When this examination is over, the results are announced in the same manner and in the same place as already described. The only added feature is that the new doctors all adjourn to the royal palace and here, in presence of the Chief Magistrates of the court and at times of the Emperor also, they write a treatise on a given subject. The results of this contest determine to which of the three grades of the magistracy the doctors will be assigned. This is a celebrated examination, and it consists entirely of a rather brief written dissertation. The one who has already been awarded first place in the regular doctorate examination is assured of at least third place in this final, and those who receive first and second places in this are marked for signal honors and have the assurance of holding high public office for the rest of their lives. The position they hold would correspond to that of duke or marquis in our country, but the title to it is not bequeathed by hereditary right.

The new doctors immediately adorn their special garb and particular hat and leggings, with the other insignia of the magistrate, and are promoted to the richer and more elevated benefices of the magistracy. From that time on they belong to a social order superseding that of the licentiates, and are counted among the ranking citizens of the kingdom. It is difficult for a stranger to appreciate how superior their rank is to that of their colleagues of the day before, who always cede them the place of honor and greet them with the most flattering titles and courtesy.

If those who failed in the examinations for the doctor's degree give up hope of obtaining it in the future, they may be admitted to public office above the lower grades, but not in the category of offices held by the doctors. If, however, they wish to take the examination again, they continue to study for the next three years, and then return to try their luck again, and they may do this as often as they please. Despite misfortune and with undying hope, some have been known to have made as many as ten attempts to gain this honor, and on the principle of all or nothing to have used up their whole lives in unsuccessful endeavor.

Here again, as in the case of the inferior order, the results are published in the form of a private volume, arranged by each of the examiners and containing the names of the successful candidates and the more distinguished dissertations. Each year, also, a book is published listing all the doctors of philosophy, giving their address, the names of their parents, the different offices they have held, and the places in which they held them. This is a sort of directory from which one may learn what offices each of the doctors has held from the year of his doctorate to the present, or to the time of his death. Besides this, a list of his promotions or demotions is given, either of which may be of daily occurrence among the Chinese, depending upon the reputation of the officeholder.

In this acquiring of degrees there really is something worthy of admiration in the relationship that grows up between candidates of the same year. Those whom fortune has brought together in attaining a higher degree look upon one another as brothers for the rest of their lives. There is mutual agreement and sympathy among them, and they help each other and one another's relatives as well, in every possible way. The friendship they enjoy with their examiners is like that of a son and father, or of a disciple and his master, and they continue to show them respect and deference though it might happen at times that the pupil is raised to even higher honors than are enjoyed by his former preceptor.

The same three grades which we have been discussing are also conferred with similar titles in military circles. These degrees are granted in the same year, but in the following month and in the same place as the former. They are conferred, however, with much less ceremony, due to the fact that military science is not highly cultivated or esteemed in this country. In fact, so few among the military aspire to these degrees that they are considered to be of little importance. Examinations for military degrees are divided into three parts. In the first part, nine arrows are shot by the soldier while he is coursing at full gallop on his charger. In the second, as many more are discharged on foot, standing still. Those who fix four arrows within the allotted space from horseback and two from afoot are admitted to the third part of the examination. In this they must answer in writing to certain questions pertaining to military tactics. The deciding judges announce the results and also the number of military licentiate degrees awarded in each province, amounting to about fifty in all. In the year in which the doctors of philosophy are named in Peking, about a hundred doctors, chosen from the military licentiates of the entire kingdom, are also named, after completing a necessary triple examination. The soldiers holding doctor's degrees are given preference over those of the licentiate grade for appointment as military prefects, but they have to make payment for the office. When one has merited the title of doctor, either in the philosophic or in the military order, his title is inscribed in large letters over the door of his home, for the prestige of his family and as an indication of the honor he has acquired.

In concluding this account of degrees awarded among the Chinese, the following should not be omitted, which to Europeans might seem to be a rather strange and perhaps a somewhat inefficient method. The judges and the proctors of all examinations, whether they be in military science, in mathematics, or in medicine, and particularly so with examinations in philosophy, are always chosen from the senate of philosophy, nor is ever a military expert, a mathematician, or a medical doctor added to their number. The wisdom of those who excel in the profession of ethics is held in such high esteem that they would seem to be competent to express a proper judgment on any subject, though it be far afield from their own particular profession.

Study Questions

1. How is the Chinese system of education as described by Ricci influenced by Confucian thought?
2. What drawbacks are inherent in the Chinese educational system owing to its insularity, cultural exclusivity, and intellectual myopia?
3. How is the system designed to maintain the traditional Chinese world order?
4. What are the differences between the education of a man or a woman of the European upper classes and someone living in China who aspires to a position in the imperial bureaucracy?

Select Writings of Ku Yen-wu

Born in the final days of the Ming dynasty, the highly influential philosopher Ku Yen-wu (1613–1682) consistently displayed an interest in
practical matters such as economics and military defense. He also expressed concern for objective truth. Hoping to prevent the mistakes of
the past, Ku Yen-wu combined his varied interests and attempted to
find out why the ancient Ming dynasty had collapsed. In the course of
his research, Ku concluded that scholars such as himself must inves-
tigate practical subjects and return to the traditional ethical principles
of primitive Confucianism. One of the following selections is taken
from his most popular work, the "Record of Daily Knowledge." Ku in
fact influenced many generations of Confucian scholars with his attention to critical research and evaluation.

A Letter to a Friend Discussing the Pursuit of Learning

It is a matter of great regret to me that for the past hundred odd years, scholars
have devoted so much discussion to the mind and human nature, all of it vague
and quite incomprehensible. We know from the **Analects** that "fate and humanity
were things which **Confucius** seldom spoke of" and that **Tzu-Kung** "had never
heard him speak on man's nature and the way of Heaven." Though he mentioned
the principle of human nature and fate in the appendices to the **Book of Changes**,
he never discussed them with others. When asked about the qualities of a gentleman, Confucius said: "In his conduct he must have a sense of shame," while with
regard to learning he spoke of a "love of antiquity" and "diligent seeking," discussing and praising Yao and Shun and transmitting their tales to his disciples.
But he never said so much as a word about the so-called theory of "the precari-
ousness [of the human mind] and the subtlety [of the mind of the **Tao**] and of the
[need for keeping one's mind] refined and undivided," but only said "sincerely
hold fast to the **Mean**—if within the four seas there be distress and poverty, your
Heaven-conferred revenues will come to a perpetual end." Ah, this is the reason
for the learning of the sage. How simple, how easy to follow! . . .

W. T. de Bary et al., ed. *Sources of Chinese Tradition* (New York: Columbia University Press, 1960), vol.
1: 553–57. Copyright © 1960 Columbia University Press. Reprinted with permission of the publisher.

But gentlemen of today are not like this. They gather a hundred or so followers and disciples about them in their studies, and though as individuals they may be as different as grass and trees, they discourse with all of them on mind and nature. They set aside broad knowledge and concentrate upon the search for a single, all-inclusive method; they say not a word about the distress and poverty of the world within the four seas, but spend all their days lecturing on theories of "the weak and subtle," "the refined and the undivided." I can only conclude that their doctrine is more lofty than that of Confucius and their disciples wiser than Tzu-kung, and that while they pay honor to the school of [Confucius] they derive their teachings on the mind from the two sage emperors Yao and Shun. . . .

What then do I consider to be the way of the sage? I would say "extensively studying all learning" and "in your conduct having a sense of shame." Everything from your own body up to the whole nation should be a matter of study. In everything from your personal position as a son, a subject, a brother, and a friend to all your comings and goings, your giving and taking, you should have things of which you would be ashamed. This sense of shame before others is a vital matter. It does not mean being ashamed of your clothing or the food you eat, but ashamed that there should be a single humble man or woman who does not enjoy the blessings that are his due. This is why **Mencius** said that "all things are complete in me" if I "examine myself and find sincerity." Alas, if a scholar does not first define this sense of shame, he will have no basis as a person, and if he does not love antiquity and acquire broad knowledge, his learning will be vain and hollow. These baseless men with their hollow learning day after day pursue the affairs of the sage, and yet I perceive that with each day they only depart further from them.

The Record of Daily Knowledge

He who is called the Son of Heaven holds supreme authority in the world. What is the nature of this supreme authority? It is authority over all the world which is vested in the men of the world but which derives ultimately from the Son of Heaven. From the highest ministers and officials down to the regional magistrates and petty officers, each holds a share of this authority of the Son of Heaven and directs the affairs of his charge, and the authority of the Son of Heaven is thereby magnified in dignity. In later ages there appeared inept rulers who gathered all authority into their own hands. But the countless exigencies of government are so broad that it is quite impossible for one man to handle them all, so that authority then shifted to the laws. With this a great many laws were promulgated to prevent crimes and violation, so that even the greatest criminals could not get around them, nor the cleverest officials accomplish anything by evading them. People thereupon expended all their efforts in merely following the laws and trying to stay out of difficulty. Thus the authority of the Son of Heaven came to reside not in the officials appointed by the government but in their clerks and assistants (who were familiar with the laws). Now what the world needs most urgently are local officials who will personally look after the people, and yet today the men who possess least authority are precisely these local officials. If local officials are not made known to the higher authorities, how can we hope to achieve peace and prosperity and prolong the life of the nation? . . .

If we understand why the feudal system changed into the prefectural system, we will also understand that as the prefectural system in turn falls into decay it too must change. Does this mean that there will be a return to **feudalism**? No, this is impossible. But if some sage were to appear who could invest the prefectural system with the essential meaning of feudalism, then the world would attain order. . . . Today the prefectural system has reached a point of extreme decay, but no such sage appears and people go on doing everything in the same old way. Therefore with each day the people become poorer, China grows weaker, and we hasten down the road to ruin. Why is this? The fault of feudalism was its concentration of power on the local level, while the fault of the prefectural system is its concentration of power at the top. The sage-rulers of antiquity were impartial and public-minded in their treatment of all men, parceling out land to them and dividing up their domains. But now the ruler considers all the territory within the four seas to be his own prefecture, and is still unsatisfied. He suspects every person, he handles every affair that comes up, so that each day the directives and official documents pile higher than the day before. On top of this he sets up supervisors, provincial governors and governors-general, supposing that in this way he can keep the local officials from tyrannizing over and harming the people. He is unaware that these officials in charge are concerned only in moving with utmost caution so as to stay out of trouble until they have the good fortune to be relieved of their posts, and are quite unwilling to undertake anything of profit to the people. Under such circumstances how can the people avoid poverty and the nation escape debilitation? If this situation is allowed to continue unchanged, I am positive that it will lead only to chaos with trouble increasing day by day. If, however, the position of local officials is accorded its proper dignity, and such officials are granted fiscal and administrative authority, if the post of supervisor is discontinued, the enticement of hereditary office held out to officials, and a method whereby they may select their own subordinates put into effect, this will achieve the goal of imbuing the prefectural system with the essential meaning of feudalism, and the decay that has come about in the last two thousand years can be remedied. Rulers hereafter will find that if they hope to improve the livelihood of the people and strengthen the power of the nation, they must heed my words.

Study Questions

1. What methods of argumentation does Ku Yen-wu employ?
2. How successful is he in demonstrating his points of view?
3. Was Ku a revolutionary or reactionary thinker within the context of his times?
4. How does Ku view the traditional order of Chinese civilization, and how does he propose to solve the problems facing the Ming dynasty?

Reading 5

Yen Yüan's *Preservation of Human Nature*

As a young man, Yen Yüan (1635–1704) took up fencing and dabbled in the military arts. However, once he settled into serious academic study of **Wang Yang-ming**'s philosophical idealism and somewhat later the rationalism of **Chu Hsi** he gave up such frivolities. Yet, in reaction to the highly speculative **Neo-Confucianism** of the Ming era and to the westernizing tendencies promoted by Jesuit scholars such as Matteo Ricci, Manchu Confucians such as Ku Yen-wu and Yen Yüan turned instead to practical knowledge and objective truth. In *Corrections of Wrong Interpretations of the Four Books,* Yen Yüan exhibits a very modern perspective that in many respects mirrors John Locke's epistemology: the true source of knowledge is concrete things, and therein knowledge and action are united. Still, Yen Yüan remained faithful to the philosophical tradition of **Confucius** and **Mencius** as is seen in his *Preservation of Human Nature,* where he argues against the Neo-Confucian view that physical nature is a source of evil. Always living on the verge of poverty until he was invited to be the director of an academy, Yen Yüan finally had the opportunity to put his theory of pragmatic learning into practice.

Master **Ch'eng [Hao]** said that in discussing human nature and material force, "It would be wrong to consider them as two." But he also said, "Due to the material force with which men are endowed, some become good from childhood and others become evil." Chu Hsi said, "As soon as there is the endowment by Heaven, there is the physical nature. They cannot be separated," but he also said, "Since there is this principle, why is there evil? What is called evil is due to material force." It is regrettable that although they were highly intelligent, they were unwittingly influenced and confused by the Buddhist doctrine of the **Six Robbers**, and said two different things in the same breath without realizing it. If we say that material force is evil, then principle is also evil, and if we say that principle is good, then material force is also good, for material force is that of principle and principle is that of material force. How can we say that principle is purely and simply good whereas material force is inclined to be evil?

Wing-Tsit Chan, trans. *A Source Book in Chinese Philosophy* (Princeton: Princeton University Press, 1963), 704–8. Copyright © 1963, renewed 1991 Princeton University Press. Reprinted with permission of Princeton University Press.

Take the eye, for example. Its socket, lid, and ball are its physical nature, whereas that which possesses vision and can perceive things is its nature. Shall we say that principle of vision sees only proper colors whereas the socket, lid, and ball see improper colors? I say that while this principle of vision is of course endowed by Heaven, the socket, lid, and ball are all endowed by Heaven. There is no need any more to distinguish which is the nature endowed by Heaven and which is physical nature. We should only say that Heaven endows man with the nature of his eyes. The fact that one can see through vision means that the nature of the eye is good. The act of seeing is due to the goodness of its feeling [which is the external expression of the nature]. Whether one sees distinctly or not and whether one sees far or not depends on the strength or weakness of its capacity. None of these can be spoken of as evil, for it is of course good to see distinctly and far, but to see near and indistinctly merely means that the goodness is not refined. How can we attribute any evil to them? It is only when vision is attracted and agitated by improper and evil colors which obstruct or becloud its clearness that there is evil vision, and only then can the term "evil" be applied. But is human nature to be blamed for the attraction and agitation? Or shall physical nature be blamed? If we blame physical nature, it surely means that the nature of the eye can be preserved only when the eye is eliminated. If this is not the Buddhist doctrine of Six Robbers, what is it? . . .

Originally Chu Hsi understood nature, but he was influenced by Buddhists and mixed up with the bad habits of people of the world. Had there been no doctrine of physical nature advocated by **Ch'eng I** and **Chang Tsai**, we would surely distinguish man's nature, feeling, and capacity, on the one hand, and attraction, obscuration, and bad influence, on the other, and the fact that man's nature, feeling, and capacity are all good and that evil originates later would be perfectly clear. But as these former scholars inaugurated this doctrine, they forthwith ascribed evil to physical nature as a concentration of the two material forces [of **yin** and **yang**] and the **Four Virtues**. How can we say that it is evil? Evil is due to attraction, obscuration, and bad influence. . . .

Scholars often compare human nature with water, material force with earth, and evil with turbidity. They regard physical nature, which is the loftiest, as the most honorable and the most useful endowment given to man by Heaven and Earth, as if it were a burden to his human nature. They did not realize that if there were no physical nature, to what will principle be attached? Furthermore, if physical nature were discarded, then human nature would become an empty principle without any function in the world. . . .

Master Ch'eng—using water as an analogy—said, "Although they differ in being clear or turbid, we cannot say that the turbid water ceases to be water." Does this not mean that although good and evil are different, it is incorrect to regard evil not as nature? Is this not precisely to regard evil as the property of physical nature? Let me ask: Is turbidity the physical nature of water? I am afraid that clearness and calmness are the physical nature of water and that what is turbid is a mixture with earth which is originally absent from the nature of water, just as human nature is subject to attraction, obscuration, and bad influence. Turbidity

33

may be of high or low degree, and may be of great or small quantity, just as attraction, obscuration, and bad influence may be heavy or light and deep or shallow. If it is said that turbidity is the physical nature of water, then it means that turbid water has physical nature but clear water is without it. How can that be? . . .

The nature of the ten thousand things is an endowment of principle, and their physical nature is a consolidation of material force. What is balanced is this principle and material force, what is unbalanced is also this principle and this material force, and what is mixed is none other than this principle and this material force. What is lofty and bright is this principle and this material force, and what is lowly and dark is also this principle and this material force. What is clear or sturdy is this principle and this material force, and what is turbid or slight is also this principle and this material force. The long and the short, the perfect and the imperfect, the penetrating and the obstructed, are none other than this principle and material force.

As to man, he is especially the purest of all things, one who "receives at birth the mean of Heaven and Earth [balanced material force]." The two material forces and the Four Virtues are man before his consolidation, and man is the two material forces and the Four Virtues after their consolidation. As the Four Virtues are preserved in man, they are humanity, righteousness, propriety, and wisdom. They are called the nature with reference to the internal existence of origination, flourish, advantage, and firmness. When externally manifested, they become commiseration, shame and dislike, deference and compliance, and the sense of right and wrong. These are called feelings with reference to the application of the Four Virtues to things. Capacity is that which manifests one's nature in feelings; it is the power of the Four Virtues. To say that feeling involves evil is to say that the Four Virtues before manifestation is not the same as the Four Virtues after manifestation. To say that capacity involves evil is to say that what is preserved is the Four Virtues but what can be aroused into action is not the Four Virtues. And to say that physical nature involves evil is to say that the principle of the Four Virtues may be called the Way of Heaven but the material force of the Four Virtues may not be so called. Alas! Is there in the world any material force without principle, or principle without material force? Are there principle and material force outside of yin and yang and the Four Virtues?

Study Questions

1. What criticisms does Yen Yüan level against earlier philosophers regarding the origin and existence of evil in the world?
2. What historical circumstances in seventeenth-century China influenced the development of Yen Yüan's thought?
3. According to Yen Yüan, what is the relationship between learning and practical experience?
4. How does he seek to maintain the status quo in Chinese intellectual circles?

Emperor Ch'ien Lung's Mandates to King George III of England

By the eighteenth century, Western merchants had made considerable headway in establishing trading centers among many of the world's ancient civilizations. At this time China was in fact a remarkably stable and prosperous nation governed by ancient traditions and a highly developed Confucian bureaucracy. When King George III of England (1738–1820) requested that diplomatic ties and commercial contacts be opened between the two countries, the Manchu emperor Ch'ien Lung (1735–1795) made it clear that "western barbarians" had little or nothing of value to offer the venerable Chinese Empire. The official letter issued to the king by Emperor Ch'ien Lung illustrates both the strengths and weaknesses of China in the period just prior to the nation's being overrun by Westerners, among whom were the British.

The Initial Mandate

You, O King, live beyond the confines of many seas, nevertheless, impelled by your humble desire to partake of the benefits of our civilization, you have dispatched a mission respectfully bearing your memorial. Your Envoy has crossed the seas and paid his respects at my Court on the anniversary of my birthday. To show your devotion, you have also sent offerings of your country's produce.

I have perused your memorial: the earnest terms in which it is couched reveal a respectful humility on your part, which is highly praiseworthy. In consideration of the fact that your Ambassador and his deputy have come a long way with your memorial and tribute, I have shown them high favor and have allowed them to be introduced into my presence. To manifest my indulgence, I have entertained them at a banquet and made them numerous gifts. I have also caused presents to be forwarded to the Naval Commander and six hundred of his officers and men, although they did not come to Peking, so that they too may share in my all-embracing kindness.

E. Backhouse and J. O. P. Bland, *Annals and Memoirs of the Court of Peking* (Boston: Houghton Mifflin, 1914), passim.

As to your entreaty to send one of your nationals to be accredited to my Celestial Court and to be in control of your country's trade with China, this request is contrary to all usage of my dynasty and cannot possibly be entertained. It is true that Europeans, in the service of the dynasty, have been permitted to live at Peking, but they are compelled to adopt Chinese dress, they are strictly confined to their own precincts and are never permitted to return home. You are presumably familiar with our dynastic regulations. Your proposed Envoy to my Court could not be placed in a position similar to that of European officials in Peking who are forbidden to leave China, nor could he, on the other hand, be allowed liberty of movement and the privilege of corresponding with his own country; so that you would gain nothing by his residence in our midst.

Moreover, our Celestial dynasty possesses vast territories, and tribute missions from the dependencies are provided for by the Department for Tributary States, which ministers to their wants and exercises strict control over their movements. It would be quite impossible to leave them to their own devices. . . .

Swaying the wide world, I have but one aim in view, namely, to maintain a perfect governance and to fulfil the duties of the State: strange and costly objects do not interest me. If I have commanded that the tribute offerings sent by you, O King, are to be accepted, this was solely in consideration for the spirit which prompted you to dispatch them from afar. Our dynasty's majestic virtue has penetrated unto every country under Heaven, and Kings of all nations have offered their costly tribute by land and sea. As your Ambassador can see for himself, we possess all things. I set no value on objects strange or ingenious, and have no use for your country's manufactures. This then is my answer to your request to appoint a representative at my Court, a request contrary to our dynastic usage, which would only result in inconvenience to yourself. I have expounded my wishes in detail and have commanded your tribute Envoys to leave in peace on their homeward journey. It behooves you, O King, to respect my sentiments and to display even greater devotion and loyalty in future, so that, by perpetual submission to our Throne, you may secure peace and prosperity for your country hereafter. Besides making gifts (of which I enclose an inventory) to each member of your Mission, I confer upon you, O King, valuable presents in excess of the number usually bestowed on such occasions, including silks and curios—a list of which is likewise enclosed. Do you reverently receive them and take note of my tender goodwill towards you! A special mandate.

Another Mandate

You, O King, from afar have yearned after the blessings of our civilization, and in your eagerness to come into touch with our converting influence have sent an Embassy across the sea bearing a memorial. I have already taken note of your respectful spirit of submission, have treated your mission with extreme favor and loaded it with gifts, besides issuing a mandate to you, O King, and honoring you with the bestowal of valuable presents. Thus has my indulgence been manifested.

Yesterday your Ambassador petitioned my Ministers to memorialize me regarding your trade with China, but his proposal is not consistent with our dynastic usage and cannot be entertained. Hitherto, all European nations, including your own country's barbarian merchants, have carried on their trade with our Celestial Empire at Canton. Such has been the procedure for many years, although our Celestial Empire possesses all things in prolific abundance and lacks no product within its own borders. There was therefore no need to import the manufactures of outside barbarians in exchange for our own produce. But as the tea, silk and porcelain which the Celestial Empire produces, are absolute necessities to European nations and to yourselves, we have permitted, as a signal mark of favor, that foreign hongs should be established at Canton, so that your wants might be supplied and your country thus participate in our beneficence. But your Ambassador has now put forward new requests which completely fail to recognize the Throne's principle to "treat strangers from afar with indulgence," and to exercise a pacifying control over barbarian tribes, the world over. Moreover, our dynasty, swaying the myriad races of the globe, extends the same benevolence towards all. Your England is not the only nation trading at Canton. If other nations, following your bad example, wrongfully importune my ear with further impossible requests, how will it be possible for me to treat them with easy indulgence? Nevertheless, I do not forget the lonely remoteness of your island, cut off from the world by intervening wastes of sea, nor do I overlook your excusable ignorance of the usages of our Celestial Empire. I have consequently commanded my Ministers to enlighten your Ambassador on the subject, and have ordered the departure of the mission. But I have doubts that, after your Envoy's return he may fail to acquaint you with my view in detail or that he may be lacking in lucidity, so that I shall now proceed . . . to issue my mandate on each question separately. In this way you will, I trust, comprehend my meaning. . . .

The next request, for a small site in the vicinity of Canton city, where your barbarian merchants may lodge or, alternatively, that there be no longer any restrictions over their movements at Aomen, has arisen from the following causes. Hitherto, the barbarian merchants of Europe have had definite locality assigned to them at Aomen for residence and trade, and have been forbidden to encroach an inch beyond the limits assigned to that locality. . . . If these restrictions were withdrawn, friction would inevitably occur between the Chinese and your barbarian subjects, and the results would militate against the benevolent regard that I feel towards you. From every point of view, therefore, it is best that the regulations now in force should continue unchanged. . . .

Regarding your nation's worship of the Lord of Heaven, it is the same religion as that of other European nations. Ever since the beginning of history, sage Emperors and wise rulers have bestowed on China a moral system and inculcated a code, which from time immemorial has been religiously observed by the myriads of my subjects. There has been no hankering after heterodox doctrines. Even the European [missionary] officials in my capital are forbidden to hold intercourse with Chinese subjects; they are restricted within the limits of their appointed residences, and may not go about propagating their religion. The distinction between Chinese and barbarian is most strict, and your Ambassador's request that barbarians shall be given full liberty to disseminate their religion is utterly unreasonable.

It may be, King, that the above proposals have been wantonly made by your Ambassador on his own responsibility, or peradventure you yourself are ignorant of our dynastic regulations and had no intention of transgressing them when you expressed these wild ideas and hopes. . . . If after the receipt of this explicit decree, you lightly give ear to the representations of your subordinates and allow your barbarian merchants to proceed to Chekiang and Tientsin, with the object of landing and trading there, the ordinances of my Celestial Empire are strict in the extreme, and the local officials, both civil and military, are bound reverently to obey the law of the land. Should your vessels touch the shore, your merchants will assuredly never be permitted to land or to reside there, but will be subject to instant expulsion. In that event your barbarian merchants will have had a long journey for nothing. Do not say that you were not warned in due time! Tremblingly obey and show no negligence!

Study Questions

1. What is the Chinese emperor's attitude concerning the status of the Celestial Empire throughout the world?
2. Why does the emperor reject the British proposals?
3. What can be ascertained from the documents about Britain's objectives and plans in China?
4. How did the Chinese adapt to changing circumstances resulting from European expansion?

Shen Chou's Poet on a Mountain

From ancient Shang bronze ritual vessels to the flurry ink technique of Ch'an painters, many Chinese objects of art express the merging of the artist's personality with the universe. The vitality of Chinese visual arts depended in great measure on imperial and aristocratic patronage. Throughout the centuries a class of professional artists was created. This was especially true of painters, among whom may be counted many talented emperors. Amateurs, mainly from the upper class literati, also flourished. These individuals had leisure time to pursue their artistic desires. Founder of the Wu School of painting, Shen Chou (1427–1509) rejected a career in public service to spend a quiet, detached life painting mostly landscapes. A highly influential and prolific artist, Shen's "Poet on a Mountain" uses the broad brush style to merge the human figure and buildings with the natural environment. The artist seeks a harmony with nature in accordance with teachings of the main schools of Chinese religion and philosophy. He represents the affinity of nature and humanity and idealizes the solitary poet as something separate from, yet in harmony with, nature.

Reading 7

Tokugawa Edicts of the Seventeenth Century

Among the first Westerners to reach the shores of Japan were Christian missionaries, one of whom, **Francis Xavier**, arrived in Japan in 1549. The remarkable advances made by the missionaries prompted considerable concern among the Tokugawa clan. In 1635 Iemitsu (1604–1651), who ruled as **shogun** from 1623 to 1651, issued the Closed Country Edict and later promulgated the Exclusion of the Portuguese Edict, both of which effectively isolated the country from Western influences. With the establishment of the Tokugawa Shogunate in the early seventeenth century, Japan entered a long period of political stability. This was partly the result of the shogunate's rigorous policy of preventing foreigners from entering and hence influencing Japanese internal affairs.

Closed Country Edict (dated 1635)

1. Japanese ships shall by no means be sent abroad.
2. No Japanese shall be sent abroad. Anyone violating this prohibition shall suffer the penalty of death, and the ship owner and crew shall be held up together with the ship.
3. All Japanese residing abroad shall be put to death when they return home.
4. All Christians shall be examined by official examiners.
5. Informers against Christians shall be rewarded.
6. The arrival of foreign ships must be reported to **Edo,** and watch kept over them.
7. [**Southern barbarians**] and any other people with evil titles propagating Christianity shall be incarcerated in the **Omura** prison as before.
8. Even ships shall not be left untouched in the matter of exterminating Christians.
9. Everything shall be done in order to see that no Christian is survived by descendants, and anyone disregarding this injunctions shall be put to death,

---

Yosoburo Takekoshi, *The Economic Aspects of the History of the Civilization of Japan* (London: George Allen & Unwin Ltd., 1930), vol. 2: 128–29. Reprinted with permission of Routledge Chapman & Hall.

while proper punishment shall be meted out to the other members of his family according to their deeds.

10. Children born of the [Southern barbarians] in Nagasaki and people adopting these Nanban children into their family shall be put to death; capital punishment shall also be meted out to those Namban descendants if they return to Japan, and their relatives in Japan, who may communicate with them, shall receive suitable punishment.

11. The **Samurai** shall not purchase goods on board foreign ships directly from foreigners.

12. The white yarns (raw silk) sent on foreign ships shall be allotted to the five privileged cities and other quarters as stipulated after establishing their prices.

13. After the settling of the price of raw silk, the sale of any goods other than raw silk may be freely carried on between the dealers concerned. It is to be added that, as Chinese ships are small and cannot, therefore, bring large consignments, the authorities may issue orders for sale at their discretion. The delivery of goods other than raw silk shall be effected within twenty days after the settling of their prices.

14. The date of departure homeward of foreign ships shall not be later than September 20th. Any ships arriving in Japan later than usual shall sail for home within fifty days after their arrival. No date is fixed for departure of Chinese ships. They shall be caused to set sail a little later than Portuguese or Spanish ships at the discretion of the authorities concerned.

15. Foreign ships shall take back with them all they are unable to sell of their cargo.

16. The arrival in Nagasaki of representatives of the five cities (representatives of the privileged silk merchants of Kyoto, Sakai, Edo, Nagasaki, and Osaka) shall not be later than July 5th. Any of them arriving at the destination later than this date shall lose the privilege of the sale of raw silk.

17. Ships arriving at Hirado shall not transact business pending the establishment of prices at Nagasaki.

Exclusion of the Portuguese Edict (dated 1639)

1. The matter relating to the proscription of Christianity is known [to the Portuguese]. However, heretofore they have secretly transported those who are going to propagate that religion.

2. If those who believe in that religion band together in an attempt to do evil things, they must be subjected to punishment.

David John Lu, ed. and trans., *Source of Japanese History* (New York: McGraw-Hill, 1974), 208–9. Copyright © 1974 McGraw-Hill. Reprinted with permission of the publisher.

3. While those who believe in the preaching of Christian priests are in hiding, there are incidents in which that country [Portugal] has sent gifts to them for their sustenance.

In view of the above, hereafter entry by the Portuguese galleon is forbidden. If they insist on coming [to Japan], the ships must be destroyed and anyone aboard those ships must be beheaded. We have received the above order and are thus transmitting it to you accordingly.

The above concerns our disposition with regard to the galleon.

Attached Memorandum

With regard to those who believe in Christianity, you are aware that there is a proscription, and thus knowing, you are not permitted to let Christian priests and those who believe in their preaching to come aboard your ships. If there is any violation, all of you who are aboard will be considered culpable. If there is anyone who hides the fact that he is a Christian and boards your ship, you may report it to us. A substantial reward will be given to you for this information.

This memorandum is to be given to those who come on Chinese [or Dutch] ships.

Study Questions

1. What contemporary circumstances caused the Tokugawa Shogunate to issue the edicts of 1635 and 1639?
2. Why were Japanese authorities initially receptive to the Christian missionaries and their message, but why by the late 1630s did the shogunate turn vehemently against them?
3. What effects did edicts such as these have on the course of Japanese cultural and political development in the late seventeenth through early nineteenth centuries?
4. What do the edicts reflect about the contemporary Japanese view of themselves and the foreigners they sought to exclude from their country?

Miura Baien's Letter to Asada Goryu

A village physician disparaged over being employed by feudal lords, Miura Baien (1723–1789) achieved wide acclaim as an advocate of the new rationalism permeating Japanese intellectual circles in the eighteenth century. A thoughtful, resourceful—if not terribly prolific— writer, Miura Baien wrote his *Discourse on Metaphysics* with an eye to educating the public, but he could not find a commercial publisher. After its thirtieth revision, his poor neighbors got together and collected enough money to have it published privately. His other significant work, *The Origin of Price,* gained considerable popularity in the West, where it was justly compared to *The Wealth of Nations* written by his contemporary Adam Smith. Unfortunately for his admirers, one year after Miura's death the shogunal premier **Matsudaira Sadanobu** issued the notorious Act of Prohibition. This ordinance severely limited public access to the works of Miura and other writers because they did not hold true to the traditional Confucianism espoused by the Chinese philosopher **Chu Hsi**. In a letter to his friend Asada Goryu (1734–1799), a renowned mathematician and astronomer of his time, Miura describes the conceptual basis of his own worldview.

From the pavilion the evening haze could be seen floating between the azure sky and blue water. The sun was gradually setting, its golden hue changing into crimson, while its evanescent glory was cast upon the clouds and reflected in the waves. Suddenly a breeze blew up out of the duckweed and vanished into the pine grove yonder; it sounded like a passing shower or like a phoenix calling to its mate.

At home, my head against a pillow, I thought of the scene that had stirred me with joy and wonder. It was made up of real things, true enough, but it was at the same time far from being real. And I thought of the sayings of those philosophers and scholars whose writings are so bulky that oxen perspire pulling them and libraries are full to overflowing with them. Are they not inspired by so many evening scenes from pavilions which aroused and delighted the senses of these philosophers? We know that sake, su, moro, and amasake are all made of rice. They are not brewed by the rice itself, but in each case the nature of rice is adapted to suit the taste and flavor [the brewer has] in mind.

W. T. de Bary, ed., *Sources of Japanese Tradition,* trans. Ryusaku Tsunoda et al. (New York: Columbia University Press, 1958), vol. 1: 495–97. Copyright © 1958 Columbia University Press. Reprinted with permission of the publisher.

The Chinese sages were sovereigns in antiquity who ruled the people well. The **Buddha** was a recluse who was adept at mind-control. So, the Classics of the sages contained the principles for ruling men and the Buddhist scriptures revealed the secret of controlling the mind. One derived from a concern for the world of men, which was going from bad to worse, and the other from compassion for the masses who were drowning themselves in passion. Out of a feeling of paternal solicitude they sought to save the people of their time from plunging to self-destruction. The ancient Chinese did use crystal orbs and jade measures for astronomical observation, it is true, but the purpose was only to give a calendar to the people. The **Bhajana-loka** was referred to by the Buddhists, but it was no more than their own mental creation. There were other schoolmen who also touched upon the problem [of the natural world] incidentally, but put it aside as a vague and remote problem, not an important one. Though occasionally skeptics have appeared, they have eventually become entangled in traditional notions; captives in the human prison, they have not penetrated into the heart of things.

Now the universe shelters all things in it, and man is just one of those things. As all things come into existence, they are provided with innumerable distinct natures. Though afforded the same means, children cannot be just like their parents; fire cannot be like water. The landlord (nature) provides what the tenant (man) occupies, but the landlord is not the tenant, and the tenant is not the landlord, each being different in character and capacity. . . . To know the world of Heaven (nature), therefore, man must put his own interests aside and enter into the world of objects; only in that way can his intellect hope to comprehend Heaven-and-earth and understand all things. All beings exist together with us, and we are just one of them. Realization that Heaven is universal, while man is individual, must be the starting point for all discussion of humanity. This is what I call opening the windows of the human sphere. The reason men have remained in the dark about the universe is that, remaining fixed in the human sphere, they have considered their own position to be of the highest dignity and their own intellect to be the most exalted. To view Heaven-and-earth in this way, or to study creation and its manifold objects with this attitude, is exactly the same as the brewers of sake, su, moro, and amasake who consider rice only in terms of taste and flavor.

In the comprehension of the universe, knowledge is most important. But as long as students approach creation without opening the windows of the human sphere, and persist in keeping a smug sense of their own importance and intelligence, their approach is certain to give rise to delusions, as a mote in the eye casts a shadow on what one sees. Concern for the world and compassion for the masses is benevolent in motive, but the study of creation in human terms is not conducive to true knowledge. Those whom the world acclaims as leaders in thought and action take humanity and human motives as the basis of their thinking and speculation in order to set up standards for what is to be believed and done. But human minds are like human faces; their preferences differ one from another. Each considers what he has arrived at to be right, a revelation from Heaven or a deposit of truth from antiquity, and thinks those who do not accept his standards should be exterminated. It is my conviction, therefore, that there is no systematic truth or logic except that which enables man to comprehend the universe without setting up standards conceived in terms of humanity or human motives. . . .

In a letter you wrote me last year, you said something to the effect that in the observation of an object, one's mind must be unfettered. If the mind is in bondage, it will drag the object into the confines of its own prejudices. Your friendly solicitude was so sincere that I was most profoundly moved. But I have an explanation for this in terms of my own method for understanding the logic of things. Suppose that a thesis is available, but not its antithesis. At least for a while something will have to be hypothesized for it. If that is found unsatisfactory, then something else will have to be hypothesized; if it fails again, still another thing must be hypothesized. Thus one hypothesis after another will be tried till at long last true accord is reached. It is just as in the case of a circle; if its true antithesis, a straight line, is not hit upon, a square will be used until the time comes when a straight line is finally hit upon. Or as in the case of the sun: if its true antithesis, shadow, is not hit upon, the moon will be tried as a hypothesis, until at last shadow is hit upon. The logic of things has never been studied before, and my lone efforts for fifty years have not sufficed to arrive at finding the true antithesis in every case. So in my *Discourse on Metaphysics* the true and the hypothetical will be found side by side. You will do me a great favor indeed by bringing the critical powers of your brilliant mind to bear on this book.

Study Questions

1. What is Miura's attitude toward the so-called philosophic and religious classics of Japanese culture?
2. Why was it in the interests of the shogun to limit people's access to works produced by Miura and other thinkers like him?
3. In what way is Miura influenced by Western science and rational philosophy?
4. How would the author's humanist perspective upset the traditional intellectual and political order of Japan?

Reading 9

Motoori Norinaga's *Arrowroot*

In the eighteenth century, the Japanese experienced a revival of **Shinto**, their native religious tradition. For despite the importation of Buddhism and Confucianism, Shinto never died out, especially among the common people. It did, however, lack intellectual vitality and substance. Indeed, the Shinto revival needs to be placed against the backdrop of **Neo-Confucianism** that served as the intellectual mainstay of the Tokugawa Shogunate. Motoori Norinaga (1730–1801) was one of the greatest leaders of the Shinto revival and for more than thirty years worked to promote a native renaissance of traditional literature and art. Motoori went so far as to suggest that foreign doctrines were subversive, and mere speculations, and contrivances, made to appeal to human credulity. In *Arrowroot* the author, rejecting the rationalistic cosmogony imported from China, details the traditional account of divine creation and also explains that human reason cannot adequately comprehend the various manifestations of the divine.

Objection: You are obstinate in insisting that the **Sun Goddess** is the sun in heaven. If this is so, perpetual darkness must have reigned everywhere before her birth. The sun must have been in heaven since the beginning of the universe [before the birth of the Goddess].

Motoori: First of all, I cannot understand why you say that I am obstinate. That the Sun Goddess is the sun in heaven is clear from the records of the **Kojiki** and the **Nihongi**. If it is so beyond any doubt, is not the person who raises an objection the one who is obstinate? This Sun Goddess casts her light to the very extremities of the universe, but in the beginning it was in our Imperial Land that she made her appearance, and as the sovereign of the Imperial Line, that is, of the Imperial Land, she has reigned supreme over the Four Seas until now. When this Goddess hid herself in a cave in heaven, closing its doors, darkness fell over the countries of the world. You ask why darkness did not reign everywhere before her birth, a question a child might well ask. It seems childish indeed when a question which might spring from the doubts of a child is asked with such insistence by you. But this very point proves that the ancient happenings of the Divine Age are

W. T. de Bary, ed., *Sources of Japanese Tradition,* trans. Ryusaku Tsunoda et al. (New York: Columbia University Press, 1958), 524–29. Copyright © 1958 Columbia University Press. Reprinted with permission of the publisher.

facts and not fabrications. Some say that the records are the fabrication of later sovereigns, but who would fabricate such shallow sounding, incredible things? This is a point you should reflect upon seriously.

The acts of the gods cannot be measured by ordinary human reasoning. Man's intellect, however wise, has its limits. It is small, and what is beyond its confines it cannot know. The acts of the gods are straightforward. That they appear to be shallow and untrue is due to the limitation of what man can know. To the human mind these acts appear to be remote, inaccessible, and difficult of comprehension and belief. Chinese teachings, on the other hand, were established within the reach of human intelligence; thus, to the mind of the listener, they are familiar and intimate and easy of comprehension and belief. The Chinese, because they believe that the wisdom of the Sage [Confucius] was capable of comprehending all the truths of the universe and of its phenomena, pretend to the wisdom of the Sage and insist, despite their small and limited minds, that they know what their minds are really incapable of knowing. But at the same time they refuse to believe in the inscrutability of the truth, for this, they conclude, is irrational. This sounds clever, but on the contrary, it betrays the pettiness of their intelligence. If my objector would rid himself of such a habit and reflect seriously, such a doubt as he has just expressed would disappear of itself.

It will be recalled that when **Izanagi** made his way to the nether region, he carried a light because of the darkness there, but while he lived in the actual world, he did not. The nether world is dark because it has to be dark; the actual world is clear because it has to be clear. Thus, there was light in the actual world before the birth of the Sun Goddess, although the reason why it is so cannot be fathomed. In the commentaries on the Nihongi there are references to luminous human beings of the days of creation who cast light about them, but these references were derived from the Buddhist scriptures. There is also mention of a deity of firefly light, but this was an evil deity, and his case cannot be taken as a typical one. There are otherwise no traditions about deities of light, and thus we have no way of knowing what light there was for illumination. But presumably there was light for reasons beyond the reach of human intelligence. Why then did darkness prevail when the Sun Goddess hid herself behind the door of the rocky cave? It was because it had been determined that with the birth of the Sun Goddess the whole space of the universe should come without her illumination. This is the same sort of inscrutable truth as the case of the descent of the Imperial Grandchild from Heaven after which communication between Heaven and earth was completely severed. There are many other strange and inscrutable happenings in the Divine Age, which should be accepted in the same way. The people of antiquity never attempted to reason out the acts of the gods with their own intelligence, but the people of a later age, influenced by the Chinese, have become addicts of rationalism. Such people appear wise, but in reality are quite foolish in their suspicion and skepticism about the strange happenings of the Divine Age which are quite different from the happenings of the human age. The fact is that even the things of the human age are, in reality, strange and wondrous, but because we are accustomed to their present form and have always lived in their midst, we cease to be aware of their wondrous quality. Consider, for example, how this universe goes on. Is the earth suspended in the sky or attached to something else? In either instance it is a wondrous thing. Suppose it is attached to something else, what is there under it to support it? This is something which cannot be understood. Thus in China, although there are many theories, they all end in wonder. Among them is a theory called the global theory which says that the earth is round and that it is enveloped in space and hangs in the sky. It sounds most plausible but ordinary reasoning tells us that despite the fullness of the ether in the sky this land and the great oceans cannot remain suspended and motionless in the sky. Thus, this theory too is nothing more than an expression of wonderment. Another theory says that space consists of ether only and that it has no form of its own. This too sounds plausible, but if ether fills the outer space, is there a limit to its extension or not? If it has no limit there is no way of determining its circumference or its center or where in it the earth is situated. The earth cannot stop except at the dead center of space. If, on the other hand, the extension of ether is limited, then it must assume the shape of a ball, raising the question about the definite point around which it condenses itself. Then again, what is there to cause it to condense? Thus we see that this theory too is an expression of the strange and the wondrous.

Man, living in such a strange and wondrous universe, wonders not about its mysteries but only about the wonders of the Divine Age, saying there is no reason for them. If this is not senseless, what is?

Consider also the human body: it has eyes to see, ears to hear, a mouth to speak, feet to walk, and hands to do a thousand things. Are they not truly wonderful? Birds and insects fly in the sky, plants and trees bloom and bear fruit—they are all wonderful. When insentient beings change into sentient beings such as birds and insects, or when foxes and badgers take on human form—are these not the strangest of all strange things? Thus, the universe and all things therein are without a single exception strange and wondrous when examined carefully. Even the Sage would be incapable of explaining these phenomena. Thus, one must acknowledge that human intelligence is limited and puny while the acts of the gods are illimitable and wondrous. But it is indeed amusing that there are people who respect and believe in this Sage as one who had illuminated every truth of the universe and its phenomena, when in fact he explained only those things within the boundaries of his own intelligence.

The beginnings of such a vastly wondrous universe and all its phenomena must be even more wonderful. The Chinese explain it in terms of **yin** and **yang**, but they have failed to explain why yin and yang operate in such a manner—which only adds to the wonder of the beginnings of the universe. Or one might say that the universe had no beginning, just as it will have no end; but if things existed which had no beginning, it would be even more strange and wondrous. If my objector would reflect upon the above things, his doubts would disappear of themselves. If his doubts are still insoluble, I shall cite examples nearer to him. Mice and martens can see in darkness as well as in broad daylight. By what manner of light do they see? There are also birds which see things well at night but cannot see them in daylight. Such things cannot be explained by the usual reasoning. The objector has said that there was no reason for light to exist in the Divine Age, but can he say that there was a reason for such light not to exist? What is your answer? Even in the case of lowly birds and animals there is a reason beyond reason. Is there any need to say more about our imperial forebears at the beginning of the universe? . . .

Objection: The scholar [Motoori] treats this country as if it were different from other countries.

Motoori: The objector also says at the end of the book that I want "to put our country outside the universe." I cannot understand what he means, but I surmise from what he says before and after that he criticizes me for my statement that the Sun Goddess, who's the sun in heaven, was born in our country. . . .

I shall not reiterate here the details of the theory that the Sun Goddess is the sun in heaven and that she was born in our land. But because of the absence of the correct transmission of this fact in foreign lands, men there do not know about the genesis of the sun and the moon. They had a theory [in China] that the sun and the moon were the eyes of **P'an Ku**, which is a remnant of the true ancient tradition, but in China, where everyone is addicted to sophistry, such an interpretation was regarded as fantastic, and it was discarded. Instead, the sun and the moon were declared to be, on pure personal conjecture, the spirits of yin and yang. The theory of P'an Ku's eyes is an instance of the transmission to and modification in a foreign country of the tradition that the Sun Goddess was born of the ablution of Izanagi's eyes. It is only a fragmentary survival, but it is superior to any conjectural theory.

Leaving aside for the moment the question as to which is superior, let us first make a distinction between the Chinese and the Japanese views. From the Chinese point of view, the Japanese view is wrong, and from the Japanese point of view, the Chinese view is wrong. But the objector advances only the Chinese view and attempts to universalize it, even denying the antiquity of our Imperial Land. Is this not prejudiced and arbitrary? To this he might reply that the universe is one, that there is no distinction between a Chinese and Japanese point of view, and that narrow partiality lies in attempting to make such distinctions. However, the objector, in advancing only the Chinese view and casting doubt on the antiquity of our Imperial Land, himself makes such a distinction and shows partiality to China. . . . Even if there were no distinctions among the countries, it would still be proper for the various countries of the world, each with its own traditions. Our Imperial Land in particular is superior to the rest of the world in its possession of the correct transmission of the ancient Way, which is that of the great Goddess who casts her light all over the world. It is treasonable malice to urge that we discard that transmission in favor of a senseless foreign view which, moreover, insists that our ancient transmission is a fantasy and a fabrication. . . .

Then again, his assertion that I represent the sun as something different from the sun of other countries is a ridiculous statement. How can the sun be different in other countries if I say that the Sun Goddess was born in our country and shines over all other countries? . . . Again, he says that the gods in Heaven regard all things equally and bestow their blessings impartially on them all. That is quite so, and yet our Imperial Land is the land where the Sky-Shining Goddess was born and where her descendants reign supreme; thus, it is superior to all other countries and cannot be regarded as the same.

Objection: The Sage, Confucius, has been looked up to as Heaven itself by tens of millions of people.

Motoori: This fact demonstrates that the Chinese, dynasty after dynasty, have been deceived by the Sage, who really does not deserve such credit. If adoration by the many is the mark of superiority, then it must be said that **Shinran**, the founder of the **Ikko Sect,** is superior to the Sage, for the present-day followers of the Ikko Sect revere their founder far more deeply than Confucians adore Confucius. . . .

Sages are superior to other people only in their cleverness. The fact is that they were all impostors. Among them the least blameworthy was Confucius. He was respectful of the Chou dynasty, for he was born in the Chou. That he deplored the impositions and irregularities of the feudal lords is a thing deserving of praise. But **Mencius**, whom the Confucianists revere as a sage in the same class with Confucius, was quite different. While professing the kingly way, he encouraged revolt wherever he went. He was no less evil person than **T'ang** and **Wu**. . . .

Study Questions

1. How does the author use Shinto mythology to discredit the rationalistic teachings of Confucius and Japanese Neo-Confucianism?
2. What methods of reasoning does Motoori employ to confirm his views?
3. How does Motoori support his conviction that Japanese civilization is superior to all others?
4. What is the author's idea of cosmic order and according to him what is the status of the Japanese people in the world?

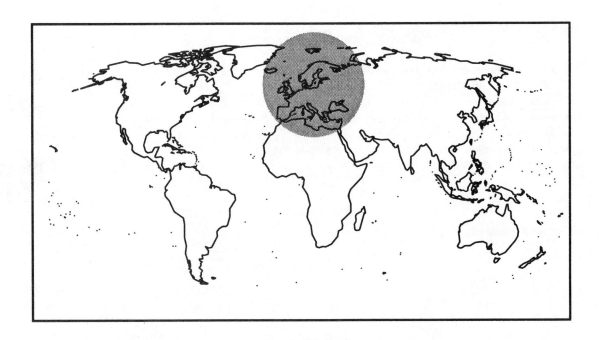

Brief Chronology for the Early Modern World
West Eurasia

1350–1550	Italian Renaissance
1394–1460	Prince Henry the Navigator of Portugal
1434	Medici begin to dominate politics in Florence, Italy
1455–1483	English War of the Roses
1483–1603	Tudor kings and queens in England (Henry VIII, 1509–1547; Elizabeth I, 1558–1603)
1487	Bartholomew Dias rounds the Cape of Good Hope
1492	Columbus's first voyage to the New World
1517	Martin Luther posts "Ninety-five Theses" and begins the Protestant Reformation
1542–1563	Council of Trent and the reform of Catholic church
1540–1700	Scientific Revolution
1555	Division of Habsburg Empire between Spanish and Austrian branches
1562–1598	French Wars of Religion
1589–1792	Bourbon monarchy in France (Louis XIV, 1643–1715; Louis XVI, 1774–1792)
1618–1648	Thirty Years' War
1642–1649	English Civil War
1653–1660	Cromwellian Protectorate in England
1660	Restoration of monarchy in England
1682–1725	Reign of Peter the Great in Russia
1687	Publication of Sir Isaac Newton's *Principia Mathematica*
1701	Rise of Kingdom of Prussia (Frederick I, 1701–1713; Frederick William I, 1713–1740; Frederick II, 1740–1786)
1701–1713	War of the Spanish Succession between England and France
1713	Treaty of Utrecht
1730–1790	The Enlightenment
1750	Industrial Revolution begins in England
1756–1763	Seven Years' War
1762–1796	Reign of Catherine the Great of Russia
1783	Treaty of Paris
1789	Outbreak of the French Revolution

All dates are C.E. and approximate unless otherwise indicated. It should be noted as well that chronologies are constantly being revised. Hence, there may be discrepancies between the dates listed above and those found in other textbooks and scholarly monographs. Throughout the text and in the Glossary, all dates are given in B.C.E. (Before the Common Era) and C.E. (the Common Era). Where there is no era designation C.E. may be assumed.

Machiavelli's *The Prince*

After the expulsion of the powerful **d'Medici** family in 1494, Niccolò Machiavelli (1469–1527) served in the new republican government of Florence. When the Medici returned to power, Machiavelli was exiled from his native city. It was then that he wrote *The Prince,* the treatise on which his popular reputation now rests. It is far from being his best work, but it does contain his revolutionary ideas on the relationship between morals and politics. Machiavelli rejected the medieval notion of the "virtuous Christian prince," and instead postulated that a ruler must not really consider whether his actions are virtuous or vicious. Furthermore, prior to Machiavelli the prevailing view held that the task of good government was the distribution and maintenance of justice. Conversely, Machiavelli believed that societies thrived when they were allowed to grow and expand. Hence, the use of force was considered an important, essential element in national and international politics. Machiavelli's works inaugurated a new stage in the development of Western political thought, a stage that viewed politics in terms of history and psychology rather than morality and justice. In his final years, Machiavelli was allowed to return to Florence and was commissioned by the Medici family to write his *History of Florence.*

Chapter Fifteen: Of the Qualities in Respect of Which Men, and Most of All Princes, Are Praised or Blamed

It now remains for us to consider what ought to be the conduct and bearing of a Prince in relation to his subjects and friends. And since I know that many have written on this subject, I fear it may be thought presumptuous of me to write of it also; the more so, because in my treatment of it I depart from the views that others have taken.

But since it is my object to write what shall be useful to whosoever understands it, it seems to me better to follow the real truth of things than an imaginary view of them. For many republics and Princedoms have been imagined that

Niccolo Machiavelli, *The Prince,* ed. Charles W. Eliot, The Harvard Classics (New York: P. F. Collier & Son, 1910), 53–54, 59–62, 83–86, passim.

were never seen or known to exist in reality. And the manner in which we live, and that in which we ought to live, are things so wide asunder, that he who quits the one to betake himself to the other is more likely to destroy than to save himself; since any one who would act up to a perfect standard of goodness in everything, must be ruined among so many who are not good. It is essential, therefore, for a Prince who desires to maintain his position, to have learned how to be other than good, and to use or not to use his goodness as necessity requires.

Laying aside, therefore, all fanciful notions concerning a Prince, and considering those only that are true, I say that all men when they are spoken of, and Princes more than others from their being set so high, are characterized by some one of those qualities which attach either praise or blame. Thus one is accounted liberal, another miserly (which word I use, rather than avaricious, to denote the man who is too sparing of what is his own, avarice being the disposition to take wrongfully what is another's); one is generous, another greedy; one cruel, another tender-hearted; one is faithless, another true to his word; one effeminate and cowardly, another haughty; one impure, another chaste; one simple, another crafty; one firm, another facile; one grave, another frivolous; one devout, another unbelieving; and the like. Every one, I know, will admit that it would be most laudable for a Prince to be endowed with all of the above qualities that are reckoned good; but since it is impossible for him to possess or constantly practice them all, the conditions of human nature not allowing it, he must be discreet enough to know how to avoid the infamy of those vices that would deprive him of his government, and, if possible, be on his guard also against those which might not deprive him of it; though if he cannot wholly restrain himself, he may with less scruple indulge in the latter. He need never hesitate, however, to incur the reproach of those vices without which his authority can hardly be preserved; for if he well considers the whole matter, he will find that there may be a line of conduct having the appearance of virtue, to follow which would be his ruin, and that there may be another course having the appearance of vice, by following which his safety and well-being are secured.

Chapter Eighteen: How Princes Should Keep Faith

Every one understands how praiseworthy it is in a Prince to keep faith, and to live uprightly and not craftily. Nevertheless, we see from what has taken place in our own days the Princes who have set little store by their word, but have known how to overreach men by their cunning, have accomplished great things, and in the end got the better of those who trusted to honest dealing.

Be it known, then, that there are two ways of contending, one in accordance with the laws, the other by force; the first of which is proper to men, the second to beasts. But since the first method is often ineffectual, it becomes necessary to resort to the second. A Prince should, therefore, understand how to use well both the man and the beast. And this lesson has been covertly taught by the ancient writers, who relate how Achilles and many other of these old Princes were given over to be brought up and trained by Chiron the Centaur; since the only meaning of their having an instructor one who was half man and half beast is, that it is necessary for a Prince to know how to use both natures, and that the one without the other has no stability.

But since a Prince should know how to use the beast's nature wisely, he ought of beasts to choose both the lion and the fox; for the lion cannot guard himself from the toils, nor the fox from wolves. He must therefore be a fox to discern toils, and a lion to drive off wolves.

To rely wholly on the lion is unwise; and for this reason a prudent Prince neither can nor ought to keep his word when to keep it is hurtful to him and the causes which led him to pledge it are removed. If all men were good, this would not be good advice, but since they are dishonest and do not keep faith with you, you, in return, need not keep faith with them; and no prince was ever at a loss for plausible reasons to cloak a breach of faith. Of this numberless recent instances could be given, and it might be shown how solemn treaties and engagements have been rendered inoperative and idle through want of faith in Princes, and that he who was best known to play the fox has had the best success.

It is necessary, indeed, to put a good color on this nature, and to be skillful in simulating and dissembling. But men are so simple, and governed so absolutely by their present needs, that he who wishes to deceive will never fail in finding willing dupes. One recent example I will not omit. **Pope Alexander VI** had no care or thought but how to deceive, and always found material to work on. No man has ever had a more effective manner of asseverating, or made promises with more solemn protestations, or observed them less. And yet, because he understood this side of human nature, his frauds always succeeded.

It is not essential, then, that a Prince should have all the good qualities which I have enumerated above, but it is most essential that he should seem to have them; I will even venture to affirm that if he has and invariably practices them all, they are hurtful, whereas the appearance of having them is useful. Thus, it is well to seem merciful, faithful, humane, religious, and upright, and also to be so; but the mind should remain so balanced that were it needful not to be so, you should be able and know how to change to the contrary.

And you are to understand that a Prince, and most of all a new Prince, cannot observe all those rules of conduct in respect whereof men are accounted good, being often forced, in order to preserve his Princedom, to act in opposition to good faith, charity, humanity, and religion. He must therefore keep his mind ready to shift as the winds and tides of Fortune turn, and, as I have already said, he ought not to quit good courses if he can help it, but should know how to follow evil courses if he must.

A Prince should therefore be very careful that nothing ever escape his lips, which is not replete with the five qualities above named, so that to see and hear him, one would think him the embodiment of mercy, good faith, integrity, humanity, and religion. And there is no virtue which it is more necessary for him to seem to possess than this last; because men in general judge rather by the eye than by the hand, for every one can see but few can touch. Every one sees what you seem, but few know what you are, and these few have the majesty of the State to back them up.

Moreover, in the actions of all men, and most of all of Princes, where there is no tribunal to which we can appeal, we look to results. Wherefore if a Prince succeeds in establishing and maintaining his authority, the means will always be judged honorable and be approved by every one. For the vulgar are always taken by appearances and by results, and the world is made up of the vulgar, the few only finding room when the many have no longer ground to stand on.

A certain Prince of our own days, whose name it is as well not to mention, is always preaching peace and good faith, although the mortal enemy of both; and both, had he practiced them as he preaches them, would, oftener than once, have lost him his kingdom and authority.

Chapter Twenty-five: What Fortune Can Effect in Human Affairs, and How She May be Withstood

I am not ignorant that many have been and are of the opinion that human affairs are so governed by Fortune and by God, that men cannot alter them by any prudence of theirs, and indeed have no remedy against them; and for this reason have come to think that it is not worth while to labor much about anything, but that they must leave everything to be determined by chance.

Often when I turn the matter over, I am in part inclined to agree with this opinion, which has had the readier acceptance in our own times from the great changes in things which we have seen, and every day see happening contrary to all human expectation. Nevertheless, that our freedom will be not wholly set aside, I think it may be the case that Fortune is the mistress of one half our actions, and yet leaves the control of the other half, or a little less, to ourselves. And I would liken her to one of those wild torrents which, when angry, overflow the plains, sweep away trees and houses, and carry off soil from one bank to throw it down upon the other. Every one flees before them, and yields to their fury without the least power to resist. And yet, though this be their nature, it does not follow that in seasons of fair weather, men cannot, by constructing weirs and moles, take such precautions as will cause them when again in flood to pass off by some artificial channel, or at least prevent their course from being so uncontrolled and destructive. And so it is with Fortune, who displays her might where there is no organized strength to resist her, and directs her onset where she knows that there is neither barrier nor embankment to confine her.

And if you look at Italy, which has been at once the seat of these changes and their cause, you will perceive that it is a field without embankment or barrier. For if, like Germany, France, and Spain, it had been guarded with sufficient skill, this inundation, if it ever came upon us, would never have wrought the violent changes which we have witnessed.

This I think enough to say generally touching resistance to Fortune. But confining myself more closely to the matter in hand, I note that one day we see a Prince prospering and the next day overthrown, without detecting any change in his nature or character. This, I believe, comes chiefly from a cause already dwelt upon, namely, that a Prince who rests wholly on Fortune is ruined when she changes. Moreover, I believe that he will prosper most whose mode of acting best adapts itself to the character of the times; and conversely that he will be unprosperous, with whose mode of acting the times do not accord. For we see that men in these matters which lead to the end that each has before him, namely, glory and wealth, proceed by different ways, one with caution, another with impetuosity, one with violence, another with subtlety, one with patience, another with its contrary; and that by one or other of these different courses each may succeed.

Again of two who act cautiously, you will find that one attains his end, the other not, and that two of different temperament, the one cautious, the other impetuous, are equally successful. All which happens from no other cause than that the character of the times accords or does not accord with their methods of acting. And hence it comes, as I have already said, that two operating differently arrive at the same result, and two operations similarly, the one succeeds the other not. On this likewise depend the vicissitudes of Fortune. For if to one who conducts himself with caution and patience, time and circumstances are propitious, so that his method of acting is good, he goes on prospering; but if these change he is ruined, because he does not change his method of acting.

For no man is found so prudent as to know how to adapt himself to these changes, both because he cannot deviate from the course to which nature inclines him, and because, having always prospered while adhering to one path, he cannot be persuaded that it would be well for him to forsake it. And so when occasion requires the cautious man to act impetuously, he cannot do so and is undone; whereas, had he changed his nature with time and circumstances, his fortune would have been unchanged.

Pope Julius II proceeded with impetuosity in all his undertakings, and found time and circumstances in such harmony with his mode of acting that he always obtained a happy result. Witness his first expedition against Bologna, when Master Giovanni Bentivoglio was yet living. The Venetians were not favorable to the enterprise; nor was the King of Spain. Negotiations respecting it with the King of France were still open. Nevertheless, the Pope with his wonted hardihood and impetuosity marched in person on the expedition, and by this movement brought the King of Spain and the Venetians to a check, the latter through fear, the former from his eagerness to recover the entire Kingdom of Naples; at the same time, he dragged after him the King of France, who, desiring to have the Pope for an ally in humbling the Venetians, on finding him already in motion saw that he could not refuse him his soldiers without openly offending him. By the impetuosity of his movements, therefore, Julius effected what no other Pontiff endowed with the highest human prudence could. For had he, as any other Pope would have done, put off his departure from Rome until terms had been settled and everything duly arranged, he never would have succeeded. For the King of France would have found a thousand pretexts to delay him, and the others would have menaced him with a thousand alarms. I shall not touch upon his other actions, which were all of a like character, and all of which had a happy issue, since the shortness of his life did not allow him to experience reverses. But if times had overtaken him, rendering a cautious line of conduct necessary, his ruin must have ensued, since he never could have departed from those methods to which nature inclined him.

To be brief, I say that since Fortune changes and men stand fixed in their old ways, they are prosperous so long as there is congruity between them, and the reverse when there is not. Of this, however, I am well persuaded, that it is better to be impetuous than cautious. For Fortune is a woman who to be kept under must be beaten and roughly handled; and we see that she suffers herself to be more readily mastered by those who so treat her than by those who are more timid in their approaches. And always, like a woman, she favors the young, because they are less scrupulous and fiercer, and command her with greater audacity.

Study Questions

1. What seems to be Machiavelli's main focus in *The Prince,* if not the despotic rule of the prince?
2. Why do religious beliefs and Christian morality have no place in the author's political doctrine?
3. According to the author, what should most concern a successful ruler?
4. What part does fortune play in politics and statecraft?

Reading 11

Thomas More's *Utopia*

Prior to writing the ever-popular *Utopia* in 1516, Thomas More (1478–1535) had long enjoyed the friendship and admiration of many European humanists. More was a lawyer and statesman rather than a philosopher; yet it was not uncommon for Renaissance humanists to bring learning and philosophical expertise to the service of the state. By the time More ended his early education at Canterbury Hall, Oxford, which he left without a degree, he was already steeped in the classics and orthodox theology. After studying at New Inn and Lincoln's Inn in London, he entered Parliament in 1504 and eventually became Chancellor of England under his patron, King Henry VIII (1491–1547). A far-reaching, highly intelligent, and entertaining treatise, *Utopia* describes the perfect society located on an island somewhere in the New World, as visited and described by the fictional character Raphael Hythlodaeus. The precision with which More details this utopian milieu allows his readers not only to envision this island of happy people but also to compare this flawless system to their own. What is most significant about *Utopia* is not its philosophical perspective nor its advocacy of communism, but rather its prescription for the ideal commonwealth. *Utopia* is thus representative of a whole genre of "utopian" literature produced in the West that may be traced to **Plato**'s *Republic*. Thomas More's opposition to both King Henry's divorce from Catherine of Aragon, and the monarch's penchant for ecclesiastical independence from Rome led to More's fall from favor. He was beheaded in 1535 but centuries later venerated as a saint of the Catholic church.

Now I will tell how the citizens behave toward each other, how the people entertain and amuse themselves, and how they distribute their goods. First, the city consists of families, the families being made up of kindred. For women, when they are married at the legal age, become part of their husband's family. But the male children and all the male offspring continue in their own family, being governed by the eldest man, unless he is senile, in which case he is replaced by the next oldest. But in order to prevent the number of citizens from increasing or decreasing, it is ordained that no family (there are 6,000 families in each city and nearby

Sir Thomas More, *Utopia*, ed. J. Rawson Lumby (Cambridge: Cambridge University Press, 1888), passim.

countryside) shall have fewer than ten children between the ages of thirteen and sixteen. Of children under this age, no number is set. This number is easily maintained by putting the children of larger families into smaller families. If by chance a city has more than can be accommodated, the excess is used in other cities. If the population of the entire island exceeds the set number, they choose citizens from every city to build up a town under their own laws in a neighboring land where there is waste land, accepting also natives of that country if they want to join and dwell with them. Thus joining and dwelling together, they easily agree on one way of life, to the great wealth of both peoples. For they manage things so by their laws that ground which was before neither good nor profitable for anyone becomes fruitful enough for both. If the natives will not dwell with them and accept their laws, they drive them out of the land they have taken for themselves. If the natives resist or rebel, they make war upon them. For they consider it a just war that if fought to dispossess people from land which they do not use and keep others from using. If by chance the number in any city is so diminished that it cannot be filled up without reducing the proper number in the other cities (which they say happened only twice, by the plague, since the beginning of the island), they replenish the number with citizens brought from their own foreign towns. They would rather see these foreign towns decay and perish than any city of the island diminish.

But to return to the behavior of the citizens toward each other: the eldest, as I have said, rules the family, the wives and their husbands; the children help their parents, and, in short, all younger people assist their elders.

Every city is divided into four equal parts or quarters. In the midst of each quarter there is a market place for all kinds of things. There the products of every family's labor are brought into certain houses, and all kinds of commodities are stored in several barns or storehouses. From thence the father of every family, or every householder, takes whatever he needs and carries it with him without money, exchange, pawn, or pledge. Why should anything be denied him—seeing that there is abundance of everything and that no one will ask for more than he needs? Why should it be thought that men who know they will never be in want would ask for more than is merely enough? Certainly, fear of want causes covetousness and greed, but only in man does it cause pride, because man thinks it a glorious thing to excel in ostentatious and vain display of possessions. This vice has no place among the Utopians. . . .

[The Utopians] keep most of the treasure at home to use for extreme danger, especially to hire at great wages foreign soldiers. For they prefer to endanger mercenaries rather than their own citizens. They know that their enemies can be bribed, and weakened by hired traitors set to fight among themselves. For this purpose they keep a great treasure on hand. This treasure is not for hoarding but for use. I am almost afraid to say this, lest I not be believed, for I would hardly believe another man's telling this, if I had not seen it myself.

It usually happens that if a thing is strange and not familiar in our experience, it is difficult to believe. However, a wise and judicious judge of matters will not be surprised, since all of their laws and customs are so different from ours, if their use of gold and silver is interpreted by their customs, not ours. I mean that they use these not as money, but keep them in case of emergency. In the meantime they are used in such a way that no one prizes them as money.

Anyone can plainly see that money is less important than iron, for men cannot live without iron any more than without fire and water. Nature has given no utility to gold and silver that we cannot do without. Only the folly of men sets them in higher esteem because of their scarcity. But nature, a most kind and loving nurse, has placed the most necessary things ready to our use, as air, water, and earth, and has hidden farthest from us all vain and unprofitable things. Therefore, if these metals should be locked up in some tower, it might be suspected that the prince and council (as the populace is always foolishly imagining) intended by some device to deceive the commons and profit themselves. Furthermore, if they should make plate of the gold and silver and other finely and cunningly wrought stuff, and if at any time they should have to melt it down again to pay their soldiers, they see that men would be loath to part from those things that they took delight in.

To remedy all of this, they have found a means which, since it conforms to all of their other laws and customs (and so different from ours, which set so much store on gold, that it is incredible except to those who are very wise) renders gold worthless. For they eat and drink of vessels of earthenware and glass, beautifully made but of small value. Of gold and silver they commonly make chamber pots and other vessels that serve for the vilest uses not only in the common halls but in every man's private house. Furthermore, of the same metals they make great chains and fetters and gyves in which they chain their bondmen. Finally, some condemned persons must wear earrings of gold, finger rings of gold, and collars of gold, and circlets of gold around their heads. Thus, by all possible means, they make gold and silver a badge of reproach and infamy. These metals, which in other nations are valued as life itself, would, if taken from the Utopians, not be missed any more than one penny.

They also gather pearls by the seashore, and diamonds and garnets from certain rocks; yet they do not seek them out, but find them by chance and cut and polish them. They give them to their children, for they make much of young children and like to dress and ornament them so that when they grow up and see that only little children wear jewels and ornaments, they put aside their own voluntarily, without being counselled to do so by their parents, even as our own children, when grown, throw away their dolls and nuts and toys.

... There are several kinds of religion, not only in different parts of the island but also within the same city. Some worship the sun as their god; some, the moon; some, other planets. There are those who worship a man, once excellently virtuous and gloriously famous, not only as god but also as the highest god. But the majority of wise people, rejecting all of these creeds, believes that there is a certain divine power, unknown, everlasting, inexplicable, far above the capacity and reach of man's knowledge, dispersed throughout the universe, not in size but in virtue. Him they call the father of all. To him alone they attribute the beginning, growth, processes, changes, and endings of all things. Nor do they worship any deity save him. All the other sects, though they differ, agree on this one point with the wisest—that there is one chief and principal god, maker and ruler of the whole world, whom they all, in their language, term "**Mythra**."

There is some disagreement, however, for some identify this god in one way, some in another fashion. For everyone takes his own god to be the one to whose divine might and majesty the power over all things is commonly attributed. However, they are beginning little by little to forsake these various superstitions and to agree in the religion which seems reasonably to excel the others. There is no doubt that the others would have been abolished long since if it had not been for the habit of ascribing any mischance befalling one who had changed his religion to the enmity of the god whom he was forsaking, as if the god were seeking revenge.

After they heard us speak of Christ, of his doctrine, laws, miracles, and the wonderful constancy of martyrs whose blood was willingly shed to bring the nations of the world into the faith, you would hardly believe how glad they were to accept the Word, either by the secret inspiration of God or because it came closest to that opinion which they already thought of among themselves as the best. I do think, however, that it helped when they heard us say that Christ bade his followers to have all things in common, and that the same communalism still exists among the best Christian groups.

Whatever the cause, many of them accepted our religion and were washed with the holy waters of baptism. Because among us four (no more of us were left alive, two having died) there was no priest, which I heartily regret, they could be instructed in all the points of our religion but lacked those sacraments which only priests can administer. They nevertheless understand them and earnestly desire them, even disputing among themselves whether, without the sending of a Christian bishop, one of their own people might receive the order of priesthood. Truly, they were intending to choose one, but at my departure had not yet done so.

Those who do not agree with Christianity fear no one who has been converted, nor do they speak against any one who has received Christianity. There was one exception, however. One of our company was severely punished. As soon as he was baptized he began, against our will, and with more earnestness than wisdom, to talk about Christ's religion, and became so vehement that he not only preferred our religion before all others but utterly despised and condemned all others, calling them profane and their followers wicked, devilish, and children of everlasting damnation. When he had argued this way for a long time, they seized him, accused and condemned him to exile, not as a despiser of religion but as a stirrer up of sedition among the people. For it is one of the most ancient laws among them that no one shall be blamed for arguing in defense of his own religion. For King Utopus, at the very beginning, heard that the inhabitants of the land were, before his coming there, in continual strife and dissension among themselves because of their religion. He also perceived that this dissension (in which several sects fought only for their own part of the country) was the only reason he was able to conquer the land. Therefore, when he had gained victory, his first decree was that it should be lawful for every man to favor and follow whatever religion he wished, and to do the best he could to bring others to his opinion so long as he did it peaceably, gently, quietly and soberly, without hasty and contentious re-buking and inveighing against others. If he could not by fair and gentle words induce others to his opinion, he must nevertheless refrain from violence and un-pleasant and seditious language. He who was guilty of vehemence and strife was banished or placed in bondage.

King Utopus made this law not only for the maintenance of peace, which he saw threatened by continual strife and mortal hatred, but also because he thought this decree would help religion. Of religion he did not define or determine anything, not knowing whether God, desiring many different kinds of respect and worship, might not inspire different men with different kinds of religious beliefs. He thought it an unwise and foolish thing, and arrogant presumption, to compel all others, by threats of violence, to agree to the same belief as yourself. Furthermore, though there may be only one true religion, and all others superstition, he foresaw that (if the matter were handled with reason and restraint) the truth of the right doctrine would at last come to light. If contention and debate were continually used, how-ever, the worst and most stubborn and obstinate men, who uphold their evil opin-ions most constantly, would win. The holiest and best religion would thus be trodden down and destroyed by violent superstition, as good corn is overgrown and choked by weeds and thorns. Therefore, he left all this matter unprescribed and gave to every man liberty and free choice to believe as he wished.

Study Questions

1. How do sixteenth-century Christian values affect More's notion of communal living?
2. How is justice relative to both the individual and society central to the author's philosophic and political objectives?
3. Explain how More's failure to fully recognize the status of the individual in *Utopia* significantly detracts from the humanist emphasis of the work.
4. What does the religion of the Utopians reveal about the author's views on the spiritual upheavals of sixteenth-century European society?

Reading 12

Martin Luther's "The Freedom of a Christian"

In 1520, Martin Luther (1483–1546) published three significant treatises that expounded his evangelical theology. Although Luther advanced an unorthodox theological perspective, "The Freedom of a Christian," published in both Latin and German, was written in a conciliatory spirit and designed to prevent a permanent rift within the Church. The treatise was meant to accompany a letter to **Pope Leo X**, but it is not known if the pope ever received the documents. If the pope did read them, he would have been shocked to discover that Luther was writing to him as an equal, with theological and spiritual advice as if he himself were the pope's personal confessor. According to Luther, a true Christian is free from sin through faith in God, yet is bound by love to serve his or her fellow human beings.

Christian faith has appeared to many an easy thing; nay, not a few even reckon it among the social virtues, as it were; and this they do because they have not made proof of it experimentally, and have never tasted of what efficacy it is. For it is not possible for any man to write well about it, or to understand well what is rightly written, who has not at some time tasted of its spirit, under the pressure of tribulation; while he who has had even a faint taste of it can never write, speak, think, or hear about it sufficiently. For it is a living fountain, springing up into eternal life, as Christ calls it in John 4[:14].

Now, though I cannot boast of my abundance, and though I know how poorly I am furnished, yet I hope that, after having been vexed by various temptations, I have attained some little drop of faith, and that I can speak of this matter, if not with more elegance, certainly with more solidity, than those literal and too subtle disputants who have hitherto discoursed upon it without understanding their own words. That I may open then an easier way for the ignorant—for these alone I am trying to serve—I first lay down these two propositions, concerning spiritual liberty and servitude:—

Martin Luther, *Ninety-Five Theses: Address to the German Nobility and Concerning Christian Liberty,* ed. Charles W. Eliot, The Harvard Classics (New York: P. F. Collier & Son, 1910), 362–377, passim.

A Christian man is the most free lord of all, and subject to none; a Christian man is the most dutiful servant of all, and subject to every one.

Although these statements appear contradictory, yet, when they are found to agree together, they will make excellently for my purpose. They are both the statement of **Paul** himself, who says, "Though I be free from all men, yet have I made myself servant unto all" (I Corinthians 9:19), and "Owe no man anything, but to love one another" (Romans 13:8). Now love is by its own nature dutiful and obedient to the beloved object. Thus even Christ, though Lord of all things, was yet made of a woman; made under the law; at once free and a servant; at once in the form of God and in the form of a servant.

Let us examine the subject on a deeper and less simple principle. Man is composed of a two-fold nature, a spiritual and a bodily. As regards the spiritual nature, which they name the soul, he is called the spiritual, inward, new man; as regards the bodily nature, which they name the flesh, he is called the fleshly, outward, old man. . . .

We first approach the subject of the inward man, that we may see by what means a man becomes justified, free, and a true Christian; that is, a spiritual, new, and inward man. It is certain that absolutely none among outward things, under whatever name they may be reckoned, has any influence in producing Christian righteousness or liberty, nor, on the other hand, unrighteousness or slavery. This can be shown by an easy argument.

What can it profit the soul that the body should be in good condition, free, and full of life; that it should eat, drink, and act according to its pleasure; when even the most impious slaves of every kind of vice are prosperous in these matters? Again, what harm can ill-health, bondage, hunger, thirst, or any other outward evil, do to the soul, when even the most pious of men and the freest in the purity of their conscience, are harassed by these things? Neither of these states of things has to do with the liberty or the slavery of the soul.

And so it will profit nothing that the body should be adorned with sacred vestments, or dwell in holy places, or be occupied in sacred offices, or pray, fast, and abstain from certain meats, or do whatever works can be done through the body and in the body. Something widely different will be necessary for the justification and liberty of the soul, since the things I have spoken of can be done by any impious person, and only hypocrites are produced by devotion to these things. On the other hand, it will not at all injure the soul that the body should be clothed in profane raiment, should dwell in profane places, should eat and drink in the ordinary fashion, should not pray aloud, should leave undone all the things above mentioned, which may be done by hypocrites.

And, to cast everything aside, even speculation, meditations, and whatever things can be performed by the exertions of the soul itself, are of no profit. One thing, and one alone, is necessary for life, justification, and Christian liberty; and that is the most holy word of God, the Gospel of Christ, as He says, "I am the resurrection and the life; he that believeth in Me shall not die eternally" (John 11:25), and also, "If the Son shall make you free, ye shall be free indeed" (John 8:36), and, "Man shall not live by bread alone, but by every word that proceedeth out of the mouth of God" (Matthew 4:4).

Let us therefore hold it for certain and firmly established that the soul can do without everything except the word of God, without which none at all of its wants are provided for. But, having the word, it is rich and wants for nothing, since that is the word of life, of truth, of light, of peace, of justification, of salvation, of joy, of liberty, of wisdom, of virtue, of grace, of glory, and of every good thing. It is on this account that the prophet is a whole Psalm (Psalms 119), and in many other places, sighs for and calls upon the word of God with so many groanings and words.

Again, there is no more cruel stroke of the wrath of God than when He sends a famine of hearing His words (Amos 8:11), just as there is no greater favor from Him than the sending forth of His word, as it is said, "He sent His word and healed them, and delivered them from their destructions" (Psalms 107). Christ was sent for no other office than that of the word; and the order of Apostles, that of bishops, and that of the whole body of the clergy, have been called and instituted for no object but the ministry of the word.

But you will ask, What is this word, and by what means is it to be used, since there are so many words of God? I answer, The Apostle Paul (Romans 1) explains what it is, namely the Gospel of God, concerning His Son, incarnate, suffering, risen, and glorified, through the Spirit, the Sanctifier. To preach Christ is to feed the soul, to justify it, to set it free, and to save it, if it believes the preaching. For faith alone and the efficacious use of the word of God, bring salvation. "If thou shalt confess with thy mouth the Lord Jesus, and shalt believe in thine heart that God hath raised Him from the dead, thou shalt be saved" (Romans 10:9); and again, "Christ is the end of the law for righteousness to every one that believeth" (Romans 10:4), and "The just shall live by faith" (Romans 1:17). For the word of God cannot be received and honored by any other works, but by faith alone. Hence it is clear that as the soul needs the word alone for life and justification, so it is justified by faith alone, and not by any works. For if it could be justified by any other means, it would have no need of the word, nor consequently of faith. . . .

But you ask how it can be the fact that faith alone justifies, and affords without works so great a treasure of good things, when so many works, ceremonies, and laws are prescribed to us in the Scriptures? I answer, Before all things bear in mind what I have said: that faith alone without works justifies, sets free, and saves, as I shall show more clearly below.

Meanwhile it is to be noted that the whole Scripture of God is divided into two parts: precepts and promises. The precepts certainly teach us what is good, but what they teach is not forthwith done. For they show us what we ought to do, but do not give us the power to do it. They were ordained, however, for the purpose of showing man to himself, that through them he may learn his own impotence for good and may despair of his own strength. For this reason they are called the Old Testament, and are so.

. . . God the Father has made everything to depend on faith, so that whosoever has it has all things, and he who has it not has nothing. "For God hath concluded them all in unbelief, that He might have mercy upon all" (Romans

11:32). Thus the promises of God give that which the precepts exact, and fulfill what the law commands; so that all things may be of God alone, both the precepts and their fulfillment. He alone commands; He alone also fulfills. Hence the promises of God belong to the New Testament; nay, are the New Testament. . . .

From all this it is easy to understand why faith has such great power, and why no good works, nor even all good works put together, can compare with it, since no work can cleave to the word of God or be in the soul. Faith alone and the word reign in it; and such as is the word, such is the soul made by it, just as iron exposed to fire glows like fire, on account of its union with the fire. It is clear then that to a Christian man his faith suffices for everything, and that he has no need of works for justification. But if he has no need of works, neither has he need of the law; and if he has no need of the law, he is certainly free from the law, and the saying is true, "The law is not made for a righteous man" (I Timothy 1:9). This is that Christian liberty, our faith, the effect of which is, not that we should be careless or lead a bad life, but that no one should need the law or works for justification and salvation.

Let us consider this as the first virtue of faith; and let us look also to the second. This also is an office of faith: that it honors with the utmost veneration and the highest reputation Him in whom it believes, inasmuch as it holds Him to be truthful and worthy of belief. For there is no honor like that reputation of truth and righteousness with which we honor Him in whom we believe. What higher credit can we attribute to any one than truth and righteousness, and absolute goodness? On the other hand, it is the greatest insult to brand any one with the reputation of falsehood and unrighteousness, or to suspect him of these, as we do when we disbelieve him.

Thus the soul, in firmly believing the promises of God, holds Him to be true and righteous; and it can attribute to God no higher glory than the credit of being so. The highest worship of God is to ascribe to Him truth, righteousness, and whatever qualities we must ascribe to one in whom we believe. In doing this the soul shows itself prepared to do His whole will; in doing this it hallows His name, and gives itself up to be dealt with as it may please God. For it cleaves to His promises, and never doubts that He is true, just, and wise, and will do, dispose, and provide for all things in the best way. . . .

The third incomparable grace of faith is this: that it unites the soul to Christ, as the wife to the husband, by which mystery, as the Apostle teaches, Christ and the soul are made one flesh (Ephesians 5:31–32). Now if they are one flesh, and if a true marriage—nay, by far the most perfect of all marriages—is accomplished between them (for human marriages are but feeble types of this one great marriage), then it follows that all they have becomes theirs in common, as well good things as evil things; so that whatsoever Christ possesses, that the believing soul may take to itself and boast of as its own, and whatever belongs to the soul, that Christ claims as His.

If we compare these possessions, we shall see how inestimable is the gain. Christ is full of grace, life, and salvation; the soul is full of sin, death, and condemnation. Let faith step in, and then sin, death, and hell will belong to Christ, and grace, life, and salvation to the soul. For, if He is a Husband, He must needs take to Himself that which is His wife's, and at the same time, impart to His wife that which is His. For, in giving her His own body and Himself, how can He but give her all that is His? And, in taking to Himself the body of His wife, how can He but take to Himself all that is hers?

In this is displayed the delightful sight, not only of communion, but of a prosperous warfare, of victory, salvation, and redemption. For, since Christ is God and man, and is such a Person as neither has sinned, nor dies, nor is condemned, nay, cannot sin, die, or be condemned, and since His righteousness, life and salvation are invincible, eternal, and almighty,—when I say, such a Person, by the wedding-ring of faith, takes a share in the sins, death, and hell of His wife, nay, makes them His own, and deals with them no otherwise than as if they were His, and as if He himself had sinned; and when He suffers, dies, and descends to hell, that He may overcome all things, and since sin, death, and hell cannot swallow Him up, they must needs be swallowed up by Him in stupendous conflict. For His righteousness rises above the sins of all men; His life is more powerful than all death; His salvation is more unconquerable than all hell.

Thus the believing soul, by the pledge of its faith in Christ, becomes free from all sins, fearless of death, safe from hell, and endowed with the eternal righteousness, life, and salvation of its Husband Christ. Thus He presents to Himself a glorious bride, without spot or wrinkle, cleansing her with the washing of water by the word [cf. Ephesians 5:26–27]; that is, by faith in the word of life, righteousness, and salvation. Thus he betroths her unto Himself "in faithfulness, in righteousness, and in judgment, and in loving kindness, and in mercies" (Hosea 2:19–20). . . .

From all this you will again understand why so much importance is attributed to faith, so that it alone can fulfill the law and justify without any works. For you see that the First Commandment, which says, "Thou shalt worship one God only," is fulfilled by faith alone. If you were nothing but good works from the soles of your feet to the crown of your head, you would not be worshipping God, nor fulfilling the First Commandment, since it is impossible to worship God without ascribing to Him the glory of truth and of universal goodness, as it ought in truth to be ascribed. Now this is not done by works, but only by faith of heart. It is not by working, but by believing, that we glorify God, and confess Him to be true. On this ground faith alone is the righteousness of a Christian man, and the fulfilling of all the commandments. For to him who fulfills the first the task of fulfilling all the rest is easy. . . .

All we who believe in Christ are kings and priests, as it is said, "Ye are a chosen generation, a royal priesthood, a holy nation, a peculiar people, that ye should show forth the praises of Him who hath called you out of darkness into His marvelous light" (I Peter 2:9).

These two things stand thus. First, as regards kingship, every Christian is by faith so exalted above all things that, in spiritual power, he is completely lord of all things, so that nothing whatever can do him any hurt; yea, all things are subject to him, and are compelled to be subservient to his salvation. Thus Paul says, "All things work together for good to them who are the called" (Romans 8:28), and also, "Whether life, or death, or things present, or things to come, all are yours; and ye are Christ's" (I Corinthians 3:22–23).

Not that in the sense of corporeal power any one among Christians has been appointed to possess and rule all things, according to the mad and senseless idea of certain ecclesiastics. That is the office of kings, princes, and men upon earth. In the experience of life we see that we are subjected to all things, and suffer many things, even death. Yea, the more of a Christian any man is, to so many the more evils, sufferings, and deaths is he subject, as we see in the first place in Christ the first-born, and in all His holy brethren.

This is a spiritual power, which rules in the midst of enemies, and is powerful in the midst of distresses. And this is nothing else than that strength is made perfect in my weakness (II Corinthians 12:9), and that I can turn all things to the profit of my salvation (Romans 8:28); so that even the cross and death are compelled to serve me and to work together for my salvation. This is a lofty and eminent dignity, a true and almighty dominion, a spiritual empire, in which there is nothing so good, nothing so bad, as not to work together for my good, if only I believe. And yet there is nothing of which I have need—for faith alone suffices for my salvation—unless that in it faith may exercise the power and empire of its liberty. This is the inestimable power and liberty of Christians. . . .

Let it suffice to say this concerning the inner man and its liberty, and concerning that righteousness of faith which needs neither laws nor good works; nay, they are even hurtful to it, if any one pretends to be justified by them. . . .

Study Questions

1. According to Luther, what is "Christian liberty"?
2. How is the author's doctrine of "by faith alone" at the heart of his theological perspective?
3. What did Martin Luther owe to the developing humanist tradition of late fifteenth- and early sixteenth-century Europe?
4. Why were Luther's beliefs and assumptions so upsetting to the Catholic church hierarchy, and how did they stimulate a reordering of Christian society?

Reading 13

Select Letters of Saint Catherine d'Ricci

Alexandrina d'Ricci (1522–1590) was born into an old noble family of Florence. At the age of thirteen, she assumed the habit of a **Dominican** nun of the Third Order at Saint Vincent's in Prato and assumed the name of Catherine. This woman of towering spirituality eventually became Mistress of Novices and was installed as prioress in 1560. The mystical Catherine experienced (like many others in this era) religious revelations. It was said that she received the stigmata and visions of Christ's passion. She was also an accomplished spiritual adviser and monastic administrator and gave counsel to many men and women who sought her out, including a few men who eventually occupied the papal throne. Catherine d' Ricci was canonized in 1746.

To the Young Nuns of the Monastery of San Vincenzio

The reason of my present letter is, that having been requested by you to say something on the occasion of your feast of **St. Catherine**, I reply as follows: It is not usual for the sub-prioress to come forward, but to leave all in the hands of the superior. But I am not able to refrain, on account of my love for you (considering that you are all my daughters), from satisfying your desire, with the same charity that has been shown to me by all in the convent. Therefore I send to you with this letter a golden shield. I am sorry I cannot give you more; but you must excuse me and accept my good will towards you. The superior will arrange all to your satisfaction; do not fear.

I exhort and pray you, my dear daughters, to imitate our glorious saint, and to practice virtue if you would be pleasing to Jesus, as she pleased Him, if not with the same degree of perfection, at least as much as your frailty allows. Remember that she was a woman, and young like yourselves; yet she did not excuse herself, and you are spouses of the same holy Spouse as she was. And if you would exercise yourselves in all the virtues, as she did, your Spouse will not fail to give you the graces and favors given to her. Be reverent and obedient to your superiors as she was. For, out of reverence and obedience to her mother she went

F. M. Capes, *St. Catherine d'Ricci* (London: n.d.), passim.

to speak to that holy hermit, whom she believed and obeyed in all simplicity; she did not say, "These things which he has told me are childish, that I am to pray to such an image and I shall see the Spouse of whom he has spoken." And by her obedience and faith she merited to see Jesus. Likewise you, my daughters, give yourselves to holy obedience, and often frequent confession and holy Communion, if you wish to see Jesus; because no one can love or see Jesus better than by uniting oneself with Him in holy Communion. In short, we come to know His goodness and mercy, and our own vileness and misery; as did that saint, who in prayer was illuminated with truth, knew her own errors, and quickly departed from them, and followed with great fervor Jesus her Spouse. And you, my daughters, have been called by your Spouse to holy Religion, so that you may follow His footsteps, and the example of His holy Mother and the saints; fly, therefore, every occasion of offending your Spouse, as did our saint. And as she had great zeal for the honor of her Spouse, and a desire to suffer for love of Him, so do you show zeal in the observance of our holy rule, first for yourselves and then for your neighbors; and desire to suffer for love of Him, and to render something to Him for what he has done for you, so far as is possible to your frailty. If you love your Spouse with all your heart, as did our glorious saint, you will not weary of obeying your superiors, but will do it in all simplicity. And I am glad when you have confidence in them, as I told you the other day; and I would on no account that you should be wanting in reverence and obedience towards them, for you would thereby displease Jesus your Spouse, and would lose many graces and spiritual favors.

My dear daughters, give yourselves joyfully to Jesus, as He willingly gave Himself wholly to you, and as did our glorious saint, who did not think it hard to go to martyrdom for love of Him. And do you joyfully and willingly bear the fatigues and observances of holy Religion, which are wearing to our senses, and are a kind of martyrdom; but to one who loves Jesus with his whole heart, everything is sweet and pleasant, as He said, "My yoke is sweet and my burden light." Therefore, my daughters, follow cheerfully your Spouse in the way of religious life, and do not be discouraged if you find you are not all you would wish to be, but humbly ask pardon of Jesus with a firm resolve to correct yourselves; and have recourse to Him with great faith and hope, because He is your Father and your Spouse and is consumed, so to say, with the desire to bestow graces upon you. But He wishes to be entreated; therefore go to Him with great confidence and doubt not that you will be heard, and take your saint as your mediator, to pray to your and her Spouse for the grace you desire. I beg you also to include me in your petitions, that Jesus may do to me as is pleasing to His Majesty. And I will continue, just as I am, to pray for all of you who are or have been my dear children; and I offer you all to Jesus, that He may make you His true spouses and fill you with His holy love. I have dictated all this to my secretary, for I am not able to write with my own hand, on account of the pain you know it gives me to write. May God bless you all.

Your Mother in Christ, Sister Catherine d'Ricci.

To a Nun (dated 18 November 1549)

Very dear daughter,—I have already sent you a letter to exhort you to the service of our Lord; and now I send you this one, in which I am going to give—first for myself, and then for you—an account of the true way of faithfully serving our Divine Spouse, and a resume of the spiritual life; so that, by following it, we shall carry out the holy will of God. If, then, my daughter, you would be the true spouse of Jesus, you must do His holy will in all things; and you will do this if you entirely give up your own will on every occasion, and if you love the divine Spouse with your whole heart, your whole soul, and your whole strength. Then you must carefully attend to the following points (but it is necessary to weigh all these words), as they contain the summary of Christian perfection:

We must force ourselves to detach the heart and the will from all earthly love; to love no fleeting things, except for the love of God; and, above all, not to love God for our own sakes for self-interest, but with a love as pure as His own goodness.

We must direct all our thoughts, words and actions to His honor; and by prayer, counsel, and good example seek his glory solely, whether for ourselves or for others, so that through our means all may love and honor God. This second thing is more pleasing to Him than the first, as it better fulfills His will.

We must aim more and more at the accomplishment of the divine will: not only desiring nothing special to happen to us, bad or even good, in this wretched life, and thus keeping ourselves always at God's disposal, with heart and soul at peace; but also believing with a firm faith that Almighty God loves us more than we love ourselves, and takes more care of us than we could take care of ourselves.

The more we conform to this way of acting, the more we shall find God present to help us, and the more we shall experience His most gentle love. But no one can reach such perfection except by constant and courageous sacrifice of self-will; and, if we would learn to practice such abnegation, it is necessary to keep ourselves in a state of great and deep humility, so that by perfect knowledge of our own misery and weakness we may rise to learn the greatness and beauty of our God. Consider how just and necessary it is to serve Him unceasingly, with love and obedience. I say just, because God being Father and Master of all things, it is just that His son and servant should obey and love Him: I say necessary, because by acting otherwise we could not be saved. Let us always remember, never doubting, that it is the eternal, sovereign, all-powerful God who does, orders, or allows everything that happens, and that nothing comes to pass without His divine will. Let us remember that He is Himself that wisdom which, in the government of the universe—of heaven, earth, and every single creature—cannot be deceived (He would be neither God nor most wise, if it were otherwise). Let us look upon Him as supremely good, loving and beneficent. If, through His mercy, this conviction becomes strongly impressed upon our wills, we shall easily take all things from His sacred hand with well-contented hearts, always thanking Him for fulfilling His most holy will in us; because, by acting thus (with the help of His holy grace) we shall unite ourselves to Him by true love in this life and by glory in eternity. May he grant it to us in His goodness! Of your charity pray for me, a wretched sinner, who commends herself to you all.

Your sister in Christ.

To Filippo Salviati (dated 4 July 1560)

Most honored and dearly-loved Father, greeting!

Two days ago, I wrote you what was necessary about Cassandra: that is, that she had rather you would leave her here until she sends you notice; so that, in talking to her yesterday evening, I said: "Cassandra, I am afraid that, as your father has been asked to leave you here, if we say nothing more to him he will suspect something, and come to fetch you as soon as possible." She replied: "I would on no account have him come for me yet. As to becoming a nun, I wish to do so; but I don't wish to speak about it to the sisters without having told him first." Then I said: "I don't think he will let you do it." "And I," she answered, "believe he will let me do what I please; but I would rather not go home so soon, so as to have too many struggles there, especially with Lucrezia." She also told Sister Maria Pia that she has determined to be a nun, but one can see that she wants to stay here just a little longer, so as to strengthen her soul, and also that she wants you to be told first of her resolution. Therefore, if you can leave her to us for another eight or ten days, I should think it a great advantage.

Be sure, my dear Father, that nobody here has ever said one word to influence her: she has been allowed to see everything connected with the Order, and with our observances, and we have noticed that she has paid great attention to it all; but the fact of her desire comes from Jesus Himself; He would have that soul entirely. I want, then, to encourage you not to take it from Him; for certainly you will have more real satisfaction in giving your daughter to our Lord for His own, than you would in refusing her to Him only to give her to a mortal spouse, subject to all the miseries of this life. Even if some fuss should be made about the matter, you ought not for that reason to act against your duty; for as you know, the things of God must always meet with opposition, especially when they clash with earthly plans. I think it would be well, when you come here, not to let Cassandra see that you know anything, but to let her be the first to speak, so as to give you her confidence spontaneously. Moreover, I think myself that you had better not discuss the matter with anyone: but this I must leave to your own judgment. We do not forget, here, to pray that all may be ordered by our Lord for both your daughter's salvation and your satisfaction.

Mother Maria Maddalena [Strozzi], from fear of you, sent you word yesterday that I had an attack of fever; but the fit has passed and I do not think it will return.

My best greetings to you, to Mona Maria, and to all. May God keep you! Mother Prioress commends herself to you,

Your daughter, Sister Catherine d'Ricci

Study Questions

1. What do Catherine's remarks suggest about the vitality of Catholic spirituality in the midst of religious upheaval in the sixteenth century?
2. How does Catherine view her own and other nuns' relationship with God?
3. According to Catherine's letters, why was the monastic life still considered valuable and also a viable means of spiritual expression during the sixteenth century?
4. What are the differences between the religious perspectives of Catherine d'Ricci and Martin Luther (Reading 12)?

Michel de Montaigne's *Essays*

Michel de Montaigne (1533–1592) was born to a French Catholic father and a Spanish-Portuguese Jewish mother. He was educated by his father until the age of six, when he heard vernacular French, instead of Latin, for the first time. After studying at the universities in Bordeaux and Toulouse, Montaigne obtained a legal post at Perigueux until he returned to his native Bordeaux in 1557. In 1561, Montaigne was sent to the king's court on a mission that lasted for a year and a half. The next year found the young scholar in Rouen, a city recently captured from the Protestant Huguenots. It was there that he saw the Brazilian natives whom he described in his essay "On Cannibals." In 1572 he began writing his most significant work, entitled the *Essays,* a series of often rambling essays that serves as a self-portrait. He continued to add material to this work until 1588, when a true "first edition" was published in Paris. A final version of the *Essays* was produced after his death in 1595. "On Cannibals" illustrates the impact of European voyages of discovery and exploration and also expresses the author's pessimistic skepticism toward what he considered the disgusting behavior of his fellow-Frenchmen. Montaigne believed his countrymen killed each other for opinions they did not hold sincerely and, hence, were not merely cruel human beings but also ignorant and hypocritical. Indeed, the following excerpt illustrates the author's view that one needs to attempt to understand and empathize with other cultures, rather than condemn them in a violent fit of ignorance. In developing his generally secular outlook, Montaigne foreshadowed the coming Age of Enlightenment.

The wording of some portions of the text has been clarified.

Michel Lord of Montaigne, *Essays,* trans. John Florio (London: J. M. Dent & Sons Ltd., 1910), 219–29, passim.

On Cannibals

I find as far as I have been informed there is nothing in that nation [of Brazil] that is either barbarous or savage, unless men call barbarism that which is not common to themselves. Indeed, most of us have no other aim of truth and reason than the example and idea of the opinions and customs of the country we live in. There is ever perfect religion, perfect policy, perfect and complete use of all things. They are even savage, as we call those fruits wild, which nature of herself, and of her ordinary progress has produced. Indeed they are those which we ourselves have altered by our artificial devices, and diverted from their common order, we should rather term savage. In those are the true and most profitable virtues, and natural properties most lively and vigorous, which in these we have bastardized applying them to the pleasure of our corrupted taste. And if nonetheless, in diverse fruits of those countries that were never tilled, we shall find that in respect of ours they are most excellent, and as delicate to our taste; there is no reason art should gain the point of honor of our great and puissant mother Nature. We have so much by our inventions surcharged the beauties and riches of her works that we have altogether overchoaked her: yet wherever her purity shines, she makes our vain and frivolous enterprises wonderfully ashamed. [According to **Propertius**:]

Ivies spring better of their own accord,
Unhaunted plots much fairer trees afford.
Birds by no art sweeter notes record.

All our endeavor or wit cannot so much as pretend to represent the nest of the least birdlet; it is texture, beauty, profit and use—no, nor the web of a seemly spider. "All things," said **Plato**, "are produced either by nature, by fortune, or by art. The greatest and fairest by one or another of the first two, the least and imperfect by the last." Those nations seem therefore so barbarous to me because they have received very little fashion from human wit and are still near their original naturality. The laws of nature do yet command them, which are but little bastardized by ours, and that with such purity as I am sometimes grieved the knowledge of it came no sooner to light at what time there were men, that better than we could have judged of it. I am sorry **Lycurgus** and Plato had it not: for it seems to me that what in those nations we see by experience does not only exceed all the pictures drawn by licentious poetry which has proudly embellished the golden age, and all her quaint inventions to fain a happy condition of man, but exceeds the conception and desire of philosophy. . . .

[The natives of Brazil] have certain prophets and priests, which commonly abide in the mountains, and very seldom show themselves to the people; but when they come down, there is a great feast prepared, and a solemn assembly of many townships together takes place. . . . The prophet speaks to the people in public, exhorting them to embrace virtue and follow their duty. All their moral discipline contains but these two articles: first, an undismayed resolution to war, [and] then an inviolable affection for their wives. He also prognosticates about things to come, and what success they shall hope for in their enterprises. He either persuades or dissuades them from war; but if he happens to miss one of his divinations, and that it succeeds otherwise than he foretold to them, if he is taken captive, he is cut into a thousand pieces and condemned as a false prophet. And therefore he who has once misreckoned himself is never seen again. Divination is the gift of God; the abusing whereof should be a punishable imposture. When the divines among the Scythians had foretold falsely, they were couched along upon hurdles full of heath or brushwood, drawn by oxen, and so manacled hand and foot, and then burned to death. Those who manage matters subject to the conduct of man's sufficiency, are excusable, although they show the utmost of their skill. But those that gull and trick us with the assurance of an extraordinary faculty, and which is beyond our knowledge, ought to be punished two-fold; first because they do not perform the effect of their promise, then for the rashness of their imposture and unadvisedness of their fraud.

They war against the nations that lie beyond their mountains, to which they go naked, having no other weapons than bows or wooden swords, sharp at one end as our broaches are. It is an admirable thing to see the constant resolution of their combats, which never end but by effusion of blood and murder: for they do not know what fear is or defeat. Every victor brings home the head of the enemy he has slain as a trophy of his victory, and fastens the same at the entrance of his dwelling place. After they have for a long time used and entreated their prisoners well, and with all the commodities they can devise, he who is the master of them and upon summoning a great assembly of his acquaintances ties a cord to one of the prisoner's arms, by the end of which he holds him fast some distance from him for fear he might offend him, and gives the other arm, bound in like manner, to the dearest friend he has. Both men in the presence of all the assembly kill him with swords—which having been done, they roast and then eat him in common and send some slices of him to such of their friends as are absent. It is not—as some imagine—to nourish themselves with it as anciently the Scythians would do, but to represent an extreme and inexpiable revenge. Which we prove thusly: some of them when they perceived the Portuguese, who had confederated themselves with their adversaries, using another kind of death when they took them prisoners—which was to bury them up to the middle, and against the upper part of the body shoot arrows, and then being almost dead, to hang them up—they supposed that these people of the other world (as they who had sowed the knowledge of many vices among their neighbors and were much more cunning in all kinds of evils and mischief than they) and undertook not this manner of revenge without cause, and that consequently it was more painful and cruel than theirs, and thereupon began to leave their old fashion to follow this. I am not sorry we note the barbarous horror of such an action, but grieved that prying so narrowly into their faults we are so blinded in ours. I think there is more barbarism in eating men alive than to feed upon them once dead; to mangle by tortures and torments a body full of lively sense, to roast him in pieces, to make dogs and swine gnaw and tear him to bits (as we have not only read, but seen very lately—yes and in our own memory!—not amongst ancient enemies, but our neighbors and fellow citizens; and which is worse, under pretense of piety and religion) than to roast and eat him after he is dead. . . .

But to return to our history, these prisoners [whom I saw at Rouen], howsoever they are dealt with, are so far from yielding, that on the contrary, during two or three months that they were kept, they always carried a cheerful countenance, and urged their keepers to hasten their trial as they outrageously defied and injured them. They upbraid them with their cowardliness, and with the number of battles, they have lost against theirs. I have a song made by a prisoner, wherein is this clause:

Let them boldly come altogether, and flock in multitudes, to feed on him; for with him they shall feed upon their fathers, and grandfathers, that heretofore have served his body for food and nourishment. These muscles, this flesh, and these veins, are your own. Fond men as you are, know you not that the substance of your forefathers' limbs is yet tied unto ours. Taste them well, for in them shall you find the relish of your own flesh.

An invention, that has no show of barbarism. Those who paint them dying and who represent this action, when they are led out to execution, portray the prisoners spitting in their executioners' faces, and making bold moves at them. Verily, so long as breath is in their body, they never cease to brave and defy them, both in speech and countenance. Surely, in respect of us these are very savage men: for either they must be so in good sooth, or we must be so indeed.

There is a wondrous distance between their form and ours. Their men have many wives, and by how much more they are reputed valiant, so much the greater is their number. The manner and beauty in their marriages is wondrous strange and remarkable: for, the same jealousy our wives have to keep us from the love and affection of other women, the same have theirs to procure it. Being more careful for their husband's honor and contentment than of anything else, they endeavor and apply all their industry to have as many rivals as possible, because this is a testimony of their husbands' virtue. . . . And least a man should think that all this is done by a simple, and servile, or awful duty to their custom and by the impression of their ancient customs, without discourse or judgment, and because they are so blockish and dull spirited that they can take no other resolution, it is not amiss, we allege some evidence of their sufficiency. Besides what I have said of one of their warlike songs, I have another amorous song, which begins like this: "Adder stay, stay good adder, that my sister may by the pattern of your party-colored coat draw the fashion and work of a rich lace, for me to give to my love; so may your beauty, your nimbleness or disposition be ever preferred before all other serpents." The first couplet is the burden of the song. I am so conversant with song style that I may judge this invention has no barbarism at all in it, but is altogether like the poetry of **Anacreon**. Their language is a kind of pleasant speech, and has a pleasing sound and some affinity with Greek. Three of that nation, ignorant of how dear the knowledge of our corruptions will one day cost their repose, security, and happiness and how their ruin shall proceed from this commerce (which I imagine is already well advanced—miserable as they are to have suffered themselves to be so cozened by a desire for novelties, and to have quit the calmness of their climate, to come and see ours) were at Rouen in the time of our late King Charles IX, who talked with them a great while. They were shown our fashions, our pomp, and the form of a fair city. Afterward, some demanded their advice, and wanted to know of them what admirable things of note they had observed amongst us. They answered three things, the last of which I have forgotten, and am very sorry for it, the other two I still remember. They said, first, they found it very strange, that so many tall men with long beards, strong and well armed, were about the King's person (it is very likely they meant the Swiss Guard) would submit themselves to obey a beardless child, and that we did not rather choose one amongst them to command the rest. Second, they had perceived, there were men amongst us fully gorged with all sorts of commodities, and others that were hunger-starved, and living in need and poverty. These begged at their gates. And they found it strange, these people could endure such an injustice, and that they did not take the others by the throat, or set fire to their houses. I talked a good while with one of them, but I had so bad an interpreter, who did not really apprehend my meaning and who through his foolishness was at great pains to conceive of what I meant that I could not draw very much information from him. Touching that point wherein I demanded of him what good he received by the superiority he had among his countrymen (for he was a captain and our sailors called him a king) he told me it was to march foremost in any war. Furthermore, I asked him, how many men followed him, and he showed me a distance of place to signify they were as many as might be contained in so much ground— which I guessed to be about four or five thousand men. Moreover I demanded if when wars were ended all his authority expired, he answered that he had only this left him— which was, that when he went on a journey and visited the villages dependent on him, the inhabitants prepared paths and high-ways among the hedges of their woods for him to pass through at ease. All that is very well; but what of it? They wear no breeches or stockings!

Study Questions

1. How did the disorder and chaos of the sixteenth century influence Montaigne's outlook?
2. What is the correlation between the author's expansive view on the nature of humanity and the discovery of new continents and peoples of the Americas?
3. How does Montaigne's work prove that European culture was influenced by native American cultures, and vice versa?
4. Did Montaigne continue to participate in the humanist tradition established during the Late Middle Ages and Renaissance, and how had it changed since about 1500 as evinced in the *Essays*?

Reading 15

Galileo's Letter to the Grand Duchess Christina

The scientific discoveries of the sixteenth and seventeenth centuries profoundly affected ideas concerning the nature of the universe. Especially significant in this regard was Copernicus's (1473–1543) *Revolution of Heavenly Bodies,* published in the year of his death. Although his theory of heliocentricism lacked substantial mathematical proof, the great astronomer had succeeded in removing the Earth from the center of the universe. Copernicus inadvertently raised serious questions concerning humanity's status within God's creation. Scientifically coherent discoveries were also made by Galileo (1564–1642), whose "Letters on Sunspots" occasioned widespread and violent controversy. The battle was ostensibly waged over the Copernican system, but in reality the fight was over the right of a scientist to teach and defend his scientific opinions. The debate between Aristotelian defenders of the Ptolemaic cosmology and the supporters of the Copernican system was summarized by Galileo in 1632 in his politically volatile *Dialogue Concerning the Two Chief World Systems.* But Galileo's most carefully considered expression of his ideas on the proper relation of science and religion is found in his letter written in 1615 to the Grand Duchess **Christina.** Like many of his later works, the public letter placed Galileo at the forefront of the debate and in grave personal danger. In 1633, the Holy Inquisition found Galileo guilty of violating church doctrine. Almost four hundred years later in 1992, **Pope John Paul II** formally proclaimed the Roman Catholic church had erred in condemning Galileo for asserting, like Copernicus, that the sun did not revolve around the earth.

The text is reproduced in the seventeenth-century English prose of Thomas Salusbury.

Some years since, as Your most Serene Highness well knows, I did discover many particulars in Heaven that had been unseen and unheard of until this our Age. Which, as well for their Novelty, as for certain consequences which depend upon

Thomas Salusbury, *Mathematical Collections and Translations,* 2 vols. (London: William Leybourn, 1661–65), 42–45, 86–88.

them, clashing with some Physical Propositions commonly received by the Schools, did stir up against me no small number of such as professed the vulgar Philosophy in the Universities; as if I with my own hand had newly placed these things in Heaven to obscure and disturb Nature and the Sciences, forgetting that the multitude of Truths contribute, and concur to the investigation, augmentation, and establishment of the Arts, and not to their diminution, and destruction. . . .

It has since come to pass, that Time has by degrees discovered to everyone the truths before by me indicated. And together with the truth of the fact, a discovery has been made of the difference of humors between those who simply and without passion did refuse to admit such like Phenomena for true, and those who to their incredulity had added some discomposed affection. For as those who were better grounded in the Science of Astronomy, and Natural Philosophy, became satisfied upon my first intimation of the news. For all those who stood not in the Negative, or in doubt for any other reason, but because it was an unlooked for Novelty, and because they had not an occasion of seeing a sensible experiment thereof, did by degrees come to satisfy themselves. But those, who besides the love they bore to their first Error, have I know not what imaginary interest to render them disaffected; not so much towards the things, as towards the author of them. . . . They persisting therefore in their first Resolution, Of ruining me and whatsoever is mine, by all imaginable ways. And knowing how that I in my Studies of Astronomy and Philosophy hold, as to the Worlds System, That the Sun, without changing place, is situated in the Center of the Conversion of the Celestial Orbs; and that the Earth, convertible about its own Axis, moves itself about the Sun. And moreover understanding, that I proceed to maintain this Position, not only by refuting the Reasons of **Ptolemy** and **Aristotle**, but by producing many on the contrary; and in particular, some Physical pertaining to Natural Effects, the causes of which perhaps can be no other way assigned. And others Astronomical depending upon many circumstances and encounters of new Discoveries in Heaven, which manifestly confute the Ptolemaic System, and admirably agree with and confirm this other Hypothesis, and possibly being ashamed to see the known truth of other Positions by me asserted, different from those that have been commonly received; and therefore distrust their defense so long as they should continue in the Field of Philosophy. For these respects, I say, they have resolved to try Arguments of the Mantle of a feigned Religion, and of the Authority of the Sacred Scriptures, applied by them with little judgment to the confutation of such Reasons of mine as they had neither understood, nor so much as heard. . . .

To facilitate the designs they seek all they can to make this opinion (at least among the vulgar) to seem new, and peculiar to myself, not owing to know that Nicholas Copernicus was its Author, or rather Restorer and Confirmer: a person who was not only a Catholic, but a priest and a canon. . . .

And having reduced the said Doctrine into six books, he published them to the World at the instance of the Cardinal of Capua, and of the Bishop of Culm. And in regard that he had re-affirmed this so laborious an enterprise by the order of The Pope. He dedicated his Book On the Celestial Revolutions to His Successor, namely **Paul III**. Which, being then also Printed, has been received by The Holy

Church, and read and studied by all the World, without any the least umbrage of scruple that has ever been conceived at his Doctrine. The which, while it is now proved manifest Experiments and necessary Demonstrations to have been well grounded, there want not persons that, though they never saw that same book intercept the rewards of those many Labors to its Author, by causing him to be censured and pronounced Heretic. And this, only to satisfy a particular displeasure conceived, without any cause, against another man, that has no other interest in Copernicus, but only as he is an approver of his Doctrine.

Now in regard to these false aspersions, which they so unjustly seek to throw upon me, I have thought it necessary for my justification before the World (of whose judgment in matters of Religion and Reputation I ought to make great esteem) to discourse concerning those Particulars, which these men produce to scandalize and subvert this Opinion, and in a word, to condemn it, not only as false, but also as Heretical; continually making a Hypocritical Zeal for Religion their Shield; going about moreover to interest the Sacred Scriptures in Dispute, and to make them in a certain sense Ministers of their Deceitful purposes. And furthermore desiring, if I mistake not, contrary to the intention of them, and of the Holy Fathers to extend (that I may not say abuse) their Authority, so as that even in Conclusions merely Natural, and not of faith, they would have us altogether leave Sense and Demonstrative Reasons, for some place of Scripture which sometimes under the apparent words may contain a different sense ... he being an Author that never treats of matters of Religion or Faith. Nor by Reasons any way depending on the Authority of Sacred Scriptures whereupon he may have erroneously interpreted them; but always insists upon Natural Conclusions belonging to the Celestial Motions, handled with Astronomical and Geometrical Demonstrations. Not that he had not a respect to the places of the Sacred Leaves, but because he knew very well that his said Doctrine being demonstrated, it could not contradict the Scriptures, rightly, and accordingly to their true meaning understood. . . .

The motive therefore that they produce to condemn the Opinion of the Mobility of the Earth, and Stability of the Sun, is, that reading in the Sacred Leaves, in many places, that the Sun moves, that the Earth stands still. And the Scripture not being capable of lying, or erring, it followed upon necessary consequence, that the Position of those is immoveable, and the Earth moveable.

Touching this Reason I think it fit in the first place, to consider, That it is both piously spoken, and prudently affirmed, That the Sacred Scripture can never lie, whenever its true meaning is understood. Which I believe none will deny to be many times very abstruse, and very different from that which the bare found of the words signifies. . . .

For (like as we have said, and as it plainly appears) out of the sole respect of condescending to Popular Capacity, the Scripture has not scrupled to shadow over most principal and fundamental Truths, attributing, even to God himself, qualities extremely remote from, and contrary unto his Essence. Who would positively affirm that the Scripture laying aside that respect, in speaking but occasionally of the Earth, of the Water, of the Sun, or of any other Creature, has chosen to confine itself, with all rigor, within the bare and narrow literal sense of the words? And especially, in mentioning of those Creatures, things not at all concerning the primary Institution of the same Sacred Volume, to wit, the Service of God, and the salvation of Souls, and in things infinitely beyond the apprehension of the Vulgar?

This therefore being granted, me thinks that in the Discussion of Natural Problems, we ought not to begin at the authority of places of Scripture; but at Sensible Experiments and Necessary Demonstrations. For, from the Divine Word, the Sacred Scripture and Nature did both alike proceed. The first, as the Holy Ghost's Inspiration; the second, as the most observant Executrix of God's Commands. And moreover it being convenient in the Scriptures (by way of condescension to the understanding of all men) to speak many things different, in appearance; and so far as concerns the naked signification of the words, from absolute truth. But on the contrary, Nature being inexorable and immutable, and never passing the bounds of the laws assigned her, as one that nothing cares whether new abstruse reasons and methods of operating be, or not be exposed to the Capacity of Men. I conceive that that, concerning Natural Effects, which either Sensible Experience sets before our eyes, or Necessary Demonstrations do prove unto us ought not, upon any account, to be called into question, much less condemned upon the Testimony of Texts of Scripture, which may, under their words, coach Senses seemingly contrary thereto. In regard that every Expression of Scripture is not tied to so strict conditions, as every Effect of Nature. Nor does God less admirably discover himself unto us in Nature's Actions, than in the Scriptures Sacred Dictions. . . .

Besides that, even in those Propositions, which are not of fact, the Authority of the same Sacred Leaves ought to be preferred to the Authority of all Humane Sciences that are not written in a Demonstrative Method, but either with bare Narrations, or else with probable Reasons. And this I hold to be so convenient and necessary, by how far the said Divine Wisdom surpassed all humane Judgment and Conjecture. But that that self same God who has endowed us with Senses, Discourse, and Understanding has intended, laying aside the use of these, to give knowledge of those things by other means, which we may attain by these. . . .

If we have it from the Mouth of the Holy Ghost, that So that man cannot find out the work that God has done from the beginning even to the end [Ecclesiastes 3:11]. One ought not, as I conceive, to stop the way to free philosophizing, touching the things of the World, and of Nature, as if that they were already certainly found, and all manifest. Nor ought it to be counted rashness, if one does not sit down satisfied with the opinions now become as it were commune. Nor ought any persons to be displeased, if others do not hold, in natural Disputes to that opinion which best pleases them; and especially touching Problems that have, for thousands of years, been controverted amongst the greatest Philosophers. . . .

But the prohibiting of Copernicus his Book, now that by many new Observations, and by the application of many of the Learned to the reading of him, his Hypothesis and Doctrine does every day appear to be more true, having admitted and tolerated it for so many years, whilst he was less followed, studied, and confirmed, would seem, in my judgment, an affront to Truth, and a seeking the more to obscure and suppress her, the more she shows her self clear and perspicuous.

The abolishing and censuring, not of the whole Book, but only so much of it as concerns this particular opinion of the Earth's Mobility, would, if I mistake not, be a greater detriment to souls, it being an occasion of great scandal, to see a Position proved, and to see it afterwards made a Heretic to believe it.

The prohibiting of the whole Science, what other would it be but an open contempt of a hundred Texts of the Holy Scriptures, which teach us, That the Glory, and the Greatness of Almighty God is admirably discerned in all his Works, and divinely read in the Open Book of Heaven? Nor let anyone think that the Lecture of the lofty conceits that are written in those Leaves finish in only beholding the Splendor of the Sun, and of the Stars, and their rising and setting, (which is the term to which the eyes of brutes and the vulgar reach) but there are couched in them mysteries so profound, and concepts so sublime, that the vigils, labors, and studies of a hundred and a hundred acute Wits, have not yet been able to thoroughly dive into them after the continual disquisition of some thousands of years. But let the unlearned believe, that like as that which their eyes discern in beholding the aspect of a human body, is very little in comparison of the stupendous Artifices, which an exquisite and curious Anatomist or Philosopher finds in the fame when he is searching for the use of so many Muscles, Tendons, Nerves, and Bones. And examining the Offices of the Heart, and of the other principal Members, seeking the feat of the vital Faculties, noting and observing the admirable structures of the Instruments of the Senses, and, without ever making an end of satisfying his curiosity and wonder, contemplating the Receptacles of the Imagination, of the Memory, and of the Understanding. So that which represents itself to the mere fight, is as nothing in comparison and proportion to the strange Wonders, that by help of long and accurate Observations the wit of Learned Men discovers in Heaven. . . .

That, in the next place, the common consent of Fathers, in receiving a Natural Proposition of Scripture, all in the same sense ought to Authorize it so far, as to make it become a matter of Faith to believe it to be so, I should think that it ought at most to be understood of those Conclusions only, which have been by the said Fathers discussed, and sifted with all possible diligence, and debated on the one side, and on the other, and all things in the end concurring to disprove the one, and prove the other. But the Mobility of the Earth, and Stability of the Sun, are not of this kind. For that the said Opinion was in those times totally buried, and never brought amongst the Questions of the Schools, and not considered, much less followed by anyone. So that it is to be believed that it never so much as entered into the thought of the Fathers to dispute it, the Places of Scripture, their own Opinion, and the assent of men having all concurred in the same judgment, without the contradiction of anyone, so far as we can find.

Besides, it is not enough to say that the Fathers all admit the stability of the Earth. Therefore to believe it is a matter of faith. But it is necessary to prove that they have condemned the contrary opinion. For I may affirm and bide by this. That their not having occasion to make satisfaction upon the fame, and to discuss it, has made them to omit and admit it, only as current, but not as resolved and proved. And I think I have very good Reason for what I say. . . .

Your highness therefore may see how preposterous those Persons proceed, who in natural Disputations do range Texts of Scripture in the Front for their Arguments. And such Texts too many times, as are but superficially understood by them.

But if these men do verily think, and absolutely believe that they have the true sense of Such a particular place of Scripture, it must needs follow of consequence, that they do likewise hold for certain, that they have found the absolute truth of that Natural Conclusion, which they intend to dispute. . . .

And thereupon, knowing that it is impossible that a Proposition should at the same time be True and Heretical; they ought, I say, to employ themselves in that work which is most proper to them, namely in demonstrating the falsity thereof. Whereby they may see how needless the prohibiting of it is, its falsehood being once discovered, for that none would follow it: or the Prohibition would be safe, and without all danger of Scandal. Therefore first let these men apply themselves to examine the Arguments of Copernicus and others; and leave the condemning of them for Erroneous and Heretical to whom it belongs. But yet let them not hope ever to find such rash and precipitous Determinations in the Wary and Holy Fathers, or in the absolute Wisdom of him that cannot err, as those into which they suffer themselves to be hurried by some particular Affection or Interest of their own.

Study Questions

1. In Galileo's opinion, what is the relationship between scripture and scientific knowledge?
2. Why would the Catholic church hierarchy as well as Protestant reformers disassociate themselves from the findings and theories of this great scientist?
3. How were Galileo's and other scientists' startling perspectives on such age-old issues as the nature of knowledge, the relationship of truth to authority, and the power of the mind different from medieval Christian views on these issues?
4. Why would proof of the heliocentric view of the solar system be so damaging to the Christian cosmological order of God's universe?

Reading 16

Descartes's *Discourse on Method*

Although René Descartes (1596–1650) was a devout Catholic throughout his life, he conceived of the universe very differently from many
of his coreligionists. Descartes believed the universe was structured
mathematically and logically. Nature was subject to mechanical operations. His preface to a book on meteors and geometry, now entitled
Discourse on Method (1637), became one of the most significant treatises on philosophy and the philosophy of science. As Descartes himself
states, his aim was to lay bare the problem of how to ascertain truth.
He refused to accept any authority other than experience and intellect.
The crux of Descartes's method was thus to accept nothing as true and
to doubt everything—with, however, the obvious exception of the acts
of doubting and thinking. Descartes freed the mind of all ideas except
those innate to the mind itself, and his *Discourse of Method* became
a cornerstone of modern thought.

Part One

Good sense is, of all things among men, the most equally distributed; for every
one thinks himself so abundantly provided with it, that those even who are the
most difficult to satisfy in everything else do not usually desire a larger measure
of this quality than they already possess. And in this it is not likely that all are
mistaken: the conviction is rather to be held as testifying that the power of judging
rightly and of distinguishing truth from error, which is properly what is called
good sense or reason, is by nature equal in all men; and that the diversity of our
opinions, consequently, does not arise from some being endowed with a larger
share of reason than others, but solely from this, that we conduct our thoughts
along different ways, and do not fix our attention on the same objects. For to be
possessed of a vigorous mind is not enough; the prime requisite is rightly to apply
it. The greatest minds, as they are capable of the highest excellencies, are open
likewise to the greatest aberrations; and those who travel very slowly may yet

J. Veitch, trans., *The Method, Meditations, and Philosophy of Descartes* (New York: Tudor Publishing,
1901), 149–50, 155, 159–64, 170–77.

make far greater progress, provided they keep always to the straight road, than those who, while they run, forsake it.

For myself, I have never fancied my mind to be in any respect more perfect than those of the generality; on the contrary, I have often wished that I were equal to some others in promptitude of thought, or in clearness and distinctness of imagination, or in fullness and readiness of memory. And besides these, I know of no other qualities that contribute to the perfection of the mind; for as to the reason or sense, inasmuch as it is that alone which constitutes us men, and distinguishes us from the brutes, I am disposed to believe that it is to be found complete in each individual; and on this point to adopt the common opinion of philosophers, who say that the difference of greater and less holds only among the accidents, and not among the forms or natures of individuals of the same species. . . .

It is true that, while busied only in considering the manners of other men, I found here, too, scarce any ground for settled conviction, and remarked hardly less contradiction among them than in the opinions of the philosophers. So that the greatest advantage I derived from the study consisted in this, that, observing many things which, however extravagant and ridiculous to our apprehension, are yet by common consent received and approved by other great nations. I learned to entertain too a decided belief in regard to nothing of the truth of which I had been persuaded merely by example and custom; and thus I gradually extricated myself from many errors powerful enough to darken our natural intelligence, and incapacitate us in great measure from listening to reason. But after I had been occupied several years in thus studying the book of the world, and in essaying to gather some experience, I at length resolved to make myself an object of study, and to employ all the powers of my mind in choosing the paths I ought to follow; an undertaking which was accompanied with greater success than it would have been had I never quitted my country or my books.

Part Two

I was led to infer that the ground of our opinions is far more custom and example than any certain knowledge.

And, finally, although such be the ground of our opinions, I remarked that a plurality of suffrages is no guarantee of truth where it is at all of difficult discovery, as in such cases it is much more likely that it will be found by one than by many.

I could, however, select from the crowd no one whose opinions seemed worthy of preference and thus I found myself constrained, as it were, to use my own reason in the conduct of my life.

But like one walking alone and in the dark, I resolved to proceed so slowly and with such circumspection, that if I did not advance far, I would at least guard against falling.

I did not even choose to dismiss summarily any of the opinions that had crept into my belief without having been introduced by reason, but first of all took sufficient time carefully to satisfy myself of the general nature of the task I was setting myself, and ascertain the true method by which to arrive at the knowledge of whatever lay within the compass of my powers. . . .

By these considerations I was induced to seek some other method which would comprise the advantages of the three and be exempt from their defects. And as one could infer from circumstances, a multitude of laws often only hampers justice, so that a state is best governed when, with few laws, these are rigidly administered; in like manner, instead of the great number of precepts of which logic is composed, I believed that the four following would prove perfectly sufficient for me, provided I took the firm and unwavering resolution never in a single instance to fail in observing them.

The first was never to accept anything for true which I did not clearly know to be such; that is to say, carefully to avoid precipitancy and prejudice, and to comprise nothing more in my judgement than what was presented to my mind so clearly and distinctly as to exclude all ground of doubt.

The second, to divide each of the difficulties under examination into as many parts as possible, and as might be necessary for its adequate solution.

The third, to conduct my thoughts in such order that, by commencing with objects the simplest and easiest to know, I might ascend by little and little, and, as it were, step by step, to the knowledge of the more complex; assigning in thought a certain order even to those objects which in their own nature do not stand in a relation of antecedence and sequence.

Finally, in every case to make enumerations so complete, and reviews so general, that I might be assured that nothing was omitted. . . .

The chief ground of my satisfaction with this method was the assurance I had of thereby exercising my reason in all matters, if not with absolute perfection, at least with the greatest attainable by me: besides, I was conscious that by its use my mind was becoming gradually habituated to clearer and more distinct conceptions of its objects; and I hoped also, from not having restricted this method to any particular matter, to apply it to the difficulties of the other sciences, with not less success than to those of algebra. I should not, however, on this account have ventured at once on the examination of all the difficulties of the sciences which presented themselves to me, for this would have been contrary to the order prescribed in the method, but observing that the knowledge of such is dependent on principles borrowed from philosophy, in which I found nothing certain, I thought it necessary, first of all to endeavor to establish its principles. And because I observed, besides, that an inquiry of this kind was of all others of the greatest moment, and one in which precipitancy and anticipation in judgement were most to be dreaded, I thought that I ought not to approach it till I had reached a more mature age (being at that time but twenty-three), and had first of all employed much of my time in preparation for the work, as well by eradicating from my mind all the erroneous opinions I had up to that moment accepted, as by amassing variety of experience to afford materials for my reasoning, and by continually exercising myself in my chosen method with a view to increased skill in its application.

Part Four

I am in doubt as to the propriety of making my first meditations, in the place above mentioned, matter of discourse; for these are so metaphysical, and so uncommon, as not, perhaps, to be acceptable to everyone. And yet, that it may be determined whether the foundations that I have laid are sufficiently secure, I find myself in a measure constrained to advert to them. I had long before remarked that, in relation to practice, it is sometimes necessary to adopt, as if above doubt, opinions which we discern to be highly uncertain, as has been already said; but as I then desired to give my attention solely to the search after truth, I thought that a procedure exactly the opposite was called for, and that I ought to reject as absolutely false all opinions in regard to which I could suppose the least ground for doubt, in order to ascertain whether after that there remained aught in my belief that was wholly indubitable. Accordingly, seeing that our senses sometimes deceive us, I was willing to suppose that there existed nothing really such as they presented to us; and because some men err in reasoning, and fall into paralogisms, even on the simplest matters of geometry, I, convinced that I was as open to error as any other, rejected as false all the reasoning I had hitherto taken for demonstrations; and finally, when I considered that the very same thoughts (presentations) which we experience when awake may also be experienced when we are asleep, while there is at that time not one of them true, I supposed that all the objects (presentations) that had ever entered into my mind when awake, had in them no more truth than the illusions of my dreams. But immediately upon this I observed that, while I thus wished to think that all was false, it was absolutely necessary that I, who thus thought, should be somewhat; and as I observed that this truth, I THINK, THEREFORE I AM, was so certain and of such evidence, that no ground of doubt, however extravagant, could be alleged by the skeptics capable of shaking it, I concluded that I might, without scruple, accept it as the first principle of the philosophy of which I was in search.

In the next place, I attentively examined what I was, and as I observed that I could suppose that I had no body, and that there was no world nor any place in which I might be; but that I could not therefore suppose that I was not; and that, on the contrary, from the very circumstance that I thought to doubt of the truth of all things, it most clearly and certainly followed that I was; while, on the other hand, if I had only ceased to think, although all the other objects which I had ever imagined had been in reality existent, I would have had no reason to believe that I existed; I thence concluded that I was a substance whose whole essence or nature consists only in thinking, and which, that it may exist, has need of no place, nor is dependent on any material thing; so that "I," that is to say, the mind by which I am what I am, is wholly distinct from the body, and is even more easily known than the latter, and is such, that although the latter were not, it would still continue to be all that it is.

After this I inquired in general into what is essential to the truth and certainty of a proposition; for since I had discovered one which I knew to be true, I thought that I must likewise be able to discover the ground of this certitude. And as I observed that in the words I THINK, THEREFORE I AM, there is nothing at all which gives me assurance of their truth beyond this, that I see very clearly that in order to think it is necessary to exist, I concluded that I might take, as a general rule, the principle, that all the things which we very clearly and distinctly conceive are true, only observing, however, that there is some difficulty in rightly determining the objects which we distinctly conceive.

In the next place, from reflecting on the circumstance that I doubted, and that consequently my being was not wholly perfect (for I clearly saw that it was a greater perfection to know than to doubt), I was led to inquire whence I had learned to think of something more perfect than myself: and I clearly recognized that I must hold this notion from some Nature which in reality was more perfect. As for the thoughts of many other objects external to me, as of the sky, the earth, light, heat, and a thousand more, I was less at a loss to know whence these came; for since I remarked in them nothing which seemed to render them superior to myself, I could believe that, if these were true, they were dependencies on my own nature, in so far as it possessed a certain perfection, and, if they were false, that I held them from nothing, that is to say, that they were in me because of a certain imperfection of my nature. But this could not be the case with the idea of a Nature more perfect than myself; for to receive it from nothing was a thing manifestly impossible; and, because it is not less repugnant that the more perfect should be an effect of, and dependence on the less perfect, than that something should proceed from nothing, it was equally impossible that I could hold it from myself: accordingly, it but remained that it had been placed in me by a Nature which was in reality more perfect than mine, and which even possessed within itself all the perfections of which I could form any idea: that is to say, in a single word, which was God. And to this I added that, since I knew some perfections which I did not possess, I was not the only being in existence, (I will here, with your permission, freely use the terms of the schools); but on the contrary, that there was of necessity some other more perfect Being upon whom I was dependent, and from whom I had received all that I possessed; for if I had existed alone, and independently of every other being, so as to have had from myself all the perfection, however little, which I actually possessed, I should have been able, for the same reason, to have had from myself the whole remainder of perfection, of the want of which I was conscious, and thus could of myself have become infinite, eternal, immutable, omniscient, all-powerful, and, in fine, have possessed all the perfections which I could recognize in God. For in order to know the nature of God (whose existence has been established by the preceding reasoning), as far as my own nature permitted, I had only to consider in reference to all the properties of which I found in my mind some idea, whether their possession was a mark of perfection; and I was assured that no one which indicated any imperfection was in him, and that none of the rest was lacking. Thus I perceived that doubt, inconstancy, sadness, and such like, could not be found in God, since I myself would have been happy to be free from them. Besides, I had ideas of many sensible and corporeal things; for although I might suppose that I was dreaming, and that all which I saw or imagined was false, I could not, nevertheless, deny that the ideas were in reality in my thoughts. But because I had already very clearly recognized in myself that the intelligent nature is distinct from the corporeal, and as I observed that all composition is an evidence of dependency, manifestly a state of imperfection, I therefore determined that it could not be a perfection in God to be compounded of these two natures, and that consequently he was not so compounded; but that if there were any bodies in the world, or even any intelligences, or other natures that were not wholly perfect, their existence depended on his power in such a way that they could not subsist without him for a single moment. . . .

But the reason which leads many to persuade themselves that there is a difficulty in knowing the truth, and even also in knowing what their mind really is, is that they never raise their thoughts above sensible objects, and are so accustomed to consider nothing except by way of imagination, which is a mode of thinking limited to material objects, that all that is not imaginable seems to them not intelligible. The truth of this is sufficiently manifest from the single circumstance, that the philosophers of the schools accept as a maxim that there is nothing in the understanding which was not previously in the senses, in which however it is certain that the ideas of God and of the soul have never been; and it appears to me that they who make use of their imagination to comprehend these ideas do exactly the same thing as if, in order to hear sounds or smell odors, they strove to avail themselves of their eyes; unless indeed that there is this a difference, that the sense of sight does not afford us an inferior assurance to those of smell or hearing; in place of which, neither our imagination nor our senses can give us assurance of anything unless our understanding intervene.

Finally, if there be still persons who are not sufficiently persuaded of the existence of God and of the soul, by the reasons I have adduced, I am desirous that they should know that all the other propositions, of the truth of which they deem themselves perhaps more assured, as that we have a body, and that there exist stars and an earth, and such like, are less certain; for, although we have a moral assurance of these things, which is so strong that there is an appearance of extravagance in doubting of their existence, yet at the same time no one, unless his intellect is impaired, can deny, when the question relates to a metaphysical certitude, that there is sufficient reason to exclude entire assurance, in the observation that when asleep we can in the same way imagine ourselves possessed of another body and that we see other stars and another earth, when there is nothing of the kind. For how do we know that the thoughts which occur in dreaming are false rather than those other which we experience when awake, since the former are often no less vivid and distinct than the latter? And though men of the highest genius study this question as long as they please, I do not believe that they will be able to give any reason which can be sufficient to remove this doubt, unless they presuppose the existence of God. For, in the first place, even the principle which I have already taken as a rule, viz., that all the things which we clearly and distinctly conceive are true, is certain only because God is or exists, and because he is a Perfect Being, and because all that we possess is derived from him: whence it follows that our ideas or notions, which to the extent of their clearness and distinctness are real, and proceed from God, must to that extent be true. Accordingly, whereas we not infrequently have ideas or notions in which some falsity is contained, this can only be the case with such as are to some extent confused and obscure, and in this proceed from nothing, (participate of negation), that is, exist in us thus confused because we are not wholly perfect. And it is evident that it is not less repugnant that falsity or imperfection, in so far as it is imperfection, should proceed from God, than that truth or perfection should proceed from nothing. But if we did not know that all which we possess of real and true proceeds from a Perfect and Infinite Being, however clear and distinct our ideas might be, we should have no ground on that account for the assurance that they possessed the perfection of being true.

Study Questions

1. What is Descartes's method for determining those "clear and distinct" ideas that form the basis of truth?
2. In what ways is this method practical, and how does it allow Descartes to arrive at the notion "I think, therefore I am" and permit the conclusion that God exists?
3. What is the essence of Cartesian dualism?
4. Why was Descartes's experiment in doubt considered revolutionary within the intellectual and social context of mid-seventeenth-century Europe?

The Putney Debates

When Queen Elizabeth I of England (1553–1603) died, her cousin King
James VI (1566–1625) of Scotland succeeded her. He soon found himself at odds with Parliament over the issue of royal finances and other
lingering problems. Many of these were religious in nature, prompted
by the Puritans who tried to reform the Church of England and make
it more Protestant. The English hoped the conflict brewing between
king and Parliament might be quickly resolved. However, exasperated
by increasing demands from Parliament, King Charles I (1600–1649)
attempted to rule in disregard of the Commons from 1629 to 1640.
When war with Scotland broke out, the king found it necessary to
summon Parliament again. The Long Parliament, which sat in session
in various forms for twenty years, wrung many parliamentary privileges
out of the king in exchange for money subsidies. However, stalwart
leaders—such as **Oliver Cromwell**—continued to be thorns in the royal
side. Charles felt compelled to enter the House of Commons to order
the arrest of some of its leaders. The result was civil war. In 1644
King Charles and the royalists were defeated at Marston Moor, and in
1645 the New Model Army and General Cromwell's cavalry, the "Iron-
sides," were victorious at Naseby. In June 1647 the political situation
was entirely transformed when the king was captured and eventually
held by the Parliamentary militants. In December 1648, Colonel
Thomas Pride (d. 1658), under orders from Cromwell and Thomas Fair-
fax (1612–1671), purged the Lower House of its irresolute members
and thereby created the **Rump Parliament**. Meanwhile, debate about
King Charles's immediate future and the nature of just government
dominated the political scene. As the confrontation between soldiers
and statesmen escalated, the army became the last resort for radical
groups whose reform programs had been earlier rejected by Parliament.
In the midst of complex negotiations, the **Leveller**'s "An Agreement
of the People" served as the focus of a four-day debate that took place
in the Council of Officers. First recorded in shorthand and later tran-
scribed by William Clarke, a secretary of the army, the so-called Putney
Debates record that among the main speakers were General Cromwell;
Henry Ireton (1611–1651), Cromwell's son-in-law and commissary-
general of the cavalry; and Colonel Thomas Rainsborough (d. 1648),
a champion of the "common man." The following portion of the transcript records the men debating the first Article of "An Agreement of
the People." It states, "the People of England being at this day very un-
equally distributed by Counties, Cities, and Burroughs, for the election of

their Deputies in Parliament, ought to be more indifferently proportioned, according to the number of Inhabitants: the circumstances whereof, for number, place, and manner, are to be set down before the end of this present Parliament."

Colonel Thomas Rainsborough: I desired that those that had engaged in [the election of representatives of Parliament], for really I think that the poorest he that is in England hath a life to live as the greatest he; and therefore truly, sir, I think it is clear, that every man that is to live under a government ought first by his own consent to put himself under that government; and I do think that the poorest man in England is not at all bound in a strict sense to that government that he hath not had a voice to put himself under; and I am confident that, when I have heard the reasons against it, that something will be said to answer those reasons, insomuch that I should doubt whether I was an Englishman or no, that should doubt of these things.

Commissary General Henry Ireton: . . . For my part, I think it is no right at all. I think that no person hath a right to an interest or share in the disposing of the affairs of the kingdom, and in determining or choosing those that shall determine what laws we shall be ruled by here, no person hath a right to this that hath not a permanent fixed interest in this kingdom, and those persons together are properly the represented of this kingdom, who taken together, and consequently are to make up the representers of this kingdom, are the representers, who taken together do comprehend whatsoever is of real or permanent interest in the kingdom, and I am sure there is otherwise (I cannot tell what), otherwise any man can say why a foreigner coming in amongst us, or as many as will come in amongst us, or by force or otherwise settling themselves here, or at least by our permission having a being here, why they should not as well lay claim to it as any other. We talk of birthright. Truly [in] birthright there is thus much claim: men may justly have by birthright, by their very being born in England, that we should not seclude them out of England. That we should not refuse to give them air and place and ground, and the freedom of the highways and other things, to live amongst us, not any man that is born here, though he in birth, or by his birth there come nothing at all that is part of the permanent interest of this kingdom to him. That I think is due to a man by birth. But that by a man's being born here he shall have a share in that power that shall dispose of the lands here, and of all things here, I do not think it a sufficient ground, but I am sure if we look upon that which is the utmost, within man's view, of what was originally the constitution of this kingdom, upon that which is most radical and fundamental, and which if you take

A. S. P. Woodehouse, *Puritanism and Liberty* (Chicago: University of Chicago Press, 1951), 99–102, passim.

away, there is no man hath any land, any goods, you take away any civil interest, and that is this: that those that choose the representers for the making of laws by which this state and kingdom are to be governed, are the persons who taken together, do comprehend the local interest of this kingdom; that is, the persons in whom all land lies, and those in corporations in whom all trading lies. This is the most fundamental constitution of this kingdom, and which if you do not allow, you allow none at all. . . .

Rainsborough: Truly, sir, I am of the same opinion I was, and am resolved to keep it till I know reason why I should not. . . . [As] to this present business, I do hear nothing at all that can convince me, why any man that is born in England ought not to have his voice in election of burgesses. . . . I do think that the main cause why Almighty God gave men reason, it was that they should make use of that reason, and that they should improve it for that end and purpose that God gave it them, and truly I think that half a loaf is better than none if a man [is] hungry; yet I think there is nothing that God hath given a man that any else can take from him, and therefore I say, that either it must be the law of God or the law of man that must prohibit the meanest man in the kingdom from having this benefit as well as the greatest.

I do not find anything in the law of God, that a lord shall choose twenty burgesses, and a gentleman but two, or a poor man shall choose none: I find no such thing in the law of nature, nor in the law of nations, but I do find that all Englishmen must be subject to English laws, and I do verily believe that there is no man but will say that the foundation of all law lies in the people, and if in the people, I am to seek for this exemption; and truly I have thought something: in what a miserable distressed condition would many a man whose zeal and affection to God and this kingdom hath carried him forth in this cause, hath so spent his estate that, in the way the state, the army are going this way, he shall not hold up his head, and when his estate is lost, and not worth forty shillings a year, a man shall not have any interest; and there are many other ways by which men have estates (if that be the rule which God in his providence does use) do fall to decay; a man, when he hath an estate, he hath an interest in making laws; when he hath none, he hath no power in it. So that a man cannot lose that which he hath for the maintenance of his family but he must lose that which God and nature hath given him; and therefore I do, and am still of the same opinion, that every man born in England cannot, ought not, neither by the law of God nor the law of nature, to be exempted from the choice of those who are to make laws and for him to live under, and for him (for aught I know) to lose his life under, and therefore I think there can be no great stick in this.

Truly I think that there is not this day reigning in England a greater fruit or effect of tyranny than this very thing would produce, for, sir, what is it, the King he grants a patent under the Broad-Seal of England to such a corporation to send burgesses. He grants to a city to send burgesses. Truly I know nothing free but only the knight of the shire, nor do I know anything in a parliamentary way that is clear from the height and fullness of tyranny, but as for this of corporations, it is as contrary to freedom as may be; when a poor base corporation from the King shall send two burgesses, when five hundred men of estate shall not send one, when those that are to make their laws are called by the King, or cannot act by such a call, truly I think that the people of England have little freedom.

Ireton: I think there was nothing that I said to give you occasion to think that I did contend for this, that such a corporation should have the electing of a man to the parliament. I think I agreed to this matter, that all should be equally distributed, but the question is, whether it should be distributed to all persons, or whether the same persons that are the electors should be the electors still, and it equally distributed amongst them. I do not see anybody else that makes this objection; and if nobody else be sensible of it I shall soon have done. Only I shall a little crave your leave to represent the consequences of it, and clear myself from one misrepresentation of the thing that was misrepresented by the gentleman that sat next me. I think, if the gentleman remember himself, he cannot but remember that what I said was to this effect: that if I saw the hand of God leading so far as to destroy King, and destroy lords, and destroy property, and no such thing at all amongst us, I should acquiesce in it; and so I did not care, if no king, no lords, or no property, how in comparison of the tender care that I have of the honor of God, and of the people of God, whose name is so much concerned in this Army. This I did deliver, and not absolutely.

The main thing that I speak for is because I would have an eye to property. I hope we do not come to contend for victory, but let every man consider with himself that he do not go that way to take away all property; for here is the case of the most fundamental part of the constitution of the kingdom, which if you take away, you take away all by that. Here are men of this and this quality are determined to be the electors of men to the parliament, and they are all those who have any permanent interest in the kingdom, and who, taken together, do comprehend the whole interest of the kingdom. I mean by permanent, local, that is not anywhere else. As for instance, he that hath a freehold, and that freehold cannot be removed out of the kingdom. And so there's a corporation, a place which hath the privilege of a market and trading, which if you should allow to all places equally, I do not see how you could preserve any peace in the kingdom, and that is the reason why in the constitution we have but some few market towns. Now those people by the former constitution were looked upon to comprehend the permanent interest of the kingdom, and those are the freemen of corporations; for he that hath his livelihood by his trade, and by his freedom of trading in such a corporation, which he cannot exercise in another, he is tied to that place, his livelihood depends upon it; and secondly, that man hath an interest, hath a permanent interest there, upon which he may live, and live a freeman without dependence. These constitutions this kingdom hath looked at.

Now I wish we may all consider of what right you will challenge, that all the people should have right to elections. Is it by the right of nature? If you will hold forth that as your ground, then I think you must deny all property too, and this is my reason. For thus: by that same right of nature, whatever it be that you pretend, by which you can say, a man hath an equal right with another to the choosing of him that shall govern him, by the same right of nature, he hath the same right in any goods he sees: meat, drink, clothes, to take and use them for his sustenance; he hath a freedom to the land, the ground, to exercise it, till it. He hath the freedom to anything that any one doth account himself to have any propriety in. Why now I say, then if you will, against the most fundamental part of civil constitution (which I have now declared), will plead the law of nature, that a man should, paramount this, and contrary to this, have a power of choosing those men that shall determine what shall be law in this state, though he himself have no permanent interest in the state, whatever interest he hath he may carry about with him, if this be allowed, we are free, we are equal, one man must have as much voice as another. Then show me what step or difference, why by the same right of necessity to sustain nature, it is for my better being, and possibly not for it neither; possibly I may not have so real a regard to the peace of the kingdom as that man who hath a permanent interest in it; but he that hath no permanent interest, that is here today and gone tomorrow, I do not see that he hath such a permanent interest. Since you cannot plead to it by anything but the law of nature, but for the end of better being, and that better being is not certain, and more destructive to another; upon these grounds, if you do, paramount all constitutions, hold up this law of nature, I would fain have any man show me their bounds, where you will end, and take away all property?

Rainsborough: I shall now be a little more free and open with you than I was before. I wish we were all true hearted, and that we did all carry ourselves with integrity; if I did mistrust you, I would use such asseverations. I think it doth go on mistrust, and things are thought too matters of reflection that were never intended for my part; as I think you forgot something that was in my speech. You forgot something in my speech, and you do not only yourselves believe, that men are inclining to anarchy, but you would make all men believe that; and, sir, to say because a man pleads that every man hath a voice, that therefore it destroys the same that there's a property, the law of God says it, else why God made that law, thou shalt not steal. I am a poor man, therefore I must be a priest; if I have no interest in the kingdom, I must suffer by all their laws, be they right or wrong. Nay thus, a gentleman lives in a county and hath three or four lordships as some men have, God knows how they got them, and when a parliament is called, he must be a man of parliament; and it may be he sees some poor men they live near, this man he can crush them. I have known an evasion to make sure he hath turned the poor man out of doors, and I would fain know whether the potency of men do not this, and so keep them under the greatest tyranny that was thought of in the world; and therefore I think that to that it is fully answered. God hath set down that thing as to property with this law of his, thou shalt not steal. And for my part I am against any such thought, and I wish you would not make the world believe that we are for anarchy, as for yourselves.

Lieutenant General Cromwell: I know nothing but this, that they that are the most yielding have the greatest wisdom; but really sir, this is not right as it should be. No man says that you have a mind to anarchy, but the consequence of this rule tends to anarchy, must end in anarchy; for where is there any bound or limit set, if you take away this, that men that have no interest but the interest of breathing [should have no voice]. Therefore I am confident of it, we should not be so hot one with another.

Rainsborough: I know that some particular men we debate with [believe—or say—we] are for anarchy.

Ireton: I have, with as much plainness and clearness of reason as I could, showed you how I did conceive the doing of this takes away that which is the most original, the most fundamental civil constitution of this Kingdom, and which is above all that constitution by which I have any property and if you will take away that and set up what ever a man may claim as a thing paramount, that by the law of nature, though it be not a thing of necessity to him for the sustenance of nature, if you do make this your rule, I desire clearly to understand where then remains property. . . .

Now then, as I say to that which is to the main answer, that it will not make the breach of property, then that there is a law, thou shalt not steal: the same law says, honor thy father, and mother: and that law doth likewise hold out that it doth extend to all that, in that place where we are in, are our governors, so that by that there is a forbidding of breaking a civil law when we may live quietly under it, and a divine law; and again it is said, indeed before, that there is no law, no divine law that tells us, that such a corporation must have the election of burgesses, of such a shire or the like. Divine law extends not to particular things; and so on the other side, if a man were to demonstrate his property by divine law, it would be very remote, but our property descends from other things, as well as our right of sending burgesses; that divine law doth not determine particulars but generals in relation to man and man, and to property, and all things else, and we should be as far to seek if we should go to prove a property in divine law as to prove that I have an interest in choosing burgesses of the parliament by divine law; and truly under favor I refer it to all whether these be any thing of solution to that objection that I made, if it be understood. I submit it to any man's judgment.

Rainsborough: To the thing itself—property—I would fain know how it comes to be the property: as for estates, and those kind of things and other things that belong to men, it will be granted that it is property, but I deny that that is a property, to a lord, to a gentleman, to any man more than another in the kingdom of England, if it be a property, it is a property by a law; neither do I think, that there is very little property in this thing by the law of the land, because I think, that the law of the land in that thing is the most tyrannical law under heaven, and I would fain know what we have fought for; and this is the old law of England and that which enslaves the people of England, that they should be bound by laws in which they have no voice at all. So the great dispute is who is a right father and a right mother. I am bound to know who is my father and mother, and I take it in the same sense you do. I would have a distinction, a character whereby God commands me to honor and for my part I look upon the people of England so, that wherein they have not voices in the choosing of their fathers and mothers, they are not bound to that commandment.

Study Questions

1. According to the main protagonists in the Putney Debates, who should be eligible to vote for members of Parliament?
2. Why was the right to vote such an important issue of the day?
3. What are the different notions of political order and authority expressed by the debaters?
4. How are the Putney Debates not only an outgrowth of seventeenth-century English politics, but also a product of the religious and intellectual revolution of the Early Modern Age?

Reading 18

John Locke's *An Essay Concerning Human Understanding*

Among his many intellectual pursuits, John Locke (1632–1704) assumed the task of investigating the limits of human knowledge, a topic intimately linked to the problem of how ideas are formed or obtained by the mind. A direct attack on René Descartes's **innatism**, Locke's *Essay Concerning Human Understanding*, published in England in 1690, broadcast the contention that there was no reason to assume the existence of innate ideas in the human mind, and that the mind was a *tabula rasa,* a "blank tablet." According to Locke, the mind obtains sense impressions through experience, and these impressions are then organized by the mind and become ideas. Knowledge was thus believed to be derived from experience in the world. With his empirical outlook, Locke was able to provide a new, rigorous framework for philosophy based on the scientific premises established by **Sir Isaac Newton**.

Book One: Chapter Two

1. The way of how we come by any Knowledge is sufficient to prove it not innate. It is an established opinion among some men, that there are in the understanding certain innate principles; some primary notions, characters, as it were stamped upon the mind of man; which the soul receives in its very first being, and brings into the world with it. It would be sufficient to convince unprejudiced readers of the falseness of this supposition, if I should only show (as I hope I shall in the following parts of this discourse) how men, barely by the use of their natural faculties, may attain to all the knowledge they have, without the help of any innate impressions; and may arrive at certainty, without any such original notions or

J. A. St. John, ed., *The Philosophical Works of John Locke* (London: George Bell & Sons, 1892), vol. 1: 134–37, 142–43, 205–8, 210–11, 221–23.

principles. For I imagine any one will easily grant that it would be impertinent to suppose the ideas of colors innate in a creature to whom God has given sight, and a power to receive them by the eyes from external objects: and no less unreasonable would it be to attribute several truths to the impressions of nature, and innate characters, when we may observe in ourselves faculties fit to attain as easy and certain knowledge of them, as if they were originally imprinted on the mind.

But because a man is not permitted without censure to follow his own thoughts in the search of truth, when they lead him ever so little out of the common road, I shall set down the reasons that made me doubt of the truth of that opinion, as an excuse for my mistake, if I be in one; which I leave to be considered by those who, with me, dispose themselves to embrace truth wherever they find it.

2. *[Concerning the] General Assent [to] the great Argument.* There is nothing more commonly taken for granted than that there are certain principles, both speculative and practical (for they speak of both), universally agreed upon by all mankind, which therefore, they argue, must needs be constant impressions, which the souls of men receive in their first beings, and which they bring into the world with them, as necessarily and really as they do any of their inherent faculties.

3. *Universal Consent proves nothing innate.* This argument, drawn from universal consent, has this misfortune in it, that if it were true in matter of fact, that there were certain truths wherein all mankind agreed, it would not prove them innate, if there can be any other way shown how men may come to that universal agreement, in the things they do consent in, which I presume may be done.

4. *"What is, is," and "it is impossible for the same Thing to be and not to be" [is] not universally assented to.* But, which is worse, this argument of universal consent, which is made use of to prove innate principles, seems to me a demonstration that there are none such; because there are none to which all mankind give universal assent. I shall begin with the speculative, and illustrate in those magnified principles of demonstration, "whatsoever is, is," and "it is impossible for the same thing to be and not to be," which, of all others, I think have the most allowed title to innate. These have so settled a reputation of maxims universally received, that it will no doubt be thought strange if any one should seem to question it. But yet I take liberty to say, that these propositions are so far from having a universal assent, that they are a great part of mankind to whom they are not so much as known.

5. *[Innate ideas are] not on the Mind naturally imprinted, because not known to Children, Idiots, and so forth.* For, first, it is evident that all children and idiots have not the least apprehension or thought of them. And the want of that is enough to destroy that universal assent which must be the necessary concomitant of all innate truths: it seems to me near a contradiction to say that there are truths imprinted on the soul, which it perceives or understands not: imprinting, if it signifies anything, being nothing else but the making of certain truths to be perceived. For to imprint anything on the mind without the mind's perceiving it, seems to me hardly intelligible. If therefore children and idiots have souls, have minds, with those impressions upon them, they must unavoidably perceive them, and necessarily know and assent to these truths; which since they do not, it is

101

evident that there are no such impressions. For if they are not notions naturally imprinted, how can they be innate? And if they are notions imprinted, how can they be unknown? To say a notion is imprinted on the mind, and yet at the same time to say that the mind is ignorant of it, and never yet took notice of it, is to make this impression nothing. No proposition can be said to be in the mind which it never yet knew, which it was never yet conscious of. . . .

15. *The steps by which the Mind attains several Truths.* The senses at first let in particular ideas, and furnish the yet empty cabinet, and the mind by degrees growing familiar with some of them, they are lodged in the memory, and names got to them. Afterwards, the mind proceeding further, abstracts them, and by degrees learns the use of general names. In this manner the mind comes to be furnished with ideas and language, the materials about which to exercise its discursive faculty. And the use of reason becomes daily more visible, as these materials that give it employment increase. But though the having of general ideas and the use of general words and reason usually grow together, yet I see not how this any way proves them innate. The knowledge of some truths, I confess, is very early in the mind; but in a way that shows them not to be innate. For, if we will observe, we shall find it still to be about ideas, not innate, but acquired; it being about those first which are imprinted by external things, with which infants have earliest to do, which make the most frequent impressions on their senses. In ideas thus got, the mind discovers that some agree and others differ, probably as soon as it has any use of memory; as soon as it is able to retain and perceive distinct ideas. But whether it be then or no, this is certain, it does so long before it has the use of words; or comes to that which we commonly call "the use of reason." For a child knows as certainly before it can speak the difference between the ideas of sweet and bitter (that is, that sweet is not bitter), as it knows afterwards (when it comes to speak) that wormwood and sugarplums are not the same thing.

Book Two: Chapter One

1. *Idea is the Object of Thinking.* Every man being conscious to himself that he thinks, and that which his mind is applied about while thinking being the ideas that are there, it is past doubt that men have in their minds several ideas,—such as are those expressed by the words whiteness, hardness, sweetness, thinking, motion, man, elephant, army, drunkenness, and others. It is in the first place then to be inquired, how he comes by them? I know it is a received doctrine that men have native ideas, and original characters, stamped upon their minds in their very first being. This opinion I have at large examined already; and, I suppose what I have (already) said . . . will be much more easily admitted, when I have shown where the understanding may get all the ideas it has; and by what ways and degrees they may come into the mind;—for which I shall appeal to every one's own observation and experience.

2. *All Ideas come from Sensation or Reflection.* Let us then suppose the mind to be, as we say, white paper, void of all characters, without any ideas. How comes it to be furnished? From where comes that vast store which the busy and boundless fancy of man has painted on it with an almost endless variety? From where has it all the materials of reason and knowledge? To this I answer, in one word, from experience. In that all our knowledge is founded; and from that it ultimately derives itself. Our observation employed either, about external sensible objects, or about the internal operations of our minds perceived and reflected on by ourselves, is that which supplies our understandings with all the materials of thinking. These two are the fountains of knowledge, from where all the ideas we have, or can naturally have, do spring.

3. *The Objects of Sensation [are] one Source of Ideas.* First, our senses, conversant about particular sensible objects, do convey into the mind several distinct perceptions of things, according to those various ways wherein those objects do affect them. And thus we come by those ideas we have of yellow, white, heat, cold, soft, hard, bitter, sweet, and all those which we call sensible qualities; which when I say the senses convey into the mind, I mean, they from external objects convey into the mind what produces there those perceptions. This great source of most of the ideas we have, depending wholly upon our senses, and derived by them to the understanding, I call sensation.

4. *Of the Operations of our Minds [and] the other Source of them.* Secondly, the other fountain from which experience furnishes the understanding with ideas is, the perception of the operations of our own mind within us, as it is employed about the ideas it has got; which operations, when the soul comes to reflect on and consider, do furnish the understanding with another set of ideas, which could not be had from things without. And such are perception, thinking, doubting, believing, reasoning, knowing, willing, and all the different actings of our own minds;—which we being conscious of, and observing in ourselves, do from these receive into our understandings as distinct ideas as we do from bodies affecting our senses. This source of ideas every man has wholly in himself; and though it be not sense, as having nothing to do with external objects, yet it is very like it, and might properly enough be called internal sense. But as I call the other sensation, so I call this reflection, the ideas it affords being such only as the mind gets by reflecting on its own operations within itself. By reflection then, in the following part of this discourse, I would be understood to mean that notice which the mind takes of its own operations, and the manner of them, by reason whereof there come to be ideas of these operations in the understanding. These two, I say, namely, external material things, as the objects of sensation, and the operations of our own minds within, as the objects of reflection are to me the only origin from where all our ideas take their beginnings. The term operations here I use in a large sense, as comprehending not barely the actions of the mind about its ideas, but some sort of passions arising sometimes from them, such as is the satisfaction or uneasiness arising from any thought.

5. *All our Ideas are of the one or the other of these.* The understanding seems to me not to have the least glimmering of any ideas which it does not

receive from one of these two. External objects furnish the mind with the ideas of sensible qualities, which are all those different perceptions they produce in us; and the mind furnishes the understanding with ideas of its own operations.

These, when we have taken a full survey of them, and their several modes, combinations, and relations, we shall find to contain all our whole stock of ideas; and that we have nothing in our minds which did not come in one of these two ways. Let any one examine his own thoughts, and thoroughly search into his understanding; and then let him tell me, whether all the original ideas he has there, are any other than of the objects of his senses, or of the operations of his mind, considered as objects of his reflection. And how great a mass of knowledge soever he imagines to be lodged there, he will, upon taking a strict view, see that he has not any idea in his mind but what one of these two have imprinted;—though perhaps, with infinite variety compounded and enlarged by the understanding, as we shall see hereafter.

22. *Follow a child from its birth, and observe the alterations that time makes, and you shall find, as the mind by the senses comes more and more to be furnished with ideas, it comes to be more and more awake; thinks more, the more it has matter to think on.* After some time it begins to know the objects which, being most familiar with it, have made lasting impressions. Thus it comes by degrees to know the persons it daily converses with, and distinguishes them from strangers; which are instances and effects of its coming to retain and distinguish the ideas the senses convey to it. And so we may observe how the mind by degrees improves in these; and advances to the exercise of those other faculties of enlarging, compounding, and abstracting its ideas, and of reasoning about them, and reflecting upon all these; of which I shall have occasion to speak more hereafter.

23. *If it shall be demanded then, when a man begins to have any ideas, I think the true answer is, when he first has any sensation.* For, since there appear not to be any ideas in the mind before the senses have conveyed any in, I conceive that ideas in the understanding are coeval with sensation; which is such an impression or motion made in some part of the body, as produces some perception in the understanding. It is about these impressions made on our senses by outward objects that the mind seems first to employ itself, in such operations as we call perception, remembering, consideration, reasoning, and so forth.

24. *The Origin of all our Knowledge.* In time the mind comes to reflect on its own operations about the ideas got by sensation, and thereby stores itself with a new set of ideas, which I call ideas of reflection. These are the impressions that are made on our senses by outward objects that are extrinsical to the mind; and its own operations, proceeding from powers intrinsical and proper to itself, which, when reflected on by itself, become also objects of its contemplation—are, as I have said, the origin of all knowledge. Thus the first capacity of human intellect is—that the mind is fitted to receive the impressions made on it; either through the senses by outward objects, or by its own operations when it reflects on them. This is the first step a man makes toward the discovery of anything, and the groundwork whereon to build all those notions which ever he shall have naturally in this world. All those sublime thoughts which tower above the clouds, and reach

as high as heaven itself, take their rise and footing here: in all that great extent wherein the mind wanders, in those remote speculations it may seem to be elevated with, it stirs not one jot beyond those ideas which sense or reflection have offered for its contemplation.

Study Questions

1. How do John Locke's philosophical investigations focus on what can be known or discovered by the mind?
2. What is the main difference between external objects and internal operations of the mind according to the author?
3. How does Locke's explanation of how the human mind functions reveal his participation in the scientific revolution of the Early Modern Age that culminated in Sir Isaac Newton's work?
4. How did the empirical emphasis found in the new science influence Locke's outlook and philosophy?

Reading 19

Mary Astell's *A Serious Proposal to the Ladies*

The daughter of an English merchant of Newcastle upon Tyne, Mary Astell (1668–1731) received her early education from a local clergyman. Later in life she settled in the vicinity of London. Astell was the author of many works, including *An Essay in Defense of the Female Sex* (1696) and *Reflections on Marriage* (1705). Her best known piece is *A Serious Proposal to the Ladies*. It was originally published as two books, the first appearing in 1694 and anonymously ascribed to "a lover of her sex." In it Astell attempted to persuade wealthy women who did not marry to use their dowries to support residential women's colleges. The second volume materialized in 1697. It offered a method for the improvement of women's minds by detailing rules of rational thought distilled from René Descartes's analytical method. Astell's general intention was to set up communities in which women would receive intellectual, moral, and religious training. In essence, she wanted to establish Protestant nunneries throughout England. An active participant in the revolution of thought taking place in the Early Modern period, her proposed colleges for women were as controversial as many ideas found in her writings.

The text has been printed, with few alterations, in its original language.

Opening Remarks

Ladies, . . . I persuade my self [that] you will not be less kind to a Proposition that comes attended with more certain and substantial Gain; whose only design is to improve your Charms and heighten your Value, by suffering you no longer to be cheap and contemptible. Its aim is to fix that Beauty, to make it lasting and permanent, which Nature with all the helps of Art cannot secure, to place it out of the reach of Sickness and Old Age, by transferring it from a corruptible Body to an immortal Mind. . . . [This proposal] would help you to surpass the Men as much in Virtue and Ingenuity, as you do in Beauty, that you may not only be as lovely,

---

Mary Astell, *A Serious Proposal to the Ladies for the Advancement of Their True and Greatest Interest* (London: n.p. 1701), passim.

but as wise as Angels. Exalt and Establish your Fame, more than the best wrought Poems and loudest Panegyrics, by ennobling your Minds with such Graces as really deserve it. And instead of the Faustian Complements and Fulsome Flatteries of your Admirers, obtain for you Him who cannot err. In a word, render you the Glory and Blessing of the present Age, and the Admiration and Pattern of the next. And sure, I shall not need many words to persuade you to close with this *Proposal.* . . .

Pardon me the seeming rudeness of this Proposal, which goes upon a supposition that there's something amiss in you, which it is intended to amend. My design is not to expose, but to rectify your Failures. To be exempt from mistake, is a privilege few can pretend to, the greatest is to be past Conviction and too obstinate to reform. Even the *Men*, as exact as they would seem, and as much as they divert themselves with our Miscarriages, are very often guilty of greater faults, and such, as considering the advantages they enjoy, are much more inexcusable. But I will not pretend to correct their Errors, who either are, or at least *think* themselves too wise to receive Instruction from a Woman's Pen. My earnest desire is, That you Ladies, would be as perfect and happy as it is possible to be in this imperfect state; for I Love you too well to endure a spot upon your Beauties, if I can by any means remove and wipe it off. I would have you live up to the dignity of your Nature, and express your thankfulness to GOD for the benefits you enjoy by a due improvement of them: As I know very many of you do, who countenance that Piety which the men decry, and are the brightest Patterns of Religion that the Age affords, it is my grief that all the rest of our Sex do not imitate such Illustrious Examples, and therefore I would have them increased and rendered more conspicuous, that Vice being put out of countenance, (because Virtue is the only thing in fashion) may sneak out of the World, and its darkness be dispelled by the confluence of so many shining Graces. . . .

Chapter One

What are Ignorance and Vice but diseases of the Mind contracted in its two principal Faculties of the Understanding and the Will? And such too as like many Bodily distempers do mutually foment each other. Ignorance disposes to Vice, and Wickedness reciprocally keeps us Ignorant, so that we cannot be free from the one unless we cure the other; . . .

Indeed if we scratch to the bottom I believe we shall find, that the Corruption of the Heart contributes *more* to the Cloudiness of the Head, than the Clearness of our Light does to the regularity of our Affections, and it is oftener seen that our vicious Inclinations keep us Ignorant, than that our Knowledge makes us Good. For it must be confessed that Purity is not *always* the product of Knowledge; though the Understanding be appointed by the Author of Nature to direct and Govern the Will, yet many times its head-strong and Rebellious Subject rushes on precipitately, without its directions. When a Truth comes to thwart our Passions, when it dares contradict our mistaken Pleasures and supposed Interests, let the Light shine never so clear we shut our Eyes against it, will not be convinced, not because there's any want of Evidence, but because we're *unwilling* to Obey. This is the Rise of all that Infidelity that appears in the world; it is not the Head but the Heart that is the Seat of Atheism. No Man without a brow of Brass, and an Impudence as strong as his Arguments are weak, could demure to the convincing Proofs of Christianity, had not he contracted such diseases in his Passions as make him believe it is his Interest to oppose *those* that he may gratify *these*. Yet this is no Objection against the Will, and shows how necessary it is to take care of both, if we would improve and advance either.

The result of all then, and what gives a satisfactory Answer to the Question where we must begin is this; that some Clearness of Head, some lower degrees of Knowledge, so much at least as will put us endeavoring after more, is necessary to obtaining Purity of Heart. For though some persons whom we vulgarly call Ignorant may be honest and Virtuous, yet they are not so in these particulars in which they are Ignorant, but their Integrity in Practicing what they know, though it be but little, causes us to overlook that wherein they Ignorantly transgress. But then any eminent degree of Knowledge, especially of Moral and Divine Knowledge, which is most excellent because most necessary and useful, can never be obtained without considerable degrees of Purity: And afterwards when we have procured a competent measure of both, they mutually assist each other; the more Pure we are the clearer will our Knowledge be, and the more we Know the more we shall Purify. . . .

Chapter Three

The perfection of the Understanding consisting in the Clearness and Largeness of its view improves proportionably as its Ideas become Clearer and more Extensive. But this is not so to be understood as if all sorts of Notices contributed to our Improvement, there are some things which make us no wiser when we know them, others which it is best to be ignorant of. But that Understanding seems to me the most exalted, which has the Clearest and most Extensive view of such Truths as are suitable to its Capacity, and Necessary or Convenient to be Known in this Present State. For being that we are but Creatures, our Understanding in its greatest Perfection has only a limited excellency. It has indeed a vast extent, and it were not amiss if we tarried a little in the Contemplation of its Powers and Capacities. . . .

As to the *Method* of Thinking, if it be proper for me to say anything of that, after those better Pens which have treated of it already, it falls in with the subject I'm now come to, which is, that *Natural Logic* I would propose. I call it natural because I shall not send you further than your Own Minds to learn it, you may if you please take in the assistance of some well chosen Book, but a good Natural Reason after all, is the best Director, without this you will scarce Argue well, though you had the Choicest Books and Tutors to Instruct you, but with it you may [argue well], though you happen to be destitute of the other. . . .

[Astell then lists various rules she believes will enhance a woman's capacity to think clearly.]

Rule 1. And therefore we should in the first place, acquaint ourselves thoroughly with the State of the Question, have a Distinct Notion of our Subject whatever it be, and of the Terms we make use of, knowing precisely what it is we drive at. . . .

Rule 2. Cut off all needless Ideas and whatever has not a Connection to the matter under Consideration, which serve only to fill up the Capacity of the Mind, and to Divide and Distract the Attention. . . .

Rule 3. . . . The next Rule is To conduct our Thoughts by Order, beginning with the most Simple and Easy Objects, and ascending as by Degrees to Knowledge of the more Composed. . . .

Rule 4. In this Method we are to practice the Fourth Rule which is, Not to leave any part of our Subject unexamined, it being as necessary to consider all that can let in Light, as to shut out what's Foreign to it. We may stop short of Truth as well as over-run it; and though we look never so attentively on our proper Object, if we view but half of it, we may be as much mistaken, as if we extended our sight beyond it. . . .

Rule 5. To which purpose we must Always keep our Subject directly in our Eye, and Closely pursue it through all our Progress; there being no better Sign of a good Understanding than Thinking Closely and Pertinently, and Reasoning dependently, so as to make the former art of our Discourse a support to the Latter, and This an Illustration of That, carrying Light and Evidence in every step we take.

Rule 6. All which being done we are in a fair way towards keeping the last Rule, which is, To judge no further than we Perceive, and not to take anything for Truth which we do not evidently Know to be so.

The Conclusion

You have, Ladies, the best Method I can at present think of for your Improvement, how well it answers by Design the World must judge. If you are so favorable as to think it comes up to it in any measure, what remains but to put it in Practice, though in the way in which you live, it is not probable that all of you either Will or Can, for reasons mentioned in the first Part, and particularly because of the great waste of your Time, without Redeeming of which there's nothing to be done. It is not my intention that you should seclude yourselves from the World, I know it is necessary that a great number of you should live in it; but it is Unreasonable and Barbarous to drive you into it, ever you are capable of doing Good in it, or at least of keeping Evil from yourselves. Nor am I so fond of my Proposal as not to lay it aside very willingly, did I think you could be sufficiently served without it. But since such Seminaries are thought proper for the Men, since they enjoy the fruits of those Noble Ladies' Bounty who were the foundress of several of their Colleges, why should we not think that such ways of Education would be as advantageous to the Ladies? Or why should we despair of finding some among them who will be as kind to their own Sex as their Ancestors have been to the other? . . .

As for those who think so Contemptibly of such a considerable part of GOD's Creation, as to suppose that we were made for nothing else but to Admire and do them Service, and to make provision for the low concerns of an Animal Life, we pity their mistake, and can calmly bear their Scoffs, for they do not express so much Contempt of us as they do of our Maker; and therefore the reproach of such incompetent Judges is not an Injury but an Honor to us. . . .

The Men therefore may still enjoy their Prerogatives for us, we mean not to intrench on any of their Lawful Privileges, our only Contention shall be that they may not out-do us in promoting his Glory who Is Lord both of them and us; And by all that appears the generality will not oppose us in this matter, we shall not provoke them by striving to be better Christians. They may busy their Heads with Affairs of State, and spend their Time and Strength in recommending themselves to an uncertain Master, or a more giddy Multitude, our only endeavor shall be to be absolute Monarchs in our own Bosoms. . . .

Let's then do what we Can, and leave the rest to our Great Benefactor and Governor, but let us set about our own part, not only when the way is open and easy, who shall give us thanks for that? but in spite of all Difficulties and Discouragement, since we have so Glorious a Leader, so indefatigable in his Labors, so boundless in his Love, such an Omnipotent Assister who neither wants Power nor Will to help us. The Peevishness and Obstinacy of such a Quarrel with our Labor of Love and set themselves against all we can do to serve them, will only add to our Laurels and enlarge our Triumphs, when our Constancy in doing Good has at last overcome those Perverse Opposers of it.

Study Questions

1. What do Mary Astell's criticisms of contemporary society reveal about the position and status of women in her time?
2. How did the remarkable changes that were taking place at the time in philosophy, metaphysics, and religion contribute to the author's writings?
3. What values does Astell suggest are the most important for women to cultivate, and what does this imply about her attitude toward her own sex?
4. How do Astell's remarks about women's position and natural capacities compare with those espoused later by Mary Wollstonecraft (Reading 38)?

Alexander Pope's "Essay on Man"

The first half of the eighteenth century was an era of relative peace and stability in Europe. As the force of the Scientific Revolution took hold of Western society, the grandiosity and emotionalism of the baroque gave way to balance and optimism. During the Age of Enlightenment, literary artists such as Alexander Pope (1688–1744) paid proper homage to human reason and the harmony of nature. In many ways, Pope's **neoclassical** poems and essays are celebrations of the order created by **Sir Isaac Newton**'s genius and Locke's brilliance. Pope's most famous work, "Essay on Man," was written in 1733–34 in the form of four epistles to the English deist, Henry St. John, Lord Bolingbroke (1678–1751). Pope's concept of universality is clearly evinced in the first epistle of his poem: in it he begins to create a rationalistic metaphysic centering on the "Great Chain of Being," a concept as old as **Plato**'s famous cosmological work *Timaeus*, but one given new life in the wake of astounding scientific discoveries.

One

Say first, of God above, or Man below,
What can we reason, but from what we know?
Of Man, what see we but his station here,
From which to reason, or to which refer?
Thro' worlds unnumber'd tho' the God be known,
'Tis ours to trace him only in our own.
He, who thro' vast immensity can pierce,
See worlds on worlds compose one universe,
Observe how system into system runs,
What other planets circle other suns,
What vary'd Being peoples ev'ry star,
May tell why Heav'n has made us as we are.
But of this frame the bearings, and the ties,

A. W. Ward, ed., *The Poetical Works of Alexander Pope* (London: Macmillan, 1907), passim.

The strong connexions, nice dependencies,
Gradations just, has thy pervading soul
Look'd thro'? or can a part contain the whole?
    Is the great chain, that draws all to agree,
And drawn supports, upheld by God, or thee?

Four

Go, wiser thou! and, in thy scale of sense,
Weigh thy Opinion against Providence;
Call imperfection what thou fancy'st such,
Say, here he gives too little, there too much:
Destroy all Creatures for thy sport or gust,
Yet cry, If Man's unhappy, God's unjust;
If Man alone engross not Heav'n's high care,
Alone made perfect here, immortal there:
Snatch from his hand the balance and the rod,
Re-judge his justice, be the God of God.
In Pride, in reas'ning Pride, our error lies;
All quit their sphere, and rush into the skies.
Pride still is aiming at the blest abodes,
Men would be Angels, Angels would be Gods.
Aspiring to be Gods, if Angels fell,
Aspiring to be Angels, Men rebel:
And who but wishes to invert the laws
Of Order, is against th' Eternal Cause.

Five

Ask for what end the heav'nly bodies shine,
Earth for whose use? Pride answers, " 'Tis for mine:
For me kind Nature wakes her genial Pow'r,
Suckles each herb, and spreads out ev'ry flow'r;
Annual for me, the grape, the rose renew
The juice nectareous, and the balmy dew;
For me, the mine a thousand treasures brings;
For me, health gushes from a thousand springs;
Seas roll to waft me, suns to light me rise;
My foot-stool earth, my canopy the skies."
    But errs not Nature from this gracious end,
From burning suns when livid deaths descend,
When earthquakes swallow, or when tempests sweep

Towns to one grave, whole nations to the deep?
"No," ('tis reply'd) the first Almighty Cause
Acts not by partial, but by gen'ral laws;
Th' exceptions few; some change since all began:
And what created perfect'?—Why then Man?
If the great end be human Happiness,
Then Nature deviates; and can Man do less?
As much that end a constant course requires
Of show'rs and sun-shine, as of Man's desires;
As much eternal springs and cloudless skies,
As Men for ever temp'rate, calm, and wise.
If plagues or earthquakes break not Heav'n's design,
Why then a **Borgia**, or a **Catiline**?
Who knows but he, whose hand the lightning forms,
Who heaves old Ocean, and who wings the storms;
Pours fierce Ambition in a **Caesar**'s mind,
Or turns young Ammon loose to scourge mankind?
From pride, from pride, our very reas'ning springs;
Account for moral, as for nat'ral things:
Why charge we Heav'n in those, in these acquit?
In both, to reason right is to submit.
      Better for Us, perhaps, it might appear,
Were there all harmony, all virtue here;
That never air or ocean felt the wind;
That never passion discompos'd the mind.
But ALL subsists by elemental strife;
And Passions are the elements of Life.
The gen'ral Order, since the whole began,
Is kept in Nature, and is kept in Man. . . .

Seven

Far as Creation's ample range extends,
The scale of sensual, mental pow'rs ascends:
Mark how it mounts, to Man's imperial race,
From the green myriads in the peopled grass:
What modes of sight betwixt each wide extreme,
The mole's dim curtain, and the lynx's beam:
Of smell, the headlong lioness between,
And hound sagacious on the tainted green:
Of hearing, from the life that fills the Flood,
To that which arbles thro' the vernal wood:
The spider's touch, how exquisitely fine!

113

Feels at each thread, and lives along the line:
In the nice bee, what sense so subtly true
From pois'nous herbs extracts the healing dew?
How Instinct varies in the grov'lling swine,
Compar'd, half-reas'ning elephant, with thine!
'Twixt that, and Reason, what a nice barrier,
For ever sep'rate, yet for ever near!
Remembrance and Reflection how ally'd;
What thin partitions Sense from Thought divide:
And Middle natures, how they long to join,
Yet never pass th' insuperable line!
Without this just gradation, could they be
Subjected, these to those, or all to thee?
The pow'rs of all subdu'd by thee alone,
Is not thy Reason all these pow'rs in one?

Eight

See, thro' this air, this ocean, and this earth,
All matter quick, and bursting into birth.
Above, how high, progressive life may go!
Around, how wide! how deep extend below!
Vast chain of Being! which from God began,
Natures ethereal, human, angel, man,
Beast, bird, fish, insect, what no eye can see,
No glass can reach; from Infinite to thee,
From thee to Nothing.—On superior pow'rs
Were we to press, inferior might on ours:
Or in the full creation leave a void,
Where, one step broken, the great scale's destroy'd:
From Nature's chain whatever link you strike,
Tenth or ten thousandth, breaks the chain alike.
          And, if each system in gradation roll
Alike essential to th' amazing Whole,
The least confusion but in one, not all
That system only, but the Whole must fall.
Let Earth unbalanc'd from her orbit fly,
Planets and Suns run lawless thro' the sky;
Let ruling Angels from their spheres be hurl'd,
Being on Being wrecked, and world on world;
Heav'n's whole foundations to their centre nod,
And Nature tremble to the throne of God.
All this dread Order break—for whom? for thee?
Vile worm!—Oh Madness! Pride! Impiety!

Nine

What if the foot, ordain'd the dust to tread,
Or hand, to toil, aspir'd to be the head?
What if the head, the eye, or ear repin'd
To serve mere engines to the ruling Mind?
Just as absurd for any part to claim
To be another, in this gen'ral frame:
Just as absurd, to mourn the tasks or pains,
The great directing Mind of All ordains.
      All are but parts of one stupendous whole,
Whose body Nature is, and God the soul;
That, chang'd thro' all, and yet in all the same;
Great in the earth, as in th' ethereal frame;
Warms in the sun, refreshes in the breeze,
Glows in the stars, and blossoms in the trees,
Lives thro' all life, extends thro' all extent,
Spreads undivided, operates unspent;
Breathes in our soul, informs our mortal part,
As full, as perfect, in a hair as heart:
As full, as perfect, in vile Man that mourns,
As the rapt Seraph that adores and burns:
To him no high, no low, no great, no small;
He fills, he bounds, connects, and equals all.

Ten

Cease then, nor Order Imperfection name:
Our proper blindness depends on what we blame.
Know thy own point: This kind, this due degree
Of blindness, weakness, Heav'n bestows on thee.
Submit.—In this, or any other sphere,
Secure to be as blest as thou canst bear:
Safe in the hand of one disposing Pow'r,
Or in the natal, or the mortal hour.
All Nature is but Art, unknown to thee;
All Chance, Direction, which thou canst not see;
All Discord, Harmony not understood;
All partial Evil, universal Good;
And, spite of Pride, in erring Reason's spite,
One truth is clear, Whatever Is, Is Right.

Study Questions

1. What does Pope mean by the term "Great Chain of Being," and how, if at all, would the "Great Chain of Being" idea obstruct eighteenth-century European efforts to discover humanity's place in the natural world?
2. How does Pope perceive the universe in all its grand complexity?
3. How did the new scientific discoveries and methods of reasoning influence poetry?
4. What aspects of the "Great Chain of Being" foreshadow what would appear a hundred years later as Darwin's "theory of evolution" (Reading 41)?

Voltaire's *Philosophical Dictionary*

François Marie Arouet (1694–1778), who used the pen name of Voltaire, was greatly influenced by **Sir Isaac Newton** and John Locke. Voltaire became aware of the writings of these brilliant Englishmen while living in exile in England from 1726 to 1729. A prolific writer, Voltaire was destined to become one of the most influential *philosophes* of the French Enlightenment. In their attempts to secularize every avenue of human life and thought, the philosophes were the great popularizers of the intellectual revolution of Early Modern Europe. Although they often disagreed among themselves regarding what is truth, they nonetheless shared the belief that civilization could be improved through education. Furthermore, it was agreed that reliable information or knowledge, upon which this education should be based, ought to be compiled in an organized way. Accordingly, works such as Voltaire's *Philosophical Dictionary* (1764) began to appear, and these compilations required laws or rules for evaluation. The philosophes thus participated in and extended the intellectual revolution to which they were heirs. Voltaire and others actively criticized contemporary society by exposing the shortcomings of old Europe's values and institutions. Only after his retirement from society in the 1760s did Voltaire launch his obsessive attack on established religion. He refused to accept all evidence from revelation and rejected any theological argumentation in developing his militant theism, as evinced in his article on "Religion" from the *Philosophical Dictionary*.

Last night I was meditating; I was absorbed in the contemplation of nature, admiring the immensity, the courses, the relations of those infinite globes, which are above the admiration of the vulgar.

I admired still more the intelligence that presides over this vast machinery. I said to myself: A man must be blind not to be impressed by this spectacle; he must be stupid not to recognize its author; he must be mad not to adore him. What tribute of adoration ought I to render him? Should not this tribute be the same throughout the extent of space, since the same Supreme Power reigns equally in all that extent?

J. Morely et al., *The Works of Voltaire: A Contemporary Version* (London: St. Hubert Guild, 1903), vol. 13, passim.

Does not a thinking being, inhabiting a star of the Milky Way, owe him the same homage as the thinking being on this little globe where we are? Light is the same to the dog-star as to us; morality, too, must be the same.

If a feeling and thinking being in the dog-star is born of a tender father and mother, who have labored for his welfare, he owes them as much love and duty as we here owe to our parents. If any one in the Milky Way sees another lame and indigent, and does not relieve him, though able to do it, he is guilty in the sight of every globe.

The heart has everywhere the same duties; on the steps of the throne of God, if He has a throne, and at the bottom of the great abyss, if there be an abyss.

I was wrapped in these reflections, when one of those genii who fill the spaces between worlds, came down to me. I recognized the same aerial creature that had formerly appeared to me, to inform me that the judgments of God are different from ours, and how much a good action is preferable to controversy.

He transported me into a desert covered all over with bones piled one upon another; and between these heaps of dead there were avenues of evergreen trees, and at the end of each avenue a tall man of august aspect gazing with compassion on these sad remains.

"Alas! my archangel," said I, "whither have you brought me?" "To desolation," answered he. "And who are those fine old patriarchs whom I see motionless and melancholy at the end of those green avenues, and who seem to weep over this immense multitude of dead?" "Poor human creature! thou shalt know," replied the genius; "but, first, thou must weep."

He began with the first heap. "These," said he, "are the twenty-three thousand Jews who danced before a calf, together with the twenty-four thousand who were slain while ravishing Midianitish women; the number of the slaughtered for similar offenses or mistakes amounts to nearly three hundred thousand.

"At the following avenues are the bones of Christians, butchered by one another on account of metaphysical disputes. They are divided into several piles of four centuries each; it was necessary to separate them; for had they been all together, they would have reached the sky."

"What!" exclaimed I, "have brethren thus treated their brethren; and have I the misfortune to be one of this brotherhood?"

"Here," said the spirit, "are the twelve millions of Americans slain in their own country for not having been baptized."

"Ah! my God! Why were not these frightful skeletons left to whiten in the hemisphere where the bodies were born, and where they were murdered in so many various ways? Why are all these abominable monuments of barbarity and fanaticism assembled here?"

"For thy instruction."

"Since thou are willing to instruct me," said I to the genius, "tell me if there be any other people than the Christians and the Jews, whom zeal and religion, unhappily turned into fanaticism, have prompted to so many horrible cruelties?"

"Yes," said he; "the Mahometans have been stained by the same inhuman acts, but rarely; and when their victims have cried out 'amman'! (mercy!) and have offered them tribute, they have pardoned them. As for other nations, not one of them, since the beginning of the world, has ever made a purely religious war. Now, follow me!" I followed.

A little beyond these heaps of dead we found other heaps; these were bags of gold and silver; and each pile had its label: "Substance of the heretics massacred in the eighteenth century, in the seventeenth, in the sixteenth," and so on. "Gold and silver of the slaughtered Americans," etc.; and all these piles were surmounted by crosses, miters, crosiers, and tiaras, enriched with jewels.

"What! my genius, was it then to possess these riches that these carcasses were accumulated?" "Yes, my son."

I shed tears; and when by my grief I had merited to be taken to the end of the green avenues, he conducted me thither.

"Contemplate," said he, "the heroes of humanity who have been the bene-factors of the earth, and who united to banish from the world, as far as they were able, violence and rapine. Question them."

I went up to the first of this band; on his head was a crown, and in his hand a small censer. I humbly asked him his name. "I," said he, "am **Numa Pompilius**; I succeeded a robber, and had robbers to govern; I taught them virtue and the worship of God; after me they repeatedly forgot both. I forbade any image to be placed in the temples, because the divinity who animates nature cannot be represented. During my reign the Romans had neither wars nor seditions; and my religion did nothing but good. Every neighboring people came to honor my funeral, which has happened to me alone."

I made my obeisance and passed on to the second. This was a fine old man, of about a hundred, clad in a white robe; his middle finger was placed on his lip, and with the other hand he was scattering beans behind him. In him I recognized **Pythagoras**. He assured me that he had never had a golden thigh, and that he had never been a cock, but that he had governed the Crotonians with as much justice as Numa had governed the Romans about the same time, which justice was the most necessary and the rarest thing in the world. I learned that the Pythagoreans examined their consciences twice a day. What good people! and how far are we behind them! Yet we, who for thirteen hundred years have been nothing but assassins, assert that these wise men were proud.

To please Pythagoras I said not a word to him, but went on to **Zoroaster**, who was engaged in concentrating the celestial fire in the focus of a concave mirror, in the center of a vestibule with a hundred gates, each one leading to wisdom. On the principal of these gates I read these words, which are the abstract of all morality, and cut short all the disputes of the casuists: "When thou art in doubt whether an action is good or bad, abstain from it."

"Certainly," said I to my genius, "the barbarians who immolated all the victims whose bones I have seen had not read these fine words."

Then we saw **Thales**, **Anaximander**, and all the other sages who had sought truth and practiced virtue.

When we came to Socrates I quickly recognized him by his broken nose. "Well," said I, "you then are among the confidants of the Most High! All the inhabitants of Europe, excepting the Turks and the Tartars, who know nothing, pronounce your name with reverence. So much is that great name venerated, so much is it loved, that it has been sought to discover those of your persecutors. Melitus and Anitus are known because of you, as **Ravallac** is known because of Henry IV; but of Anitus I know only the name. I know not precisely who that villain was by whom you were calumniated, and who succeeded in procuring your condemnation to the hemlock."

"I have never thought of that man since my adventure," answered Socrates; "but now that you put me in mind of him, I pity him much. He was a wicked priest, who secretly carried on a trade in leather, a traffic reputed shameful amongst us. He sent his two children to my school; the other disciples reproached them with their father's being a courier, and they were obliged to quit. The incensed father was unceasing in his endeavors until he had stirred up against me all the priests and all the sophists. They persuaded the council of the five hundred that I was an impious man, who did not believe that the moon, Mercury, and Mars were deities. I thought indeed, as I do now, that there is but one God, the master of all nature. The judges gave me up to the republic's poisoner, and he shortened my life a few days. I died with tranquility at the age of seventy years, and since then I have led a happy life with all these great men whom you see, and of whom I am the least."

After enjoying the conversation of Socrates for some time, I advanced with my guide into a bower, situated above the groves, where all these sages of antiquity seemed to be tasting the sweets of repose.

Here I beheld a man of mild and simple mien, who appeared to me to be about thirty-five years old. He was looking with compassion upon the distant heaps of whitened skeletons through which I had been led to the abode of the sages. I was astonished to find his feet swelled and bloody, his hands in the same state, his side pierced, and his ribs laid bare by flogging. "Good God!" said I, "is it possible that one of the just and wise should be in this state? I have just seen one who was treated in a very odious manner; but there is no comparison between his punishment and yours. Bad priests and bad judges poisoned him. Was it also by priests and judges that you were so cruelly assassinated?"

With great affability he answered—"Yes."

"And who were those monsters?"

"They were hypocrites."

"Ah! you have said all! By that one word I understand that they would condemn you to the worst of punishments. You then had proved to them, like Socrates, that the moon was not a goddess, and that Mercury was not a god?"

"No; those planets were quite out of the question. My countrymen did not even know what a planet was; they were all arrant ignoramuses. Their superstitions were quite different from those of the Greeks."

"Then you wished to teach them a new religion?"

"Not at all; I simply said to them—'Love God with all your hearts, and your neighbor as yourselves; for that is all.' Judge whether this precept is not as old as the universe; judge whether I brought them a new worship. I constantly told them that I had come, not to abolish their law, but to fulfill it; I had observed all their rites; I was circumcised as they all were; I was baptized like the most zealous of them; like them I paid the corban; like them I kept the Passover; and ate, standing, lamb cooked with lettuce. I and my friends went to pray in their temple; my friends, too, frequented the temple after my death. In short, I fulfilled all their laws without one exception."

"What! Could not these wretches even reproach you with having departed from their laws?"

"Certainly not."

"Why, then, did they put you in the state in which I now see you?"

"Must I tell you?—They were proud and selfish; they saw that I knew them; they saw that I was making them known to the citizens; they were the strongest; they took away my life; and such as they will always do the same, if they can, to whoever shall have done them too much justice."

"But did you say nothing; did you do nothing, that could serve them as a pretext?"

"The wicked find a pretext in everything."

"Did you not once tell them that you were come to bring, not peace, but the sword?"

"This was an error of some scribe. I told them that I brought, not the sword, but peace. I never wrote anything; what I said might be miscopied without any ill intent."

"You did not then contribute in anything, by your discourses, either badly rendered or badly interpreted, to those frightful masses of bones which I passed on my way to consult you?"

"I looked with horror on those who were guilty of all these murders."

"And those monuments of power and wealth—of pride and avarice—those treasures, those ornaments, those ensigns of greatness, which, when seeking wisdom, I saw accumulated on the way—do they proceed from you?"

"It is impossible; I and mine lived in poverty and lowliness; my greatness was only in virtue."

I was on the point of begging of him to have the goodness just to tell me who he was; but my guide warned me to refrain. He told me that I was not formed for comprehending these sublime mysteries. I conjured him to tell me only in what true religion consisted.

"Have I not told you already? Love God and your neighbor as yourself."

"What! Can we love God and yet eat meat on Friday?"

"I always ate what was given me; for I was too poor to give a dinner to any one."

"Might we love God and be just, and still be prudent enough not to entrust all the adventures of one's life to a person one does not know?"

"Such was always my custom."

"Might not I, while doing good, be excused from making a pilgrimage to St. James of Compostello?"

"I never was in that country."

"Should I confine myself in a place of retirement with blockheads?"

"For my part, I always made little journeys from town to town."

"Must I take part with the Greek or with the Latin Church?"

"When I was in the world, I never made any difference between the Jew and the Samaritan."

"Well, if it be so, I take you for my only master."

Then he gave me a nod, which filled me with consolation. The vision disappeared, and I was left with a good conscience.

Study Questions

1. What does Voltaire as a contemporary social critic espouse?
2. What is the author's conception of "truth"?
3. According to the author, how does traditional Christianity stifle human progress and understanding?
4. What do Voltaire's criticisms suggest about institutional religion in the Age of Enlightenment?

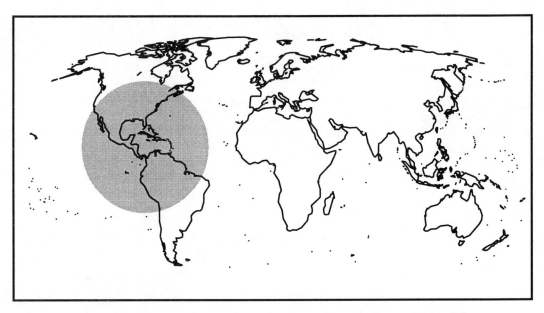

Brief Chronology for the Early Modern World

The Americas

1000–1550	Inca civilization in South America
1325–1521	Aztec Empire (Tlatoani Montezuma Ilhuicamina, 1440–1468; Montezuma, 1502–1520)
1425–1428	The Mexica's Rebellion against Azcapotzalco
1487	20,000 people sacrificed to god Huitzilopochtli on site of present cathedral of Mexico City
1492	Columbus's first voyage to the New World
1497	John Cabot, from Bristol, reaches Newfoundland
1500	Pedro Alvares Cabral discovers coast of Brazil
1507	Name of "America" first appears on a German map
1510	Spaniards begin reconnaissance along east coast in Mexico
1513	Balboa sights Pacific Ocean
1521	Conquest of the Aztec capital of Tenochtitlan by Cortés
1524	Giovanni Verrazano reaches Newfoundland, apparently the first to realize that America is a continent
1529	Mexico City becomes capital of the viceroyalty of New Spain
1530–1535	Pizzaro conquers Inca Empire
1565	St. Augustine, Florida, founded by Spanish colonists

1607	Jamestown, Virginia, founded
1619	House of Burgesses of Virginia, first American parliamentary institution, meets at Jamestown
1620	Mayflower reaches North America, New Plymouth founded
1643	Indian massacre in New York
1680–1726	2,130,000 slaves imported into British colonies in America and West Indies
1713	Treaty of Utrecht, and henceforth British dominant in North America
1732–1799	George Washington
1756–1763	Seven Years' War (French-Indian Wars)
1773	Boston Tea Party
1775	Meeting of the Second Continental Congress and American Continental Army organized with Washington in command; beginning of American War of Independence
1776	American Declaration of Independence drawn up
1783	Treaty of Paris concludes American War of Independence

All dates are C.E. and approximate unless otherwise indicated. It should be noted as well that chronologies are constantly being revised. Hence, there may be discrepancies between the dates listed above and those found in other textbooks and scholarly monographs. Throughout the text and in the Glossary, all dates are given in B.C.E. (Before the Common Era) and C.E. (the Common Era). Where there is no era designation C.E. may be assumed.

Letters of Discovery and Exploration of the Americas

The twin discoveries of a new route to India and of the New World at the end of the fifteenth century resulted in enormous changes in the Americas and Western Europe. Although many Western nations participated in voyages of exploration, the Italian cities of Venice and Genoa and the kingdoms of Portugal and Spain were initially in the forefront of the movement. Spanish ambitions are indeed illustrated by the attempts of Columbus (1446?–1506) and others to find new trade routes to east Eurasia and in the systematic exploration of the interiors of the American continents by the conquistadors. Since Europeans looked upon the Americas as areas to be exploited, they closed the door on understanding and appreciating the alien civilizations they discovered. Only after a generation or so were the "Indians" considered "human" and capable of receiving God's grace, an attitude exemplified in **Pope Paul III**'s (r. 1534–1549) decree *Sublimis Deus* of 1537. Some Westerners, such as **Bartholomew Las Casas** (1474–1566) were appalled at the treatment of Native Americans and began to champion the notion of treating them empathetically and humanely.

Columbus's Letter to de Santangel (dated 1493)

Knowing that it will afford you [Lord **Raphael Sanchez de Santangel**], pleasure to learn I have brought my undertaking to a successful termination, I have decided upon writing you this letter to acquaint you with all the events which have occurred in my voyage, and the discoveries which have resulted from it. Thirty-three days after my departure from Cadiz I reached the Indian sea, where I discovered many islands, thickly peopled, of which I took possession without resistance in the name of our most illustrious monarch, by public proclamation and with unfurled banners. To the first of these islands, which is called Guanahani by the Indians, I gave the name of the blessed Saviour [San Salvador], relying upon whose protection I had reached this as well as the other islands [mainly of the Bahamas island chain]; to

R. H. Major, ed. and trans., *Select Letters of Christopher Columbus, With Other Original Documents Relating to His Four Voyages to the New World* (London: Hakluyt Society, 1847), 1–8, 15–17.

each of these I also gave a name, ordering that one should be called Santa Maria de la Concepcion, another Fernandina, the third Isabella, the fourth Juana, and so with all the rest respectively.

As soon as we arrived at that, which as I have said was named Juana, I proceeded along its coast a short distance westward, and found it to be so large and apparently without termination, that I could not suppose it to be an island, but the continental province of **Cathay**. Seeing, however, no towns or populous places on the sea coast, but only a few detached houses and cottages, with whose inhabitants I was unable to communicate, because they fled as soon as they saw us, I went further on, thinking that in my progress I should certainly find some city or village. At length, after proceeding a great way and finding that nothing new presented itself, and that the line of coast was leading us northwards (which I wished to avoid, because it was winter, and it was my intention to move southward; and because moreover the winds were contrary), I resolved not to attempt any further progress, but rather to turn back and retrace my course to a certain bay that I had observed, and from which I afterwards dispatched two of our men to ascertain whether there were a king or any cities in that province. These men reconnoitred the country for three days, and found a most numerous population, and great numbers of houses, though small, and built without any regard to order; with which information they returned to us.

In the mean time I had learned from some Indians whom I had seized, that that country was certainly an island: and therefore I sailed towards the east, coasting to the distance of three hundred and twenty-two miles, which brought us to the extremity of it; from this point I saw lying eastward another island, fifty-four miles distant from Juana, to which I gave the name of **Espanola**: I went thither, and steered my course eastward as I had done at Juana, even to the distance of five hundred and sixty-four miles along the north coast. . . .

The trees, herbage, and fruits of Espanola are very different from those of Juana, and moreover it abounds in various kinds of spices, gold, and other metals. The inhabitants of both sexes in this island, and in all the others which I have seen, or of which I have received information, go always naked as they were born, with the exception of some of the women, who use the covering of a leaf, or small bough, or an apron of cotton which they prepare for that purpose. None of them, as I have already said, are possessed of any iron, neither have they weapons, being unacquainted with, and indeed incompetent to use them, not from any deformity of body (for they are well-formed), but because they are timid and full of fear. They carry however in lieu of arms, canes dried in the sun, on the ends of which they fix heads of dried wood sharpened to a point, and even these they dare not use habitually; for it has often occurred when I have sent two or three of my men to any of the villages to speak with the natives, that they have come out in disorderly troop, and have fled in such haste at the approach of our men, that the fathers forsook their children and the children their fathers. This timidity did not arise from any loss or injury that they had received from us; for, on the contrary, I gave to all I approached whatever articles I had about me, such as cloth and many other things, taking nothing of theirs in return: but they are naturally timid and fearful. As soon however as they see that they are safe, and have laid aside all fear, they are very simple and honest, and exceedingly liberal with all they have; none of them refusing any thing he possess when he is asked for it, but on the contrary inviting us to ask them. They exhibit great love towards all others in preference to themselves: they also give objects of great value for trifles, and content themselves with very little or nothing in return. I however forbad that these trifles and articles of no value (such as pieces of dishes, plates, and glass, keys, and leather straps) should be given to them, although if they could obtain them, they imagined themselves to be possessed of the most beautiful trinkets in the world. It even happened that a sailor received for a leather strap as much gold as was worth three golden nobles, and for things of more trifling value offered by our men, especially-newly coined blancas, or any gold coins, the Indians would give whatever the seller required; as, for instance, an ounce and a half or two ounces of gold, or thirty or forty pounds of cotton, with which commodity they were already acquainted. Thus they bartered, like idiots, cotton and gold for fragments of bows, glasses, bottles, and jars; which I forbad as being unjust, and myself gave them many beautiful and acceptable articles which I had brought with me, taking nothing from them in return; I did this in order that I might the more easily conciliate them, that they might be led to become Christians, and be inclined to entertain a regard for the King and Queen, our Princes and all Spaniards, and that I might induce them to take an interest in seeking out, and collecting, and delivering to us such things as they possessed in abundance, but which we greatly needed. . . .

They assure me that there is another island larger than Espanola, whose inhabitants have no hair, and which abounds in gold more than any of the rest. I bring with me individuals of this island and of the others that I have seen, who are proofs of the facts which I state.

Finally, to compress into few words the entire summary of my voyage and speedy return, and of the advantages derivable thereof, I promise, that with a little assistance afforded me by our most invincible sovereigns, I will procure them as much gold as they need, as great a quantity of spices, of cotton, and of mastic (which is only found in **Chios**), and as many men for the service of the navy as their Majesties may require. I promise also rhubarb and other sorts of drugs, which I am persuaded the men whom I have left in the aforesaid fortress have found already and will continue to find; for I myself have tarried no where longer than I was compelled to do by the winds, except in the city of Navidad, while I provided for the building of the fortress, and took the necessary precautions for the perfect security of the men I left there.

Although all I have related may appear to be wonderful and unheard of, yet the results of my voyage would have been more astonishing if I had had at my disposal such ships as I required. But these great and marvelous results are not to be attributed to any merit of mine, but to the holy Christian faith, and to the piety and religion of our Sovereigns; for that which the unaided intellect of man could not compass, the spirit of God has granted to human exertions, for God is wont to hear the prayers of his servants who love his precepts even to the performance of apparent impossibilities. Thus it has happened to me in the present instance, who have accomplished a task to which the powers of mortal men had never hitherto attained; for if there have been those who have anywhere written or spoken of these islands, they have done so with doubts and conjectures, and no one has ever asserted that he has seen them, on which account their writings have been looked upon as little else than fables.

Therefore let the King and Queen, our princes and their most happy kingdoms, and all the other provinces of Christendom, render thanks to our Lord and Saviour Jesus Christ, who has granted us so great a victory and such prosperity. Let processions be made, and sacred feasts be held, and the temples be adorned with festive boughs. Let Christ rejoice on earth, as he rejoices in heaven in the prospect of the salvation of the souls of so many nations hitherto lost. Let us also rejoice, as well on account of the exaltation of our faith, as on account of the increase of our temporal prosperity, of which not only Spain, but all Christendom will be partakers. Such are the events which I have briefly described. Farewell. [Dated from] Lisbon, [on] the 14th of March.

The Papal Bull *Sublimis Deus* (dated 1537)

Paul III, Pope to all faithful Christians to whom this writing may come, health in Christ our Lord and the apostolic benediction.

The sublime God [*Sublimis Deus*] so loved the human race that He created man in such a way that he might participate, not only in the good that other creatures enjoy, but endowed him with capacity to attain to the inaccessible and invisible Supreme Good and behold it face to face; and since man, according to the testimony of the sacred scriptures, has been created to enjoy eternal life and happiness, which none may obtain save through faith in our Lord Jesus Christ, it is necessary that he should possess the nature and faculties enabling him to receive that faith; and that whoever is thus endowed should be capable of receiving that same faith. Nor is it credible that any one should possess so little understanding as to desire the faith and yet be destitute of the most necessary faculty to enable him to receive it. Hence Christ, who is the Truth itself, that has never failed and can never fail, said to the preachers of the faith whom He chose for that office "Go ye and teach all nations." He said all, without exception, for all are capable of receiving the doctrines of the faith.

The enemy of the human race, who opposes all good deeds in order to bring men to destruction, beholding and envying this, invented a means never before heard of, by which he might hinder the preaching of God's word of Salvation to the people: he inspired his satellites who, to please him, have not hesitated to

F. A. MacNutt, trans. and ed., *Bartholomew de Las Casas: His Life, His Apostolate, and His Writings* (New York: G. P. Putnam's Sons, 1909), 311–57, passim, 427–31.

publish abroad that the Indians of the West and the South, and other people of whom We have recent knowledge should be treated as dumb brutes created for our service, pretending that they are incapable of receiving the catholic faith.

We, who, though unworthy, exercise on earth the power of our Lord and seek with all our might to bring those sheep of His flock who are outside, into the fold committed to our charge, consider, however, that the Indians are truly men and that they are not only capable of understanding the catholic faith but, according to our information, they desire exceedingly to receive it. Desiring to provide ample remedy for these evils, we define and declare by these our letters, or by any translation thereof signed by any notary public and sealed with the seal of any ecclesiastical dignitary, to which the same credit shall be given as to the originals, that, notwithstanding whatever may have been or may be said to the contrary, the said Indians and all other people who may later be discovered by Christians, are by no means to be deprived of their liberty or the possession of their property, even though they be outside the faith of Jesus Christ; and that they may and should, freely and legitimately, enjoy their liberty and the possession of their property; nor should they be in any way enslaved; should the contrary happen, it shall be null and of no effect.

By virtue of our apostolic authority We define and declare by these present letters, or by any translation thereof signed by any notary public and sealed with the seal of any ecclesiastical dignitary, which shall thus command the same obedience as the originals, that the said Indians and other peoples should be converted to the faith of Jesus Christ by preaching the word of God and by the example of good and holy living.

Given in Rome in the year of our Lord 1537. The fourth of June and of our Pontificate, the third year.

Las Casas's *Brief Description on the Destruction of the Indies* (dated 1552)

To the Most High and Mighty Lord, the Prince of the Spanish States. **Don Philip** our Lord. Most High, and Mighty Lord.

As divine Providence has ordained that in his world, for its government, and for the common utility of the human race, kingdoms and countries should be constituted in which kings are almost fathers and pastors (as **Homer** calls them), they being consequently the most noble, and most generous members of the Republics, there neither is nor can be reasonable doubt as to the rectitude of their royal hearts. If any defect, wrong, and evil is suffered, there can be no other cause than that the kings are ignorant of it; for if such were manifested to them, they would extirpate them with supreme industry and watchful diligence.

It is seemingly this that the divine Scriptures mean in the Proverbs of Solomon, . . . because it is thus assumed from the innate and peculiar virtue of the king namely, that the knowledge alone of evil in his kingdom is absolutely sufficient that he should destroy it; and that not for one moment, as far as in him lies, can he tolerate it.

As I have fifty, or more, years of experience in those countries, I have therefore been considering the evils, I have seen committed, the injuries, losses, and misfortunes, such as it would not have been thought could be done by man; such kingdoms, so many, and so large, or to speak better, that most vast and new world of the Indies, conceded and confided by God and his Church to the kings of Castile, that they should rule and govern it; that they should convert it, and should prosper it temporally, and spiritually.

When some of their particular actions are made known to Your Highness, it will not be possible to forbear supplicating His Majesty with importunate insistence, that he should not concede nor permit that which the tyrants have invented, pursued, and put into execution, calling it Conquests; which if permitted, will be repeated; because these acts in themselves, done against those pacific, humble, and mild Indian people, who offend none, are iniquitous, tyrannous, condemned and cursed by every natural, divine, and human law. So as not to keep criminal silence concerning the ruin of numberless souls and bodies that these persons cause, I have decided to print some, though very few, of the innumerable instances I have collected in the past and can relate with truth, in order that Your Highness may read them with greater facility. . . .

The daring and unreasonable cupidity of those who count it as nothing to unjustly shed such an immense quantity of human blood, and to deprive those enormous countries of their natural inhabitants and possessors, by slaying millions of people and stealing incomparable treasures, increase every day; and they insist by various means and under various feigned pretexts, that the said Conquests are permitted, without violation of the natural and divine law, and, in consequence, without most grievous mortal sin, worthy of terrible and eternal punishment. I therefore esteemed it right to furnish Your Highness with this very brief summary of a very long history that could and ought to be composed, of the massacres and devastation that have taken place. . . .

Having seen and understood the monstrous injustice done to these innocent people in destroying and outraging them, without cause or just motive, but out of avarice alone, and the ambition of those who design such villainous operations, may Your Highness be pleased to supplicate and efficaciously persuade His Majesty [King Charles V] to forbid such harmful and detestable practices to those who seek license for them: may he silence this infernal demand for ever, with so much terror, that from this time onward there shall be no one so audacious as to dare but to name it. . . .

When [**Pedro de Alvarado**] reached [the kingdom of Guatemala], he began with a great massacre. Nevertheless the principal lord, accompanied by many other lords of **Ultatlan**, the chief town of all the kingdom went forth with trumpets, tambourines and great festivity to receive him with litters; they served him with all that they possessed, and especially by giving him ample food and everything else they could.

The Spaniards lodged outside the town that night because it seemed to them to be strong, and that they might run some risk inside it. The following day, the captain called the principal lord and many others, and when they came like tame lambs, he seized them and demanded so many loads of gold. They replied that they had none, because that country does not produce it. Guiltless of other fault and without trial or sentence, he immediately ordered them to be burned alive.

When the rulers throughout all those provinces saw that the Spaniards had burnt that one and all those chief lords, only because they gave them no gold, they all fled from their towns and hid in the mountains; they commanded all their people to go to the Spaniards and serve them as their lords, but that they should not, however, reveal to them their hiding place.

All the inhabitants came to offer themselves to his men and to serve them as their lords. This compassionate captain replied that he would not receive them; on the contrary, he would kill them all, if they did not disclose the whereabouts of their chiefs. The Indians answered that they knew nothing about them but that the Spaniards should make use of them, of their wives and children whom they would find in their houses, where they could kill them or do with them what they wished. And this the Indians declared and offered many times.

Stupefying to relate, the Spaniards went to the houses where they found the poor people working in safety at their occupations with their wives and children, and there they wounded them with their lances and cut them to pieces. They also went to a quiet, large and important town, where the people were ignorant of what had happened to the others and were safe in their innocence; within barely two hours they destroyed it, putting women, children, and the aged to the sword, and killing all who did not save themselves by flight.

Seeing that with such humility, submission, patience and suffering they could not break nor soften hearts so inhuman and brutal, and that they were thus cut to pieces contrary to every show or shadow of right, and that they must inevitably perish, the Indians determined to summon all their people together and to die fighting, avenging themselves as best they could on such cruel and infernal enemies; they well knew, however, that being not only unarmed but also naked and on foot, they could not prevail against such fierce people, mounted and so well armed, but must in the end be destroyed.

They constructed some pits in the middle of the streets, covered over with broken boughs of trees and grass, completely concealing them: they were filled with sharp stakes hardened by fire which would be driven into the horses's bellies if they fell into the pits. Once, or twice, did some horses fall in but not often, because the Spaniards knew how to avoid them. In revenge, the Spaniards made a law, that all Indians of whatsoever rank and age whom they captured alive, they would throw into the pits. And so they threw in pregnant and confined women, children, old men and as many as they could capture who were left stuck on the stakes, until the pits were filled: It excited great compassion to see them, particularly the women with their children.

They killed all the others with lances and knives; they threw them to savage dogs, that tore them to pieces and ate them; and when they came across some lord, they accorded him the honour of burning in live flames. This butchery lasted about seven years from 1524 to 1531. From this may be judged what numbers of people they destroyed.

Among the numberless horrible operations that this unhappy and accursed tyrant performed in this kingdom, together with his brothers, (for his captains and the others who helped him, were not less unhappy and senseless than he) was one very notorious one. He went to the province of Cuzcatan, in which, or not far distant, there is the town of San Salvador, which is a most delightful place extending all along the coast of the South Sea from forty to fifty leagues: and the town of Cuzcatan, which was the capital of the province, gave him the kindest of welcomes, sending him more than twenty or thirty Indians loaded with fowls and other provisions.

When he arrived, and had received the gift, he commanded that each Spaniard should take from that multitude of people, as many Indians as he pleased for his service during their stay there, whose duty should be to bring them everything they needed. Each Spaniard took a hundred, or fifty or as many as he reckoned would be sufficient for his service, and those innocent lambs bore with the distribution, and served with all their strength, and almost adored them. . . .

He and his brothers, together with the others, have killed more than four or five million people in fifteen or sixteen years, from the year 1524 till 1540, and they continue to kill and destroy those who are still left; and so they will kill the remainder.

It was his custom when he went to make war on some town or province, to take with him as many of the Indians as he could, to fight against the other; and as he led ten or twenty thousand and gave them nothing to eat, he allowed them to eat the Indians they captured. And so a solemn butchery of human flesh took place in his army where, in his presence, children were killed and roasted; and they would kill a man only to eat his hands and feet, which were esteemed the best bits. And all the people of the other countries, hearing of these villainies, were so terror stricken they knew not where to hide themselves.

They killed numberless people with the labor of building boats. From the South Sea to the North, a distance of a hundred and thirty leagues, they led the Indians loaded with anchors weighing seventy and eighty pounds each—some of which wore into their shoulders and loins. They also carried much artillery in this way on the shoulders of those poor naked creatures; and I saw many of them loaded with artillery, suffering along the roads.

They deprived the husbands of their wives and daughters, and gave them to the sailors and soldiers, to keep them contented and bring them on board the ships. They crowded Indians into the ships, where they all perished of hunger and thirst. And in truth, were I to recount his cruelties one by one, I could make a big book that would astonish the world.

He built two fleets, each composed of many ships, with which he burnt, as though with fire from heaven, all those countries. Of how many did he make orphans! Of how many did he take away the children! How many did he deprive of their wives! How many wives did he leave without husbands! Of what adulteries, rapes and violence was he the cause! How many did he deprive of liberty! What anguish and calamity were suffered by many people because of him! What tears did he cause to be shed! What sighs! What groans! What solitude in this life and of how many has he caused the eternal damnation in the next! not only of the Indians—who were numberless—but of the unhappy Christians, of whose company he made himself worthy, with such outrages, most grave sins and execrable abominations. And I pray God, that He may have had compassion on [Pedro de Alvarado] and be appeased with the bad death to which He at last brought him.

Study Questions

1. What does Columbus's letter suggest about what Spain was really after when her rulers agreed to finance his voyage to the Indies?
2. How was Columbus's record of what he saw in the New World conditioned by what he wanted and expected to see?
3. What does Pope Paul's decree suggest about Europeans' conception of humanity?
4. How was Christianity compromised by the material motives of Europeans who traveled to the New World, and why did Las Casas choose to detail the barbarous behavior of Europeans in his history?

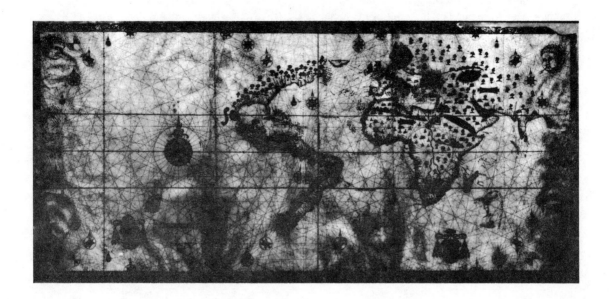

Salviati's Planisphere Map

Mapmaking is a significant activity of nearly all civilized peoples. The earliest extant world maps, in fact, date from the mid-first millennium B.C.E. Prior to the late fifteenth-century voyages of discovery and exploration, the geographical lore of Ptolemy of Alexandria (87–150) governed the mapmaker's art in west Eurasia, especially after the recovery of Ptolemy's *Geography* earlier in the century. By the early 1700s, however, European explorers had reached the New World. Ptolemaic maps quickly became anachronistic as De Gama, Balboa, Pizzaro, and others sent dispatches to their royal and noble patrons. German and Italian printing presses in particular not only produced maps, but also books of letters and other documents written and collected by explorers.

Salviati's "Planisphere Map" of 1527 illustrates how far global exploration had gone and the extent to which geographic knowledge had been disseminated throughout Europe. The absence of information concerning the interiors of North and South America is notable, as is the lack of detail for the islands of the Pacific Ocean. The geographical knowledge of east Eurasia is not derived from recent voyages of exploration, but is dependent upon older works of Ptolemy, Marco Polo, and others.

The Fundamental Orders of Connecticut of 1639

In 1636, the Reverend Thomas Hooker (1586–1647) led his New Town congregation into the inviting Connecticut valley to establish the town of Hartford. These pioneers were soon followed by other adventurous folks from Massachusetts Bay. In January 1639, the free men from the towns of Hartford, Wynsor, and Wethersfield assembled at Hartford and drew up the so-called Fundamental Orders, the first written constitution that created a European-style government in the New World. The document is reproduced in the original English language of the early seventeenth century.

Forasmuch as it hath pleased the Allmighty God by the wise disposition of his divyne providence so to Order and dispose of things that we the Inhabitants and Residents of Wynsor, Harteford and Wethersfield are now cohabiting and dwelling in and uppon the River of Conectecotte and the Lands thereunto adioyneing; And well knowing where a people are gathered together the word of God requires that to mayntayne the peace and union of such a people there should be an orderly and decent Government established according to God, to order and dispose of the affayres of the people at all seasons as occation shall require; doe therefore assotiate and conioyne our selves to be as one Publike State or Commonwelth; and doe, for our selves and our Successors and such as shall be adioyned to us att any tyme hereafter, enter into Combination and Confederation togather, to mayntayne and presearve the liberty and purity of the gospell of our Lord Jesus which we now professe, as also the disciplyne of the Churches, which according to the truth of the said gospell is now practised amongst us; As also in our Civell Affaires to be guided and governed according to such Lawes, Rules, Orders and decrees as shall be made, ordered & decreed, as followeth:—

1. It is Ordered . . . that there shall be yerely two generall Assemblies or Courts, the one the second thursday in Aprill, the other the second thursday in September, following; the first shall be called the Courte of Election, wherein shall be yerely Chosen . . . soe many Magestrats and other publike Officers as shall be

Benjamin P. Poore, ed., *The Federal and State Constitutions,* 2nd ed. (Washington, DC: Government Printing Office, 1878), passim.

found requisitte: Whereof one to be chosen Governour for the yeare ensueing and untill another be chosen, and noe other Magestrate to be chosen for more than one yeare; provided allwayes there be six chosen besids the Governour; which being chosen and sworne according to an Oath recorded for that purpose shall have power to administer justice according to the Lawes here established, and for want thereof according to the rule of the word of God; which choise shall be made by all that are admitted freemen and have taken the Oath of Fidellity, and doe cohabitte within this Jurisdiction, (having beene admitted Inhabitants by the major part of the Towne wherein they live,) or the major parte of such as shall be then present.

4. It is Ordered ... that noe person be chosen Governor above once in two yeares, and that the Governor be alwayes a member of some approved congregation, and formerly of the Magestracy within this Jurisdiction; and all the Magestrats Freemen of this Commonwelth: ...

5. It is Ordered ... that to the aforesaid Courte of Election the severall Townes shall send their deputyes, and when the Elections are ended they may proceed in any publike searvice as at other Courts. Also the other Generall Courte in September shall be for makeing of lawes, and any other publike occation, which conserns the good of the Commonwelth.

7. It is Ordered ... that after there are warrants given out for any of the said Generall Courts, the Constable ... of ech Towne shall forthwith give notice distinctly to the inhabitants of the same, ... that at a place and tyme by him or them lymited and sett, they meet and assemble them selves togather to elect and chuse certen deputyes to be att the Generall Courte then following to agitate the afayres of the commonwelth; which said Deputyes shall be chosen by all that are admitted Inhabitants in the severall Townes and have taken the oath of fidellity; provided that non be chosen a Deputy for any Generall Courte which is not a Freeman of this Commonwelth....

8. It is Ordered ... that Wynsor, Harteford and Wethersfield shall have power, ech Towne, to send fower of their freemen as their deputyes to every Generall Courte; and whatsoever other Townes shall be hereafter added to this Jurisdiction, they shall send so many deputyes as the Courte shall judge meete, a resonable proportion to the number of Freemen that are in the said Townes being to be attended therein; which deputyes shall have the power of the whole Towne to give their voats and alowance to all such lawes and orders as may be for the publike good, and unto which the said Townes are to be bownd.

9. It is Ordered ... that the deputyes thus chosen shall have power and liberty to appoynt a tyme and a place of meeting togather before any Generall Courte to advise and consult of all such things as may concerne the good of the publike, as also to examine their owne Elections....

10. It is Ordered ... that every Generall Courte ... shall consist of the Governor, or some one chosen to moderate the Court, and four other Magestrats at lest, with the major parte of the deputyes of the severall Townes legally chosen; and in case the Freemen or major parte of them, through neglect or refusall of the Governor and major parte of the magestrats, shall call a Courte, it shall consist of

the major parte of Freemen that are present or their deputyes, with a Moderator chosen by them: In which said Generall Courts shall consist the supreme power of the commonwelth, and they only shall have power to make lawes or repeale them, to graunt levyes, to admitt of Freemen, dispose of lands undisposed of, to severall Townes or persons, and also shall have power to call ether Courte or Magestratte or any other person whatsoever into question for any misdemeanour, and may for just causes displace or deale otherwise according to the nature of the offence; and also may deale in any other matter that concerns the good of this commonwelth, excepte election of Magestrats, which shall be done by the whole boddy of Freemen.

In which Courte the Governour or Moderator shall have power to order the Courte to give liberty of spech, and silence unreasonable and disorderly speakeings, to put all things to voate, and in case the voate be equall to have the casting voice. But non of these Courts shall be adjorned or dissolved without the consent of the major parte of the Courte.

11. It is Ordered . . . that when any Generall Courte uppon the occasions of the Commonwealth have agreed uppon any summe or sommes of mony to be levyed uppon the severall Townes within this Jurisdiction, that a Committee be chosen to sett out and appoynt what shall be the proportion of every Towne to pay of the said levy, provided the Committees be made up of an equall number out of each Towne.

Study Questions

1. According to the document, what is the basis of civil order?
2. What most concerned the Reverend Hooker and his fellow colonists as they attempted to create a viable government for their colony?
3. What powers and authority are granted in the document to government and its various officials in the town assemblies?
4. What does the document suggest concerning people's motives behind traveling to the New World to establish colonies?

Part 2

The Modern World

An Age of Revolutionaries and Reactionaries

TOWARD THE CREATION OF A GLOBAL COMMUNITY   The course of events in the Modern Age flowed along from preceding centuries toward the creation of the global community, precipitating new perceptions of world order. In the late eighteenth through early twentieth centuries, the pace of transition from regional isolation to globalization quickened. Many reactionary potentates and uncompromising bureaucrats still attempted to exist in relative seclusion from the rest of the civilized world, but anachronistic institutions and sacrosanct traditions gave way as all humanity labored under the ambiguities and disorder brought on by rapid change.

Some people were more agile than others when dealing with anomalies brought about by global modernization. Although some native African tribes, for example, had already been tainted by Christian and Islamic influences, other people wholly or partially rejected such influences in favor of the customs and lifestyles of their ancestors (Readings 24, 25). While Mughal kings and their vassal princes continued to lord over the Indian subcontinent, their empire, like many Muslim states, was hard pressed to maintain its former power and grandeur. By the mid-eighteenth century Mughal authority in India had diminished to the point of impotency, and the region once again descended into the familiar abyss of political disunity and foreign conquest. In reaction to British intrusions into the subcontinent, Indian culture, especially among Hindus, was reborn and ancient values revived and embellished (Reading 27). This cultural renaissance nourished a heightened sense of the uniqueness of the Indian experience, and with it the birth of Indian nationalism (Readings 28, 29). Islamic civilization also flourished in India and elsewhere. Muslims continued to dictate the course of events in southwestern Eurasia and Africa, at least until the arrival of Western imperialists (Reading 26).

A few thousand miles to the east in China, vigorous Manchu tribesmen deposed the last Ming emperor in 1644 and consequently established the Ch'ing dynasty, the last imperial regime to govern the Celestial Empire. Ch'ing rulers successfully consolidated China's imperial system and ushered in an age of prosperity and extraordinary geographic expansion. Confucian political ideals embodied in the ancient civil service examination system (aptly described centuries before by Matteo Ricci) ensured enlightened government until the early nineteenth century, even while incorporating some Occidental ideas (Reading 31). Despite constant criticism and scrutiny, the Chinese heritage continued to influence political and cultural developments in many east Eurasian countries. The Japanese supported a lively, unique civilization derived in part from Chinese roots long before the establishment of the Tokugawa Shogunate in the early seventeenth century. It was the pragmatic policies of the isolationist Tokugawa shoguns, however, that yielded a distinctly Japanese urban culture. Japan had been officially segregated from all foreigners for centuries until the 1850s, when American gunboat diplomacy exacted a treaty from the emperor, which granted the United States trading rights at specific ports. Unsullied by external influences, the Japanese had developed a dynamic, brilliant culture; they were nevertheless capable of absorbing alien features and adapting them to suit their own purposes (Reading 33).

MODERNIZATION OF THE WESTERN WORLD Devastating wars and other age-old calamities continued to plague Europeans and Americans in the Modern Age. Revolutionaries and reactionaries in the West and in fact throughout the world grappled with problems facing their respective countries. Despite the calamities they faced, Europeans and Americans became excessively enamored with their achievements, and consequently instilled in themselves an overwhelming sense of intellectual and technological virtuosity, military prowess, and new economic power (Reading 36). Westerners became firmly convinced their cultural and religious values were vastly superior to all others. In effect, they prepared themselves well to dominate the world they had explored and only partially subjugated in the preceding era.

The intellectual revolution that began in the early sixteenth century now spurred Europeans and their descendants in the Americas to question and reevaluate traditional institutions and fundamental principles and beliefs. The American and French Revolutions of the late eighteenth century were especially significant events with far-reaching consequences. Echoing the sentiments of the French philosophes and their concern for the natural rights of citizens and the national sovereignty (Reading 35), American patriots fanned the flames of political dissent and proved that the ideals of the Enlightenment were practical as well as necessary. The War of Independence fought by the American colonists against the British not only justified acts of rebellion against established authority, but made the ideal of "life, liberty, the pursuit of happiness" of individual citizens and constitutional government practical realities (Reading 43). A generation later, French revolutionaries took similar aspirations and made them permanent features of national politics. The French Revolution swept away everything associated with absolutism, feudalism, and inherited rights.

In the West, the rights of "man" were henceforth guaranteed by republics, democracies, or constitutional monarchies (Reading 37). It should be noted, however, that only during the most radical phase of the French Revolution and never during the course of the American War of Independence was the status of female

139

citizens seriously scrutinized, much to the dismay and disgust of some women and men (Readings 38, 45). Still, by affirming principles of individual liberty and modern democratic society, the so-called Atlantic Revolutions of the late eighteenth century ushered in an era of radical change. This continued beyond mid-century and came to shape events and political movements in different parts of the world well into the twentieth century. In Central and South America, movements for independence gained momentum as revolutionaries in the old colonies dissolved their ties with an obsolete Spanish Empire (Reading 44).

The world in the eighteenth and nineteenth centuries appeared to be a smaller place than when ships from European seaports embarked on voyages of exploration and discovery at the end of the fifteenth century. Although further exploration of unknown continents lay in the immediate future, by the nineteenth century there was truly a sense that different parts of the globe were connected. Despite the enormous differences among people, the world was viewed as a global community. At the same time, however, the universe seemed to be growing larger owing to the tremendous strides made in the theoretical and practical sciences. The word "scientist" itself was coined in 1841, indicating the important role of science in Western culture (Reading 41). A consequence of scientific progress was the belief that since various aspects of the physical universe were endowed with such properties as mass, shape, and motion, it naturally followed that human beings possessed innate characteristics that varied according to race and ethnic background. Politicians, diplomats, and social scientists used seemingly objective, theoretical conclusions not only to justify domination of foreign peoples, but also to rationalize the oppression of the lower classes in their own countries (Reading 40).

Throughout the nineteenth century European nations and the United States were occupied not only with their overseas empires but also the social and political effects of modernization (Readings 39, 42, 46). Increasingly rapid industrialization brought in its wake the proliferation of industrial capitalism, class conflict, and the rise of new, sometimes belligerent nation-states. This certainly tested the efficacy of Western traditions and people's resolve to endure change. The invention of labor-saving machines, discovery of new sources of power, improvements in manufacturing techniques, and innovations in business and banking organization enhanced the capacity and symbolized the necessity for Western industrialized nations to expand beyond their boundaries. Europe's and the United States's indisputable technological superiority and sharply rising populations created a need for new markets and abundant sources of raw materials. These are also reasons why overseas empires were established with such haste at the end of the nineteenth century. Thus, the economic modernization of the West greatly affected the global community.

"NEW IMPERIALISM" OF THE LATE NINETEENTH CENTURY During the early days of expansion, direct forms of colonization and exploitation readily took hold in the Americas and along the coast of tropical Africa. These were vast areas, where no recognizable "states" existed; their tribal associations garnered little respect from the interlopers. Conversely, European governments used their diplomatic and military power to influence the policies of sophisticated foreign states in eastern and southeast Eurasia. Chinese, Japanese, and other east and southeast Eurasian rulers were eventually not sufficiently powerful to curb foreign aggression or to stem the tide of Occidental ideas (Reading 30). Of course, native reactions to the influx of foreigners differed from place to place, the variety of responses falling anywhere between outright rejection of their influence to sincere admiration of any novelty from abroad. Indeed, many people throughout the world believed Europe and the United States offered many things of considerable value (Readings 32, 34). Furthermore, it is ironic that some local leaders, many of whom gained prominence after the turn of the century, traveled to the West to receive advanced educations and were consequently inspired by its political and social doctrines. They eventually became extreme opponents of imperial entanglements in their mother countries.

The latter part of the nineteenth century saw the Western imperialist nations suddenly partition most of the world among themselves. Coupled with intense economic modernization, an important ingredient in the equation of New Imperialism was the rise of nationalism. With the establishment of viable national states in Germany and Italy as well as in the United States, especially after the Civil War of the 1860s, imperialism became closely tied to the modernization of the nation-state and the need to create a political consensus otherwise lacking, owing to rapidly changing sociopolitical and economic conditions. Acquiring and governing foreign territory meant, of course, controlling the productive life of a country and forcing large numbers of natives to serve the needs of the home country. New Imperialism not only brought with it significant changes for Western nations, but it also altered the sociopolitical and economic structures of foreign countries. European and American statesmen and diplomats did not fully recognize (or did not want to acknowledge) the real dangers brought on by this heated competition for overseas colonies. The cries for independence and freedom by oppressed peoples in east Eurasia, Africa, and elsewhere fell on deaf ears. Only the outbreak of World War I in 1914 made imperialists think twice about the consequences of their global aspirations.

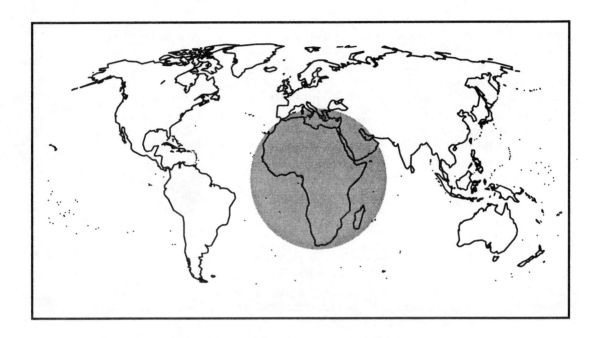

Brief Chronology for the Modern World
Southwest Eurasia and Africa

1700	Transatlantic slave trade at its height	**1879–1880**	Henry Stanley obtains the Congo for King Leopold of Belgium
1741–1856	United Sultanate of Oman and Zanzibar in East Africa	**1882**	Establishment of British protectorate in Egypt
1769	Ali Bey (1728–1773) declares Egyptian independence from Ottoman Empire	**1884–1885**	International Conference in Berlin to discuss African affairs
1774	Ottomans lose the Crimea to Russian czar	**1893–1913**	Mohandas K. Gandhi works as a lawyer in South Africa
1795	British dominate Cape Colony, replacing the Dutch	**1899–1902**	Boer War in South Africa
1816–1827	Reign of Chief Shaka Zulu (1787–1828) in southern Africa	**1907**	Orange Free State, the Transvaal, Natal, and Cape Colony form the Union of South Africa
1823–1831	Ashanti tribes at war with British in Africa	**1908**	"Young Turk" revolt in Ottoman Empire
1830–1847	French conquest of Algeria	**1911**	Liberia becomes U.S. protectorate in all but name
1839–1880	*Tanzimat* reforms in Ottoman Empire, initial rescripts proclaim all citizens guaranteed equality under the law	**1922–1938**	Mustafa Kemal, "Ataturk," reigns as first president of Turkey
1848–1885	Muhammad Ahmad, the "Madhi," active in the Sudan	**1935**	Italian dictator Mussolini orders the invasion of Ethiopia
1854–1856	Crimean War		
1854–1862	Sir Richard Burton (1821–1890) and John H. Speke (1827–1864) mount expeditions to discover the source of the Nile in Africa		
1859–1869	Building of the Suez Canal		
1871	Dr. David Livingstone (1813–1873) rescued by Henry Stanley in Ujiji, Africa		

All dates are C.E. and approximate unless otherwise indicated. It should be noted as well that chronologies are constantly being revised. Hence, there may be discrepancies between the dates listed above and those found in other textbooks and scholarly monographs. Throughout the text and in the Glossary, all dates are given in B.C.E. (Before the Common Era) and C.E. (the Common Era). Where there is no era designation C.E. may be assumed.

142

Edward Blyden's "The Aims and Methods of a Liberal Education for Africans"

Unlike the majority of native Africans in the middle of the nineteenth century, the Americo-Liberian settlers of Liberia were recognized by Western imperialists as an independent people. Nevertheless, the United States government frequently intervened in Liberian affairs and by the end of the century exercised a kind of informal protectorate over the country. Even American blacks who had settled in this part of western Africa wanted to validate their African heritage and ensure their continued independence by exploring their native culture. Edward Blyden (1832–1912) was born in St. Thomas, West Indies, and traveled to Liberia in 1851 to study at the new Alexander High School in Monrovia. He remained active in the nation's affairs for the rest of his life, serving in various capacities, including secretary of state and minister of the interior. In 1880, Blyden became president of Liberia College in Monrovia. At his inauguration on 5 January 1881, he delivered the following address, in which he discussed his vision of an educational system that was Pan-African in scope and contained an African rather than a European bias. Such an education was designed to develop an African rather than European personality. Blyden's Liberia College for Africans, located in the rural interior of the country, fostered self-reliance and promoted relevant links between land, people, and cultural traditions and history.

A college in West Africa, for the education of African youth by African instructors, under a Christian government conducted by Negroes, is something so unique in the history of Christian civilization, that wherever in the civilized world the existence of such an institution is heard of, there will be curiosity as to its character, its work, and its prospects. A college suited, in all respects, to the exigencies of this nation and to the needs of the race cannot come into existence all at once. It must be the result of years of experience, of trial, of experiment.

Every thinking man will allow that all we have been doing in this country so far, whether in church, in state, or in school—our forms of religion, our politics, our literature, such as it is—is only temporary and transitional. When we advance

---

Edward W. Blyden, *Christianity, Islam, and the Negro Race* (London: W. B. Whittingham, 1887), 71–93, passim.

further into Africa, and become one with the great tribes on the continent, these things will take the form which the genius of the race shall prescribe.

The civilization of that vast population, untouched by foreign influence, not yet affected by European habits, is not to be organized according to foreign patterns, but will organize itself according to the nature of the people and the country. Nothing that we are doing now can be absolute or permanent, because nothing is normal or regular. Everything is provisional or tentative.

The college is only a machine, an instrument to assist in carrying forward our regular work—devised not only for intellectual ends, but for social purposes, for religious duty, for patriotic aims, for racial development; and when as an instrument, as a means, it fails, for any reason whatever, to fulfill its legitimate functions, it is the duty of the country, as well as in the interest of the country, to see that it is stimulated into healthful activity, . . .

The object of all education is to secure growth and efficiency, to make a man all that his natural gifts will allow him to become; to produce self-respect, a proper appreciation of our own powers and of the powers of other people; to beget a fitness for one's sphere of life and action, and ability to discharge the duties it imposes. Now, if we take these qualities as the true outcome of a correct education, then everyone who is acquainted with the facts must admit that, as a rule, in the entire civilized world, the Negro, not withstanding his two hundred years' residence with Christian and civilized races, has nowhere received anything like a correct education. We find him everywhere—in the United States, in the West Indies, in South America—largely unable to cope with the responsibilities which devolve upon him.

To a certain extent—perhaps to a very important extent— Negroes trained on the soil of Africa have the advantage of those trained in foreign countries; but in all, as a rule, the intellectual and moral results, thus far, have been far from satisfactory. There are many men of book-learning, but few, very few, of any capability—even fewer who have that amount, or that sort, of culture, which produces self-respect, confidence in oneself, and efficiency in work. Now, why is this? The evil, it is considered, lies in the system and methods of European training to which Negroes are, everywhere in Christian lands, subjected, and which everywhere affects them unfavorably. Of a different race, different susceptibility, different bent of character from that of the European, they have been trained under influences in many respects adapted only to the Caucasian race. Nearly all the books they read, the very instruments of their culture, have been such as to force them from the groove which is natural to them, where they would be strong and effective, without furnishing them with any avenue through which they may move naturally and free from obstruction. Christian and so-called civilized Negroes live, for the most part, in foreign countries, where they are only passive spectators of the deeds of a foreign race; and where, with other impressions which they receive from without, and element of doubt as to their own capacity and their own destiny is fastened upon them, and inheres in their intellectual and social constitution. They deprecate their own individuality, and would escape from it if they could. And in countries like this, where they are free from the hampering surroundings of an alien race, they still read and study the books of foreigners, and form their idea

144

of everything that man may do, or ought to do, according to the standard held up in those teachings. Hence, without the physical or mental aptitude for the enterprises which they are taught to admire and revere, they attempt to copy and imitate them, and share the fate of all copyists and imitators. Bound to move on a lower level, they acquire and retain a practical inferiority, transcribing, very often, the faults rather than the virtues of their models.

Besides this result of involuntary impressions, they often receive direct teachings which are not only incompatible with, but destructive of, their self-respect.

In all English-speaking countries the mind of the intelligent Negro child revolts against the descriptions given in elementary books—geographies, travels, histories—of the Negro; but, though he experiences an instinctive revulsion from these caricatures and misrepresentations, he is obliged to continue, as he grows in years, to study pernicious teachings. After leaving school he finds the same things in newspapers, in reviews, in novels, in quasi scientific works; and after a while they begin to seem to him the proper things to say and to feel about his race, and he accepts what, at first, his fresh and unbiased feelings naturally and indignantly repelled. Such is the effect of repetition. . . .

Black men, and especially black women, in such communities, experience the greatest imaginable inconvenience. They never feel at home. In the depth of their being they always feel themselves strangers in the land of their exile, and the only escape from this feeling is to escape from themselves. And this feeling of self-depreciation is not diminished, as I have intimated above, by the books they read. Women, especially, are fond of reading novels and light literature; and it is in these writings that flippant and eulogistic reference is constantly made to the superior physical and mental characteristics of the Caucasian race, which, by contrast, suggest the inferiority of other races—especially of that race which is furthest removed from it in appearance.

It is painful in America to see the efforts which are made by Negroes to secure outward conformity to the appearance of the dominant race.

This is by no means surprising; but what is surprising is that, under the circumstances, any Negro has retained a particle of self-respect. Now in Africa, where the color of the majority is black, the fashion in personal matters is naturally suggested by the personal characteristics of the race, and we are free from the necessity of submitting to the use of "incongruous feathers awkwardly stuck on." Still, we are held in bondage by our indiscriminate and injudicious use of a foreign literature; and we strive to advance by the methods of a foreign race. In this effort we struggle with the odds against us. We fight at the disadvantage which **David** would have experienced in Saul's armor. The African must advance by methods of his own. He must possess a power distinct from that of the European. It has been proved that he knows how to take advantage of European culture, and that he can be benefitted by it. This proof was perhaps necessary, but it is not sufficient. We must show that we are able to go alone, to carve out our own way. We must not be satisfied that, in this nation, European influence shapes our polity, makes our laws, rules in our tribunals, and impregnates our social atmosphere. We must not suppose that the Anglo-Saxon methods are final, that there is nothing for us to find for our own guidance, and that we have nothing to teach the world. There is inspiration for us also. We must study our brethren in the interior, who know better than we do the laws of growth for the race. We see among them the rudiments of that which, with fair play and opportunity, will develop into important and effective agencies for our work. We look too much to foreigners, and are dazzled almost to blindness by their exploits—so as to fancy that they have exhausted the possibilities of humanity. . . .

Matthew Arnold reminds us that when someone talked to **Themistocles** of an art of memory, he answered, "Teach me rather to forget." The full meaning of this aspiration must be realized in the life of the Christian Negro before he can become a full man, or a successful worker in his fatherland. . . .

The true principle of mental culture is perhaps this: to preserve an accurate balance between the studies which carry the mind out of itself, and those which recall it home again. When we receive impressions from without we must bring from our own consciousness the idea that gives them shape; we must mold them by our own individuality. Now, in looking over the whole civilized world I see no place where this sort of culture for the Negro can be better secured than in Liberia—where he may, with less interruption from surrounding influences, find out his place and his work, develop his peculiar gifts and powers; and for the training of Negro youth upon the basis of their own idiosyncracy, with a sense of race individuality, self-respect, and liberty, there is no institution so well adapted as Liberia College with its Negro faculty and Negro students. . . .

The instruments of [European] culture which we shall employ in the college will be chiefly the Classics and Mathematics. By Classics I mean the Greek and Latin languages and their literature. In those languages there is not, as far as I know, a sentence, a word, or a syllable disparaging to the Negro. He may get nourishment from them without taking in any race-poison. They will perform no sinister work upon his consciousness, and give no unholy bias to his inclinations.

It will be our aim to introduce into our curriculum also the Arabic, and some of the principal native languages—by means of which we may have intelligent intercourse with the millions accessible to us in the interior, and learn more of our own country. We have young men who are experts in the geography and customs of foreign countries; who can tell all about the proceedings of foreign statesmen in countries thousands of miles away; can talk glibly of London, Berlin, Paris, and Washington; know all about **Gladstone**, **Bismarck**, **Gambetta**, and **Hayes**; but who knows anything about Musahdu, Medina, Kankan, or Sego—only a few hundred miles from us? Who can tell anything of the policies or doings [of statesmen] . . . only a few steps from us? These are hardly known. Now as Negroes, allied in blood and race to these people, this is disgraceful; and as a nation, if we intend to grow and prosper in this country, it is impolitic, it is shortsighted, it is unpatriotic; but it has required time for us to grow up to these ideas, to understand our position in this country. In order to accelerate our future progress, and to give to the advance we make the element of permanence, it will be our aim in the college to produce men of ability. Ability or capability is the power to use with effect the instruments in our hands. The bad workman complains of his tools; but, even when he is satisfied with the excellence of his tools, he cannot produce the results which an able workman will produce, even with indifferent tools. . . .

As those who have suffered affliction in a foreign land, we have no antecedents from which to gather inspiration. Now, if we are to make an independent nation—a strong nation—we must listen to the songs of our unsophisticated brethren as they sing of their history, as they tell of their traditions, of the wonderful and mysterious events of their tribal or national life, of the achievements of what we call their superstitions; we must lend a ready ear to the ditties of the Kroomen who pull our boats, of the Pessah and Golah men who till our farms; we must read the compositions, rude as we may think them, of the Mandingoes and the Veys. We shall in this way get back the strength of the race, like the giant of the ancients, who always gained strength, for his conflict with Hercules, whenever he touched his mother earth.

And this is why we want the college away from the seaboard—with its constant intercourse with foreign manners and low foreign ideas—that we may have free and uninterrupted intercourse with the intelligent among the tribes of the interior; that the students, even from the books to which they will be allowed access, may conveniently flee to the forests and fields of Manding and the River Niger, and mingle with our brethren and gather fresh inspiration and fresh and living ideas.

We have a great work before us, a work unique in the history of the world, which others who appreciate its vastness and importance, envy us the privilege of doing. The world is looking at this republic to see whether "order and law, religion and morality, the rights of conscience, the rights of persons and the rights of property," may all be secured and preserved by a government administered entirely by Negroes.

Let us show ourselves equal to the task.

The time is past when we can be content with putting forth elaborate arguments to prove our equality with foreign races. Those who doubt our capacity are more likely to be convinced of their error by the exhibition, on our part, of those qualities of energy and enterprise which will enable us to occupy the extensive field before us for our own advantage and the advantage of humanity—for the purposes of civilization, of science, of good government, and of progress generally—than by any mere abstract argument about the equality of races. The suspicions disparaging to us will be dissipated only by the exhibition of the indisputable realities of a lofty manhood as they may be illustrated in successful efforts to build up a nation, to wrest from Nature her secrets, to lead the van of progress in this country, and to regenerate a continent.

Study Questions

1. What kind of educational curriculum does Blyden seek for Liberia College?
2. Why does he reject some but not all of the classics of Western literature?
3. How does Blyden view the position and status of blacks in African countries and throughout the world?
4. What is Blyden's theory of education, and how does he define "real purpose"?

Janus Headpiece of Ekoi tribe for Ekkpe Society, Ekparabrong clan, West Africa

A sense of oneness with the visible and unseen order of things was portrayed in African masks, which had varied public and private functions in their societies. Whether enacting fertility rituals, dramatizing cosmogonic events, or performing initiation rites, masks such as this Ekoi "Janus" headpiece used by the Ekkpe Society of the Ekparabrong clan helped to ensure the proper order of existence. The Ekoi tribe inhabited the Cross River area of Cameroon and southeastern Nigeria. According to native tradition, sometime in the eighteenth century the Efut tribe sold the secrets of their Ngbe Society to the Ekoi, who renamed it after their own word for leopard, *ekkpe*. As a source of secret vengeance and as an ultimate, mysterious authority, the society promulgated or canceled laws, forced resolution of civil conflicts, and defied western European arrogance and aggression. The male Ekkpe Society has survived among the Ekoi of the Cross River area. This Janus mask, made of wood covered by animal skin and decorated with antelope horn, is about 23 inches in height. The masks are common among many tribes, the dark face representing a male, a lighter, often yellow-brown face, a female. They are construed as cosmic symbols representing, respectively, the Sky-Father and Earth-Mother, life and death, and other aspects of the duality of human existence. Regardless of the many functions served by the masks, the socio-religious ceremonies in which they were used aimed at maintaining the cohesion and order of the community.

Traditional Oral Texts from Africa

Many "primitive" cultures of Africa support worldviews that imply a well-ordered, communal, and integrated way of life. Although the ethnic diversity of Africa is enormous, its people live in harmony with nature by surrendering the self to the rhythms of existence. This fusion of the internal and external results in a philosophy requiring a kind of mystical participation in life through contemplation of nature and transcendence of egoism. These aspects of the African way of life might very well be likened to the "cosmic religious feeling" spoken of by the great European scientist Albert Einstein or to Sigmund Freud's psychologically loaded concept of "oceanic feeling." The following stories and folktales, recorded by Western anthropologists and derived from the oral traditions of native tribes, illustrate the African sense of harmonious existence. The Nyanga folktale comes from the people inhabiting the forest region of northwestern Kivu Province in the old Republic of the Congo. It is part of *mushinga* oral literature, that is, pieces that were recited but not sung. The two Lugbara myths come from the people living in Uganda's extreme northwest territory. The first story relates how lightning visited the people of the Aiiku clan. Lightning was regarded as a manifestation of divine power, and a person killed by it was considered to have been marked out in a special way by divine forces. The second story, "The First People to Have Lived Here," is a creation myth. In this myth and many others like it, Arube and O'duru are construed as the first children of the original couple Gborogboro and Meme, who were themselves created by divine forces. These figures are thus miraculous and not wholly human. Furthermore, the incest that occurs between Arube and O'duru signifies that the two did not comprehend the importance of kinship and, therefore, existed before society was formed. Derived from Somali tradition, the final tale, entitled "**Garaad** Muhammed," is somewhat different in nature from the others and obviously reflects strong Islamic influence.

A Nyanga Folktale

"Sun and Rain"

Sun and Rain started an argument with one another.

A young Monkey had begotten a daughter in another village. Rain arrived there, looking for this young girl. After he had arrived there, he talked to Monkey about his daughter. The father of the girl refused. After Rain had received this answer, he returned without anything and covered with shame.

When Sun had seen that Rain failed to get the girl, he, Sun, arrived there, asked for the girl, got her, and so became son-in-law of Monkey. War [danger] arrived, pursued Monkey. This war killed Monkey's wife and all his children, and he also had finished fleeing. There, where Monkey had fled, he shouted, "You, Sun, because of the way you shone therefore I lose a lot of people."

One day again, they hunted and hunted at Monkey's place. Rain also fell. They left him above, he had finished climbing up into the trees. Rain did not stop, it fell very hard. The hunters went home because of too much rain. After Rain has finished falling and Monkey has been saved, Rain came to where he was and told him, "You have given your daughter to Sun, saying he can save you, but I here have saved you and this although you have denied me your daughter."

After he had thus been saved by Rain, Monkey took away his daughter from Sun, gave her to Rain because he had saved him. Rain went home with the daughter of Monkey where before he had been refusing her. His strength and his strong intelligence, it is because of that that he got her.

Two Lugbara Myths

"How Lightning Bore Children on Earth"

Long ago a man of this country dug a large field. The field produced a very large amount of millet. Seeing that he had so much millet he decided to make a very big granary for storing it. When harvest came the millet was collected and stored in the granary. The big granary they made was too small for all the millet. They therefore compressed it by using logs and other heavy objects. When the millet was all stored and the work completed a heavy rain fell. As it was falling lightning came down in the form of a sheep; its body and wool were all white.

W. H. Whitely, ed., *A Selection of African Prose: Traditional Oral Texts* (Oxford: Oxford University Press, 1964), vol. 1:60, 129–30, 148–49.

The lightning opened the granary with its wings and entered it. The owner of the granary then opened it so that the lightning could get out. The lightning then prepared a very good place on top of the stored millet for laying eggs. This was said to be the mother lightning, and the father was up in the sky. The father then threw a white substance like cloth to the ground for the mother to be taken up again. The following day nothing happened. The lightning rested and the next day it descended to that village and again opened the granary with its wings, entered it and laid an egg. After that it flew up to the father. After that it again took a day's rest. The following day it laid a second egg. It repeated these actions until they amounted to three.

When there were three eggs the mother lightning descended every day to visit the eggs in the granary. It was fed on unsqueezed beer. The owner of the millet therefore had to collect that kind of food from the surrounding villages. Besides that, his wife made beer every day. They were very careful to do this because when the lightning came down and found no food it destroyed very many things like pots and granaries and even set huts on fire. For that reason the people feared it very much. They kept on bringing the food for the lightning and were waiting for the time when the eggs would hatch. No one knew how long it would take. When three weeks had passed the eggs then hatched. The eggs were divided into six magnificent calabashes. When the eggs had hatched both the mother lightning and the father lightning came down every day to their children to teach them how to fly. Each day they flew a short distance until they were well trained. When the children were strong enough they flew up. The six beautiful calabashes were left at the village. By then the owner of the millet had made beer and had made a great feast for his people. The elders had gathered, questioning each other why the lightning had done these things.

Immediately after the feast the lightning divided the calabashes among the people. It gave two to the owner of the millet. Two calabashes were then given to the next-door village, one to another small village, and the other to another small village. It also gave the people a kind of medicine which was to be planted and kept for ever. It was to be used when a man was struck by lightning. Another day the lightning came down and set fire to a large area of grass. The man who was to take care of the lightning shouted and said, "Put out all the fire you have with you at home, come and fetch this fire brought to us by the lightning." The fire was very bright and all of the people of that place took it and for a long time people talked of it.

The lightning used to come down to his people but these days it does not.

"The First People to Have Lived Here"

Ever since the world was created no man had lived in this country. After a long time a man by the name Arube and a woman O'duru came to this country by the way of Kakwa, [from the North]. As they were coming they did not know where they were going, but thought they would find human beings. As they were coming along their way they slept in caves and the only food they ate was [wild] fruit. When they arrived here they went everywhere to search for human beings. As they wandered about they did not meet anyone. When they found out that there was no one who lived in this country they decided to settle in a place and to rest. Arube was O'duru's brother, but finding no one to marry he married his sister.

When the two had married they had many children. Those children took their sisters as wives. Each one had children and in that way people became numerous. Being many in one home quarrels soon arose between them.

When Arube saw that his children were quarrelling he decided to separate them. He divided them into groups and opened new homes near the main home so as to stop quarrels. The people of those new homes also did the same as did Arube, and they married their sisters. This continued until many of their children spread all over the country.

A Somali Story

"Garaad Muhammed"

When Muhammed was a small boy his father died, and being an orphan he went to live with his stepmother, the widow of his father, and she looked after him. His own mother had died before his father. His stepmother was the daughter of Muumin, the Ugaas of the Ogaden. She, the daughter of Muumin, was married, after she was widowed, by 'Adduur 'Ali, who was Muhammed's uncle. 'Adduur 'Ali was the brother of Muhammed's father, [Garaad] Mahamuud, and he also had another brother called Samakaab.

Now Samakaab said to 'Adduur 'Ali, "Listen, man. Our brother the Garaad is dead, and the children he left are certainly too young to take his place as Garaad. You must either take it yourself, or marry the young woman who is his widow."

"I shall think about it and take counsel," replied 'Adduur 'Ali. He went to the woman and told her about the matter, and she said, "Do not give any answer to Samakaab 'Ali until you hear further news from me." Then she called young Muhammed and said to him, "Listen, boy. People are planning to prevent you from becoming Garaad!"

"What do you think I should do?" he asked.

"If you do what I tell you, you will become Garaad!"

"What must I do?"

"What you must do is this: every day, go to the assembly, put on good clothes, and do what your father used to do when he went to the assembly. When people ask you for something, grant it to them, and then tell me and I will pay whatever you have granted."

When for some time the boy had granted whatever was asked of him, the people said, "Listen, men! This one is even more noble than his father!" He soon gained a great reputation, all the people loving him and planning that he should be Garaad.

When matters had been like this for some time, Samakaab 'Ali said, "Listen, 'Adduur. Did I not say to you, either take the kingdom for yourself, or marry the widow?" 'Adduur 'Ali then said, "I shall marry the widow," and Samakaab said, "And I shall take the kingdom for myself."

'Adduur 'Ali and the woman he was going to marry, the stepmother of Muhammed, wanted to outwit Samakaab 'Ali by having young Muhammed, the rightful heir, made Garaad. To this end they did all they could to spread Muhammed's good reputation all over the country and to blacken the character of Samakaab 'Ali, who wanted to deprive him of his kingdom. When they were satisfied that their design had gone well, and that the people did not want Samakaab 'Ali, but Muhammed, who was young, to become Garaad, they one day called an assembly. They told Samakaab 'Ali, "You must come to the assembly because the question of Garaad-making will be dealt with."

All the people gathered for the assembly, and while Samakaab 'Ali was saying to himself, "It is you whom they are going to make Garaad!" A man was chosen to perform the ceremony and this man got up. The people had agreed together that Samakaab should not know that Muhammed was going to be made Garaad until the moment of crowning, and now the man who was to bestow the crown stood with it in his hands. He said three times: "Let his be the Garaad!" and, while Samakaab 'Ali was still thinking mistakenly that it was he who would be crowned, the man put the crown on Muhammed. All the people cried: "Accept him as your Garaad!" but Samakaab 'Ali, dumbfounded, left the assembly in anger.

Study Questions

1. What proper modes of behavior for native Africans are prescribed in the Nyanga folktale and the Somali story, and what exemplary human characteristics are described in these pieces?
2. What role do such tales play in preliterate, tribal societies?
3. What foreign influences are reflected in these African folktales and myths?
4. Would Edward Blyden (Reading 24) have included or excluded these types of literature in his curricula for Liberia College?

Reading 26

Abdul Mejid's Imperial Rescript of 1856

The once great Ottoman Empire established by Muslim Turks in the late fifteenth century fell on very difficult times in the decades preceding the **Crimean War** of the mid-nineteenth century. In the wake of a series of military disasters, Abdul Mejid (1823–1861) succeeded to the Ottoman sultanate he would rule from 1839 until his death. Four months after his accession, the new sultan issued the Illustrious Rescript that was designed to initiate a new political era for the empire by restructuring the judicial, legislative, and taxation systems. Foreign minister and sometime Grand Vizier Mustafa Reshid (1800–1858) helped to move the reforms forward by initiating *Tanzimat,* a movement for further reorganization that was rooted not in foreign intervention but in internal pressures and discontent. This process of gradual change was greatly expedited by the Crimean War. When the war ended, Sultan Abdul Mejid issued on 18 February 1856 his famous Imperial Rescript, a proclamation sanctioning the earlier Illustrious Rescript and the entire Tanzimat movement.

All the Privileges and Spiritual Immunities granted by my ancestors from ancient times, and at subsequent dates, to all Christian communities or other non-Moslem persuasions established in my Empire under my protection shall be confirmed and maintained.

Every Christian or other non-Moslem community shall be bound within a fixed period, and with the concurrence of a Commission composed ad hoc of members of its own body, to proceed with my high approbation and under the inspection of my **Sublime Porte**, to examine into its actual Immunities and Privileges, and to discuss and submit to my Sublime Porte the Reforms required by the progress of civilization and of the age. The powers conceded to the Christian Patriarchs and Bishops by the **Sultan Mahomet II** and his successors, shall be made to harmonize with the new position which my generous and beneficent intentions insure to these communities. . . . In the towns, small boroughs, and villages, where the whole population is of the same Religion, no obstacle shall be offered to the repair, according to their original plan, of buildings set apart for Religious Worship, for Schools, for Hospitals, and for Cemeteries. . . .

 E. Hertslet, *The Map of Europe by Treaty* (London: Butterworth, 1875–91), vol. 2:1243–49.

Every distinction or designation tending to make any class whatever of the subjects of my Empire inferior to another class, on account of their Religion, Language, or Race, shall be for ever effaced from the Administrative Protocol. The laws shall be put in force against the use of any injurious or offensive term, either among private individuals or on the part of the authorities.

As all forms of Religion shall be freely professed in my dominions, no subject of my Empire shall be hindered in the exercise of the Religion that he professes. . . . No one will be compelled to change their Religion. . . . All the subjects of my Empire, without distinction of nationality, shall be admissible to public employments. . . . All the subjects of my Empire, without distinction, shall be received into the Civil and Military Schools of the Government. . . . Moreover, every community is authorized to establish Public Schools of Science, Art, and Industry. . . .

All Commercial, Correctional, and Criminal Suits between Moslems and Christians or other non-Moslems of different sects, shall be referred to Mixed Tribunals. The proceedings of these Tribunals shall be public: the parties shall be confronted, and shall produce their witnesses, whose testimony shall be received, without distinction, upon oath taken according to the religious law of each sect. . . .

Penal, Correctional, and Commercial Laws, and Rules of Procedure for the Mixed Tribunals, shall be drawn up as soon as possible, and formed into a code. . . . Proceedings shall be taken, for the reform of the Penitentiary System. . . .

The organization of the Police . . . shall be revised in such a manner as to give to all the peaceable subjects of my Empire the strongest guarantees for the safety both of their persons and property. . . . Christian subjects, and those of other non-Moslem sects, . . . shall, as well as Moslems, be subject to the obligations of the Law of Recruitment. The principle of obtaining substitutes, or of purchasing exemption, shall be admitted. . . .

Proceedings shall be taken for a Reform in the Constitution of the Provincial and Communal Councils, in order to ensure fairness in the choice of the Deputies of the Moslem, Christian, and other communities, and the freedom of voting in the Councils. . . .

As the Laws regulating the purchase, sale, and disposal of Real Property are common to all the subjects of my Empire, it shall be lawful for Foreigners to possess Landed Property in my dominions. . . .

The Taxes are to be levied under the same denomination from all the subjects of my Empire, without distinction of class or of Religion. The most prompt and energetic means for remedying the abuses in collecting the Taxes, and especially the Tithes, shall be considered. The system of direct collection shall gradually, and as soon as possible, be substituted for the plan of Farming, in all the branches of the Revenues of the State.

A special Law having been already passed, which declared that the Budget of the Revenue and Expenditure of the State shall be drawn up and made known every year, the said law shall be most scrupulously observed. . . .

The heads of each Community and a Delegate, designated by my Sublime Porte, will be summoned to take part in the deliberations of the Supreme Council of Justice on all occasions which might interest the generality of the subjects of my Empire. . . .

Steps shall be taken for the formation of Banks and other similar institutions, so as to effect a reform in the monetary and financial system, as well as to create Funds to be employed in augmenting the sources of the material wealth of my Empire.

Steps shall also be taken for the formation of Roads and Canals to increase the facilities of communication and increase the sources of the wealth of the country. Everything that can impede commerce or agriculture shall be abolished. . . .

Study Questions

1. What kind of reforms are undertaken by Abdul Mejid and his government?
2. What glaring problems were apparently inherent in the old Ottoman Empire that attracted the Sultan's attention?
3. What advantages were gained by the non-Muslim peoples of the empire as a result of this legislation?
4. To what degree and how has the Imperial Rescript been influenced by the liberal political ideology of the West?

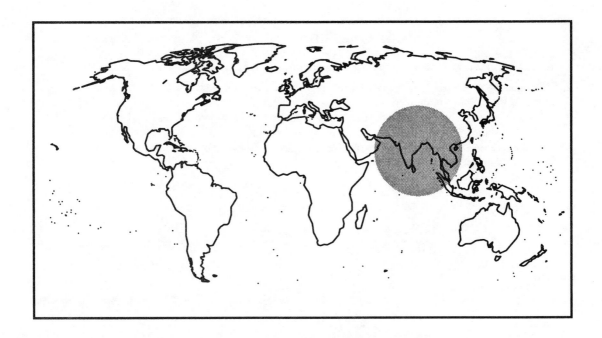

Brief Chronology for the Modern World

South and Southeast Eurasia

1756–1763	Seven Years' War in Europe
1757	Robert Clive's (1725–1774) victory at Plassey gives English control of Bengal
1769	Captain James Cook (1728–1779) reaches New Zealand
1784	Prime Minister Pitt's "India Act" placing British East India Company under government Board of Control; Asiatick Society founded in Calcutta by Sir William Jones
1788	Sydney Cove, Australia, and Port Jackson, New Zealand, established as British penal colonies
1800	Revival of Hindu culture begins
1835	Introduction of English system of education in India
1844–1845	Maori revolt against the British in New Zealand

1857–1858	Sepoy Mutiny in India
1858	India placed under direct governance of Great Britain
1869–1948	Mohandas K. Gandhi
1877	Queen Victoria (1819–1901) of England proclaimed empress of India
1886	First Indian National Congress formed in Bombay
1905	Partition of Bengal arouses nationalist agitation (partition annulled in 1911)
1919	Amritsar massacre in India

All dates are C.E. and approximate unless otherwise indicated. It should be noted as well that chronologies are constantly being revised. Hence, there may be discrepancies between the dates listed above and those found in other textbooks and scholarly monographs. Throughout the text and in the Glossary, all dates are given in B.C.E. (Before the Common Era) and C.E. (the Common Era). Where there is no era designation C.E. may be assumed.

Rammohun Roy's "In Defense of Hindu Theology"

Rammohun Roy (1772–1833), the son of devout Bengali **brahmin** parents, is considered the "father of modern India" by many Indians. After spending several years studying Buddhism in Tibet and many more wandering about India, Roy finally entered the British civil service in Bengal. Retiring from active duty at age 42, he spent the remainder of his life founding and editing newspapers (one of the first Indians to do so), establishing several secondary schools, campaigning against many social injustices that plagued his native country, and organizing the religious society of *Brahmo Samaj* (Society of the Worshipers of Brahma). Rammohun Roy was one of the first Indian Hindus whose ideas were critically affected by modern Western culture. Although Roy recognized the merits of Christian ethics, he remained a devoted Hindu. Roy's great service to modern Hinduism was his recovering from obscurity the supreme religious ideals and beliefs embodied in original Hinduism. He wrote the following letter in response to one by a man who signed himself Sankara Sastri (Roy believed him to be an Englishman regardless of his Indian-sounding name). Sastri's letter appeared in the *Madras Courier* in December 1816. In his reply, Roy defends his positions concerning Hindu theology, which he enunciated with his translations of the Isa and Kena Upanishads, two of the greatest texts in the Hindu canon.

The learned gentleman commences by objecting to the terms "discoverer" and "reformer," in which the Editor of the Calcutta Gazette was pleased to make mention of me. . . .

In none of my writings, nor in any verbal discussion, have I ever pretended to reform or to discover the doctrines of the unity of God, nor have I ever assumed the title of reformer or discoverer; so far from such an assumption, I have urged

Raja Rammohun Roy, *The English Works*, ed. O. C. Ghose (Calcutta, India: Oriental Press, 1885), vol. 1: 102–18, passim.

in every work that I have hitherto published, that the doctrines of the unity of God are real Hinduism, as that religion was practiced by our ancestors, and as it is well known even at the present age to many learned Brahmin [priests]. I beg to repeat a few of the passages to which I allude.

In the introduction to the abridgment of the *Vedanta,* I have said, "In order, therefore, to vindicate my own faith and that of our forefathers, I have been endeavoring, for some time past, to convince my countrymen of the true meaning of our sacred books, and prove that my aberration deserves not the opprobrium which some unreflecting persons have been so ready to throw upon me." In another place of the same introduction, I wrote that "The present is an endeavor to render an abridgment of the [Vedanta] into English, by which I expect to prove to my European friends, that the superstitious practices which deform the Hindu religion, have nothing to do with the pure spirit of its dictates." In the introduction of the "Kena" Upanishad, I said that "This work will, I trust, by explaining to my countrymen the real spirit of the Hindu scriptures, which is but the declaration of the unity of God, tend in a great degree to correct the erroneous conceptions which have prevailed with regard to the doctrines they inculcate;" and in the Preface of the "Isa" Upanishad I wrote "many learned Brahmins are perfectly aware of the absurdity of idol worship, and are well informed of the nature of the pure mode of divine worship." A reconsideration of these passages will, I hope, convince the learned gentleman, that I never advanced any claim to the title either of a reformer, or of a discoverer of the doctrines of the unity of the Godhead. . . .

The learned gentleman states that "the difficulty of attaining a knowledge of the Invisible and Almighty Spirit is evident . . ." [from the various texts/verses I have cited]. I agree with him in that point; that the attainment of perfect knowledge of the nature of the Godhead is certainly difficult, or rather impossible; but to read the existence of the Almighty Being in his works of nature, is not, I will dare to say, so difficult to the mind of a man possessed of common sense, and unfettered by prejudice, as to conceive artificial images to be possessed, at once, of the opposite natures of human and divine beings, which idolaters constantly ascribe to their idols, strangely believing that things so constructed can be converted by ceremonies into constructors of the universe. . . .

The learned gentleman is of the opinion that the attributes of God exist distinctly from God, and he compares the relation between God and these attributes to that of a king to his ministers. . . . This opinion, I am extremely sorry to find, is directly contrary to all the doctrines of the **Vedas** interpreted to us by the most revered **Sankaracharya,** . . . They affirm that God has no second that may be possessed of eternal existence, either of the same nature with himself or of a different nature from him, nor any second of that nature that might be called either his part or his quality. . . . The [Vedic scripture] very often calls the Supreme Existence by the epithets of Existent, Wise, and Eternal; and assigns as the reason for adopting such epithets, that the **Rig Veda** in the first instance speaks of God according to human idea, which views quality separately from person, in order to facilitate our comprehension of objects. In case these attributes should be supposed, as the learned gentleman asserts, to be separate existences, it necessarily follows, that they must be either eternal or non-eternal. The former case, vis. the existence of a plurality of beings imbued like God himself with the property of eternal duration, strikes immediately at the root of all the doctrines relative to the unity of the Supreme Being contained in the *Vedanta.* By the latter sentiment, namely, that the power and attributes of God are not eternal, we are led at once into the belief that the nature of God is susceptible of change, and consequently that He is not eternal, which makes no inconsiderable step toward atheism itself. These are the obvious and dangerous consequences, resulting from the learned gentleman's doctrine, that the attributes of the Supreme Being are distinct existences. I am quite at a loss to know how these attributes of the pure and perfect Supreme Being (as the learned gentleman declares them to exist really and separately, and not fictitiously and allegorically,) can be so sensual and destitute of morality, as the creating attribute of "**Brahma**" is [sometimes] said to be, which represents him in one instance as attempting to commit a rape upon his own daughter. The protecting attribute, or **Vishnu**, is in another place affirmed to have fraudulently violated the chastity of Brinda, in order to kill her husband. **Shiva**, the destroying attribute, is said to have had a criminal attachment to Mohini, disregarding all ideas of decency. And a thousand similar examples must be familiar to every reader of the **Puranas**. . . . Although the learned gentleman in [various] instances considers these attributes to be separate existences, yet in another place he seems to view them as parts of the Supreme Being, as he says, "If one part of the ocean be adored, the ocean is adored." I am somewhat at a loss to understand how the learned gentleman proposed to reconcile this apparent contradiction. I must observe, however, in this place that the comparison drawn between the relation of God and those attributes, and that of a king and his ministers, is totally inconsistent with the faith entertained by Hindus of the present day; who, so far from considering these objects of worship as mere instruments by which they may arrive at the power of contemplating the God of Nature, regard them in the light of independent gods, to each of whom, however absurdly, they attribute almighty power, and a claim to worship, solely on his own account.

The learned gentleman is dissatisfied with the objection mentioned in my translation to worshipping these fictitious representations, . . . I consequently repeat the following authorities, which I hope may answer my purpose. The following are the declarations of the *Rig Vedas:* "He, who worships any god excepting the Supreme Being, and thinks that he himself is distinct and inferior to that God, knows nothing, and is considered as a domestic beast of these gods." Again, "A state even so high as that of Brahma does not afford real bliss." And again, "Adore God alone." And, "None but the Supreme Being is to be worshipped; nothing excepting him should be adored by a wise man." I repeat also the following text of the *Vedanta:* "The declaration of the *Rig Veda,* that those who worship the celestial gods are the food of such gods, is an allegorical expression, and only means that they are comforts to the celestial gods as food to mankind; for he who has no faith in the Supreme Being is rendered subject to these gods. The *Rig Veda* affirms the same." . . .

To these authorities a thousand others might be added. But should the learned gentleman require some practical grounds for objecting to the idolatrous worship of the Hindus, I can be at no loss to give him numberless instances, where the ceremonies that have been instituted under the pretext of honoring the all-perfect Author of Nature, are of a tendency utterly subversive of every moral principle.

I begin with **Krishna** as the most adored of the incarnations, the number of whose devotees is exceedingly great. . . . His devotees very often personify (in the same manner as European actors upon stages do) him and his female companions, dancing with indecent gestures and singing songs relative to his love and debaucheries. . . . In the worship of Kali, human sacrifices, the use of wine, criminal intercourse, and licentious songs, are included: the first of these practices has become generally extinct; but it is believed that there are parts of the country where human victims are still offered.

Debauchery, however, universally forms the principal part of the worship of her [Kali's] followers. Nigam and other **Tantras** may satisfy every reader of the horrible tenets of the worshippers of the latter two deities. The modes of worship of almost all the inferior deities are pretty much the same. Having so far explained the nature of worship adopted by Hindus in general, for the propitiation of their allegorical attributes, in direct opposition to the mode of pure divine worship inculcated by the Vedas, I cannot but entertain a strong hope that the learned gentleman, who ranks even monotheistical songs among carnal pleasures, and consequently rejects their admittance in worship, will no longer stand forward as an advocate for the worship of separate and independent attributes and incarnations.

The learned gentleman says, "that the Saviour," meaning Jesus Christ, "should be considered a personification of the mercy and kindness of God, by which I mean actual not allegorical personification." From what little knowledge I had acquired of the tenets of Christians and those of anti-Christians, I thought there were only three prevailing opinions respecting the nature of Christ, vis., that he was considered by some as the expounder of the laws of God, and the mediator between God and man; by many to be one of the three mysterious persons of the Godhead; whilst others, such as the Jews, say that he was a mere man. But to consider Christ as a personification of the mercy of God is, if I mistake not, a new doctrine in Christianity, the discussion of which, however, has no connection with the present subject. I, however, must observe that this opinion which the learned gentleman has formed of Christ being a personification of the mercy of God, is similar to that entertained by Moslems, for a period of upwards of a thousand years, respecting Mohammed, whom they call mercy of God upon all his creatures. The learned gentleman in his conclusion of his observations has left, as he says, the doctrines of pure allegory to me. It would have been more consistent with justice had he left pure allegory also to the Vedas, which declare "appellations and figures of all kinds are innovations," and which have allegorically represented God in the figure of the universe: "Fire is his head, the sun and the moon are his two eyes," etc., and which have also represented human internal qualities by different earthly objects. . . .

Study Questions

1. What is Roy's understanding of religion, and how balanced are his opinions of non-Hindu spirituality?
2. Why does Roy think it is necessary to defend his interpretation of his native religion?
3. What is the author's main objective in his response to the criticisms of the "learned gentleman"?
4. How does Roy's discussion of the gentleman's criticisms reflect the problems and issues associated with Britain's dominance of India during the nineteenth and early twentieth centuries?

Reading 28

Tilak's "Tenets of the New Party in India"

While Rammohun Roy is known as the "father of modern India," Bal Gangadhar Tilak (1856–1920) is often labeled the "father of Indian unrest." Born into the **brahmin** caste, which tended to accommodate the British presence in India, Tilak maintained throughout his life an uncompromising hostility toward foreign domination. A well-educated and self-reliant man, he wrote and spoke forcefully not only against the British but also against the Muslim minority in his native country. His extremist activities landed Tilak in jail on not a few occasions, and during such times he studied and wrote. He produced his greatest work, a commentary on the **Bhagavad Gita**, while imprisoned in Mandalay, Upper Burma. At the end of the **Indian National Congress** of 1906, extremists and moderates were further away than ever from agreement on how to proceed toward independence. It was at this point in the session that Tilak delivered this speech summarizing the aims and methods of a new political party under his leadership.

Two new words have recently come into existence with regard to our politics, and they are Moderates and Extremists. These words have a specific relation to time, and they, therefore, will change with time. The Extremists of today will be Moderates tomorrow, just as the Moderates today were Extremists yesterday. When the National Congress was first started and Mr. **Dadabhai Naoroji**'s views, which now go for Moderates, were given to the public, he was styled an Extremist, so that you will see that the term Extremist is an expression of progress. We are Extremists today and our sons will call themselves Extremists and us Moderates. Every new Party begins as Extremists and ends as Moderates. The sphere of practical politics is not unlimited. We cannot say what will or will not happen 1,000 years hence—perhaps during that long period, the whole of the white race will be swept away in another glacial period. We must, therefore, study the present and work out a program to meet the present condition. . . .

One fact is that this alien Government has ruined the country. In the beginning, all of us were taken by surprise. We were almost dazed. We thought that everything that the rulers did was for our good and that this English Government has descended from the clouds to save us from the invasions of **Tamerlane** and

Bal Gangadhar Tilak, *His Writings and Speeches* (Madras, India: Ganesh, 1923), 39–45, 48–51. Reprinted by permission.

Gengis Khan, and, as they say, not only from foreign invasions but from inter-necine warfare, or the internal or external invasions, as they call it. . . .

[Naoroji] has come here at the age of 82 to tell us that he is bitterly dis-appointed. Mr. **Gokhale**, I know, is not disappointed. He is a friend of mine and I believe that this is his honest conviction. Mr. Gokhale is not disappointed but is ready to wait another 80 years till he is disappointed like Mr. Naoroji.

He is young, younger than myself, and I can very well see that disappoint-ment cannot come in a single interview, from interviews which have lasted only for a year or so. If Naoroji is disappointed, what reason is there that Gokhale shall not, after 20 years? It is said there is a revival of Liberalism, but how long will it last? Next year it might be, they are out of power, and are we to wait till there is another revival of Liberalism, and then again if that goes down and a third revival of Liberalism takes place; and after all what can a liberal Government do? . . . I laughed when I read the proceedings of the meeting in Calcutta, con-gratulating people on the appointment of Mr. **Morley** to the Secretaryship of State for India. Passages were read from Mr. Morley's books. Mr. Morley had said so and so in Mr. **Gladstone**'s Life; Mr. Morley had said this and had said that; he was the editor of a certain paper 30 years ago, and he said so and so. . . . A states-man is bound to look to the present circumstances and see what particular con-cessions are absolutely necessary, and what is theoretically true or wrong. He has to take into consideration both the sides. . . . So then it comes to this that the whole British electorate must be converted. So you are going to convert all persons who have a right to vote in England, so as to get the majority on your side, and when this is done and when by that majority the Liberal party is returned to Parliament bent upon doing good to India and it appoints a Secretary of State as good as Mr. Morley, then you hope to get something of the old methods. The new Party has realized this position. The whole electorate of Great Britain must be converted by lectures. You cannot touch their pocket or interest, and that man must be a fool indeed who would sacrifice his own interest on hearing a philosophical lecture. . . .

The New Party perceives that this is futile. To convert the whole electorate of England to your opinion and then to get indirect pressure to bear upon the Parliament, they in their turn to return a Cabinet favorable to India and the whole Parliament, the Liberal party and the Cabinet to bring pressure on the bureaucracy to yield. We say this is hopeless. . . .

There is no empire lost by a free grant of concessions by the rulers to the ruled. History does not record any such event. Empires are lost by luxury, by being too much bureaucratic or overconfident or from other reasons. But an empire has never come to an end by the rulers conceding power to the ruled. . . .

We have come forward with a scheme which if you accept, shall better enable you to remedy this state of things than the scheme of the Old school. Your industries are ruined utterly, ruined by foreign rule; your wealth is going out of the country and you are reduced to the lowest level which no human being can occupy. In this state of things, is there any other remedy by which you can help yourself? The remedy is not petitioning but boycott. We say prepare your forces,

165

organize your power, and then go to work so that they cannot refuse you what you demand. . . . Are you prepared in this way to fight if your demand is refused? If you are, be sure you will not be refused; but if you are not, nothing can be more certain than that your demand will be refused, and perhaps, for ever. We are not armed, and there is no necessity for arms either. We have a stronger weapon, a political weapon, in boycott. We have perceived one fact, that the whole of this administration, which is carried on by a handful of Englishmen, is carried on with our assistance. We are all in subordinate service. The whole Government is carried on with our assistance and they try to keep us in ignorance of our power of co-operation between ourselves by which that which is in our own hands at present can be claimed by us and administered by us. The point is to have the entire control in our hands. I want to have the key of my house, and not merely one stranger turned out of it. Self-Government is our goal; we want control over our administrative machinery. . . . What the New Party wants you to do is to realize the fact that your future rests entirely in your own hands. If you mean to be free, you can be free; if you do not mean to be free, you will fall and be for ever fallen. So many of you need not like arms; but if you have not the power of active resistance, have you not the power of self-denial and self-abstinence in such a way as not to assist the foreign Government to rule over you? This is boycott and this is what is meant when we say, boycott is a political weapon. We shall not give them assistance to collect revenue and keep peace. We shall not assist them in fighting beyond the frontiers or outside India with Indian blood and money. We shall not assist them in carrying on the administration of justice. We shall have our own courts, and when time comes we shall not pay taxes. . . .

I do not ask you to blindly follow us. Think over the whole problem for yourselves. If you accept our advice, we feel sure, we can achieve our salvation thereby. This is the advice of the New Party. Perhaps we have not obtained a full recognition of our principles. Old prejudices die very hard. Neither of us wanted to wreck the Congress, so we compromised, and were satisfied that our principles were recognized, and only to a certain extent. That does not mean that we have accepted the whole situation. We may have a step in advance next year, so that within a few years our principles will be recognized, and recognized to such an extent that the generations who come after us may consider us Moderates. This is the way in which a nation progresses. . . .

Study Questions

1. Why does Tilak consider it necessary to form a new political coalition in India?
2. According to the speaker, how and why must India gain its independence from Great Britain?
3. If Tilak's views had been accepted by the Congress and Indian people, how would they have overturned the established political order throughout the Indian sub-continent?
4. What problems inherent in Indian society are not addressed by Tilak's proposed reforms?

Select Writings of Sarojini Naidu

Like her contemporary Tilak, Sarojini Chattopadhyaya (1879–1949), known as "the nightingale of India," was born into the privileged **brahmin** caste. Her father, who received his Ph.D. in 1877 from the University of Edinburgh, Scotland, was a pioneer in Indian education and one of India's leading scientists. Sarojini herself was educated at King's College, London, and at Girton College, Cambridge, but she never completed her graduate studies. Sarojini began her public life as a poet and published numerous collections of her verse shortly after the turn of the century. As evinced in the following selections, Sarojini became involved in various social and political causes and was especially influenced by **Gopal Gokhale**, whom she met at the **Indian National Congress** of 1906. It was there that she delivered a moving speech and became recognized as one of the leaders of India's independence movement. In 1918 she married Dr. Govindarajulu Naidu and raised their four children herself, even while traveling extensively to lecture on humanitarian themes. In fact, Sarojini Naidu became the first Indian woman to be elected president of the Indian National Congress in 1925. A friend and colleague of some of the great figures of the age, including **Tagore, Jinnah**, and Mohandas K. Gandhi, she, like them, was arrested and jailed by British authorities on many occasions. Upon her death on 2 March 1949 Jawaharlal Nehru, India's first prime minister, remarked that she "infused artistry and poetry into India's national struggle."

True Brotherhood (dated 1903)

You know that you are provincial—and you are more limited than that—because your horizon is bounded almost by your city, your own community, your own sub-caste, your own college, your own homes, your own relations, your own self. (Loud cheers.) I know I am speaking rightly, because I also in my earlier youth was afflicted with the same sort of short-sightedness of the love. Having travelled, having conceived, having hoped, having enlarged my love, having widened my sympathies, having come in contact with different races, different communities, different religions, different civilizations, friends, my vision is clear. I have no prejudice of race, creed, caste or color. Though, as is supposed, every Brahmin is an aristocrat by instinct, I am a real democrat, because to me there is no difference

Sarojini Naidu, *Speeches and Writings of Sarojini Naidu* (Madras, India: G. A. Natesan, n.d.), 7–11, 12–16, 17–20.

between a king on his throne and a beggar in the street. And until, you, students have acquired and mastered that spirit of brotherhood, do not believe it possible that you will ever cease to be provincial, that you will cease to be sectarian—if I may use such a word—that you will ever be national. If it were otherwise, there should have been no necessity for all those Resolutions in the Social Conference yesterday. I look to you and not to the generation that is passing; it is the young that would have the courage to cast aside that bondage to make it impossible for the Social Conference of ten years hence to proclaim its disgrace in the manner in which it was proclaimed yesterday and in which I took part. (Continued cheers.) Students, if facilities come in your way, travel; because the knowledge that comes from living contact with men and minds, the inestimable culture that comes through interchange of ideas, can never be equalled and certainly not surpassed by that knowledge between the covers of textbooks. You read the poems of **Shelley** on "Liberty." You read the lecture of **Keats** on the "Brotherhood of Man," but do you put them all in practice? Reading is one thing. It is a very different thing to put it into practice by your deeds. It is difficult to follow in reality the proverb that all men are brethren. Therefore, to you, young men, we look to the fulfillment of the dreams that we have dreamed. To you we look to rectify the mistakes we have made. To you we look to redeem the pledges we have given to posterity. I beg of you, young men, nay, I enjoin upon you that duty that you dare not, if you are men, separate from your hearts and mind and spirit. I say that it is not your pride that you are a Madrassee, that it is not your pride that you are a Brahmin, that it is not your pride that you belong to the South of India, that it is not your pride that you are a Hindu, but that it is your pride that you are an Indian. I was born in Bengal. I belong to the Madras Presidency. In a Mahomedan city I was brought up and married and there I lived; still I am neither a Bengalee, nor Madrassee, nor Hyderabadee but I am an Indian, (cheers) not a Hindu, not a Brahmin, but an Indian to whom my Mahomedan brother is as dear and as precious as my Hindu brother. I was brought up in a home, that would never have tolerated the least spirit of difference, in the treatment given to people of different classes. There you will find that genuine spontaneous love shown to them. I was brought up in a home over which presided one of the greatest men of India and who is an embodiment of all great lores and ideal truth, of love, of justice and patriotism. That great teacher of India, had come to us to give immortal inspiration. That is a home of Indians and not of Hindus or Brahmins. It is because that my beloved father said, "Be not limited even to the Indians, but let it be your pride that you are a citizen of the world," that I should love my country. I am ready to lay down my life for the welfare of all India. I beg of you, my brothers, not to limit your love only to India, because it is better that your ideals of patriotism should extend for the welfare of the world and not be limited to the prosperity of India and so to achieve that prosperity for your country; because, if the ideals be only for the prosperity of your country, it would end where it began, by being a profit to your own community and very probably to your own self. You have inherited great dreams. You have had great duties laid upon you. You have been bequeathed legacies for whose suffrage and whose growth and accumulation you are responsible. It does not matter where you are and who you are. Even a sweeper of streets can be a patriot. You can find in him a moralizing spirit that can inspire your mind. There is not one of you who is so humble and so insignificant that can evade the duties that belong to you, that are predestined to you and which nobody but you can perform. Therefore each of you is bound to dedicate his life to the up-lifting of his country.

Personal Element in Spiritual Life (dated 1906)

The title of the Lecture is the "Personal Element in Spiritual Life," and by the word "spiritual" I do not mean merely the religious or ethical side but even the highest ideal of manhood or womanhood. At this great moment, when there is abroad so much enthusiasm and when all the best energies and ambitions of the people of India are directed towards the re-establishing of the social and political ideals of the country, it is well for us to remember that no results are of any lasting value that are not obtained by the light of the spirit. I say that all the glories of Greece and all the grandeur that was of Rome have perished because of want of this light of the spirit. But the advancing hope for the salvation of India lies in this magnificent fact that our civilization in the past was highly spiritual and the powers of the spirit, though they may be dimmed, can never die. (Applause.) I want you to realize, all of you who are here present, that each of you is an indispensable spark in the rekindling of the manifold fires of the National life. Many of you, I have no doubt, are acquainted with that great Persian poet and astronomer, **Omar Khayyam**, whose beautiful poetry is equally the wonder and delight of East and West. Some there are who say he is somewhat of a **Sufi** and more that he was merely a dreamer of dreams, but whether he was a Sufi or a dreamer of dreams, his teachings and his singings of lore among the roses and bulbuls of the Persian gardens have contributed to the literature of the world one immortal phrase which might stand for the very epigram of the scriptures. It might stand for the very essence of all the spiritual and secular doctrine and traditions handed down to man about the personal element in spiritual life. He says in his wonderful Rubaiyat:—

> I sent my soul into the invisible,
> Some letter of that after life to spell,
> And by and by my soul returned to me
> Answered, myself am heaven and hell.

Turn where you will, to the scriptures of the Hindus or the mandates of **Zoroaster**, the Koran of the Mahomedans, to the teachings of Christ or the teachings of Lord **Buddha** under the Bodi Tree, you will find this great point of unity among them, that in all these religions the greatest emphasis is laid on two essential points. First, terrible individual responsibility of every human being for his own destiny; and, secondly, the unique and incommunicable personal relationship with its Master Spirit. The life of the Spirit is not a thing that we can attain, but it is interwoven like a golden thread through the very fabric of our existence. I want you to realize, my friends, that even so there is a state of divinity which it is possible, nay, it is necessary, that we must develop up to its full fire of godhead. There is no one among you so weak or so small that he is not necessary to the divine scheme of eternal life. There is no one among you so small, so frail, so insignificant that he cannot contribute to the divinity of the world. If he should fail let him fail. Does success or failure count for anything in the life of the spirit? No; it is endeavor that is the very soul of life. You all remember that when Napoleon, the greatest hero of the 19th century, was taunted with his lack of ancestry, how superbly he held up his head and said, "I am the ancestor." I hope that each of you has that self-knowledge and that self-reverence that enable you to say, "I am the ancestor." For it is the bounden duty of every human being to contribute something individual and distant to the sum-total of the world's progress to justify his existence (hear, and applause)—and is there any among you so small in spirit that he will not realize the dictum that **Plato** sent forth into the world—Man, know thyself. Self-knowledge is only the first step in the ultimate destiny of man. You, sons of India, whom I speak to today, and you, daughters, whom I am also addressing, know that you are responsible for the call upon you for ennobled lives, not merely for the glory and prosperity of your country, but for the higher patriotism that says the world is my country, and all men are my brothers. You must ask for the larger vision that looks beyond the fleeting pomps and glories of today and knows that the destiny of the souls lies in immortality and eternity. Friends, it is not for me to speak to you, no better that I can tell you, what an infinity of the divinity is hidden within you. It is not for me to point the way to you, it is for you to pray in secret, and to reverence that beauty within your lives, those divine principles that inspire us. It is for you to be the prisms of the love of God.

Education of Indian Women (dated 1906)

It seems to me a paradox, at once touched with humor and tragedy, that on the very threshold of the twentieth century, it should still be necessary for us to stand upon platforms and pass resolutions in favor of what is called female education in India—in all places in India, which, at the beginning of the first century was already ripe with civilization and had contributed to the world's progress radiant examples of women of the highest genius and widest culture. But as by some irony of evolution the paradox stands to our shame, it is time for us to consider how best we can remove such a reproach, how best we can achieve something more fruitful than the passing of empty resolutions from year to year. At this great moment of stress and striving, when the Indian races are seeking for the ultimate unity of a common national ideal, it is well for us to remember that the success of the whole movement lies centered in what is known as the woman question. It is not you but we who are the true nation-builders. But it seems to me that there is not even an unanimous acceptance of the fact that the education of women is an essential factor in the process of nation-building. Many of you will remember that, some years ago, when Mrs. Sathianadhan first started "The Indian Ladies' Magazine," a lively correspondence went on as to whether we should or should not educate our women. The women themselves with one voice pleaded their own cause most eloquently, but when it came to the men there was more division in the camp. Many men doubtless proved themselves true patriots by proving themselves the true friends of education for the mothers of the people. But others there were who took fright at the very word. "What," they cried, "educate our women? What then will become of the comfortable domestic ideals as exemplified by the luscious 'halwa' and the savory 'omelette'?" Others again were neither "for Jove nor for Jehovah," but were for compromise, bringing forward a whole syllabus of compromises. "Teach this," they said, "and not that." But, my friends, in the matter of education you cannot say thus far and no further. Neither can you say to the winds of Heaven "Blow not where ye list," nor forbid the waves to cross their boundaries, nor set the human soul to soar beyond the bounds of arbitrary limitations. The word education is the worst misunderstood word in any language. The Italians, who are an imaginative people, with their subtle instinct for the inner meaning of words have made a positive difference between instruction and education and we should do well to accept and acknowledge that difference. Instruction being merely the accumulation of knowledge might, indeed, lend itself to conventional definition, but education is an immeasurable, beautiful, indispensable atmosphere in which we live and move and have our being. Does one man dare to deprive another of his birthright to God's pure air which nourishes his body? How then shall a man dare to deprive a human soul of its immemorial inheritance of liberty and life? And yet, my friends, man has so dared in the case of Indian women. That is why you men of India are today what you are: because your fathers, in depriving your mothers of that immemorial birthright, have robbed you, their sons, of your just inheritance. Therefore, I charge you, restore to your women their ancestral rights, for, as I have said it is we, and, not you, who are the real nation-builders, and without our active co-operation at all points of progress all your Congresses and Conferences are in vain. Educate your women and the nation will take care of itself, for it is true today as it was yesterday and will be to the end of human life that the hand that rocks the cradle is the power that rules the world.

Study Questions

1. What does Sarojini Naidu mean by "true brotherhood"?
2. Why would India's acceptance of the ideal of "true brotherhood" further the cause of nationalism?
3. How does the Hindu spiritual tradition serve as the basis for Sarojini Naidu's social and political rhetoric?
4. What does Naidu see as the most dire problem confronting Indian women, and what does she propose to overcome it?

171

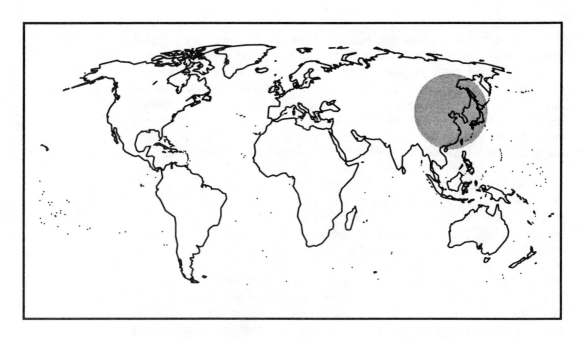

Brief Chronology for the Modern World

East Eurasia

1603–1867	Tokugawa Shogunate in Japan (Ieysau, 1603–1605; Iyemitsu, 1623–1651; Tsunayoshi, 1680–1709; Kei-ki, 1867)
1644–1911	Ch'ing (Manchu) dynasty in China (Shun-chih, 1644–1662; Chi'en-lung, 1736–1796; Hsüan-t'ung, 1909–1911)
1784	U.S. traders arrive in China
1798–1802	White Lotus Rebellion in China
1800	British begin importation of opium into China
1835–1908	Empress Dowager Tz'u-hsi
1839–1842	Opium Wars in China
1850–1873	Era of internal rebellion (Taiping Uprising, 1850–1864; Muslim Rebellion, 1868–1873) in China
1853–1854	U.S. Commodore Perry opens Japan to the West
1856–1860	Arrow War
1866–1925	Sun Yat-sen, Chinese statesman and first provisional president of the Republic (1912)
1868	Beginning of Meiji Reform in Japan (Emperor Meiji, 1867–1912)
1889	New constitution in Japan that follows imperial German model
1894–1895	War between China and Japan
1898	Hundred Days' Reform Movement
1898–1900	Boxer Rebellion in China
1904–05	Japan defeats Russia in brief war
1905	Traditional civil service examination system ends
1910	Japanese annexation of Korea
1911	Beginning of Republican Revolution in China
1916–1928	Era of the warlords in China
1921	Foundation of Chinese Communist Party
1928–1937	Nationalist government in China under Kuomintang

All dates are C.E. and approximate unless otherwise indicated. It should be noted as well that chronologies are constantly being revised. Hence, there may be discrepancies between the dates listed above and those found in other textbooks and scholarly monographs. Throughout the text and in the Glossary, all dates are given in B.C.E. (Before the Common Era) and C.E. (the Common Era). Where there is no era designation C.E. may be assumed.

The Treaties of Nanking and Tientsin

As Westerners began to make their presence acutely known in China during the nineteenth century, various miscalculations by China's ruling elite resulted in a situation that, at least from the Chinese perspective, got totally out of hand. The opium trade in the late eighteenth and nineteenth centuries increased in proportions alarming to Chinese authorities. The unwillingness of many Western governments to stop the supply and smuggling of the dreaded commodity eventually resulted in the British-Chinese **Opium Wars** of 1839–1842. The Treaty of Nanking of 1842 concluded the Opium Wars on terms very advantageous to Great Britain. The opium trade in China continued to flourish. Britain thus led the way in forcibly changing Western relations with China by being the first nation to exact an "unequal treaty." In the following decade, Western interlopers gained considerably more advantages in their relations with China; for example, the Treaty of Tientsin of 1858 was finally ratified after the French and British (in a rare act of collaboration) defeated the Chinese in the **Arrow War** of 1856–1860.

The Treaty of Nanking (dated 1842)

1. There shall henceforward be Peace and Friendship between . . . [England and China] and between their respective Subjects, who shall enjoy full security and protection for their persons and property within the Dominions of the other.

    2. His Majesty the Emperor of China agrees that British Subjects, with their families and establishments, shall be allowed to reside, for the purpose of carrying on their Mercantile pursuits, without molestation or restraint at the Cities and Towns of Canton, Amoy, Roochow-fu, Ningpo, and Shanghai, and Her Majesty the Queen of Great Britain, etc., will appoint Superintendents or Consular Officers, to reside at each of the above-named Cities or Towns, to be the medium of communication between the Chinese Authorities and the said Merchants, and to see that the just

Inspectorate General of Customs Statistical Department, *The Maritime Customs of China, Treaties, Conventions, Between China and Foreign States* (Shanghai, China: Inspectorate General of Customs Statistical Department, 1917), vol. 1: passim.

Duties and other Dues of the Chinese Government as hereafter provided for, are duly discharged by Her Britannic Majesty's Subjects.

3. It being obviously necessary and desirable, that British Subjects should have some Port whereat they may careen and refit their Ships, when required, and keep Stores for that purpose, His Majesty the Emperor of China cedes to Her Majesty the Queen of Great Britain, etc., the Island of Hong Kong, to be possessed in perpetuity by Her Britannic Majesty, Her Heirs and Successors, and to be governed by such Laws and Regulations as Her Majesty the Queen of Great Britain, etc., shall see fit to direct.

4. The Emperor of China agrees to pay the sum of Six Millions of Dollars as the value of Opium which was delivered up at Canton in the month of March, 1839, as a Ransom for the lives of Her Britannic Majesty's Superintendent and Subjects, who had been imprisoned and threatened with death by the Chinese High Officers.

5. The Government of China having compelled the British merchants trading at Canton to deal exclusively with certain Chinese Merchants called Hong Merchants who had been licensed by the Chinese Government for that purpose, the Emperor of China agrees to abolish that practice in future at all Ports where British Merchants may reside, and to permit them to carry on their mercantile transactions with whatever persons they please, and His Imperial Majesty further agrees to pay to the British Government the sum of Three Millions of Dollars, on account of Debts due to British Subjects by some of the said Hong Merchants, who have become insolvent, and who owe very large sums of money to Subjects of Her Britannic Majesty.

6. The Government of Her Britannic Majesty having been obliged to send out an Expedition to demand and obtain redress for the violent and unjust Proceedings of the Chinese High Authorities towards Her Britannic Majesty's Officer and Subjects, the Emperor of China agrees to pay the sum of Twelve Millions of Dollars on account of the Expenses incurred, and Her Britannic Majesty's Plenipotentiary voluntarily agrees, on behalf of Her Majesty, to deduct from the said amount of Twelve Millions of Dollars, any sums which may have been received by Her Majesty's combined Forces as Ransom for Cities and Towns in China, subsequent to the 1st day of August 1841.

8. The Emperor of China agrees to release unconditionally all Subjects of Her Britannic Majesty (whether Natives of Europe or India) who may be in confinement at this moment, in any part of the Chinese Empire.

9. The Emperor of China agrees to publish and promulgate, under His Imperial Sign Manual and Seal, a full and entire amnesty and act of indemnity, to all Subjects of China on account of their having resided under, or having had dealings and intercourse with, or having entered the Service of Her Britannic Majesty, or of Her Majesty's Officers, and His Imperial Majesty further engages to release all Chinese Subjects who may be at this moment in confinement for similar reasons.

10. His Majesty the Emperor of China agrees to establish at all the Ports which are by the 2nd Article of this Treaty to be thrown open for the resort of

British Merchants, a fair and regular Tariff of Export and Import Customs and other Dues, which Tariff shall be publicly notified and promulgated for general information, and the Emperor further engages, that when British Merchandise shall have once paid at any of the said Ports the regulated Customs and Dues agreeable to the Tariff, to be hereafter fixed, such Merchandise may be conveyed by Chinese Merchants, to any Province or City in the interior of the Empire of China on paying a further amount as Transit Duties. . . .

The Treaty of Tientsin (dated 1858)

5. His Majesty the Emperor of China agrees to nominate one of the Secretaries of State, or a President of one of the Boards, as the High Officer with whom the Ambassador, Minister, or other Diplomatic Agent of Her Majesty the Queen shall transact business, either personally or in writing, on a footing of perfect equality.

7. Her Majesty the Queen may appoint one or more Consuls in the dominions of the Emperor of China, and such Consul or consuls shall be at liberty to reside in any of the Open Ports. . . . They shall be treated with due respect by the Chinese authorities, and enjoy the same privileges and immunities as the Consular Officers of the most favored nation. Consuls and Vice-Consuls in charge shall rank with Intendants of Circuits; Vice-Consuls, Acting Vice-Consuls and Interpreters with Prefects. . . .

8. The Christian religion as professed by Protestants or Roman Catholics, inculcates the practice of virtue and teaches man to do as he would be done by. Persons teaching it, or professing it, therefore, shall alike be entitled to the protection of the Chinese authorities, nor shall any such, peaceably pursuing their calling, and not offending against the laws, be persecuted or interfered with.

9. British subjects are hereby authorized to travel for their pleasure or for purposes of trade, to all parts of the Interior, under Passports, which will be issued by the Consuls and countersigned by the Local Authorities. . . . If he be without a Passport, or if he commits an offense against the Law, he shall be handed over to the nearest Consul for punishment, but he must not be subjected to any ill-usage in excess of necessary restraint. No Passport need be applied for by persons going on excursions from the Ports open to trade to a distance not exceeding one hundred *li,* and for a period not exceeding five days. . . .

10. British merchant ships shall have authority to trade upon the [Yangtze]. The Upper and Lower Valley being, however, disturbed by outlaws, no Port shall be for the present opened to trade, with the exception of Chinkiang, which shall be opened in a year from the date of the signing of this Treaty. . . .

11. In addition to the Cities and Towns of Canton, Amoy, Foochow, Ningpo and Shanghai, opened by the Treaty of Nanking, it is agreed that British subjects may frequent the Cities and Ports of Newchwang, Tangchow, Taiwan [Formosa], Chawchow [Swatow] and Kiungchow [Hainan]. . . .

15. All questions in regard to rights, whether of property or person, arising between British subjects, shall be subject to the jurisdiction of the British authorities.

16. Chinese subjects who may be guilty of any criminal act towards British subjects shall be arrested and punished by the Chinese authorities according to the Laws of China.

British subjects who may commit any crime in China shall be tried and punished by the Consul or other Public Functionary authorized thereto according to the Laws of Great Britain. Justice shall be equitably and impartially administered on both sides.

Study Questions

1. What political and economic advantages are gained by the British in the Treaty of Nanking?
2. How do the two treaties compromise the governing authority of the Chinese empire?
3. What does a comparison of the two documents reveal about the changing historical circumstances in China?
4. From the Chinese perspective, how did the treaties contradict the traditional view of world order?

Hung Hsiu-ch'üan's "Imperial Declaration of the Taipings"

The Taiping Rebellion lasted from 1850 to 1864 and posed a serious threat to the stability of the Manchu dynasty. Earlier dynasties had their own difficulties with dissident movements and upheavals, including the **Yellow Turbans** and the **White Lotus** that were under Taoist and Buddhist auspices respectively. The Taiping Rebellion was unique, however, in that it was greatly influenced by Christian ideals. The Heavenly Kingdom of Great Peace (*Taiping Tienguo*), the new dynasty founded in 1851 by Hung Hsiu-ch'üan (1814–1864), clearly reflected the impact of Western religion on east Eurasian culture and politics. A valuable source of information on Taiping ideology in its formative stages, the "Taiping Imperial Declaration" of 1852 was written by the rebellion's prophet and leader Hung Hsiu-ch'üan, who earlier had assumed the title of Heavenly King. This declaration has three parts: the first part is entitled "An Ode on the Origin of Virtue and the Saving of the World" and is reprinted below. In it Hung discusses the worship of God and warns against various moral offenses. The last two sections of the declaration preach tolerance and harmony in society while promoting the notion that God is the true deity and the worship of demons will result in suffering in hell.

The great origin of virtue is Heaven;
Let us reverently take Heaven's way to arouse the multitudes of the virtuous.
The way of Heaven is to punish the licentious, bless the good;
Repent while it is early; be the first.
The root and source of the true Way lies only in rectitude;
Successive generations have all observed this without distinction.
Enjoy heavenly bliss; free yourselves from worldly considerations;
Be not entangled by any of the common feelings.
Abandon at once every vicious view;
The true creating Spirit is God alone.
Without distinction between noble or lowly, all must reverently worship him;

God, the Heavenly Father, is shared by everyone.
That the world is one family has been passed down from of old,
In high antiquity China was like the foreign nations,
Both princes and people as one body honored August heaven.
During that time when the sovereigns honored God,
Nobles, scholars, and commoners all did the same.
It might be compared, among men, to children serving their father;
For whether worthy or unworthy, all must follow the Domestic Rules.

Heaven and man were of one mind, there were no two principles;
How could monarchs and sovereigns let their private views prevail?
Let God be worshipped;
Let all in this unite,
Whether west or north,
Whether south or east.
Every fibre and thread depends on God;
Every sip and morsel comes from the Heavenly Majesty.
It is your duty every morning to adore and every evening to worship him;
Reason demands that you should praise his goodness and sing his merits.
Should men set this aside, and worship another,
Or worship all other things, it would all be in vain.
Not only would there be no gain, there would also be harm;
And thus deluding the natural conscience the sin would be beyond redemption.
If man's natural conscience is not yet lost,
Certainly he knows that every breath depends on Heaven.
The five elements and the ten thousand things were Heaven-created;
How could other spirits rule within this realm?
Even if God had needed assistance,
Certainly no Buddha could have helped in the transformation.
If the transformation had depended on the Buddha,
Since it took place before he had come, the logic is hard to follow.
He warms with the sun, moistens with the rain;
He drives the thunderbolt, he scatters the winds.
All these are God's spiritual wonders;
Those who can repay Heaven's favor will obtain glory.
Do not worship evil spirits,
Act like upright men;
That which is not upright, Heaven abhors;
That which is upright, Heaven favors.

Of all wrong things Licentiousness is the chief;
When man becomes demon, Heaven is most enraged.
Debauch others and debauch oneself, and both are monstrous.
Why not sing of the footprints of the gentle deer, and celebrate a virtuous
posterity.

Depraved customs change men; who can set them aright?
All that is needed is a reformation of faults;
His four cautions against improprieties stimulate the spirit.
Only he who can reform his errors will be free from errors;
On this the ancients gave repeated instructions.
From of old princes and teachers had no other duties
Than merely to employ the true **Way** to awaken the people.
From of old the good and upright had no other virtue
Than merely to employ the true Way to perfect their conduct.
All who possess bodily vigor and mental intelligence—
How can they outrage virtues and debase human relations?
All who uphold Heaven and stand erect upon the earth
Should instantly return to the pure, and revert to the true.
The devilish heart thus reformed,
The *Hsiao Ching* one should know.

The second kind of wrong is Disobedience to parents,
A great violation of the Heavenly Commandments; make haste to reform
    yourselves.
The lamb kneels to reach the teat, the crow returns the food to its dam;
When men are not equal to brutes, they disgrace their origin.
The dweller at Li-shan howled and wept, and Heaven was moved,
The birds aided him in weeding, and the elephants in ploughing.
Though exalted as the Son of Heaven and rich in the possession of the four
    seas,
His filial virtues moved Heaven; how could they be viewed lightly!
Our fathers have given us life; our mothers have nursed us;

The travail and anxiety they endured in rearing us cannot be described.
Benevolence supreme that reaches to heaven is difficult to repay.
Can we not be filial in sustaining them, exhausting loyalty and sincerity?
The man of true filial virtue loves his parents all his life;
He discerns their formless wishes and hears them, unexpressed.
To be filial to one's parents is to be filial to God;
The cutting and maiming of one's own origin alone will cause the self to fall.
The *Liao Ngo ode* should be read;
Brotherhood and magnanimity should be all-inclusive.

The third kind of wrong is to Kill;
To slay our fellow men is the worst of crimes.
Under heaven all are brothers;
The souls of all come alike from heaven.
God looks upon all men as his children;
For men to destroy one another is extremely lamentable,

Hence in former days there was no wanton killing.
Their virtue accorded with Heaven's will, and Heaven watched over them.
Cherishing and tranquilizing the four quarters, they aided the Supreme;
Therefore they were able to unite the whole and enjoy Heaven's blessing.
Yu of Hsia wept over offenders, and **Wen** surrendered the Lo territory;
Heaven responded and the people returned without suspicion.
All who want only to kill the people returned without suspicion.
All who want only to kill the people are abandoned robbers;
In the end how can they escape calamity?
Pai Ch'i and **Hsiang Yu** ended by committing suicide;
Huang Ch'ao and **Li Ch'uang**, where are they now?
From of old those who have killed others have afterwards killed themselves;
Who will say that the eyes of Heaven are not opened wide?
From of old those who have saved others have thereby saved themselves,
And their souls have been taken up to heaven.
From of old those who have benefitted others have benefitted themselves;
Happiness is of one's own seeking, and is easily obtained.
From of old, those who have injured others have injured themselves;
Misery is of one's own making, and is difficult to undo.
Do not say that having no enemies is a virtue to be rewarded;
To practice forgiveness throughout life is your duty.
Make faith and charity your masters,
Modesty must be known.

The fourth kind of wrong is Robbery and Thievery;
Injustice and inhumanity are not proper.
Those who form gangs and are disorderly, Heaven will not protect;
When iniquities are excessive, calamity will surely follow.
A good man, meeting with wealth, does not take it illicitly.
Yang Chen, though in the depth of night, could not be deceived.
Kuan Ning cut the mat because Hsin looked away,
And solitarily roamed the hills and valleys, his will never changing.
I and Ch'i, yielding the throne to one another, willingly died of hunger,
And at the foot of Shou-yang hill their names were handed down.
From of old, the good and upright have striven for Heaven's honor;
Riches and honors are but fleeting clouds, not to be cherished.
To kill one innocent person is an act of unrighteousness,
And even if one can thereby obtain the empire, he should not do it.
If men would but reverently fear God
And rest contented with the Heavenly mandate, what further need of anxiety?
How can one bear to kill men and plunder their goods,
And seize that which one does not own?
In trade, cherish the way of justice;
In learning, heed the rules and examples.

The fifth kind of wrong is Witchcraft;
By the evil arts of deceiving the multitude, Heaven's penalty is incurred.
Death and life, calamity and sickness, all are determined by Heaven;
Why then deceive the people by the useless manufacture of charms?
Incantations to procure luck, vows to the demons, services to the devils,
Fastings and processions, all are of no avail.
From of old, death and nature have been difficult to defend oneself against;
How can anyone by intercession guard against harm?
From of old, wizards, witches, and necromancers
Have for numerous generations lived in poverty because Heaven will not
    sustain them.
The devils' agents, having served the devils, are eventually possessed by the
    devils;
The gates of hell are ever open to receive such heretic-followers.
Wishing to fatten one's own purse, one only adds to one's sin;
Why not then repent and early seek salvation?
Arts and skills must be exact;
Human conduct must all the more be regulated.

The sixth kind of wrong is Gambling;
He who uses the hidden blade to kill a man is evil at heart.
Beware! Beware! Beware!
For it is opposed to reason.
The seeking of wealth has its way, and its acquisition lies in fate.
Do not by deceit and fraud destroy the heart.
If fate provides for you, why need you gamble?
If fate does not, although you gamble, you will not obtain your wish.
In the end, poverty and riches are arranged by Heaven.
Follow your proper avocations, and you shall be at ease.
Confucius and **Yen-tzu** were happy on water and thin gruel;
Knowing their fate they were content in poverty, and their spirits soared.
Man's life in this world is like a dream at the third watch.
Why ponder? Why worry? Why hope?
Small wealth comes from diligence and great wealth from fate.
From of old, to be a man one must exert himself.
Oh you multitudes!
Do not say it does not matter;
There is nothing one might not do because of gambling.
Heroes, why do you sink and stray?
Unrighteous gain is like quenching one's thirst with poison;
Scholars, farmers, artisans, and merchants long forbear.
Of one thousand who gamble, one thousand are mean;
I implore you to change your thoughts and carefully deliberate.
There are others who drive on till they fall into a snare,
And cooking and smoking opium, they become mad.

In the present day so many brave men
Have wounded themselves with the opium gun.
With regard to the love of wine, this is also a wrong.
Successful families ought to warn themselves against the family-destroying
     juice.
I ask you to look at **Chieh** and **Chou** who ruled the empire;
With iron they bound rivers and hills; yet because of wine they perished.
Moreover there are the geomancers and the fortunetellers,
Who deceive God and contract endless guilt.
Riches and honors rest with Heaven, life and death are sealed by fate;
Wherefore then deceive the world, with a view to fattening your purse?
All the rest of the wrong things are too numerous to mention;
It is up to man himself to distinguish the obscure and indistinct;
If the small matters are not attended to, eventually this will prejudice your
     virtue.
Before the solid ice is formed, be careful in treading on the hoar frost.
Yu and Chi were diligent, and anxious to starve or drown.
Hence one became emperor, and the descendants of the other became rulers.
Wen of Chou and Confucius in their own persons were upright;
Hence their souls were permitted to advance and retreat in the presence of God.
True words, without affectation.
My soul has previously been allowed to ascend to heaven,
My words are true and real, without the slightest extravagance.
My parental feelings are strong, and I cannot forget;
Finding my words insufficient, I have thus spoken at length.
Those families which accumulate goodness will have a surplus of blessings;
Those families which accumulate wickedness will have excessive misfortune.
Those who obey Heaven will be preserved; those who disobey Heaven perish.
So honor God and you will obtain glory and honor.

Study Questions

1. To what virtues does Hung subscribe, how is Hung's ideology—and, hence, the Taiping Rebellion—influenced by Christian thought and doctrine?
2. How does moral regeneration underlie the Taipings' political and social philosophy?
3. How and why does Hung integrate foreign ideas within the traditional Chinese outlook?
4. What kind of world does Hung envision, and how did it conflict with the worldview espoused by Chinese traditionalists?

K'ang Yu-wei's Philosophical Commentaries

Like many contemporary Chinese academics and philosophers, K'ang Yu-wei (1858–1927) tried to put Confucian teachings to work in government and society. He was, however, somewhat more successful than most in influencing efforts toward reform in the anachronistic bureaucracy. In a dramatic attempt to reconstruct his beloved China, K'ang spearheaded the **Hundred Days' Reform** of 1898. But, he and other reform-minded Chinese were defeated by the supporters of the radically conservative **dowager empress**. K'ang fled for his life and remained in exile, traveling throughout the world until his return to China in 1917 when he and other reformers took part in an abortive attempt to restore the deposed emperor Hsüan-t'ung (r. 1909–1912). However traditional he may have been, K'ang Yu-wei's Confucian outlook was conditioned by the liberal view that history was an evolutionary, not a cyclical, process. The origin of his perspective was undoubtedly Western ideology that penetrated China during the nineteenth century. Nevertheless, K'ang insisted on attributing the notion to Confucius. In fact, K'ang's ideas about the Confucian "Age of Great Unity," formulated in the 1880s, were so radical that the book in which they are found was not published until 1935. A radical Confucian reformer turned arch-reactionary, K'ang died in disgrace in 1927.

Commentary on *the Analects* of Confucius

In the progress of mankind there have always been definite stages. From the clan system come tribes, from which in time come nations, and from nations the Great Unification comes into existence. From the individual man the rule of tribal chieftains gradually becomes established, and from the rule of tribal chieftains the correct relationship between ruler and minister is gradually defined. From autocracy gradually comes [monarchic] constitutionalism, and from constitutionalism gradually comes republicanism. From men living as individuals gradually comes the relationship between husband and wife, and from this the relationship between

Wing-Tsit Chan, trans., *A Source Book in Chinese Philosophy* (Princeton: Princeton University Press, 1963), 725–35, passim. Copyright © 1963, renewed 1991 Princeton University Press. Reprinted with permission of Princeton University Press.

father and son is gradually fixed. From the relationship between father and son gradually comes the system in which blessings are also extended to all the rest of mankind. And from this system, that of Great Unity comes into being, whereby individuals again exist as individuals [in a harmonious world without the bonds of father and son, husband and wife, and so forth].

Thus in the progress from the Age of Disorder to the Age of Rising Peace, and from the Age of Rising Peace to the Age of Great Peace, their evolution is gradual and there are reasons for their continuation or modification. Examine this process in all countries and we shall find that the pattern is the same. By observing the infant one can foretell the future adult and further the future old man, and by observing the sprout one can foretell the future tree large enough to be enclosed with both arms and further the future tree high enough to reach the sky. . . .

Confucius was born in the Age of Disorder. Now that communications have extended throughout the great earth and important changes have taken place in Europe and America, the world has entered upon the Age of Rising Peace. Later, when all groups throughout the great earth, far and near, big and small, are like one, when nations will cease to exist, when racial distinctions are no longer made, and when customs are unified, all will be one and the Age of Great Peace will have come. Confucius knew all this in advance.

However, within each age there are Three Rotating Phases. In the Age of Disorder, there are the phases of Rising Peace and Great Peace, and in the Age of Great Peace are the phases of Rising Peace and Disorder. Thus there are barbarian red Indians in progressive America and primitive Miao, Yao, T'ung, and Li tribes in civilized China. Each age can further be divided into three ages. These three can further be extended (geometrically) into nine ages, then eighty-one, then thousands and tens of thousands, and then innumerable ages. After the arrival of the Age of Great Peace and Great Unity, there will still be much progress and many phases. It will not end after only a hundred generations. . . .

The Book of Great Unity

In consciousness and perception, forms and sounds of objects are transmitted to my eyes and ears. They rush against my soul. Chilly and cold, they attack the active aspects (**yang**) of my existence. Dark and quiet, they enter my negative aspects (**yin**). They continue at moderate speed as if they could not stop. Of what are they the clue? Is it what Europeans call ether? Is it what the ancients called the "mind that cannot bear [to see the suffering of] others"? Do all people have this mind that cannot bear to see the suffering of others? Or do I alone have it? And why should I be deeply affected by this clue?

Thereupon Master K'ang says: Do I not have a body? If not, how do I have knowledge or affection? Since I have a body, can that which permeates my body as well as the material force of Heaven, the concrete stuff of Earth, and the breath of man be cut off or not? If it could be cut off, then one could draw a knife and cut water to pieces. If it cannot be cut off, then it is like material force filling space and being possessed by all things, like electricity operating through material force and penetrating everything, like water spreading all over the land and permeating everything, and like blood-vessels spreading through the body and penetrating every part of it. Cut the material force off the mountain and it will collapse. Cut the blood-vessels off the body and it will die. And cut the material force off the earth and it will disintegrate. Therefore if man cuts off the substance of love which is the mind that cannot bear to see the suffering of others, moral principles of mankind will be destroyed and terminated. If these are destroyed and terminated, civilization will stop and mankind will revert to barbarism. Furthermore, barbarism will stop and men will revert to their original animal nature.

Great is the material force of origination. It created Heaven and Earth. By Heaven is meant the spiritual substance of a thing (the universe), and by man is also meant the spiritual substance of a thing (the body). Although they differ in size, they are no different in partaking the great force of great origination, just as if both were scooping up small drops of water from the great sea. Confucius said [in the *Book of Rites*], "Earth contains spiritual energy, which produces the wind and thunder. As a result of movements of wind and thunder, a countless variety of things in their changing configurations ensue, and the myriad things show the appearance of life." Spirit is electricity with consciousness. The electric light can be transmitted everywhere, and spiritual energy can act on everything. It makes spiritual beings and gods spiritual. It produces Heaven and Earth. In its entirety it is origination; divided, it becomes man. How subtle and how wonderful does spirit act on things! There is nothing without electricity, and there is nothing without spirit. Spirit is the power of consciousness, the consciousness of the soul, spiritual intelligence, clear intelligence, and clear character. These are different in name but the same in actuality. As there is consciousness, there is attraction. This is true of the lodestone. How much more is it with man! Not being able to bear to see the suffering of others is an instance of this power of attraction. Therefore both humanity and wisdom are stored in the mind, but wisdom comes first. Both humanity and wisdom are exercised (in action), but humanity is nobler. . . .

The love of those whose consciousness is small is also small, and the humanity of those whose consciousness is great is also great. . . .

All living creatures in the world only aim at seeking happiness and avoiding suffering. They follow no other course. There are some who take a roundabout way, take an expedient [borrowed] way, or zig-zag in their course, going through painful experiences without getting tired. They, too, only aim at seeking happiness. Although men differ in their nature, we can decidedly say that the way of mankind is never to seek suffering and avoid happiness. To establish institutions and inaugurate doctrines so as to enable men to have happiness but no suffering is the highest of goodness. To enable men to have much happiness and little suffering is good but not perfectly good. And to cause men to have much suffering and little happiness is no good. . . .

Having been born in an age of disorder, and seeing with my own eyes the path of suffering in the world, I wish to find a way to save it. I have thought

185

deeply and believe the only way is to practice the way of Great Unity and Great Peace. Looking over all ways and means in the world, I believe that aside from the way of Great Unity there is no other method to save living men from their sufferings or to seek their great happiness. The way of Great Unity is perfect equality, perfect impartiality, perfect humanity, and good government in the highest degree. Although there are good ways, none can be superior.

The sufferings of mankind are so innumerable as to be unimaginable, changing from place to place and from time to time. They cannot be all listed, but let us roughly mention the major ones that are readily apparent:

(1) Seven sufferings from living: rebirth, premature death, physical debilities, being a barbarian, living in frontier areas (on the fringe of civilization), being a slave, and being a woman.

(2) Eight sufferings from natural calamities: famines resulting from floods or droughts, plagues of locusts, fire, flood, volcanic eruptions (including earthquakes and landslides), collapse of buildings, shipwrecks (including collisions of carts), and epidemics.

(3) Five sufferings from conditions of life: being a widow or widower, being an orphan or childless, being ill without medical care, being poor, and being humble in social station.

(4) Five sufferings from government: punishment and imprisonment, oppressive taxation, military conscription, the existence of the state, and the existence of the family.

(5) Eight sufferings from human feelings: stupidity, hatred, sexual love, burden imposed by others, toil, desires, oppression, and class distinction.

(6) Eight sufferings from being objects of honor and esteem: a rich man, a man of high station, a man of longevity, a king or emperor, and a god, a sage, an immortal, or a Buddha.

All these are sufferings of human life, not to mention the conditions of sufferings of the feathered, furred, or scaly animals. But if we broadly survey the miseries of life, we shall find that all sufferings originate from nine spheres of distinction. What are these nine? The first is the distinction between states [as a cause of suffering], because it divides the world into territories and tribes. The second is class distinction, because it divides people into the honored and the humble, the pure and the impure. The third is racial distinction, which divides people into yellows, whites, browns, and blacks. The fourth is the distinction between physical forms, because it makes the divisions between male and female. The fifth is the distinction between families, because it confines the various affections between father and son, husband and wife, and brothers to those personal relations. The sixth is the distinction between occupations, because it considers the products of farmers, artisans, and merchants as their own. The seventh is the sphere of chaos, because it has systems that are unfair, unreasonable, non-uniform, and unjust. The eighth is the distinction between species, because it divides them into human beings, birds, animals, insects, and fish. And the ninth is the sphere of suffering. Suffering gives rise to suffering, and so passes on without end and which is beyond imagination. . . .

My way of saving people from these sufferings consists in abolishing these nine spheres of distinction. First, to do away with the distinction between states in order to unify the whole world. Second, do away with class distinction so as to bring about equality of all people. Third, do away with racial distinction so there will be one universal race. Fourth, do away with the distinction between physical forms so as to guarantee the independence of both sexes. Fifth, do away with the distinction between families so men may become citizens of Heaven. Sixth, do away with the distinction between occupations so that all productions may belong to the public. Seventh, do away with the spheres of chaos so that universal peace may become the order of the day. Eighth, do away with the distinction between species so we may love all sentient beings. And ninth, do away with the sphere of suffering so happiness may reach its height. . . .

Commentary on the Subtle Meanings of the *Book of Mencius*

The mind that cannot bear to see the suffering of others is humanity. It is electricity. It is ether. Everyone has it. This is why it is said that the nature of all men is originally good. Since there is already this mind that cannot bear to see the suffering of others, when it is aroused and applied externally, it results in a government that cannot bear to see the people's suffering. If man were without this mind that cannot bear to see the suffering of others, then the sage ruler would be without this seed and that means that none of the benevolent governmental measures can be produced. Therefore we know that all benevolent governmental measures proceed from this mind that cannot bear to see the suffering of others. It is the seat of all transformations, the root of all things, the source of all things, the seed that will become the tree reaching up to the sky, the drop of water that will become the great sea. Man's feeling of love, human civilization, the progress of mankind, down to Great Peace and Great Unity all originate from it. . . .

The mind that cannot bear to see the suffering of others is a humane mind. The government that cannot bear to see the people's suffering is a human government. Although they differ as inner and outer and as substance and function, their constituting the **Way** is the same. It is humanity, that is all. Humanity means "people living together." **Chuang Tzu** said that in an empty valley "One is happy when he sees someone similar in appearance." It is the natural feeling of men that when they see someone with a similar appearance, a similar form, or a similar voice, the feeling is inevitably aroused in their minds to love each other. . . . All people have the mind to love each other. All people work for each other. . . .

Confucius instituted the scheme of Three Ages. In the Age of Disorder, humanity cannot be extended far and therefore people are merely affectionate to their parents. In the Age of Rising Peace, humanity is extended to one's kind and therefore people are humane to all people. In the Age of Great Peace, all creatures form a unity and therefore people feel love for all creatures as well. There are

187

distinctions and gradations in humanity because of stages in historical progress.
... History goes through an evolution, and humanity has its path of development.
As the path may be large or small, so humanity may be large or small. Before the
time is ripe, it cannot be forced.

Study Questions

1. Bearing in mind the Confucian view of history as a series of hills and valleys,
   explain how K'ang perpetuates this traditional outlook in his cyclical theory of
   history.
2. How was K'ang's thought influenced by the modern science he learned from
   Western intellectuals living in China?
3. What notion of social and political dynamics underlies K'ang's theory of reform?
4. What is the social and political significance of K'ang's understanding of the idea
   of the "Age of Great Unity"?

Reading 33

Select Writings of Sato Nobuhiro

Sato Nobuhiro (1769–1850) was one of Tokugawa Japan's most eclectic thinkers. His interests ranged from natural science to ancient mythology. He adamantly believed that because of Japan's tremendous
economic difficulties during the early nineteenth century it was crucial
that a dramatic reformation of the country occur. These difficulties
were caused in part by the presence of Western traders in Japanese
waters. A practical man with eclectic intellectual tastes, Sato proposed
the most complete and detailed reform program of any of his contemporaries, calling for the total use and control of Japan's natural and
human resources. As evinced in his *Essays on Creation and Cultivation,*
Sato employs philosophical rationalism to bolster **Shinto** vitalism, and
views economic productivity and the technological transformation of
nature as a part of the natural order of things. In effect, Sato Nobuhiro
advocated the development of authoritarian government for Japan based
on Western science and model institutions. Though much of what he
wrote was pleasing to the Tokugawa shoguns, passages from his *Con-
fidential Plan of World Unification* were kept from public view because
they detailed how various governmental agencies would control the
nation's economy.

Essays on Creation and Cultivation

For rulers to employ every means in their power for the sake of agriculture—including the study of natural law, astronomy, surveying of land and sea, determining
latitude and longitude, examining climate, distinguishing the nature of soils, re-
claiming paddy fields and farms, rectifying boundaries, repairing irrigation ditches,
building and repairing embankments, preparing for drought and rain, tilling and
harrowing with infinite care, and cultivating with earnestness—is the way to carry
out the divine will of creation and to assist in the cultivation of nature. These are
what we call the thirteen laws of agricultural management.

W. T. de Bary, ed., *Sources of Japanese Tradition,* trans. Ryusake Tsunoda et al. (New York: Columbia
University Press, 1958), vol 2: 67–73. Copyright © 1958 Columbia University Press. Reprinted with
permission of the publisher.

If the thirteen laws of agricultural management were conscientiously carried out, then all things would produce an abundant harvest. These products would then be brought under the control of a system of allocation and distribution. In this manner the goods and wealth of the land would be accumulated, and the way would be opened for civilizing the countries of the world. If we strive to teach service to Heaven, all living people will enjoy the benefits of benevolent rule. To be well-versed in agricultural management, to bring all products under a single control, and to endeavor to spread education are what we call the Three Essentials of Economics.

When the head of a nation carries out satisfactorily these Three Essentials, production will increase greatly, there will be a flow of money and wealth, the whole country will prosper, all the people will be rich and happy, and suffering due to poverty will be unknown. Then what harm would there be in having a large family? Then and only then can the teaching of gratitude for divine favors be promoted and the foul custom of infanticide be eradicated. Only in this way can talents be developed, military defense be perfected, and laws enforced. Therefore if the government is conscientious in this respect, the innate goodness of all men will assert itself. Acts of violence will decrease gradually, moral discipline will gradually improve, and the population increase greatly. . . .

Let us respectfully examine the annals of the Divine Age [*Nihongi*]. Prior to the creation of heaven and earth there were three godheads: the Lord of the Center of Heaven, the Spirit of Vitality, and the Spirit of Fertility. These three together were the fountainhead of all creation.

Then in the beginning of creation one original energy manifested itself in the midst of the great void of fusion and confusion. Because of the divine act of creation what was heavy was separated from what was light, and what was clear was separated from what was foul. The ethereal essence was condensed in the center, whereby the upper heaven was completed. . . .

Confidential Plan of World Unification

Our Imperial Land came into existence at the very beginning of the earth and it is the root and basis of all other countries of the world. Thus, if the root is attended to with proper care, the entire world will become its prefectures and counties, and the heads and rulers of the various countries will all become its ministers and servants. According to the scriptures of the Divine Age, the imperial progenitors, **Izanagi** and **Izanami**, instructed **Susanoo** that "our rule extends over the eight hundred folds of the blue immense." And thus we learn that to make clear the divine teaching of production and procreation and thereby to set the peoples of the entire world at peace was, from the very beginning, the principal and urgent mission of our heavenly country. My earlier works, the *Compendium of Economics* and the *Outline of Heaven's Law,* examined the divine teaching of creation with the purpose of uniting the entire world in peace.

The salvation of the people of the world is an immense task which requires, first of all, a clear knowledge of geography and the state of affairs in the countries of the world. If measures are not taken to bring the actual state of affairs into harmony with Heaven's will, the principle and teaching of production and procreation cannot be put into effect. And therefore the study of geography is imperative.

Let us now examine the situation of our country in terms of the geography of the countries of the world. It extends from 30 degrees North latitude to 45 degrees North latitude. Its climate is temperate, its soil fertile, and it is not without a variety of crops which produce abundant harvests. Facing the ocean on four sides, for convenience of ocean transportation it has no equal among the nations of the world. Its people, living on sacred land, are superior, excelling those of other countries for bravery and resoluteness. In truth they are fully capable of holding the reins of the world. From this position of strength they could majestically command the world in every direction, and by virtue of the awesome prestige of this Imperial Land they could readily subjugate the puny barbarians and unify the world under their control. Ah, how boundless have been the blessings of the creator on our Imperial Land!

However, even in our Imperial Land, since the descent from heaven of the Imperial Grandson, rulers have disobeyed the laws and teachings of the Divine Age. They have squandered many years in pleasure, idleness, and unbridled dissipation, setting their hearts on beautiful women instead of heroic women, and thus shortening their own lives. They have also neglected their duties toward the industry and economy of the nation, while they indulged instead in useless undertakings. There has been no harmony between husband and wife, and household management has suffered. Brothers have quarreled with each other and relatives have killed one another, resulting in the decline of state and society. The ruler did not act like a ruler, nor the subject like a subject. The providential plan initiated by Onamochi and Sukuna-hikone was abandoned and the national polity remained in a state of decline for a long time. Thus magic and **Buddha**'s teachings came into vogue, and no one was left who knew the true teaching of old. The ignorant masses of this corrupt age, having been informed of the vastness of China and India on the one hand, while seeing on the other the smallness of their heavenly land and the weakness of its power, have been convulsed with laughter when they heard my arguments for the unification of the world, telling me that I lack a sense of proportion. They have no awareness that heaven has ordained our country to command all nations. . . .

In terms of world geography our Imperial Land would appear to be the axis of the other countries of the world, as indeed it is. Natural circumstances favor the launching of an expedition from our country to conquer others, whereas they are adverse to the conquest of our country by an expedition from abroad. The reason why an expedition from our country could be executed more easily than one from abroad is as follows. Among the nations of the world today, no country compares with China in immensity of territorial domain, in richness of products, and in military prestige. Yet, even though China is our neighbor and very close to us, there is no way for her to inflict harm on us, try as she might to conquer us

191

with all the resources of her country. Should a reckless despot dare to send a great force against us—like **Kublai Khan** of the barbarous Mongols who mobilized the entire manpower of his country to send against us—we in our heavenly land need have no fear. On the contrary, we will inflict great damage on China. She may make a second attempt but will be incapable of making any more. If our nation should attempt to conquer China, however, with proper spirit and discipline on our part China would crumble and fall like a house of sand within five to seven years. This is because the cost to our country of dispatching a military expedition will be small while for China it would be so great as to be prohibitive. Moreover, her people would be exhausted with ceaseless running from one end of the country to another. Thus, for Japan to attempt to open other countries, her first step must be the absorption of China.

As already noted above, China, despite her great strength, cannot oppose our country. Needless to say, the other countries likewise cannot oppose us, for by the grace of nature Japan is so situated as to be able to unify the countries of the world. I am, therefore, going to explain in this work how China can be subjugated. After China is brought within our domain, the Central Asian countries, as well as Burma, India, and other lands where different languages are spoken and curious costumes are worn, who yearn for our virtues and fear our power, will come to us with bowed heads and on hands and knees to serve us. . . .

The Six Ministries should be the Ministry of Fundamental Affairs [agriculture], Ministry of Development, Ministry of Manufacture, Ministry of Finance, Ministry of the Army, and Ministry of the Navy. This system is similar to the Six Offices of the Chou government and the Six Departments of the T'ang dynasty in China. However, the systems of the Chou and T'ang dynasties governed the people by dividing them into four classes: the ruling class, the farmer, the artisan, and the merchant. After much thought, I conclude that in a four-class system there are some matters which do not come under effective control of the government and possibilities for the development of industry cannot be exploited to their fullest extent. In this way, we neglect some of the great resources which nature has bestowed upon us.

In order to promote government "in the service of Heaven" (and in accordance with natural law), it should be done on the basis of the occupations of all the people, who should be classified into groups with similar functions. The country's industries should be divided into eight groups, namely: plant-cultivation, forestry, mining, manufacturing, trading, unskilled occupations, shipping, and fishing. The people, once classified into these eight groups, would then be assigned to the Six Ministries. Each person would be assigned to one occupation and attend diligently to his own occupation. The law should strictly prohibit anyone from trying his hand at another occupation. Those who cultivate plants should be assigned to the Ministry of Fundamental Affairs, foresters and miners to the Ministry of Development, craftsmen to the Ministry of Manufacture, traders to the Ministry of Finance, unskilled labor to the Ministry of the Army, and the boatmen and fishermen to the Ministry of the Navy. Thus, the six Ministries will care for the groups of people assigned to them, inducing them to study their occupations and making them devote their attention constantly and exclusively to the performance of their occupations without faltering or becoming negligent, and to the fullest extent of their energies. In this way, as the months and the years pass, each industry will acquire proficiency and perfect itself, providing steadily increased benefits for the greater wealth and prosperity of the state.

If, as in the systems of the Chou and the T'ang, the people are divided into four classes for purposes of administration, the division, although clear and distinct in appearance, in practice leads inevitably to confusion. This is because the ruling class concerns itself exclusively with the administration of government and national defense, giving no attention to the production of goods from land or sea, and placing the burden of production for the entire country on the other three groups: the farmers, craftsmen, and the merchants. As a small number of groups must assume a large number of industries, the merchant has to take on some of the functions of the farmer, forester, artisan, and the fisherman. Each trade is left largely uncontrolled, and thus is unable to develop any skill and ingenuity. Profits dwindle from year to year, and some people have to turn over their businesses to others losing house and home as well. The number of homeless destitutes gradually increases, and leads in the end to the decline of the nation itself. This is a matter of the greatest magnitude, requiring serious thought and investigation.

Moreover, when the people are divided into eight groups, each group should be segregated and mixed residence not permitted, as in the ancient rule of **Kuan Chung** of Ch'i. If this system is followed the people will learn their trades from the period of their adolescence, and even without being formally instructed they will become familiar with their trades. Thus, the number of specialists will naturally increase. . . .

Study Questions

1. What kind of government and society does Sato envision?
2. How were Sato's views on government different from those of the Tokugawa Shogunate?
3. How does Sato root a Western notion of progress in the tradition of Japanese Shintoism?
4. How do Sato's ideas presage the course of Japanese history in the late nineteenth and early twentieth centuries?

The Meiji Constitution of 1868 and the Imperial Rescript on Education

By the mid-nineteenth century, the Tokugawa Shogunate had run its course, and imperial rule in Japan was restored under the young **Emperor Meiji** and a handful of men whose attitudes and ideals guided a new reform movement. The overall aim of the Meiji Restoration was to enrich Japan and strengthen its military. These reforms contributed to Japan's emergence as a modern state with a constitutional government, political parties, and a powerful military. The Constitution of 1868 sheds light on the original intentions of the reformers, who were influenced by Western concepts of government. The first section of the constitution, known as the "Charter Oath," was drawn up in April 1868. The remaining articles were designed to implement that covenant. The Emperor Meiji himself came to symbolize progress and, ironically, tradition as well. In fact, his Imperial Rescript on Education, published in 1890, is a reaction to some westernizing tendencies.

The Constitution of 1868

I. By this oath we set up as our aim the establishment of the national weal on a broad basis and the framing of a constitution and laws.

1. Deliberative assemblies shall be widely established and all matters decided by public discussion.
2. All classes, high and low, shall unite in vigorously carrying out the administration of affairs of state.
3. The common people, no less than the civil and military officials, shall each be allowed to pursue his own calling so that there may be no discontent.
4. Evil customs of the past shall be broken off and everything based upon the just laws of Nature.
5. Knowledge shall be sought throughout the world so as to strengthen the foundations of imperial rule.

W. W. McLaren, *Japanese Government Documents, Transactions of the Asiatic Society of Japan,* 1st series (1914), vol. 42, pt. 1.

II. All power and authority in the empire shall be vested in a Council of State, and thus the grievances of divided government shall be done away with. The power and authority of the Council of State shall be threefold, legislative, executive, and judicial. Thus the imbalance of authority among the different branches of the government shall be avoided.

III. The legislative organ shall not be permitted to perform executive functions, nor shall the executive organ be permitted to perform legislative functions. However, on extraordinary occasions the legislative organ may still perform such functions as tours of inspection of cities and the conduct of foreign affairs.

IV. Attainment to offices of the first rank shall be limited to princes of the blood, court nobles, and territorial lords, and shall be by virtue of [the sovereign's] intimate trust in the great ministers of state. A law governing ministers summoned from the provinces shall be adopted, clan officials of whatever status may attain offices of the second rank on the basis of worth and talent.

V. Each great city, clan, and imperial prefecture shall furnish qualified men to be members of the Assembly. A deliberative body shall be instituted so that the views of the people may be discussed openly.

VI. A system of official ranks shall be instituted so that each [official] may know the importance of his office and not dare to hold it in contempt.

VII. Princes of the blood, court nobles, and territorial lords shall be accompanied by [no more than] six two-sworded men and three commoners, and persons of lower rank by [no more than] two two-sworded men and one commoner, so that the appearance of pomp and grandeur may be done away with and the evils of class barriers may be avoided.

VIII. Officers shall not discuss the affairs of the government in their own houses with unofficial persons. If any persons desire interviews with them for the purpose of giving expression to their own opinions, they shall be sent to the office of the appropriate department and the matter shall be discussed openly.

IX. All officials shall be changed after four years' service. They shall be selected by means of public balloting. However, at the first expiration of terms hereafter, half of the officials shall retain office for two additional years, after which their terms shall expire, so that [the government] may be caused to continue without interruption. Those whose relief is undesirable because they enjoy the approval of the people may be retained for an additional period of years.

X. A system shall be established for levying taxes on territorial lords, farmers, artisans, and merchants, so that government revenue may be supplemented, military installations strengthened, and public security maintained. For this purpose, even persons with rank or office shall have taxes levied upon them equivalent to one thirtieth of their income or salaries.

XI. Each large city, clan, and imperial prefecture shall promulgate regulations, and these shall comply with the Charter Oath. The laws peculiar to one locality shall not be generalized to apply to other localities. There shall be no private conferral of titles or rank, no private coinage, no private employment of foreigners, and no conclusion of alliances with neighboring clans or with foreign countries, lest inferior authorities be confounded with superior and the government be thrown into confusion.

Imperial Rescript on Education

Know you, Our subjects:

Our Imperial Ancestors have founded Our Empire on a basis broad and everlasting, and have deeply and firmly implanted virtue; Our subjects ever united in loyalty and filial piety have from generation to generation illustrated the beauty thereof. This is the glory of the fundamental character of Our Empire, and herein also lies the source of Our education. Ye, Our subjects, be filial to your parents, affectionate to your brothers and sisters; as husbands and wives be harmonious, as friends true; bear yourselves in modesty and moderation; extend your benevolence to all; pursue learning and cultivate arts, and thereby develop intellectual faculties and perfect moral powers; furthermore, advance public good and promote common interests; always respect the constitution and observe the laws; should emergency arise, offer yourselves courageously to the State; and thus guard and maintain the prosperity of Our Imperial Throne coeval with heaven and earth. So shall ye not only be Our good and faithful subjects, but render illustrious the best traditions of your forefathers.

The Way here set forth is indeed the teaching bequeathed by Our Imperial Ancestors, to be observed alike by Their Descendants and the subjects, infallible for all ages and true in all places. It is Our wish to lay it to heart in all reverence, in common with you, Our subjects, that we may all attain to the same virtue.

Study Questions

1. How does the Meiji Constitution reflect Japan's positive response to Western influence?
2. What kind of government does the document prescribe?
3. On what political ideology is the constitution based?
4. What in the document can be attributed to Japan's traditional worldview?

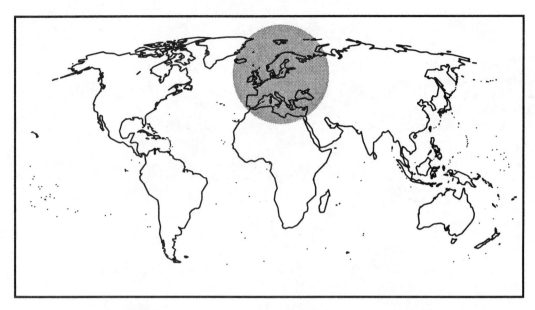

Brief Chronology for the Modern World

West Eurasia

1730–1790	The Enlightenment
1750	Industrial Revolution begins in England
1751	Publication of first volume of Diderot's *Encyclopedia*
1756–1763	Seven Years' War
1762–1796	Reign of Catherine the Great of Russia
1769	Scottish inventor James Watt obtains patent for condensing steam engine
1783	Treaty of Paris
1789	Outbreak of the French Revolution
1793	French adopt Constitution of 1793, but it does not go into effect
1794	Fall of Robespierre and end of the "Terror" in France
1804–1814	Napoleon's French Empire
1806	Dissolution of the Holy Roman Empire
1814–1815	Congress of Vienna
1815	Napoleon defeated at Waterloo
1818–1883	Karl Marx, political philosopher
1825	Stockton and Darlington Railway, world's first line, opened in England
1831	English chemist and physicist Michael Faraday (1791–1867) demonstrates electromagnetic induction, laying foundations for practical electrical science
1832	Great Reform Bill passes in England
1848–1849	Revolutions throughout Europe
1854–1856	Crimean War
1855–1881	Reign of Alexander II of Russia
1859	Publication of Charles Darwin's *The Origin of Species*
1861	Unification of Italy
1862–1890	Otto von Bismarck (1815–1898) serves as prime minister for king of Prussia
1866	Alfred Nobel (1833–1898) invents dynamite
1871	Proclamation of German Empire; Paris Commune
1880	French parasitologist Charles Laveran (1845–1922) discovers the malaria germ
1900	Publication of Sigmund Freud's *The Interpretation of Dreams*
1903	Bolshevik-Menshevik schism in Russian Social-Democratic Communist Party
1905	Revolution in Russia; Albert Einstein's first papers on theory of relativity published
1913	Danish physicist Niels Bohr (1885–1962) proposes theory of atomic structure
1914–1918	World War I

All dates are C.E. and approximate unless otherwise indicated. It should be noted as well that chronologies are constantly being revised. Hence, there may be discrepancies between the dates listed above and those found in other textbooks and scholarly monographs. Throughout the text and in the Glossary, all dates are given in B.C.E. (Before the Common Era) and C.E. (the Common Era). Where there is no era designation C.E. may be assumed.

Rousseau's *The Social Contract*

Jean Jacques Rousseau's (1712–1778) great influence on Western political thought may be attributed in part to his judicious combination of idealism and realism. Yet, like many French philosophes, he was also a vehement critic of the social and political order of his day. In 1762 Rousseau published *The Social Contract,* a masterwork of political science that describes a just society in which liberty and legality are drawn from what he terms the general will. According to Rousseau, a society consists of a collection of free and rational beings living in a given community. It is the collective action of this group that determines its contribution to social development and to humanity. Since only those individuals who are free and equal under the law can enter into a contract to form the general will, the general will becomes the moral force or authority, and in turn, the final arbiter of right and wrong.

Book One

1. Man is born free, and everywhere he is in chains. Many a one believes himself the master of others, and yet he is a greater slave than they. How has this change come about? I do not know. What can render it legitimate? I believe that I can settle this question.

　　If I considered only force and the results that proceed from it, I should say that so long as a people is compelled to obey and does obey, it does well; but that, so soon as it can shake off the yoke and does shake it off, it does better; for, if men recover their freedom by virtue of the same right by which it was taken away, either they are justified in resuming it, or there was no justification for depriving them of it. But the social order is a sacred right which serves as a foundation for all others. This right, however, does not come from nature. It is

Jean Jacques Rousseau, *The Social Contract,* in *Ideal Empires and Republics,* ed. C. M. Andrews (New York: M. Walter Dunne, 1901), 4, 13–15, 17–18, 21–22, 24–28, 92–94.

therefore based on conventions. The question is to know what these conventions are. . . .

6. I assume that men have reached a point at which the obstacles that endanger their preservation in the state of nature overcome by their resistance the forces which each individual can exert with a view to maintaining himself in that state. Then this primitive condition can no longer subsist, and the human race would perish unless it changed its mode of existence.

Now, men cannot create any new forces, but only combine and direct those that exist, they have no other means of self-preservation than to form by aggregation a sum of forces which may overcome the resistance, to put them in action by a single motive power, and to make them work in concert.

This sum of forces can be produced only by the combination of many; but the strength and freedom of each man being the chief instruments of his preservation, how can he pledge them without injuring himself, and without neglecting the cares which he owes to himself? This difficulty, applied to my subject, may be expressed in these terms: "To find a form of association which may defend and protect with the whole force of the community the person and property of every associate, and by means of which each coalescing with all may nevertheless obey only himself, and remain as free as before." Such is the fundamental problem of which the social contract furnishes the solution.

The clauses of this contract are so determined by the nature of the act that the slightest modification would render them vain and ineffectual; so that, although they have never perhaps been formally enunciated, they are everywhere the same, everywhere tacitly admitted and recognized, until, the social pact being violated, each man regains his original rights and recovers his natural liberty, while losing the conventional liberty for which he renounced it.

These clauses, rightly understood, are reducible to one only, namely, the total alienation to the whole community of each associate with all his rights; for, in the first place, since each gives himself up entirely, the conditions are equal for all; and, the conditions being equal for all, no one has any interest in making them burdensome to others.

Further, the alienation being made without reserve, the union is as perfect as it can be, and an individual associate can no longer claim anything; for, if any rights were left to individuals, since there would be no common superior who could judge between them and the public, each, being on some point his own judge, would soon claim to be so on all; the state of nature would still subsist, and the association would necessarily become tyrannical or useless.

In short, each giving himself to all, gives himself to nobody; and as there is not one associate over whom we do not acquire the same rights which we concede to him over ourselves, we gain the equivalent of all that we lose, and more power to preserve what we have.

If, then, we set aside what is not of the essence of the social contract, we shall find that it is reducible to the following terms: "Each of us puts in common his person and his whole power under the supreme direction of the general will; and in return we receive every member as an indivisible part of the whole."

Forthwith, instead of the individual personalities of all the contracting parties, this act of association produces a moral and collective body, which is composed of as many members as the assembly has voices, and which receives from this same act its unity, its common self, its life, and its will. This public person, which is thus formed by the union of all the individual members, formerly took the name of city, and now takes that of republic or body politic, which is called by its members state when it is passive, sovereign when it is active, power when it is compared to similar bodies. With regard to the associated, they take collectively the name of people, and are called individually citizens, as participating in the sovereign power, and subjects, as subjected to the laws of the State. But these terms are often confused and are mistaken one for another; it is sufficient to know how to distinguish them when they are used with complete precision.

Book Two

1. The first and most important consequence of the principles above established is that the general will alone can direct the forces of the State according to the object of its institution, which is the common good; for if the opposition of private interests has rendered necessary the establishment of societies, the agreement of these interests has rendered it possible. That which is common to these different interests forms the social bond; and unless there were some point in which all interests agree, no society could exist. Now, it is solely with regard to this common interest that the society should be governed.

I say, then, that sovereignty, being nothing but the exercise of the general will, can never be alienated, and that the sovereign power, which is only a collective being, can be represented by itself alone; power indeed can be transmitted, but not will.

In fact, if it is not impossible that a particular will should agree on some point with the general will, it is at least impossible that this agreement should be lasting and constant; for the particular will naturally tends to preferences, and the general will to equality. It is still more impossible to have security for this agreement; even though it should always exist, it would not be a result of art, but of chance. The sovereign may indeed say: "I will now what a certain man wills, or at least what he says that he wills"; but he cannot say: "What that man wills tomorrow, I shall also will," since it is absurd that the will should bind itself as regards to future, and since it is not incumbent on any will to consent to anything contrary to the welfare of the being that wills. If, then, the nation simply promises to obey, it dissolves itself by that act and loses its character as a people; the moment there is a master, there is no longer a sovereign, and forthwith the body politic is destroyed.

This does not imply that the orders of the chiefs cannot pass for decisions of the general will, so long as the sovereign, free to oppose them, refrains from doing so. In such a case the consent of the people should be inferred from the universal silence.

3. It follows from what precedes that the general will is always right and always tends to the public advantage; but it does not follow that the resolutions of the people have always the same rectitude. Men always desire their own good, but do not always discern it; the people are never corrupted, though often deceived, and it is only then that they seem to will what is evil.

There is often a great deal of difference between the will of all and general will; the latter regards only the common interest, while the former has regard to private interests, and is merely a sum of particular wills; but take away from these same wills the pluses and minuses which cancel one another, and the general will remains as the sum of the differences.

If the people came to a resolution when adequately informed and without any communication among the citizens, the general will would always result from the great number of slight differences, and the resolution would always be good. But when factions, partial associations, are formed to the detriment of the whole society, the will of each of these associations becomes general with reference to its members, and particular with reference to the State; it may then be said that there are no longer as many voters as there are men, but only as many voters as there are associations. The differences become less numerous and yield a less general result. Lastly, when one of these associations becomes so great that it predominates over all the rest, you no longer have as the result a sum of small differences, but a single difference; there is then no longer a general will, and the opinion which prevails is only a particular opinion. . . .

4. If the State or city is nothing but a legal person, the life of which consists in the union of its members, and if the most important of its cares is that of self-preservation, it needs a universal and compulsive force to move and dispose every part in the manner most expedient for the whole. As nature gives every man an absolute power over all his limbs, the social pact gives the body politic an absolute power over all its members; and it is this same power which, when directed by the general will, bears the name of sovereignty. . . .

From this we must understand that what generalizes the will is not so much the number of voices as the common interest which unites them; for, under this system, each necessarily submits to the conditions which he imposes on others—an admirable union of interest and justice, which gives to the deliberations of the community a spirit of equity that seems to disappear in the discussion of any private affair, for want of a common interest to unite and identify the ruling principle of the judge with that of the party.

By whatever path we return to our principle we always arrive at the same conclusion, namely, that the social compact establishes among the citizens such an equality that they all pledge themselves under the same conditions and ought all to enjoy the same rights. Thus, by the nature of the compact, every act of sovereignty, that is, every authentic act of the general will, binds or favors equally all the citizens; so that the sovereign knows only the body of the nation, and distinguishes none of those that compose it. . . .

Book Four

1. ... When the social bond begins to be relaxed and the State weakened, when private interests begin to make themselves felt and small associations to exercise influence on the State, the common interest is injuriously affected and finds adversaries; unanimity no longer reigns in the voting; the general will is no longer the will of all; opposition and disputes arise, and the best counsel does not pass uncontested.

Also, when the State, on the verge of ruin, no longer subsists except in a vain and illusory form, when the social bond is broken in all hearts, when the basest interest shelters itself impudently under the sacred name of the public welfare, the general will becomes dumb; all, under the guidance of secret motives, no more express their opinions as citizens than if the State had never existed: and, under the name of laws, they deceitfully pass unjust decrees which have only private interest as their end.

Does it follow from this that the general will is destroyed or corrupted? No; it is always constant, unalterable, and pure; but it is subordinated to others which get the better of it. Each, detaching his own interest from the common interest, sees clearly that he cannot completely separate it; but his share in the injury done to the State appears to him as nothing in comparison with the exclusive advantage which he aims at appropriating to himself. This particular advantage being excepted, he desires the general welfare for his own interests quite as strongly as any other. Even in selling his vote for money, he does not extinguish in himself the general will, but eludes it. The fault that he commits is to change the state of the question, and to answer something different from what he was asked; so that, instead of saying by a vote: "It is beneficial to the State," he says: "It is beneficial to a certain man or a certain party that such or such a motion should pass." Thus the law of public order in assemblies is not so much to maintain in them the general will as to ensure that it shall always be consulted and always respond. ...

Study Questions

1. How does Rousseau arrive at the conclusion that the social order is "a sacred right" that serves as the foundation for all order?
2. Describe the "social contract" and explain how it relates to the notion of the "general will."
3. How was Rousseau influenced by the Age of Enlightenment's climate of opinion?
4. Why would *The Social Contract* be considered inflammatory and revolutionary by some people of the late eighteenth century?

Reading 36

Adam Smith's *The Wealth of Nations*

The French **physiocrats** of the Age of Enlightenment brought new insights to the analysis of economics. Among others notably influenced by them was the British social philosopher Adam Smith (1732–1790). Building national wealth through government regulation and intervention, or mercantilism—a term that does not accurately describe the complex commercial system of pre-Industrial Europe—had come under heavy criticism as Adam Smith was putting the finishing touches on his masterful *Wealth of Nations*. It was first published in 1776. Endorsing a program of natural liberty in an attempt to teach Western nations better economic manners, Smith postulated that deregulation and the end of government subsidies would eliminate many social and commercial inequities and evils in Europe. He prescribed division of labor and economic specialization as the best means of improving large-scale enterprise. Furthermore, removing barriers and obstacles to world trade would foster streamlined industrial production, open up new markets, and hence promote fiscal growth. His principle of **laissez-faire** was eventually heralded as a hallmark in Western economic theory.

Introduction

The annual labor of every nation is the fund which originally supplies it with all the necessaries and conveniences of life which it annually consumes, and which consist always either in the immediate produce of that labor, or in what is purchased with that produce from other nations. Accordingly, therefore, as this produce or what is purchased with it bears a greater or smaller proportion to the number of those who are to consume it, the nation will be better or worse supplied with all the necessaries and conveniences for which it has occasion. But this proportion must in every nation be regulated by two different circumstances; first, by the skill, dexterity, and judgement with which its labor is generally applied; and, secondly, by the proportion between the number of those who are employed in useful

Adam Smith, *An Inquiry into the Nature and Causes of the Wealth of Nations,* ed. J. E. T. Rogers (Oxford: Oxford University Press, 1869), passim.

labor, and that of those who are not so employed. Whatever be the soil, climate, or extent of territory of any particular nation, the abundance or scantiness of its annual supply must, in that particular situation, depend upon those two circumstances.

The abundance or scantiness of this supply too seems to depend more upon the former of those two circumstances than upon the latter. Among the savage nations of hunters and fishers, every individual who is able to work is more or less employed in useful labor and endeavors to provide, as well as he can, the necessaries and conveniences of life, for himself and such of his family or tribe as are either too old, or too young, or too infirm to go hunting or fishing. Such nations, however, are so miserably poor that from mere want, they are frequently reduced, or, at least, think themselves reduced to the necessity sometimes of directly destroying, and sometimes of abandoning their infants, their old people, and those afflicted with lingering diseases, to perish with hunger, or to be devoured by wild beasts. Among civilized and thriving nations, on the contrary, though a great number of people do not labor at all, many of whom consume the produce of ten times, frequently of a hundred times more labor than the greater part of those who work; yet the produce of the whole labor of the society is so great, that all are often abundantly supplied, and a workman, even of the lowest and poorest order, if he is frugal and industrious, may enjoy a greater share of the necessaries and conveniences of life than it is possible for any savage to acquire. . . .

Whatever be the actual state of the skill, dexterity, and judgement with which labor is applied in any nation, the abundance or scantiness of its annual supply must depend, during the continuance of that state, upon the proportion between the number of those who are annually employed in useful labor, and that of those who are not so employed. The number of useful and productive laborers, it will hereafter appear, is every where in proportion to the quantity of capital stock which is employed in setting them to work, and to the particular way in which it is so employed. . . .

Nations tolerably well advanced as to skill, dexterity, and judgement, in the application of labor, have followed very different plans in the general conduct or direction of it; and those plans have not all been equally favorable to the greatness of its produce. The policy of some nations has given extraordinary encouragement to the industry of the country; that of others to the industry of towns. Scarcely any nation has dealt equally and impartially with every sort of industry. Since the downfall of the Roman empire, the policy of Europe has been more favorable to arts, manufactures, and commerce—the industry of towns—than to agriculture—the industry of the country. . . .

Though those different plans were, perhaps, first introduced by the private interests and prejudices of particular orders of men, without any regard to or foresight of their consequences upon the general welfare of the society; yet they have given occasion to very different theories of political economy; of which some magnify the importance of that industry which is carried on in towns, others of that which is carried on in the country. Those theories have had a considerable influence, not only upon the opinions of men of learning, but upon the public conduct of princes and sovereign states. . . .

Of the Principle of the Commercial or Mercantile System

That wealth consists in money, or in gold and silver, is a popular notion which naturally arises from the double function of money, as the instrument of commerce, and as the measure of value. In consequence of its being the instrument of commerce, when we have money we can more readily obtain whatever else we have occasion for, than by means of any other commodity. The great affair, we always find is to get money. When that is obtained, there is no difficulty in making any subsequent purchase. In consequence of its being the measure of value we estimate that of all other commodities by the quantity of money which they will exchange for. . . .

The gold and silver which can properly be considered as accumulated or stored up in any country, may be distinguished into three parts; first, the circulating money; secondly, the plate of private families; and last of all, the money which may have been collected by many years of parsimony, and laid up in the treasury of the prince. . . .

The importation of gold and silver is not the principal, much less the sole benefit which a nation derives from its foreign trade. Between whatever places foreign trade is carried on, they all of them derive two distinct benefits from it. It carries out that surplus part of the produce of their land and labor for which there is no demand among them, and brings back in return for it something else for which there is a demand. It gives a value to their superfluities, by exchanging them for something else, which may satisfy a part of their wants, and increase their enjoyments. By means of it, the narrowness of the home market does not hinder the division of labor in any particular branch of art or manufacture from being carried to the highest perfection. By opening a more extensive market for whate/er part of the produce of their labor may exceed the home consumption, it encourages them to improve its productive powers, and to augment its annual produce to the utmost, and thereby to increase the real revenue and wealth of the society. . . .

It is not by the importation of gold and silver that the discovery of America has enriched Europe. By the abundance of the American mines, those metals have become cheaper. A service of plate can now be purchased for about a third part of the corn, or a third part of the labor, which it would have cost in the fifteenth century. With the same annual expense of labor and commodities, Europe can annually purchase about three times the quantity of plate which it could have purchased at that time. But when a commodity comes to be sold for a third part of what had been its usual price, not only those who purchased it before can purchase three times their former quantity, but it is brought down to the level of a much greater number of purchasers, perhaps to more than ten, perhaps to more than twenty times the former number. So that there may be in Europe at present not only more than three times, but more than twenty or thirty times the quantity of plate which would have been in it, even in its present state of improvement, had the discovery of the American mines never been made. So far Europe has, no doubt, gained a real convenience, though surely a very trifling one. The cheapness of gold and silver renders those metals rather less fit for the purposes of money than they were before. In order to make the same purchases, we must load ourselves with a greater quantity of them, and carry about a shilling in our pocket where a groat would have done before. It is difficult to say which is most trifling, this inconvenience, or the opposite convenience. Neither the one nor the other could have made any very essential change in the state of Europe. The discovery of America, however, certainly made a most essential one. By opening a new and inexhaustible market to all the commodities of Europe, it gave occasion to new divisions of labor and improvements of art, which, in the narrow circle of the ancient commerce, could never have taken place for want of a market to take off the greater part of their produce. The productive powers of labor were improved, and its produce increased in all the different countries of Europe, and together with it the real revenue and wealth of the inhabitants. The commodities of Europe were almost all new to America, and many of those of America were new to Europe. A new set of exchanges, therefore, began to take place which had never been thought of before, and which should naturally have proved as advantageous to the new, as it certainly did to the old continent. Savage injustice of the Europeans rendered an event, which ought to have been beneficial to all, ruinous and destructive to several of those unfortunate countries. . . .

The two principles being established, however, that wealth consisted in gold and silver, and that those metals could be brought into a country which had no mines only by the balance of trade, or by exporting to a greater value than it imported; it necessarily became the great object of political economy to diminish as much as possible the importation of foreign goods for home consumption, and to increase as much as possible the exportation of the produce of domestic industry. Its two great engines for enriching the country, therefore, were restraints upon importation and encouragements to exportation.

The restraints upon importation were of two kinds.

First, restraints upon the importation of goods of almost all kinds from those particular countries with which the balance of trade was supposed to be disadvantageous.

Those different restraints consisted sometimes in high duties, and sometimes in absolute prohibitions.

Exportation was encouraged sometimes by drawbacks, sometimes by bounties, sometimes by advantageous treaties of commerce with foreign states, and sometimes by the establishment of colonies in distant countries.

Drawbacks were given upon two different occasions. When the home-manufactures were subject to any duty or excise, either the whole or a part of it was frequently drawn back upon their exportation; and when foreign goods liable to a duty were imported in order to be exported again, either the whole or a part of this duty was sometimes given back upon such exportation.

Bounties were given for the encouragement either of some beginning manufactures, or of such sorts of industry of other kinds as were supposed to deserve particular favor.

207

By advantageous treaties of commerce, particular privileges were procured in some foreign state for the goods and merchants of the country, beyond what were granted to those of other countries.

By the establishment of colonies in distant countries, not only particular privileges, but a monopoly was frequently procured for the goods and merchants of the country which established them.

The two sorts of restraints upon importation above-mentioned, together with these four encouragements to exportation, constitute the six principal means by which the commercial system proposes to increase the quantity of gold and silver in any country by turning the balance of trade in its favor. I shall consider each of them in a particular chapter, and without taking much further notice of their supposed tendency to bring money into the country, I shall examine chiefly what are likely to be the effects of each of them upon the annual produce of its industry. According as they tend either to increase or diminish the value of this annual produce, they must evidently tend either to increase or diminish the real wealth and revenue of the country.

Conclusion of the Mercantile System

... If any artificer has gone beyond the seas, and is exercising or teaching his trade in any foreign country, upon warning being given to him by any of his majesty's ministers or consuls abroad, or by one of his majesty's secretaries of state for the time being, if he does not, within six months after such warning, return into this realm, and from thenceforth abide and inhabit continually within the same, he is from thenceforth declared incapable of taking any legacy devised to him within this kingdom, or of being executor or administrator to any person, or of taking any lands within this kingdom by descent, devise, or purchase. He likewise forfeits to the king, all his lands, goods and chattels, is declared an alien in every respect, and is put out of the king's protection.

It is unnecessary, I imagine, to observe, how contrary such regulations are to the boasted liberty of the subject, of which we affect to be so very jealous; but which, in this case, is so plainly sacrificed to the futile interests of our merchants and manufacturers.

The laudable motive of all these regulations, is to extend our own manufactures, not by their own improvement, but by the depression of those of all our neighbors, and by putting an end, as much as possible, to the troublesome competition of such odious and disagreeable rivals. Our master manufacturers think it reasonable, that they themselves should have the monopoly of the ingenuity of all their countrymen. Though by restraining, in some trades, the number of apprentices which can be employed at one time, and by imposing the necessity of a long apprenticeship in all trades, they endeavor, all of them, to confine the knowledge of their respective employments to as small a number as possible; they are unwilling, however, that any part of this small number should go abroad to instruct foreigners.

Consumption is the sole end and purpose of all production; and the interest of the producer ought to be attended to, only so far as it may be necessary for promoting that of the consumer. The maxim is so perfectly self-evident, that it would be absurd to attempt to prove it. But in the mercantile system, the interest of the consumer is almost constantly sacrificed to that of the producer; and it seems to consider production, and not consumption, as the ultimate end and object of all industry and commerce.

In the restraints upon the importation of all foreign commodities which can come into competition with those of our own growth, or manufacture, the interest of the home-consumer is evidently sacrificed to that of the producer. It is altogether for the benefit of the latter, that the former is obliged to pay that enhancement of price which this monopoly almost always occasions.

It is altogether for the benefit of the producer that bounties are granted upon the exportation of some of his productions. The home-consumer is obliged to pay, first, the tax which is necessary for paying the bounty, and secondly, the still greater tax which necessarily arises from the enhancement of the price of the commodity in the home market.

By the famous treaty of commerce with Portugal, the consumer is prevented by high duties from purchasing of a neighboring country, a commodity which our own climate does not produce, but is obliged to purchase it of a distant country, though it is acknowledged, that the commodity of the distant country is of a worse quality than that of the near one. The home-consumer is obliged to submit to this inconvenience, in order that the producer may import into the distant country some of his productions upon more advantageous terms than he would otherwise have been allowed to do. The consumer, too, is obliged to pay, whatever enhancement in the price of those very productions, this forced exportation may occasion in the home market.

But in the system of laws which has been established for the management of our American and West Indian colonies, the interest of the home-consumer has been sacrificed to that of the producer with a more extravagant profusion than in all our other commercial regulations. A great empire has been established for the sole purpose of raising up a nation of customers who should be obliged to buy from the shops of our different producers, all the goods with which these could supply them. For the sake of that little enhancement of price which this monopoly might afford our producers, the home-consumers have been burdened with the whole expense of maintaining and defending that empire. For this purpose, and for this purpose only, in the two last wars, more than two hundred millions have been spent, and a new debt of more than a hundred and seventy millions has been contracted over and above all that had been expended for the same purpose in former wars. The interest of this debt alone is not only greater than the whole extraordinary profit, which, it ever could be pretended, was made by the monopoly of the colony trade, but than the whole value of that trade, or than the whole value of the goods, which at an average have been annually exported to the colonies.

It cannot be very difficult to determine who have been the contrivers of this whole mercantile system; not the consumers, we may believe, whose interest has been entirely neglected; but the producers, whose interest has been so carefully attended to; and among this latter class our merchants and manufacturers have been by far the principal architects. In the mercantile regulations, which have been taken notice of in this chapter, the interest of our manufacturers has been most peculiarly attended to; and the interest, not so much of the consumers, as that of some other sets of producers, has been sacrificed to it.

Study Questions

1. What are Adam Smith's main objections to mercantilism?
2. How does the author attempt to prove that gold and silver bullion does not constitute the true wealth of a nation, and what is implied in this hypothesis for the economic well-being of nations?
3. How does Smith justify the premise that when the individual works for his or her own betterment, the whole society benefits?
4. If Smith's theories had been put into practice at the end of the eighteenth century, how would they have influenced the conventional economic order throughout Europe and the world?

Two Documents of the French Revolution

Modeled on similar documents issued by American patriots some years before, the **Constituent Assembly** of France voted its **bourgeoisie** preference for the "Declaration of the Rights of Man and Citizen" in late August 1789. The concepts of liberty, equality, and fraternity espoused in the declaration of 1789, which eventually served as the preamble to the constitution of 1791, outlined a new order for French society. This "Declaration of the Rights of Man and Citizen" failed to address France's immediate problems effectively; the one promulgated in 1793, however, makes a more ambitious attempt at social and political reform and, hence, captures France's overt revolutionary spirit. **Maximilien Robespierre** and his **Jacobin** compatriots advocated many of the goals expressed in the 1793 declaration's redefinition of public rights. But they also sought to defend the violent regime of "the Terror" by proclaiming its right to change the French constitution and overlook the declaration's precepts. Interestingly, the constitution of 1793, for which this declaration served as a preamble, was never enforced because the **Convention** of the Republic proclaimed in October 1793 that the French government was to remain "revolutionary" until peace was secured at home and abroad.

Declaration of the Rights of Man and Citizen of 1789

The representatives of the French people, organized in **National Assembly**, considering that ignorance, forgetfulness or contempt of the rights of man are the sole causes of the public miseries and of the corruption of governments, have resolved to set forth in a solemn declaration the natural, inalienable, and sacred rights of man, in order that this declaration, being ever present to all the members of the social body, may unceasingly remind them of their rights and duties: in order that the acts of the legislative power and those of the executive power may be each

---

E. L. Higgins, ed., *The French Revolution as Told by Contemporaries* (New York: Houghton Mifflin, 1938), 432–33. Copyright © 1938 Houghton Mifflin. Reprinted with permission of the publisher.

moment compared with the aim of every political institution and thereby may be more respected; and in order that the demands of the citizens, grounded henceforth upon simple and incontestable principles, may always take the direction of maintaining the constitution and the welfare of all.

In consequence, the National Assembly recognizes and declares, in the presence and under the auspices of the Supreme Being, the following rights of man and citizen.

1. Men are born and remain free and equal in rights. Social distinctions can be based only upon public utility.
2. The aim of every political association is the preservation of the natural and imprescriptible rights of man. These rights are liberty, property, security, and resistance to oppression.
3. The source of all sovereignty is essentially in the nation; no body, no individual can exercise authority that does not proceed from it in plain terms.
4. Liberty consists in the power to do anything that does not injure others; accordingly, the exercise of the natural rights of each man has for its only limits those that secure to the other members of society the enjoyment of these same rights. These limits can be determined only by law.
5. The law has the right to forbid only such actions as are injurious to society. Nothing can be forbidden that is not interdicted by the law and no one can be constrained to do that which it does not order.
6. Law is the expression of the general will. All citizens have the right to take part personally or by their representatives in its formation. It must be the same for all, whether it protects or punishes. All citizens being equal in its eyes, are equally eligible to all public dignities, places, and employments, according to their capacities, and without other distinction than that of their virtues and their talents.
7. No man can be accused, arrested, or detained except in the cases determined by the law and according to the forms that it has prescribed. Those who procure, expedite, execute, or cause to be executed arbitrary orders ought to be punished: but every citizen summoned or seized in virtue of the law ought to render instant obedience; he makes himself guilty by resistance.
8. The law ought to establish only penalties that are strictly and obviously necessary and no one can be punished except in virtue of a law established and promulgated prior to the offence and legally applied.
9. Every man being presumed innocent until he has been pronounced guilty, if it is thought indispensable to arrest him, all severity that may not be necessary to secure his person ought to be strictly suppressed by law.
10. No one ought to be disturbed on account of his opinions, even religious, provided their manifestation does not derange the public order established by law.
11. The free communication of ideas and opinions is one of the most precious of the rights of man; every citizen then can freely speak, write, and print, subject to responsibility for the abuse of this freedom in the cases determined by law.
12. The guarantee of the rights of man and citizen requires a public force; this force then is instituted for the advantage of all and not for the personal benefit of those to whom it is entrusted.

13. For the maintenance of the public force and for the expense of administration a general tax is indispensable; it ought to be equally apportioned among all the citizens according to their means.

14. All the citizens have the right to ascertain, by themselves or by their representatives, the necessity of the public tax, to consent to it freely, to follow the employment of it, and to determine the assessment, the collection, and the duration of it.

15. Society has the right to call for an account from every public agent of its administration.

16. Any society in which the guarantee of the rights is not secured or the separation of powers is not determined has no constitution at all.

17. Property being a sacred and inviolable right, no one can be deprived of it unless a legally established public necessity demands it, under the condition of a just and prior indemnity.

Declaration of the Rights of Man and Citizen of 1793

The French people, convinced that forgetfulness of, and contempt for, the natural rights of man are the only causes of the misfortunes of the world, have resolved to expose, in a declaration, their sacred and inalienable rights, in order that all citizens, being able always to compare the acts of government with the end of every social institution, may never suffer themselves to be oppressed and degraded by tyranny; and that the people may always have before their eyes the basis of their liberty and happiness; the magistrates the rule of their duty; and the legislature the object of their mission.

They acknowledge therefore and proclaim, in the presence of the Supreme Being, the following:

1. The end of society is common happiness. Government is instituted to secure to man the enjoyment of his natural and imprescriptible rights.

2. These rights are equality, liberty, safety, and property.

3. All men are equal by nature, and before the law.

4. The law is the free and solemn expression of the general will. It ought to be the same for all, whether it protects or punishes. It cannot order but what is just and useful to society. It cannot forbid but what is hurtful.

5. All citizens are equally admissible to public employments. Free people avow no other motives of preference in their elections than virtues and talents.

6. Liberty is that power which belongs to a man doing everything that does not hurt the rights of another: its principle is nature; its rule is justice; its protection the law; and its moral limits are defined by the maxim, "Do not to another what you would not wish done to yourself."

F. M. Anderson, ed., *The Constitutions and Other Select Documents Illustrative of the History of France* (Minneapolis: H. W. Wilson, 1904), 58–60.

7. The right of manifesting one's thoughts and opinions, either by the press, or in any other manner; the right of assembling peaceably and the free exercise of religious worship cannot be forbidden. The necessity of announcing these rights supposes either the presence or the recent remembrance of despotism.

8. Whatever is not forbidden by law cannot be prevented. No one can be forced to do what it does not order.

9. Safety consists in the protection granted by society to each citizen for the preservation of his person, his rights, and his property.

10. The law avenges public and individual liberty of the abuses committed against them by power.

11. No person can be accused, arrested, or confined but in cases determined by the law, and according to the forms which it prescribes. Every citizen summoned or seized by the authority of the law ought immediately to obey; he renders himself culpable by resistance.

12. Every act exercised against a man to which the cases in the law do not apply, and in which its forms are not observed, is arbitrary and tyrannical. Respect for the law forbids him to submit to such acts; and if attempts are made to execute them by violence, he has a right to repel force by force.

13. Those who shall solicit, dispatch, sign, execute, or cause to be executed, arbitrary acts, are culpable, and ought to be punished.

14. Every man being supposed innocent until he has been declared guilty, if it is judged indispensable to arrest him, all severity not necessary to secure his person ought to be strictly repressed by law.

15. No one ought to be tried and punished until he has been legally summoned, and in virtue of a law published previous to the commission of a crime. A law which should punish crimes committed before it existed would be tyrannical. The retroactive effect given to a law would be a crime.

16. The law ought not to decree any punishments but such as are strictly and evidently necessary; punishment ought to be proportioned to the crime, and useful to society.

17. The right of property is that right which belongs to every citizen to enjoy and dispose of according to his pleasure his property, revenues, labor, and industry.

18. No labor, culture, or commerce can be forbidden to the industrious citizen.

19. Every man may engage his services and his time, but he cannot sell himself—his person is not alienable property. The law does not acknowledge servitude—there can exist only an engagement of care and acknowledgment between the man who labors and the man who employs him.

20. No one can be deprived of the smallest portion of his property without his consent, except when the public necessity, legally ascertained, evidently requires it, and on condition of a just and previous indemnification.

21. No contribution can be established but for general utility, and to relieve the public wants. Every citizen has the right to concur in the establishment to contributions, to watch over the use made of them, and to call for a statement of their expenditure.

22. Public aids are a sacred debt. Society is obliged to provide for the subsistence of the unfortunate, either by procuring them work, or by securing the means of existence to those who are unable to labor.

23. Instruction is the want of all, and society ought to favor, with all its power, the progress of public reason; and to place instruction within the reach of every citizen.

24. The social guarantee consists in the actions of all to secure to each the enjoyment and preservation of his rights. The guarantee rests on the national sovereignty.

25. The social guarantee cannot exist if the limits of public functions are not clearly defined by the law, and if the responsibility of all public functionaries is not secured.

26. The sovereignty resides in the people. It is one and indivisible, imprescriptible and inalienable.

27. No portion of the people can exercise the power of the whole, but each section of the sovereign assembled ought to enjoy the right of expressing its will in perfect liberty. Every individual who arrogates to himself the sovereignty, or who usurps the exercise of it, ought to be put to death by free men.

28. A people have always the right of revising, amending, and changing their constitution. One generation cannot subject to its laws future generations.

29. Every citizen has an equal right of concurring in the formation of the law, and in the nomination of his mandataries or agents.

30. Public function cannot be considered as distinctions or rewards, but as duties.

31. Crimes committed by the mandataries of the people and their agents ought never to remain unpunished. No one has a right to pretend to be more inviolable than other citizens.

32. The right of presenting petitions to the depositories of public authority belongs to every individual. The exercise of this right cannot, in any case, be forbidden, suspended, or limited.

33. Resistance to oppression is the consequence of the other rights of man.

34. Oppression is exercised against the social body when even one of its members is oppressed. Oppression is exercised against each member when the social body is oppressed.

35. When the government violates the rights of the people, insurrection becomes to the people, and to every portion of the people, the most sacred, and the most indispensable of duties.

Study Questions

1. What citizens' rights and obligations do both declarations emphasize?
2. How do the documents reflect changes in the historical conditions and circumstances in France between 1789 and 1793?
3. Although the declaration of 1789 was not intended to be merely a philosophical statement on citizen's rights, why does it succeed best on an ideological rather than a politically pragmatic level?
4. What are the "revolutionary" aspects of the documents, and how does a comparison of the declarations of 1789 and 1793 reflect the ideological and historical progression of the French Revolution?

Reading 38

Mary Wollstonecraft's *Vindication of the Rights of Woman*

Always sensitive to the plight of women, Mary Wollstonecraft (1759–1797) founded a school for them in 1784 in the vicinity of London. Her sister Eliza, who eventually obtained a divorce from her abusive husband, and Fanny Blood, a long-time companion, joined in this endeavor. Within two years the school closed owing to financial difficulties, and Wollstonecraft turned her hand to writing. In 1786, she produced her first work, *Thoughts on the Education of Daughters*. This was followed by a novel, a children's book, various pamphlets, and a series of translations of foreign social and philosophical treatises. She published her early writings with the help of **Samuel Johnson** and other English literati. In 1790 her friend and publisher, Joseph Johnson, printed her *Vindication of the Rights of Men,* the first published response to **Edmund Burke**'s famous *Reflections on the Revolution in France.* The principles in *Vindication of the Rights of Woman,* first published in 1792, were derived in part from **Catherine Macaulay**'s influential *Letters on Education* (1790), which Wollstonecraft discusses at length. A second, revised edition appeared at the end of that same year. In 1795, on the heels of a disastrous three-year relationship with a philandering American named Gilbert Imlay, Wollstonecraft married William Godwin (1756–1836), a left-wing radical known affectionately as the only man to make the English poet Samuel Coleridge (1772–1834) lose his temper. Two weeks after the birth of their daughter Mary, who years later became the wife of **Percy Bysshe Shelley** and a well-known author in her own right, Mary Wollstonecraft died of puerperal fever. *Vindication of the Rights of Woman* continues to challenge the traditional notions of the subjugation of women even today.

Introduction

My own sex, I hope, will excuse me, if I treat them like rational creatures, instead of flattering their fascinating graces, and viewing them as if they were in the state of perpetual childhood, unable to stand alone. I earnestly wish to point out in what true dignity and human happiness consists. I wish to persuade women to endeavor to acquire strength, both of mind and body, and to convince them that the soft phrases, susceptibility of heart, delicacy of sentiment, and refinement of taste, are almost synonymous with epithets of weakness, and these beings who are only the objects of pity, and that kind of love which has been termed its sister, will soon become objects of contempt. . . .

The education of women has of late been more attended to than formerly; yet they are still reckoned a frivolous sex, and ridiculed or pitied by the writers who endeavored by satire or instruction to improve them. It is acknowledged that they spend many of the first years of their lives in acquiring a smattering of accomplishments; meanwhile strength of body and mind are sacrificed to libertine notions of beauty, to the desire of establishing themselves—the only way women can rise in the world—by marriage. And this desire making mere animals out of them, when they marry they act as such children may be expected to act—they dress, they paint, and nickname God's creatures. Surely these weak beings are only fit for a seraglio! Can they be expected to govern a family with judgment, or take care of the poor babes whom they bring into the world?

If, then, it can be fairly deduced from the present conduct of the sex, from the prevalent fondness for pleasure which takes place of ambition and those nobler passions that open and enlarge the soul, that the instruction which women have hitherto received has only tended, with the constitution of civil society, to render them insignificant objects of desire—mere propagators of fools!—if it can be proved that in aiming to accomplish them, without cultivating their understandings, they are taken out of their sphere of duties, and made ridiculous and useless when the short-lived bloom of beauty is over, I assume that rational men will excuse me for endeavoring to persuade them to become more masculine and respectable. . . .

Women are, in fact, so much degraded by mistaken notions of female excellence, that I do not mean to add a paradox when I assert that this artificial weakness produces a propensity to tyrannize, and gives birth to cunning, the natural opponent of strength, which leads them to play off those contemptible infantile airs that undermine the esteem even whilst they excite desire. Let men become more chaste and modest, and if women do not grow wiser in the same ration it will be clear that they have weaker understandings. It seems scarcely necessary to say that I now speak of the sex in general. Many individuals have more sense than

Mary Wollstonecraft, *Vindication of the Rights of Woman,* 2nd ed. (London: Joseph Johnson Publisher, 1792), passim.

their male relatives; and, as nothing preponderates where there is a constant struggle for an equilibrium without having naturally more gravity, some women govern their husbands without degrading themselves, because intellect will always govern.

Chapter Four

That woman is naturally weak, or degraded by a concurrence of circumstances, is, I think, clear. But this position I shall simply contrast with a conclusion, which I have frequently heard fall from sensible men in favor of an aristocracy: that the mass of mankind cannot be anything, or the obsequious slaves, who patiently allow themselves to be driven forward, would feel their own consequence, and spurn their chains. Men, they further observe, submit everywhere to oppression, when they have only to lift up their heads to throw off the yoke; yet, instead of asserting their birthright, they quickly lick the dust, and say, "Let us eat and drink, for tomorrow we may die." Women, I argue from analogy, are degraded by the same propensity to enjoy the present moment, and at last despise the freedom which they have not sufficient virtue to struggle to attain. But I must be more explicit.

With respect to the culture of the heart, it is unanimously allowed that sex is out of the question; but the line of subordination in the mental powers is never to be passed over. Only "absolute in loveliness," the portion of rationality granted to woman is, indeed, very scanty; for denying her genius and judgment, it is scarcely possible to divine what remains to characterize intellect.

The stamen of immortality, if I may be allowed the phrase, is the perfectibility of human reason; for, were man created perfect, or did a flood of knowledge break in upon him, when he arrived at maturity, that precluded error, I should doubt whether his existence would be continued after the dissolution of the body. But, in the present state of things, every difficulty in morals that escapes from human discussion, and equally baffles the investigation of profound thinking, and the lightning glance of genius, is an argument on which I build my belief of the immortality of the soul. Reason is, consequentially, the simple power of improvement; or, more properly speaking, of discerning truth. Every individual is in this respect a world in itself. More or less may be conspicuous in one being than another; but the nature of reason must be the same in all, if it be an emanation of divinity, the tie that connects the creature with the Creator; for, can that soul be stamped with the heavenly image, that is not perfected by the exercise of its own reason? Yet outwardly ornamented with elaborate care, and so adorned to delight man, "that with honour he may love," the soul of woman is not allowed to have this distinction, and man, ever placed, between her and reason, she is always represented as only created to see through a gross medium, and to take things on trust. But dismissing these fanciful theories, and considering woman as a whole, let it be what it will, instead of a part of man, the inquiry is whether she have reason or not. If she have, which, for a moment, I will take for granted, she was not created merely to be the solace of man, and the sexual should not destroy the human character.

Into this error men have, probably, been led by viewing education in a false light; not considering it as the first step to form a being advancing gradually towards perfection; but only as a preparation for life. On this sensual error, for I must call it so, has the false system of female manners been reared, which robs the whole sex of its dignity, and classes the brown and fair with the smiling flowers that only adorn the land. This has ever been the language of men, and the fear of departing from a supposed sexual character, has made even women of superior sense adopt the same sentiments. Thus understanding, strictly speaking, has been denied to woman; and instinct, sublimated into wit and cunning, for the purposes of life, has been substituted in its stead.

The power of generalizing ideas, of drawing comprehensive conclusions from individual observations, is the only acquirement, for an immortal being, that really deserves the name of knowledge. Merely to observe, without endeavouring to account for anything, may (in a very incomplete manner) serve as the common sense of life; but where is the store laid up that is to clothe the soul when it leaves the body?

This power has not only been denied to women; but writers have insisted that it is inconsistent, with a few exceptions, with their sexual character. Let men prove this, and I shall grant that woman only exists for man. I must, however, previously remark, that the power of generalizing ideas, to any great extent, is not very common amongst men or women. But this exercise is the true cultivation of the understanding; and everything conspires to render the cultivation of the understanding more difficult in the female than the male world.

Chapter Thirteen

It is not necessary to inform the sagacious reader, now [that] I enter on my concluding reflections, that the discussion of my subject merely consists in opening a few simple principles, and clearing away the rubbish which obscured them. But, as all readers are not sagacious, I must be allowed to add some explanatory remarks to bring the subject home to reason—to that sluggish reason, which supinely takes opinions on trust, and obstinately supports them to spare itself the labour of thinking.

Moralists have unanimously agreed, that unless virtue be nursed by liberty, it will never attain due strength—and what they say of man I extend to mankind, insisting that in all cases morals be fixed on immutable principles; and, that the being cannot be termed rational or virtuous, who obeys any authority, but that of reason.

To render women truly useful members of society, I argue that they should be led, by having their understandings cultivated on a large scale, to acquire a rational affection for their country, founded in knowledge, because it is obvious that we are little interested about what we do not understand. And to render this general knowledge of due importance, I have endeavoured to show that private duties are never properly fulfilled unless the understanding enlarges the heart; and that public virtue is only an aggregate of private. But, the distinctions established in society undermine both, by beating out the solid gold of virtue, till it becomes only the tinsel-covering of vice; for whilst wealth renders a man more respectable than virtue, wealth will be sought before virtue; and, whilst women's persons are caressed, when a childish simper shows an absence of mind—the mind will lie fallow. Yet, true voluptuousness must proceed from the mind—for what can equal the sensations produced by mutual affection, supported by mutual respect? What are the cold, or feverish caresses of appetite, but sin embracing death, compared with the modest overflowings of a pure heart and exalted imagination? Yes, let me tell the libertine of fancy when he despises understanding in woman—that the mind, which he disregards, gives life to the enthusiastic affection from which rapture, short-lived as it is, alone can blow! And, that, without virtue, a sexual attachment must expire, like a tallow candle in the socket, creating intolerable disgust. To prove this, I need only observe, that men who have wasted great part of their lives with women, and with whom they have sought for pleasure with eager thirst, entertain the meanest opinion of the sex. Virtue, true refiner of joy!—if foolish men were to fright thee from earth, in order to give loose to all their appetites without a check—some sensual weight of taste would scale the heavens to invite thee back, to give a zest to pleasure!

That women at present are by ignorance rendered foolish or vicious is, I think, not to be disputed; and, that the most salutary effects tending to improve mankind might be expected from a revolution in female manners, appears, at least, with a face of probability, to rise out of the observation. For as marriage has been termed the parent of those enduring charities which draw man from the brutal herd, the corrupting intercourse that wealth, idleness, and folly, produce between the sexes, is more universally injurious to morality than all the other vices of mankind collectively considered. To adulterous lust the most sacred duties are sacrificed, because before marriage, men, by a promiscuous gratification—learned to separate it not only from esteem, but from the gratification merely built on habit, which mixes little humanity with it. Justice and friendship are also set at defiance, and that purity of taste is vitiated which would naturally lead a man to relish an artless display of affection rather than affect airs. But that noble simplicity of affection, which dares to appear unadorned, has few attractions for the libertine, though it be the charm, which by cementing the matrimonial tie, secures to the pledges of a warmer passion than necessary parental attention; for children will never be properly educated till friendship subsists between parents. Virtue flies from a house divided against itself—and a whole legion of devils take up their residence there.

The affection of husbands and wives cannot be pure when they have so few sentiments in common, and when so little confidence is established at home, as must be the case when their pursuits are so different. That intimacy from which tenderness should flow, will not, cannot subsist between the vicious.

Contending, therefore, that the sexual distinction which men have so warmly insisted upon, is arbitrary, I have dwelt on an observation, that several sensible men, with whom I have conversed on the subject, allowed to be well founded; and it is simply this, that the little chastity to be found amongst men, and consequent disregard of modesty, tend to degrade both sexes; and further, that the modesty of women, characterized as such, will often be only the artful veil of wantonness instead of being the natural reflection of purity, till modesty be universally respected.

From the tyranny of man, I firmly believe, the greater number of female follies proceed; and the cunning, which I allow makes at present a part of their character, I likewise have repeatedly endeavored to prove, is produced by oppression.

Were not dissenters, for instance, a class of people, with strict truth, characterized as cunning? And may I not lay some stress on this fact to prove, that when any power but reason curbs the free spirit of man, dissimulation is practiced, and the various shifts of art are naturally called forth? Great attention to decorum, which was carried to a degree of scrupulosity, and all that puerile bustle about trifles and consequential solemnity, which **Butler**'s caricature of a dissenter brings before the imagination, shaped their persons as well as their minds in the mould of prim littleness. I speak collectively, for I know how many ornaments in human nature have been enrolled amongst sectaries; yet, I assert, that the same narrow prejudice for their sect, which women have for their families, prevailed in the dissenting part of the community, however worthy in other respects; and also that the same timid prudence, or headstrong efforts, often disgraced the exertions of both. Oppression thus formed many of the features of their character perfectly to coincide with that of the oppressed half of mankind; for it is not notorious that dissenters were, like women, fond of deliberating together, and asking advice of each other, till by a complication of little contrivances, some little end was brought about? A similar attention to preserve their reputation was conspicuous in the dissenting and female world, and was proud by a similar cause.

Asserting the rights which women have in common with men ought to contend for, I have not attempted to extenuate their faults; but to prove them to be the natural consequence of their education and station in society. If so, it is reasonable to suppose that they will change their character, and correct their vices and follies, when they are allowed to be free in a physical, moral, and civil sense.

Let women share the rights, and she will emulate the virtues of man; for she must grow more perfected when emancipated, or justify the authority that chains such a weak being to her duty. If the latter, it will be expedient to now open afresh trade with Russia for whips: a present which a father should always make to his son-in-law on his wedding day, that a husband may keep his whole family in order by the same means; and without any violation of justice reign, wielding this sceptre, solo master of his house, because he is the only thing in it who has reason:—the divine, indefeasible earthly sovereignty breathed into man by the Master of the universe. Allowing this position, women have not any inherent rights to claim; and, by the same rule, their duties vanish, for rights and duties are inseparable.

Be just then, ye of understanding; and mark not more severely what women do amiss than the vicious tricks of the horse or the ass for whom ye provide provender—and allow her the privilege of ignorance, to whom ye deny the rights of reason, or ye will be worse than Egyptian task-masters, expecting virtue where Nature has not given understanding.

Study Questions

1. What does Wollstonecraft cite as the major distinctions existing between the sexes?
2. How is this treatise clearly a product of the Age of Enlightenment and the revolutionary activities that consumed France and America in the late eighteenth century?
3. According to Wollstonecraft, what factors determine the status of women, and how do education and the perfection of human reason influence their position in society?
4. What are the apparent differences in Wollstonecraft's and Astell's (Reading 19) conceptions of "womanhood"?

The Communist Manifesto of Marx and Engels

Few will deny the importance of Karl Marx's (1818–1883) contribution to philosophy and political theory. The political revolution that he stimulated and came to symbolize has shaped much twentieth-century history. Marx's major works include *The German Ideology* (1846), *The Communist Manifesto* (1848), which he wrote with Frederick Engels (1820–1895), and *Capital* (1867)—with Engels completing volumes two and three (1885, 1894) after Marx's death. Neither man began life as a revolutionary political economist. As a university student in Berlin in the 1830s, Marx studied literature, wrote poetry to his future wife Jenny von Westphalen, and dabbled in classical metaphysics, later writing a thesis on early Greek philosophy. Initially a philosophical idealist, Marx's study of the works of **Georg Hegel** and **Ludwig Feuerbach** eventually pointed him in the direction of historical materialism, a position clearly presented in *The Communist Manifesto*. Engels's association with Marx dates from their involvement in the Young Hegelians Society. The well-to-do Engels in fact largely supported Marx from the time of their collaboration on *The Communist Manifesto*. This work is a direct appeal to all workers to emancipate themselves and fight against the unjust division of wealth in society. Contemporary circumstances particularly in the Western world were viewed by Marx and Engels as contrary to basic human decency.

A spectre is haunting Europe—the spectre of Communism. All the Powers of old Europe have entered into a holy alliance to exorcise this spectre: Pope and Czar, **Metternich** and **Guizot**, French Radicals and German police-spies.

Where is the party in opposition that has not been decried as Communistic by its opponents in power? Where the Opposition that has not hurled back the

Karl Marx and Frederick Engels, *The Manifesto of the Communist Party,* trans. F. Engels (London: William Reeves Bookseller, 1888), passim.

branding reproach of Communism, against the more advanced opposition parties, as well as against its reactionary adversaries?

Two things result from this fact.

Communism is already acknowledged by all European Powers to be itself a Power.

It is high time that Communists should openly, in the face of the whole world, publish their views, aims, and tendencies, and meet this nursery tale of the Spectre of Communism with a Manifesto of the party itself. . . .

The history of all hitherto existing society is the history of class struggles.

Freeman and slave, patrician and plebeian, lord and serf, guild-master and journeyman, in a word, oppressor and oppressed, stood in constant opposition to one another, carried on an uninterrupted, now hidden, now open fight, a fight that each time ended, either in a revolutionary re-constitution of society at large, or in the common ruin of the contending classes. . . .

Our epoch, the epoch of the **bourgeoisie**, possesses, however, this distinctive feature: it has simplified class antagonisms. Society as a whole is more and more splitting up into two great hostile camps, into two great classes directly facing each other: Bourgeoisie and **Proletariat**. . . .

Modern bourgeois society with its relations of production, of exchange, and of property, a society that has conjured up such gigantic means of production and of exchange, is like the sorcerer, who is no longer able to control the powers of the nether world whom he has called up by his spells. For many a decade past the history of industry and commerce is but the history of the revolt of modern productive forces against modern conditions of production, against the property relations that are the conditions for the existence of the bourgeoisie and of its rule. . . .

The weapons with which the bourgeoisie felled **feudalism** to the ground are now turned against the bourgeoisie itself.

But not only has the bourgeoisie forged the weapons that bring death to itself; it has also called into existence the men who are to wield those weapons—the modern working class—the proletarians. . . .

In what relation do the Communists stand to the proletarians as a whole?

The Communists do not form a separate party opposed to other working-class parties.

They have no interests separate and apart from those of the proletariat as a whole.

They do not set up any sectarian principles of their own, by which to shape and mould the proletarian movement.

The Communists are distinguished from the other working-class parties by this only: (1) In the national struggles of the proletarians of the different countries, they point out and bring to the front the common interests of the entire proletariat independently of all nationality. (2) In the various stages of development which the struggle of the working class against the bourgeoisie has to pass through, they always and everywhere represent the interests of the movement as a whole.

The Communists, therefore, are on the one hand, practically, the most advanced and resolute section of the working-class parties of every country, that section which pushes forward all others; on the other hand, theoretically, they have over the great mass of the proletariat the advantage of clearly understanding the line of march, the conditions, and the ultimate general results of the proletarian movement.

The immediate aim of the Communists is the same as that of all the other proletarian parties: the formation of the proletariat into a class, the overthrow of the bourgeois supremacy, conquest of political power by the proletariat. . . .

In this sense, the theory of the Communists may be summed up in a single phrase: Abolition of private property. . . .

You are horrified at our intending to do away with private property. But in your existing society, private property is already done away with for nine-tenths of the population; its existence for the few is solely due to its non-existence in the hands of those nine-tenths. You reproach us, therefore, with intending to do away with a form of property, the necessary condition for whose existence is the non-existence of any property for the immense majority of society.

In one word, you reproach us with intending to do away with your property. Precisely so; that is just what we intend.

From the moment when labor can no longer be converted into capital, money, or rent, into a social power capable of being monopolized, i.e., from the moment when individual property can no longer be transformed into bourgeois property, into capital, from that moment, you say, individuality vanishes.

You must, therefore, confess that by "individual" you mean no other person than the bourgeois, than the middle-class owner of property. This person must, indeed, be swept out of the way, and made impossible.

Communism deprives no man of the power to appropriate the products of society; all that it does is to deprive him of the power to subjugate the labor of others by means of such appropriation. . . .

Abolition of the family! Even the most radical flare up at this infamous proposal of the Communists.

On what foundation is the present family, the bourgeois family, based? On capital, on private gain. In its completely developed form this family exists only among the bourgeoisie. But this state of things finds its complement in the practical absence of the family among the proletarians, and in public prostitution.

The bourgeois family will vanish as a matter of course when its complement vanishes, and both will vanish with the vanishing of capital.

Do you charge us with wanting to stop the exploitation of children by their parents? To this crime we plead guilty.

But, you will say, we destroy the most hallowed of relations, when we replace home education by social.

And your education! Is not that also social, and determined by the social conditions under which you educate, by the intervention, direct or indirect, of society, by means of schools, etc.? The Communists have not invented the intervention of society in education; they do but seek to alter the character of that intervention, and to rescue education from the influence of the ruling class. . . .

The Communists are further reproached with desiring to abolish countries and nationality.

The working men have no country. We cannot take from them what they have not got. Since the proletariat must first of all acquire political supremacy, must rise to be the leading class of the nation, must constitute itself the nation, it is, so far, itself national, though not in the bourgeois sense of the word.

National differences and antagonisms between peoples are daily more and more vanishing, owing to the development of the bourgeoisie, to freedom of commerce, to the world-market, to uniformity in the mode of production and in the conditions of life corresponding thereto.

The supremacy of the proletariat will cause them to vanish still faster. United action, of the leading civilized countries at least, is one of the first conditions for the emancipation of the proletariat.

In proportion as the exploitation of one individual by another is put an end to, the exploitation of one nation by another will also be put an end to. In proportion as the antagonism between classes within the nation vanishes, the hostility of one nation to another will come to an end.

The charges against Communism made from a religious, a philosophical, and, generally, from an ideological standpoint, are not deserving of serious examination.

Does it require deep intuition to comprehend that man's ideas, views and conceptions, in one word, man's consciousness, changes with every change in the conditions of his material existence, in his social relations and in his social life?

What else does the history of ideas prove, than that intellectual production changes its character in proportion as material production is changed? The ruling ideas of each age have ever been the ideas of its ruling class.

When people speak of ideas that revolutionize society, they do but express the fact, that within the old society, the elements of a new one have been created, and that the dissolution of the old ideas keeps even pace with the dissolution of the old conditions of existence. . . .

The Communist revolution is the most radical rupture with traditional property relations; no wonder that its development involves the most radical rupture with traditional ideas.

But let us have done with the bourgeois objections to Communism.

We have seen above, that the first step in the revolution by the working class, is to raise the proletariat to the position of ruling class, to win the battle of democracy.

The proletariat will use its political supremacy to wrest, by degrees, all capital from the bourgeoisie, to centralize all instruments of production in the hands of the State, i.e., of the proletariat organized as the ruling class; and to increase the total of productive forces as rapidly as possible.

Of course, in the beginning, this cannot be effected except by means of despotic inroads on the rights of property, and on the conditions of bourgeois production; by means of measures, therefore, which appear economically insufficient and untenable, but which, in the course of the movement, outstrip themselves, necessitate further inroads upon the old social order, and are unavoidable as a means of entirely revolutionizing the mode of production.

These measures will of course be different in different countries.

Nevertheless in the most advanced countries, the following will be pretty generally applicable: (1) Abolition of property in land and application of all rents of land to public purposes; (2) A heavy progressive or graduated income tax; (3) Abolition of all right of inheritance; (4) Confiscation of the property of all emigrants and rebels; (5) Centralization of credit in the hands of the State, by means of a national bank with State capital and exclusive monopoly; (6) Centralization of the means of communication and transport in the hands of the State; (7) Extension of factories and instruments of production owned by the State, the bringing into cultivation of waste-lands, and the improvement of the soil generally in accordance with a common plan; (8) Equal liability of all to labor. Establishment of industrial armies, especially for agriculture; (9) Combination of agriculture with manufacturing industries; gradual abolition of the distinction between town and country, by a more equable distribution of the population over the country; (10) Free education for all children in public schools. Abolition of children's factory labor in its present form. Combination of education with industrial production, etc., etc.

When, in the course of development, class distinctions have disappeared, and all production has been concentrated in the hands of a vast association of the whole nation, the public power will lose its political character. Political power, properly so called, is merely the organized power of one class for oppressing another. If the proletariat during its contest with the bourgeoisie is compelled by force of circumstances, to organize itself as a class, if, by means of a revolution, it makes itself the ruling class, and, as such, sweeps away by force the old conditions of production, then it will, along with these conditions, have swept away the conditions for the existence of class antagonisms and of classes generally, and will thereby have abolished its own supremacy as a class.

In place of the old bourgeois society, with its classes and class antagonisms, we shall have an association, in which the free development of each is the condition for the free development of all. . . .

In short, the Communists everywhere support every revolutionary movement against the existing social and political order of things.

In all these movements they bring to the front, as the leading question in each, the property question, no matter what its degree of development at the time.

Finally, they labor everywhere for the union and agreement of the democratic parties of all countries.

The Communists disdain to conceal their views and aims. They openly declare that their ends can be attained only by the forcible overthrow of all existing social conditions. Let the ruling classes tremble at the Communistic revolution. The proletarians have nothing to lose but their chains. They have a world to win.

Working men of all countries, unite!

Study Questions

1. What do the authors of *The Communist Manifesto* mean by the terms "revolution" and "class struggle" in both a practical as well as a theoretical sense?
2. According to Marx and Engels, why is the destruction of the bourgeoisie inevitable?
3. How is *The Communist Manifesto* clearly a product of the nineteenth century?
4. What kind of future for humanity does the treatise envision, and why was this vision so appealing to the working classes in the late nineteenth and early twentieth centuries?

Gobineau's *Essay on the Inequality of the Human Races*

Arthur de Gobineau (1816–1882), known as the "father of modern racism," framed his theory of racial inequality in the mid-nineteenth century. A frightened Gobineau observed the changes occurring in Europe at that time. In the name of democratic liberalism, Europeans were rejecting true nobility and placing political power into what Gobineau considered the irresponsible hands of the **bourgeoisie** and **proletariat**. Gobineau's *Essay on the Inequality of the Human Races* reflects a profound pessimism in the author's attitude toward race and class and expresses, in fact, his own dire sense of racist class-consciousness. Published between 1853 and 1855, Gobineau's most famous work is founded on the belief that there are innate inequalities among the races, a sentiment similarly detailed with catastrophic consequences in Adolf Hitler's *Mein Kampf.*

Human history is like an immense tapestry. The earth is the frame over which it is stretched. The successive centuries are the tireless weavers. As soon as they are born they immediately seize the shuttle and operate it on the frame, working at it until they die. The broad fabric thus goes on growing beneath their busy fingers. The two most inferior varieties of the human species, the black and yellow races, are the crude foundation, the cotton and wool, which the secondary families of the white race make supple by adding their silk; while the Aryan group, circling its finer threads through the noble generations, designs on its surface a dazzling masterpiece of arabesques in silver and gold. . . .

The birth, growth and decline of a society and its civilization involve factors which go far beyond the normal concerns of historians. These factors have nothing to do, fundamentally, with human passions or popular movements, materials too fragile to figure in developments of such long duration. The most decisive influences in this are the different kinds of intelligence allotted to different races and racial mixtures. These are still seen only in those manifestations which are most basic, innate and pure, most emancipated from the authority of free will, in short,

M. Biddiss, ed., *Gobineau: Selected Political Writings* (London: Jonathan Cape, 1970), 37–42, 162–76, passim. Reprinted with permission.

in those which are the most fateful, those over which individuals and nations are completely powerless to exercise control. Thus, transcending any transitory or voluntary action of either an individual or a nation, these fundamental determining factors in life operate with imperturbable independence and impassiveness. In the sphere of total freedom where they operate and interact no caprice of an individual or nation brings about any fortuitous result. . . .

A society does not, in the first instance, depend on man for its creation or preservation, and thus there is nothing for which he can be held responsible. It therefore carries with it no morality. A society is not, in itself, virtuous or vicious, wise or foolish: it simply exists. The foundation of a society does not depend on any individual or collective action. The environmental conditions to which it must be subjected before reaching any positive kind of existence must be rich in the necessary ethnic elements, just as certain bodies (to use again a comparison which constantly springs to mind) easily absorb electrical energy and can effectively distribute it, while others have difficulty in absorbing it and have even more difficulty in making it radiate around them. It is not the will of a monarch or his subjects which modifies the essence of a society: it is, by virtue of the same laws, a subsequent ethnic mixture. A society, then, envelops its component nations as the sky envelops the earth, and this sky, which neither the fumes of swamps nor the flames of volcanoes can reach, is still, in its serenity, the perfect image of those societies which could not be immediately affected by the upsets of their constituent parts, but are, however, insidiously and inevitably influenced by them.

These racial elements impose their modes of existence on nations, circumscribing them within limits from which, like blind slaves, they do not even wish to escape, although they would not even have the strength to do so. They dictate their laws, inspire their wishes, control their sympathies and stir up their hatreds and contempt. Always subject to ethnic influence, they create local triumphs by this immediate means; by the same means they implant the germ of national disasters. Eventually, such a situation is reached that only a new ethnic development can prevent total catastrophe.

They govern individuals as rigorously as nations. In giving them (and, it is vital to note, without reservations) the benefits of a morality which they nevertheless control, they mold and shape their minds, in some way, from the moment they are born, and, while indicating certain courses, they shut off others in such a manner that they do not even allow their conclusions to be seen.

Thus, before attempting to write the history of a particular country and to explain the problems involved in such a task, it is indispensable to examine and gain full familiarity with the sources and nature of the society of which the country in question is only a small part. One must study its constituent elements, the changes it has undergone, the causes of these changes, and the ethnic state produced by the successive racial intermixtures which have taken place within it. . . .

Omnipresent and everlasting racial intermixture—this is the clearest, most inevitable and lasting product of our great societies and powerful civilizations; the more extensive the territory and the more powerful the will to conquer, the greater will be the degree to which the resultant wave of ethnic intermixture with other originally foreign elements will effect transformations in the nature of both parties. . . .

Under their influence Europe had seen the disappearance into complete submersion of the yellow essence and of white purity. Through the strongly Semitized intermediary of the Greeks, reinforced by Roman colonization, its peoples gradually became more and more influenced by the closest regions of Asia. The latter, in their turn, were influenced by Europe; for while the European groups were becoming marked by an Oriental influence in Spain, southern France, Italy and Illyria, those of Asia and Africa were undergoing the influence of the Roman West on the Propontis and in Anatolia, Arabia and Egypt. When this intermixture had taken place, the influence of the Slavs and Celts, having been combined with that of the Greeks and been brought to its logical conclusion, could be carried no further. The civilization of Rome, the sixth [civilization] in history and whose overriding purpose was to concentrate and fuse the ethnic principles of the Western world, did not have the strength for any independent activity after the third century.

In order to enlarge the area in which so many multitudes were already intermixing, intervention by a very powerful ethnic agent was necessary—the product, for example, of a new union between the best human variety and races already civilized. In short, there was needed an infusion of Aryans into the social center best situated to influence the rest of the world—for without this all the sporadic kinds of life which were scattered over the earth would have continued to be completely isolated from each other.

The Germans thus appeared in the midst of Roman society. At the same time they occupied the extreme north-west of Europe, which gradually became the pivot of their influence. Successive unions with the Celts and Slavs, and with the Gallo-Roman peoples, increased their strength without prejudicing too seriously their natural instinct for initiative. Thus modern society was born and resolutely devoted itself to fostering and developing the aggregative work of its predecessors. . . .

I said above that [the life of humanity] was comparable to a vast tapestry composed of different textiles, displaying the most variegated and distorted patterns; it is even more comparable to a chain of mountains with several peaks representing civilizations, and with the geological composition of these peaks representing the different mixtures produced by the multiple combinations of the three great primordial divisions of the human species and their secondary blends. Such is the fruit of human striving. All that serves civilization acts on society; all that attracts it extends it; all which extends it carries it further geographically; and the last stage of this development is the addition or removal of several more Negroes or Finns at the heart of the already amalgamated masses. Let us take it as axiomatic that the ultimate aim of the toil and suffering, the pleasures and triumphs of humanity is to attain, one day, supreme unity. Once this is accepted everything else we should know follows naturally.

Viewed abstractly, the white race has disappeared from the face of the earth. It has lived through the age of the gods, when it was absolutely pure; the age of heroes, when intermixture was restricted in strength and scope; and the age of nobility, in which its capacities, though still considerable, could not be replenished from barren sources. It then progressed more or less immediately (varying according to the particular areas concerned) towards the definitive blending of all its principles as a result of its heterogeneous intermixture. Consequently, it is now only represented by hybrids; those who occupy the territory of the first mixed societies have naturally had most time and opportunity to become degenerate. As to the masses in western Europe and North America who now represent the last possible form of culture, they still seem quite vigorous, and are in fact less degenerate than the inhabitants of Campania, Susiana and Yemen. This relative superiority, however, constantly tends to disappear; the last remaining Aryan blood, already diluted so many times, and which alone supports the edifice of our society, moves closer each day towards total absorption.

When this happens the age of unity will begin. The white principle, held in check in each individual person, will be one against two in relation to its rivals—a sad proportion which would be enough to paralyze it almost completely. It is even more deplorable when we reflect that this state of fusion, far from being the result of the direct union of the three main racial types in their pure state, will be only the useless residue of an infinite series of mixtures, and consequently of grave blemishes. This will lead eventually to mediocrity in all fields: mediocrity of physical strength, mediocrity of beauty, mediocrity of intellectual capacities—we could almost say, to nothingness. Everyone will share this sad heritage in equal measure; there is no reason why one man should have a larger share than another; and, just as in the Polynesian islands, where the Malayan half-breeds equally represent a type whose initial composition has never been disturbed by any infusion of new racial blood, men will all resemble each other. Their size, features and bodily habits will all be the same. They will have the same amount of physical strength, the same instinctive urges and abilities; and their general level will be revoltingly low.

Nations, or rather human herds, oppressed beneath a mournful somnolence, will thenceforth live benumbed in their nullity, like the buffalo grazing in the stagnant waters of the Pontine marshes. Perhaps they will think themselves the wisest and cleverest beings that ever existed; as for ourselves, when we contemplate the great monuments of Egypt and India, which we would be so incapable of imitating, are we not convinced that our very impotence proves our superiority? Our shameful descendants will have no difficulty in finding some similar argument which will justify them giving us their pity and priding themselves on their barbarity. Disdainfully pointing to the tottering ruins of our last remaining buildings, they will say "That was how our ancestors so senselessly employed their strength. What can we do with this useless legacy?" The legacy we leave will indeed be useless to them; for vigorous nature will have regained universal domination over the earth, and humanity will no longer be its master, but simply a guest, like the inhabitants of the forests and the waters.

Nor will this sad situation last for a long time; for one side effect of indefinite racial intermixture is a progressive reduction in population. When we look at ancient civilizations we see that the world used to be far more densely populated than it is today. China has never had less inhabitants than at present; Central Asia used to be a veritable ant-nest and is now quite deserted. Scythia, according to **Herodotus**, was teeming with nations, but Russia is now a desert. Germany is well-populated, but was not less so in the second, fourth and fifth centuries, when it endlessly threw hordes of warriors at the Roman world, followed by their wives and children. France and England seem to us neither empty nor uncultivated; but Gaul and Great Britain were not more so at the time of the Cymric emigrations. Spain and Italy no longer have a quarter of the people who covered their lands in antiquity. Greece, Egypt, Syria, Asia Minor and Mesopotamia were overflowing with people, and towns were as numerous as ears of corn in a field; they are now like a deathly wilderness. And India, although still populous, is in this respect only the shadow of its former self. West Africa, which nourished Europe and where so many colonial powers displayed their splendors, no longer contains anything but the scattered tents of nomads and the moribund towns of a few merchants. The rest of Africa similarly languishes everywhere that the Europeans and Moslems brought what the former call progress and the latter faith, and it is only the interior of these lands, where scarcely anyone has penetrated, which still retains a compact nucleus of people. But this will not last. As for America, Europe is pouring into it what blood it has; but, if one is enriched, the other is impoverished. Thus, humanity is disappearing at the same time that it is declining.

We cannot accurately calculate the number of centuries which still separate us from final obliteration. However, it is possible to hazard a rough estimate. The Aryans and, with greater reason, the rest of the white species, had lost their complete purity by the time of Christ. If we accept that the world was created in its present state six or seven thousand years before Christ, then we see that this period was enough to wither the seed of the visible principles governing societies. When this period was over, the forces of degeneration had already taken control of the world. Just as the white race had become absorbed by the two inferior races so as to lose its true purity, the latter had undergone corresponding changes, particularly extreme in the case of the yellow race. In the eighteen hundred years which have since elapsed, the process of intermixture, although unrelenting and moving irrevocably towards its ultimate triumph, has nevertheless not been as directly effective. But, besides its influence on the future, it has greatly increased ethnic intermixture within all societies and accordingly has hastened the ultimate realization of total amalgamation. This time has thus certainly not been wasted, and, since it has laid the groundwork for future developments, and since, moreover, the three racial varieties have lost their essential purity, it would not be an exaggeration to estimate that total amalgamation will be effected in a little less time than we needed for its preparatory stages to reach their present point of development. It would thus be tempting to assign to man's domination of the earth a total of twelve to fourteen thousand years, divided into two periods: the first, which has passed, will have seen and possessed the youth, vigor and intellectual greatness of humanity; the other, which has already begun, will see its waning and inevitable decline.

I do not know whether we would be entitled to regard as the end of the world the less distant age when humanity will not quite have disappeared but will have completely degenerated—a time before that age of death when the earth, silent and without us, will continue to describe its impassive orbits in space. Nor would it be easy to show sympathy and interest in the destinies of people deprived of strength, beauty and intelligence, if one did not remember that they will at least retain their religious faith, their last link with, and sole reminder of, the precious heritage of better days.

But even religion has not promised eternity. Science, however, while revealing our beginnings, has seemed to assure us that we must also reach an end. There is thus no reason to be surprised or moved at discovering yet another confirmation of what is already an undeniable fact. What is truly sad is not death itself but the certainty of our meeting it as degraded beings. And perhaps even that shame reserved for our descendants might leave us unmoved, if we did not feel, and secretly fear, that the rapacious hands of destiny are already upon us.

Study Questions

1. How does Gobineau justify his theory and views of racial superiority?
2. What is Gobineau's outlook on the nature of society, and how did this view of society influence the development of his ideas on race relations?
3. What outcomes does the author predict will occur when people from different classes and race intermingle?
4. Explain how the success of Western imperialism in the nineteenth century contributed to fostering the attitudes of racial and ethnic superiority.

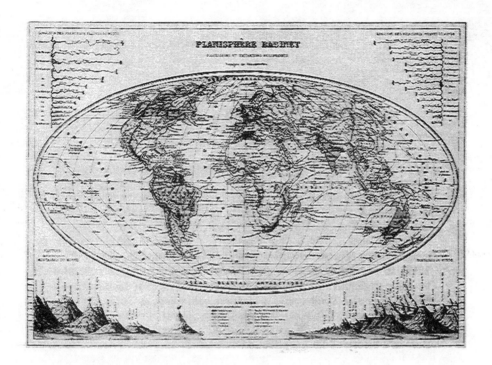

Babinet's Planisphere Projection Map, dated 1860

It is estimated that in 1885 not more than six million square miles, or approximately one-ninth of the earth's surface, had been properly surveyed. Instrumental land surveys were extremely expensive, so parochial attitudes prevailed among nations and mapmakers. Vast lands inhabited by millions of people remained virtually unknown territories. Inexact knowledge of the earth did not, however, forestall cartographers from producing numerous world atlases during the nineteenth century. In this era of Western imperialism the shapes of the world's land masses were well known, but much of the topography—indeed, most of it beyond the great landmarks such as mountains, and rivers—was a mystery. In fact, scientific global cartography did not reach maturity until about 1890. Perhaps as a consequence of Western expansion and "New Imperialism," European and American cartographers thought in grand terms. *Nouveaux Atlas de Géographie Moderne Physique et Politique* of 1860 includes a typical representation of the world. Produced under the auspices of the French Ministry of Education and Culture for use in public schools, the Babinet planisphere projection exhibits many features of other nineteenth-century world maps. A color wash is used to indicate the extension of Western political influence around the world, while the stereographic projection continues the age-old tradition of distorting the sizes and shapes of continents. Major voyages of discovery and exploration are also detailed, which further emphasizes the mapmaker's Eurocentricism. Additional information is projected in the plate by the inclusion of principle rivers and mountains. Like some other parts of the world, the interior of Africa—the exploration and exploitation of which would occupy many European states throughout the second half of the nineteenth century—is virtually terra incognita.

235

Charles Darwin's *Origin of Species*

The revolution in science that began in the sixteenth century continued to flourish in succeeding centuries. As the processes of modernization took firm root in the West, tremendous advances were made not only in astronomy, physics, and mechanics, but also in chemistry, botany, and biology. The sensational *On the Origin of Species by Means of Natural Selection,* published in England in 1859, combined many new insights from diverse fields of inquiry. In it, Charles Darwin (1809–1882) formulated a view of the natural world that differed radically from the traditional perspective held by early nineteenth-century Europeans. It is still sometimes considered controversial. Scientists like **Lyell, Lamarck, Wallace**—the man who almost simultaneously arrived at the same conclusions as Darwin—helped pave the way for Darwin's theory of natural selection, known as "survival of the fittest." In fact, Charles Darwin did not originate the theory of evolution or the idea of the mutability of species; but it was he who provided a wealth of evidence to support these hypotheses and proposed the notion of natural selection to account for it. To many of his contemporaries, Darwin seemed persuasive when others were not because the evidence he amassed was empirical and the arguments he advanced were logical.

Nothing at first can appear more difficult to believe than that the more complex organs and instincts have been perfected, not by means superior to though analogous with, human reason, but by the accumulation of innumerable slight variations, each good for the individual possessor. Nevertheless, this difficulty, though appearing to our imagination insuperably great cannot be considered real if we admit the following propositions, namely, that all parts of the organization and instincts offer, at least, individual differences—that there is a struggle for existence leading to the preservation of profitable deviations of structure or instinct—and, lastly, that gradations in the state of perfection of each organ may have existed, each good of its kind. The truth of these propositions cannot, I think, be disputed.

It is, no doubt, extremely difficult even to conjecture by what gradations many structures have been perfected, more especially amongst broken and failing

Charles Darwin, *The Origin of Species* (London: John Murray, 1859), passim.

groups of organic beings, which have suffered much extinction; but we see so many strange gradations in nature, that we ought to be extremely cautious in saying that any organ or instinct, or any whole structure, could not have arrived at its present state by many graduated steps. There are, it must be admitted, cases of special difficulty opposed to the theory of natural selection; . . . but I have attempted to show how these difficulties can be mastered. . . .

Under domestication we see much variability, caused, or at least excited, by changed conditions of life; but often in so obscure a manner, that we are tempted to consider the variations as spontaneous. Variability is governed by many complex laws,—by correlated growth, compensation, the increased use and disuse of parts, and the definite action of the surrounding conditions. There is much difficulty in ascertaining how largely our domestic productions have been modified; but we may safely infer that the amount has been large, and that modifications can be inherited for long periods. As long as the conditions of life remain the same, we have reason to believe that a modification, which has already been inherited for many generations, may continue to be inherited for an almost infinite number of generations. On the other hand, we have evidence that variability when it has once come into play, does not cease under domestication for a very long period; nor do we know that it ever ceases, for new varieties are still occasionally produced by our oldest domesticated productions. . . .

There is no reason why the principles which have acted so efficiently under domestication should not have acted under nature. In the survival of favored individuals and races, during the constantly-recurrent struggle for Existence, we see a powerful and ever-acting form of Selection. The struggle for existence inevitably follows from the high geometrical ratio of increase which is common to all organic beings. This high rate of increase is proved by calculation,—by the rapid increase of many animals and plants during a succession of peculiar seasons, and when naturalized in new countries. More individuals are born than can possibly survive. A grain in the balance may determine which individuals shall live and which shall die,—which variety or species shall increase in number, and which shall decrease, or finally become extinct. As the individuals of the same species come in all respects into the closest competition with each other, the struggle will generally be most severe between them; it will be almost equally severe between the varieties of the same species, and next in severity between the species of the same genus. On the other hand the struggle will often be severe between beings remote in the scale of nature. The slightest advantage in certain individuals, at any age or during any season, over those with which they come into competition, or better adaptation in however slight a degree to the surrounding physical conditions, will, in the long run, turn the balance.

With animals having separated sexes, there will be in most cases a struggle between the males for the possession of the females. The most vigorous males, or those which have most successfully struggled with their conditions of life, will generally leave most progeny. But success will often depend on the males having special weapons, or means of defence, or charms; and a slight advantage will lead to victory. . . .

If then, animals and plants do vary, let it be ever so slightly or slowly, why should not variations or individual differences, which are in any way beneficial, be preserved and accumulated through natural selection, or the survival of the fittest? If man can by patience select variations useful to him, why, under changing and complex conditions of life, should not variations useful to nature's living products often arise, and be preserved or selected? What limit can be put to this power, acting during long ages and rigidly scrutinising the whole constitution, structure, and habits of each creature,—favoring the good and rejecting the bad? I can see no limit to this power, in slowly and beautifully adapting each form to the most complex relations of life. The theory of natural selection, even if we look no farther than this, seems to be in the highest degree probable. . . .

On the view that species are only strongly marked and permanent varieties, and that each species first existed as a variety, we can see why it is that no line of demarcation can be drawn between species, commonly supposed to have been produced by special acts of creation, and varieties which are acknowledged to have been produced by secondary laws. On this same view we can understand how it is that in a region where many species of a genus have been produced, and where they now flourish, these same species should present many varieties; for where the manufactory of species has been active, we might expect, as a general rule, to find it still in action; and this is the case if varieties have incipient species. Moreover, the species of the larger genera, which afford the greater number of varieties or incipient species, retain to a certain degree the character of varieties; for they differ from each other by a less amount of difference than do the species of smaller genera. The closely allied species also of the larger genera apparently have restricted ranges, and in their affinities they are clustered in little groups round other species—in both respects resembling varieties. These are strange relations on the view that each species was independently created, but are intelligible if each existed first as a variety. . . .

As natural selection acts solely by accumulating slight, successive, favorable variations, it can produce no great or sudden modification; it can act only by short and slow steps. . . .

We can see why throughout nature the same general end is gained by an almost infinite diversity of means, for every peculiarity when once acquired is long inherited, and structures already modified in many different ways have to be adapted for the same general purpose. We can, in short, see why nature is prodigal in variety, though niggard in innovation. But why this should be a natural law if each species has been independently created, man can explain. . . .

If we admit that the geological record is imperfect to an extreme degree, then the facts, which the record does give, strongly support the theory of descent with modification. New species have come on the stage slowly and at successive intervals; and the amount of change, after equal intervals of time, is widely different in different groups. The extinction of species and of whole groups of species, which has played so conspicuous a part in the history of the organic world, almost inevitably follows from the principle of natural selection; for old forms are supplanted by new and improved forms. Neither single species nor groups of species reappear when the chain of ordinary generation is once broken. The gradual diffusion of dominant forms, with the slow modification of their descendants, causes the forms of life, after long intervals of time, to appear as if they had changed simultaneously throughout the world. The fact of the fossil remains of each formation being in some degree intermediate in character between the fossils in the formations above and below, is simply explained by their intermediate position in the chain of descent. . . .

The similar framework of bones in the hand of a man, wing of a bat, fin of the porpoise, and leg of the horse,—the same number of vertebrae forming the neck of the giraffe and of the elephant,—and innumerable other such facts, at once explain themselves on the theory of descent with slow and slight successive modifications. The similarity of pattern in the wing and in the leg of a bat, though used for such different purpose—in the jaws and legs of a crab—in the petals, stamens, and pistils of a flower, is likewise, to a large extent, intelligible on the view of the gradual modification of parts or organs, which were aboriginally alike in an early progenitor in each of these classes. On the principle of successive variations not always supervening at an early age, and being inherited at a corresponding not early period of life, we clearly see why the embryos of mammals, birds, reptiles, and fishes should be so closely similar, and so unlike the adult forms. We may cease marvelling at the embryo of an air-breathing mammal or bird having branchial slits and arteries running in loops, like those of a fish which has to breathe the air dissolved in water by the aid of well-developed branchiae. . . .

I have now recapitulated the facts and considerations which have thoroughly convinced me that species have been modified, during a long course of descent. This has been effected chiefly through the natural selection of numerous successive, slight, favorable variations; aided in an important manner by the inherited effects of the use and disuse of parts; and in an unimportant manner, that is in relation to adaptive structures, whether past or present, by the direct action of external conditions, and by variations which seem to us in our ignorance to arise spontaneously. It appears that I formerly underrated the frequency and value of these latter forms of variation, as leading to permanent modifications of structure independently of natural selection. But as my conclusions have lately been much misrepresented, and it has been stated that I attribute the modification of species exclusively to natural selection, I may be permitted to remark that in the first edition of this work, and subsequently, I placed in a most conspicuous position—namely, at the close of the Introduction—the following words: "I am convinced that natural selection has been the main but not the exclusive means of modification." This has been of no avail. Great is the power of steady misrepresentation; but the history of science shows that fortunately this power does not long endure. . . .

I see no good reason why the views given in this volume should shock the religious feelings of anyone. It is satisfactory, as showing how transient such impressions are, to remember that the greatest discovery ever made by man, namely, the law of the attraction of gravity, was also attacked by **Leibnitz**, "as subversive of natural, and inferentially of revealed, religion." A celebrated author and divine has written to me that "he has gradually learnt to see that it is just as noble a conception of the Deity to believe that He created a few original forms capable of self-development into other and needful forms, as to believe that He required a fresh act of creation to supply the voids caused by the action of His laws. . . ."

Although I am fully convinced of the truth of the views given in this volume under the form of an abstract, I by no means expect to convince experienced naturalists whose minds are stocked with a multitude of facts all viewed, during a long course of years, from a point of view directly opposite to mine. It is so easy to hide our ignorance under such expressions as "the plan of creation," "unity of design," etc., and to think that we give an explanation when we only re-state a fact. Any one whose disposition leads him to attach more weight to unexplained difficulties than to the explanation of a certain number of facts will certainly reject the theory. A few naturalists, endowed with much flexibility of mind, and who have already begun to doubt the immutability of species, may be influenced by this volume; but I look with confidence to the future,—to young and rising naturalists, who will be able to view both sides of the question with impartiality. Whoever is led to believe that species are mutable will do good service by conscientiously expressing his conviction; for thus only can the load of prejudice by which this subject is overwhelmed be removed. . . .

Authors of the highest eminence seem to be fully satisfied with the view that each species has been independently created. To my mind it accords better with what we know of the laws impressed on matter by the Creator, that the production and extinction of the past and present inhabitants of the world should have been due to secondary causes, like those determining the birth and death of the individual. When I view all beings not as special creations, but as the lineal descendants of some few beings which lived long before the first bed of the Cambrian system was deposited, they seem to me to become ennobled. Judging from the past, we may safely infer that not one living species will transmit its unaltered likeness to a distant futurity. And of the species now living very few will transmit progeny of any kind to a far distant futurity; for the manner in which all organic beings are grouped, shows that the greater number of species in each genus, and all the species in many genera, have left no descendants, but have become utterly extinct. We can so far take a prophetic glance into futurity as to foretell that it will be the common and widely-spread species, belonging to the larger and dominant groups within each class, which will ultimately prevail and procreate new and dominant species. As all the living forms of life are the lineal descendants of those which lived long before the Cambrian epoch, we may feel certain that the ordinary succession by generation has never once been broken, and that no cataclysm has desolated the whole world. Hence we may look with some confidence to a secure future of great length. And as natural selection works solely by and for the good of each being, all corporeal and mental endowments will tend to progress towards perfection.

It is interesting to contemplate a tangled bank, clothed with many plants of many kinds, with birds singing on the bushes, with various insects flitting about, and with worms crawling through the damp earth, and to reflect that these elaborately constructed forms, so different from each other, and dependent upon each other in so complex a manner, have all been produced by laws acting around us. These laws, taken in the largest sense, being Growth with Reproduction; Inheritance which is almost implied by reproduction; Variability from the indirect and direct action of the conditions of life, and from use and disuse; a Ration of Increase so high as to lead to a Struggle for Life, and as a consequence to Natural Selection, entailing Divergence of Character and the Extinction of less-improved forms. Thus, from the war of nature, from famine and death, the most exalted object which we are capable of conceiving, namely, the production of the higher animals, directly follows. There is grandeur in this view of life, with its several powers, having been originally breathed by the Creator into a few forms or into one; and that, whilst this planet has gone cycling on according to the fixed law of gravity, from so simple a beginning endless forms most beautiful and most wonderful have been, and are being evolved.

Study Questions

1. How does Darwin use the notion of "survival of the fittest" to support the theory of natural selection?
2. How did people of the late nineteenth century use (or perhaps misuse) Darwin's scientific theories to explain and justify the sociopolitical and economic conditions of their time?
3. Why did Darwin's theories disturb nineteenth-century religious conservatives, and how does the author go out of his way in an attempt to mollify any criticisms that might be leveled against him?
4. How did Darwin's scientific ideas change the ways people conceived the world and the universe?

Reading 42

Pope Leo XIII's *Rerum Novarum*

Pope Leo XIII (1878–1903), known popularly as "the workingman's pope," expressed the sincere desire of many in the hierarchy of the Catholic church to come to terms with the vast social and economic changes occurring in the West during the nineteenth century. His encyclical *Rerum Novarum,* "Of New Things," issued on 15 May 1891, reflects in particular the Church's concern for social justice and places the pope himself on the side of labor in the fast-paced industrialization of the West. Pope Leo condemns socialism as a barren remedy for the evil conditions prompted by economic modernization, rejects the Marxist theory of the inevitability of class warfare, and insists that religion forbids employers to overburden workers. The pope also makes a point of favoring the rights of both employers and workers to organize themselves and therefore supports the concept of the labor union. Although this papal bull was attacked by the political right as too subversive and criticized by those on the left as too timid, the pronouncement continued to exert great influence throughout Europe in succeeding decades.

It is not surprising that the spirit of revolutionary change, which has long been predominant in the nations of the world, should have passed beyond politics and made its influence felt in the cognate field of practical economy. The elements of a conflict are unmistakable: the growth of industry, and the surprising discoveries of science; the changed relations of masters and workmen; the enormous fortunes of individuals and the poverty of the masses; the increased self-reliance and the closer mutual combination of the working population; and, finally, a general moral deterioration. The momentous seriousness of the present state of things just now fills every mind with painful apprehension; wise men discuss it; practical men propose schemes; popular meetings, legislatures, and sovereign princes, all are occupied with it—and there is nothing which has a deeper hold on public attention. . . .

Now we have thought it useful to speak on the Condition of Labor. It is a matter on which we have touched once or twice already. But in this letter the

Pope Leo XIII, *Rerum Novarum* (New York: The Paulist Press, 1939), 3–5, 8–13, 15, 19–20, 23–31, 36–37, passim.

responsibility of the apostolic office urges Us to treat the question expressly and at length, in order that there may be no mistake as to the principles which truth and justice dictate for its settlement. The discussion is not easy, nor is it free from danger. It is not easy to define the relative rights and the mutual duties of the wealthy and of the poor, of capital and of labor. And the danger lies in this, that crafty agitators constantly make use of these disputes to pervert men's judgments and to stir up the people to sedition. . . .

Public institutions and the laws have repudiated the ancient [Christian] religion. Hence by degrees it has come to pass that working men have been given over, isolated and defenseless, to the callousness of employers and the greed of unrestrained competition. The evil has been increased by rapacious usury, which, although more than once condemned by the Church, is nevertheless, under a different form but with the same guilt, still practiced by avaricious and grasping men. And to this must be added the custom of working by contract, and the concentration of so many branches of trade in the hands of a few individuals, so that a small number of very rich men have been able to lay upon the masses of the poor a yoke little better than slavery itself.

To remedy these evils the Socialists, working on the poor man's envy of the rich, endeavor to destroy private property, and maintain that individual possessions should become the common property of all, to be administered by the State or by municipal bodies. . . .

It is surely undeniable that, when a man engages in remunerative labor, the very reason and motive of his work is to obtain property, and to hold it as his own private possession. If one man hires out to another his strength or his industry, he does this for the purpose of receiving in return what is necessary for food and living; he thereby expressly proposes to acquire a full and real right, not only to the remuneration, but also to the disposal of that remuneration as he pleases. Thus, if he lives sparingly, saves money, and invests his savings, for greater security, in land, the land in such a case is only his wages in another form; and, consequently, a working man's little estate thus purchased should be as completely at his own disposal as the wages he receives for his labor. But it is precisely in this power of disposal that ownership consists, whether the property be land or movable goods. The Socialists, therefore, in endeavoring to transfer the possessions of individuals to the community, strike at the interests of every wage earner, for they deprive him of the liberty of disposing of his wages, and thus of all hope and possibility of increasing his stock and of bettering his condition in life.

What is of still greater importance, however, is that the remedy they propose is manifestly against justice. Every man has by nature the right to possess property as his own. . . .

It is clear that the main tenet of Socialism, the community of goods, must be utterly rejected; for it would injure those whom it is intended to benefit, it would be contrary to the natural rights of mankind, and it would introduce confusion, and disorder into the commonwealth. Our first and most fundamental principle, therefore, when we undertake to alleviate the condition of the masses, must be the inviolability of private property. . . .

Let it be laid down, in the first place, that humanity must remain as it is. It is impossible to reduce human society to a level. The Socialists may do their utmost, but all striving against nature is vain. There naturally exists among mankind innumerable differences of the most important kind; people differ in capability, in diligence, in health, and in strength; and unequal fortune is a necessary result of inequality in condition. Such inequality is far from being disadvantageous either to individuals or to the community; social and public life can only go on by the help of various kinds of capacity and the playing of many parts, and each man, as a rule, chooses the part which peculiarly suits his case. As regards bodily labor, even had man never fallen from the state of innocence, he would not have been wholly unoccupied; but that which would then have been his free choice, his delight, became afterwards compulsory, and the painful expiation of his sin. "Cursed be the earth in your work; in your labor you shall eat of it all the days of your life" [Genesis 3:17]. In like manner, the other pains and hardships of life will have no end or cessation on this earth; for the consequences of sin are bitter and hard to bear, and they must be with man as long as life lasts. To suffer and endure, therefore, is the lot of humanity; let men try as they may, no strength and no artifice will ever succeed in banishing from human life the ills and troubles which beset it. If any there are who pretend differently—who hold out to a hard-pressed people freedom from pain and trouble, undisturbed repose, and constant enjoyment—they cheat the people and impose upon them, and their lying promises will only make the evil worse than before. There's nothing more useful than to look at the world as it really is—and at the same time look elsewhere for a remedy to its troubles.

The great mistake that is made in the matter now under consideration, is to possess oneself of the idea that class is naturally hostile to class; that rich and poor are intended by nature to live at war with one another. So irrational and so false is this view, that the exact contrary is the truth. Just as the symmetry of the human body is the result of the disposition of the members of the body, so in a State it is ordained by nature that these two classes should exist in harmony and agreement, and should, as it were, fit into one another, to maintain the equilibrium of the body politic. . . . [The] rich must religiously refrain from cutting down the workman's earning, either by force, fraud, or by usurious dealing; and with the more reason because the poor man is weak and unprotected, and because his slender means should be sacred in proportion to their scantiness.

Were such precepts carefully obeyed and followed would not strife die out and cease? . . .

It cannot, however, be doubted that to attain the purpose of which We treat, not only the Church, but all human means must conspire. All who are concerned in the matter must be of one mind and must act together. It is in this, as in the Providence which governs the world; results do not happen save where all the causes cooperate. . . .

The first duty, therefore, of the rulers of the State should be to make sure that the laws and institutions, the general character and administration of the commonwealth, shall be such as to produce of themselves public well-being and private prosperity. This is the proper office of wise statesmanship and the work of the heads of the State. Now a State chiefly prospers and flourishes by morality, well-regulated family life, by respect for religion and justice, by the moderation and equal distribution of public burdens, by the progress of the arts and of trade, by the abundant yield of the land—by everything which makes the citizens better and happier....

Rights must be religiously respected wherever they are found; and it is the duty of the public authority to prevent and punish injury, and to protect each one in the possession of his own....

It must be borne in mind that the chief thing to be secured is the safe-guarding, by legal enactment and policy, of private property. Most of all it is essential in these times of covetous greed, to keep the multitude within the line of duty; for all may justly strive to better their condition, yet neither justice nor the common good allows anyone to seize that which belongs to another, or, under the pretext of futile and ridiculous equality, to lay hands on other people's fortunes. It is most true that by far the larger part of the people who work prefer to improve themselves by honest labor rather than by doing wrong to others. But there are not a few who are imbued with bad principles and are anxious for revolutionary change, and whose great purpose it is to stir up tumult and bring about a policy of violence. The authority of the State should intervene to put restraint upon these disturbers, to save the workmen from their seditious arts, and to protect lawful owners from spoilation....

If we turn now to things exterior and corporal, the first concern of all is to save the poor workers from the cruelty of grasping speculators, who use human beings as mere instruments for making money. It is neither justice nor humanity so to grind men down with excessive labor as to stupefy their minds and wear out their bodies. Man's powers, like his general nature, are limited, and beyond such limits he can't go.... In regard to children, great care should be taken not to place them in workshops and factories until their bodies and minds are sufficiently ma-ture. For just as rough weather destroys the buds of spring, so too early an expe-rience of life's hard work blights the young promise of a child's powers, and makes any real education impossible. Women, again, are not suited to certain trades; for a woman is by nature fitted for home-work, and it is that which is best adapted at once to preserve her modesty, and to promote the good bringing up of children and the well-being of the family. As a general principle, it may be laid down, that a workman ought to have leisure and rest in proportion to the wear and tear of his strength; for the waste of strength must be repaired by the cessation of work....

We now approach a subject of very great importance and one on which, if extremes are to be avoided, right ideas are absolutely necessary. Wages, we are told, are fixed by free consent; and, therefore, the employer when he pays what was agreed upon, has done his part, and is not called upon for anything further. The only way, it is said, in which injustice could happen, would be if the master refused to pay the whole of the wages, or the workman would not complete the work undertaken; when this happens the State should intervene, to see that each obtains his own, but not under any other circumstances....

Let it be granted, then, that as a rule workman and employer should make free agreements, and in particular should freely agree as to wages; nevertheless, there is a dictate of nature more imperious and more ancient than any bargain between man and man, that the remuneration must be enough to support the wage-earner in reasonable and frugal comfort. If through necessity or fear of a worse evil, the workman accepts harder conditions because an employer or contractor will give him no better, he is the victim of force and injustice. . . .

If a workman's wages be sufficient to enable him to maintain himself, his wife, and his children in reasonable comfort, he will not find it difficult, if he is a sensible man, to study economy; and he will not fail, by cutting down expenses, to put by a little property. Nature and reason would urge him to do this. We have seen that this great labor question cannot be solved except by assuming as a principle that private ownership must be held sacred and inviolable. The law, therefore, should favor ownership, and its policy should be to induce as many people as possible to become owners.

Many excellent results will follow from this; and first of all, property will certainly become more equitably divided. For the effect of civil change and revolution has been to divide society into two widely different castes. On the one side there is the party which holds the power because it holds the wealth; which has in its grasp all labor and all trade; which manipulates for its own benefit and its own purposes all the sources of supply, and which is powerfully represented in the councils of the State itself. On the other side there is the needy and powerless multitude, sore and suffering, always ready for disturbance. If working people can be encouraged to look forward to obtaining a share in the land, the result will be that the gulf between vast wealth and deep poverty will be bridged over, and the two orders will be brought nearer together. Another consequence will be the great abundance of the fruits of the earth. Men always work harder and more readily when they work on that which is their own; nay, they learn to love the very soil which yields in response to the labor of their hands, not only to food to eat, but an abundance of the good things for themselves and those that are dear to them. It is evident how such a spirit of willing labor would add to the produce of the earth and to the wealth of the community. And a third advantage would arise from this: men would cling to the country in which they were born; for no one would exchange his country for foreign land if his own afforded him the means of living a tolerable and happy life. These three important benefits, however, can only be expected on the condition that a man's means be not drained and exhausted by excessive taxation. The right to possess private property is from nature, not from man; and the State has only right to regulate its use in the interests of the public good, but by no means to abolish it altogether. The State is, therefore, unjust and cruel, if, in the name of taxation, it deprives the private owner of more than is just.

In the first place—employers and workmen may themselves effect much in the matter of which We treat, by means of those institutions and organizations which afford opportune assistance to those in need, and which draw the two orders more closely together. Among these may be numerated: societies for mutual help;

various foundations established by private persons for providing for the workman, and for his widow or his orphans, in sudden calamity, in sickness, and in the event of death; and what are called "patronages," or institutions for the care of boys and girls, and also for those of more mature age. . . .

The experience of his own weakness urges man to call in help from without. We read in the pages of Holy Writ: "It is better that two should be together than one; for they have the advantage of their society. If one falls he shall be supported by the other. Woe to him that is alone, for when he falls he has none to lift him up" [Ecclesiastes 4:9–10]. And further: "A brother that is helped by his brother is like a strong city" [Proverbs 18:19]. It is this natural impulse which unites men in civil society; and it is this also which makes them band themselves together in associations of citizen with citizen; associations which, it is true, cannot be called societies in a complete sense, but are societies nevertheless. . . .

Particular societies, then, although they exist within the State, and are each a part of the State, nevertheless cannot be prohibited by the State absolutely and as such. For to enter into a "society" of this kind is the natural right of man; and the State must protect natural rights, not destroy them; and if it forbids its citizens to form associations, it contradicts the very principle of its own existence; for both they and it exist in virtue of the same principle, which is, the natural propensity of man to live in society. . . .

We have now laid before you, Venerable Brethren, who are the persons, and what are the means, by which this most difficult question must be solved. Every one must put his hand to work which falls to his share, and that at once and immediately, lest the evil which is already so great may by delay become absolutely beyond remedy. Those who rule the State must use the law and the institutions of the country; masters and rich men must remember their duty; the poor, whose interests are at stake, must make every lawful and proper effort; since religion alone, as We said at the beginning, can destroy the evil at its root, all men must be persuaded that the primary thing needful is to return to real Christianity, in the absence of which all the plans and devices of the wisest will be of little avail.

As far as regards the Church, its assistance will never be wanting, be the time or the occasion what it may; and it will intervene with great effect in proportion as its liberty of action is the more unfettered; let this be carefully noted by those whose office it is to provide for the public welfare. Every minister of holy religion must throw into the conflict all the energy of his mind, and all the strength of his endurance; with your authority, Venerable Brethren, and by your example, they must never cease to urge upon all men of every class, upon the high as well as the lowly, the gospel doctrines of Christian life; by every means in their power they must strive for the good of the people; and above all they must earnestly cherish in themselves, and try to arouse in others, charity, the mistress and queen of virtues. For the happy results we all long for must be chiefly brought about by the plenteous outpouring of charity; of that true Christian charity which is the fulfilling of the whole gospel law, which is always ready to sacrifice itself for other's sake, and which is man's surest antidote against worldly pride and immoderate love of self; that charity whose office is described and whole God-like features are drawn by the apostle St. Paul in these words: "Charity is patient, is kind, . . . seeks not her own, . . . suffers all things, . . . endures all things" [I Corinthians 13:4–7].

Study Questions

1. What societal ills are exposed in Pope Leo's *Rerum Novarum*?
2. On what grounds does the pope reject Marxism and socialism as viable remedies for the evils of nineteenth-century European society?
3. Why did the pope's remarks incite the anger of both conservatives and radicals?
4. How do the ideas expressed in this document fall in line with the venerable Western tradition of elevating the status of the individual at the expense of the masses?

Albert Robida's Demolition of the Old World

The pace of scientific progress in the West accelerated rapidly during the nineteenth century and this caused much speculation concerning the future of humanity and civilization. Renowned novelists such as H.G. Wells (1866–1946) wrote fantastic futuristic romances combining scientific projections and social idealism. From the early 1880s until his death in 1926, French novelist and illustrator Albert Robida exerted a significant influence on the futuristic literature of his times. He worked as the principal illustrator for the French magazine *La Caricature*. In his own books and articles, he provided his large audiences with artistic creations of the future world, including drawings and illustrations of fantastic devices and technologies. Robida's novels, including *Le Vigtième Siècle* set in 1952 and *Le Vie Electrique* placed in 1955, also brought his conception of the future to the public. In his "Demolition of the Old World," Robida takes a serious look at the contemporary world. The gothic palace, representing the old world, is being dismantled. As tradition and history are carted away to a museum, the old ideal is discarded along with other curiosities. The violent effects of industrialization are portrayed in the background. Above this woeful scene is a robotic figure with a T-square and electric light in hand.

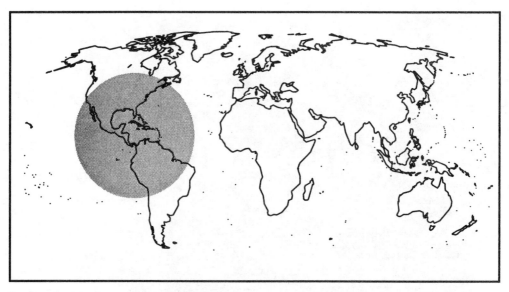

Brief Chronology for the Modern World

The Americas

1732–1799	George Washington
1756–1763	Seven Years' War (French-Indian Wars)
1773	Boston Tea Party
1775	Meeting of the Second Continental Congress and American Continental Army organized with Washington in command; beginning of American War of Independence
1776	American Declaration of Independence drawn up
1783	Treaty of Paris concludes American War of Independence
1803	France sells Louisiana to U.S.
1808–1824	Wars of independence in South America
1847	U.S. and Mexico at War
1850–1860	2.45 million immigrants into U.S.
1855	Henry Bessemer invents process for mass-producing steel
1855–1876	*La Reforma* period in Mexico
1859	Opening of Drake's oil well in Pennsylvania, U.S., marking beginning of commercial exploitation of petroleum
1861–1865	Abraham Lincoln serves as U.S. president; U.S. Civil War
1865–1877	Reconstruction Era in U.S.
1876	Alexander Graham Bell (1847–1922) invents the telephone
1876–1911	Dictatorship of Porfirio Diaz (1830–1915) in Mexico
1881	Foundation of the American Federation of Labor
1882	Thomas Edison (1847–1931) constructs first electricity generating and distributing station in New York
1886	Gottlieb Daimler (1834–1900) invents an internal combustion engine that uses gasoline
1891–1930	Republican government in Brazil
1893	U.S. makes Hawaii a protectorate
1896	Supreme Court of U.S. declares racial segregation to be constitutional
1898	Spanish-American War
1903	Wright Brothers make four sustained flights in first really successful airplane
1909	W. E. B. du Bois (1868–1963) and others attend conference out of which emerges in 1910 the National Association for the Advancement of Coloured People
1910–1917	Mexican Revolution
1917	U.S. enters World War I

All dates are C.E. and approximate unless otherwise indicated. It should be noted as well that chronologies are constantly being revised. Hence, there may be discrepancies between the dates listed above and those found in other textbooks and scholarly monographs. Throughout the text and in the Glossary, all dates are given in B.C.E. (Before the Common Era) and C.E. (the Common Era). Where there is no era designation C.E. may be assumed.

250

Thomas Jefferson's Declaration of Independence

One of America's most learned men and one of Virginia's wealthiest, Thomas Jefferson (1743–1826) was a moving force behind the American War of Independence. Although regarded a junior member of the **Continental Congress** of 1776, Jefferson's unassuming point of view and rhetorical style led to his being entrusted with the writing of the Declaration of Independence. Focusing on both general principles and particular grievances, this important document of American history later influenced French revolutionaries. When approached by **General Lafayette** and others for counsel, Jefferson advised moderation rather than overt revolutionary activity, even though he himself was a true revolutionary. The text of the Declaration printed below is Jefferson's original version from the summer of 1776 and includes Congress's final corrections. The parts stricken by the Congress appear in brackets, those inserted are shown in italics.

When, in the course of human events, it becomes necessary for one people to dissolve the political bands which have connected them with another, and to assume among the powers of the earth the separate and equal station to which the laws of nature and of nature's God entitle them, a decent respect to the opinions of mankind requires that they should declare the causes which impel them to the separation.

We hold these truths to be self-evident; that all men are created equal; that they are endowed by their creator with *certain* [inherent and] inalienable rights; that among these are life, liberty, and the pursuit of happiness; that to secure these rights, governments are instituted among men, deriving their just powers from the consent of the governed; that whenever any form of government becomes destructive of these ends, it is the right of the people to alter or to abolish it, and to institute new government, laying its foundation on such principles, and organizing its powers in such form, as to them shall seem most likely to effect their safety and happiness. Prudence, indeed, will dictate that governments long established should not be changed for light and transient causes; and accordingly all experience

Saul K. Padover, ed. *The Complete Jefferson* (New York: Tudor Publishing for Duell, Sloan, & Pearce, 1943), 28, 30–34.

hath shown that mankind are more disposed to suffer while evils are sufferable, than to right themselves by abolishing the forms to which they are accustomed. But when a long train of abuses and usurpations [begun at a distinguished period and] pursuing invariably the same object, evinces a design to reduce them under absolute despotism, it is their right, it is their duty to throw off such government, and to provide new guards for their future security. Such has been the patient sufferance of these Colonies; and such is now the necessity which constrains them to *alter* [expunge] their former systems of government. The history of the present King of Great Britain is a history of *repeated* [unremitting] injuries and usurpations, *all having* [among which appears no solitary fact to contradict the uniform tenor of the rest, but all have] in direct object the establishment of an absolute tyranny over these States. To prove this, let facts be submitted to a candid world [for the truth of which we pledge a faith yet unsullied by falsehood].

He has refused his assent to laws the most wholesome and necessary for the public good.

He has forbidden his governors to pass laws of immediate and pressing importance, unless suspended in their operation till his assent should be obtained; and, when so suspended, he has utterly neglected to attend to them.

He has refused to pass other laws for the accommodation of large districts of people, unless those people would relinquish the right of representation in the Legislature, a right inestimable to them, and formidable to tyrants only.

He has called together legislative bodies at places unusual, uncomfortable, and distant from the depository of their public records, for the sole purpose of fatiguing them into compliance with his measures.

He has dissolved representative houses repeatedly [and continually] for opposing with manly firmness his invasions on the rights of the people.

He has refused for a long time after such dissolutions to cause others to be elected, whereby the legislative powers, incapable of annihilation, have returned to the people at large for their exercise, the State remaining, in the meantime, exposed to all the dangers of invasion from without and convulsions within.

He has endeavored to prevent the population of these States; for that purpose obstructing the laws for naturalization of foreigners, refusing to pass others to encourage their migrations hither, and raising the conditions of new appropriations of lands.

He has *obstructed* [suffered] the administration of justice [totally to cease in some of these States] *by* refusing his assent to laws for establishing judiciary powers.

He has made [our] judges dependent on his will alone for the tenure of their offices, and the amount and payment of their salaries.

He has erected a multitude of new offices, [by a self-assumed power] and sent hither swarms of new officers to harass our people and eat out their substance.

He has kept among us in times of peace standing armies [and ships of war] without the consent of our Legislatures.

He has affected to render the military independent of, and superior to, the civil power.

He has combined with others to subject us to a jurisdiction foreign to our constitutions and unacknowledged by our laws, giving his assent to their acts of pretended legislation for quartering large bodies of armed troops among us; for protecting them by a mock trial from punishment for any murders which they should commit on the inhabitants of these States; for cutting off our trade with all parts of the world; for imposing taxes on us without our consent; for depriving us *in many cases* of the benefits of trial by jury; for transporting us beyond seas to be tried for pretended offences; for abolishing the free system of English laws in a neighboring province, establishing therein an arbitrary government, and enlarging its boundaries, so as to render it at once an example and fit instrument for introducing the same absolute rule into these *Colonies* [States]; for taking away our charters, abolishing our most valuable laws, and altering fundamentally the forms of our governments; for suspending our own Legislatures, and declaring themselves invested with power to legislate for us in all cases whatsoever.

He has abdicated government here by *declaring us out of his protection, and waging war against us* [withdrawing his governors, and declaring us out of his allegiance and protection].

He has plundered our seas, ravaged our coasts, burnt our towns, and destroyed the lives of our people.

He is at this time transporting large armies of foreign mercenaries to complete the works of death, desolation, and tyranny already begun with circumstances of cruelty and perfidy *scarcely paralleled in the most barbarous ages, and totally* unworthy of the head of a civilized nation.

He has constrained our fellow-citizens taken captive on the high seas to bear arms against their country, to become the executioners of their friends and brethren, or to fall themselves by their hands.

He has *excited domestic insurrection among us, and has* endeavored to bring on the inhabitants of our frontiers the merciless Indian savages, whose known rule of warfare is an undistinguished destruction of all ages, sexes, and conditions [of existence].

[He has incited treasonable insurrections of our fellow-citizens, with the allurements of forfeiture and confiscation of our property.

He has waged cruel war against human nature itself, violating its most sacred rights of life and liberty in the persons of a distant people who never offended him, captivating and carrying them into slavery in another hemisphere, or to incur miserable death in their transportation thither. This piratical warfare, the opprobrium of INFIDEL powers, is the warfare of the CHRISTIAN King of Great Britain. Determined to keep open a market where MEN should be bought and sold, he has prostituted his negative for suppressing every legislative attempt to prohibit or to restrain this execrable commerce. And that this assemblage of horrors might want no fact of distinguished die, he is now exciting those very people to rise in arms among us, and to purchase that liberty of which he has deprived them, by murdering the people on whom he also obtruded them: thus paying off former crimes committed against the LIBERTIES of one people with crimes which he urges them to commit against the LIVES of another.]

253

In every stage of these oppressions we have petitioned for redress in the most humble terms: our repeated petitions have been answered only by repeated injuries.

A Prince whose character is thus marked by every act which may define a tyrant is unfit to be the ruler of a *free* people [who mean to be free. Future ages will scarcely believe that the hardiness of one man adventured, within the short compass of twelve years only, to lay a foundation so broad and so undisguised for tyranny over a people fostered and fixed in principles of freedom].

Nor have we been wanting in attentions to our British brethren. We have warned them from time to time of attempts by their legislature to extend *an unwarrantable* [a] jurisdiction over *us* [these our States]. We have reminded them of the circumstances of our emigration and settlement here, [no one of which could warrant so strange a pretension: that these were effected at the expense of our own blood and treasure, unassisted by the wealth or the strength of Great Britain: that in constituting indeed our several forms of government, we had adopted one common king, thereby laying a foundation for perpetual league and amity with them: but that submission to their parliament was no part of our Constitution, nor ever in idea, if history may be credited: and,] we *have* appealed to their native justice and magnanimity *and we have conjured them by* [as well as to] the ties of our common kindred to disavow these usurpations which *would inevitably* [were likely to] interrupt our connection and correspondence. They too have been deaf to the voice of justice and of consanguinity, [and when occasions have been given them, by the regular course of their laws, of removing from their councils the disturbers of our harmony, they have, by their free election, reestablished them in power. At this very time too, they are permitting their chief magistrate to send over not only soldiers of our common blood, but Scotch and foreign mercenaries to invade and destroy us. These facts have given the last stab to agonizing affection, and manly spirit bids us to renounce forever these unfeeling brethren. We must endeavor to forget our former love for them, and hold them as we hold the rest of mankind, enemies in war, in peace friends. We might have been a free and a great people together; but a communication of grandeur and of freedom, it seems, is below their dignity. Be it so, since they will have it. The road to happiness and to glory is open to us too. We will tread it apart from them, and] *We must therefore* acquiesce in the necessity which denounces our [eternal] separation *and hold them as we hold the rest of mankind, enemies in war, in peace friends.*

We therefore the representatives of the United States of America in General Congress assembled, appealing to the supreme judge of the world for the rectitude of our intentions, do in the name, and by the authority of the good people of these Colonies, solemnly publish and declare, that these united Colonies are, and of right ought to be, free and independent States; that they are absolved from all allegiance to the British crown, and that all political connection between them and the state of Great Britain is, and ought to be, totally dissolved; [do in the name, and by the authority of the good people of these States reject and renounce all allegiance and subjection to the kings of Great Britain and all others who may hereafter claim by, through, or under them; we utterly dissolve all political connection which may heretofore have subsisted between us and the people or parliament of Great Britain: and finally we do assert and declare these Colonies to be free and independent States,] and that as free and independent States, they have full power to levy war, conclude peace, contract alliances, establish commerce, and to do all other acts and things which independent States may of right do.

And for the support of this declaration, with a firm reliance on the protection of divine providence, we mutually pledge to each other our lives, our fortunes, and our sacred honor.

Study Questions

1. In Jefferson's opinion, why are the American people declaring their independence from Great Britain?
2. What are the major charges leveled by Americans against the British king and—implicitly—against Parliament?
3. What may be discerned from this version of the document regarding Jefferson's personal views and Congress's outlook on the matters discussed in the Declaration of Independence?
4. How was Jefferson influenced by the philosophes of the Age of Enlightenment?

Reading 44

Simón Bolívar's Address to the Second National Congress of Venezuela

After the first voyages of discovery and exploration to the Americas, many imperial colonies were established in the New World. Spain's enormous holdings in the Americas were at first economically beneficial owing to the gold and silver bullion that flowed into the king's coffers. By the late eighteenth century, however, the Spanish Empire—though still impressive on maps—was only a shadow of what it had been at the time of King Philip II (1527–1598). In effect, Spain had become an anachronism, a relic of the past, her rulers having failed to acknowledge the birth of modern nationalism during the late eighteenth century. The empire was further weakened during the reign of the French emperor Napoleon (1769–1821) as many Spanish-American colonies sought liberation from the imperial yoke. Simón Bolívar (1783–1830), known as *El Liberador,* was a South American soldier and statesman of the first order. Bolívar was instrumental in bringing independence to New Granada (modern Colombia), where he served as president and military dictator in 1819. A few years later he helped obtain final victory and freedom for his native Venezuela as well as Peru. Despite exercising nearly dictatorial powers, his address of 1819 to the National Congress of Venezuela describes his plan for the kind of conservative government he thought best for the newly independent nation of Colombia.

America, in separating from the Spanish monarchy, found herself in a situation similar to that of the Roman Empire when its enormous framework fell to pieces in the midst of the ancient world. Each Roman division then formed an independent nation in keeping with its location or interests; but this situation differed from America's in that those members proceeded to re-establish their former associations. We, on the contrary, do not even retain the vestiges of our original being. We are not Europeans; we are not Indians; we are but a mixed species of aborigines and Spaniards. Americans by birth and Europeans by law, we find ourselves engaged in a dual conflict: we are disputing with the natives for titles of ownership,

Simon Bolivar, *Selected Writings,* ed. H. A. Bierck, Jr., trans. L. Bertrand (New York, Colonial Press, 1951), 175–77, 179–80, 184–85, 187–91.

and at the same time we are struggling to maintain ourselves in the country that gave us birth against the opposition of the invaders. Thus our position is most extraordinary and complicated. But there is more. As our role has always been strictly passive and our political existence nil, we find that our quest for liberty is now even more difficult of accomplishment; for we, having been placed in a state lower than slavery, had been robbed not only of our freedom but also of the right to exercise an active domestic tyranny. Permit me to explain this paradox....

Subject to the threefold yoke of ignorance, tyranny, and vice, the [Latin] American people have been unable to acquire knowledge, power, or [civic] virtue. The lessons we received and the models we studied, as pupils of such pernicious teachers, were most destructive. We have been ruled more by deceit than by force, and we have been degraded more by vice than by superstition. Slavery is the daughter of Darkness: an ignorant people is a blind instrument of its own destruction. Ambition and intrigue abuse the credulity and experience of men lacking all political, economic, and civic knowledge; they adopt pure illusion as reality; they take license for liberty, treachery for patriotism, and vengeance for justice. This situation is similar to that of the robust blind man who, beguiled by his strength, strides forward with all the assurance of one who can see, but, upon hitting every variety of obstacle, finds himself unable to retrace his steps.

If a people, perverted by their training, succeed in achieving their liberty, they will soon lose it, for it would be of no avail to endeavor to explain to them that happiness consists in the practice of virtue; that the rule of law is more powerful than the rule of tyrants, because, as the laws are more inflexible, everyone should submit to their beneficent austerity; that proper morals, and not force, are the bases of law; and that to practice justice is to practice liberty. Therefore, Legislators, your work is so much the more arduous, inasmuch as you have to reeducate men who have been corrupted by erroneous illusions and false incentives. Liberty, says Rousseau, is a succulent morsel, but one difficult to digest. Our weak fellow-citizens will have to strengthen their spirit greatly before they can digest the wholesome nutriment of freedom. Their limbs benumbed by chains, their sight dimmed by the darkness of dungeons, and their strength sapped by the pestilence of servitude, are they capable of marching toward the august temple of Liberty without faltering? Can they come near enough to bask in its brilliant rays and to breathe freely the pure air which reigns therein?

Legislators, meditate well before you choose. Forget not that you are to lay the political foundation for a newly born nation which can rise to the heights of greatness that Nature has marked out for it if you but proportion this foundation in keeping with the high plane that it aspires to attain. Unless your choice is based upon the peculiar tutelary experience of the Venezuelan people—a factor that should guide you in determining the nature and form of government you are about to adopt for the well-being of the people—and, I repeat, unless you happen upon the right type of government, the result of our reforms will again be slavery....

The more I admire the excellence of the federal Constitution of Venezuela, the more I am convinced of the impossibility of its application to our state. And, to my way of thinking, it is a marvel that its prototype in North America endures so successfully and has not been overthrown at the first sign of adversity or danger. Although the people of North America are a singular model of political virtue and moral rectitude; although that nation was cradled in liberty, reared on freedom, and maintained by liberty alone; and—I must reveal everything—although those people, so lacking in many respects, are unique in the history of mankind, it is a marvel, I repeat, that so weak and complicated a government as the federal system has managed to govern them in the difficult and trying circumstances of their past. But, regardless of the effectiveness of this form of government with respect to North America, I must say that it has never for a moment entered my mind to compare the position and character of two states as dissimilar as the English-American and the Spanish-American. Would it not be most difficult to apply to Spain the English system of political, civil, and religious liberty? Hence, it would be even more difficult to adapt to Venezuela the laws of North America. Does not **L'Esprit des lois** state that laws should be suited to the people for whom they are made; that it would be a major coincidence if those of one nation could be adapted to another; that laws must take into account the physical conditions of the country, climate, character of the land, location, size, and mode of living of the people; that they should be in keeping with the degree of liberty that the Constitution can sanction respecting the religion of the inhabitants, their inclinations, resources, number, commerce, habits, and customs? This is the code we must consult, not the code of Washington! . . .

We must never forget that the excellence of a government lies not in its theories, not in its form or mechanism, but in its being suited to the nature and character of the nation for which it is instituted.

Among the ancient and modern nations, Rome and Great Britain are the most outstanding. Both were born to govern and to be free and both were built not on ostentatious forms of freedom, but upon solid institutions. Thus I recommend to you, Representatives, the study of the British Constitution, for that body of laws appears destined to bring about the greatest possible good for people that adopt it; but, however perfect it is, I by no means propose that you imitate it slavishly. . . .

No matter how closely we study the composition of the English executive power, we can find nothing to prevent its being judged as the most perfect model for a kingdom, for an aristocracy, or for a democracy. Give Venezuela such an executive power in the person of a president chosen by the people or their representatives, and you will have taken a great step toward national happiness. . . .

Therefore, let the entire system of [our] government be strengthened, and let the balance of power be drawn up in such a manner that it will be permanent and incapable of decay because of its own tenuity. Precisely because no form of government is so weak as the democratic, its framework must be firmer, and its institutions must be studied to determine their degree of stability. Unless this is done, we must plan on the establishment of an experimental rather than a permanent system of government; and we will have to reckon with an ungovernable, tumultuous, and anarchic society, not with a social order where happiness, peace and justice prevail. . . .

My desire is for every branch of government and administration to attain that degree of vigor which alone can insure equilibrium, not only among the members of the government, but also among the different factions of which our society is composed. It would matter little if the springs of a political system were to relax because of its weakness, so long as this relaxation itself did not contribute to the dissolution of the body social and the ruination of its membership. The shouts of humanity, on the battlefields or in tumultuous crowds, denounce to the world the blind, unthinking legislators who imagined that experiments with chimerical institutions could be made with impunity. All the peoples of the world have sought freedom, some by force of arms, others by force of law, passing alternately from anarchy to despotism, or from despotism to anarchy. Few peoples have been content with moderate aims, establishing their institutions according to their means, their character, and their circumstances. We must not aspire to the impossible, lest, in trying to rise above the realm of liberty, we again descend into the realm of tyranny. Absolute liberty invariably lapses into absolute power, and the mean between these two extremes is supreme social liberty. Abstract theories create the pernicious idea of unlimited freedom. Let us see to it that the strength of the public is kept within the limits prescribed by reason and interest; that the national will is confined within the bonds set by a just power; that the judiciary is rigorously controlled by civil and criminal laws, analogous to those in our present Constitution—then an equilibrium between the powers of government will exist, the conflicts that hamper the progress of the estate will disappear, and those complications which tend to hinder rather than unite society will be eliminated.

Study Questions

1. According to Bolívar, what are the most significant problems facing the people of Spanish America in the early nineteenth century?
2. What is the speaker's concept of "liberty"?
3. Why does Bolívar believe a government must reflect the culture of its people?
4. How do Bolívar's remarks illustrate the popular late eighteenth- and early nineteenth-century notion that the old world order was quickly becoming outmoded and anachronistic?

Reading 45

The Seneca Falls Declaration of 1848

The American and French Revolutions brought the concepts of liberty and equality to the forefront of public and legal affairs in the West. Many women and men actively participated in a variety of reform movements; even as reformers, however, women were required to assume a subordinate position. In July 1848, the first organized meeting for women's rights was held in Seneca Falls, New York. In attendance were some two hundred delegates, the vast majority of whom were women. Using the Declaration of Independence as a model, **Elizabeth Cady Stanton** (1815–1902) drew up the Declaration of Sentiments and drafted a series of resolutions that were adopted by the convention. Stanton was later joined by the likes of **Susan B. Anthony** (1820–1906) in working for women's rights and suffrage.

Declaration of Sentiments

When, in the course of human events, it becomes necessary from one portion of the family of man to assume among the people of the earth a position different from that which they have hitherto occupied, but one to which the laws of nature and of nature's God entitle them, a decent respect to the opinions of mankind requires that they should declare the causes that impel them to such a course.

We hold these truths to be self-evident: that all men and women are created equal; that they are endowed by their Creator with certain inalienable rights; that among these are life, liberty and the pursuit of happiness; that to secure these rights governments are instituted, deriving their powers from the consent of the governed. Whenever any form of government becomes destructive of these ends, it is the right of those who suffer from it to refuse allegiance to it, and to insist upon the institution of a new government, laying its foundations on such principles, and organizing its powers in such form, as to them shall seem most likely to effect their safety and happiness. Prudence, indeed, will dictate that governments long established should not be changed for light and transient causes; and accordingly all experience hath shown that mankind are more disposed to suffer, while evils are sufferable, than to right themselves by abolishing the forms to which they were

Susan B. Anthony, Elizabeth Cady Stanton, and Matilda Joslyn Gage, eds., *History of Woman Suffrage* (Rochester, NY: Susan B. Anthony, Publisher, 1889), vol 1: 75–80.

accustomed. But when a long train of abuses and usurpations, pursuing invariably the same object evinces a design to reduce them under absolute despotism, it is their duty to throw off such government, and to provide new guards for their future security. Such has been the patient sufferance of the women under this government, and such is now the necessity which constrains them to demand the equal station to which they are entitled.

The history of mankind is a history of repeated injuries and usurpations on the part of the man toward woman, having in direct object the establishment of an absolute tyranny over her. To prove this, let facts be submitted to a candid world.

He has never permitted her to exercise her inalienable right to the elective franchise.

He has compelled her to submit to laws, in the formation of which she had no voice.

He has withheld from her rights which are given to the most ignorant and degraded men—both natives and foreigners.

Having deprived her of this first right of a citizen, the elective franchise, thereby leaving her without representation in the halls of legislation, he has opposed her on all sides.

He has made her, if married, in the eye of the law, civilly dead.

He has taken from her all right in property, even to the wages she earns.

He has made her, morally, an irresponsible being, as she can commit many crimes with impunity, provided that they be done in the presence of her husband. In the covenant of marriage, she is compelled to promise obedience to her husband, he becoming, to all intents and purposes, her master—the law giving him power to deprive her of her liberty, and to administer chastisement.

He has so framed the laws of divorce, as to what shall be the proper causes, and in case of separation, to whom the guardianship of the children shall be given, as to be wholly regardless of the happiness of women—the law, in all cases, going upon a false supposition of the supremacy of man, and giving all power in his hands.

After depriving her of all rights as a married woman, if single, and the owner of property, he has taxed her to support a government which recognizes her only when her property can be made profitable to it.

He has monopolized nearly all the profitable employments, and from those she is permitted to follow, she receives but a scanty remuneration. He closes against her all the avenues to wealth and distinction which he considers most honorable to himself. As a teacher of theology, medicine, or law, she is not known.

He has denied her the facilities for obtaining a thorough education, all colleges being closed against her.

He allows her in Church, as well as State, but a subordinate position, claiming Apostolic authority for her exclusion from the ministry, and, with some exceptions, from any public participation in the affairs of the Church.

He has created a false public sentiment by giving to the world a different code of morals for men and women, by which moral delinquencies which exclude women from society, are not only tolerated, but deemed of little account in man.

He has usurped the prerogative of Jehovah himself, claiming it as his right to assign for her a sphere of action, when that belongs to her conscience and to her God.

He has endeavored, in every way that he could, to destroy her confidence in her own powers, to lessen her self-respect, and to make her willing to lead a dependent and abject life.

Now, in view of this entire disfranchisement of one-half the people of this country, their social and religious degradation—in view of the unjust laws above mentioned, and because women do not feel themselves aggrieved, oppressed, and fraudulently deprived of their most sacred rights, we insist that they have immediate admission to all the rights and privileges which belong to them as citizens of the United States.

In entering upon the great work before us, we anticipate no small amount of misconception, misrepresentation, and ridicule; but we shall use every instrumentality within our power to effect our object. We shall employ agents, circulate tracts, petition the State and National legislatures, and endeavor to enlist the pulpit and the press in our behalf. We hope this Convention will be followed by a series of Conventions embracing every part of the country.

Resolutions

WHEREAS, the great precept of nature is conceded to be, that "man shall pursue his own true and substantial happiness." **Blackstone** in his *Commentaries* remarks, that this law of Nature being coequal with mankind, and dictated by God himself, is of course superior in obligation to any other. It is binding over all the globe, in all countries and at all times; no human laws are of any validity if contrary to this, and such of them as are valid, derive all their force, and all their validity, and all their authority, mediately and immediately, from this original; therefore,

Resolved, That such laws as conflict, in any way, with the true and substantial happiness of woman, are contrary to the great precept of nature and of no validity, for this is "superior in obligation to any other."

Resolved, That all laws which prevent woman from occupying such a station in society as her conscience shall dictate, or which place her in a position inferior to that of man, are contrary to the great precept of nature, and therefore of no force or authority.

Resolved, That woman is man's equal—was intended to be so by the Creator, and the highest good of the race demands that she should be recognized as such.

Resolved, That the women of this country ought to be enlightened in regard to the laws under which they live, that they may no longer publish their degradation by declaring themselves satisfied with their present position, nor their ignorance, by asserting that they have all the rights they want.

Resolved, That inasmuch as man, while claiming for himself intellectual superiority, does not accord to woman moral superiority, it is pre-eminently his duty to encourage her to speak and teach, as she has an opportunity, in all religious assemblies.

Resolved, That the same amount of virtue, delicacy, and refinement of behavior that is required of woman in the social state, should also be required of man, and the same transgressions should be visited with equal severity on both man and woman.

Resolved, That the objection of indelicacy and impropriety, which is so often brought against woman when she addresses a public audience, comes with a very ill-grace from those who encourage, by their attendance, her appearance on the stage, in the concert, or in feats of the circus.

Resolved, That woman has too long rested satisfied in the circumscribed limits which corrupt customs and a perverted application of the Scriptures have marked out for her, and that it is time she should move in the enlarged sphere which her great Creator has assigned her.

Resolved, That it is the duty of the women of this country to secure to themselves their sacred right to the elective franchise.

Resolved, That the equality of human rights results necessarily from the fact of the identity of the race in capabilities and responsibilities.

Resolved, therefore, That, being invested by the Creator with the same capabilities, and the same consciousness of responsibility for their exercise, it is demonstrably the right and duty of woman, equally with man, to promote every righteous cause by every righteous means; and especially in regard to the great subjects of morals and religion, it is self-evidently her right to participate with her brother in teaching them, both in private and in public, by writing and by speaking, by any instrumentalities proper to be used, and in any assemblies proper to be held; and this being a self-evident truth growing out of the divinely implanted principles of human nature, any custom or authority adverse to it, whether modern or wearing the hoary sanction of antiquity, is to be regarded as a self-evident falsehood, and at war with mankind.

Study Questions

1. Why did the authors of the Seneca Falls declaration use the American Declaration of Independence (Reading 43) as their model?
2. Did Elizabeth Cady Stanton want to emphasize women's legal, political, or economic rights?
3. What are the truly radical aspects of the Seneca Falls declaration, and why did such controversy develop over the issue of women's suffrage rather than other, equally significant issues?
4. If the document had become law in the mid-nineteenth century, what would be different about the sociopolitical order in the United States today?

Reading 46

Lincoln's "Gettysburg Address" and "Second Inaugural Address"

In the mid-nineteenth century, national unity in the United States was severely tested. Sectional struggles grew more embittered and possible compromise with southern states became more remote. After Abraham Lincoln (1809–1865) was elected president, the nation stumbled toward disintegration. Events moved rapidly, and with the secession of many southern states from the Union, the Civil War began in April 1861. Soon after the northern victory at Gettysburg in early July, Lincoln went to the battlefield to deliver his "Gettysburg Address," which he hastily wrote on the back of an envelope, and to dedicate a national cemetery. Regardless of the North's military advantages, the South obstinately refused to end the fighting through negotiations. Faced with not being renominated for a second term as president of the Union, Lincoln offered to end the war if the South returned to the Union and abolished slavery. Jefferson Davis (1808–1889), the president of the Confederacy, however, was unwilling to oblige; the end of the war seemed as distant as ever. On 4 March 1865, President Lincoln delivered his "Second Inaugural Address," which anticipated the day when all Americans would live with a "just and lasting peace." On 14 April 1865, Lincoln was assassinated, a victim of the hatred and revenge he sought to overcome.

The Gettysburg Address

Four score and seven years ago our fathers brought forth on this continent, a new nation, conceived in Liberty, and dedicated to the proposition that all men are created equal.

Now we are engaged in a great civil war, testing whether that nation or any nation so conceived and so dedicated, can long endure. We are met on a great battle-field of that war. We have come to dedicate a portion of that field, as a final

James D. Richardson, ed., *A Compilation of the Messages and Papers of Presidents* (Washington, DC: Government Printing Office, 1897–1907), passim.

resting place for those who here gave their lives that that nation might live. It is altogether fitting and proper that we should do this.

But, in a larger sense, we can not dedicate—we can not consecrate—we can not hallow—this ground. The brave men, living and dead, who struggled here, have consecrated it, far above our poor power to add or detract. The world will little note, nor long remember what we say here, but it can never forget what they did here. It is for us the living, rather, to be dedicated here to the unfinished work which they who fought here have thus far so nobly advanced. It is rather for us to be here dedicated to the great task remaining before us—that from these honored dead we take increased devotion to that cause for which they gave the last full measure of devotion—that we here highly resolve that these dead shall not have died in vain—that this nation, under God, shall have a new birth of freedom—and that government of the people, by the people, for the people, shall not perish from the earth.

The Second Inaugural Address

Fellow-Countrymen: At this second appearing to take the oath of the presidential office there is less occasion for an extended address than there was at the first. Then a statement somewhat in detail of a course to be pursued seemed fitting and proper. Now, at the expiration of four years, during which public declarations have been constantly called forth on every point and phase of the great contest which still absorbs the attention and engrosses the energies of the nation, little that is new could be presented. The progress of our arms, upon which all else chiefly depends, is as well known to the public as to myself, and it is, I trust, reasonably satisfactory and encouraging to all, with high hope for the future, no prediction in regard to it is ventured.

On the occasion corresponding to this four years ago all thoughts were anxiously directed to an impending civil war. All dreaded it, all sought to avert it. While the inaugural address was being delivered from this place, devoted altogether to *saving* the Union without war, insurgent agents were in the city seeking to *destroy* it without war—seeking to dissolve the Union and divide effects by negotiation. Both parties depreciated war, but one of them would *make* war rather than let the nation survive, and the other would *accept* war rather than let it perish, and the war came.

One eighth of the whole population was colored slaves, not distributed generally over the Union, but localized in the southern part of it. These slaves constituted a peculiar and powerful interest. All knew that this interest was somehow the cause of the war. To strengthen, perpetuate, and extend this interest was the object for which the insurgents would rend the Union even by war, while the Government claimed no right to do more than to restrict the territorial enlargement of it. Neither party expected for the war the magnitude or the duration which it has already attained. Neither anticipated that the *cause* of the conflict might cease

265

with or even before the conflict itself should cease. Each looked for an easier triumph, and a result less fundamental and astounding. Both read the same Bible and pray to the same God, and each invokes His aid against the other. It may seem strange that any men should dare to ask a just God's assistance in wringing their bread from the sweat of other men's faces, but let us judge not, that we be not judged. The prayers of both could not be answered. That of neither has been answered fully. The Almighty has His own purposes. "Woe unto the world because of offenses; for it must needs be that offenses come, but woe to that man by whom the offense cometh." If we shall suppose that American slavery is one of those offenses which, in the providence of God, must needs come, but which, having continued through His appointed time, He now wills to remove, and that He gives to both North and South this terrible war as the owe due to those by whom the offense came, shall we discern therein any departure from those divine attributes which the believers in a living God always ascribe to Him? Fondly do we hope, fervently do we pray, that this mighty scourge of war may speedily pass away. Yet, if God wills that it continue until all the wealth piled by the bondsman's two hundred and fifty years of unrequited toil shall be sunk, and until every drop of blood drawn with the lash shall be paid by another drawn with the sword, as was said three thousand years ago, so still it must be said, "The judgments of the Lord are true and righteous altogether."

With malice toward none, with charity for all, with firmness in the right as God gives us to see the right, let us strive on to finish the work we are in, to bind up the nation's wounds, to care for him who shall have borne the battle and for his widow and his orphan, to do all which may achieve and cherish a just and lasting peace among ourselves and with all nations.

Study Questions

1. What in Lincoln's opinion is the main cause of the American Civil War?
2. Explain the president's views of nationalism and how he applied it to the future of the American people?
3. How and why does the president interject religion and the use of the Bible into his political rhetoric?
4. In what way does Lincoln appear as both social reformer and political reactionary in these two speeches?

Part 3

The Contemporary World
An Age of Politicians and the Masses

THE FADING OF WESTERN SUPREMACY Throughout the twentieth century, the world has had to adapt to rapid, far-reaching changes. In spite of constant material, technological, and intellectual progress, the depth and scope of today's crises and challenges have sometimes resulted in extraordinary pain and misery. Some malcontents have suggested that the ordeals humanity has suffered in this age of politicians and the masses have severely dimmed the chances of surviving into the next century. Apocalyptic visions are nothing new to the history of the world: many people proclaimed similar views at the dawn of the twentieth century, a time when Western political supremacy throughout the world was beginning to fade.

The people of western Europe and the United States in fact emerged from the nineteenth century conscious of their scientific advancements and technological proficiency. Rapid industrialization and the desire to expand overseas brought them to the brink of global domination and instilled in them an overwhelming confidence in the r economic, political, and cultural achievements. Of all the world's emerging nations only Japan could even remotely challenge the West's attempts to dominate the globe. Japan's remarkable transition from the archaic Tokugawa Shogunate to a modern nation-state during the Meiji era is clearly manifested in its surprising victory over czarist Russia in 1905. The Japanese had succeeded where other east Eurasian and African peoples had failed: the armed forces of their Empire of the Rising Sun had defeated a Western power in war. Yet even this significant victory betokens the fact that the West had succeeded in one way or another in imposing its image on the world. At the turn of the century the majority of the world's population still labored under the yoke of New Imperialism. World War I was, however, destined to bring traditional Europe down in ruins and to put extraordinary strains on its position in the global community that Westerners had helped to create.

WORLD WAR IN THE TWENTIETH CENTURY At the outbreak of the first world war in the autumn of 1914, Great Britain's foreign minister, Sir Edward Grey (1862–1933), aptly remarked that "the lamps are going out all over Europe." By the time it ended, empires had crumbled or were about to be dismantled by the victorious allies, and new nations emerged in place of obsolete states. An estimated 18 million civilians and soldiers lost their lives in this so-called war to end all wars. In its aftermath, many people in the West became disillusioned with Western liberal democracy, which provided a fertile breeding ground for new political doctrines such as Bolshevik Communism and fascism (Readings 57, 61). The failure of progressive government in the West had repercussions elsewhere as well. It was viewed by many activists as a great anomaly that Western nations, which had for some time extolled enlightened government for their own citizens, were morally and politically bankrupt colonial powers, yet nevertheless continued to control the destinies of foreign territories. Indeed, such convictions fueled the fires of nationalism and independence movements on a global scale (Readings 50, 53). The postwar settlements and treaties of 1919 through 1923 lasted less than a generation, confirming in the minds of many that the Great War of 1914–1918 was the kind of debacle signaling the decline, if not total collapse, of Western civilization. The harsh experiences of world war left even the victors demoralized and shattered (Readings 59, 60).

During the 1920s, the balance of power and authority in the West and throughout the world began to shift dramatically. With the creation of the USSR in 1922, a new superpower gradually emerged. Movements of national liberation and independence in southwest Eurasia, China, and India began to gather momentum. These events presaged an analogous series of occurrences that would dominate global politics and diplomacy after the second world war of the century. Clearly, many people during and after the two world wars considered conventional culture and traditional institutions as patently unjust and uncompromising. Unrelenting cries for reform or revolution resounded throughout the world. Following World War I, people who had been subjected to Western imperialist policies intensified their quest for independence from outside authority and influence (Readings 51, 54). Paradoxically, many of their leaders were inspired by Western notions of freedom and liberty.

No sooner had the first global war become a memory than another global conflagration erupted. The rise of fascist, totalitarian regimes in Germany, Italy, and Japan during the 1920s and 1930s precipitated the global conflict that once again consumed the material and human resources of the world's nations (Readings 55, 66). Western democracies, led by Great Britain, the United States, and their totalitarian ally, the USSR, fought against the terror and barbarism of these blatantly aggressive nations. Soon, however, wartime cooperation among the victorious nations yielded to further tensions between the two emergent superpowers, the United States and the USSR. The creation of the Soviet bloc and America's support of various "friendly" nations in Europe and elsewhere only served to heighten the possibility of another global armed conflict. Many newly independent countries and other sovereign nations avoided commitment to the two superpowers by developing a policy of nonalignment. That the world would not become polarized by the two dominant political forces of the late twentieth century was amply illustrated by the Bandung Conference of nonaligned nations held in 1955. China's break with the Soviets in 1959 and Japan's remarkable recovery following its unconditional surrender in 1945 ensured that the former USSR and the United States would play a restricted role, at least in East Asian affairs (Reading 56).

The world as a whole is, however, a different matter. The cold war, along with limited warfare in Korea in the early 1950s and Vietnam in the 1960s and 1970s, severely compromised global political stability for decades. The breakup of African colonial empires, continuous strife in southwestern Eurasia between Israel and Muslim states, and turmoil among factions within the Islamic community of nations demonstrated that the world's political climate was extremely volatile (Readings 48, 49, 68). More recently, the fall of the iron curtain in eastern Europe and the dissolution of the USSR itself have engendered new dilemmas as well as appeals for a new world order whereby the rights and privileges of all human beings might be realized.

CRISIS AND CREATIVITY IN THE CONTEMPORARY WORLD   Throughout this century, political and diplomatic crises have corresponded to upheavals in thought and culture. For example, issues such as civil liberties and human rights (Readings 47, 63, 69) and women's status and position in society (Readings 58, 64), which in prior centuries were considered trifling to established authorities, assumed tremendous importance. Along with the havoc and destruction of life and property caused by the two world wars—including the collapse of Western colonial empires in east Eurasia and Africa and economic ruin throughout the world—came significant changes in attitudes toward traditional values and beliefs. Many artists and intellectuals had little or no interest in supporting conventional ideas and modes of thought. In the West, underlying almost every aspect of human life and activity was the feeling that humankind—living as it did in a world devoid of real values—appeared to possess an enormous capacity for self-destruction. It was thought necessary to develop new mores and ideas that would sustain humanity's capacity to understand itself and the world (Reading 62). Some non-Western political and spiritual leaders also repudiated that which they considered responsible for the moral and physical carnage and chaos wrought by global conflict and the problems of their own people, by affirming ancestral values and beliefs. Regardless of the extreme pessimism and sense of helplessness manifested during this turbulent era, an urgent desire to improve not only one's own society but also the global community has thrived (Readings 52, 65, 67).

LIVING IN THE CONTEMPORARY WORLD   The challenges facing humanity in this Age of Politicians and the Masses are as varied as they are great. Whatever issue or crisis must be met—whether nuclear destruction, racial or sexual discrimination, the population explosion, preserving the environment, global peace and prosperity, or the meaning of existence itself—people throughout the world must continue to search for realistic solutions. The late Geoffrey Barraclough, a historian of considerable distinction, suggested the following in his *Turning Points in World History*, published in 1977:

In the long run, salvation is the result of recognizing the fundamental unity of mankind, the fact that, in spite of different social organizations, different values, different cultural traditions, everywhere there are basic similarities of human nature, human thinking and human responses. To recognize that seems to me the challenge of the twenty-first century, a challenge to build an international order based on equality, not on power, based on cooperation, not on conflict, based on reason, not on fear.

Many multinational organizations, sovereign states, and individuals have accepted the challenge issued by Dr. Barraclough. People worldwide have made the future of civilization on Earth less precarious than it was even a generation ago by offering a variety of viable solutions to the multifarious problems confronting them. To understand the present and positively shape the immediate future, students of history must not only discern and analyze historical processes with objectivity and empathy; they must join the global community in which they live and which was created by the history we all share. Indeed, the study of world history, if it has any meaning, will lift our eyes from our small, provincial selves to the magnificence of the world and all humanity. In the words of American poet Maya Angelou:

> History, despite its wrenching pain,
> Cannot be unlived, but if faced
> With courage, need not be lived again.

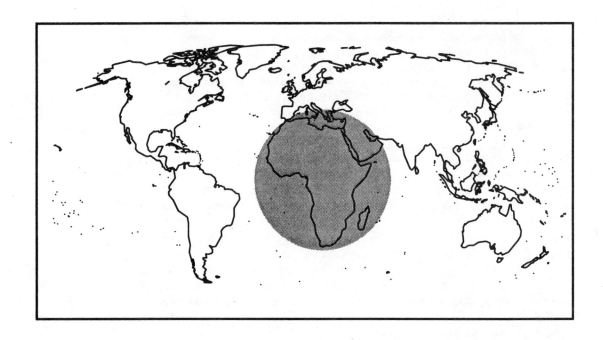

Brief Chronology for the Contemporary World
Southwest Eurasia and Africa

1893–1913	Mohandas K. Gandhi works as lawyer in South Africa
1899–1902	Boer War in South Africa
1907	Orange Free S ate, the Transvaal, Natal, and Cape Colony form the Union of South Africa
1908	"Young Turk" revolt in Ottoman Empire
1911	Liberia becomes U.S. protectorate in all but name
1914–1918	World War I
1916–1918	Arab Revolt against Ottoman Empire
1919	Paris Peace Conference
1920	San Remo Conference of victorious allies deny Arab nations' sovereignty
1922–1938	Mustafa Kemal, "Ataturk," reigns as first president of Turkey
1923	Egypt becomes sovereign nation with certain British restrictions
1936	Italian dictator Mussolini conquers Ethiopia
1939–1945	World War II
1948	State of Israel founded
1954–1970	Gamal Nasser premier of Egypt
1955–1962	French and Algerian Wars of Independence
1957	Beginning of decolonization in sub-Saharan Africa
1960	UN orders peacekeeping forces into the Congo to help end civil war
1967	Arab-Israeli "Six-Day War"
1979	Ayatollah Khomeini engineers the fall of the Shah of Iran; Egyptian-Israeli Peace Treaty signed at Camp David, U.S.
1980–1988	Iran-Iraq War
1990	Antiapartheid activist Nelson Mandela released from South African prison
1991	Persian Gulf War

All dates are c.e. and approximate unless otherwise indicated. It should be noted as well that chronologies are constantly being revised. Hence, there may be discrepancies between the dates listed above and those found in other textbooks and scholarly monographs. Throughout the text and in the Glossary, all dates are given in b.c.e. (Before the Common Era) and c.e. (the Common Era). Where there is no era designation c.e. may be assumed.

The African National Congress's "Freedom Charter"

The government of the Republic of South Africa recently rescinded some of its laws and constitutional pronouncements on apartheid—the legal segregation of black and "colored" non-citizens from white citizens—with a view to holding national elections in which blacks and whites will participate. This comes as the culmination of a long, bitter struggle. In the decades following World War II, only minor advances were made against the brutality of white minority rule. In 1955, the African National Congress convened a "Peoples' Congress" that for the first time called together representatives of different races. In 1955, the delegates of the A.N.C. adopted the so-called Freedom Charter by an overwhelming majority. The initial steps toward dismantling apartheid thus began with the A.N.C.'s activities nearly forty years ago. In March 1992, South African president F. W. de Klerk proposed a referendum to end white rule before the white minority of the country. The measure passed, receiving 68.7 percent of the vote. For the first time in the history of South Africa, blacks and people of color obtained voting rights. The efforts of Nelson Mandela and other black leaders are slowly changing the status quo, and the tide of violence and repression is gradually abating. Moreover, the world community has saluted the roles of South Africa's leaders: Mandela and de Klerk have jointly received the 1993 Nobel Peace Prize.

We, the people of South Africa, declare for all our country and the world to know:

That South Africa belongs to all who live in it, black and white, and that no government can justly claim authority unless it is based on the will of the people;

That our people have been robbed of their birthright to land, liberty and peace by a form of government founded on injustice and inequality;

That our country will never be prosperous or free until all our people live in brotherhood, enjoying equal rights and opportunities;

Nelson Mandela, *The Struggle Is My Life: His Speeches and Writings Brought Together with Historical Documents and Accounts of Mandela in Prison by Fellow Prisoners* (New York: Pathfinder Press, 1986), passim. Copyright © 1990 Pathfinder Press. Reprinted with permission.

That only a democratic state, based on the will of all of the people, can secure to all their birthright without distinction of color, race, sex or belief;

And therefore, we, the people of South Africa, black and white, together—equals, countrymen and brothers—adopt this FREEDOM CHARTER. And we pledge ourselves to strive together, sparing nothing of our strength and courage, until the democratic changes here set out have been won.

The People Shall Govern!

Every man and woman shall have the right to vote for and stand as a candidate for all bodies which make laws.

All the people shall be entitled to take part in the administration of the country.

The rights of the people shall be the same regardless of race, color or sex.

All bodies of minority rule, advisory boards, councils and authorities shall be replaced by democratic organs of self-government.

All National Groups Shall Have Equal Rights!

There shall be equal status in the bodies of state, in the courts, and in the schools for all national groups and races;

All people shall have equal rights to use their own languages and to develop their own folk culture and customs;

All national groups shall be protected by law against insults to their race and national pride;

The preaching and practice of national, race or color discrimination and contempt shall be a punishable crime;

All apartheid laws and practices shall be set aside.

The People Shall Share in the Country's Wealth!

The national wealth of our country, the heritage of all South Africans, shall be restored to the people;

The mineral wealth beneath the soil, the banks and monopoly industry shall be transferred to the ownership of the people as a whole;

All other industries and trade shall be controlled to assist the well-being of the people;

All people shall have equal rights to trade where they choose, to manufacture and to enter all trades, crafts and professions.

The Land Shall Be Shared Among Those Who Work It!

Restriction of land ownership on a racial basis shall be ended, and all the land re-divided amongst those who work it, to banish famine and land hunger;

The state shall help the peasants with implements, seed, tractors and dams to save the soil and assist the tillers;

Freedom of movement shall be guaranteed to all who work on the land;

All shall have the right to occupy land wherever they choose;

People shall not be robbed of their cattle, and forced labor and farm prisons shall be abolished.

All Shall Be Equal Before the Law!

No one shall be imprisoned, deported or restricted without a fair trial;

No one shall be condemned by the order of any Government official;

The courts shall be representative of all the people;

Imprisonment shall be only for serious crimes against the people, and shall aim at re-education, not vengeance;

The police force and army shall be open to all on an equal basis and shall be the helpers and protectors of the people;

All laws which discriminate on grounds of race, color or belief shall be repealed.

All Shall Enjoy Equal Human Rights!

The law shall guarantee to all their right to speak, to organize, to meet together, to publish, to preach, to worship and to educate their children;

The privacy of the house from police raids shall be protected by law;

All shall be free to travel without restriction from countryside to town, from province to province, and from South Africa abroad;

Pass laws, permits and all other laws restricting these freedoms shall be abolished.

There Shall Be Work and Security!

All who work shall be free to form trade unions, to elect their officers and to make wage agreements with their employers;

The state shall recognize the right and duty of all to work; and to draw full unemployment benefits;

Men and women of all races shall receive equal pay for equal work;

There shall be a forty-hour working week, a national minimum wage, paid annual leave, and sick leave for all workers, and maternity leave on full pay for all working mothers;

Miners, domestic workers, farm workers and civil servants shall have the same rights as all others who work;

Child labor, compound labor, the tot system and contract labor shall be abolished.

The Doors of Learning and of Culture Shall Be Opened!

The government shall discover, develop and encourage national talent for the enhancement of our cultural life;

All the cultural treasures of mankind shall be open to all, by free exchange of books, ideas and contact with other lands;

The aim of education shall be to teach the youth to love their people and their culture, to honor human brotherhood, liberty and peace;

Education shall be free, compulsory, universal and equal for all children;

Higher education and technical training shall be opened to all by means of state allowances and scholarships awarded on the basis of merit;

Adult illiteracy shall be ended by a mass state education plan;

Teachers shall have all the rights of other citizens;

The color bar in cultural life, in sport and in education shall be abolished.

There Shall Be Houses, Security and Comfort!

All people shall have the right to live where they choose, to be decently housed, and to bring up their families in comfort and security;

Unused housing space to be made available to the people;

Rent and prices shall be lowered, food plentiful and no one shall go hungry;

A preventive health scheme shall be run by the state;

Free medical care and hospitalization shall be provided for all, with special care for mothers and young children;

Slums shall be demolished, and new suburbs built where all have transport, roads, lighting, playing fields, creches and social centers;

The aged, the orphans, the disabled and the sick shall be cared for by the state;

Rest, leisure and recreation shall be the right of all;

Fenced locations and ghettos shall be abolished, and laws which break up families shall be repealed.

South Africa shall be a fully independent state, which respects the rights and sovereignty of all nations;

South Africa shall strive to maintain world peace and the settlement of all international disputes by negotiations—not war;

Peace and friendship amongst all our people shall be secured by upholding the equal rights, opportunities and status of all;

The people of the protectorates, Basutoland, Bechuanaland and Swaziland, shall be free to decide for themselves their own future;

The right of all the peoples of Africa to independence and self-government shall be recognized, and shall be the basis of close cooperation.

Let all who love their people and their country now say, as we say here: "THESE FREEDOMS WE WILL FIGHT FOR, SIDE BY SIDE, THROUGHOUT OUR LIVES, UNTIL WE HAVE WON OUR LIBERTY."

Study Questions

1. According to the A.N.C., what are some of the major problems blacks face in South Africa?
2. What can be ascertained from the document regarding apartheid's effect on the lives of South Africans?
3. How do the authors of the charter define freedom and liberty?
4. Are there any similarities between the A.N.C.'s charter and the United Nations Declaration of 1948 (Reading 63)?

Reading 48

Kwame Nkrumah's "African Socialism Revisited"

Ghana on the old Gold Coast was the first nation in sub-Saharan Africa to throw off the yoke of white imperialism after World War II. Its leader, Kwame Nkrumah (1909–1972), and his new government became symbols of liberalism and democracy for all Africans. Nkrumah, however, soon developed into a classic dictator. In *Consciencism,* his first major work published in 1964, he advocated a socialist-Marxist doctrine with particular reference to Africa's needs and traditions. In his slightly later "African Socialism Revisited," Nkrumah berates African nationalists who fail to grasp the vital importance of socialist institutions and perspectives. Nkrumah's megalomania eventually led to his downfall; the government in which he served as president beginning in 1960 was toppled by an army coup in 1966.

The term "socialism" has become a necessity in the platform diction and political writings of African leaders. It is a term which unites us in the recognition that the restoration of Africa's humanist and egalitarian principles of society calls for socialism. All of us, therefore, even though pursuing widely contrasting policies in the task of reconstructing our various nation-states, still use "socialism" to describe our respective efforts. The question must therefore be faced: What real meaning does the term retain in the context of contemporary African politics? . . .

Some African political leaders and thinkers certainly use the term "socialism" as it should in my opinion be used: to describe a complex of social purposes and the consequential social and economic policies, organizational patterns, state structure, and ideologies which can lead to the attainment of those purposes. For such leaders, the aim is to remold African society in the socialist direction; to reconsider African society in such a manner that the humanism of traditional African life reasserts itself in a modern technical community. Consequently, socialism in Africa introduces a new social synthesis in which modern technology is reconciled with human values, in which the advanced technical society is realized without the staggering social malefactions and deep schisms of capitalist industrial society. For true economic and social development cannot be promoted without

    Kwame Nkrumah, "African Socialism Revisited," *African Forum* (Winter 1966), 3–9, passim.

the real socialization of productive and distributive processes. Those African leaders who believe these principles are the socialists in Africa. . . .

Some years ago, African political leaders and writers used the term "African socialism" in order to label the concrete forms that socialism might assume in Africa. But the realities of the diverse and irreconcilable social, political, and economic policies being pursued by African states today have made the term "African socialism" meaningless and irrelevant. It appears to be much more closely associated with anthropology than with political economy. . . . The uncertainties concerning the meaning and specific policies of "African socialism" have led some of us to abandon the term because it fails to express its original meaning and because it tends to obscure our fundamental socialist commitment.

Today, the phrase "African socialism" seems to espouse the view that the traditional African society was a classless society imbued with the spirit of humanism and to express a nostalgia for that spirit. Such a conception of socialism makes a fetish of the communal African society. But an idyllic, African classless society (in which there were no rich and no poor) enjoying a drugged serenity is certainly a facile simplification; there is no historical or even anthropological evidence for any such a society. I am afraid the realities of African society were somewhat more sordid. . . .

All this notwithstanding, one could still argue that the basic organization of many African societies in different periods of history manifested a certain communalism and that the philosophy and humanist purposes behind that organization are worthy of recapture. A community in which each saw his well-being in the welfare of the group certainly was praiseworthy, even if the manner in which the well-being of the group was pursued makes no contribution to our purposes. Thus, what socialist thought in Africa must recapture is not the structure of the "traditional African society" but its spirit, for the spirit of communalism is crystallized in its humanism and in its reconciliation of individual advancement with group welfare. Even if there is incomplete anthropological evidence to reconstruct the "traditional African society" with accuracy, we can still recapture the rich human values of that society. In short, an anthropological approach to the "traditional African society" is too much unproven; but a philosophical approach stands on much firmer ground and makes generalization feasible.

One predicament in the anthropological approach is that there is some disparity of view concerning the manifestations of the "classlessness" of the "traditional African society." While some hold that the society was based on the equality of its members, others hold that it contained a hierarchy and division of labor in which the hierarchy—and therefore power—was founded on spiritual and democratic values. Of course, no society can be founded on the equality of its members, although some societies are founded on egalitarianism, which is something quite different. Similarly, a classless society that at the same time rejoices in a hierarchy of power (as distinct from authority) must be accounted a marvel of socio-political finesse.

We know that the "traditional African society" was founded on principles of egalitarianism. In its actual workings, however, it had various shortcomings. Its humanist impulse, nevertheless, is something that continues to urge us toward our all-African socialist reconstruction. We postulate each man to be an end in himself, not merely a means; and we accept the necessity of guaranteeing each man equal opportunities for his development. The implications of this for socio-political practice have to be worked out scientifically, and the necessary social and economic policies pursued with resolution. Any meaningful humanism must begin from egalitarianism and must lead to objectively chosen policies for safeguarding and sustaining egalitarianism. Hence, socialism, [or] scientific socialism. . . .

We know, of course, that the defeat of colonialism and even neocolonialism will not result in the automatic disappearance of the imported patterns of thought and social organization. For those patterns have taken root, and are in unvarying degrees sociological features of our contemporary society. Nor will a simple return to the communalistic society of ancient Africa offer a solution either. To advocate a return, as it were, to the rock from which we were hewn is a charming thought, but we are faced with contemporary problems, which have arisen from political subjugation, economic exploitation, educational and social backwardness, increases in population, familiarity with the methods and products of industrialization, modern agricultural techniques. These—as well as a host of other complexities—can be resolved by no mere communalistic society, however sophisticated, and anyone who so advocates must be caught in insoluble dilemmas of the most excruciating kind. All available evidence from socio-political history discloses that such a return to a status quo ante is quite unexampled in the evolution of societies. There is, indeed, no theoretical or historical reason to indicate that it is at all possible.

When one society meets another, the observed historical trend is that acculturation results in a balance of forward movement, a movement in which each society assimilates certain useful attributes of the other. Social evolution is a dialectical process; it has ups and downs, but, on balance, it always represents an upward trend.

Islamic civilization and European colonialism are both historical experiences of the traditional African society, profound experiences that have permanently changed the complexion of the traditional African society. They have introduced new values and a social, cultural, and economic organization into African life. Modern African societies are not traditional, even if backward, and they are clearly in a state of socio-economic disequilibrium. They are in this state because they are not anchored to a steadying ideology.

The way out is certainly not to regurgitate all Islamic or Euro-colonial influences in a futile attempt to recreate a past that cannot be resurrected. The way out is only forward, forward to a higher and reconciled form of society, in which the quintessence of the human purposes of traditional African society reasserts itself in a modern context—forward, in short, to socialism, through policies that are scientifically devised and correctly applied. . . .

To be sure, there is a connection between communalism and socialism. Socialism stands to communalism as capitalism stands to slavery. In socialism, the principles underlying communalism are given expression in modern circumstances. Thus, whereas communalism in a nontechnical society can be laissez-faire, in a technical society where sophisticated means of production are at hand, the situation is different; for if the underlying principles of communalism are not given correlated expression, class cleavages will arise, which are connected with economic disparities and thereby with political inequalities. Socialism, therefore, can be, and is, the defense of the principles of communalism in a modern setting; it is a form of social organization that, guided by the principles underlying communism, adopts procedures and measures made necessary by demographic and technological developments. Only under socialism can we reliably accumulate the capital we need for our development and also ensure that the gains of investment are applied for the general welfare.

Socialism is not spontaneous. It does not arise of itself. It has abiding principles according to which the major means of production and distribution ought to be socialized if exploitation of the many by the few is to be prevented; if, that is to say, egalitarianism in the economy is to be protected. Socialist countries in Africa may differ in this or that detail of their policies, but such differences themselves ought not to be arbitrary or subject to vagaries of taste. They must be scientifically explained, as necessities arising from differences in the particular circumstances of the countries themselves.

There is only one way of achieving socialism: by the devising of policies aimed at the general socialist goals, each of which takes its particular state at a definite historical period. Socialism depends on dialectical and historical materialism, upon the view that there is only one nature subject in all its manifestations to natural laws and that human society is, in this sense, part of nature and subject to its own laws of development.

It is the elimination of fancifulness from socialist action that makes socialism scientific. To suppose that there are tribal, national, or racial socialisms is to abandon objectivity in favor of chauvinism.

Study Questions

1. Why does Nkrumah think that socialist doctrines are practical for African nations?
2. Why would communism and/or socialism appeal to African leaders such as Nkrumah as well as to organizations such as the A.N.C. (Reading 47)?
3. What is Nkrumah's understanding of African nationalism, and why does he consider it so important to African societies?
4. What do the author's remarks suggest about Africans' views of their customs and cultural traditions?

Reading 49

Two Declarations of Ayatollah Khomeini

Imam Ruhullah Al-Musavi Al-Khomeini (1902–1989) was the moving force behind the Islamic Revolution in Iran. After decades of agitation and polemical writing while living in exile, Khomeini and his followers forced Shah Mohammad Reza Pahlavi (1919–1980) to leave the country on 16 January 1979. Shortly after returning to Iran the Imam assumed control of Iran's government. The main goal of Khomeini and the other clerical revolutionaries was to establish a social order founded on fundamentalist **Shi'a** Islam. Government agencies, schools and universities, and radio and television stations were purged of so-called satanic (Western oriented) influences and revolutionized by the Islamic Republican party and the **ulama**, headed by Khomeini himself. A period of continued internal strife, a devastating war with Iraq in the 1980s, and very poor foreign relations with many Western countries followed. These factors curbed the further growth and development of Iran. Today the country is coming out of its isolation and seems on the verge of overcoming the military, economic, social, and religious problems that arose when Khomeini founded the Islamic Republic and when the Imam died.

Proclamation of the Islamic Republic
(dated 1 April 1979)

We desired to grant Our favor to those that were oppressed in the land, and to make of them leaders and the inheritors.

(*Koran,* 28:4)

I offer my sincere congratulations to the great people of Iran, who were despised and oppressed by arrogant kings throughout the history of the monarchy. God Almighty has granted us His favor and destroyed the regime of arrogance by His powerful hand, which has shown itself as the power of the oppressed. He has made our great people into leaders and exemplars for all the world's oppressed,

H. Algar, trans., *Islam and Revolution* (Berkeley, CA: Mizan Press, 1981), 265–67, 275–77. Reprinted with permission of the publisher.

and He has granted them their just heritage by the establishment of this Islamic Republic.

On this blessed day, the day the Islamic community assumes leadership, the day of the victory and triumph of our people, I declare the Islamic Republic of Iran.

I declare to the whole world that never has the history of Iran witnessed such a referendum, where the whole country rushed to the polls with ardor, enthusiasm, and love in order to cast their affirmative votes and bury the tyrannical regime forever in the garbage heap of history. I value highly this unparalleled solidarity by virtue of which the entire population—with the exception of a handful of adventurers and godless individuals—responded to the heavenly call of "Hold firm to the rope of God, all together" (*Koran,* 3:103) and cast a virtually unanimous vote in favor of the Islamic Republic, thus demonstrating its political and social maturity to both the East and the West.

Blessed for you be the day on which, after the martyrdom of your upright young people, the sorrow of their grieving mothers and fathers, and the suffering of the whole nation, you have overthrown your ghoulish enemy, the pharaoh of the age. By casting a decisive vote in favor of the Islamic Republic, you have established a government of divine justice, a government in which all segments of the population shall enjoy equal consideration, the light of divine justice shall shine uniformly on all, and the divine mercy of the Koran and the Sunna shall embrace all, like life-giving rain. Blessed for you be this government that knows no difference of race, whether between black and white, or between Turk, Persian, Kurd, and Baluch. All are brothers and equal; nobility lies only in the fear of God, and superiority may be attained only by acquiring virtues and performing good deeds. Blessed for you be the day on which all segments of the population have attained their legitimate rights; in the implementation of justice, there will be no difference between women and men, or between the religious minorities and the Muslims. Tyranny has been buried, and all forms of transgression will be buried along with it.

The country has been delivered from the clutches of domestic and foreign enemies, from the thieves and plunderers, and you, courageous people, are now the guardians of the Islamic Republic. It is you who must preserve this divine legacy with strength and determination and must not permit the remnants of the putrid regime of the Shah who now lie in wait, or the supporters of the international thieves and oil bandits, to penetrate your serried ranks. You must now assume control of your own destiny and not give the opportunists any occasion to assert themselves. Relying on the divine power that is manifested in communal solidarity, take the next steps by sending virtuous, trustworthy representatives to the Constituent Assembly, so that they may revise the Constitution of the Islamic Republic. Just as you voted with ardor and enthusiasm for the Islamic Republic, vote, too, for your representatives, so that the malevolent will have no excuse to object.

This day of Farvardin 12, the first day of God's government, is to be one of our foremost religious and national festivals; the people must celebrate this day and keep its remembrance alive, for it is the day on which the battlements of the twenty-five hundred-year old fortress of tyrannical government crumbled, a satanic power departed forever, and the government of the oppressed—which is the government of God—was established in its place.

Beloved people! Cherish and protect the rights you have attained through the blood of your young people and help to enact Islamic justice under the banner of Islam and the flag of the *Koran*. I stand ready to serve you and Islam with all the strength at my disposal during these last days of my life, and I expect the nation to devote itself similarly to guarding Islam and the Islamic Republic.

I ask the government that, fearing neither East nor West and cultivating an independent outlook and will, it purge all remnants of the tyrannical regime, which left deep traces upon all the affairs of our country. It should transform our educational and judicial systems, as well as all the ministries and government offices that are now run on Western lines or in slavish imitation of Western models, and make them compatible to Islam, thus demonstrating to the world true social justice and true cultural, economic, and political independence.

I ask God Almighty that He grant dignity and independence to our country and the nation of Islam.

Peace be upon you, and the blessings and mercy of God.

Message to the Pilgrims (dated 24 September 1979)

Abundant greetings and infinite salutations to all Muslims in the world, whether in the East or the West. Warm greetings to the pilgrims to the sacred House of God: may God grant them success!

It is undeniable and requires no reminder that the great religion of Islam, the religion of divine unity, destroys polytheism, unbelief, idolatry, and self-worship. It is the religion of man's essential nature, which liberates him from the bonds and fetters of material nature and from the temptations of demons in jinn and human form, both in his inner being and in his outward life. It is a religion that provides guidance for conducting the affairs of state and a guide to the straight path, which is neither Eastern nor Western. It is a religion where worship is joined to politics and political activity is a form of worship.

Now that Muslims from different countries of the world have set out toward the **Ka'ba** of their desires on the pilgrimage to God's House, so that this great act of worship decreed by God, this vast Islamic congress, is taking place at a blessed time and in a blessed place, the Muslims must strive not to content themselves with mere observance of form, but to benefit also from the political and social aspects of the pilgrimage as well as the devotional aspect. Everyone knows that no human authority or state is capable of convening such a vast gathering; it is only God's command that can bring about this great assembly. But unfortunately, the Muslims throughout history have never been able to make proper use of the divine power represented in this congress of Islam for the sake of Islam and the Muslims.

All assemblies of Muslims—for congregational prayer, Friday prayer, and especially the precious gathering of the **hajj**—have many political aspects. One of them is that through the coming together of religious leaders, intellectuals, and all committed Muslims visiting God's House, the problems of the Muslims may be discussed and solved on a basis of consultation. Then, when the pilgrims return home to their respective countries, they may give reports at public meetings so that all may contribute to the solution of problems.

Another duty that must be fulfilled in this vast gathering is to summon the people, as well as all Islamic groups, to unity, overlooking the differences between the various Muslim groups. Preachers, speakers, and writers must undertake this vital step and attempt to bring into being a front of the oppressed and deprived peoples. Such a united front, proclaiming the slogan, *La ilaha illa 'Llah* could then proceed to deliver the Muslims from their servitude to the diabolical powers represented by the foreigners, the imperialists and exploiters, and overcome all their problems on the basis of Islamic brotherhood.

Dear sisters and brothers, in whatever country you may live, defend your Islamic and national honor! Defend fearlessly and unhesitatingly the peoples and countries of Islam against their enemies—America, international **Zionism**, and all the superpowers of East and West. Loudly proclaim the crimes of the enemies of Islam.

My Muslim brothers and sisters! You are aware that the superpowers of East and West are plundering all our material and other resources, and have placed us in a situation of political, economic, cultural, and military dependence. Come to your senses; rediscover your Islamic identity! Endure oppression no longer, and vigilantly expose the criminal plans of the international bandits, headed by America!

Today the first *qibla* of the Muslims has fallen into the grasp of Israel, that cancerous growth in the Middle East. They are battering and slaughtering our dear Palestinian and Lebanese brothers with all their might. At the same time, Israel is casting dissension among the Muslims with all the diabolical means at its disposal. Every Muslim has a duty to prepare himself for battle against Israel.

Today our African Muslim countries are writhing beneath the yoke of American imperialism and other foreign powers and their agents. Muslim Africa calls out for help against its oppressors. Now, the philosophy of the hajj contains within it the answer to these cries for help. Our circling the House of God indicates that we seek aid only from God, and our stoning of the pillars is in reality a stoning of demons, whether in jinn or human form. When you cast your stones at the pillars, vow to God that you will expel the superpowers—those demons in human form—from our beloved Islamic lands. Today the Islamic world is caught in the clutches of America. So convey to all Muslims in all continents of the globe this message from God: "Refuse all servitude except servitude to God."

O Muslims, followers of the school of *tauhid!* The ultimate reason for all the troubles that afflict the Muslim countries is their disunity and lack of harmony, and the secret of future victory will lie in unity and the creation of harmony. There is a verse in which God Almighty says: "Hold fast to the rope of God all together and fall not into disunity" (*Koran,* 3:103). Holding fast to the rope of God means creating harmony among the Muslims. Let us all act for the sake of Islam and the welfare of the Muslims and shun disunity, separation, and sectarianism, for these are the source of all our misfortunes and weaknesses.

I beseech God Almighty that He exalt Islam and the Muslims and grant unity to all Muslims in the world.

Study Questions

1. What is the essence of Islam according to the Ayatollah?
2. How is the theocratic nature of the Iranian state proclaimed in the Ayatollah's speeches?
3. How do Islamic fundamentalism and Muslim nationalism serve as the basis for Khomeini's government in Iran?
4. Why does the Ayatollah think it is necessary for all Muslims to unite and end their internal conflicts?

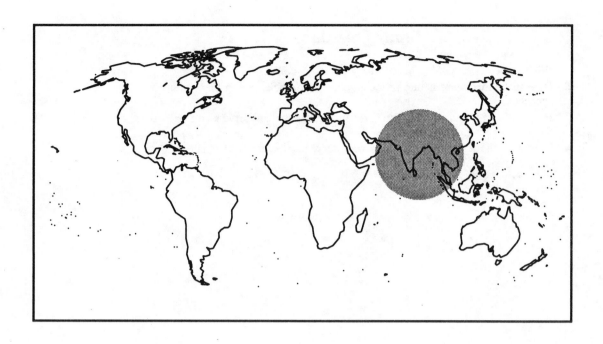

Brief Chronology for the Contemporary World
South and Southeast Eurasia

1869–1948 Mohandas K. Gandhi

1877 Queen Victoria of England proclaimed empress of India

1886 First Indian National Congress formed in Bombay

1905 Partition of Bengal arouses nationalist agitation (partition annulled in 1911)

1919 Gandhi's campaign for India's independence begins; Amritsar massacre in India

1930 Communists begin opposition to French rule in Indochina

1930–1934 Second nationwide civil disobedience movement in India

1947 India and Pakistan gain their independence from Great Britain

1947–1964 Jawaharlal Nehru dominates Indian politics

1956 Pakistan adopts Islamic constitution

1964–1975 Vietnam War

1966–1977 Indira Gandhi's first term as prime minister of India

1971 Bangladesh, formerly East Pakistan, established as independent state

1975 Communist victories in Vietnam, Laos, and Cambodia

All dates are C.E. and approximate unless otherwise indicated. It should be noted as well that chronologies are constantly being revised. Hence, there may be discrepancies between the dates listed above and those found in other textbooks and scholarly monographs. Throughout the text and in the Glossary, all dates are given in B.C.E. (Before the Common Era) and C.E. (the Common Era). Where there is no era designation C.E. may be assumed.

Gandhi's Articles on *Satyagraha*

Mohandas K. Gandhi (1869–1948), universally known as the Mahatma, "great soul," was one of the most powerful personalities in Indian history and the world's greatest advocate of nonviolent political protest. Soon after he reached his eighteenth birthday, Gandhi left his wife and infant son to study law in England. Three years later he returned to his native India but found little professional success there. Gandhi and his family then moved to South Africa, where there happened to be a large Indian population. Owing to the blatant racial prejudice he and other people of color experienced in South Africa, Gandhi decided to dedicate his life to the elimination of fear, injustice, and prejudice. This decision impelled him toward what he called *satyagraha,* "firmness in truth." After spending twenty years in Africa, he returned to India and became a moving force in the **Indian National Congress**. After serving as president of the Indian National Congress in 1925, Gandhi never again held an official position in the Indian government. But his inspired, enlightened guidance of Indian affairs throughout thirty troubled years helped enormously to bring about political independence with membership in the British Commonwealth. Britain granted independence to the subcontinent in 1947. But Gandhi's dream of a free, unified India was shattered when the country was partitioned into Muslim Pakistan and the predominantly Hindu state of India. A massive upheaval followed, intensifying the brutal strife between the two religious communities. On 30 January 1948, a right-wing Hindu militant enraged by Gandhi's attempts to unite Muslims and Hindus shocked the world community by assassinating this great humanitarian.

What Satyagraha Is

Satyagraha is literally holding on to Truth and it means, therefore, Truth-force. Truth is soul or spirit. It is, therefore, known as soul force. It excludes the use of violence because man is not capable of knowing the absolute truth and, therefore,

M. K. Gandhi, "Satyagraha," *Young India* (23 March 1921). Reprinted with permission of Navajivan Trust, Ahmedabad, India.

not competent to punish. The word was coined in South Africa to distinguish the non-violent resistance of the Indians of South Africa from the contemporary "passive resistance" of the suffragettes and others. It is not conceived as a weapon of the weak.

Passive resistance is used in the orthodox English sense and covers the suffragette movement as well as the resistance of the Non-conformists. Passive resistance has been conceived and is regarded as a weapon of the weak. Whilst it avoids violence, being not open to the weak, it does not exclude its use if, in the opinion of a passive resister, the occasion demands it. However, it has always been distinguished from armed resistance and its application was at one time confined to Christian martyrs.

Civil Disobedience is civil breach of immoral statutory enactments. The expression was, so far as I am aware, coined by **Thoreau** to signify his own resistance to the laws of a slave State. He has left a masterly treatise on the duty of Civil Disobedience. But Thoreau was not perhaps an out and out champion of non-violence. Probably, also, Thoreau limited his breach of statutory laws to the revenue law, i.e. payment of taxes. Whereas the term Civil Disobedience as practiced in 1919 covered a breach of any statutory and immoral law. It signified the resister's outlawry in a civil, i.e., non-violent manner. He invoked the sanctions of the law and cheerfully suffered imprisonment. It is a branch of Satyagraha.

Non-co-operation predominantly implies withdrawing of co-operation from the State that in the non-co-operator's view has become corrupt and excludes Civil Disobedience of the fierce type described above. By its very nature, non-co-operation is even open to children of understanding and can be safely practiced by the masses. Civil Disobedience presupposes the habit of willing obedience to laws without fear of their sanctions. It can, therefore, be practiced only as a last resort and by a select few in the first instance at any rate. Non-co-operation, too, like Civil Disobedience is a branch of Satyagraha which includes all non-violent resistance for the vindication of Truth.

The Theory and Practice of Satyagraha

Carried out to its utmost limit, Satyagraha is independent of pecuniary or other material assistance; certainly, even in its elementary form, of physical force or violence. Indeed, violence is the negation of this great spiritual force, which can only be cultivated or wielded by those who will entirely eschew violence. It is a force that may be used by individuals as well as by communities. It may be used as well in political as in domestic affairs. Its universal applicability is a demonstration of its permanence and invincibility. It can be used alike by men, women

M. K. Gandhi, "Theory and Practice of Satyagraha," *Young India* (1914). Reprinted with permission of Navajivan Trust, Ahmedabad, India.

and children. It is totally untrue to say that it is a force to be used only by the weak so long as they are not capable of meeting violence by violence. This superstition arises from the incompleteness of the English expression, passive resistance. It is impossible for those who consider themselves to be weak to apply this force. Only those who realize that there is something in man which is superior to the brute nature in him and that the latter always yields to it, can effectively be Satyagrahis. This force is to violence, and, therefore, to all tyranny, all injustice, what light is to darkness. In politics, its use is based upon the immutable maxim, that government of the people is possible only so long as they consent either consciously or unconsciously to be governed. We did not want to be governed by the **Asiatic Act** of 1907 of the Transvaal, and it had to go before this mighty force. Two courses were open to us: to use violence when we were called upon to submit to the Act, or to suffer the penalties prescribed under the Act, and thus to draw out and exhibit the force of the soul within us for a period long enough to appeal to the sympathetic chord in the governors or the law-makers. We have taken long to achieve what we set about striving for. That was because our Satyagraha was not of the most complete type. All Satyagrahis do not understand the full value of the force, nor have we men who always from conviction refrain from violence. The use of this force requires the adoption of poverty, in the sense that we must be indifferent whether we have the wherewithal to feed or clothe ourselves. During the past struggle, all Satyagrahis, if any at all, were not prepared to go that length. Some again were only Satyagrahis so called. They came without any conviction, often with mixed motives, less often with impure motives. Some even, whilst engaged in the struggle, would gladly have resorted to violence but for most vigilant supervision. Thus it was that the struggle became prolonged; for the exercise of the purest soul-force, in its perfect form, brings about instantaneous relief. For this exercise, prolonged training of the individual soul is an absolute necessity, so that a perfect Satyagrahi has to be almost, if not entirely, a perfect man. We cannot all suddenly become such men, but if my proposition is correct— as I know it to be correct—the greater the spirit of Satyagraha in us, the better men will we become. Its use, therefore, is, I think, indisputable, and it is a force, which, if it became universal, would revolutionize social ideals and do away with despotisms and the ever-growing militarism under which the nations of the West are groaning and are being almost crushed to death, and which fairly promises to overwhelm even the nations of the East. If the past struggle has produced even a few Indians who would dedicate themselves to the task of becoming Satyagrahis as nearly perfect as possible, they would not only have served themselves in the truest sense of the term, they would also have served humanity at large. Thus viewed, Satyagraha is the noblest and best education. It should come, not after the ordinary education in letters, of children, but it should precede it. It will not be denied, that a child, before it begins to write its alphabet and to gain worldly knowledge, should know what the soul is, what truth is, what love is, what powers are latent in the soul. It should be an essential of real education that a child should learn, that in the struggle of life, it can easily conquer hate by love, untruth by truth, violence by self-suffering.

Faith in Non-Violence

I have found that life persists in the midst of destruction and, therefore, there must be a higher law than that of destruction. Only under that law would a well-ordered society be intelligible and life worth living. And if that is the law of life, we have to work it out in daily life. Wherever there are wars, wherever you are confronted with an opponent, conquer him with love. In a crude manner I have worked it out in my life. That does not mean that all my difficulties are solved. I have found, however, that this law of love has answered as the law of destruction has never done. In India we have had an ocular demonstration of the operation of this law on the widest scale possible. I do not claim therefore that non-violence has necessarily penetrated the three hundred millions, but I do claim that it has penetrated deeper than any other message, and in an incredibly short time. We have not been all uniformly non-violent; and with the vast majority, non-violence has been a matter of policy. Even so, I want you to find out if the country has not made phenomenal progress under the protecting power of non-violence.

It takes a fairly strenuous course of training to attain to a mental state of non-violence. In daily life it has to be a course of discipline though one may not like it, like for instance, the life of a soldier. But I agree that, unless there is a hearty co-operation of the mind, the mere outward observance will be simply a mask, harmful both to the man himself and to others. The perfect state is reached only when mind and body and speech are in proper co-ordination. But it is always a case of intense mental struggle. It is not that I am incapable of anger, for instance, but I succeed on almost all occasions to keep my feelings under control. Whatever may be the result, there is always in me a conscious struggle for following the law of non-violence deliberately and ceaselessly. Such a struggle leaves one stronger for it. Non-violence is a weapon of the strong. With the weak it might easily be hypocrisy. Fear and love are contradictory terms. Love is reckless in giving away, oblivious as to what it gets in return. Love wrestles with the world as with the self and ultimately gains a mastery over all other feelings. My daily experience, as of those who are working with me, is that every problem lends itself to solution if we are determined to make the law of truth and non-violence the law of life. For truth and non-violence are, to me, faces of the same coin.

The law of love will work, just as the law of gravitation will work, whether we accept it or not. Just as a scientist will work wonders out of various application of the law of nature, even so a man who applies the law of love with scientific precision can work greater wonders. For the force of non-violence is infinitely more wonderful and subtle than the material forces of nature, like, for instance, electricity. The men who discovered for us the law of love were greater scientists than any of our modern scientists. Only our explorations have not gone far enough and so it is not possible for every one to see all its working. Such, at any rate, is

M. K. Gandhi, "Faith in Non-Violence," *The Nation's Voice,* part 2: 109–10. Reprinted with permission of Navajivan Trust, Ahmedabad, India.

the hallucination, if it is one, under which I am laboring. The more I work at this law the more I feel the delight in life, the delight in the scheme of this universe. It gives me a peace and a meaning of the mysteries of nature that I have no power to describe.

Study Questions

1. Why does Gandhi believe that love is more powerful and resilient than physical force?
2. How is Gandhi's satyagraha distinct in certain respects from the common understanding of passive or non-violent resistance?
3. How is satyagraha rooted in Gandhi's understanding of the sacred nature of humanity?
4. How have Gandhi's views influenced other political dissidents, such as Martin Luther King, Jr. (Reading 69)?

Reading 51

Nehru's "The Last Lap of Our Long Journey"

India's first seventeen years as an independent nation were dominated by the dynamic leadership of its first prime minister, Jawaharlal Nehru (1889–1964). Nehru was one of the most prominent leaders of the Indian National Congress in pre-Independence India and at the forefront of the freedom struggle. Like Gandhi and others, he was jailed several times. A benevolent despot in socialist garb, Nehru guided the Indian ship of state from 1947 to 1964. His government's foreign policy brought India to the forefront of the world's nonaligned countries, while his inspired domestic strategy, epitomized in the **Five-Year Economic Plans**, helped modernize India's underdeveloped economy. The following speech, delivered on 8 November 1948 at the Constituent Assembly in New Delhi, was occasioned by Nehru's public endorsement of the Indian constitution framed by the Drafting Committee. (His resolution was eventually approved by the assembly.) Nehru's vision of India's greatness made him immensely popular throughout his long and distinguished political career. It was undoubtedly his popularity and achievements that afforded both his daughter **Indira Gandhi** and his grandson **Rajiv** the opportunity to become prime ministers of India after his death. Sadly, both were assassinated. The significance of Jawaharlal Nehru's legacy is not diminished by the fact that he accomplished less than he intended; he was a prime minister with great aspirations for this very troubled nation.

Mr. Vice-President, Sir, we are on the last lap of our long journey. Nearly two years ago, we met in this hall and on that solemn occasion it was my high privilege to move a Resolution which has come to be known as the Objectives Resolution. That is rather a prosaic description of that Resolution, because it embodied something more than mere objectives, although objectives are big things in the life of a nation. It tried to embody, in so far as it is possible in cold print to embody, the spirit that lay behind the Indian people at the time. It is difficult to maintain the spirit of a nation or a people at a high level all the time and I do not know

Jawaharlal Nehru, *Independence and After* (Freeport, NY: Books for Libraries Press, 1950), 375–84, passim.

if we have succeeded in doing that. Nevertheless, I hope that it is in that spirit that we have to approach the framing of this Constitution and it is in that spirit that we shall consider it in detail, always using that Objectives Resolution as the yard measure with which to test every clause and phrase in this Constitution. It may be, of course, that we can improve even on that Resolution; if so, certainly we should do it, but I think that Resolution in some of its clauses laid down the fundamental and basic content of what our Constitution should be. The Constitution is after all some kind of legal body given to the ways of Governments and the life of a people. A Constitution if it is out of touch with the people's life, aims and aspirations, becomes rather empty: if it falls behind those aims, it drags the people down. It should be something ahead to keep people's eyes and minds up to a certain high mark. I think that the Objectives Resolution did that. . . .

I had thought that I could [contribute to the debate] even more, because in recent days and weeks, I have been beyond the shores of India, have visited foreign lands, met eminent people and statesmen of other countries and had the advantage of looking at this beloved country of ours from a distance. That is some advantage. It is true that those who look from a distance do not see many things that exist in this country. But it is equally true that those who live in this country and are surrounded all the time with our numerous difficulties and problems sometimes fail to see the picture as a whole. We have to do both; to see our problems in their intricate detail in order to understand them and also to see them in some perspective so that we may have that picture as a whole before our eyes. . . .

We have, ever since I moved this Objectives Resolution before this House (a year and eleven months ago almost exactly), passed through strange transitions and changes. We function here far more independently than we did at that time. We function as a sovereign independent nation, but we have also gone through a great deal of sorrow and bitter grief during this period and all of us have been powerfully affected by it. The country for which we were going to frame this Constitution was partitioned and split into two. And what happened afterwards is fresh in our minds and will remain fresh with all its horrors for a very long time to come. All that has happened, and yet, in spite of all this, India has grown in strength and in freedom, and undoubtedly this growth of India, this emergence of India as a free country, is one of the significant facts of this generation, significant for us and for the vast numbers of our brothers and sisters who live in this country, significant for Asia, and significant for the world, and the world is beginning to realize—chiefly I think and I am glad to find this—that India's role in Asia and the world will be a beneficent role; sometimes it may be with a measure of apprehension, because India may play some part which some people, some countries, with other interests may not particularly like. All that is happening, but the main thing is this great significant factor that India after being dominated for a long period has emerged as a free sovereign democratic independent country, and that is a fact which changes and is changing history. How far it will change history will depend upon us, this House in the present and other Houses like this coming in the future who represent the organized will of the Indian people.

That's a tremendous responsibility. Freedom brings responsibility; of course, there is no such thing as freedom without responsibility. Irresponsibility itself means lack of freedom. Therefore, we have to be conscious of this tremendous burden of responsibility which freedom has brought: the discipline of freedom and the organized way of working freedom. But there is something even more than that. The freedom that has come to India by virtue of many things, history, tradition, resources, our geographical position, our great potential and all that, inevitably leads India to play an important part in all the world affairs. It is not a question of choosing this or that; it is an inevitable consequence of what India is and what free India must be. . . .

It is in this way that I would like this House to consider this constitution: first of all to keep the Objective Resolution before us and to see how far we are going to act up to it, how far we are going to build up, as we said in that Resolution: "an Independent Sovereign Republic, wherein all power and authority of the sovereign Independent India, its constituent parts and organs of Government, are derived from the people, and wherein shall be guaranteed and secured to all of the people of India justice, social, economic and political; equality of status, of opportunity, and before the law; freedom of thought and expression, belief, faith, worship, vocation, association and action, subject to law and public morality: and this ancient land attain its rightful and honored place in the world and make its full and willing contribution to the promotion of world peace and the welfare of mankind."

I read that last clause in particular, because that brings to our mind India's duty to the world. I should like this House when it considers the various controversies—there are bound to be controversies and there should be controversies, because we are a living and vital nation, and it is right that people should think differently—to realize that it is also right that, thinking differently when they come to decisions, they should act unitedly in furtherance of those decisions. There are various problems, some very important problems, on which there is very little controversy and we pass them—they are of the greatest importance—with a certain unanimity. There are other problems, important no doubt, possibly of a lesser importance, on which we spend a great deal of time and energy and passion also, and do not arrive at agreements in the spirit and which we should arrive at agreements. In the country today, reference is made . . . to the question of language in this Assembly and the country. . . . Now, it is an obvious thing and a vital thing that any country, much more so a free and independent country, must function in its own language. Unfortunately, the mere fact that I am speaking to this House in a foreign language and so many of our colleagues here have to address the House in a foreign language itself shows that something is lacking. It is lacking, let us recognize it; we shall get rid of that lacuna undoubtedly. But, if in trying to press for a change, an immediate change, we get wrapped up in numerous controversies and possibly even delay the whole Constitution, I submit to this House it is not a very wise step to take. Language is and has been a vital factor in an individual's and a nation's life and because it is vital, we have to give it every thought and consideration. Because it is vital, it is also an urgent matter;

and because it is vital, it is also a matter in which urgency may ill-serve our purpose. There is a slight contradiction. Because, if we proceed in an urgent matter to impose something, maybe by a majority, on an unwilling minority in parts of the country or even in this House, we do not really succeed in what we have started to achieve. Powerful forces are at work in the country which will inevitably lead to the substitution of the English language by an Indian language or Indian languages in so far as the different parts of the country are concerned; but there will always be one all-India language. Powerful forces are also at work in the formation of that all-India language. A language ultimately grows from the people; it is seldom that it can be imposed. Any attempt to impose a particular form of language on an unwilling people has usually met with the strongest opposition and has actually resulted in something the very reverse of what the promoters thought. I would beg this House to consider the fact and to realize, if it agrees with me, that the surest way of developing a natural all-India language is not so much to pass resolutions and laws on the subject, but to work to that end in other ways. For my part I have a certain conception of what an all-India language should be. Other people's conception may not be quite the same as mine. I cannot impose my conception on this House or on the country just as any other person will not be able to impose his or her conception unless the country accepts it. I would much rather avoid trying to impose my or anyone else's conception and instead work to that end in co-operation and amity and see how, after we have settled these major things about the Constitution, after we have attained an even greater measure of stability, we can take up each one of these questions and dispose of them in a much better atmosphere. . . .

Now, may I beg again to repeat what I said earlier? Destiny has cast a certain role on this country. Whether anyone of us present here can be called men or women of destiny or not I do not know. That is a big word which does not apply to average human beings, but whether we are men or women of destiny or not, India is a country of destiny and so far as we represent this great country with a great destiny stretching out in front of her, we also have to act as men and women of destiny, viewing all our problems in that long perspective of destiny and of the world and of Asia, never forgetting the great responsibility that freedom, that this great destiny of our country has cast upon us, not losing ourselves in petty controversies and debates which might be useful, but which would in this context be either out of place or out of tune. Vast numbers of minds and eyes look in this direction. We have to remember them. Hundreds of millions of our own people look to us and hundreds of millions of others also look to us; and remember this that while we want this Constitution to be as solid and as permanent a structure as we can make it, nevertheless, there is no permanence in constitutions. There should be a certain flexibility. If you make a thing rigid and permanent, you stop a nation's growth, the growth of a living, vital, organic people. Therefore, it has to be flexible. So also, when you pass this Constitution you will, and I think it is so proposed, lay down a period of years—whatever that period may be—during which changes to that constitution can easily be made without any difficulty. That is a very necessary proviso for a number of reasons. One is this: that while we, who are assembled in this House, undoubtedly represent the people of India, nevertheless, I think it can be said, and truthfully, that when a new House, by whatever name it goes, is elected in terms of this Constitution, and every adult in India has the right to vote—man and woman—the House that emerges then will certainly be fully representative of every section of the Indian people. It is right that the House so elected—under this Constitution, of course, it will have the right to do anything—should have an easy opportunity to make such changes as it wants easily. But in any event, we should not, as some other great countries have, make a Constitution so rigid that it cannot be easily adapted to changing conditions. Today especially, when the world is in turmoil and we are passing through a very swift period of transition, what we do today may not be wholly applicable tomorrow. Therefore, while we make a Constitution which is sound and as basic as we can make it, it should also be flexible and for a period we should be in a position to change it with relative facility.

May I say one word again about certain tendencies in the country which still think in terms of separatist existence or separate privileges and the like? This very Objectives Resolution has set out adequate safeguards to be provided for minorities, for tribal areas, depressed and other backward classes. Of course, that must be done, and it is the duty and responsibility of the majority to see that this is done and to see that they win over all minorities which may have suspicions against them, which may suffer from fear. It is right and important that we should raise the level of the backward groups in India and bring them up to the level of the rest. But it is not right that in trying to do this we create further barriers, or even keep existing barriers, because the ultimate objective is not separatism, but building up an organic nation, not necessarily a uniform nation, because we have a varied culture, and in this country, ways of living differ in various parts of the country, habits differ and cultural traditions differ. I have no grievance against that. Ultimately in the modern world there is a strong tendency for the prevailing culture to influence others. That may be a natural influence. But I think the glory of India has been the way in which it has managed to keep two things going at the same time: that is, its infinite variety and at the same time its unity in that variety. Both have to be kept, because if we have only variety, then that means separatism and going to pieces. If we seek to impose some kind of regimented unity that makes a living organism rather lifeless. Therefore, while it is our bounden duty to do everything we can to give full opportunity to every minority or group and to raise every backward group or class, I do not think it will be the right thing to go the way this country has gone in the past by creating barriers and by calling for protection. As a matter of fact, nothing can protect such a minority or a group less than a barrier which separates it from the majority. It makes it a permanently isolated group and it prevents it from coming closer to the other groups in the country.

I trust, Sir, that what I have ventured to submit to the House will be borne in mind when these various clauses are considered and that ultimately we shall pass this Constitution in the spirit of the solemn moment when we started this great endeavor.

Study Questions

1. What does Nehru mean by the phrase "the last lap of our long journey"?
2. What is the author's strategy for building a national political consensus of all inhabitants of India?
3. A devoted follower of Gandhi (Reading 50), how did Nehru remain true to the essential philosophy of his spiritual and political mentor?
4. According to Nehru, what is India's role and destiny in the global community?

Reading 52

Mother Teresa's Nobel Peace Prize Lecture of 1979

Agnes Gonxha Bojaxhiu was born in 1910 in what was once Yugo-slavia. As a young woman she was enthusiastic about Christian missionary work, and when she turned 21 Agnes Bojaxhiu took holy vows, and with them the name Teresa. She served her novitiate with the Congregation of Loreto Sisters, a community of Catholic nuns working in West Bengal, India. After teaching at the Loreto girls' schools in Calcutta for fifteen years, Sister Teresa believes she received a call from God to work in Calcutta's slums. She thereupon applied for release from her teaching duties to begin her new work. She established the Congregation of the Missionaries of Charity and received Pope Pius XII's (1876–1958) approval for the organization on 7 October 1950. The order's charter prescribes the foundation of a Home for the Dying, which Mother Teresa opened in Calcutta in 1952. Her simple goal is to give medical attention to anyone on the verge of death; those who cannot be treated are given the opportunity to die with dignity. In 1965, Mother Teresa's religious order was recognized as a papal congregation under protection of the Vatican. Houses of the Missionaries of Charity, made up of nuns who "give whole-hearted and free service to the poorest of the poor," have since spread to every corner of the world and now more than 150 foundations offer a wide variety of services to society's forgotten underclass. According to her many admirers, Mother Teresa teaches and embodies an acceptance of God's will that goes beyond the common pale of human actions and thoughts. Interestingly, some of Mother Teresa's comments in her 1979 Nobel Peace Prize Lecture—especially her condemnation of abortion—were not well received.

As we have gathered here together to thank God for the Nobel Peace Prize, I think it will be beautiful that we pray the prayer of **St. Francis of Assisi** which always surprises me very much. We pray this prayer every day after Holy Communion, because it is very fitting for each one of us. And I always wonder that 400–500 years ago when St. Francis of Assisi composed this prayer, they had the same

Mother Teresa, "The Nobel Lecture," *Vital Speeches of the Day* (Mt. Pleasant, SC: City News Publishing, 1941), vol. 46: no. 16.

difficulties that we have today as we compose this prayer that fits very nicely for us also. I think some of you already have got it—so we will pray together:

Let us thank God for the opportunity that we all have together today, for this gift of peace that reminds us that we have been created to live that peace, and that Jesus became man to bring that good news to the poor. He, being God, became man in all things like us except in sin, and he proclaimed very clearly that he had come to give the good news.

The news was peace to all of good will and this is something that we all want—the peace of heart. And God loved the world so much that he gave his son—it was a giving; it is as much as if to say it hurt God to give, because he loved the world so much that he gave his son. He gave him to the Virgin Mary, and what did she do with him?

As soon as he came in her life, immediately she went in haste to give that good news, and as she came into the house of her cousin, the child—the unborn child—the child in the womb of Elizabeth, leapt with joy. He was, that little unborn child was, the first messenger of peace. He recognized the Prince of Peace, he recognized that Christ had come to bring the good news for you and for me. And as if that was not enough—it was not enough to become a man—he died on the cross to show that greater love, and he died for you and for me and for that leper and for that man dying of hunger and that naked person lying in the street not only of Calcutta, but of Africa, and New York, and London, and Oslo—and insisted that we love one another as he loves each one of us. And we read that in the Gospel very clearly: "love as I have loved you; as I love you; as the Father has loved me, I love you." And the harder the Father loved him, he gave him to us, and how much we love one another, we too must give to each other until it hurts.

It is not enough for us to say: "I love God, but I do not love my neighbor." St. John says that you are a liar if you say you love God and you don't love your neighbor. How can you love God whom you do not see, if you do not love your neighbor whom you see, whom you touch, with whom you live? And so this is very important for us to realize that love, to be true, has to hurt.

It hurt Jesus to love us. It hurt him. And to make sure we remember his great love, he made himself the bread of life to satisfy our hunger for his love—our hunger for God—because we have been created for that love. We have been created in his image. We have been created to love and be loved, and he has become man to make it possible for us to love as he loved us. He makes himself the hungry one, the naked one, the homeless one, the sick one, the one in prison, the lonely one, the unwanted one, and he says: "You did it to me." He is hungry for our love, and this is the hunger of our poor people. This is the hunger that you and I must find. It may be in our own home.

I never forget an opportunity I had in visiting a home where they had all these old parents of sons and daughters who had just put them in an institution and forgotten, maybe. And I went there, and I saw in that home they had everything, beautiful things, but everybody was looking toward the door. And I did not see a single one with a smile on their face. And I turned to the sister and I asked; How is that? How is it that these people who have everything here, why are they all looking toward the door? Why are they not smiling?

I am so used to seeing the smiles on our people, even the dying ones smile. And she said: "This is nearly every day. They are expecting, they are hoping that a son or daughter will come to visit them. They are hurt because they are forgotten." And see—this is where love comes. That poverty comes right there in our own home, even neglect to love. Maybe in our own family we have somebody who is feeling lonely, who is feeling sick, who is feeling worried, and these are difficult days for everybody. Are we there? Are we there to receive them? Is the mother there to receive the child?

I was surprised in the West to see so many young boys and girls given into drugs. And I tried to find out why. Why is it like that? And the answer was: "Because there is no one in the family to receive them." Father and mother are so busy they have no time. Young parents are in some institution and the child goes back to the street and gets involved in something. We are talking of peace. These are things that break peace.

But I feel the greatest destroyer of peace today is abortion, because it is a direct war, a direct killing, direct murder by the mother herself. And we read in the scripture, for God says very clearly: "Even if a mother could forget her child, I will not forget you. I have curved you in the palm of my hand." We are curved in the palm of his hand; so close to him, that unborn child has been curved in the hand of God. And that is what strikes me most, the beginning of that sentence, that even if a mother could forget, something impossible—but even if she could forget—I will not forget you.

And today the greatest means, the greatest destroyer of peace is abortion. And we who are standing here—our parents wanted us. We would not be here if our parents would do that to us.

Our children, we want them, we love them. But what of the other millions? Many people are very, very concerned with the children of India, with the children of Africa where quite a number die, maybe of malnutrition, of hunger and so on, but millions are dying deliberately by the will of the mother. And this is what is the greatest destroyer of peace today. Because if a mother can kill her own child, what is left for me to kill you and you to kill me? There is nothing between.

And this I appeal in India, I appeal everywhere—"Let us bring the child back"—and this year being the child's year: What have we done for the child? At the beginning of the year I told, I spoke everywhere and I said: Let us ensure this year that we make every single child born, and unborn, wanted. And today is the end of the year. Have we really made the children wanted?

I will tell you something terrifying. We are fighting abortion by adoption. We have saved thousands of lives. We have sent word to all the clinics, to the hospitals, police stations: "Please don't destroy the child; we will take the child." So every hour of the day and night there is always somebody—we have quite a number of unwedded mothers—tell them: "Come, we will take care of you, we will take the child from you, and we will get a home for the child." And we have a tremendous demand for families who have no children, that is the blessing of

God for us. And also, we are doing another thing which is very beautiful. We are teaching our beggars, our leprosy patients, our slum dwellers, our people of the street, natural family planning.

And in Calcutta alone in six years—it is all in Calcutta—we have had 61,273 babies less from the families who would have had them because they practice this natural way of abstaining, of self-control, out of love for each other. We teach them the temperature method which is very beautiful, very simple. And our poor people understand. And you know what they have told me? "Our family is healthy, our family is united, and we can have a baby whenever we want." So clear—those people in the street, those beggars—and I think that if our people can do like that how much more you and all the others who can know the ways and means without destroying the life that God has created in us.

The poor people are very great people. They can teach us so many beautiful things. The other day one of them came to thank us and said: "You people who have evolved chastity, you are the best people to teach us family planning because it is nothing more than self-control out of love for each other." And I think they said a beautiful sentence. And these are people who maybe have nothing to eat, maybe they have not a home where to live, but they are great people.

The poor are very wonderful people. One evening we went out and we picked up four people from the street. And one of them was in a most terrible condition. And I told the Sisters: "You take care of the other three; I will take care of this one that looks worse." So I did for her all that my love can do. I put her in bed, and there was such a beautiful smile on her face. She took hold of my hand, as she said one word only: "thank you"—and she died.

I could not help but examine my conscience before her. And I asked: "What would I say if I was in her place?" And my answer was very simple. I would have tried to draw a little attention to myself. I would have said: "I am hungry, I am dying, I am cold, I am in pain," or something. But she gave me much more—she gave me her grateful love. And she died with a smile on her face—like that man who we picked up from the drain, half eaten with worms, and we brought him to the home—"I have lived like an animal in the street, but I am going to die like an angel, loved and cared for." And it was so wonderful to see the greatness of that man who could speak like that, who could die like that without blaming anybody, without cursing anybody, without comparing anything. Like an angel—this is the greatness of our people.

And that is why we believe what Jesus has said: "I was hungry, I was naked, I was homeless; I was unwanted, unloved, uncared for—and you did it to me."

I believe that we are not really social workers. We may be doing social work in the eyes of the people. But we are really contemplatives in the heart of the world. For we are touching the body of Christ twenty-four hours. We have twenty-four hours in his presence, and so you and I. You too must try to bring that presence of God into your family, for the family that prays together stays together. And I think that we in our family, we don't need bombs and guns, to destroy or to bring peace—just get together, love one another, bring that peace, that joy, that strength of presence of each other in the home. And we will be able to overcome all the evil that is in the world. There is so much suffering, so much hatred, so much misery, and we with our prayer, with our sacrifice are beginning at home. Love begins at home, and it is not how much we do, but how much love we put in the action that we do. It is to God almighty—how much we do does not matter, because he is infinite, but how much love we put in that action. How much we do to him in the person that we are serving.

Sometime ago in Calcutta we had great difficulty in getting sugar. And I don't know how the word got around to the children, and a little boy of four years old, a Hindu boy, went home and told his parents: "I will not eat sugar for three days. I will give my sugar to Mother Teresa for her children." After three days his father and mother brought him to our house. I had never met them before, and this little one could scarcely pronounce my name. But he knew exactly what he had come to do. He knew that he wanted to share his love.

And this is why I have received such a lot of love from all. From the time that I have come here I have simply been surrounded with love, and with real, real understanding love. It could feel as if everyone in India, everyone in Africa is somebody very special to you. And I felt quite at home. I was telling Sister today. I feel in the convent with the Sisters as if I am in Calcutta with my own Sisters. So completely at home here, right here.

And so here I am talking with you. I want you to find the poor here, right in your own home first. And begin love there. Be that good news to your own people. And find out about your next-door neighbor. Do you know who they are?

I had the most extraordinary experience with a Hindu family who had eight children. A gentleman came to our house and said: "Mother Teresa, there is a family with eight children; they have not eaten for so long; do something." So I took some rice and I went there immediately. And I saw the children—their eyes shining with hunger. I don't know if you have ever been hungry. But I have seen it very often. And she took the rice, she divided the rice, and she went out. When she came back I asked her: "Where did you go, what did you do?" And she gave me a very simple answer: "They are hungry also." What struck me most was that she knew. I didn't bring more rice that evening because I wanted them to enjoy the joy of sharing.

But there were those children, radiating joy, sharing the joy with their mother because she had the love to give. And you see, this is where love begins—at home. And I love you—and I am very grateful for what I have received. It has been a tremendous experience and I go back to India—I will be back by next week, the 15th I hope, and I will be able to bring your love.

And I know well that you have not given from your abundance, but you have given until it has hurt you. Today the little children, they gave—I was so surprised—there is so much joy for the children that are hungry. That the children like themselves will need love and get so much from their parents.

So let us thank God that we have had this opportunity to come to know each other, and that this knowledge of each other has brought us very close. And we will be able to help the children of the whole world, because as you know our

Sisters are all over the world. And with this prize that I have received as a prize of peace, I am going to try to make the home for many people that have no home. Because I believe that love begins at home, and if we can create a home for the poor, I think that more and more love will spread. And we will be able through this understanding love to bring peace, be the good news to the poor. The poor in our own family first, in our country and in the world.

To be able to do this, our Sisters, our lives have to be woven with prayer. They have to be woven with Christ to be able to understand, to be able to share. Today there is so much suffering and I feel that the passion of Christ is being relived all over again. Are we there to share that passion, to share that suffering of people—around the world, not only in the poor countries? But I found the poverty of the West so much more difficult to remove.

When I pick up a person from the street, hungry, I give him a plate of rice, a piece of bread, I have satisfied. I have removed that hunger. But a person that is shut out, that feels unwanted, unloved, terrified, the person that has been thrown out from society—that poverty is so hurtful and so much, and I find that very difficult. Our Sisters are working amongst that kind of people in the West.

So you must pray for us that we may be able to be that good news. We cannot do that without you. You have to do that here in your country. You must come to know the poor. Maybe our people here have material things, everything, but I think that if we all look into our own homes, how difficult we find it sometimes to smile at each other, and that the smile is the beginning of love.

And so let us always meet each other with a smile, for the smile is the beginning of love, and once we begin to love each other, naturally we want to do something. So you pray for our Sisters and for me and for our Brothers, and for our Co-workers that are around the world. Pray that we may remain faithful to the gift of God, to love him and serve him in the poor together with you. What we have done we would not have been able to do if you did not share with your prayers, with your gifts, this continual giving. But I don't want you to give me from your abundance. I want that you give me until it hurts.

The other day I received $15 from a man who has been on his back for twenty years and the only part that he can move is his right hand. And the only companion that he enjoys is smoking. And he said to me: "I do not smoke for one week, and I send you this money." It must have been a terrible sacrifice for him but see how beautiful, how he shared. And with that money I bought bread and I gave to those who are hungry with a joy on both sides. He was giving and the poor were receiving.

This is something that you and I can do—it is a gift of God to us to be able to share our love with others. And let it be able to share our love with others. And let it be as it was for Jesus. Let us love one another as he loved us. Let us love him with undivided love. And the joy of loving him and each other—let us give now that Christmas is coming so close.

Let us keep that joy of loving Jesus in our hearts, and share that joy with all that we come in touch with. That radiating joy is real, for we have no reason not to be happy because we have Christ with us. Christ in our hearts, Christ in the poor that we meet, Christ in the smile that we give and the smile that we receive. Let us make that one point—that no child will be unwanted, and also that we meet each other always with a smile, especially when it is difficult to smile.

I never forget some time ago about fourteen professors came from the United States from different universities. And they came to Calcutta to our house. Then we were talking about the fact that they had been to the home for the dying. (We have a home for the dying in Calcutta, where we have picked up more than 36,000 people only from the streets of Calcutta, and out of that big number more than 18,000 have died a beautiful death. They have just gone home to God.) And they came to our house and we talked of love, of compassion. And then one of them asked me: "Say, Mother, please tell us something that we will remember." And I said to them: "Smile at each other, make time for each other in your family. Smile at each other."

And then another one asked me: "Are you married?" And I said: "Yes, and I find it sometimes very difficult to smile at Jesus because he can be very demanding sometimes." This is really something true. And there is where love comes—when it is demanding, and yet we can give it to him with joy.

Just as I have said today, I have said that if I don't go to heaven for anything else I will be going to heaven for all the publicity because it has purified me and sacrificed me and made me really ready to go to heaven.

I think that this is something, that we must live life beautifully, we have Jesus with us and he loves us. If we could only remember that God loves us, and we have an opportunity to love others as he loves us, not in big things, but in small things with great love, then Norway becomes a nest of love. And how beautiful it will be that from here a center for peace from war has been given. That from here the joy of life of the unborn child comes out. If you become a burning light of peace in the world, then really the Nobel Peace Prize is a gift of the Norwegian people. God bless you!

Study Questions

1. Why did Mother Teresa's remarks on certain sensitive issues such as abortion make some people uncomfortable?
2. How does Mother Teresa maintain her unbounded optimism while living amid India's dire poverty and death, and what seems to be at the core of her extraordinary faith in humanity?
3. According to Mother Teresa, what above all else plagues the modern world?
4. How have Mother Teresa's spiritual beliefs been influenced by Indian culture and religion?

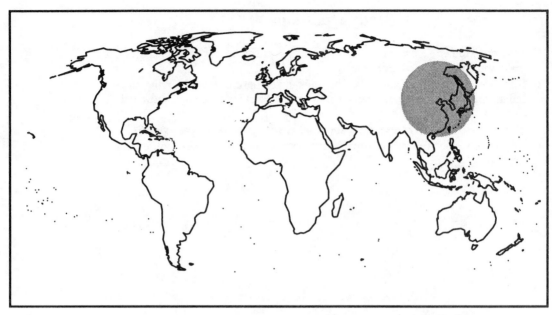

Brief Chronology for the Contemporary World

East Eurasia

1868	Beginning of Meiji Reform in Japan (Emperor Meiji, 1867–1912)
1889	New constitution in Japan that follows imperial German model
1893–1976	Mao Zedong
18¦4–1895	War between China and Japan
18¦8	Chinese Hundred Days' Reform Movement
1898–1900	Boxer Rebellion in China
1904–1905	Japan defeats Russia in brief war
1905	Traditional civil service examination system ends in China
1910	Japanese annexation of Korea
1911	Beginning of Republican Revolution in China
1916–1928	Era of the warlords in China
1921	Foundation of Chinese Communist Party
1921–1925	Sun Yat-sen controls Chinese republican government from Canton
1928–1937	Nationalist government in China under Kuomintang
1931	Japan invades Manchuria
1937	Japan, Germany, and Italy form Anti-Comintern Pact
1937–1945	China and Japan at war
1938	Japan proclaims New Order in Asia
1941	Tojo becomes premier of Japan
1941–1945	World War II in the Pacific theater
1945	Two atomic bombs dropped on Japan; Japanese unconditional surrender to Allied forces
1946–1949	Civil war in China ends with establishment of Communist People's Republic of China
1950–1953	Korean War
1952	End of military occupation of Japan by Allied Powers
1954	French suffer major defeat at Dien Bien Phu, Vietnam
1966	Beginning of the Cultural Revolution in China
1971	People's Republic of China given the China seat at the United Nations
1972	U.S. president Richard M. Nixon visits China
1979	U.S. and People's Republic of China establish formal diplomatic ties
1988	Japan's GNP becomes second largest in the world
1989	Massacre in Tiananmen Square in China

All dates are C.E. and approximate unless otherwise indicated. It should be noted as well that chronologies are constantly being revised. Hence, there may be discrepancies between the dates listed above and those found in other textbooks and scholarly monographs. Throughout the text and in the Glossary, all dates are given in B.C.E. (Before the Common Era) and C.E. (the Common Era). Where there is no era designation C.E. may be assumed.

308

Sun Yat-sen's *Three Principles of the People*

Sun Yat-sen (1866–1925) was educated in China, the British colony of Hong Kong, and the United States. Dr. Sun practiced medicine for a short time but gave it up following China's defeat in its war against Japan in 1894–95. He came to believe that the imperial government was thoroughly rotten, and nothing short of a revolution would restore China's greatness. After the **Boxer Rebellion** (1898–1900), revolutionary forces gained momentum among Chinese patriots. As a result, the Manchu dynasty was overthrown in 1911 and the Republic of China was established. One of the founders of modern China, Dr. Sun delivered a series of lectures at the Senior Normal School in Canton between January and August of 1924. He presented six lectures on nationalism, six on democracy, and four on Chinese people's livelihood. On the day before his death, Sun Yat-sen wrote, "The work of the Revolution is not yet done." Little did he realize that his prophetic words would ring true: when Mao Zedong arrived on the Chinese political scene about ten years later, he continued the work Sun Yat-sen had begun.

On Nationalism (27 January 1924)

What is the Principle of Nationalism? I would say briefly that the Principle of Nationalism is equivalent to the "doctrine of the state." The Chinese people have shown the greatest loyalty to family and clan with the result that in China there have been family-ism and clanism but no real nationalism. The unity of the Chinese people has stopped short at the clan and has not extended to the nation.

My statement that the principle of nationalism is equivalent to the doctrine of the state is applicable in China but not in the West. For the reason that China, since the Ch'in and Han dynasties, has been developing a single state out of a single race, while foreign countries have developed many states from one race and have included many nationalities within one state. For example, England, now the world's most powerful state, has, upon the foundation of the white race, added

---

Sun Yat-sen, *The Three Principles of the People* (Taipei: China Cultural Service, 1981), 1–5, 39–45, 99–109, passim.

brown, black, and other races to form the British Empire. Hence, to say that the race or nation is the state is not true of England.

There is a definite line between them. In simple terms, the race or nationality has developed through natural forces, while the state has developed through force of arms. To use an illustration from China's political history: Chinese say that the wang-tao, royal way or way of right, followed nature; in other words, natural force was the royal way. The group molded by the royal way is the race, the nationality. Armed force is the *pa-tao,* or "the way of might"; the group formed by the way of might is the state. Since of old, no state has been built up without force. But the development of a race or nationality is quite different: it grows entirely by nature, in no way subject to force. Therefore, we say that a group united and developed in the royal way, by forces of nature, is a race; a group united and developed by the way of might, by human forces, is a state. This, then, is the difference between a race or nationality and a state.

Again, as to the origin of races. Man was originally a species of animal, yet he is far removed from the common fowl and the beasts; he is "the soul of all creation." Dividing further, we have many subraces. The forces which developed these races were, in general, natural forces, but when we try to analyze them we find they are very complex. The greatest force is common blood. The blood of ancestors is transmitted by heredity down through the race, making blood kinship a powerful force.

The second great force is livelihood; when the means used to obtain a living vary, the races developed show differences. The abode of the Mongolians, for instance, followed water and grass; they lived the life of nomads, roaming and tenting by water and grass, and out of these common nomadic habits there developed a race, which accounts for the sudden rise of Mongol power.

The third great force in forming races is language. If foreign races learn our language, they are more easily assimilated by us and in time become absorbed into our race. So language is also one of the great forces for the development of a race.

The fourth force is religion. People who worship the same gods or the same ancestors tend to form one race. Religion is also a very powerful factor in the development of races.

The fifth force is customs and habits. If people have markedly similar customs and habits, they will, in time, cohere and form one race. When, therefore, we discover dissimilar peoples or stocks amalgamating and forming a homogeneous race, we must attribute the development to these five forces—blood kinship, common language, common livelihood, common religion, and common customs— which are products not of military occupation but of natural evolution. The comparison between these five natural forces and armed force helps us to distinguish between the race or nationality and the state.

Considering the law of survival of ancient and modern races, if we want to save China and to preserve the Chinese race, we must certainly promote Nationalism. To make this principle luminous for China's salvation, we must first understand it clearly. The Chinese race totals four hundred million people; for the most part, the Chinese people are of the Han or Chinese race with common blood, common language, common religion, and common customs—a single, pure race.

What is the standing of our nation in the world? In comparison with other nations we have the greatest population and the oldest culture, of four thousand years' duration. We ought to be advancing in line with the nations of Europe and America. But the Chinese people have only family and clan groups; there is no national spirit. Consequently, in spite of four hundred million people gathered together in one China, we are in fact but a sheet of loose sand. We are the poorest and weakest state in the world, occupying the lowest position in international affairs; the rest of mankind is the carving knife and the serving dish, while we are the fish and the meat. Our position now is extremely perilous; if we do not earnestly promote nationalism and weld together our four hundred millions into a strong nation, we face a tragedy—the loss of our country and the destruction of our race. To ward off this danger, we must espouse Nationalism and employ the national spirit to save the country.

On Democracy (9 March 1924)

What is the People's Sovereignty? In order to define this term we must first understand what a "people" is. Any unified and organized body of men is called a "people." What is "sovereignty"? It is power and authority extended to the area of the state. The power to execute orders and to regulate public conduct is called "sovereignty," and when "people" and "sovereignty" are linked together, we have the political power of the people. To understand "political power" we must know what government is. Briefly, government is a thing of the people and by the people; it is control of the affairs of all the people. The power of control is political sovereignty, and where the people control the government we speak of the "people's sovereignty."

The word democracy—popular sovereignty—has only lately been introduced into China. All of you who have come here today to support my revolution are naturally believers in democracy. Which, autocracy or democracy, is really better suited to modern China? If we base our judgment upon the intelligence and the ability of the Chinese people, we come to the conclusion that the sovereignty of the people would be far more suitable for us. **Confucius** and **Mencius** two thousand years ago spoke for people's rights. Confucius said, "When the Great Doctrine prevails, all under heaven will work for the common good." . . . Thus China more than two millenniums ago had already considered the idea of democracy, but at that time she could not put it into operation. Democracy was then what foreigners call a Utopia, an ideal which could not be immediately realized.

Now that Europe and America have founded republics, we whose ancients dreamed of these things should certainly follow the tide of world events and make use of the people's power if we expect our state to rule long and peacefully and our people to enjoy happiness. . . .

Since the beginning of human history, the kind of power which government has wielded has inevitably varied according to the circumstances and tendencies of the age. In an age which reverenced gods, theocratic power had to be used; in an age of princes autocratic power had to be used. But now the currents of the world's life have swept into the age of democracy and it behooves us quickly to study what democracy means. Because some of the treatises upon democracy, such as the *Social Contract* of Rousseau, have been a bit inconsistent with true principles, is no reason why we should oppose all that is good in democracy as well. Nor must we think that democracy is impracticable because the monarchy was restored after the revolution of **Cromwell** in England or because the revolution stretched out for so long a time in France. The French Revolution lasted eighty years before it succeeded. The American Revolution accomplished its aims in eight years, but England after two hundred years of revolution still has a king. However, if we observe the steady progress of the world from many angles, we are assured the day of democracy is here; and that, no matter what disappointments and defeats democracy may meet, it will maintain itself for a long time to come upon the earth.

Thirty years ago, therefore, we fellow revolutionists firmly resolved that, if we wanted China to be strong and our revolution to be effective, we must espouse the cause of democracy. Those Chinese who opposed democracy used to ask what strength there was in our Revolutionary Party to be able to overthrow the Manchu emperor. But in 1911 he fell with one push, another victim of the world tide. This world tendency has flowed from theocracy on to autocracy and from autocracy now on to democracy, and there is really no way to stem the current. . . .

Today I am speaking about the people's sovereignty and I want you all to understand clearly what it really means. Unless we do understand clearly, we can never get rid of imperial ambitions among us, ambitions which will make even brethren in a cause and citizens of the same country fight one another. The whole land will be torn year after year with civil strife and there will be no end to the sufferings of the people. Because I wanted us to avert such calamities, I lifted up the banner of democracy as soon as the revolution began and determined that we should found a republic. When we have a real republic, who will be king? The people, our four hundred millions, will be king. This will prevent everybody from struggling for power and will reduce the war evil in China.

On Livelihood (3 August 1924)

The subject of my lecture today is *Min Sheng Chu I,* the "Principle of the People's Livelihood." *Min Sheng* is a worn phrase in China. We talk about *Kuo Chi Min Sheng,* "national welfare and the people's livelihood," but I fear that we pay only lip service to these words and have not really sought to understand them. I cannot see that they have held much meaning for us. But if, in this day of scientific knowledge, we will bring the phrase into the realm of scientific discussion and study its social and economic implications, we shall find that it takes on an immeasurable significance. I propose today a definition for *Min Sheng,* the People's Livelihood. It denotes the livelihood of the people—the existence of society, the welfare of the nation, the life of the masses. And now I shall use the phrase *Min Sheng* to describe one of the greatest problems that has emerged in the West during the past century or more, and that is a social problem.

The problem of livelihood is now rising like a tide in every country. Yet the problem is comparatively new, with a history of not much over a century. What has caused the sudden emergence of this question in the last hundred years? Briefly, the rapid progress of material civilization all over the world, the great development of industry and the sudden increase in the productive power of the human race. Candidly speaking, the problem arose with the invention of machinery and with the gradual substitution of natural power for human labor in the most civilized nations. . . .

On account of this [industrial] revolution the workers suffered greatly. This is why, during the last few decades, a social problem has come into existence, the result of an effort to relieve this kind of suffering.

It is this social problem that I am discussing today in the Principle of Livelihood. Why not follow the West and speak directly of socialism? Why use the old Chinese term *Min Sheng* in its stead? There is a very significant reason for this which we shall consider. Since its first development, and especially since the Industrial Revolution, machinery has become a serious social problem and has stimulated the rise of socialistic theories. But although socialism has been a growing force for several decades, Western nations have not yet found a solution for the questions involved in it, and a severe dispute is still raging over them.

Is the Principle of Livelihood really different from socialism? Socialism deals primarily with the economic problems of society; that is, the common problem of living. Since the introduction of machinery, a large number of people have had their work taken away from them and workers generally have been unable to maintain their existence. Socialism arose as an effort to solve the living problem, and from this standpoint, the social question is also the economic question, and the principle of livelihood is the main theme of socialism. But now every country's socialism has different theories and different proposals for social reconstruction.

[Karl] Marx worked out the theory that all human activity upon the globe which has been preserved in written records for succeeding generations can be called history; and all human history, viewed in this way, gravitates about material forces. This latter point was the new emphasis which Marx gave to history. If the material basis of life changes, the world also changes; human behavior, moreover, is determined by the material environment, and so the history of human civilization is the story of adaptation to material environment. . . . But the facts of Western history, in the seventy-odd years since Marx, have directly contradicted his theory.

The world now is making steady progress and initiating new reforms daily. Take, for example, the new practice of socialized distribution, also called co-operative societies. These societies are organized by a union of many workers. If the workers buy the clothing and food which they need indirectly through retail merchants, the merchants will demand a profit and make a lot of money, while the workers will have to spend much more upon their purchases. In order to buy good articles at a low price the workers themselves effect an organization and open their own store to sell them what they need. In this way they can buy all goods which they ordinarily use from their own store. The supplies are handy and cheap and at the end of every year the surplus profit which the store makes is divided among the customers according to the proportion of their purchases. It is on account of this division of profits in proportion to the amount of purchase that the stores are called consumers' cooperative societies. A large number of banks and productive factories in Great Britain are now managed by these co-operative societies. The rise of these societies has eliminated a great many commercial stores. Those who once looked upon these stores as unimportant commercial shops now regard them as powerful organizations. For due to the rapid spread of such organizations the big British merchants have now all become producers. The development of these co-operative societies as a solution for the social problem is a side issue, yet it has disproved Marx's conclusion that capitalists would be destroyed before the merchant class. This inconsistency of Marx's deductions with modern facts is another evidence that my theory—that knowledge is difficult, action easy—cannot be effaced. . . .

Livelihood is the center of government, the center of economics, the center of all historical movements. Just as men once misjudged the center of the solar system, so the old socialists mistook material forces for the center of history. The confusions which have resulted may be compared to those which followed the convulsions of the old astronomers that the earth was the center of our solar system. If we want to clear away the confusions from within the social problem, we must correct this mistake in social science. We can no longer say that material issues are the central force in history. We must let the political, social, and economic movements of history gravitate about the problem of livelihood. We must recognize livelihood as the center of social history. When we have made a thorough investigation of this central problem, then we can find a way to a solution of the social problem.

Study Questions

1. According to Sun Yat-sen, how are nationalism, democracy, and livelihood pragmatically related?
2. How did the ideals of Western liberal democracy influence Sun's thinking?
3. According to Sun, why is a state only as strong as its national economy?
4. How do Sun's convictions about his country differ from the traditional views of imperial Chinese bureaucrats and literati?

Two Documents from Maoist China

Mao Zedong (1893–1976), chairman of the People's Republic of China from 1949 until his death, was perceived by many Chinese as someone who could be trusted and who would get things done. Born into a well-to-do peasant family from Hunan, at an early age he was caught up in the revolutionary activity characteristic of many young Chinese in the early twentieth century. As Mao Zedong rose in stature in the Chinese Communist Party—which he helped to establish in 1921—he eventually assumed a position within the Party that was quite unique and removed from its official leadership. By the end of the war against Japan in 1945, Mao had proved his mettle. His military escapades, efforts of internal reform, and penchant for clever, pithy sayings, which seemed to capture the essence of a situation or philosophical principle, led to his assuming the Party's chairmanship. He and his followers eventually triumphed in the civil wars of the late 1940s when the Communists fought against the forces of the autocratic **Chiang Kai-shek**. Mao's first speech to the Chinese People's Political Consultative Conference (CPPCC) was delivered at its initial Plenary session convened on 21 September 1949, about two weeks before the People's Republic of China was proclaimed a political reality. The speech reflects the enormous changes that took place in China at the end of World War II. As the years passed Mao's control over the Party began to wane. Appealing to local and provincial Communist officials, the army, and the youth of China, Mao launched a national campaign known as the Cultural Revolution. Its central aim was to reinvigorate the revolutionary principles in the Party and the nation. At the Eleventh Plenary Session of the Central Committee held in August 1966, Mao's supporters issued the "Sixteen-Point Decision" that officially sanctioned the beginning of the Cultural Revolution.

Opening Speech at the First Plenary Session of the CPPCC (dated 21 September 1949)

Our conference is composed of more than six hundred delegates, representing all the democratic parties and people's organizations of China, the People's Liberation Army, the various regions and localities, and the nationalities all over China as well as the overseas Chinese. This shows that ours is a conference of great unity of the people of the whole country.

The achievement of this great unity among the people throughout the entire country has been made possible by our defeat of the reactionary **Kuomintang** government, which was aided by U.S. imperialism. In a period of just over three years, the heroic Chinese People's Liberation Army, [an army] such as the world has rarely seen, crushed the offensive of the several million troops of the U.S.-aided Kuomintang reactionary government and turned to [launching] its own counter-offensive and offensive. At present, several million troops of the field armies of the People's Liberation Army are already striking at areas close to Taiwan, Guangdong, Guangxi, Guizhou, Sichuan, and Xinjiang, and the majority of the Chinese people have already been liberated. In just over three years' time, the people all over the country have united together to aid the People's Liberation Army and oppose their own enemy, and they have won basic victory. It is on this foundation the current People's Political Consultative Conference is convened. . . .

Within a period of just over three years, the Chinese people, led by the Communist Party of China, have quickly awakened and organized themselves into a nationwide united front to fight against imperialism, feudalism, bureaucratic capitalism, and the Kuomintang reactionary government, which represents these things in a concentrated form. They aided the People's War of Liberation, basically struck down the Kuomintang reactionary government, toppled the rule of imperialism in China, and resurrected the Political Consultative Conference. . . .

Fellow delegates, we all share the feeling that our work will be written down in the history of humanity; it will show that the Chinese people, forming one quarter of humanity, have now stood up. The Chinese have always been a great, courageous, and industrious nation, and it is only in modern times that they have fallen behind. This falling behind came entirely as a result of the oppression and exploitation by foreign imperialism and domestic reactionary governments. For over a century our forbearers have never stopped waging tenacious struggles against domestic and foreign oppressors, including the Revolution of 1911 led by Mr. Sun Yat-sen, the great forerunner of the Chinese revolution. Our forebears have instructed us to fulfill their behest, and we have now done so accordingly. We have united and have overthrown both domestic and foreign oppressors through the People's War of Liberation and the people's great revolution, and now proclaim the establishment of the People's Republic of China. From now on our nation will

Mao Tse-tung, "Opening Speech at the First Plenary Session of the CPPCC," *Daily Bulletin* 634 (2 October 1952) (New China News Agency), 3–4, 5.

join the great family of peace- and freedom-loving nations of the world. We will work with courage and diligence to create our own civilization and well-being, and at the same time promote world peace and freedom. Our nation will never again be a nation insulted by others. We have stood up. Our revolution has won the sympathy and acclamation of the broad masses of the people throughout the world. Our friends are all over the world.

Our revolutionary work has not yet been completed; the People's War of Liberation and the people's revolutionary movement are still surging forward, and we must continue our efforts. Imperialists and domestic reactionaries will certainly not take their defeat lying down; they will undertake a last-ditch struggle. After there is peace and order in the entire country, they will nevertheless engage in sabotage and cause disturbances in any and every way; they will try every day and every minute to stage a comeback in China. This is inevitable and will, without a doubt, happen; we must never relax our vigilance.

Our state system of the people's democratic dictatorship is a powerful weapon for safeguarding the fruits of the victory of the people's revolution and for thwarting the foreign and domestic enemies in their plots to stage a comeback. We must firmly grasp this weapon. Internationally, we must unite with all countries and peoples who cherish peace and freedom, first of all with the Soviet Union and the various New Democracies, so that we will not become isolated in our struggle to safeguard the fruits of the victory of the people's revolution and to thwart the plots of the foreign and domestic enemies to stage a comeback. So long as we uphold the people's democratic dictatorship and unite with our international friends, we shall forever be victorious.

The people's democratic dictatorship and unity with our international friends will enable us to achieve speedy success in our work of construction. The task of national economic construction already lies before us. . . . As long as we maintain the work-style of plain living and hard struggle, as long as we unite as one, and as long as we uphold the people's democratic dictatorship and unite with international friends, we are sure to win swift victory on the economic front.

Following the advent of an upsurge in economic construction, there will inevitably appear an upsurge of cultural construction. The era in which the Chinese people were regarded as uncivilized is now over. We will emerge in the world as a highly civilized nation.

Our national defense will be consolidated, and no imperialist will be allowed to invade our territory again. Our people's armed forces must be preserved and developed with the heroic and tested People's Liberation Army as the foundation. We will not only have a powerful army but also a powerful air force and a powerful navy.

Let the domestic and foreign reactionaries tremble before us! Let them say that we are no good at this and no good at that, but, through indomitable effort, the Chinese people will steadily achieve their goal.

Eternal glory to the people's heroes who have given their lives to the People's War of Liberation and to the people's revolution!

Hail to the victory of the People's War and people's revolution!

Hail to the establishment of the People's Republic of China!

Hail to the success of the Chinese People's Political Consultative Conference!

Decision of the Central Committee of the Chinese Communist Party Concerning the Great Proletarian Revolution (dated 8 August 1966)

I. A new stage of the socialist revolution

The current great **proletarian** cultural revolution is a great revolution that touches people to their very souls, representing a more intensive and extensive new stage of the development of socialist revolution in our country. . . .

Although the **bourgeoisie** have been overthrown, yet they attempt to use the old ideas, old culture, old customs, and old habits of the exploiting classes to corrupt the mind of man and conquer his heart in a bid to attain the goal of restoring their challenges of the bourgeoisie in the ideological sphere, and use its own new ideas, new culture, new customs and new habits to transform the spiritual aspect of the whole society.

At present, our aim is to knock down those power holders who take the capitalist road, criticize the bourgeois reactionary academic "authorities," criticize the ideologies of the bourgeoisie and all exploiting classes, reform education and literature and the arts, and reform all superstructure which is incompatible with the socialist economic base in order to facilitate the consolidation and development of the socialist system.

II. The main stream and twists and turns

The broad masses of workers, peasants and soldiers, revolutionary intellectuals and revolutionary cadres constitute the main force in this great cultural revolution. Large numbers of revolutionary youngsters, hitherto unknown, have become brave vanguards. They have energy and wisdom. Using big-character posters and debates, they are airing their views and opinions in a big way, exposing and criticizing in a big way, firmly launching an attack against those open and covert bourgeois representatives. . . .

The cultural revolution, being a revolution, will unavoidably meet with resistance, which stems mainly from those power holders who have sneaked into the Party and who take the capitalist road. It also comes from the force of old

"Decision of the Central Committee of the Chinese Communist Party Concerning the Great Proletarian Revolution," *Survey of the China Mainland Press,* 16 August 1966.

social habits. Such resistance is still rather great and stubborn at present. But the great proletarian cultural revolution is a general trend of the time and cannot be resisted. A mass of facts show that if only the masses are fully aroused to action, such resistance will break down quickly....

III. The word "courage" must be given first place and the masses mobilized with a free hand

Whether the leadership of the Party dares to mobilize the masses with a free hand will decide the fate of this great cultural revolution....

The Party Central Committee requires Party committees at various levels to uphold correct leadership, be courageous, mobilize the masses with a free hand, change their state of weakness and impotency, encourage those comrades who have made mistakes but who are willing to make amends to lay down their packs and join the battle, and dismiss the power holders who take the capitalist road, so as to let the leadership return to the hands of proletarian revolutionaries.

IV. Let the masses educate themselves in the movement

In the great proletarian cultural revolution, it is the masses who must liberate themselves. We cannot do the things for them which they should do themselves.

We must trust the masses, rely on them, and respect their creative spirit. We must get rid of the word "fear." We must not be afraid of trouble. Chairman Mao has always told us that revolution is not an elegant, gentle, kind and genial thing. In this great revolutionary movement the masses must be told to educate themselves, to discern what is right and what is wrong, and which ways of doing things are correct and which are incorrect....

V. Party's class line must be executed with resolve

Who is our enemy and who is our friend? This question is a primary question of the revolution, as well as a primary question of the cultural revolution.

The Party leadership must be good at discovering the leftists, developing and expanding the ranks of the leftists, and resolutely relying on the revolutionary leftists. Only in this way can we in the movement completely isolate the mass of reactionary rightists, win over the middle-of-the-roaders, and rally the great majority. Through the movement we shall then ultimately unite with over 95 percent of the cadres and with over 95 percent of the masses....

The focus of this movement is on the purge of those power holders within the Party who take the capitalist road....

VI. Contradictions among the people must be correctly handled

It is necessary to strictly separate the two kinds of contradictions of different character—those among the people and those between the enemy and ourselves. Contradictions among the people must be treated as contradictions between the enemy and ourselves or the other way round.

That differing opinions are found among the people is a normal phenomenon. Controversy between various kinds of opinion is not only unavoidable but necessary and beneficial. In the course of normal and unreserved debates the masses are capable of affirming what is correct and rectifying what is wrong, and gradually attaining unanimity.

In the course of the debate, it is essential to adopt the method of putting facts on the table, explaining the reasons, and convincing people with truth. To the minority of people who hold different opinions the method of suppression must not be applied. The minority must be protected because sometimes truth is in the hands of the minority. Even if the opinions of the minority were wrong, they should be permitted to put forward their arguments and to reserve their own opinions.

In the course of the debates, people may argue with one another but must not use their fists. . . .

VII. Be alert against those who label revolutionary masses as "counter-revolutionaries"

In some schools, some units and some work teams, responsible members have organized a counter-attack against the masses who posted big-character wall newspapers against them. They even intimated that to oppose the leaders of their own units or work teams was to oppose the Party Central Committee, the Party and socialism, and that any slogan shouted in this regard was a counter-revolutionary slogan. By so doing they will necessarily attack some real revolutionary activists. This is a wrong direction to take and a wrong line to follow. It is impermissible to do so. . . .

VIII. The **Cadre** question

Cadres may generally be classified into four types:

(1) The good.
(2) The relatively good.
(3) Those with serious mistakes but who are not anti-Party and anti-socialist elements.
(4) A small number of anti-Party and anti-socialist rightists.

Under general conditions, the first two types of cadres (the good and the relatively good) are in the majority.

Anti-Party and anti-socialist rightists must be fully exposed and knocked down, their influence must be eliminated and at the same time they should be given a chance to start anew.

IX. Cultural revolutionary groups, committees, and congresses

In the course of the great proletarian cultural revolution, many new things have begun to appear. In many schools and units, such organizational forms as cultural revolutionary groups and cultural revolutionary committees created by the masses are new things of great historic significance.

Cultural revolutionary groups, cultural revolutionary committees and cultural revolutionary congresses are the best new organizational forms for the self-education of the masses under the leadership of the Communist Party. They are the best bridges for strengthening the contact between the Party and the masses. They are power organs of the proletarian cultural revolution.

The struggle of the proletariat against old ideas, old culture, old customs and old habits left over from all exploiting classes for the past thousands of years will take a very long time. In view of this, cultural revolutionary groups, cultural revolutionary committees, and cultural revolutionary congresses should not be temporary organizations but should be permanent mass organizations. They are applicable not only to schools and organs but basically also to industrial and mining enterprises, streets and the countryside.

Members of the cultural revolutionary groups and cultural revolutionary committees and delegates to the cultural revolutionary congresses must be fully elected as in the **Paris Commune**. . . .

X. Teaching reform

Reforming the old educational system and the old policy and method of teaching is an extremely vital task of the great proletarian cultural revolution.

In this great cultural revolution, it is necessary to completely change the situation where our schools are dominated by bourgeois intellectuals.

In schools of all types, it is imperative to carry out the policy, advanced by Comrade Mao Tse-tung, of making education serve proletarian politics and having education integrated with productive labor, so that those who get an education may develop morally, intellectually and physically and become socialist-minded, cultured laborers.

The academic course must be shortened and the curricula simplified. Teaching materials must be thoroughly reformed, and the more complex material must be simplified first of all. Students should take as their main task the study of their proper courses and also learn other things. Besides studying academic subjects, they should also learn to do industrial, agricultural and military work. They must also be prepared to participate in the cultural revolutionary struggle for criticizing the bourgeoisie.

XI. The question of criticism by name in the press

... Criticism by name in the press must first be discussed by the Party committees at the corresponding levels, and in some cases approved by the higher Party committees.

XII. Policy toward scientists, technicians, and working personnel in general

Toward scientists, technicians and [scientific and technical] working personnel in general, provided that they love their country, work actively, are not against the Party and socialism, and do not secretly collaborate with any foreign power(s), the policy of unity-criticism-unity should continue to be adopted in this movement. Scientists and scientific and technical personnel who have made valuable contributions should be protected. They may be assisted in gradually transforming their world outlook and styles of work.

XIII. The question of arrangements for combining [the cultural revolution] education movement in town and countryside

In big and medium cities cultural and educational units and Party and government leadership organs are the key points of the present proletarian cultural revolution.

The great cultural revolution has made the socialist education movement in town and countryside even richer in content and better. It is necessary to combine the two. . . .

XIV. Grasp the revolution and promote production

The great proletarian cultural revolution is aimed at enabling man to revolutionize his thinking and consequently enabling work in all fields to be done with greater, faster, better and more economical results. Provided the masses are fully mobilized and satisfactory arrangements are made, it is possible to guarantee that the cultural revolution and production will not impede each other and that a high quality of work in all fields will be attained.

The great proletarian cultural revolution is a mighty motive force for developing our country's social productivity. It is wrong to set the great cultural revolution against the development of production.

XV. The army

The cultural revolutionary movement and the socialist education movement in the armed forces should be conducted in accordance with the directives of the Military Commission of the Party Central Committee and the General Political Department of the P[eople's] L[iberation] A[rmy].

XVI. The thought of Mao Tse-tung is the guide for the proletarian cultural revolution

In the course of the great proletarian cultural revolution, it is necessary to hold high the great red banner of the thought of Mao Tse-tung and to place proletarian politics in command. The movement for creatively studying and applying Chairman Mao's works must be launched among the broad masses of workers, peasants and soldiers, cadres and intellectuals. The thought of Mao Tse-tung must be regarded as a compass to the cultural revolution. . . .

Party committees of various levels must abide by the successive directives of Chairman Mao, implement the mass line of coming from the masses and returning to the masses, and be pupils first and teachers later. They must make an effort to avoid one-sidedness and limitations. They must promote materialist dialectics and oppose metaphysics and scholasticism.

Under the leadership of the Party center headed by Comrade Mao Tse-tung, the great proletarian cultural revolution will surely win a grand victory.

Study Questions

1. According to Mao, why were the Communists victorious over the Kuomintang regime in China?
2. What does Mao's notion of "dictatorship of the people" owe to Lenin's idea of "dictatorship of the proletariat" (Reading 57)?
3. In what ways do Mao's remarks in 1949 foreshadow the Chinese Cultural Revolution of the mid-1960s?
4. What were Mao's real objectives in promoting the Cultural Revolution?

Reading 55

Cardinal Principles of the National Entity of Japan

The original text of Kokutai no hongi, *or* Cardinal Principles of the National Entity of Japan *was written by Dr. Hisamatsu Sen-ichia, a professor of Tokyo Imperial University, shortly before its official publication in 1937. His work was rewritten and edited by a committee of "technical experts" and Zto Enkichi, chief of the Imperial Bureau of Thought Control of the Ministry of Education. The Japanese Empire issued* Kokutai no hongi *through the ministry, hoping it would serve as an effective means of state propaganda. The book, in fact, sold two million copies and was apparently very successful in informing the Japanese people of the ideological basis of their government and society. Professor Hisamatsu eventually disavowed the published version of his treatise because of the numerous adulterations made by ministry officials in his original text.*

Introduction

The various ideological and social evils of present-day Japan are the result of ignoring the fundamental and running after the trivial, of lack of judgment, and a failure to digest things thoroughly; and this is due to the fact that since the days of **Meiji** so many aspects of European and American culture, systems, and learning, have been imported, and that, too rapidly. As a matter of fact, the foreign ideologies imported into our country are in the main ideologies of the [European] Enlightenment that have come down from the eighteenth century, or extensions of them. The views of the world and of life that form the basis of these ideologies are a rationalism and a **positivism**, lacking in historical views, which on the one hand lay the highest value on, and assert the liberty and equality of, individuals, and on the other hand lay value on a world by nature abstract, transcending nations and races. . . .

Paradoxical and extreme conceptions, such as socialism, anarchism, and communism, are all based in the final analysis on individualism, which is the root

J. O. Gauntlet, trans., and R. K. Hall, ed., *Kokutai No Hongi: Cardinal Principles of the National Entity of Japan* (Cambridge, MA: Harvard University Press, 1949), 52–183, passim. Copyright © 1949 by the President and Fellows of Harvard College. Reprinted with permission.

of modern Occidental ideologies and of which they are no more than varied manifestations. Yet even in the Occident, where individualism has formed the basis of their ideas, when it has come to communism, they have found it unacceptable; so that now they are about to do away with their traditional individualism, and this has led to the rise of totalitarianism and nationalism and to the springing up of Fascism and Nazism. That is, it can be said that both in the Occident and in our country the deadlock of individualism has led alike to a season of ideological and social confusion and crisis.... This means that the present conflict seen in our people's ideas, the unrest of their modes of life, the confused state of their civilization, can be put right only by a thorough investigation by us of the intrinsic nature of Occidental ideologies and by grasping the true meaning of our national polity. Then, too, this should be done not only for the sake of our nation but for the sake of the entire human race which is struggling to find a way out of the deadlock with which individualism is faced....

Loyalty and Patriotism

Our country is established with the emperor, ... to serve the emperor and to receive the emperor's great august Will as one's own is the rationale of making our historical "life" live in the present; and on this is based the morality of the people.

Loyalty means to reverence the emperor as [our] pivot and to follow him implicitly. By implicit obedience is meant casting ourselves aside and serving the emperor intently. To walk this Way of loyalty is the sole Way in which we subjects may "live," and the fountainhead of all energy. Hence, offering our lives for the sake of the emperor does not mean so-called self-sacrifice, but the casting aside of our little selves to live under his august grace and the enhancing of the genuine life of the people of a State....

From the point of individualistic personal relationships, the relationship between sovereign and subject in our country may [perhaps] be looked upon as that between non-personalities. However, this is nothing but an error arising from treating the individual as supreme, from the notion that has individual thoughts for its nucleus, and from personal abstract consciousness. Our relationship between sovereign and subject is by no means a shallow, horizontal relationship such as implies a correlation between ruler and citizen, but is a relationship springing from a basis transcending this correlation, and is that of "dying to self and returning to [the] One," in which this basis is not lost. This is a thing that can never be understood from an individualistic way of thinking. In our country, this great Way has seen a natural development since the founding of the nation, and the most basic thing that has manifested itself as regards the subjects is in short this Way of loyalty....

Harmony

When we trace the marks of the facts of the founding of our country and the progress of our history, what we always find there is the spirit of harmony. Harmony is a product of the great achievements of the founding of the nation, and is the power behind our historical growth; it is also a humanitarian Way inseparable from our daily lives. The spirit of harmony is built on the concord of all things. When people determinedly count themselves as masters and assert their egos, there is nothing but contradictions and the setting of one against the other; and harmony is not begotten. In individualism it is possible to have cooperation, compromise, sacrifice, etc., so as to regulate and mitigate this contradiction and the setting of one against the other; but after all there exists no true harmony. That is, a society of individualism is one of clashes between [masses of] people . . . and all history may be looked upon as one of class wars. Social structure and political systems in such a society, and the theories of sociology, political science, statecraft, etc., which are their logical manifestations, are essentially different from those of our country which makes harmony its fundamental Way. . . .

Harmony as in our nation is a great harmony of individuals who, by giving play to their individual differences, and through difficulties, toil and labor, converge as one. Because of individual differences and difficulties, this harmony becomes all the greater and its substance rich. Again, in this way individualities are developed, special traits become beautiful, and at the same time they even enhance the development and well-being of the whole.

The Martial Spirit

And then, this harmony is clearly seen also in our nation's martial spirit. Our nation is one that holds bushido in high regard, and there are shrines deifying warlike spirits. . . . But this martial spirit is not [a thing that exists] for the sake of itself but for the sake of peace, and is what may be called a sacred martial spirit. Our martial spirit does not have for its objective the killing of men, but the giving of life to men. This martial spirit is that which tries to give life to all things, and is not that which destroys. That is to say, it is a strife which has peace at its basis with a promise to raise and to develop; and it gives life to things through its strife. Here lies the martial spirit of our nation. War, in this sense, is not by any means intended for the destruction, overpowering, or subjugation of others; and it should be a thing for the bringing about of great harmony, that is, peace, doing the work of creation by following the Way. . . .

Bushido

Bushido may be cited as showing an outstanding characteristic of our national morality. In the world of warriors one sees inherited the totalitarian structure and spirit of the ancient clans peculiar to our nation. Hence, though the teachings of Confucianism and Buddhism have been followed, these have been transcended. That is to say, though a sense of obligation binds master and servant, this has developed into a spirit of self-effacement and meeting death with a perfect calmness. In this, it was not that death was made light of so much as that man tempered himself to death and in a true sense regarded it with esteem. In effect, man tried to fulfill true life by the way of death. . . .

The warrior's aim should be, in ordinary times, to foster a spirit of reverence for the deities and his own ancestors in keeping with his family tradition; to train himself to be ready to cope with emergencies at all times; to clothe himself with wisdom, benevolence, and valor; to understand the meaning of mercy; and to strive to be sensitive to the frailty of Nature. . . .

Every type of foreign ideology that has been imported into our country may have been quite natural in China, India, Europe, or America, in that it has sprung from their racial or historical characteristics; but in our country, which has a unique national polity, it is necessary as a preliminary step to put these types to rigid judgment and scrutiny so as to see if they are suitable to our national traits. . . .

To put it in a nutshell, while the strong points of Occidental learning and concepts lie in their analytical and intellectual qualities, the characteristics of Oriental learning and concepts lie in their intuitive and aesthetic qualities. These are natural tendencies that arise through racial and historical differences; and when we compare them with our national spirit, concepts, or mode of living, we cannot help recognizing further great and fundamental differences. Our nation has in the past imported, assimilated, and sublimated Chinese and Indian ideologies, and has therewith supported the Imperial Way, making possible the establishment of an original culture based on her national polity. . . .

Only where the people one and all put heart and soul into their respective occupations, and there is coherence or order in each of their activities, with their minds set on guarding and maintaining the prosperity of the Imperial Throne, is it possible to see a healthy development in the people's economic life.

The same thing holds true in the case of education. Since the Meiji Restoration our nation has adapted the good elements of the advanced education seen among European and American nations, and has exerted efforts to set up an educational system and materials for teaching. The nation has also assimilated on a wide scale the scholarship of the West, not only in the fields of natural science, but of the mental sciences, and has thus striven to see progress made in our scholastic pursuits and to make education more popular. . . .

However, at the same time, through the infiltration of individualistic concepts, both scholastic pursuits and education have tended to be taken up with a world in which the intellect alone mattered, and which was isolated from historical and actual life; so that both intellectual and moral culture drifted into tendencies in which the goal was the freedom of man, who had become an abstract being, and the perfecting of the individual man. At the same time, these scholastic pursuits and education fell into separate parts, so that they gradually lost their synthetic coherence and concreteness.

In order to correct these tendencies, the only course open to us is to clarify the true nature of our national polity, which is at the very source of our education, and to strive to clear up individualistic and abstract ideas. . . .

Our Mission

Our present mission as a people is to build up a new Japanese culture by adopting and sublimating Western cultures with our national polity as the basis, and to contribute spontaneously to the advancement of world culture. Our nation early saw the introduction of Chinese and Indian cultures, and even succeeded in evolving original creations and developments. This was made possible, indeed, by the profound and boundless nature of our national polity; so that the mission of the people to whom it is bequeathed is truly great in its historical significance.

Study Questions

1. According to the document, what are the primary features of Japanese culture?
2. What are the role and status of the individual in Japanese society according to the compilers of the text?
3. How do the editors of the text combine traditional Japanese values and customs with modern, essentially Western, notions of political sovereignty and nationalism?
4. How could the views expressed in the text justify Japanese aggression against Manchuria and other Asian states in the late 1920s and 1930s?

Japanese Leaflet Entitled "Rise of Asia"

Throughout history, propaganda has served the valuable function of supporting military strength and expert negotiation. Owing to the development of mass media techniques and technology, visual images have been especially effective in modern psychological warfare. Whether referring to films, works of art, posters, or leaflets, associative images were meant either to confirm or affect the feelings and behavior of citizens. This was certainly the major task of the Japanese Bureau of Thought Supervision (BTS), founded by the Ministry of Education in 1932. Unlike the Cabinet Information Bureau, whose main function was to influence public opinion at home, the BTS directed its efforts abroad. Contrived to propagate the empire's "Asia for Asians" campaign, this 1943 leaflet designed by an unknown artist proclaims Japan's leading role as Asia's liberator. The empire, disguised under the name of "The Greater East Asia Co-Prosperity Sphere," worked toward the common goal of freeing Asia from Western control. Although the Japanese Foreign Office did not exploit the full potential of propaganda in the cinema and other art forms, leaflets were effective at least for a time, before many Asians realized that their national destinies were not the same as that of the Japanese Empire.

Reading 56

Oyama Ikuo's *Japan's Future Course*

Oyama Ikuo (1880–1956) was a professor of political science who won a national reputation in Japan while serving as chairman of the Labor-Farmer Party in 1927. When Japan occupied the Chinese province of Manchuria in 1931, an act that brought the world close to war, Oyama went into self-imposed exile in the United States. He taught at Northwestern University during the war years and did not return to his native country until 1947, when he immersed himself in socialist and pacifist activities. His progressive ideas were set forth in his *Nihon no shinro,* or *Japan's Future Course,* published in 1948 during the American occupation of his native country.

Since the **Meiji** Restoration, the ruling class in Japan has built up a system of nationalistic ethics called "the essence of national polity" and based on the ideology of the family state inherited from the feudal age. It has indoctrinated the nation with this type of thought through universal conscription and uniform national education. By this method, the ruling class has tried, on the one hand, to check the trend toward the awakening of individuals that was engendered by the modernization of society, and, on the other, to expel the democratic and socialistic ideas that were rushing in from the outside world. However, this attempt was not entirely successful. For, despite the fact that it was backed by many suppressive laws and the threat of brutal oppression by the military and the police, there were widespread movements of resistance of various kinds, which it succeeded in eliminating only immediately beforehand during the Second World War. Unfortunately these resistance movements came too late. They were smashed before they could develop into nationwide insurrection by the suppressive policy of the ruling class—a policy that hardened greatly in anticipation of the war. Nevertheless these movements clearly disproved the idea that the Japanese were an essentially authoritarian people.

Still, the policy of ideological seclusion inherited from the Meiji era was continued to the end. There was a short break during the decade after the First World War, a period of rising liberalism in Japan. But after the outbreak of the Manchurian Incident, it was increasingly strengthened until it reached its peak

---

during the Second World War. During this war, the militarists established complete control over national public opinion. Thereby the intelligence and conscience of the people were completely benumbed. Thus, world-disturbing actions by Japan, which reached their climax in the attack on Pearl Harbor, had nation-wide support. At home, furthermore, even a number of former leaders of movements for the emancipation of the proletariat joined the camp of the ruling class and became supporters and propagators of the imperialistic policy; abroad, soldiers left the worst stains on our history by their atrocities. Truly, in this period, the intellectual and moral standard of the Japanese was at its worst. A sample of the propaganda used by the militarists was "War is the father of creation and the mother of culture." But the contrary has proved to be the case. At this point, the Japanese have to criticize themselves thoroughly. They must re-examine every nook and corner of their souls. The most important thing for a new Japan is moral reflection. Without it, a new Japan is impossible and her return to international society is out of the question. . . .

As a result of defeat, the wall that secluded the Japanese mind from the outside world broke down. The Japanese people could see the world as it was for the first time. There they saw the great structure of the United Nations. This is the only existing organ for international cooperation for the maintenance of world peace. It embodies the ideals of international democracy and international ethics, which are based upon the concept of human solidarity, and which have gradually developed among the allied powers since the time of the League of Nations. Its present form may not be perfect. But the fact that such a thing has been realized is of the greatest historical significance.

When the Japanese people began to realize that democratization and international cooperation were a single historical necessity for Japan, the new Constitution was established in the full view of the public. Formally, it has some of the marks of a constitution granted by the sovereign, but in its content it contains a number of principles for which we fought in our struggles for political freedom. By and large, it is a democratic constitution. It may not be perfect, but it leaves the way open to correct its deficiencies. Even as it is, it is quite useful as an instrument for our present task: the establishment of democracy.

The new Constitution of Japan has two major principles: a proclamation that sovereignty lies in the people and a declaration to renounce war. Naturally, it corresponds to the United Nations Charter in many respects. In the process of establishing a democratic social order, we must try to make use of this Constitution so that it may not remain a mere piece of paper. But first we have to start by getting rid of the traditional nationalistic doctrine based upon the ideology of the family state and try to acquire an international political ethics corresponding to the concept of human solidarity.

We also have to realize fully the significance of the declaration renouncing war. This declaration is not a mere accessory, but a guiding principle to regulate our future national life. With this ideal, Japan is going to enter the international stage as an unarmed nation. This is a new role for the Japan that until yesterday was armed from top to toe as one of the imperialistic powers. A nation without

331

arms is a nation without power. The political science of the past taught that a nation consists of land, people and power. . . .

According to Section Eight of the new constitution, Japan is not to possess an army, navy, air force, or other military forces (except for police forces). From the point of view of a cynic, a state without power cannot be a nation. But for a student who earnestly accepts the new concept of sovereignty expressed in the United Nations Charter, it is undoubtedly a new type of nation. As such a new type of nation, Japan will live and develop in the new political surroundings of a world that has acquired the United Nations. If she succeeds in the experiment of existing as such a nation, her contribution to the world will be immensely great. For it will set a concrete example of the ideal of universal disarmament that mankind has been dreaming of for centuries. . . .

If Japan holds to absolute pacifism, she must ultimately rely upon science in order to build the material foundations for her national existence. In the past, the ruling class of Japan has tried to justify her thoughtless expansionist policy on the grounds of her so-called "over-population." We have to make it our central industrial policy to promote production through the utilization of science, discarding the idea of territorial expansion. Only by this policy can Japan make her "over-population" an asset instead of a liability. Especially if the peaceful use of atomic energy should start in the next few years, as nuclear scientists confidently predict, the establishment of the material foundations of Japan's existence may be hopefully expected. . . .

Lastly we have to study and do something about the problem of preventing a third world war, which is a continuous threat to the people of the world. I believe it of the utmost importance to start a powerful peace movement throughout the entire nation, in order to inform progressive people in the world of the fact that the Japanese people too have a fervent desire to establish world peace. I will do my best to contribute to this movement.

Let me repeat again. Establishment of a democratic Japan cannot be separated from establishment of a pacifistic Japan. Today the development of the democratic ideal has reached its peak in the concept of international democracy.

Study Questions

1. How, in Oyama Ikuo's opinion, was the Japanese imperial government responsible for Japan's defeat in World War II?
2. According to the author, why is it necessary for the Japanese to end their self-imposed isolation from the rest of the world and to abolish their ethnocentric attitudes?
3. What sort of relationship between democracy and pacificism does Oyama Ikuo want to establish?
4. How prophetic were the author's remarks concerning Japan's postwar requirements, obligations, and needs?

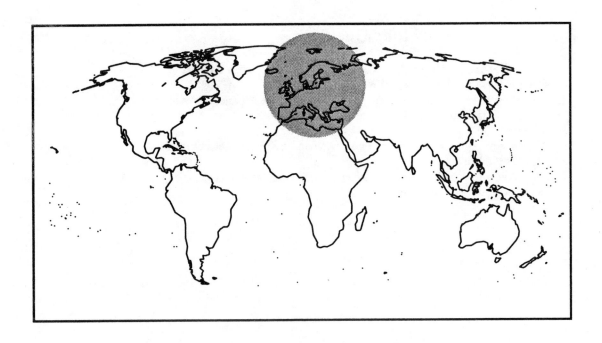

Brief Chronology for the Contemporary World
West Eurasia

1900	Publication of Sigmund Freud's *The Interpretation of Dreams*
1903	Bolshevik-Menshevik schism in Russian Social-Democratic Party Communist party
1905	Revolution in Russia; Albert Einstein's first papers on theory of relativity published
1913	Danish physicist Niels Bohr (1885–1962) discovers atomic structure
1914–1918	World War I
1917	Beginning of Bolshevik Revolution
1918–1922	Civil war in Russia ends with establishment of USSR
1919	Paris Peace Conference and establishment of League of Nations
1921	Establishment of Irish Free State in southern Ireland
1922	Mussolini seizes government in Italy
1927–1953	Stalin era in USSR
1933	Hitler becomes dictator in Germany and proclaims the Third Reich
1936–1939	Spanish Civil War
1936	Rome-Berlin Axis formed
1939–1975	Dictatorship of Franco in Spain
1939–1945	World War II
1945	Establishment of the United Nations
1947	Introduction of the U.S. Marshall Plan; Beginning of the cold war
1949	Explosion of first Soviet atomic bomb
1957	Creation of European Economic Community; Space Age begins with Soviet launch of Sputnik
1958–1964	Khrushchev era in USSR
1961	Berlin Wall constructed
1981	Government crackdown on Solidarity Union in Poland
1985–1991	Gorbachev era in USSR, policies of *glasnost* and *perestroika* eventually announced
1988	The iron curtain begins to fall
1989	Berlin Wall dismantled
1991	Dissolution of USSR

All dates are C.E. and approximate unless otherwise indicated. It should be noted as well that chronologies are constantly being revised. Hence, there may be discrepancies between the dates listed above and those found in other textbooks and scholarly monographs. Throughout the text and in the Glossary, all dates are given in B.C.E. (Before the Common Era) and C.E. (the Common Era). Where there is no era designation C.E. may be assumed.

Reading 57

Select Writings of Lenin

Born Vladimir Ilyich Ulyanov, Lenin (1870–1924) was one of the supreme political architects of the former Soviet Union. In 1895, Lenin began serving a prison term for his involvement in radical politics, and from his cell he wrote the "Draft and Explanation of the Program of the Social-Democratic Party." He was eventually released by Russian imperial authorities and exiled to Siberia in 1897. Two decades later and after a prolonged exile abroad, this leader of the **Bolshevik** faction of the Russian Social-Democratic Party returned to Russia in the hope of establishing his "dictatorship of the **proletariat**" there. World War I precipitated the collapse of czarist Russia, and in 1917 Lenin moved quickly to consolidate his position. When civil war erupted he grasped the opportunity not only to seize power (he remained head of the new government from 1918 until his death), but to put into effect his radical ideas. Always a strong opponent of Western imperialism—which he considered a major cause of the Great War—Lenin viewed the exploitation of foreign peoples as evil, but the era of New Imperialism as a natural and necessary phase in evolutionary history. In *Imperialism: The Highest Stage of Capitalism,* written in 1916, Lenin develops the ideas that the concentration of capital and creation of economic monopolies and financial oligarchies create a kind of predatory expansionism. This activity leads imperialist groups to divide the world among themselves. Lenin continues by suggesting that territorial division eventually intensifies international conflict among capitalist nations; and such strife, he conjectures, will cause the collapse of capitalism.

Draft and Explanation of the Program of the Social-Democratic Party

Section A

1. Large factories and works are developing more and more rapidly in Russia, ruining the small **kustars** and peasants and converting them into propertyless workers,

V. I. Lenin, *Selected Works* (London: Martin Lawrence Limited, n.d.), vol. 1:467–71. Reprinted with permission of International Publishers, New York.

driving more and more people into the towns and into factory and industrial villages.

2. This growth of capitalism implies an enormous increase in wealth and luxury among a handful of manufacturers, merchants and landowners and a still more rapid increase of poverty and oppression among the workers. The improvements in production and machinery introduced by the large factories, while serving to increase the productivity of social labor, at the same time serves to increase the power of capital over the workers, to increase unemployment and, simultaneously, the defenselessness of the workers.

3. But, while increasing the oppression of labor by capital to the highest degree, the big factories have created a special class of workers who obtain the opportunity of waging a struggle against capital because the very conditions of their lives destroy all their ties with their own enterprises and, combining the workers by common labor and shifting them from factory to factory, unite together large masses of workers. The workers begin to wage their struggle against the manufacturers by means of strikes, and a strong desire to unite springs up among them. Out of separate uprisings of workers arises the struggle of the Russian working class.

4. The working class struggle against the capitalist class is a struggle against all classes that live on the labor of others, and against all exploitation. This struggle can end only in the transition of political power to the hands of the working class and the transference of all the land, implements, factories, machines and mines to the whole of society for the purpose of organizing socialist production, under which all that which is produced by the workers and all improvements in production will be for the benefit of the toilers themselves.

5. In its nature and aims the Russian working class movement forms part of the international working class movement.

6. The principal obstacle in the struggle of the Russian working class for its emancipation is the absolutist, autocratic government with its irresponsible officials. Relying on the privileges enjoyed by the landlords and capitalists, and on pandering to their interests, it keeps the lower orders in a state of complete lack of rights, and by that hampers the labor movement and retards the development of the whole of the people. For that reason, the struggle of the Russian working class for its emancipation inevitably gives rise to a struggle against the absolute power of the autocratic government.

Section B

1. The Russian Social-Democratic Party declares its tasks to be to assist this struggle of the Russian working class by developing the class consciousness of the workers, by helping them to organize and by teaching them the real aims of the struggle.

2. The struggle of the Russian working class for its emancipation is a political struggle and its first aim is to achieve political liberty.

3. For that reason, the Russian Social-Democratic Party, while remaining part of the labor movement, will support every social movement against the absolute power of the autocratic government, against the privileged class of landed aristocracy and against the survivals of serfdom and the estate system which restrict free competition.

4. On the other hand, the Russian Social-Democratic Party will wage war against all attempts to bestow on the toiling classes the guardianship of the absolutist government and its officials and to retard the development of capitalism and hence, the development of the working class.

5. The emancipation of the working class must be the task of the working class itself.

6. The Russian people need not assistance from the absolutist government and its officials, but emancipation from their tyranny.

Section C

On the basis of these views, the Russian Social-Democratic Party demands first of all:

1. The convocation of a **Zemski Sobor** of the representatives of all citizens for the purpose of drawing up a Constitution.

2. Universal and direct suffrage for all Russian citizens who have reached the age of 21, without distinction of religion and nationality.

3. Freedom of assembly, right of association and the right to strike.

4. Freedom of the press.

5. Abolition of the estates and complete equality of all citizens before the law.

6. Liberty of conscience and equal rights for all nationalities. The transference of the registration of births and deaths to independent civil officials who shall be independent of the police.

7. The right of every citizen to lay a charge against any official in the courts without having first to complain to the higher officials.

8. The abolition of passports, complete liberty to move from place to place and to settle in other parts of the country.

9. Liberty to engage in any trade or occupation and the abolition of the guilds.

Section D

For the workers, the Russian Social-Democratic Party demands:

1. The establishment of industrial courts in all branches of industry, the judges to be elected in equal number by the capitalists and the workers respectively.

2. The legal restriction of the working day to eight hours.

3. The legal prohibition of night work and night shifts. Prohibition of the employment of children under fifteen years of age.

4. The legislative enactment of rest days and holidays.

5. The extension of factory laws and factory inspection to all branches of industry over the whole of Russia and also to state factories and to kustars working in their own homes.

6. The factory inspectors occupy an independent position and shall not be subordinate to the Ministry of Finance. That members of the industrial courts will enjoy equal rights with the factory inspectors in regard to the supervision of the application of the factory laws.

7. That payment of wages in goods be everywhere completely prohibited.

8. That representatives of the workers be elected to supervise the proper drawing up of wage rates, the rejection of bad work, the expenditure of money collected in fines, and the housing conditions of the workers at the factories.

That a law be passed to the effect that the total deductions from wages for whatever purposes (fines, deductions for bad work, etc.) shall not exceed ten kopeks per ruble of wages earned.

9. That a law be passed making the employer responsible for injury to the workers, the onus of proof that the injury was due to the fault of the worker to be placed on the employer.

10. That a law be passed making it compulsory for employers to maintain schools and provide medical service for the workers.

Section E

For the peasants, the Russian Social-Democratic Party demands:

1. The abolition of land purchase payments, the peasants to be compensated for payments already made. The peasants to be compensated for all payments made to the state in excess of what was due.

2. The restoration to the peasants of the land that was cut off from their holdings in 1861.

3. Complete equality of dues and taxes on peasant and landlord lands.

4. The abolition of the system of collective responsibility and the repeal of all laws that restrict the peasants in the disposal of their lands.

Imperialism: The Highest Stage of Capitalism

Private property based on the labor of the small proprietor, free competition, democracy, i.e., all the catchwords with which the capitalists and their press deceive the workers and the peasants—are things of the past. Capitalism has grown into

V. I. Lenin, *Imperialism: The Highest Stage of Capitalism* (New York: International Publishers, 1939), 9–14, 109–11, 123–28 passim. Copyright © 1939 International Publishers. Reprinted with permission of the publisher.

a world system of colonial oppression and of the financial strangulation of the overwhelming majority of the people of the world by a handful of "advanced" countries. And this "booty" is shared between two or three powerful world marauders armed to the teeth (America, Great Britain, Japan), who involve the whole world in their war over the sharing of their booty.

The Brest-Litovsk Peace Treaty dictated by monarchist Germany, and later on, the much more brutal and despicable Versailles Treaty dictated by the "democratic" republics of America and France and also by "free" England, have rendered very good service to humanity by exposing both the hired coolies of the pen of imperialism and the petty-bourgeois reactionaries, although they call themselves pacifists and socialists, who sang praises to "Wilsonianism," and who insisted that peace and reform were possible under imperialism.

The tens of millions of dead and maimed left by the war—a war for the purpose of deciding whether the British or German group of financial marauders is to receive the lion's share—and the two "peace treaties," mentioned above, open the eyes of the millions and tens of millions of people who are downtrodden, oppressed, deceived and duped by the bourgeoisie with unprecedented rapidity. Thus, out of the universal ruin caused by the war a world-wide revolutionary crisis is arising which, in spite of the protracted and difficult stages it may have to pass, cannot end in any other way than in a proletarian revolution and in its victory. . . .

Not the slightest progress can be made toward the solution of the practical problems of the Communist movement and of the impending social revolution unless the economic roots of this phenomenon are understood and unless its political and sociological significance is appreciated.

Imperialism is the eve of the proletarian social revolution. This has been confirmed since 1917 on a world-wide scale.

The Critique of Imperialism

By the critique of imperialism, in the broad sense of the term, we mean the attitude towards imperialist policy of the different classes of society as part of their general ideology.

The enormous dimensions of finance capital concentrated in a few hands and creating an extremely extensive and close network of ties and relationships which subordinate not only the small and medium, but also even the very small capitalists and small masters, on the one hand, and the intense struggle waged against other national state groups of financiers for the division of the world and domination over other countries, on the other hand, cause the wholesale transition of the possessing classes to the side of imperialism. The signs of the times are a "general" enthusiasm regarding its prospects, a passionate defense of imperialism, and every possible embellishment of its real nature. The imperialist ideology also penetrates the working class. There is no Chinese Wall between it and the other classes. The leaders of the so-called "Social-Democratic" Party of Germany are today justly called "social-imperialists," that is, socialists in words and imperialists in deeds; but as early as 1902, Hobson noted the existence of "Fabian imperialists" who belonged to the opportunist Fabian Society in England.

Bourgeois scholars and publicists usually come out in defense of imperialism in a somewhat veiled form, and obscure its complete domination and its profound roots; they strive to concentrate attention on partial and secondary details and do their very best to distract attention from the main issue by means of ridiculous schemes for "reform," such as police supervision of the trusts and banks, etc. Less frequently, cynical and frank imperialists speak out and are bold enough to admit the absurdity of the idea of reforming the fundamental features of imperialism.

We will give an example. The German imperialists attempt, in the magazine *Archives of World Economy*, to follow the movements for national emancipation in the colonies, particularly, of course, in colonies other than those belonging to Germany. They note the ferment and protest movements in India, the movement in Natal [South Africa], the movement in the Dutch East Indies, etc. One of them, commenting on an English report of the speeches delivered at a conference of subject peoples and races, held on June 28–30, 1910, at which representatives of various peoples subject to foreign domination in Africa, Asia, and Europe were present, writes as follows in appraising the speeches delivered at this conference:

> "We are told that we must fight against imperialism; that the dominant states should recognize the right of subject peoples to home rule; that an international tribunal should supervise the fulfillment of treaties concluded between the great powers and weak peoples. One does not get any further than the expression of these pious wishes. We see no trace of understanding of the fact that imperialism is indissolubly bound up with capitalism in its present form" (!!) "and therefore also no trace of the realization that an open struggle against imperialism would be hopeless, unless, perhaps, the fight is confined to protests against certain of its especially abhorrent excesses." (*Archives of World Economy*, Vol. II, pp. 194–95)

Since the reform of the basis of imperialism is a deception, a "pious wish," since the bourgeois representatives of the oppressed nations go no "further" forward, the bourgeois representatives of the oppressing nation go "further" backward, to servility, towards imperialism, concealed by the cloak of "science." "Logic," indeed!

The question as to whether it is possible to reform the basis of imperialism, whether to go forward to the accentuation and deepening of the antagonisms which it engenders, or backwards, towards allaying these antagonisms, is a fundamental question in the critique of imperialism. As a consequence of the fact that the political features of imperialism are reaction all along the line, and increased national oppression, resulting from the oppression of the financial oligarchy and the elimination of free competition, a petty-bourgeois—democratic opposition has been rising against imperialism in almost all imperialist countries since the beginning of the twentieth century. . . .

In the United States, the imperialist war waged against Spain in 1898 stirred up the opposition of the "anti-imperialists," the last of the Mohicans of bourgeois democracy. They declared this war to be "criminal"; they denounced the annexation of foreign territories as being a violation of the Constitution, and denounced the "Jingo treachery" by means of which Aguinaldo, leader of the native Filipinos, was deceived (the Americans promised him the independence of his country, but later they landed troops and annexed it). They quoted the words of Lincoln in his speech "On the Repeal of the Missouri Compromise" [delivered at Peoria, Illinois, October 16, 1854]: "When the white man governs himself, that is self-government; but when he governs himself and also governs another man, that is more than self-government—that is despotism."

But while all this criticism shrank from recognizing the indissoluble bond between imperialism and the trusts, and, therefore, between imperialism and the very foundations of capitalism; while it shrank from joining up with the forces engendered by large-scale capitalism and its development—it remained a "pious wish." . . .

The Place of Imperialism in History

We have seen that the economic quintessence of imperialism is monopoly capitalism. This very fact determines its place in history, for monopoly that grew up on the basis of free competition, and precisely out of free competition, is the transition from the capitalist system to a higher social-economic order. We must take special note of the four principal forms of monopoly, or the four principal manifestations of monopoly capitalism, which are characteristic of the epoch under review.

Firstly, monopoly arose out of the concentration of production at a very advanced stage of development. This refers to the monopolist capitalist combines, cartels, syndicates and trusts. We have seen the important part that these play in modern economic life. At the beginning of the twentieth century, monopolies acquired complete supremacy in the advanced countries. And although the first steps towards the formation of the cartels were first taken by countries enjoying the protection of high tariffs (Germany, America), Great Britain, with her system of free trade, was not far behind in revealing the same basic phenomenon, namely, the birth of monopoly out of the concentration of production.

Secondly, monopolies have accelerated the capture of the most important sources of raw materials, especially for the coal and iron industries, which are the basic and most highly cartelized industries in capitalist society. The monopoly of the most important sources of raw materials has enormously increased the power of big capital, and has sharpened the antagonism between cartelized and non-cartelized industry.

Thirdly, monopoly has sprung from the banks. The banks have developed from modest intermediary enterprises into the monopolists of finance capital. Some three or five of the biggest banks in each of the foremost capitalist countries have achieved the "personal union" of industrial and bank capital, and have concentrated

341

in their hands the disposal of thousands upon thousands of millions which form the greater part of the capital and income of entire countries. A financial oligarchy, which throws a close net of relations of dependence over all the economic and political institutions of contemporary bourgeois society without exception—such is the most striking manifestation of this monopoly.

Fourthly, monopoly has grown out of colonial policy. To the numerous "old" motives of colonial policy, finance capital has added the struggle for the sources of raw materials, for the export of capital, for "spheres of influence," i.e., for spheres for profitable deals, concessions, monopolist profits and so on; in fine, for economic territory in general. When the colonies of the European powers in Africa, for instance, comprised only one-tenth of that territory (as was the case in 1876), colonial policy was able to develop by methods other than those of monopoly—by the "free grabbing" of territories, so to speak. But when nine-tenths of Africa had been seized (approximately by 1900), when the whole world had been divided up, there was inevitably ushered in a period of colonial monopoly and, consequently, a period of particularly intense struggle for the division and the redivision of the world.

The extent to which monopolist capital has intensified all the contradictions of capitalism is generally known. It is sufficient to mention the high cost of living and the oppression of the cartels. This intensification of contradictions constitutes the most powerful driving force of the transitional period of history, which began from the time of the definite victory of world finance capital.

Monopolies, oligarchy, the striving for domination instead of the striving for liberty, the exploitation of an increasing number of small or weak nations by an extremely small group of the richest or most powerful nations—all these have given birth to those distinctive characteristics of imperialism which compel us to define it as parasitic or decaying capitalism. More and more prominently there emerges, as one of the tendencies of imperialism, the creation of the "bondholding" (rentier) state, the usurer state, in which the bourgeoisie lives on the proceeds of capital exports and by "clipping coupons." It would be a mistake to believe that this tendency to decay precludes the possibility of the rapid growth of capitalism. It does not. In the epoch of imperialism, certain branches of industry, certain strata of the bourgeoisie, and certain countries betray, to a more or less degree, one or other of these tendencies. On the whole, capitalism is growing far more rapidly than before. But this growth is not only becoming more and more uneven in general; its unevenness also manifests itself, in particular, in the decay of the countries which are richest in capital (such as England). . . .

In its turn, this finance capital which has grown so rapidly is not unwilling (precisely because it has grown so quickly) to pass on to a more "tranquil" possession of colonies which have to be seized—and not only by peaceful methods—from richer nations. In the United States, economic development in the last decades has been even more rapid than in Germany, and for this very reason the parasitic character of modern American capitalism has stood out with particular prominence. On the other hand, a comparison of, say, the republican American bourgeoisie with the monarchist Japanese or German bourgeoisie shows that the most pronounced political distinctions diminish to an extreme degree in the epoch of imperialism—not because they are unimportant in general, but because in all these cases we are discussing a bourgeoisie which has definite features of parasitism.

The receipt of high monopoly profits by the capitalists in one of the numerous branches of industry, in one of numerous countries, etc., makes it economically possible for them to corrupt certain sections of the working class, and for a time a fairly considerable minority, and win them to the side of the bourgeoisie of a given industry or nation against all the others. The intensification of antagonisms between imperialist nations for the division of the world increases this striving. And so there is created that bond between imperialism and opportunism, which revealed itself first and most clearly in England, owing to the fact that certain features of imperialist development were observable there much earlier than in other countries. . . .

From all that has been said in this book on the economic nature of imperialism, it follows that we must define it as capitalism in transition, or, more precisely, as moribund capitalism. It is very instructive in this respect to note that the bourgeois economists, in describing modern capitalism, frequently employ terms like "interlocking," "absence of isolation," etc.; "in conformity with their functions and course of development," banks are "not purely private business enterprises; they are more and more outgrowing the sphere of purely private business regulation." And this very Riesser, who uttered the words just quoted, declares with all seriousness that the "prophecy" of the Marxists concerning "socialization" has "not come true"!

What then does this word "interlocking" express? It merely expresses the most striking feature of the process going on before our eyes. It shows that the observer counts the separate trees, but cannot see the wood. It slavishly copies the superficial, the fortuitous, the chaotic. It reveals the observer as one who is overwhelmed by the mass of raw material and is utterly incapable of appreciating its meaning and importance. Ownership of shares and relations between owners of private property "interlock in a haphazard way." But the underlying factor of this interlocking, its very base, is the changing social relations of production. When a big enterprise assumes gigantic proportions, and, on the basis of exact computation of mass data, organizes according to plan the supply of primary raw materials to the extent of two-thirds, or three-fourths of all that is necessary for tens of millions of people; when the raw materials are transported to the most suitable place of production, sometimes hundreds or thousands of miles away, in a systematic and organized manner; when a single center directs all the successive stages of work right up to the manufacture of numerous varieties of finished articles; when these products are distributed according to a single plan among tens and hundreds of millions of consumers (as in the case of the distribution of oil in America and Germany by the American "oil trust")—then it becomes evident that we have socialization of production, and not mere "interlocking"; that private economic relations and private property relations constitute a shell which is no longer suitable for its contents; a shell which must inevitably begin to decay if its destruction be delayed by artificial means; a shell which may continue in a state of decay for a fairly long period (particularly if the cure of the opportunist abscess is protracted), but which will inevitably be removed.

Study Questions

1. How is Lenin's idea of "dictatorship of the proletariat" manifested in these works?
2. According to the author, why are capitalism and imperialism detrimental to the working classes?
3. What reasons does Lenin offer in justification of the need for political, economic, and social change and reform in Russia?
4. How has Lenin modified various crucial tenets of Marxism as espoused in *The Communist Manifesto* (Reading 39)?

Alexandra Kollontai's "Theses on Communist Morality in the Sphere of Marital Relations"

Alexandra Mikhailovna Domontovich (1873–1952), the daughter of a czarist general, rebelled against parental authority in 1895 when she married her distant cousin, Vladimir Kollontai. Immediately after her marriage and the birth of a son, she seemed content to live the life of a typical Russian wife. A visit to a factory near Narva in late 1896, however, sparked her desire to improve the lot of the working classes. The oppression and inequality she observed soon led her to ally with Marxists. By 1915 Kollontai was a prominent participant in the Russian Social-Democratic movement. When the **Bolsheviks** assumed power in Russia, she was named Commissar of Social Welfare. She eventually worked as the People's Commissar of Propaganda and Agitation in the Ukraine, and by the early 1920s was serving as a Deputy of the International Women's Secretariat and an adviser to the Soviet delegation in Norway. In 1930 she was transferred to Sweden, where she remained until 1945. Kollontai ultimately attained the rank of ambassador in 1943, the first woman in the world to achieve this distinction. She lived the last few years of her life in Moscow as a private Soviet citizen. An orthodox Marxist, Alexandra Kollontai always worked for the full emancipation of women. Many of her writings—including "Theses on Communist Morality in the Sphere of Marital Relations," published in 1921—dealt with women's issues. Many ideas expressed in her works were branded as libertine both in the Soviet Union and the West, yet Kollontai helped to expand the concept of "women's issues." She considered family, sex and sexuality, and personal politics as important to the betterment of women's status and role in society as the right to vote.

Family and marriage are historical categories, phenomena which develop in accordance with the economic relations that exist at the given level of production. The form of marriage and of the family is thus determined by the economic system

Alix Holt, trans., *Selected Writings of Alexandra Kollontai,* with an introduction and commentaries by Alix Holt (London: Allison & Busby, 1977), 225–231, passim. Copyright © 1977 Alix Holt. Reprinted with permission of Lawrence Hill Books, New York, NY.

of the given epoch, and it changes as the economic base of society changes. The family, in the same way as government, religion, science, morals, law and customs, is part of the superstructure which derives from the economic system of society.

Where economic functions are performed by the family rather than by society as a whole, family and marital relations are more stable and possess a vital capacity: "The less the development of labor, and the more limited its volume of production ... the more preponderantly does the social order appear to be dominated by ties of sex" (Engels, *Origins of the Family*). In the period of natural economy the family formed an enclosed economic unit which was necessary for humankind and thus had a vital capacity. The family was at the time a unit of both production and consumption. Outside the family/economic unit the individual had no means, especially at the earliest levels of development of society, of sustaining the conditions necessary for life. In some areas and in some countries where capitalism is weakly developed (among the peoples of the East, for example) the peasant family is still fundamentally a family/economic union. With the transition, however, from a natural economy to a merchant capitalist economy based on trade and exchange, the family ceases to be necessary for the functioning of society and thus loses its strength and vital capacity.

The fact that with the consolidation of the capitalist system of production, the marital/family union develops from a production unit into a legal arrangement concerned only with consumption, leads inevitably to the weakening of marital/family ties. In the era of private property and the bourgeois-capitalist economic system, marriage and the family are grounded in (a) material and financial considerations, (b) economic dependence of the female sex on the family breadwinner—the husband—rather than the social collective, and (c) the need to care for the rising generation. Capitalism maintains a system of individual economies; the family has a role to play in performing economic tasks and functions within the national capitalist economy. Thus under capitalism the family does not merge with or dissolve into the national economy but continues to exist as an independent economic unit, concerned with production in the case of the peasant family and consumption in the case of the urban family. The individual economy which springs from private property is the basis of the bourgeois family.

The communist economy does away with the family. In the period of the dictatorship of the **proletariat** there is a transition to the single production plan and collective social consumption, and the family loses its significance as an economic unit. The external economic functions of the family disappear, and consumption ceases to be organized on an individual family basis; a network of social kitchens and canteens is established, and the making, mending, and washing of clothes and other aspects of housework are integrated into the national economy. In the period of the dictatorship of the proletariat the family economic unit should be recognized as being, from the point of view of the national economy, not only useless but harmful. The family economic unit involves (a) the uneconomic expenditure of products and fuel on the part of small domestic economies, and (b) unproductive labor, especially by women, in the home—and is therefore in conflict with the interest of the worker's republic in a single economic plan and the expedient use of the labor force (including women). . . .

In the period of the dictatorship of the proletariat, the workers' state has to concern itself not with the economic and social unit of the family, since this unit dies as the bonds of communism are consolidated, but with the changing forms of marital relations. The family as an economic unit and as a union of parents and children based on the need to provide for the material welfare of the latter is doomed to disappear. Thus the workers' collective has to establish its attitude not to economic relationships but to the form of relationships between the sexes. What kind of relations between the sexes are in the best interests of the workers' collective? What forms of relations would strengthen, not weaken, the collective in the transitional stage between capitalism and communism would thus assist the construction of the new society? The laws and the morality that the workers' system is evolving are beginning to give an answer to this question.

Once relations between the sexes cease to perform economic and social functions of the former family, they are no longer the concern of the workers' collective. It is not the relationships between the sexes but the result—the child—that concerns the collective. The workers' state recognizes its responsibility to provide for maternity, i.e. to guarantee the well-being of the woman and of the child, but it does not recognize the couple as a legal unit separate from the workers' collective. The decrees on marriage issued by the workers' republic establishing the mutual rights of the married couple (the right to demand material support from the partner for yourself or the child), and thus giving legal encouragement to the separation of this unit and its interests from the general interests of the workers' social collective (the right of wives to be transferred to the town or village where their husbands are working), are survivals of the past; they contradict the interests of the collective and weaken its bonds, and should therefore be reviewed and changed.

The law ought to emphasize the interest of the workers' collective in maternity and eliminate the situation where the child is dependent on the relationship between its parents. The law of the workers' collective replaces the right of the parents, and the workers' collective keeps a close watch, in the interests of the unified economy and of present and future labor resources. In the period of the dictatorship of the proletariat there must, instead of marriage law, be regulation of the relationship of the government to maternity, of the relationship between mother and child and of the relationship between the mother and the workers' collective (i.e. legal norms must regulate the protection of female labor, the welfare of the expectant and nursing mothers, the welfare of the children and their social education). Legal norms must regulate the relationship between the mother and the socially educated child, and between the father and child. Fatherhood should not be established through marriage or a relationship of a material nature. The man should be able to choose whether or not to accept the role of fatherhood (i.e. the right which he shares equally with the mother to decide on a social system of education for the child, and the right, where this does not conflict with the interests of the collective, of intellectual contact with the child and the opportunity to influence its development. . . .

In the period of the dictatorship of the proletariat, communist morality—and not the law—regulates sexual relationships in the interest of the workers' collective of future generations.

Each historical (and therefore economic) epoch in the development of society has its own ideal of marriage and its own sexual morality. Under the tribal system, with its ties of kinship, the morality was different from that which developed with the establishment of private property and the rule of the husband and father (patriarchy). Different economic systems have different moral codes. Not only each stage in the development of society, but each class has its corresponding sexual morality (it is sufficient to compare the morals of the feudal landowning class and of the bourgeois in one and the same epoch to see that this is true). The more firmly established the principles of private property, the stricter the moral code. The importance of virginity before legal marriage sprang from the principles of private property and the unwillingness of men to pay for the children of others.

Hypocrisy (the outward observance of decorum and the actual practice of depravity), and the double code (one code of behavior for the man and another for the woman) are the twin pillars of bourgeois morality. Communist morality must, above all, resolutely spurn all the hypocrisy inherited from bourgeois society in relationships between the sexes, and reject the double standard of morality.

In the period of the dictatorship of the proletariat, relations between the sexes should be evaluated only according to the criteria mentioned above—the health of the working population and the development of inner bonds of solidarity within the collective. The sexual act must be seen not as something shameful and sinful but as something which is as natural as the other needs of healthy organisms, such as hunger and thirst. Such phenomena cannot be judged as moral or immoral. The satisfaction of healthy and natural instincts only ceases to be normal when the boundaries of hygiene are overstepped. In such cases, not only the health of the person concerned but the interests of the work collective, which needs the strength and energy and health of its members, are threatened. Communist morality, therefore, while openly recognizing the normality of sexual interests, condemns unhealthy and unnatural interest in sex (excesses, for example, or sexual relations before maturity has been reached, which exhaust the organism and lower the capacity of men and women for work).

As communist morality is concerned for the health of the population, it also criticizes sexual restraint. The preservation of health includes the full and correct satisfaction of all man's needs; norms of hygiene should work to this end, and not artificially suppress such an important function of the organism as the sex drive ([**August**] **Bebel**, *Woman and Socialism*). Thus both early sexual experience (before the body has developed and grown strong) and sexual restraint must be seen as equally harmful. This concern for the health of the human race does not establish either monogamy or polygamy as the obligatory form of relations between the sexes, for excesses may be committed in the bounds of the former, and a frequent change of partners by no means signifies sexual intemperance. Science has discovered that when a woman has relationships with many men at one time, her ability to have children is impaired; and relationships with a number of women drain the man and affect the health of his children negatively. Since the workers' collective needs strong and healthy men and women, such arrangements of sexual life are not in its interests. . . .

In the view of the need to encourage the development and growth of feelings of solidarity and to strengthen the bonds of the work collective, it should above all be established that the isolation of the "couple" as a special unit does not answer the interests of communism. Communist morality requires the education of the working class in comradeship and the fusion of the hearts and minds of the separate members of this collective. The needs and interests of the individual must be subordinated to the interests and aims of the collective. On the one hand, therefore, the bonds of family and marriage must be weakened, and on the other, men and women need to be educated in solidarity and the subordination of the will of the individual to the will of the collective. Even at this present, early stage, the workers' republic demands that mothers learn to be the mothers not only of their own child but of all workers' children; it does not recognize the couple as a self-sufficient unit, and does not therefore approve of wives deserting work for the sake of this unit.

As regards sexual relations, communist morality demands first of all an end to all relations based in financial or other economic considerations. The buying and selling of sexual favors destroys the sense of equality between the sexes, and thus undermines the basis of solidarity without which communist society cannot exist. Moral censure is consequently directed at prostitution in all its forms and at all types of marriage of convenience, even when recognized by Soviet law. The preservation of marriage regulations creates the illusion that the workers' collective can accept the "couple" with its special, exclusive interests. The stronger the ties between the members of the collective as a whole, the less the need to reinforce marital relations. Secondly, communist morality demands the education of the younger generation in responsibility to the collective and in the consciousness that love is not the only thing in life (this is especially important in the case of women, for they have been taught the opposite for centuries). Love is only one aspect of life, and must not be allowed to overshadow the other facets of the relationships between individual and collective. The ideal of the bourgeois was the married couple, where the partners complemented each other so completely that they had no need of contact with society. Communist morality demands, on the contrary, that the younger generation be educated in such a way that the personality of the individual is developed to the full, and the individual with his or her many interests has contact with a range of persons of both sexes. Communist morality encourages the development of many and varied bonds of love and friendship among people. The old ideal was "all for the loved one"; communist morality demands all for the collective.

Though sex love is seen in the context of the interests of the collective, communist morality demands that people are educated in sensitivity and understanding and are psychologically demanding both to themselves and to their partners. The bourgeois attitude to sexual relations as simply a matter of sex must be criticized and replaced by an understanding of the whole gamut of joyful love-experience that enriches life and makes for great happiness. The greater intellectual and emotional development of the individual the less place will there be in his or her relationship for the bare physiological side of love, and the brighter will be the love experience.

In the transitional period, relations between men and women must, in order to meet the interests of the workers' collective, be based on the following considerations. (1) All sexual relationships must be based on mutual inclination, love, infatuation, or passion, and in no case on financial or material motivations. All calculation in relationships must be subject to merciless condemnation. (2) The form and length of the relationship are not regulated, but the hygiene of the race and communist morality require that relationships be based not on the sexual act alone, and that it should not be accompanied by any excesses that threaten health. (3) Those with illnesses, etc. that might be inherited should not have children. (4) A jealous and proprietary attitude to the person loved must be replaced by a comradely understanding of the other and an acceptance of his or her freedom. Jealousy is a destructive force of which communist morality cannot approve. (5) The bonds between the members of the collective must be strengthened. The encouragement of the intellectual and political interests of the younger generation assists the development of healthy and bright emotions in love.

The stronger the collective, the more firmly established becomes the communist way of life. The closer the emotional ties between the members of the community, the less they need to seek refuge from loneliness in marriage. Under communism the blind strength of matter is subjugated to the will of the strongly welded and thus unprecedentedly powerful workers' collective. The individual has the opportunity to develop intellectually and emotionally as never before. In this collective, new forms of relationships are maturing and the concept of love is extended and expanded.

Study Questions

1. Why does Kollontai consider it important to expand the concept of "women's issues"?
2. How does Kollontai relate various problems and issues confronting women to the class struggle of classic Marxist doctrine (Reading 39)?
3. According to Kollontai, what must women do if they wish to achieve equal status with men?
4. Why were Kollontai's views, especially on women, marriage, sexuality, and the family, considered too radical by some Soviet Communists?

Poems From W. B. Yeats's *Michael Robartes and the Dancer*

When World War I ended in 1918, people in the West felt deeply disillusioned. Many writers, poets, and artists expressed a profound sense of despair and disgust at the physical and moral carnage the Great War had wrought. The people of Ireland had reason to bemoan their predicament long before the cruelties of war became an ever-present reality. With the Act of Union of 1800, Ireland became part of the United Kingdom of Great Britain. This did not resolve the problem of Irish emancipation from English overlordship, but exacerbated it. During the nineteenth century, Irish political activities reached new heights with the formation of the Catholic Association, Irish National Land League, and Gaelic League. But hope for home rule as a final solution to Ireland's national aspirations quickly evaporated. Consequently many people began to place greater importance on poetry, drama, and narrative literature to achieve their goals. The Anglo-Irish literary revival, led by W. B. Yeats (1865–1939) and others, focused on the intellectual rather than the material needs of their fellow countrymen. They argued that the Irish could not preserve their nationality without a national literature. These ideas found full expression in Yeats's poetry and plays, many of which were produced at The Abbey Theatre that he helped to establish in 1904. With his complex poetic imagery in poems such as "Easter 1916" (1916), "The Second Coming" (1920), and "A Meditation in Time of War" (1921), Yeats echoes the fearful, pessimistic, and almost apocalyptic sentiments expressed not only by the Irish, but by many Europeans in the aftermath of war and revolution. He received the Nobel Prize for literature in 1923 because his poetry spoke to people throughout the world.

Easter 1916

I have met them at close of day
Coming with vivid faces
From counter or desk among grey

Richard J. Finneran, ed., *The Poems of W. B. Yeats: A New Edition* (New York: Macmillan, 1924). Copyright © 1924 Macmillan Publishing Company, renewed 1952 by Bertha Georgie Yeats. Reprinted with permission of Macmillan Publishing Company.

Eighteenth-century houses.
I have passed with a nod of the head
Or polite meaningless words,
Or have lingered awhile and said
Polite meaningless words,
And thought before I had done
Of a mocking tale or a gibe
To please a companion
Around the fire at the club,
Being certain that they and I
But lived where motley is worn:
All changed, changed utterly:
A terrible beauty is born.

That woman's days were spent
In ignorant good-will,
Her nights in argument
Until her voice grew shrill.
What voice more sweet than hers
When, young and beautiful,
She rode to harriers?
This man had kept a school
And rode our wingèd horse;
This other his helper and friend
Was coming into his force;
He might have won fame in the end,
So sensitive his nature seemed,
So daring and sweet his thought.
This other man I had dreamed
A drunken, vainglorious lout.
He had done most bitter wrong
To some who are near my heart,
Yet I number him in the song;
He, too, has resigned his part
In the casual comedy;
He, too, has been changed in his turn,
Transformed utterly:
A terrible beauty is born.

Hearts with one purpose alone
Through summer and winter seem
Enchanted to a stone
To trouble the living stream.
The horse that comes from the road,
The rider, the birds that range

From cloud to tumbling cloud,
Minute by minute they change;
A shadow of cloud on the stream
Changes minute by minute;
A horse-hoof slides on the brim,
And a horse plashes within it;
The long-legged moor-hens dive,
And hens to moor-cocks call;
Minute by minute they live:
The stone's in the midst of all.

Too long a sacrifice
Can make a stone of the heart.
O when may it suffice?
That is Heaven's part, our part
To murmur name upon name,
As a mother names her child
When sleep at last has come
On limbs that had run wild.
What is it but nightfall?
No, no, not night but death;
Was it needless death after all?
For England may keep faith
For all that is done and said.
We know their dream; enough
To know they dreamed and are dead;
And what if excess of love
Bewildered them till they died?
I write it out in a verse—
MacDonagh and **MacBride**
And **Connolly** and **Pearse**
Now and in time to be,
Wherever green is worn,
Are changed, changed utterly:
A terrible beauty is born.

The Second Coming

Turning and turning in the widening gyre
The falcon cannot hear the falconer;
Things fall apart; the centre cannot hold;
Mere anarchy is loosed upon the world,
The blood-dimmed tide is loosed, and everywhere

The ceremony of innocence is drowned;
The best lack all conviction, while the worst
Are full of passionate intensity.
Surely some revelation is at hand;
Surely **the Second Coming** is at hand.
The Second Coming! Hardly are those words out
When a vast image out of *Spiritus Mundi*
Troubles my sight: somewhere in sands of the desert
A shape with lion body and the head of a man,
A gaze blank and pitiless as the sun,
Is moving its slow thighs, while all about it
Reel shadows of the indignant desert birds.
The darkness drops again; but now I know
That twenty centuries of stony sleep
Were vexed to nightmare by a rocking cradle,
And what rough beast, its hour come round at last,
Slouches towards Bethlehem to be born?

A Meditation in Time of War

For one throb of the artery,
While on that old grey stone I sat
Under the old wind-broken tree,
I knew that One is animate,
Mankind inanimate phantasy.

Study Questions

1. How do Yeats's poetic images, such as the anarchy in "The Second Coming," epitomize the despair and hardship people experienced during the war years?
2. What consolation—if any—does the poet find in religion?
3. Explain the refrain of "Easter 1916," "A terrible beauty is born."
4. How does "A Meditation in Time of War" reflect attitudes characteristic of the postwar era?

Freud's *Civilization and Its Discontents*

The attitude of extreme pessimism that pervaded Western society during the 1920s and 1930s is echoed in Sigmund Freud's (1856–1939) descriptions of the destructive instincts inherent in human beings. Freud believed the development of civilization was dependent upon subordinating humanity's natural desires—and, hence, repressing sexual instincts. He was particularly interested in the negative aspects of sexuality, which he believed were the antithesis of **Eros**. Freud hypothesized that it was sex as an act of aggression and the instinct for destruction that generated a heightened sense of guilt and negated life-giving Eros. According to the great Viennese psychoanalyst, the natural happiness of the race, as evinced in primitive societies, is sacrificed in sophisticated social structures. People in the latter groups subdue their natural instincts and conform to cultural restrictions and impositions. Freud's last major work, *Civilization and Its Discontents*, published in 1930, details his thoughts on humanity's place in the world and on the world itself, which he concludes is in a state of perpetual conflict. The final sentence of this piece was added in 1931, when the menace of Hitler was already apparent.

Our enquiry concerning happiness has not so far taught us much that is not already common knowledge. And even if we proceed from it to the problem of why it is so hard for men to be happy, there seems no greater prospect of learning anything new. We have given the answer already by pointing to the three sources from which our suffering comes: the superior power of nature, the feebleness of our own bodies and the inadequacy of the regulations which adjust the mutual relationships of human beings in the family, the state and society. In regard to the first two sources, our judgement cannot hesitate long. It forces us to acknowledge those sources of suffering and to submit to the inevitable. We shall never completely master nature; and our bodily organism, itself a part of that nature, will always remain a transient structure with a limited capacity for adaptation and achievement. This recognition does not have a paralysing effect. On the contrary, it points the direction for our activity. If we cannot remove all suffering, we can remove some, and we can mitigate some: the experience of many thousands of years has convinced us of that. As regards the third source, the social source of suffering, our attitude is a different one. We do not admit it at all; we cannot see why the regulations made by ourselves should not, on the contrary, be a protection and a benefit for every one of us. And yet, when we consider how unsuccessful we have been in precisely this field of prevention of suffering, a suspicion dawns on us that here, too, a piece of unconquerable nature may lie behind—this time a piece of our own psychical constitution.

When we start considering this possibility, we come upon a contention which is so astonishing that we must dwell upon it. This contention holds that what we call our civilization is largely responsible for our misery, and that we should be much happier if we gave it up and returned to primitive conditions. I call this contention astonishing because, in whatever way we may define the concept of civilization, it is a certain fact that all the things with which we seek to protect ourselves against the threats that emanate from the sources of suffering are part of that very civilization.

How has it happened that so many people have come to take up this strange attitude of hostility to civilization? I believe that the basis of it was a deep and long-standing dissatisfaction with the then existing state of civilization and that on that basis a condemnation of it was built up, occasioned by certain specific historical events. I think I know what the last and the last but one of those occasions were. I am not learned enough to trace the chain of them far back enough in the history of the human species; but a factor of this kind hostile to civilization must already have been at work in the victory of Christendom over the heathen religions. For it was very closely related to the low estimation put upon earthly life by the Christian doctrine. The last but one of these occasions was when the progress of voyages of discovery led to contact with primitive peoples and races. In consequence of insufficient observation and a mistaken view of their manners and customs, they appeared to Europeans to be leading a simple, happy life with few wants, a life such as was unattainable by their visitors with their superior civilization. Later experience has corrected some of those judgements. In many cases the observers had wrongly attributed to the absence of complicated cultural demands what was in fact due to the bounty of nature and the ease with which the major human needs were satisfied. The last occasion is especially familiar to us. It arose when people came to know about the mechanism of the neuroses, which threaten to undermine the modicum of happiness enjoyed by civilized men. It was discovered that a person becomes neurotic because he cannot tolerate the amount of frustration which society imposes on him in the service of its cultural ideals, and it was inferred from this that the abolition or reduction of those demands would result in a return to possibilities of happiness.

There is also an added factor of disappointment. During the last few generations mankind has made an extraordinary advance in the natural sciences and in their technical application and has established his control over nature in a way never before imagined. The single steps of this advance are common knowledge and it is unnecessary to enumerate them. Men are proud of those achievements, and have a right to be. But they seem to have observed that this newly-won power over space and time, this subjugation of the forces of nature, which is the fulfillment of a longing that goes back thousands of years, has not increased the amount of pleasurable satisfaction which they may expect from life and has not made them feel happier. From the recognition of this fact we ought to be content to conclude that power over nature is not the *only* precondition of human happiness, just as it is not the *only* goal of cultural endeavour; we ought not to infer from it that technical progress is without value for the economics of our happiness. . . .

It seems certain that we do not feel comfortable in our present-day civilization, but it is very difficult to form an opinion whether and in what degree men of an earlier age felt happier and what part their cultural conditions played in the matter. We shall always tend to consider people's distress objectively—that is, to place ourselves, with our own wants and sensibilities, in *their* conditions, and then to examine what occasions we should find in them for experiencing happiness or unhappiness. This method of looking at things, which seems objective because it ignores the variations in subjective sensibility, is, of course, the most subjective possible, since it puts one's own mental states in the place of any others, unknown though they may be. Happiness, however, is something essentially subjective. No matter how much we may shrink with horror from certain situations—of a galley-slave in antiquity, of a peasant during the Thirty Years' War, of a victim of the Holy Inquisition, of a Jew awaiting a **pogrom**—it is nevertheless impossible for us to feel our way into such people—to divine the changes which original obtuseness of mind, a gradual stupefying process, the cessation of expectations, and cruder or more refined methods of narcotization have produced upon their receptivity to sensations of pleasure and unpleasure. Moreover, in the case of the most extreme possibility of suffering, special mental protective devices are brought into operation. . . .

The existence of this inclination to aggression, which we can detect in ourselves and justly assume to be present in others, is the factor which disturbs our relations with our neighbour and which forces civilization into such a high expenditure [of energy]. In consequence of this primary mutual hostility of human beings, civilized society is perpetually threatened with disintegration. The interest of work in common would not hold it together; instinctual passions are stronger than reasonable interests. Civilization has to use its utmost efforts in order to set limits to man's aggressive instincts and to hold the manifestations of them in check by physical reaction-formations. Hence, therefore, the use of methods intended to incite people into identifications and aim-inhibited relationships of love, hence the restriction upon sexual life, and hence too the ideal's commandment to love one's neighbour as oneself—a commandment which is really justified by the fact that nothing else runs so strongly counter to the original nature of man. In spite of every effort, these endeavours of civilization have not so far achieved very much. It hopes to prevent the crudest excesses of brutal violence by itself assuming the right to use violence against criminals, but the law is not able to lay hold of the more cautious and refined manifestations of human aggressiveness.

The time comes when each one of us has to give up as illusions the expectations which, in his youth, he pinned upon his fellow-men, and when he may learn how much difficulty and pain has been added to his life by their ill-will. At the same time, it would be unfair to reproach civilization with trying to eliminate strife and competition from human activity. These things are undoubtedly indispensable. But opposition is not necessarily enmity; it is merely misused and made an *occasion* for enmity. . . .

It is clearly not easy for men to give up the satisfaction of this inclination to aggression. They do not feel comfortable without it. The advantage which a comparatively small cultural group offers of allowing this instinct an outlet in the form of hostility against intruders is not to be despised. It is always possible to bind together a considerable number of people in love, so long as there are other people left over to receive the manifestations of their aggressiveness. I once discussed the phenomenon that it is precisely communities with adjoining territories, and related to each other in other ways as well, who are engaged in constant feuds and in ridiculing each other—like the Spaniards and Portuguese, for instance, the North Germans and South Germans, the English and Scotch and so on. I gave this phenomenon the name of 'the narcissism of minor differences', a name which does not do much to explain it. We can now see that it is a convenient and relatively harmless satisfaction of the inclination to aggression, by means of which cohesion between the members of the community is made easier. In this respect the Jewish people, scattered everywhere, have rendered most useful services to the civilizations of the countries that have been their hosts; but unfortunately all the massacres of the Jews in the Middle Ages did not suffice to make that period more peaceful and secure for their Christian fellows. When once the Apostle **Paul** had posited universal love between men as the foundation of his Christian community, extreme intolerance on the part of Christendom towards those who remained outside it became the inevitable consequence. To the Romans, who had not founded their communal life as a State upon love, religious intolerance was something foreign, although with them religion was a concern of the State and the State was permeated by religion. Neither was it an unaccountable chance that the dream of a Germanic world-dominion called for antisemitism as its complement; and it is intelligible that the attempt to establish a new, communist civilization in Russia should find its psychological support in the persecution of the bourgeois. One only wonders, with concern, what the Soviets will do after they have wiped out their bourgeois. . . .

In all that follows I adopt the standpoint, therefore, that the inclination to aggression is an original, self-subsisting instinctual disposition in man, and I return to my view . . . that it constitutes the greatest impediment to civilization. At one point in the course of this enquiry . . . I was led to the idea that civilization was a special process which mankind undergoes, and I am still under the influence of that idea. I may now add that civilization is a process in the service of Eros, whose purpose is to combine single human individuals, and after that families, then races, peoples and nations, into one great unity, the unity of mankind. Why this has to happen, we do not know; the work of Eros is precisely this. These collections of men are to be libidinally bound to one another. Necessity alone, the advantages of work in common, will not hold them together. But man's natural aggressive instinct, the hostility of each against all and of all against each, opposes this programme of civilization. This aggressive instinct is the derivative and the main representative of the death instinct which we have found alongside of Eros and which shares world-dominion with it. And now, I think, the meaning of the evolution of civilization is no longer obscure to us. It must present the struggle between Eros and Death, between the instinct of life and the instinct of destruction, as it works itself out in the human species. This struggle is what all life essentially consists of, and the evolution of civilization may therefore be simply described as the struggle for life of the human species. And it is this battle of the giants that nurse-maids try to appease with their lullaby about Heaven. . . .

The fateful question for the human species seems to me to be whether and to what extent their cultural development will succeed in mastering the disturbance of their communal life by the human instinct of aggression and self-destruction. It may be that in this respect precisely the present time deserves a special interest. Men have gained control over the forces of nature to such an extent that with their help they would have no difficulty in exterminating one another to the last man. They know this, and hence comes a large part of their current unrest, their unhappiness and their mood of anxiety. And now it is to be expected that the other of the two 'Heavenly Powers' . . . , eternal Eros, will make an effort to assert himself in the struggle with his equally immortal adversary. But who can foresee with what success and with what result?

Study Questions

1. How does Freud use the struggle between Eros and Death to explain the strains and turmoil of people living in his or any other society?
2. Why does the author think that civilization itself is the main cause of human misery and suffering?
3. According to Freud, why has modern society with its advanced technologies failed to make men and women truly happy?
4. What is Freud's psychological interpretation of historical events?

Reading 61

Select Documents of European Fascism

Following the conclusion of World War I in 1918, Western politics and diplomacy seemed to revolve around the survival of liberal democracy in Europe and the United States, the propagation of communism throughout the old Russian Empire, and the evolution of fascism in Italy, Germany, and Spain. As a product of the twentieth century, fascism used psychology, science and technology, and mass communication techniques to win converts and to make sure that the national consciousness fell in line with party policies. German national socialism and Italian fascism had much in common. Both Benito Mussolini (1883–1945), one of the originators of fascist totalitarianism, and Adolf Hitler (1889–1945) stressed charismatic leadership and **Nietzschean** superman activism while promoting the idea that the state, the supreme ethical ideal, was superior to the individual. German Nazis dwelt on their country's defeat in World War I, its national humiliation exemplified by the **Treaty of Versailles**, and the general disorders of the postwar era. Hitler and his cohorts denounced everything from capitalism, communism, and Judaism to those "traitors"—pacifists and liberals—who had engineered Germany's defeat in 1918. Mussolini and Hitler created political movements that were profoundly anti-intellectual and that exploited the irrationality of the masses, whom they publicly glorified but privately scorned.

Mussolini's Political and Social Doctrine of Fascism
(dated 1932)

Fascism, the more it considers and observes the future and the development of humanity quite apart from political considerations of the moment, believes neither in the possibility nor the utility of perpetual peace. It thus repudiates the doctrine of Pacifism—born of a renunciation of the struggle and an act of cowardice in the face of sacrifice. War alone brings up to its highest tension all human energy and puts the stamp of nobility upon the peoples who have the courage to meet it. All

Benito Mussolini, "Political and Social Doctrine of Fascism," *International Conciliation* 306 (January 1935): 5–17. Reprinted with permission of Carnegie Endowment for International Peace.

other trials are substitutes, which never really put men into the position where they have to make the great decision—the alternative of life or death. Thus a doctrine which is founded upon this harmful postulate of peace is hostile to Fascism. And thus hostile to the spirit of Fascism, though accepted for what use they can be in dealing with particular political situations, are all the international leagues and societies which, as history will show, can be scattered to the winds when once strong national feeling is aroused by any motive—sentimental, ideal, or practical. This anti-pacifist spirit is carried by Fascism even into the life of the individual; the proud motto of the Squadrista, "Me ne frego" ["I do not fear"], written on the bandage of the wound, is an act of philosophy not only stoic, the summary of a doctrine not only political—it is the education to combat, the acceptance of the risks which combat implies, and a new way of life for Italy. Thus the Fascist accepts life and loves it, knowing nothing of and despising suicide: he rather conceives of life as duty and struggle and conquest, life which should be high and full, lived for oneself, but above all for others—those who are here, those who are far distant, contemporaries, and the men and women who will come after. . . .

Given that the nineteenth century was the century of Socialism, Liberalism, and Democracy: political doctrines pass, but humanity remains; and it may rather be expected that this will be a century of Fascism. For if the nineteenth century was the century of individualism (Liberalism always signifying individualism) it may be expected that this will be the century of collectivism, and hence the century of the State. It is a perfectly logical deduction that a new doctrine can utilize the vital elements of previous doctrines. . . .

Every doctrine tends to direct human activity towards a determined objective; but the action of men also reacts upon the doctrine, transforms it, adapts it to new needs, or supersedes it with something else. A doctrine then must be no mere exercise in words, but a living act; and thus the value of Fascism lies in the fact that it is veined with pragmatism, but at the same time has a will to exist and a will to power, a firm front in face of the reality of "violence."

The foundation of Fascism is the conception of the State, its character, its duty, and its aim. Fascism conceives of the State as an absolute, in comparison with which all individuals or groups are relative, only to be conceived of in their relation to the State. The conception of the Liberal State is not that of a directing force guiding the play and development, both material and spiritual, of a collective body, but merely a force limited to the function of recording results. Conversely, the Fascist State is itself conscious, and has itself a will and a personality—thus it may be called the "ethic" State.

In 1929, at the first five-year assembly of the Fascist regime, I said: "For us Fascists, the State is not merely a guardian, preoccupied solely with the duty of assuring the personal safety of the citizens; nor is it an organization with purely material aims, such as to guarantee a certain level of well-being and peaceful conditions of life; for a mere council of administration would be sufficient to realize such objects. Nor is it a purely political creation, divorced from all contact with the complex material reality which makes up the life of the individual and the life of the people as a whole. The State, as conceived of and as created by

361

Fascism, is a spiritual and moral fact in itself, since its political, juridical, and economic organization of the nation is a concrete thing. Such an organization must be in its origins and development a manifestation of the spirit. The State is the guarantor of security both internal and external, but it is also the custodian and transmitter of the spirit of the people, as it has grown up through the centuries in language, in customs, and in faith. And the State is not only a living reality of the present, it is also linked with the past and above all with the future, and thus transcending the brief limits of individual life, it represents the immanent spirit of the nation. The forms in which States express themselves may change, but the necessity for such forms is eternal. It is the State which educates its citizens in civic virtue, gives them a consciousness of their mission and welds them into unity; harmonizing their various interests through justice, and transmitting to future generations the mental conquests of science, of art, of law and the solidarity of humanity. It leads men from primitive tribal life to the highest expression of human power which is Empire. It links up through the centuries the names of those of its members who have died for its existence and in obedience to its laws. It holds up the memory of the leaders who have increased its territory and the geniuses who have illuminated it with glory as an example to be followed by future generations. When the conception of the State declines, and disunifying and centrifugal tendencies prevail, whether of individuals or of particular groups, the nations where such phenomena appear are in their decline."

From 1929 until today, evolution, both political and economic, has everywhere gone to prove the validity of these doctrinal premises. Of such gigantic importance is the State. It is the force which alone can provide a solution to the dramatic contradictions of capitalism. . . . Fascism desires the State to be a strong and organic body, at the same time reposing upon broad and popular support. The Fascist State has drawn into itself even the economic activities of the nation, and through the corporative social and educational institutions created by it, its influence reaches every aspect of the national life and includes, framed in their respective organizations, all the political, economic and spiritual forces of the nation. A State which reposes upon the support of millions of individuals who recognize its authority, are continually conscious of its power and are ready at once to serve it, is not the old tyrannical State of the medieval lord nor has it anything in common with the absolute governments either before or after 1789. The individual in the Fascist State is not annulled but rather multiplied, just in the same way that a soldier in a regiment is not diminished but rather increased by the number of his comrades. The Fascist State organizes the nation, but leaves a sufficient margin of liberty to the individual; the latter is deprived of all useless and possibly harmful freedom, but retains what is essential; the deciding power in this question cannot be the individual, but the State alone.

The Fascist State is not indifferent to the fact of religion in general, or to that particular and positive faith which is Italian Catholicism. The State professes no theology, but a morality, and in the Fascist State religion is considered as one of the deepest manifestations of the spirit of man; thus it is not only respected but defended and protected. The Fascist State has never tried to create its own God, as at one moment **Robespierre** and the wildest extremists of the Convention tried to do; nor does it vainly seek to obliterate religion from the hearts of men as does **Bolshevism**; Fascism respects the God of the ascetics, the saints and heroes, and equally, God, as He is perceived and worshipped by simple people.

The Fascist State is an embodied will to power and government; the Roman tradition is here an ideal of force in action. According to Fascism, government is not so much a thing to be expressed in territorial or military terms as in terms of morality and the spirit. It must be thought of as an empire—that is to say, a nation which directly or indirectly rules other nations, without the need for conquering a single square yard of territory. For Fascism, the growth of empire, that is to say the expansion of the nation, is an essential manifestation of vitality, and its opposite a sign of decadence. Peoples which are rising, or rising again after a period of decadence, are always imperialist: any renunciation is a sign of decay and of death.

Fascism is the doctrine best adapted to represent the tendencies and the aspirations of a people, like the people of Italy, who are rising again after many centuries of abasement and foreign servitude. But empire demands discipline, the co-ordination of all forces and a deeply felt sense of duty and sacrifice: this fact explains many aspects of the practical working of the regime, the character of many forces in the State, and the necessarily severe measures which must be taken against those who would oppose this spontaneous and inevitable movement of Italy in the twentieth century, and would oppose it by recalling the outworn ideology of the nineteenth century—repudiated wheresoever there has been the courage to undertake great experiments of social and political transformation: for never before has the nation stood more in need of authority, of direction, and of order.

If every age has its own doctrine, there are a thousand signs which point to Fascism as the characteristic doctrine of our time. For if a doctrine must be a living thing, this is proved by the fact that Fascism has created a living faith; and that this faith is very powerful in the minds of men, is demonstrated by those who have suffered and died for it.

Fascism has henceforth in the world the universality of all those doctrines which, in realizing themselves, have represented a stage in the history of the human spirit.

Hitler's Program of the German Workers' Party
(dated 1920)

The Program of the German Workers' Party is limited as to period. The leaders have no intention, once the aims announced in it have been achieved, of setting up fresh ones, in order to ensure the continued existence of the Party by the artificially increased discontent of the masses.

Gottfried Feder, *Hitler's Official Programme and Its Fundamental Ideas* (London: Allen & Unwin, 1938), 38–43.

1. We demand the union of all Germans, on the basis of the right of the self-determination of peoples, to form a Great Germany.

2. We demand equality of rights for the German People in its dealings with other nations, and abolition of the Peace Treaties of **Versailles** and **Saint-Germain**.

3. We demand land and territory (colonies) for the nourishment of our people and for settling our surplus population.

4. None but members of the nation may be citizens of the State. None but those of German blood, whatever their creed, may be members of the nation. No Jew, therefore, may be a member of the nation.

5. Anyone who is not a citizen of the State may live in Germany only as a guest and must be regarded as being subject to the Alien laws.

8. All further non-German immigration must be prevented. We demand that all non-Germans who entered Germany subsequently to 2 August 1914, shall be required forthwith to depart from the Reich.

9. All citizens of the State shall possess equal rights and duties.

WE DEMAND THEREFORE:

11. Abolition of incomes unearned by work. Abolition of the thraldom of interest.

13. We demand the nationalization of all businesses which have (hitherto) been amalgamated (into Trusts).

15. We demand a generous development of provision for old age.

16. We demand the creation and maintenance of a healthy middle class, immediate communalization of wholesale warehouses, and their lease at a low rate to small traders, and that the most careful consideration shall be shown to all small purveyors to the State, the provinces, or smaller communities.

17. We demand a land-reform suitable to our national requirements, the passing of a law for the confiscation without compensation of land for communal purposes, the abolition of interest on mortgages, and prohibition of all speculation in land.

18. We demand ruthless war upon all those whose activities are injurious to the common interest. Common criminals against the nation, usurers, profiteers, etc., must be punished with death, whatever their creed or race.

19. We demand that the Roman Law, which serves the materialistic world order, shall be replaced by a German common law.

20. With the aim of opening to every capable and industrious German the possibility of higher education and consequent advancement to leading positions the State must consider a thorough reconstruction of our national system of education. The curriculum of all educational establishments must be brought into line with the requirements of practical life. Directly as the mind begins to develop the schools must aim at teaching the pupil to understand the idea of the State (State sociology). We demand the education of specially gifted children of poor parents, whatever their class or occupation, at the expense of the State.

21. The State must apply itself to raising the standard of health in the nation by protecting mothers and infants, prohibiting child labor, and increasing bodily

efficiency by legally obligatory gymnastics and sports, and by extensive support of clubs engaged in the physical training of the young.

22. We demand the abolition of mercenary troops and the formation of a national army.

23. We demand legal warfare against conscious political lies and their dissemination in the Press. In order to facilitate the creation of a German national Press we demand:

That all editors and contributors to newspapers employing the German language must be members of the nation;

That special permission from the State shall be necessary before non-German newspapers may appear. These need not necessarily be printed in the German language;

That non-Germans shall be prohibited by law from participating financially in or influencing German newspapers, and that the penalty for contravention of the law shall be suppression of any such newspaper, and immediate deportation of the non-German involved.

It must be forbidden to publish newspapers which do not conduce to the national welfare. We demand the legal prosecution of all tendencies in art and literature of a kind likely to disintegrate our life as a nation, and the suppression of institutions which militate against the above-mentioned requirements.

24. We demand liberty for all religious denominations in the State, so far as they are not a danger to it and do not militate against the morality and moral sense of the German race. The Party, as such, stands for positive Christianity, but does not bind itself in the matter of creed to any particular confession. It combats the Jewish-materialist spirit within and without us, and is convinced our nation can achieve permanent health from within only on the principle: the common interest before self-interest.

25. That all the foregoing requirements may be realized we demand the creation of a strong central power of the Reich. Unconditional authority of the politically central Parliament over the entire Reich and its organization in general. . . .

Nazi Party Organization Book (dated 1940)

The National Socialist commandments:

The Führer is always right!

Never go against discipline!

Don't waste your time in idle chatter or in self-satisfying criticism, but take
     hold and do your work!

Be proud but not arrogant!

Let the program be your dogma. It demands of you the greatest devotion to the
     movement.

You are a representative of the party; control your bearing and your manner
     accordingly!

Let loyalty and unselfishness be your highest precepts!
Practice true comradeship and you will be a true socialist!
Treat your racial comrades as you wish to be treated by them!
In battle be hard and silent! Spirit is not unruliness!
That which promotes the movement, Germany, and your people, is right!
If you act according to these commandments, you are a true soldier of your
      Führer.

Study Questions

1. According to Mussolini, why must the state remain dominant and its needs supersede the desires of individual citizens?
2. What do Hitler's demands, as set out in his Program of the German Workers' Party, suggest about his political views?
3. How did Hitler's political and racial beliefs exploit the fear and discontent of the German people following their defeat and humiliation in World War I?
4. What do the Nazi commandments of 1940 have in common with the notions espoused in Hitler's Program of the German Workers' Party of 1920?

Pablo Picasso's "Guernica"

The Spanish Civil War began in 1936 when General Francisco Franco invaded his native Spain from Spanish Morocco, North Africa. He headed a coalition of the middle and upper classes, conservatives in the Spanish Catholic church, and most of the national army of Spain. With the help of the fascist dictators of Italy and Germany, Franco's forces gained final victory over the leftist Popular Front government of the Spanish Republic in 1939. The cruelties and atrocities committed by both sides in the conflict resulted in the deaths of an estimated one million people. Fascist regimes in Europe viewed the conflict as a symbolic test, whose outcome would predict the immediate direction of European affairs. Hence, both Mussolini and Hitler gave Franco more than mere moral support. On 26 April 1937, the Condor Legion, a German air force unit that had bombed many Spanish cities, destroyed the Basque town of Guernica, killing or wounding the majority of people living there. The brutal attack not only outraged world opinion, but inspired the most famous and successful artist of the twentieth century, Pablo Picasso (1881–1973), to create "Guernica," one of the most significant paintings of the twentieth century. Working furiously, Picasso completed his anguished protest against the brutality of war after one month and 27 sketches. It was painted not in full color, but in stark black, white, and gray. The crucial symbol is the wounded horse representing the people. The bull symbolizes fascism, brutality, and darkness. The pessimistic tone of the work is mitigated slightly by the symbol of the light bulb in the center of the sun and a small, fragile flower above the broken sword. Picasso decreed the work to remain on loan to the Museum of Modern Art in New York until the restoration of democracy in Spain. This condition was satisfied in 1982, so that this massive oil on canvas measuring 25 feet 5¾ inches × 11 feet 5½ inches is now the property of the Prado Museum, Madrid, Spain.

Reading 62

Jean-Paul Sartre's *Being and Nothingness*

The roots of existentialism may be traced to the nineteenth-century philosophies of **Kierkegaard, Dostoevsky, Nietzsche,** and others. As it evolved in the twentieth century, this system of thought (it is more a philosophical attitude than a systematic philosophy) greatly appealed to many desperate and disillusioned people after World War II. One of its foremost proponents was Jean-Paul Sartre (1905–1980). Sartre showcased existentialism in many plays, short stories, and philosophical treatises, such as *Being and Nothingness*, published in 1943. (He was awarded the Nobel Prize for literature in 1964 but did not accept it.) In *Being and Nothingness* Sartre postulates that humanity must turn to itself to find new values. For him, existentialist philosophy is a means to understand all the consequences of human existence without a reference to God. He begins with the premise that existence precedes essence: that what a person "is" is determined by the course of existence and not by something innate in an individual. Sartre goes on to suggest that human beings create themselves and are defined by individual acts and choices. It is thus the responsibility and choice of every person to make life meaningful and valuable.

The essential consequence of our earlier remarks is that man being condemned to be free carries the weight of the whole world on his shoulders; he is responsible for the world and for himself as a way of being. We are taking responsibility in the ordinary sense as "consciousness (of) being the incontestable author of an event or of an object." In this sense the responsibility of the **for-itself** is overwhelming since he is the one by whom it happens that there is a world; since he is also the one who makes himself be, then whatever may be the situation in which he finds himself, the for-itself must wholly assume this situation with its peculiar coefficient of adversity, even though it be insupportable. He must assume the situation with the proud consciousness of being the author of it, for the very worst disadvantages or the worst threats which can endanger my person have meaning only in and through my project; and it is on the ground of the engagement which I am planning since nothing foreign has decided what we feel, what we live, or what we are.

Jean-Paul Sartre, *Being and Nothingness,* trans. H. E. Barnes (New York: Philosophical Library, 1956), 707–11, passim. Copyright © 1956 Philosophical Library. Reprinted with permission.

Furthermore this absolute responsibility is not resignation; it is simply the logical requirement of the consequences of our freedom. What happens to me happens through me, and I can neither affect myself with it nor revolt against it nor resign myself to it. Moreover everything which happens to me is mine. By this we must understand first of all that I am always equal to what happens to me qua man, for what happens to a man through other men and through himself can be only human. The most terrible situations of war, the worst tortures do not create a non-human state of things; there is no non-human situation. It is only through fear, flight, and recourse to magical types of conduct that I shall decide on the non-human, but this decision is human, and I shall carry the entire responsibility for it. But in addition the situation is mine because it is the image of my free choice of myself, and everything which it presents to me is mine in that this represents me and symbolizes me. Is it not I who decide the coefficient of adversity in things and even their unpredictability by deciding myself?

Thus there are no accidents in a life; a community event which suddenly bursts forth and involves me in it does not come from the outside. If I am mobilized in a war, this war is my war; it is in my image and I deserve it. I deserve it first because I could always get out of it by suicide or by desertion; these ultimate possibilities are those which must always be present for us when there is a question of envisioning a situation. For lack of getting out of it, I have chosen it. This can be due to inertia, to cowardice in the face of public opinion, or because I prefer certain other values to the value of the refusal to join in the war (the good opinion of my relatives, the honor of my family, etc.). Any way you look at it, it is a matter of a choice. This choice will be repeated later on again and again without a break until the end of the war. Therefore we must agree with the statement by **J. Romains**, "In war there are no innocent victims." If therefore I have preferred war to death or to dishonor, everything takes place as if I bore the entire responsibility for this war. Of course others have declared it, and one might be tempted perhaps to consider me as a simple accomplice. But this notion of complicity has only a juridical sense, and it does not hold here. For it depended on me that for me and by me this war should not exist, and I have decided that it does exist. There was no compulsion here, for the compulsion could have got no hold on a freedom. I did not have any excuse; for as we have said repeatedly in this book, the peculiar character of human-reality is that it is without excuse. Therefore it remains for me only to lay claim to this war.

But in addition the war is mine because by the sole fact that it arises in a situation which I cause to be and that I can discover it there only by engaging myself for or against it, I can no longer distinguish at present the choice which I make of myself from the choice which I make of the war. To live this war is to choose myself through it and to choose it through my choice of myself. There can be no question of considering it as "four years of vacation" or as a "reprieve," as a "recess," the essential part of my responsibilities being elsewhere in my married, family, or professional life. In this war which I have chosen I choose myself from day to day, and I make it mine by making myself. If it is going to be four empty years, then it is I who bear the responsibility for this.

Finally, as we pointed out earlier, each person is an absolute choice of self from the standpoint of a world of knowledge and of techniques which this choice both assumes and illumines; each person is an absolute upsurge at an absolute date and is perfectly unthinkable at another date. It is therefore a waste of time to ask what I should have been if this war had not broken out, for I have chosen myself as one of the possible meanings of the epoch which imperceptibly led to war. I am not distinct from this same epoch; I could not be transported to another epoch without contradiction. Thus I am this war which restricts and limits and makes comprehensible the period which preceded it. In this sense we may define more precisely the responsibility of the for-itself if to the earlier quoted statement, "There are no innocent victims," we add the words, "We have the war we deserve." Thus, totally free, undistinguishable from the period for which I have chosen to be the meaning, as profoundly responsible for the war as if I had myself declared it, unable to live without integrating it in my situation, engaging myself in it wholly and stamping it with my seal, I must be without remorse or regrets as I am without excuse; for from the instant of my upsurge into being, I carry the weight of the world by myself alone without anything or any person being able to lighten it.

Yet this responsibility is of a very particular type. Someone will say, "I did not ask to be born." This is a naive way of throwing greater emphasis on our facticity. I am responsible for everything, in fact, except for my very responsibility, for I am not the foundation of my being. Therefore everything takes place as if I were compelled to be responsible. I am abandoned in the world, not in the sense that I might remain abandoned and passive in a hostile universe like a board floating on the water, but rather in the sense that I find myself suddenly alone and without help, engaged in a world for which I bear the whole responsibility without being able, whatever I do, to tear myself away from this responsibility for an instant For I am responsible for my very desire of fleeing responsibilities. To make myself passive in the world, to refuse to act upon things and upon others is still to choose myself, and suicide is one mode among others of being-in-the-world. Yet I find an absolute responsibility for the fact that my facticity (here the fact of my birth) is directly inapprehensible and even inconceivable, for this fact of my birth never appears as a brute fact but always across a projective reconstruction of my for-itself. I am ashamed of being born or I am astonished at it or I rejoice over it, or in attempting to get rid of my life I affirm that I live and I assume this life as bad. Thus in a certain sense I choose being born. This choice itself is integrally affected with facticity since I am not able not to choose, but this facticity in turn will appear only in so far as I surpass it toward my ends. Thus facticity is everywhere but inapprehensible; I never encounter anything except my responsibility. That is why I cannot ask, "Why was I born?" or curse the day of my birth or declare that I did not ask to be born, for these various attitudes toward my birth—i.e., toward the fact that I realize a presence in the world—are absolutely nothing else but ways of assuming this birth in full responsibility and of making it mine. Here again I encounter only myself and my projects so that finally my abandonment—i.e., my facticity—consists simply in the fact that I am condemned to be wholly responsible for myself. I am the being which is in such a way that in its being its being is in question. And this "is" of my being is as present and inapprehensible.

Under these conditions since every event in the world can be revealed to me only as an opportunity (an opportunity made use of, lacked, neglected, etc.), or better yet since everything which happens to us can be considered as a chance (i.e., can appear to us only as a way of realizing this being which is in question in our being) and since others as transcendences-transcended are themselves only opportunities and chances, the responsibility of the for-itself extends to the entire world as a peopled-world. It is precisely thus that the for-itself apprehends itself in anguish; that is, as a being which is neither the foundation of its own being nor of the Other's being nor of the **in-itselfs** which form the world, but a being which is compelled to decide the meaning of being—within it and everywhere outside of it. The one who realizes in anguish his condition as being thrown into a responsibility which extends to his very abandonment has no longer either remorse or regret or excuse; he is no longer anything but a freedom which perfectly reveals itself and whose being resides in this very revelation. But as we pointed out at the beginning of this work, most of the time we flee anguish in bad faith. . . .

Study Questions

1. What does Sartre mean when he remarks that human beings are "condemned to be free"?
2. How is establishing a relationship between "being-in-itself" and "being-for-itself" essential for understanding the author's notion of perfect responsibility?
3. How does Sartre's existentialism lead to a new, humanistic perception of the universe and humanity?
4. How is Sartre's perception of freedom generated by the anguish and despair people feel and experience, and how does this viewpoint encourage individual self-awareness?

Reading 63

The United Nations Universal Declaration of Human Rights

When the United Nations Charter was signed on 26 June 1945, the world appeared to be a more humane, hospitable place. The charter established the initial charges and duties of the UN and set up its organizational structure. The 11 member states of the first Security Council—including the United States, Great Britain, France, the USSR, and the Republic of China—were given various functions and powers that enabled them to work on behalf of the UN's entire membership. The cold war significantly compromised the UN's major goals: namely, international cooperation and world peace. There have been instances, however, when this institution has played an important role in handling sundry global crises, the most recent examples being Iraq's invasion of Kuwait and the civil strife in Somalia. Many actions that the UN undertakes are based on Resolution 217 [III] A, better known as the Universal Declaration of Human Rights. This resolution was written to establish a global consensus on the meaning of individual liberty and freedom within the modern nation-state. It was adopted by the General Assembly on 10 December 1948; 58 nations voted in favor of the proclamation, while 8 countries (Poland, Saudi Arabia, South Africa, Yugoslavia, the USSR, the Soviet Socialist Republics of the Ukraine and Byelorussia, and Czechoslovakia) abstained.

Whereas recognition of the inherent dignity and of the equal and inalienable rights of all members of the human family is the foundation of freedom, justice and peace in the world,

Whereas disregard and contempt for human rights have resulted in barbarous acts which have outraged the conscience of mankind, and the advent of a world in which human beings shall enjoy freedom of speech and belief and freedom

United Nations. *The Universal Declaration of Human Rights,* UN Publication 63. 1. 13 (New York: United Nations, 1963), 33–38. Reprinted with permission.

from fear and want has been proclaimed as the highest aspiration of the common people,

Whereas it is essential, if man is not to be compelled to have recourse, as a last resort, to rebellion against tyranny and oppression, that human rights should be protected by the rule of law,

Whereas it is essential to promote the development of friendly relations between nations,

Whereas the peoples of the United Nations have in the Charter reaffirmed their faith in fundamental human rights, in the dignity and worth of the human person and in the equal rights of men and women and have determined to promote social progress and better standards of life in larger freedom,

Whereas Member States have pledged themselves to achieve, in cooperation with the United Nations, the promotion of universal respect for and observance of human rights and fundamental freedoms,

Whereas a common understanding of these rights and freedoms is of the greatest importance for the full realization of this pledge,

Now therefore, THE GENERAL ASSEMBLY proclaims this Universal Declaration of Human Rights as a common standard of achievement for all peoples and all nations, to the end that every individual and every organ of society, keeping this Declaration constantly in mind, shall strive by teaching and education to promote respect for these rights and freedoms and by progressive measures, national and international, to secure their universal and effective recognition and observance, both among the people of Member States themselves and among the people of territories under their jurisdiction.

Article 1. All human beings are born free and equal in dignity and rights. They are endowed with reason and conscience and should act towards one another in a spirit of brotherhood.

Article 2. Everyone is entitled to all the rights and freedoms set forth in this Declaration, without distinction of any kind, such as race, color, sex, language, religion, political or other opinion, national or social origin, property, birth or other status. Furthermore, no distinction shall be made on the basis of the political, jurisdictional or international status of the country or territory to which a person belongs, whether it be independent, trust, non-self-governing or under any other limitation of sovereignty.

Article 3. Everyone has the right to life, liberty and security of person.

Article 4. No one shall be held in slavery or servitude; slavery and slave trade shall be prohibited in all their forms.

Article 5. No one shall be subjected to torture or to cruel, inhuman or degrading treatment or punishment.

Article 6. Everyone has the right to recognition everywhere as a person before the law.

Article 7. All are equal before the law and are entitled without any discrimination to equal protection of the law. All are entitled to equal protection against any discrimination in violation of this Declaration and against any incitement to such discrimination. . . .

Article 8. Everyone has the right to an effective remedy by the competent rational tribunals for acts of violating the fundamental rights granted him by the constitution of the law.

Article 9. No one shall be subjected to arbitrary arrest, detention or exile.

Article 10. Everyone is entitled in full equality to a fair and public hearing by an independent and impartial tribunal, in the determination of his rights and obligations and of any criminal charge against him.

Article 11. Everyone charged with a penal offence has the right to be presumed innocent until proved guilty, according to law in a public trial at which he has had all the guarantees necessary for his defence.

No one shall be held guilty of any penal offence on account of any act or omission which did not constitute a penal offence, under national or international law, at the time when it was committed. Nor shall a heavier penalty be imposed than the one that was applicable at the time that penal offence was committed.

Article 12. No one shall be subjected to arbitrary interference with his privacy, family, correspondence, nor to attacks upon his honor and reputation. Every person has the right to the protection of the law against such interference and attacks.

Article 13. Everyone has the right to freedom of movement and residence within the borders of each state.

Everyone has the right to leave any country, including his own, and to return to his country.

Article 14. Everyone has the right to seek and to enjoy in other countries asylum from persecution.

This right may not be invoked in the case of prosecutions genuinely arising from non-political crimes or from acts contrary to the purposes and principles of the United Nations.

Article 15. Everyone has the right to a nationality.

No one shall be arbitrarily deprived of his nationality nor denied the right to change his nationality.

Article 16. Men and women of full age, without any limitation due to race, nationality or religion, have the right to marry and to found a family. They are entitled to equal rights as to marriage, during marriage and at its dissolution.

Marriage shall be entered into only with free and full consent of the intending spouses.

The family is the natural and fundamental group unit of society and is entitled to protection by society and the State.

Article 17. Everyone has the right to own property alone and in association with others.

No one shall be arbitrarily deprived of his property.

Article 18. Everyone has the right to freedom of thought, conscience and religion; this right includes freedom to change his religion or belief, and freedom, either alone or in community with others and in public or private, to manifest his religion or belief in teaching, practice, worship and observance.

Article 19. Everyone has the right to freedom of opinion and expression; this right includes freedom to hold opinions without interference and to seek, receive and impart information and ideas through any media and regardless of frontiers.

Article 20. Everyone has the right to freedom of peaceful assembly and association.

No one may be compelled to belong to an association.

Article 21. Everyone has the right to take part in the government of his country, directly or through freely chosen representatives.

Everyone has the right of equal access to public service in his country.

The will of the people shall be the basis of the authority of government; this will shall be expressed in periodic and genuine elections which shall be by universal and equal suffrage and shall be held by secret vote or by equivalent free voting procedures.

Article 22. Everyone, as a member of society, has the right to social security and is entitled to realization, through national effort and international cooperation and in accordance with the organization and resources of each State, of the economic, social and cultural rights indispensable for his dignity and the free development of his personality.

Article 23. Everyone has the right to work, to free choice of employment, to just and favorable conditions of work and to protection against unemployment.

Everyone, without any discrimination, has the right to equal pay for equal work.

Everyone who works has the right to just and favorable remuneration insuring for himself and his family an existence worthy of human dignity, and supplemented, if necessary, by other means of social protection.

Everyone has the right to form and to join trade unions for the protection of his interests.

Article 24. Everyone has the right to rest and leisure, including reasonable limitation of working hours and periodic holidays with pay.

Article 25. Everyone has the right to a standard of living adequate for the health and well-being of himself and of his family, including food, clothing, housing and medical care and necessary social services, and the right to security in the event of unemployment, sickness, disability, widowhood, old age or other lack of livelihood in circumstances beyond his control.

Motherhood and childhood are entitled to special care and assistance. All children, whether born in or out of wedlock, shall enjoy the same social protection.

Article 26. Everyone has the right to education, which shall be free, at least in the elementary and fundamental stages. Elementary education shall be compulsory. Technical and professional education shall be made generally available and higher education shall be equally accessible to all on the basis of merit.

Education shall be directed to the full development of the human personality and to the strengthening of respect for human rights and fundamental freedoms. It shall promote understanding, tolerance, and friendship among all nations, racial or religious groups, and shall further the activities of the United Nations for the maintenance of peace.

Parents have a prior right to choose the kind of education that shall be given to their children.

Article 27. Everyone has the right freely to participate in the cultural life of the community, to enjoy the arts and to share in scientific advancement and its benefits.

Everyone has the right to the protection of the moral and material interests resulting from any scientific, literary or artistic production of which he is the author.

Article 28. Everyone is entitled to a social and international order in which the rights and freedoms set forth in this Declaration can be fully realized.

Article 29. Everyone has duties to the community in which alone the free and full development of his personality is possible. In the exercise of his rights and freedoms, everyone shall be subject only to such limitations as are determined by law solely for the purpose of securing due recognition and respect for the rights and freedoms of others and of meeting the just requirements of morality, public order and the general welfare in a democratic society.

These rights and freedoms may in no case be exercised contrary to the purposes and principles of the United Nations.

Article 30. Nothing in this Declaration may be interpreted as implying for any State, group or person any right to engage in any activity or to perform any act aimed at the destruction of any of the rights and freedoms set forth herein.

Study Questions

1. In what ways is the Universal Declaration of Human Rights based on the political and socioeconomic ideology of Western liberal democracy?
2. How comprehensive is the UN's statement on universal human rights?
3. How does the UN's resolution on human rights establish the sovereignty of the individual?
4. What is the notion of universal order underlying the Declaration's stand on human liberty and freedom?

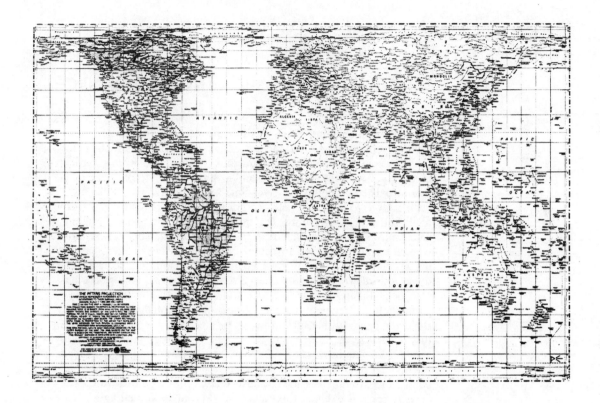

The Peters Projection Map of the World

Atlases and maps have always presented a somewhat distorted picture of the world. This results from both political and cultural biases, as well as from the attempt to represent the spherical earth on flat paper according to inconsistent scales. According to cartographer Arno Peters, since the sixteenth century many atlases have been published that differ significantly from the world-famous Mercator projection map, but all tend to adhere to Mercator's Eurocentric view of the world. In the foreword to *Peters Projection,* 1973, he wrote: "All of [the maps] represent their own country, their own continent, as larger than the non-European countries through the use of different scales. If, together with the age of colonialism, the Eurocentric way of thinking is also to come to an end, we need a new geographical picture of the world based on the equal status of all the peoples of the earth. . . . This equal presentation of the world is the expression of the worldwide consciousness of solidarity which is beginning to overcome traditional Eurocentric thinking." In the Peters Atlas all topographic maps have equal area scale: one square centimeter on the map equals six thousand square kilometers.

377

Reading 64

Simone de Beauvoir's *The Second Sex*

Existentialism examines some of life's most basic, concrete problems. This is perhaps its most significant contribution to philosophy. One such issue is the conventional perception of men and women's roles in society. The roots of modern feminism certainly predate the evolution of existential philosophy; yet Simone de Beauvoir's (1908–1986) contributions to both twentieth-century movements establish many mutually related considerations. Feminism is in part an attempt to eliminate faulty stereotypes of female intellect and behavior, to transform women's self-image, and to better appreciate those qualities that are innate to women alone. If these goals are accomplished, society's attitude toward women would change dramatically, and as a result, human behavior itself would be affected in a positive way. Influenced particularly by Jean-Paul Sartre's brand of existentialism, Simone de Beauvoir believed that human beings realize true freedom only when they recognize the ambiguous nature of life. Protection against these ambiguities requires individuals to choose values to live by, which bestows on them the kind of personal freedom and responsibility espoused by existentialists and feminists alike. Simone de Beauvoir's *The Second Sex* was published in France in 1949; in 1953 the English language version first appeared. Various aspects of femininity, including sexual differentiation between women and men, are explored within its pages from the perspective of existentialist ethics. According to de Beauvoir, the status of women as the "Other" is the antithesis of the male "Absolute."

To state the question [what is a woman?] is, to me, to suggest, at once, a preliminary answer. The fact that I ask it is in itself significant. A man would never get the notion of writing a book on the peculiar situation of the human male. But if I wish to define myself, I must first of all say: "I am a woman"; on this truth must be based all further discussion. A man never begins by presenting himself as an individual of a certain sex; it goes without saying that he is a man. The terms masculine and feminine are used symmetrically only as a matter of form, as on legal papers. In actuality the relation of the two sexes is not quite like that of two electrical poles, for man represents both the positive and the neutral, as is indicated by the common use of man to designate human beings in general; whereas woman represents only the negative, defined by limiting criteria, without reciprocity. In the midst of an abstract discussion it is vexing to hear a man say: "You think thus and so because you are a woman"; but I know that my only defense is to reply: "I think thus and so because it is true," thereby removing my subjective self from the argument. It would be out of the question to reply: "And you think the contrary because you are a man," for it is understood that the fact of being a man is no peculiarity. A man is in the right in being a man; it is the woman who is in the wrong. It amounts to this: just as for the ancients there was an absolute vertical with reference to which the oblique was defined, so there is an absolute human type, the masculine. . . .

Thus humanity is male and man defines woman not in herself but as relative to him; she is not regarded as an autonomous being. [Woman] is defined and differentiated with reference to man and not he with reference to her; she is the incidental, the inessential as opposed to the essential. He is the Subject, he is the Absolute—she is the Other.

The category of Other is as primordial as consciousness itself. In the most primitive societies, in the most ancient mythologies, one finds the expression of a duality—that of the Self and the Other. This duality was not originally attached to the division of the sexes; it was not dependent upon any empirical facts. . . . Otherness is a fundamental category of human thought. Thus it is that no group ever sets itself up as the One without immediately setting up the Other over against itself. . . .

But the other consciousness, the other ego, sets up a reciprocal claim. The native traveling abroad is shocked to find himself in turn regarded as a "stranger" by the natives of neighboring countries. As a matter of fact, wars, festivals, trading, treaties, and contests among tribes, nations, and classes tend to deprive the concept of Other of its absolute sense and to make manifest its relativity; willy-nilly, individuals and groups are forced to realize the reciprocity of their relations. How is it, then, that this reciprocity has not been recognized between the sexes, that one of the contrasting terms is set up as the sole essential, denying any relativity in regard to its correlative and defining the latter as pure otherness? Why is it that women do not dispute male sovereignty? No subject will readily volunteer to become the object, the inessential; it is not the Other who, in defining himself as the Other, establishes the One. The Other is posed as such by the One in defining himself as the One. But if the Other is not to regain the status of being the One, he must be submissive enough to accept this alien point of view. . . .

Now, woman has always been man's dependent, if not his slave; the two sexes have never shared the world in equality. And even today woman is heavily handicapped, though her situation is beginning to change. Almost nowhere is her legal status the same as man's, and frequently it is much to her disadvantage. Even when her rights are legally recognized in the abstract, long-standing custom prevents their full expression in the mores. In the economic sphere men and women can almost be said to make up two castes; other things being equal, the former

379

hold the better jobs, get higher wages, and have more opportunity for success than their new competitors. In industry and politics men have a great many more positions and they monopolize the most important posts. In addition to all this, they enjoy a traditional prestige that the education of children tends in every way to support, for the present enshrines the past—and in the past all history has been made by men. At the present time, when women are beginning to take part in the affairs of the world, it is still a world that belongs to men—they have no doubt of it at all and women have scarcely any. To decline to be the Other, to refuse to be a party to the deal—this would be for women to renounce all the advantages conferred upon them by their alliance with the superior caste.

Man-the-sovereign provides woman-the-liege with material protection and will undertake the moral justification of her existence; thus she can evade at once both economic risk and the metaphysical risk of a liberty in which ends and aims must be contrived without assistance. Indeed, along with the ethical urge of each individual to affirm his subjective existence, there is also the temptation to forgo liberty and become a thing. This is an inauspicious road, for he who takes it—passive, lost, ruined—becomes henceforth the creature of another's will, frustrated in his transcendence and deprived of every value. But it is an easy road; on it one avoids the strain involved in undertaking an authentic existence. When man makes of woman the Other, he may, then, expect her to manifest deep-seated tendencies toward complicity. Thus, woman may fail to lay claim to the status of subject because she lacks definite resources, because she feels the necessary bond that ties her to man regardless of reciprocity, and because she is often very well pleased with her role as the Other. . . .

Now, what peculiarly signalizes the situation of woman is that she—a free and autonomous being like all human creatures—nevertheless finds herself living in a world where men compel her to assume the status of the Other. They propose to stabilize her as object and to doom her to immanence since her transcendence is to be overshadowed and forever transcended by another ego (conscience) which is essential and sovereign. The drama of woman lies in the conflict between the fundamental aspirations of every subject (ego)—who always regards the self as the essential—and the compulsions of a situation in which she is the inessential. How can a human being in woman's situation attain fulfillment? What roads are open to her? Which are blocked? How can independence be recovered in a state of dependency? What circumstances limit woman's liberty and how can they be overcome? These are the fundamental questions on which I would fain throw some light. This means that I am interested in the fortunes of the individual defined not in terms of happiness but in terms of liberty. . . .

Indeed, the struggle cannot be clearly drawn between them, since woman is opaque in her very being; she stands before man not as a subject but as an object paradoxically imbued with subjectivity; she takes herself simultaneously as self and as other, a contradiction that entails baffling consequences. When she makes weapons at once of her weakness and of her strength, it is not a matter of designing calculation: she seeks salvation spontaneously in the way that has been imposed on her, that of passivity, at the same time when she is actively demanding her sovereignty: and no doubt this procedure is unfair tactics, but it is dictated to her by the ambiguous situation assigned her. Man, however, becomes indignant when he treats her as a free and independent being and then realizes that she is still a trap for him; if he gratifies and satisfies her in her posture as prey, he finds her claims to autonomy irritating; whatever he does, he feels tricked and she feels wronged. . . .

A world where men and women would be equal is easy to visualize, for that precisely is what the Soviet Revolution promised: women raised and trained exactly like men were to work under the same conditions and for the same wages. Erotic liberty was to be recognized by custom, but the sexual act was not to be considered a "service" to be paid for; woman was to be obliged to provide herself with other ways of earning a living; marriage was to be based on a free agreement that the spouses could break at will; maternity was to be voluntary, which meant that contraception and abortion were to be authorized and that, on the other hand, all mothers and their children were to have exactly the same rights, in or out of marriage: pregnancy leaves were to be paid for by the State, which would assume charge of the children, signifying not that they would be taken away from their parents, but that they would not be abandoned to them.

But is it enough to change laws, institutions, customs, public opinion, and the whole social context, for men and women to become truly equal? "Women will always be women," say the skeptics. Other seers prophesy that in casting off their femininity they will not succeed in changing themselves into men and they will become monsters. This would be to admit that the woman of today is a creation of nature; it must be repeated once more that in human society nothing is natural and that woman, like much else, is a product elaborated by civilization. The intervention of others in her destiny is fundamental: if this action took a different direction, it would produce a quite different result. Woman is determined not by her hormones or by mysterious instincts, but by the manner in which her body and her relation to the world are modified through the action of others than herself. The abyss that separates the adolescent boy and girl has been deliberately opened out between them since earliest childhood; later on, woman could not be other than what she was made, and that past was bound to shadow her for life. If we appreciate its influence, we see clearly that her destiny is not predetermined for all eternity.

We must not believe, certainly, that a change in woman's economic condition alone is enough to transform her, though this factor has been and remains the basic factor in her evolution; but until it has brought about the moral, social, cultural, and other consequences that it promises and requires, the new woman cannot appear. At this moment they have been realized nowhere, in Russia no more than in France or the United States; and this explains why the woman of today is torn between the past and the future. She appears most often as a "true woman" disguised as a man, and she feels herself as ill at ease in her flesh as in her masculine garb. She must shed her old skin and cut her own new clothes. This she could do only through a social evolution. No single educator could fashion a female human being today who would be the exact homologue of the male human being; if she is raised like a boy, the young girl feels she is an oddity and thereby she is given a new kind of sex specification. **Stendhal** understood this when he said: "The forest must be planted all at once." But if we imagine, on the contrary, a society in which the equality of the sexes would be concretely realized this equality would find new expression in each individual. . . .

To emancipate woman is to refuse to confine her to the relations she bears to man, not to deny them to her; let her have her independent existence and she will continue none the less to exist for him also: mutually recognizing each other as subject, each will yet remain for the other an other. The reciprocity of their relations will not do away with the miracles—desire, possession, love, dream, adventure—worked by the division of human beings into two separate categories; and the words that move us—giving, conquering, uniting—will not lose their meaning. On the contrary, when we abolish the slavery of hypocrisy that it implies, then the "division" of humanity will reveal its genuine significance and the human couple will find its true form. "The direct, natural, necessary relation of human creatures is the relation of man to woman," Marx has said. "The nature of this relationship determines to what point man himself is to be considered as a generic being, as mankind; the relation of man to woman is the most natural relation of human being to human being. By it is shown, therefore, to what point the natural behavior of man has become human or to what point the human being has become his natural being, to what point his human nature has become his nature."

The case could not be better stated. It is for man to establish the reign of liberty in the midst of the world of the given. To gain the supreme victory, it is necessary, for one thing, that by and through their natural differentiation men and women unequivocally affirm their brotherhood.

Study Questions

1. How does de Beauvoir define "woman"?
2. Why would the author's view that people must develop a new outlook on humanity's biological destiny upset traditional thinking on relations between men and women?
3. What does de Beauvoir's thinking owe to earlier writings on the status and position of women (Readings 19, 38, 45) and also to existential philosophy (Reading 62)?
4. What aspects of women's role and status in society concerned both Kollontai (Reading 58) and de Beauvoir?

Gorbachev's Nobel Peace Prize Lecture of 1991

A political storm had been brewing in eastern Europe and the Soviet Union for years before Mikhail Gorbachev (b. 1931) unleashed its force. A political visionary who exhibited both desperation and self-confidence, Gorbachev significantly changed the late twentieth-century world through his notions of *perestroika* and *glasnost*. Early in his career, he combined political skills and intelligence to maneuver his way up through a stifling Soviet bureaucracy. By 1985, as head of the Communist Party and the Soviet government, Gorbachev began to move toward a more open press and other democratic reforms. As a result of his actions, tremendous changes occurred throughout the tottering communist world; for example, the Soviet bloc in eastern Europe collapsed in 1989, and the Soviet Union itself was dismantled when a military coup failed in 1991. Mikhail Gorbachev received the Nobel Peace Prize in 1990 in recognition of his efforts to bring about a more open society in his native country and throughout the Soviet bloc. He delivered his acceptance speech in the summer of 1991 in Oslo, Norway. Now a private citizen of the Republic of Russia, Gorbachev heads a political think tank with offices in Moscow.

This moment is no less emotional for me than when I first learned about the Nobel Committee's decision. For on similar occasions great men addressed mankind—men renowned for their courage in working to bring together morality and politics. My compatriots were among their number.

The award of the Nobel Peace Prize makes one think once again about a seemingly simple and obvious question: what is peace?

When preparing my address I found in an old Russian encyclopedia a definition of "peace" as a "commune"—the traditional cell of Russian peasant life. I saw in that definition the people's profound understanding of peace as harmony, concord, mutual help, and cooperation.

This understanding is embodied in the canons of world religions and in the works of philosophers from antiquity up to present times. The names of many of

Reprinted with permission of the Information Department, Embassy of the Union of Soviet Socialist Republics, Washington, DC.

them have been mentioned here before. Let me add another one of them. Peace "propagates wealth and justice, which constitute the prosperity of nations," a peace which is "just a respite from wars . . . is not worthy of the name," peace implies "general counsel." This was written almost 200 years ago by Malinovsky—the dean of the Tsarskoye Selo Lyceum where the great **Pushkin** was educated.

Since then, of course, history has added a great deal to the specific content of the concept of peace. In this nuclear age it also means a condition for the survival of the human race. But the essence, as understood both by popular wisdom and intellectual leaders, is the same.

Today, peace means the ascent from simple coexistence to cooperation and common creativity among countries and nations.

Peace is a movement towards globality and the universality of civilization. Never before has the idea that peace is indivisible been so true as it is now.

Peace is not unity in similarity but unity in diversity, in the comparison and conciliation of differences.

And, ideally, peace means the absence of violence. It is an ethical value. And here we have to recall **Rajiv Gandhi**, who died so tragically a few days ago.

I consider the decision of your Committee a recognition of the great international importance of the changes now under way in the Soviet Union, and an expression of confidence in our policy of new thinking, which is based on the conviction that at the end of the twentieth century force and arms will have to give way as a major instrument in world politics.

I also consider the decision to award me the Nobel Peace Prize an act of solidarity with the monumental undertaking which has already placed enormous demands on the Soviet people in terms of effort, cost, hardship, willpower, and character. And solidarity is a universal value which is becoming indispensable for progress and the survival of mankind.

But a modern state has to be worthy of solidarity, in other words, it should pursue, in both domestic and international affairs, policies that bring together the interests of its people and those of the world community. This task, however obvious, is not a simple one. Life is much richer and more complex than even the most perfect plans to make it better. It ultimately takes vengeance on attempts to impose abstract schemes, even with the best of intentions. Perestroika has made us understand this about our past, and the actual experience of recent years has indeed taught us to reckon with the most general laws of civilization. . . .

I began my book about perestroika and new thinking with the following words: "We want to be understood." After a while I felt that it was already happening. But now I would like once again to repeat those words here, from this world rostrum because, in order to really understand us—to understand and consequently believe us—proved to be not at all that easy, owing to the immensity of the changes under way in our country. Their magnitude and character are such as to require in-depth analysis. Applying conventional wisdom to perestroika is unproductive. It is also futile and dangerous to stipulate conditions, to say: we'll understand and believe you as soon as you, the Soviet Union, come completely to resemble "us," the West.

No one is in a position to describe in detail what perestroika will finally produce. But it would certainly be a self-delusion to expect that perestroika will produce "a copy" of anything else.

Of course, learning from the experience of others is something we have been doing and will continue to do. But this does not mean that we will come to be exactly like other countries. Our state will preserve its own identity within the international community. A country like ours, with its uniquely close-knit ethnic composition, cultural diversity and tragic past, the greatness of its historic endeavors and the exploits of its peoples—such a country will find its own path to the civilization of the twenty-first century, and its own place in it. Perestroika has to be conceived solely in this context, otherwise it will fail and be rejected. After all, it is impossible to "shed" the country's thousand-year history—a history, which we still have to subject to serious analysis in order to find the truth that we shall take to the future.

We want to be an integral part of modern civilization, to live in harmony with mankind's universal values, abide by the norms of international law, follow the "rules of the game" in our economic relations with the outside world. We want to share with all other peoples the burden of responsibility for the future of our common home.

A period of transition to a new quality in all spheres of society's life is accompanied by painful phenomena. When we were initiating perestroika, we failed to properly assess and foresee everything. Our society turned out to be hard to move off the ground, not ready for the major changes which affect people's vital interests and make them leave behind everything which they had become accustomed to over many years. In the beginning we imprudently generated great expectations, without taking into account the fact that it takes time for people to realize that all have to live and work differently, to stop expecting that new life would be given from above.

Perestroika has entered its most dramatic phase. . . .

[Yet] as to the fundamental choice, I long ago made a final and irrevocable decision. Nothing and no one, no pressure, either from the right or from the left, will make me abandon the positions of perestroika and new thinking. I do not intend to change views or convictions. My choice is a final one.

It is my profound conviction that the problems arising in the course of our transformations can be solved solely by constitutional means. That is why I make every effort to keep this process within the confines of democracy and reforms.

This applies also to the problem of self-determination of nations, which is a challenging one for us. We are looking for mechanisms to solve that problem within the framework of a constitutional process, we recognize the people's legitimate choice, with the understanding that if a people really decides, through a fair referendum, to withdraw from the Soviet Union, a certain agreed transition period will then be needed.

Our democracy is going through labor pains. A political culture is emerging—one that presupposes debate and pluralism, but also legal order and, if democracy is to work, strong government authority based on one law for all. This process is gaining strength. Resolution in the pursuit of perestroika, a subject of much debate these days, must be measured by the commitment to democratic change. Resolution does not mean a return to repression or the suppression of rights and freedoms. I will never agree to having our society split once again into **Reds and Whites**, into those who claim to speak and act "on behalf of the people" and those who are "enemies of the people." Being resolute today means to act within the framework of political and social pluralism and the rule of law to provide conditions for continued reform and prevent a breakdown of the state and economic collapse and prevent the elements of chaos from becoming catastrophic. . . .

We will seek answers to the questions we face only by moving forward, only by continuing and even radicalizing reforms, by consistently democratizing our society. But we will proceed very prudently, carefully weighing every step we take. . . .

The stormy and contradictory process of perestroika, particularly in the past two years, has made us face squarely the problem of criteria to measure the effectiveness of state leadership. In the new environment of a multiparty system, freedom of thought, rediscovered ethnic identity and sovereignty of the republics, the interests of society must be put above those of various parties or groups, or any other sectional, parochial or private interests, even though they also have the right to exist and to be represented in the political process and in public life, and, of course, must be taken into account in the policies of the state.

Ladies and Gentlemen, international politics is another area where a great deal depends on the correct interpretation of what is now happening in the Soviet Union. This is true today, and it will remain so in the future. . . .

The more I reflect on current world developments, the more I become convinced that the world needs perestroika no less than the Soviet Union needs it. Fortunately, the present generation of policy-makers, for the most part, are becoming increasingly aware of this interrelationship, and also of the fact that now that perestroika has entered its crucial phase the Soviet Union is certainly entitled to expect large-scale support to ensure its success. . . .

In other words, we are thinking of a fundamentally new phase in our international cooperation. . . .

If we fail to reach an understanding regarding a new phase of cooperation, we will have to look for other ways, for time is of the essence. But if we are to move to that new phase, those who participate in and even shape world politics must also continue to review their philosophic perception of the changing realities of the world and of its imperatives. Otherwise, there is no point in drawing up a joint program of practical action. . . .

Clearly, as the Soviet Union proceeds with perestroika, its contribution to the construction of a new world order will become more constructive and significant. What we have done on the basis of new thinking has made it possible to channel international cooperation along new, peaceful lines. Over the years we have come a long way in general political cooperation with the West. It faced a difficult test at a time of momentous change in Eastern Europe and of the search for a solution to the German problem. It has withstood the crushing stress of the crisis in the Persian Gulf. There is no doubt that this cooperation, which all of us need, will become more effective and indispensable if our economics become more integrated and start working more or less in synchronized rhythm.

To me, it is self-evident that if Soviet perestroika succeeds, there will be a real chance of building a new world order. And if perestroika fails, the prospect of entering a new peaceful period in history will vanish, at least for the foreseeable future.

I believe that the movement that we have launched towards that goal has fairly good prospects of success. After all, mankind has already derived great benefits in recent years, and this has created a certain positive momentum.

The Cold War is over. The risk of a global nuclear war has practically disappeared. The iron curtain is gone. Germany has united, which is a momentous milestone in the history of Europe. There is not a single country on our continent which would not regard itself as fully sovereign and independent.

The USSR and the USA, the two nuclear superpowers, have moved from confrontation to interaction and, in some important cases, partnership. This has had a decisive effect on the entire international climate. This should be preserved and filled with new substance. The climate of Soviet–U.S. trust should be protected, for it is a common asset of the world community. Any revision of the direction and potential of the Soviet–U.S. relationship would have grave consequences for the entire global process.

The ideas of the **Helsinki Final Act** have begun to acquire real significance. They are being transformed into real policies and have found a more specific and topical expression in the **Charter of Paris** for a new Europe. Institutional forms of European security are beginning to take shape.

Real disarmament has begun. Its first phase is nearing completion, and following the signing, I hope shortly, of the **START Treaty**, the time will come to give practical consideration to the ideas which have already been put forward for the future. There seems, however, to be a need to develop a general concept for this new phase, which would embrace all negotiations concerning the principal components of the problem of disarmament and new ideas reflecting the changes in Europe, the Middle East, Africa and Asia, a concept that would incorporate recent major initiatives of President [George] Bush and President **Mitterrand**. We are now thinking about it. . . .

The new integrity of the world, in our view, can be built only on the principles of the freedom of choice and balance of interests. Every state, and now also a number of existing or emerging regional interstate groups, have their own interests. They are all equal and deserve respect. . . .

Progress towards the civilization of the twenty-first century will certainly not be simple or easy. One cannot get rid of overnight of the heavy legacy of the past or the dangers created in the post-war years. We are experiencing a turning point in international affairs and are only at the beginning of a new, and I hope mostly peaceful, lengthy period in the history of civilization.

With reduced East-West confrontation, or even none at all, old contradictions resurfaced, which seemed of secondary importance compared to the threat of nuclear war. The melting ice of the Cold War reveals old conflicts and claims, and entirely new problems accumulate rapidly.

We can already see many obstacles and dangers on the road to durable peace, including:

—increased nationalism, separatism, and disintegration processes in a number of countries and regions,

—the growing gap in the level and quality of socio-economic development between the "rich" and "poor" countries, the dire consequences of poverty of hundreds of millions of people who can, owing to the dissemination worldwide of information, see how people live in developed countries. Hence the unprecedented passions and brutality and even fanaticism of mass protests. Poverty is also the breeding ground for the spread of terrorism and for the emergence and persistence of dictatorial regimes with their unpredictable behavior in relations among states,

—the dangerously rapid accumulation of the "costs" of previous forms of progress, such as the threat of environmental catastrophe and of the depletion of energy and primary resources, uncontrollable overpopulation, pandemics, drug abuse, and so on,

—the gap between basically peaceful policies and selfish economies bent on achieving a kind of "technological hegemony." Unless these two vectors are brought together, civilization will tend to break down into incompatible sectors,

—further improvement in modern weaponry, even if under the pretext of strengthening security. This may result not only in a new arms race and a dangerous overabundance of arms in many states, but may also lead to a final divorce between the process of disarmament and development, and, what is more, to an erosion of the foundations and criteria of the emerging new world order in politics.

How can the world community cope with all this? All these tasks are enormously complex. They cannot be postponed. Tomorrow may be too late.

I am convinced that, in order to solve these problems, there is no other way but to seek and implement new forms of interaction. We are simply doomed to such interaction, or we will be unable to consolidate positive trends which have emerged and are emerging, and which we simply must not sacrifice.

However, to accomplish this, all members of the world community should resolutely discard old stereotypes and motivations nurtured by the Cold War, and give up the habit of seeking each other's weak points and exploiting them in their own interests. We have to respect the peculiarities and differences which will always exist, even when human rights and freedoms are observed throughout the world. I keep repeating that after the end of confrontation differences can be made a source of healthy competition, an important factor for progress. This is an incentive to study each other, to engage in exchanges, a prerequisite for the growth of mutual trust.

For knowledge and trust are the foundations of a new world order. Hence the necessity, in my view, to learn how to forecast the course of events in various regions of the globe, by pooling the efforts of scientists, philosophers and humanitarian thinkers within the UN framework. Policies, even the most prudent and precise, are made by man. We need the maximum insurance to ensure that decisions taken by members of the world community should not affect the security, sovereignty and vital interests of its other members or damage the natural environment and the moral climate of the world.

I am an optimist and I believe that together we shall be able now to make the right historical choice and not miss the great chance provided by the turn of each century and millennium and make the current extremely difficult transition to a peaceful world order. A balance of interests rather than a balance of power, a search for compromise and concord rather than a search for advantages at other people's expense, and respect for equality rather than claims to leadership—such are the elements which can provide the groundwork for world progress and which should be readily acceptable for reasonable people informed of the experience of the twentieth century.

The future prospect of truly peaceful global politics lies in the creation through joint efforts of a single international democratic space where states shall be guided by the priority of human rights and welfare for their own citizens and the promotion of the same rights and similar welfare elsewhere. This is an imperative of the growing integrity of the modern world and the interdependence of its components.

I have been suspected of utopian thinking more than once, most particularly five years ago, when I proposed the elimination of nuclear weapons by the year 2000 and joint efforts to create a system of international security. It may well be that by that date it will not have happened. But look, merely five years have passed and have we not actually and noticeably moved in that direction? Have we not been able to cross the barrier of mistrust, though mistrust has not completely disappeared? Has not the political thinking in the world changed substantially? Does not most of the world community already regard weapons of mass destruction as an unacceptable way of achieving political objectives? . . .

In conclusion let me say again that I view the award of the Nobel Prize to me as an expression of the understanding of my intentions, my aspirations, the objectives of the profound transformation we have begun in our country, and the ideas of new thinking. I see it as your acknowledgment of my commitment to peaceful ways of implementing the objectives of perestroika.

I am extremely grateful to the members of the committee and wish to assure them that I understand correctly their motives, and that they were not mistaken.

Study Questions

1. What in Gorbachev's opinion are the most pressing problems that face people in the Soviet Union and Eastern bloc countries?
2. How democratic are perestroika, glasnost, and the other reforms suggested by Gorbachev?
3. According to Gorbachev, the success of his domestic and international reforms is dependent on what crucial factors?
4. What is Gorbachev's conception of world order?

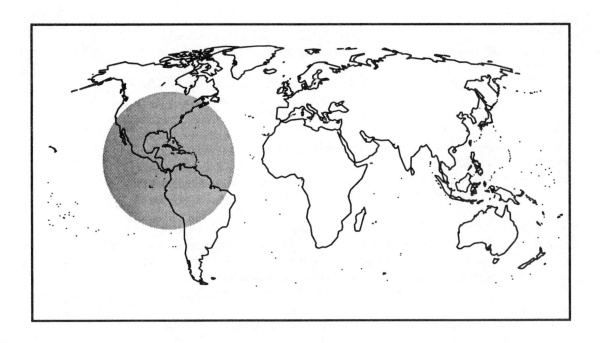

Brief Chronology for the Contemporary World
The Americas

1893	U.S. makes Hawaii a protectorate
1896	Supreme Court of U.S. declares racial segregation to be constitutional
1893	Spanish-American War
1909	W. E. B. du Bois (1868–1963) and others attend conference out of which emerges in 1910 the National Association for the Advancement of Coloured People
1910–1917	Mexican Revolution
1917	U.S. enters World War I
1929	U.S. stock market crash initiates the Great Depression, with worldwide repercussions
1933–1945	Franklin D. Roosevelt president of the U.S., begins by inaugurating New Deal
1941	Japanese attack on Pearl Harbor brings U.S. into World War II
1941–1945	World War II
1946–1955	Juan Peron's first term as president of Argentina
1947	Beginning of the cold war

1959	Cuban Revolution ends Batista regime
1962	Cuban missile crisis
1963	Civil rights march on Washington, D.C.; assassination of John F. Kennedy (1917–1963)
1964–1975	Vietnam War era in U.S.
1968	Assassinations of Martin Luther King and Robert F. Kennedy
1969	U.S. astronauts land on the moon
1979	Civil war in Nicaragua ends with establishment of Sandinista rule
1982	"Equal Rights Amendment" fails state ratification in U.S.
1989	U.S. invades Panama
1990	Democratic elections in Nicaragua
1991	Persian Gulf War

All dates are c.e. and approximate unless otherwise indicated. It should be noted as well that chronologies are constantly being revised. Hence, there may be discrepancies between the dates listed above and those found in other textbooks and scholarly monographs. Throughout the text and in the Glossary, all dates are given in b.c.e. (Before the Common Era) and c.e. (the Common Era). Where there is no era designation c.e. may be assumed.

Roosevelt's "Four Freedoms Address"

Franklin D. Roosevelt (1882–1945) ran a successful bid for president in 1932 when the United States and the world were in the throes of the Great Depression. His New Deal stressed economic recovery as well as relief and reform. Although supported by the democratic majority he helped to forge, economic turmoil did not dissipate until the advent of World War II. With the rise of aggressive governments in Germany, Italy, and Japan, Roosevelt and his administration steered the country away from global detachment. When Pearl Harbor was attacked by the Japanese on 7 December 1941—"a day that will live in infamy"—the United States entered the war. Delivered about a month after the attack on Pearl Harbor, Roosevelt's annual message to a joint session of Congress is a succinct, powerful statement that assures the global community that the American people are prepared for another world war. Roosevelt was reelected in 1936, 1940, and 1944 (a record never duplicated, since in 1951 it became unconstitutional to hold the presidency for more than two terms). He died in office in Warm Springs, Georgia, and was immediately succeeded by Vice President Harry S. Truman (1884–1972).

Mr. Speaker, members of the 77th Congress: I address you, the members of this new Congress, at a moment unprecedented in the history of the nation. I use the word "unprecedented" because at no previous time has American security been as seriously threatened from without as it is today. . . .

Therefore, as your President, performing my constitutional duty to "give to the Congress information of the state of the union," I find it unhappily necessary to report that the future and the safety of our country and democracy are overwhelmingly involved in events far beyond our own borders. . . .

Franklin D. Roosevelt, "Message to Congress," *Vital Speeches of the Day* (Mt. Pleasant, SC: City News Publishing, 1941).

I have recently pointed out how quickly the tempo of modern warfare could bring into our very midst the physical attack which we must eventually expect if the dictator nations were to win this war. . . .

As long as the aggressor nations maintain the offensive they, not we, will choose the time and the place and the method of their attack.

And that is why the future of all the American Republics is today in serious danger. That is why this annual message to the Congress is unique in our history. That is why every member of the executive branch of the government and every member·of the Congress face great responsibility—great accountability.

The need of the moment is that our actions and our policy should be devoted primarily—almost exclusively—to meeting this foreign peril. For all our domestic problems are now a part of the great emergency.

Just as our national policy in internal affairs has been based upon a decent respect for the rights and the dignity of all of our fellow men within our gates, so our national policy in foreign affairs has been based on a decent respect for the rights and the dignity of all nations, large and small. And the justice of morality must and will win in the end.

Our national policy is this:

First, by an impressive expression of the public will and without regard to partisanship, we are committed to all-inclusive national defense.

Second, by an impressive expression of the public will and without regard to partisanship, we are committed to full support of all those resolute people everywhere who are resisting aggression and are thereby keeping war away from our hemisphere. By this support we express our determination that the democratic cause shall prevail, and we strengthen the defense and the security our own nation.

Third, by an impressive expression of the public will and without regard to parti.sanship, we are committed to the proposition that principles of morality and considerations for our own security will never permit us to acquiesce in a peace dictated by aggressors and sponsored by appeasers. We know that enduring peace cannot be bought at the cost of other people's freedom.

In the recent national election there was no substantial difference between the two great parties in respect to that national policy. No issue was fought out on this line before the American electorate. And today it is abundantly evident that American citizens everywhere are demanding and supporting speedy and complete action in recognition of obvious danger.

Therefore, the immediate need is a swift and driving increase in our armament production. Leaders of industry and labor have responded to our summons. Goals of speed have been set. In some cases these goals are being reached ahead of time. In some cases we are on schedule; in other cases there are slight but not serious delays. And in some cases—and, I am sorry to say, very important cases— we are still concerned by the slowness of the accomplishment of our plans.

The Army and Navy, however, have made substantial progress during the past year. Actual experience is improving and speeding up our methods by production with every passing day. And today's best is not good enough for tomorrow.

I am not satisfied with the progress thus far made. The men in charge of the program represent the best in training, in ability and in patriotism. They are not satisfied with the progress thus far made. None of us will be satisfied until the job is done. . . .

To change a whole nation from a basis of peacetime production of implements of peace to a basis of wartime production of implements of war is no small task. The greatest difficulty comes at the beginning of the program, when new tools, new plant facilities, new assembly lines, new shipways must first be constructed before the actual material begins to flow steadily and speedily from them.

The Congress, of course, must rightly keep itself informed at all times of the progress of the program. However, there is certain information, as the Congress itself will readily recognize, which, in the interests of our own security and those of the nations that we are supporting, must of needs be kept in confidence.

New circumstances are constantly begetting new needs for our safety. I shall ask this Congress for greatly increased new appropriations and authorizations to carry on what we have begun.

I also ask this Congress for authority and for funds sufficient to manufacture additional munitions and war supplies of many kinds, to be turned over to those nations which are now in actual war with aggressor nations. Our most useful and immediate role is to act as an arsenal for them as well as for ourselves. They do not need manpower, but they do need billions of dollars' worth of the weapons of defense. . . .

For what we send abroad we shall be repaid, repaid within a reasonable time following the close of hostilities, repaid in similar materials, or at our option in other goods of many kinds which they can produce and which we need.

Let us say to the democracies: "We Americans are vitally concerned in your defense of freedom. We are putting forth our energies, our resources and our organizing powers to give you the strength to regain and maintain a free world. We shall send you in ever-increasing numbers, ships, planes, tanks, guns. That is our purpose and our pledge."

In fulfillment of this purpose we will not be intimidated by the threats of dictators that they will regard as a breach of international law or as an act of war our aid to the democracies which dare to resist their aggression. Such aid is not an act of war, even if a dictator should unilaterally proclaim it so to be.

And when the dictators—if the dictators—are ready to make war upon us, they will not wait for an act of war initiated by our part. . . .

Yes, and we must prepare, all of us prepare, to make the sacrifices that the emergency—almost as serious as war itself—demands. Whatever stands in the way of speed and efficiency in defense, in defense preparations at any time, must give way to the national need.

A free nation has the right to expect full cooperation from all groups. A free nation has the right to look to the leaders of business, of labor and of agriculture to take the lead in stimulating effort, not among other groups but within their own groups.

393

The best way of dealing with the few slackers or troublemakers in our midst is, first, to shame them by patriotic example, and if that fails, to use the sovereignty of government to save government.

As men do not live by bread alone, they do not fight by armaments alone. Those who man our defenses and those behind them who build our defenses must have the stamina and the courage which come from unshakable belief in the manner of life which they are defending. The mighty action that we are calling for cannot be based on a disregard of all the things worth fighting for.

The nation takes great satisfaction and much strength from the things which have been done to make its people conscious of their individual stake in the preservation of democratic life in America. Those things have toughened the fiber of our people and have renewed their faith and strengthened their devotion to the institutions we make ready to protect.

Certainly this is no time for any of us to stop thinking about the social and economic problems which are the root cause of the social revolution which is today a supreme factor in the world. For there is nothing mysterious about the foundations of a healthy and strong democracy.

The basic things expected by our people of their political and economic systems are simple. They are equal opportunity for youth and for others; jobs for those who can work; security for those who need it; the ending of special privilege for the few; the preservation of civil liberties for all; the enjoyment of the fruits of scientific progress in a wider and constantly rising standard of living.

These are the simple, the basic things that must never be lost sight of in the turmoil and unbelievable complexity of our modern world. The inner and abiding strength of our economic and political systems is dependent upon the degree to which they fulfill these expectations.

Many subjects connected with our social economy call for immediate improvement. For example: we should bring more citizens under the cover of old-age pensions and unemployment insurance; we should widen the opportunities for adequate medical care; we should plan a better system by which persons deserving or needing gainful employment may obtain it.

I have called for personal sacrifice, and I am assured of the willingness of almost all Americans to respond to that call. A part of the sacrifice means the payment of more money in taxes. In my budget message I will recommend that a greater portion of this great defense program be paid for from taxation than we are paying for today. No person should try, or be allowed to get rich out of the program, and the principle of tax payments in accordance with ability to pay should be constantly before our eyes to guide our legislation.

If the Congress maintains these principles the voters, putting patriotism ahead of pocketbooks, will give you their applause.

In the future days which we seek to make secure, we look forward to a world founded upon four essential human freedoms.

The first is freedom of speech and expression—everywhere in the world.

The second is freedom of every person to worship God in his own way—everywhere in the world.

The third is freedom from want, which, translated into world terms, means economic understandings which will secure to every nation a healthy peacetime life for its inhabitants—everywhere in the world.

The fourth is freedom from fear, which, translated into world terms, means a world-wide reduction of armaments to such a point and in such a thorough fashion that no nation will be in a position to commit an act of physical aggression against any neighbor—anywhere in the world.

That is no vision of a distant millennium. It is a definite basis for a kind of world attainable in our own time and generation. That kind of world is the very antithesis of the so-called "new order" of tyranny which the dictators seek to create with the crash of a bomb.

To that new order we oppose the greater conception—the moral order. A good society is able to face schemes of world domination and foreign revolutions alike without fear.

Since the beginning of our American history we have been engaged in change, in a perpetual, peaceful revolution, revolution which goes on steadily, quietly, adjusting itself to changing conditions without the concentration camp or the quicklime in the ditch. The world order which we seek is the cooperation of free countries, working together in friendly, civilized society.

This nation has placed its destiny in the hands, heads and hearts of its millions of free men and women, and its faith in freedom under the guidance of God. Freedom means the supremacy of human rights everywhere. Our support goes to those who struggle to gain those rights and keep them. Our strength is our unity of purpose.

To that high concept there can be no end save victory.

Study Questions

1. What are Roosevelt's "four freedoms," and in his opinion how do they serve as the foundation for domestic and foreign policy initiatives?
2. How is the moral order implied in Roosevelt's remarks the antithesis of the "new order" promoted by the tyrannical dictators against whom the allied powers fought in World War II?
3. How does Roosevelt's speech to Congress promote morality within a sound political context?
4. How do the basic tenets of Roosevelt's ideology compare with those of Mussolini and Hitler (Reading 61)?

Reading 67

Albert Einstein's "Atomic War or Peace"

Albert Einstein (1879–1955), one of the most creative and brilliant scientists in history, published papers on his Special Theory of Relativity in 1905. He postulates that time and space have no objective reality, and that the speed of light is constant for all uniformly moving systems throughout the universe. This theory would later serve as the basis for his famous equation concerning the relationship of energy and matter and his theory of **General Relativity**. The practical validity of Einstein's ideas was graphically demonstrated by the explosion of the first experimental atomic bomb on 16 July 1945 in New Mexico. He witnessed the great destructive reality of atomic power when two nuclear devices were dropped on Japan at the end of World War II. As a result, this remarkable man devoted much of his energy to addressing the awesome dangers of nuclear power. Einstein was convinced that the problems facing humanity—including the existence of the bomb—would best be solved through the use of reason. He explained his perspective on the human condition by stating that the goal of existence is to become a community "of free and happy human beings who by constant inward endeavor strive to liberate destructive instincts. In this effort the intellect can be the most powerful aid." Einstein's collected essays on humanistic subjects, including "Atomic War or Peace," written in 1947, were published in 1950.

Since the completion of the first atomic bomb nothing has been accomplished to make the world more safe from war, while much has been done to increase the destructiveness of war. I am not able to speak from any firsthand knowledge about the development of the atomic bomb, since I do not work in this field. But enough has been said by those who do to indicate that the bomb has been made more effective. Certainly the possibility can be envisaged of building a bomb of far greater size, capable of producing destruction over a larger area. It also is credible that an extensive use could be made of radioactivated gases which would spread over a wide region, causing heavy loss of life without damage to buildings.

I do not believe it is necessary to go on beyond these possibilities to contemplate a vast extension of bacteriological warfare. I am skeptical that this form presents dangers comparable with those of atomic warfare. Nor do I take into account a danger of starting a chain reaction of a scope great enough to destroy part or all of this planet. I dismiss this on the ground that if it could happen from a man-made atomic explosion it would already have happened from the action of the cosmic rays which are continually reaching the earth's surface.

But it is not necessary to imagine the earth being destroyed like a nova by a stellar explosion to understand vividly the growing scope of atomic war and to recognize that unless another war is prevented it is likely to bring destruction on a scale never before held possible and even now hardly conceived, and that little civilization would survive it.

In the first two years of the atomic era another phenomenon is to be noted. The public, having been warned of the horrible nature of atomic warfare, has done nothing about it, and to a large extent has dismissed the warning from its consciousness. A danger that cannot be averted had perhaps better be forgotten; or a danger against which every possible precaution has been taken also had probably better be forgotten. That is, if the United States had dispersed its industries and decentralized its cities, it might be reasonable for people to forget the peril they face.

I should say parenthetically that it is well that this country has not taken these precautions, for to have done so would make atomic war still more probable, since it would convince the rest of the world that we are resigned to it and are preparing for it. But nothing has been done to avert war, while much as been done to make atomic war more horrible; so there is no excuse for ignoring the danger.

I say that nothing has been done to avert war since the completion of the atomic bomb, despite the proposal for supranational control of atomic energy put forward by the United States in the United Nations. This country has made only a conditional proposal, and on conditions which the Soviet Union is now determined not to accept. This makes it possible to blame the failure on the Russians.

But in blaming the Russians the Americans should not ignore the fact that they themselves have not voluntarily renounced the use of the bomb as an ordinary weapon in the time before the achievement of supranational control, or if supranational control is not achieved. Thus they have fed the fear of other countries that they consider the bomb a legitimate part of their arsenal so long as other countries decline to accept their terms for supranational control.

Americans may be convinced of their determination not to launch an aggressive or preventive war. So they may believe it is superfluous to announce publicly that they will not a second time be the first to use the atomic bomb. But this country has been solemnly invited to renounce the use of the bomb—that is, to outlaw it—and has declined to do so unless its terms for supranational control are accepted.

I believe this policy is a mistake. I see a certain military gain from not renouncing the use of the bomb in that this may be deemed to restrain another country from starting a war in which the United States might use it. But what is gained in one way is lost in another. For an understanding over the supranational control of atomic energy has been made more remote. That may be no military drawback so long as the United States has the exclusive use of the bomb. But the moment another country is able to make it in substantial quantities, the United States loses greatly through the absence of an international agreement, because of the vulnerability of its concentrated industries and its highly developed urban life.

In refusing to outlaw the bomb while having the monopoly of it, this country suffers in another respect, in that it fails to return publicly to the ethical standards of warfare formally accepted previous to the last war. It should not be forgotten that the atomic bomb was made in this country as a preventive measure; it was to head off its use by the Germans, if they discovered it. The bombing of civilian centers was initiated by the Germans and adopted by the Japanese. To it the Allies responded in kind—as it turned out, with greater effectiveness—and they were morally justified in doing so. But now, without any provocation and without the justification of reprisal or retaliation, refusal to outlaw the use of the bomb save in reprisal is making a political purpose of its possession. This is hardly pardonable. . . .

But I do not suggest that the American failure to outlaw the use of the bomb except in retaliation is the only cause of the absence of an agreement with the Soviet Union over atomic control. The Russians have made it clear that they will do everything in their power to prevent a supranational regime from coming into existence. They not only reject it in the range of atomic energy: they reject it sharply on principle, and thus have spurned in advance any overture to join a limited world government.

Mr. **Gromyko** has rightly said that the essence of the American atomic proposal is that national sovereignty is not compatible with the atomic era. He declares that the Soviet Union cannot accept this thesis. The reasons he gives are obscure, for they quite obviously are pretexts. But what seems to be true is that the Soviet leaders believe they cannot preserve the social structure of the Soviet state in a supranational regime. The Soviet government is determined to maintain its present social structure, and the leaders of Russia, who hold their great power through the nature of that structure, will spare no effort to prevent a supranational regime from coming into existence, to control atomic energy or anything else.

The Russians may be partly right about the difficulty of retaining their present social structure in a supranational regime, though in time they may be brought to see that this is a far lesser loss than remaining isolated from a world of law. But at present they appear to be guided by their fears, and one must admit that the United States has made ample contributions to these fears, not only as to atomic energy but in many other respects. Indeed this country has conducted its Russian policy as though it were convinced that fear is the greatest of all diplomatic instruments.

That the Russians are striving to prevent the formation of a supranational security system is no reason why the rest of the world should not work to create one. It has been pointed out that the Russians have a way of resisting with all their arts what they do not wish to have happen; but once it happens, they can be flexible and accommodate themselves to it. So it would be well for the United States and other powers not to permit the Russians to veto an attempt to create supranational security. They can proceed with some hope that once the Russians see they cannot prevent such a regime they may join it.

So far the United States has shown no interest in preserving the security of the Soviet Union. It has been interested in its own security, which is characteristic of the competition which marks the conflict for power between sovereign states. But one cannot know in advance what would be the effect on Russian fears if the American people forced their leaders to pursue a policy of substituting law for the present anarchy of international relations. In a world of law, Russian security would be equal to our own, and for the American people to espouse this whole-heartedly, something that should be possible under the workings of democracy, might work a kind of miracle in Russian thinking.

At present the Russians have no evidence to convince them that the American people are not contentedly supporting a policy of military preparedness which they regard as a policy of deliberate intimidation. If they had evidences of a passionate desire by Americans to preserve peace in the one way it can be maintained, by a supranational regime of law, this would upset Russian calculations about the peril to Russian security in current trends of American thought. Not until a genuine, convincing offer is made to the Soviet Union, backed by an aroused American public, will one be entitled to say what the Russian response would be.

It may be that the first response would be to reject the world of law. But if from that moment it began to be clear to the Russians that such a world was coming into existence without them, and that their own security was being increased, their ideas necessarily would change.

I am in favor of inviting the Russians to join a world government authorized to provide security, and if they are unwilling to join, to proceed to establish supranational security without them. Let me admit quickly that I see great peril in such a course. If it is adopted it must be done in a way to make it utterly clear that the new regime is not a combination of power against Russia. It must be a combination that by its composite nature will greatly reduce the chances of war. It will be more diverse in its interests than any single state, thus less likely to resort to aggressive or preventive war. It will be larger, hence stronger than any single nation. It will be geographically much more extensive, and thus more difficult to defeat by military means. It will be dedicated to supranational security, and thus escape the emphasis on national supremacy which is so strong a factor in war.

If a supranational regime is set up without Russia, its service to peace will depend on the skill and sincerity with which it is done. Emphasis should always be apparent on the desire to have Russia take part. . . .

Membership in a supranational security system should not, in my opinion, be based on any arbitrary democratic standards. The one requirement from all should be that the representatives to supranational organization—assembly and council—must be elected by the people in each member country through a secret ballot. These representatives must represent the people rather than any government—which would enhance the pacific nature of the organization.

To require that other democratic criteria be met is, I believe, inadvisable. Democratic institutions and standards are the result of historic developments to an extent not always appreciated in the lands which enjoy them. Setting arbitrary standards sharpens the ideological differences between the Western and Soviet systems.

But it is not the ideological differences which now are pushing the world in the direction of war. Indeed, if all the Western nations were to adopt socialism, while maintaining their national sovereignty, it is quite likely that the conflict for power between East and West would continue. The passion expressed over the economic systems of the present seems to me quite irrational. Whether the economic life of America should be dominated by relatively few individuals, as it is, or these individuals should be controlled by the state, may be important, but it is not important enough to justify all the feelings that are stirred up over it. . . .

I should like to see the authority of the supranational regime restricted altogether to the field of security. Whether this would be possible I am not sure. Experience may point to the desirability of adding some authority over economic matters, since under modern conditions these are capable of causing national upsets that have in them the seeds of violent conflict. But I should prefer to see the function of the organization altogether limited to the tasks of security. I also should like to see this regime established through the strengthening of the United Nations, so as not to sacrifice continuity in the search for peace.

I do not hide from myself the great difficulties of establishing a world government, either a beginning without Russia or one with Russia. I am aware of the risks. Since I should not wish it to be permissible for any country that has joined the supranational organization to secede, one of these risks is a possible civil war. But I also believe that world government is certain to come in time, and that the question is how much it is to be permitted to cost. It will come, I believe, even if there is another world war, though after such a war, if it is won, it would be world government established by the victor, resting on the victor's military power, and thus to be maintained permanently only through the permanent militarization of the human race.

But I also believe it can come through agreement and through the force of persuasion alone, hence at low cost. But if it is to come in this way it will not be enough to appeal to reason. One strength of the communist system of the East is that it has some of the character of a religion and inspires the emotions of a religion. Unless the cause of peace based on law gathers behind it the force and zeal of a religion, it hardly can hope to succeed. Those to whom the moral teaching of the human race is entrusted surely have a great duty and a great opportunity. The atomic scientists, I think, have become convinced that they cannot arouse the American people to the truths of the atomic era by logic alone. There must be added that deep power of emotion which is a basic ingredient of religion. It is to be hoped that not only the churches but the schools, the colleges, and the leading organs of opinion will acquit themselves well of their unique responsibility in this regard.

Study Questions

1. How do Einstein's remarks concerning atomic war and world peace mirror the fears and anxieties that people felt at the end of World War II and the beginning of the cold war?
2. What solutions does Einstein offer to secure world peace, and how viable were these solutions in the late 1940s and 1950s?
3. Why does Einstein think it necessary to create a world government?
4. What are the author's views on the relationship between science and politics?

Reading 68

Fidel Castro's "Why We Fight"

The Cuban constitution of 1901 gave the United States the right to intervene in Cuba's internal affairs, when the constituent assembly affixed to the constitution the Platt Amendment. Direct interference by the United States in Cuban affairs thus began in the late nineteenth century and continued throughout the era of the cold war. In the decades following World War II, the United States became secretly involved in Latin American politics in order to deny the Soviets a possible foothold in the western hemisphere. This covert policy was especially resented by Cuban nationalists. Cuba's corrupt, inefficient government seemed to encourage revolutionary movements, and in the 1940s and 1950s such activity gained momentum. Fidel Castro (b. 1927) and his fellow revolutionaries fought for years to eliminate the government of **Fulgencio Batista**, which was something of a dictatorship supported by the United States. After a period of imprisonment (1953–1955) and exile (1955–1957), Castro began a decisive assault on Cuba's dictatorial regime. Shortly before his final victory, Fidel Castro was given the opportunity to publicize the goals of his movement in the February 1958 issue of *Coronet Magazine* in a short piece entitled "Why We Fight." When Castro finally came to power in 1959, the U.S. government, then under the direction of President Dwight D. Eisenhower (1890–1969), adopted a hard line toward Cuba that helped drive it into the Soviet orbit. This in turn led to further covert actions with U.S. support against Castro's newly-formed Marxist government.

As this is written, our armed campaign on Cuban soil against Cuba's dictatorial regime is entering its second year. Though it has been given many meanings and many interpretations, it is essentially a political struggle. In this struggle, we have sustained few reverses and a good many victories, while dictator Batista can point to a single successful achievement: he has effectively muzzled all public communications in our country, silenced TV, radio, and the press, and so intimidated our news publishers that not a single Cuban reporter has ever been assigned to *our* side of what is, in effect, a spreading civil war.

One of the unexpected results of this iron censorship, augmented by a military blockade around the combat zone, has been that our program—the aims, plans, and aspirations of the **26th of July Movement**—has never been published or explained adequately. In obtaining and publishing this exclusive article—the only first-person story written by me since we landed in Cuba on December 2, 1956—*Coronet Magazine* has given us the opportunity to state our aims and to correct the many errors and distortions circulating about our revolutionary struggle.

Though dictatorship, ignorance, military rule, and police oppression have spawned a great many evils among our people, all these evils have a common root: the lack of liberty. The single word most expressive of our aim and spirit is simply—freedom. First of all and most of all, we are fighting to do away with dictatorship in Cuba and to establish the foundations of genuine representative government.

To attain this, we intend to eject from office Fulgencio Batista and all his cabinet officers; to place them under arrest and impeach them before special revolutionary tribunals. To replace the unconstitutional Batista regime, we will aid in setting up a provisional government to be nominated by a special convention made up of the delegates of our various civic organizations: Lions, Rotarians, professional bodies such as the physicians' or engineers' guilds, religious associations, and so forth. This will be a break with established procedure, but we feel certain that it will prove workable. Once appointed, the provisional government's chief task will be to prepare and conduct truly honest general elections within twelve months.

The question has presented itself whether I aspire to the presidential office of this provisional government or the elected government which will succeed it. The truth is that, quite apart from my personal reluctance to enter the presidential competition so soon, our Constitution, as it now stands, would prohibit it. Under its age requirement clause, I am, at 31, far too young to be eligible for the presidency, and will remain so for another ten years.

We do have, however, a number of program points which might serve as a basis for action by the provisional government. They are the following:

1. Immediate freedom for all political prisoners, civil as well as military. Although the outside world knows little about it, Batista has imprisoned dozens of officers and hundreds of enlisted men from his own armed forces who have shown revulsion or resistance to his bloody suppression of political discontent.

2. Full and untrammeled freedom of public information for all communication media—broadcasting, TV, the daily and periodical press. Arbitrary censorship and systematic corruption of journalists has long been one of the festering sores of our nation.

3. We want to reestablish for all citizens the personal and political rights set forth in our much-ignored Constitution.

4. We want to wipe out corruption in Cuban public life. Those who have grown accustomed over the years to dealing with venal policemen, thieving tax collectors, and rapacious army bosses here in Cuba may think this an optimistic resolution. But we intend to attack this problem at its very roots, by creating a career civil service beyond the reach of politics and nepotism and by making sure

403

that our career functionaries get paid enough to be able to live without having to accept bribes.

5. We want to sponsor an intensive campaign against illiteracy. Though no one knows the exact number of our illiterates, they run into the hundreds of thousands, perhaps even up to a million. Our farm children get little schooling at best; many of them get none at all. Hundreds of thousands of small farmers feed their families on roots and rice, simply because no one has ever taught them how to grow tomatoes, lettuce, or corn. No one has ever shown them how to utilize water. No one has ever told them how to choose a wholesome diet or how to protect their health.

6. We are in favor of land reform bills adjusting the uncertain owner-tenant relations that are a peculiar blight of rural Cuba. Hundreds of thousands of small farmers occupy parcels which they do not own under the law. Thousands of absentee owners claim title to properties they have hardly ever seen. The titles, in fact, have been seen by no one and it is often impossible to establish who actually owns a particular property. We feel that in settling the question of legal ownership, preferential treatment should be given to those who actually occupy and cultivate the land. We will support no land reform bill, however, which does not provide for the just compensation of expropriated owners.

7. Finally, we support speedy industrialization of our national economy and the raising of employment levels.

Apart from the political misconceptions about my ambitions and those of our movement—we have often been accused of plotting to replace military dictatorship with revolutionary dictatorship—nothing has been so frequently misunderstood as our economic program. Various influential U.S. publications have identified me as a tool of big business, as a dangerous radical, and as a narrow reactionary manipulated by the clergy. U.S. companies with business interests in Cuba have been repeatedly warned that I have secret plans in my pocket for seizing all foreign holdings.

Let me say for the record that we have no plans for the expropriation or nationalization of foreign investments here. True, the extension of government ownership to certain public utilities—some of them, such as the power companies, U.S.-owned—was a point of our earliest programs; but we have currently suspended all planning on this matter. I personally have come to feel that nationalization is, at best, a cumbersome instrument. It does not seem to make the state any stronger, yet it enfeebles private enterprise. Even more importantly, any attempt at wholesale nationalization would obviously hamper the principal point of our economic platform—industrialization at the fastest possible rate. For this purpose, foreign investments will always be welcome and secure here.

Industrialization is at the heart of our economic progress. Something must be done about the staggering mass of over one million unemployed who cannot find jobs during eight months out of twelve. They can hope to work only during the four months of the cane harvest. A million unemployed in a nation of six million bespeaks a terrible economic sickness which must be cured without delay, lest it fester and become a breeding ground for communism.

Fortunately, improvement is by no means as difficult as Cuba's present rulers would lead us to believe. Our country is rich in natural resources. What we need is an adequate canning industry to utilize our superb fruit crops; expanded industrial facilities for the processing of sugar and its important by-products; expanded consumer industries for the production of light metal, leather, paper, and textile goods which would go far toward improving our trade balance; and the beginnings of a long-range cargo fleet.

The state would not need to resort to expropriation to take a guiding part in such economic developments. By reforming its tax collection system, which now consists of paying off the revenue collector instead of paying the state, it could increase its budget many times and turn its attention to the sorely needed extension of our road network.

And with rising living standards and growing confidence in government will come rapid progress toward political stability under a representative, truly democratic government. That, ultimately, is what we are fighting for.

As long as we are forced to fight, however, our constructive projects must wait. Our immediate task is something entirely different: it is the burning of Cuba's entire sugar crop. It was a terrible decision, and now that we are about to carry it out, it is a terrible job. Sugar is Cuba's principal source of revenue; it contributes about one-third of the total national income and employs two-fifths of the labor force. Half of our farm income is dependent on sugar. Yet it is the very importance of the cane crop that compels us to destroy it.

If the cane goes up in flames, the army will grind to a standstill; the police will have to disband, for none of them will get paid; and the Batista regime will have to capitulate. What is more, we will gain this decisive victory with comparatively little bloodshed by expending this year's crop.

I know well the heavy personal losses involved. My family has sizable holdings here in **Oriente**, and my instructions to our clandestine action groups state clearly that our crop must be the first one to burn, as an example to the rest of the nation. Only one thing can save the cane, and that is Batista's surrender.

But even if the crop will have to burn down to the last single cane, the flames will set fire to the dictatorship which weighs heavily on us now. Once the tyranny has gone up in smoke, we will see the way to a decent, democratic future.

Study Questions

1. According to Fidel Castro, how have Cuba's citizens suffered under Batista's regime?
2. What is Castro's understanding of liberty?
3. What goals does the author establish for any provisional government that succeeds the dictatorship of Batista?
4. How does Castro combine political, social, and economic reforms in his revolutionary ideology?

405

Reading 69

Martin Luther King, Jr.'s "I Have a Dream"

Throughout his life as a civil rights activist, Dr. Martin Luther King, Jr. (1929–1968) brought to a large audience of blacks and whites alike the challenging idea that it was both desirable and proper to break morally unjust laws by nonviolent means. Many leaders of the Southern Christian Leadership Conference, which King helped to organize in 1957, fell under the influence of Mohandas K. Gandhi's philosophy of nonviolent civil disobedience. Inspired by King and other civil rights workers, President John F. Kennedy (1917–1963) presented a new civil rights bill to Congress in February 1963, but it failed to pass due to a lack of broad public support. On 28 August 1963, however, Kennedy's rejected bill received a stirring mandate when a quarter of a million people marched to the Lincoln Memorial in Washington, D.C., and heard Dr. King deliver his now-famous "I Have a Dream" speech. In the wake of the Kennedy assassination and growing civil rights agitation, the civil rights act was spearheaded through Congress by President Lyndon B. Johnson (1908–1973).

I am happy to join with you today in what will go down in history as the greatest demonstration for freedom in the history of our nation.

Five score years ago, a great American, in whose symbolic shadow we stand today, signed the **Emancipation Proclamation**. This momentous decree came as a great beacon of hope to millions of slaves, who had been seared in the flames of withering injustice. It came as a joyous daybreak to end the long night of their captivity.

But one hundred years later the colored American is still not free. One hundred years later the life of the colored American is still sadly crippled by the manacle of segregation and the chains of discrimination.

One hundred years later the colored American lives on a lonely island of poverty in the midst of a vast ocean of material prosperity. One hundred years later, the colored American is still languishing in the corners of American society and finds himself an exile in his own land. So we have come here today to dramatize a shameful condition.

In a sense we have come to our Nation's Capital to cash a check. When the architects of our great republic wrote the magnificent words of the Constitution and the Declaration of Independence, they were signing a promissory note to which every American was to fall heir.

This note was a promise that all men, yes, black men as well as white men, would be guaranteed the inalienable rights of life, liberty, and the pursuit of happiness.

It is obvious today that America has defaulted on this promissory note insofar as her citizens of color are concerned. Instead of honoring this sacred obligation, America has given its colored people a bad check, a check that has come back marked "insufficient funds."

But we refuse to believe that the bank of justice is bankrupt. We refuse to believe that there are insufficient funds in the great vaults of opportunity of this nation. So we have come to cash this check, a check that will give us upon demand the riches of freedom and security of justice.

We have also come to this hallowed spot to remind America of the fierce urgency of Now. This is no time to engage in the luxury of cooling off or to take the tranquilizing drug of gradualism.

Now is the time to make the promise of democracy.

Now is the time to rise from the dark and desolate valley of segregation to the sunlit path of racial justice.

Now is the time to lift our nation from the quicksand of racial injustice to the solid rock of brotherhood.

Now is the time to make justice a reality to all of God's children.

It would be fatal for the nation to overlook the urgency of the moment and to underestimate the determination of its colored citizens. This sweltering summer of the colored people's legitimate discontent will not pass until there is an invigorating autumn of freedom and equality. Nineteen sixty-three is not an end but a beginning. Those who hope that the colored Americans needed to blow off steam and will now be content, will have a rude awakening if the nation returns to business as usual.

There will be neither rest nor tranquillity in America until the colored citizen is granted his citizenship rights. The whirlwinds of revolt will continue to shake the foundations of our nation until the bright day of justice emerges.

But there is something that I must say to my people who stand on the threshold which leads into the palace of justice. In the process of gaining our rightful place we must not be guilty of wrongful deeds.

Let us not seek to satisfy our thirst for freedom by drinking from the cup of bitterness and hatred.

We must forever conduct our struggle on the high plane of dignity and discipline. We must not allow our creative protest to degenerate into physical violence.

Again and again we must rise to the majestic heights of meeting physical force with soul force. The marvelous new militancy which has engulfed the colored community must not lead us to a distrust of all white people, for many of our white brothers, evidenced by their presence here today, have come to realize that their destiny is tied up with our destiny and their freedom is inextricably bound to our freedom.

We cannot walk alone.

As we walk, we must make the pledge that we shall always march ahead. We cannot turn back. There are those who are asking the devotees of civil rights, "When will you be satisfied?"

We can never be satisfied as long as the colored person is the victim of the unspeakable horrors of police brutality.

We can never be satisfied as long as our bodies, heavy with the fatigue of travel, cannot gain lodging in the motels of the highways and the hotels of the cities.

We cannot be satisfied as long as the colored person's basic mobility is from a smaller ghetto to a larger one.

We can never be satisfied as long as our children are stripped of their selfhood and robbed of their dignity by signs stating "for white only."

We cannot be satisfied as long as a colored person in Mississippi cannot vote and a colored person in New York believes he has nothing for which to vote.

No, no we are not satisfied and we will not be satisfied until justice rolls down like waters and righteousness like a mighty stream.

I am not unmindful that some of you have come here out of your trials and tribulations. Some of you have come straight from narrow jail cells. Some of you have come from areas where your quest for freedom left you battered by storms of persecutions and staggered by the winds of police brutality.

You have been the veterans of creative suffering. Continue to work with the faith that unearned suffering is redemptive.

Go back to Mississippi, go back to Alabama, go back to South Carolina, go back to Georgia, go back to Louisiana, go back to the slums and ghettos of our modern cities, knowing that somehow this situation can and will be changed.

Let us not wallow in the valley of despair. I say to you, my friends, we face the difficulties of today and tomorrow.

I still have a dream. It is a dream deeply rooted in the American dream. I have a dream that one day this nation will rise up and live out the true meaning of its creed. We hold these truths to be self-evident that all men are created equal.

I have a dream that one day out in the red hills of Georgia the sons of former slaves and the sons of former slave owners will be able to sit down together at the table of brotherhood.

I have a dream that one day even the state of Mississippi, a state sweltering with the heat of oppression, will be transformed into an oasis of freedom and justice.

I have a dream that my four little children will one day live in a nation where they will not be judged by the color of their skin but by their character.

I have a dream today.

I have a dream that one day down in Alabama, with its vicious racists, with its governor having his lips dripping with the words of interposition and nullification; that one day right down in Alabama little black boys and black girls will be able to join hands with little white boys and white girls as sisters and brothers.

I have a dream today.

I have a dream that one day every valley shall be engulfed, every hill shall be exalted, and every mountain shall be made low, the rough places will be made plain, and the crooked places will be made straight, and the glory of the Lord shall be revealed and all flesh shall see it together.

This is our hope. This is the faith that I will go back to the South with. With this faith we will be able to hew out of the mountain of despair a stone of hope.

With this faith we will be able to transform the jangling discords of our nation into a beautiful symphony of brotherhood.

With this faith we will be able to work together, to pray together, to struggle together, to go to jail together, to climb up for freedom together, knowing that we will be free one day.

This will be the day when all of God's children will be able to sing with new meaning "My country 'tis of thee, sweet land of liberty, of thee I sing. Land where my fathers died, land of the Pilgrim's pride, from every mountainside, let freedom ring!"

And if America is to be a great nation, this must become true. So, let freedom ring from the hilltops of New Hampshire.

Let freedom ring from the mighty mountains of New York.

Let freedom ring from the heightening Alleghenies of Pennsylvania.

Let freedom ring from the snow-capped Rockies of Colorado.

Let freedom ring from the curvaceous slopes of California.

But not only that, let freedom ring from the Stone Mountain of Georgia.

Let freedom ring from every hill and molehill of Mississippi and every mountainside.

When we let freedom ring, when we let it ring from every tenement and every hamlet, from every state and every city, we will be able to speed up that day when all of God's children, black men and white men, Jews and Gentiles, Protestants and Catholics, will be able to join hands and sing in the words of the old spiritual, "Free at last, free at last! Thank God Almighty, we are free at last."

Study Questions

1. What in essence is Martin Luther King's "dream"?
2. How does the speech epitomize the movement of nonviolent civil disobedience begun by King and other American civil rights activists in the 1950s?
3. Why would militant African Americans of 1963 consider King's remarks to be too deferential and submissive?
4. What rhetorical images does King employ and how effective are they?

Quick Reference Guide to Standard World History Textbooks

This table serves to facilitate the use of the primary historical sources found in volume two of *The Search for Order* in conjunction with the narrative textbooks listed below. The reference numbers detailed below each textbook indicate the relevant chapter(s) and page number(s). Occasional reference is also made to the first of two volumes of authors' works. The following books are hereafter represented: William McNeill, *A History of the Human Community, Volume 2, 1500 to the Present*, 4th ed., Prentice Hall (1993); Peter Stearns et al., *World Civilizations: The Global Experience*, HarperCollins (1992); Anthony Esler, *Human Venture, A World History from Prehistory to the Present*, 2nd ed., Prentice Hall (1992); Stanley Chodorow et al., *The Mainstream of Civilization*, 5th ed., Harcourt Brace Jovanovich (1989); Albert M. Craig et al., *The Heritage of World Civilizations*,

Reading Number in Meyer	McNeill	Stearns et al.	Esler	Chodorow et al.	Craig et al.	Wallbank et al.
1	17:431-35	23:536-38	34:540-42	19:553	19:571-74	22:570-76
2	17:415	26:608-10	23:372-73	15:420-22	24:733-35	14:372-73
3	17:421-22	28:656	30:474	15:435	20:597-98	14:379
4	17:419-22	28:656-57	30:471-72	15:433-34	20:599	14:374-79
5	17:422	28:656-57	30:471-72	15:434-35	20:598-99	14:374-79
6	19:481	32:772	30:474	15:434-35	20:593-94, 597	22:586
7	17:422-26	28:661	30:475-76	15:437-38	20:606-15	22:588-90
8	19:484-87	33:791-93	30:475-76	15:437-38	20:619-20	22:588-90
9	19:484-87	33:792	30:475-76	15:436-38	20:620	22:588-90
10	I:14:338-9	22:499	22:354	16:453-54	I:17:504-6	12:309-10
11	16:404	22:499-501	22:354	17:475	I:18:515-16	12:329-31
12	16:385-88	22:501-02	22:357-58	17:476-82	I:18:517-22	13:342-48
13	16:392	22:502-07	22:358	17:489-92	I:18:527-29	13:360
14	16:404-05	22:514-15	22:355-56	18:523	25:761	12:331-32
15	16:401-04	22:508	29:459	21:594-95	25:752-54	20:524
16	16:400	22:508-09	29:460-61	21:592-93	18:547-48	20:523
17	18:455	22:511	29:456	19:536-39	21:629-30	17:466-67
18	18:460-61	22:509-11	29:461	21:601	25:756-57	20:534, 539
19	18:461-63	22:506-7	29:458-59	18:519-20	22:661	20:540
20	18:461-63	22:514-15	29:461	21:611	25:757	20:532
21	18:461-63	22:514-16	29:460	21:603-4	25:758	20:533-35
22	15:366-74	25:567-89	28:434-38	18:502-6	23:687-700	16:423-33
23	17:430-31	23:538-41	33:516	19:553-55	23:712	16:444
24	23:597-602	30:719	31:483-84	27:761-65	19:582-83	28:735-36
25	23:597-602	14:321-25	27:420-21	27:761-65	8:229-54	22:570-76
26	23:596-97	32:759-60	30:469	26:740-41	28:846-50	26:687-88
27	19:477-79	30:711	41:670	27:759-60	33:990	29:740-42
28	23:594	39:945-46	41:670	27:759-60	33:993	29:740-42
29	23:594	39:945-46	41:670	27:759-60	33:989-92	29:740-42
30	19:483-84	32:773-74	34:546	27:778	34:1018	29:748-49

Volume 2 (since 1500) 3rd ed., Macmillan (1994); T. Walter Wallbank et al., *Civilization: Past and Present*, 7th ed., HarperCollins (1992); J. L. Upshur et al., *World History: Since 1500, Age of Global Integration*, West Publishing (1991); Kevin Reilly, *The West and the World: A History of Civilization*, 2nd ed., HarperCollins (1989); F. Roy Willis, *World Civilizations, From the Sixteenth Century to the Contemporary Age, Volume 2*, 2nd ed., D. C. Heath (1986); L. Stavrianos, *The World Since 1500: A Global History*, 5th ed., Prentice Hall (1991); Robert W. Strayer et al., *The Making of the Modern World: Connected Histories, Divergent Paths, 1500 to the Present*, 1st ed., St. Martin's Press (1989); and Richard L. Greaves et al., *Civilizations of the World: The Human Adventure, Volume 2*, 2nd ed., HarperCollins (1993); and John McKay et al., *A History of World Societies*, 3rd ed., Houghton Mifflin (1992).

Upshur et al.	Reilly	Willis	Stavrianos	Strayer et al.	Greaves et al.	McKay et al.	Reading Number in Meyer
9:406	1:54-58	17:58-61	34:572-73	19:450-69	34:904-06	22:725-39	1
9:376-78	I:9	17:20-22	19:336-37	10:259	I:19:548-5	23:753-56	2
10:444	1:33-34	17:43	20:348-49	15:358	I:18:492-94	18:578	3
10:439	1:34-37	17:37	20:347	14:348-49	I:21:579-84	24:779-82	4
10:443-51	1:37	17:40-43	20:347	14:349	29:765-72	24:779-82	5
10:452-55	I:13-14	17:43	20:347-49	15:356-59	29:771-73	24:779-82	6
10:460-61	I:15-17	17:48-50	20:353	15:374	29:776-83	24:785-87	7
10:461-63	I:15-17	17:55-56	20:350-52	15:374	29:776-83	24:787-90	8
10:461-63	I:15-17	17:55-56	20:350	15:374-77	29:782-84	11:323	9
11:482-83	3:74-83	I:13:582	22:389-90	2:52	I:16:427-29	17:519-20	10
8:363	6:164	23:309	22:373	2:52	I:17:454-56	17:525	11
9:376-78	1:30-32	I:15:745-53	22:374-75	1:41-43	I:17:456-61	17:537-45	12
11:479-82	1:30-33	I:15:677-81	22:377-79	1:41-43	I:17:469-74	17:535-37	13
8:364	1:29-30	20:166-75	22:373	2:52	24:645	18:598-99	14
11:480-82	3:82	20:167-78	28:473	2:47	24:636-39	20:664-65	15
11:481	9:278	20:170	29:498-500	2:49	24:640-42	20:667-68	16
9:387-91	3:87	19:143-45	29:496-98	3:74-75	I:19:528-31	19:645-47	17
11:484	3:94-99	20:172	29:499	2:53	24:645, 684	20:671	18
11:484-85	1:25	19:134-36	22:379	3:79	I:19:531	17:593	19
11:482-85	9:274	20:170	29:498-500	2:54	26:688-89	20:671-77	20
11:483	9:275-76	20:171	29:498-500	2:54	26:687-93	20:672-76	21
9:409-15	I:3-5	I:16:687-712	16:301-12	9:210-16	I:18:483-500	18:563-75	22
9:414-16	3:85-88	21:198-203	25:427	7:162-64	25:660-63	25:798	23
13:584-85	7:207	25:397-401	35:576	18:447	34:904-06	30:972-79	24
9:404-05	I:20-22	I:9:423-40	21:356-61	18:429-40	34:904-10	15:461-81	25
12:548	II:137-38	17:13-15	29:510	8:188	32:860-61	29:492	26
13:589-92	8:225	25:376	32:551-52	11:269	28:754	30:981-83	27
13:594-97	8:225-27	25:362-81	32:553	11:275	34:917	30:981-83	28
13:594-97	8:225-27	25:362-81	32:553	11:273-77	34:912-18	30:981-93	29
13:599	8:229	25:406-17	33:557	15:360-62	29:772-76	30:966	30

Reading Number in Meyer	McNeill	Stearns et al.	Esler	Chodorow et al.	Craig et al.	Wallbank et al.
31	21:544-46	32:774	34:547	27:778	34:1020-22	29:749-50
32	23:588-91	32:774-75	34:546	27:778	34:1026	29:751
33	21:546-49	33:791-92	30:476	27:778-80	34:1037-39	29:752-58
34	23:591-94	33:795	35:565	27:780	34:1040-43	29:754-56
35	18:461	22:514-16	29:460	21:609-11	25:764-65	20:533
36	18:461	22:515	32:503	21:608-9	25:761-62	20:536-37
37	20:498-503	29:675-77	32:499	23:652-53	26:783	21:560
38	20:498-501	22:515	32:508	25:721-22	30:920	20:541, 534
39	22:556	29:689-90	32:504	25:712-16	27:832-33	25:649-50
40	22:568-71	29:688-90	32:506-7	25:700	31:951-52	26:680
41	22:568-70	29:692	32:512	25:703	31:936-37	26:675-77
42	22:562-65	29:688-90	32:512	25:705	31:943-44	26:682-83
43	20:496-98	29:674	33:516-19	22:642-43	23:713-17	21:553
44	20:509-12	31:737-39	33:527-28	27:775	27:816-17	22:602
45	21:549-50	29:690	32:507-08	25:721-22	29:877	20:540-41
46	21:549-51	29:668, 688	33:520-22	27:769-73	29:879-81	20:540-41
47	25:646-48	40:988	45:745-46	35:1033-36	39:1202	36:967
48	25:646-48	40:980	45:745-46	35:1033-36	39:1199	36:964
49	25:649-53	40:985-86	43:708-10	36:1051-53	39:1207	36:960-61
50	24:624-25	39:950-52	38:621-23	31:888	33:993-94	33:856-58
51	25:646	40:983	43:711	35:1026	33:993-95	36:955
52	25:646, 659	40:983-84	45:743-44	35:1026-28	39:1207-9	36:954-56
53	23:591	41:992-97	38:615-17	31:889	34:1028-33	33:850-51
54	24:624, 639	37:995-1006	45:742-43	35:1022-23	34:1031-36	36:943-47
55	25:641-43	37:901-02	42:681	31:982	34:1043-53	36:940-43
56	25:641-43	37:901-02	42:681	31:892	34:1043-53	36:940-43
57	24:614-17	36:869-73	38:608-10	28:794-95	30:927-29	32:819-24
58	24:621-23	36:869-73	36:637-39	25:713-16	36:1114-18	32:822
59	26:677-78	34:820-23	41:667-68	31:901	35:1094-95	37:990
60	22:570-71	35:860	41:664-65	31:900-04	31:948-50	31:811
61	24:623-26	35:842-43	39:628-35	32:915-16	36:1100-12	32:832-43
62	26:680-81	35:859-61	41:669	36:1069	38:1194	37:992
63	25:638-41	34:834	42:681-82	33:963, 969	37:1154	35:906-07
64	26:680-81	35:858	44:720	36:1069	38:1194	37:990-92
65	25:644	36:887-90	44:731-32	36:1062-64	38:1182-85	37:979-80
66	24:622-38	34:834, 842	37:598-600	31:894-96	37:1142, 1152-54	34:894-99
67	26:670	35:844	41:663	31:896-97	31:945-46, 94	31:809-11
68	25:646-49	38:927-29	45:747-48	34:984	39:1212-13	35:969
69	25:645-46	35:851	44:725	34:1003-6	38:1174-76	35:926

Upshur et al.	Reilly	Willis	Stavrianos	Strayer et al.	Greaves et al.	McKay et al.	Reading Number in Meyer
13:597-600	8:245	25:410-11	33:561	15:366-71	34:921-25	30:985	31
13: 597-600	II:141-42	25:416	33:561	16:383	34:921-25	30:987	32
13:601	II:142-43	25:420-25	33:564-66	15:374-77	29:782-86	30:983-85	33
13:601	II:142-43	25:421-22	33:566-67	15:375	34:925-27	30:983-85	34
11:485	6:167-68	20:175-76	29:499	2:53	26:688-90	20:676-77	35
11:485	8:228	23:306	29:498-99	3:80-81	26:689; 30:801	27:872	36
12:528	6:165-78	23:207-23	29:505-6	3:77	27:708-23	25:802-10	37
11:484	6:165-69	23:307	28:486-89	4:102-4	26:703-04	25:810-11	38
12:543	6:186	23:313-15	29:512-13	4:98-9	31:835-37	27:875-76	39
12:570-71	2:41-69	26:454-57	36:596	4:97-101	35:939	28:906	40
12:570-71	9:279-80	26:461	28:474	2:57-58	33:887-89	28:923	41
12:564-65	6:190-94	23:300-05	29:511	4:97-104	33:889-92	29:949	42
11:506-10	8:225	21:203-7	29:502	7:168-69	25:672-75	25:801	43
12:539-41	2:58	25:425-29	35:587-90	9:221	25:677-78	31:999-1000	44
12:553	7:205	23:310-11	29:514-15	4:102	33:883-87	28:916-19	45
12:564	7:203	23:292	35:587	7:172-73	32:864-65	31:1013-15	46
14:643	13:407	31:701-11	43:713	20:486	41:1114-22	37:1248-49	47
16:729-30	III:361-62	31:705-6	43:709	20:481	41:1115-20	37:1239-40	48
16:753	III:360	31:717-18	45:759	13:325-26	40:1101-04	37:1233	49
14:645-46	13:395-96	31:684-86	38:7632	11:277-83	36:986-89	33:1086-88	50
16:724-25	13:395-96	31:688-90	38:633-34	11:281-88	40:1078-85	33:1089	51
15:709	13:395-97	31:688-92	43:704-05	12:301-06	40:1089	28:1255-73	52
14:647-49	10:302-03	31:660-61	33:562-64	16:381-86	36:980-82	33:1090-92	53
14:647-49	10:308-12	31:662-70	38:636	16:390-403	39:1056-67	37:1213-16	54
15:692-93	13:397-98	31:680-83	41:667-70	5:512-18	39:1051-56	33:1095-97	55
15:710	13:397-98	31:674-78	41:669	16:393-94	38:1026	27:1219-20	56
14:652-53	10:304-07	28:536-53	37:615-19	8:191-98	36:969-75	32:1056-57	57
14:655	6:185-90	28:540-41	39:639-46	8:196	36:975-76	35:1144	58
13:625-26	II:322-23	29:574-79	37:623-24	5:113-14	35:958	34:1112-13	59
15:704	9:281	26:458-59	39:639-51	2:59	35:935-36	34:1111-12	60
14:660-61	11:340-43	29:586-90	37:646-48	5:115-19	37:996-1013	35:1145-55	61
15:712-13	9:280-83	32:732	45:746-50	5:111-15	35:957-59	34:1108-09	62
15:691	8:224	29:612	44:725-26	5:122-23	38:1044-45	36:1174	63
15:712-13	9:280-83	29:603	45:746-50	5:124-27	42:1147-48	34:1108-09	64
16:748	13:387-88	32:743-50	45:741-42	8:208	42:1163-69	36:1194-95	65
13:637-26	13:388-91	29:599-612	41:690	7:178	38:1031-44	35:1161	66
15:702-03	9:287	26:463-64	42:683	2:60	35:936-37	34:1110	67
16:742-44	III:362-63	31:723	44:731-32	9:228	41:1132-35	36:1206-07	68
16:747	2:41-58	32:736-37	45:739-40	7:181	42:1149-50	33:1090	69

Glossary

The first occurrence in a Reading of select terms, concepts, and names that may not be readily familiar to readers or that may not necessarily appear in standard world history textbooks have been identified by boldface typescript throughout the text. A brief explanation of each item is provided below to allow for better comprehension of the materials. All dates in the glossary and throughout the text are given in B.C.E. (Before the Common Era) and C.E. (the Common Era). Where there is no era designation, C.E. may be assumed. Abbreviations used pertaining to dates are: ca. (approximately), d. (died), r. (reigned), fl. (flourished).

Alexander VI: one of the most corrupt popes of the Catholic church on record, Roderigo Borgia reigned as Alexander VI from 1492–1503.

Alvarado, Pedro de: Spanish soldier who lived from 1485 to 1541; captain of Spanish explorer Hernando Cortés, who was sent to subdue the Indians of Guatemala in the 1520s; he visited Spain in 1527 and returned to America a knight of Santiago, with his government of Guatemala confirmed by royal decrees; he was kicked to death by a horse while on a military campaign.

Anacreon: classical Greek poet from Teos who flourished from 535 to 490 B.C.E.; his verse is often provocative and symbolic.

Analects: collection of the sayings of Confucius compiled by his disciples shortly after his death in 479 B.C.E.; central proposition in the work consists of *chun tzu*, an ideal man, or "gentleman," whose character embodies the virtue of benevolence.

Anaximander: Greek Pre-Socratic philosopher from Miletus who lived from 610–547 B.C.E.; first Greek to write his views on nature in prose; used the concept of *Aperion*, "quasi-physical stuff," rather than an item of human experience as his principle of explanation.

Anthony, Susan B.: cofounder with Elizabeth Cady Stanton of the women's rights movement in the United States, who lived from 1820 to 1906.

Aristotle: famous Greek philosopher who lived from 384 to 322 B.C.E.; pupil of Plato, and teacher of Alexander the Great (356–323 B.C.E.).

Arnold, Matthew: British poet and critic who lived from 1822–1888.

Arrow War: war fought from 1856 to 1860 between the combined French and British forces and the Chinese; conflict began with the seizure by a Chinese official of the Arrow, a Chinese-owned vessel with British registry that was engaged in the opium trade; incident used as a pretext by the British and French for renewing hostilities against the Chinese.

Asiatic Act of 1907: South African racial dictate prescribing, among other things, that non-whites must carry identification cards.

Babur: founder of the Mughal dynasty in India who lived from 1483 to 1530; traced his lineage and hence his right of conquest to Genghis Khan and Tamerlane; ruled in north India from 1526 to 1530.

Batista, Fulgencio: Cuban president (1940–1944) and dictator (1952–1959) who lived from 1901 to 1973.

Bebel, August: Russian author who lived from 1840 to 1913; his *Women under Socialism* was published in 1883.

Bhagavad Gita: lit., "Song of the Lord"; Hindu religious classic compiled between the fifth

415

century B.C.E. and the fourth century C.E.; story focuses on a conversation between the god Krishna and the nobleman Arjuna in which they discuss fulfilling one's duty, or *dharma*, and reconciling it with human actions.

bhajana-loka: Buddhist term for the physical environment or innate world.

Bismarck, Otto von: Prussian statesman and influential European diplomat who lived from 1815 to 1898; engineered the unification of Germany in the mid-nineteenth century.

Blackstone, Sir William: English judge and author of influential legal commentaries on English common law who lived from 1723 to 1780.

bolsheviks, bolshevism: lit., "the majority" party of V. I. Lenin; one of two main segments of the Russian Social-Democratic Party; victorious in the Russian Revolution and civil wars of the early twentieth century.

Book of Changes: the mystical *I Ching*, one of the Confucian classics.

Book of Rites: the *Li Chi*, one of the Confucian classics.

Borgia, Cesare: influential Italian cardinal of the Catholic church and military leader who lived from about 1476 to 1507; son of Pope Alexander VI.

bourgeoisie: the expansive middle class in Western society made up of merchants, industrialists, bankers, and other professionals; in Marxist terms, the class of modern capitalists, owners of the means of social production and employers of wage-labor.

Boxer Rebellion: anti-foreign rebellion of 1898 to 1900 initiated by a secret society known as *I Ho Ch'uan*, "Righteous and Harmonious Fists," and supported by the party of the empress dowager of China and her followers.

Brahma: Hindu male creator god.

brahmin: a member of the priestly caste, the highest group in the order of traditional Hindu society.

Buddha: lit., "awakened one"; title applied to Siddhartha Gautama (563–479 B.C.E.), founder of Buddhism, after his enlightenment, and to others who achieved perfect illumination.

Burke, Edmund: famous British political conservative and author of *Reflections on the Revolution in France* (1790) who lived from 1729 to 1797.

Butler, Samuel: English poet and essayist who lived from 1612 to 1680; author of *Hudibras* and "A Hypocritical Non-Conformist."

cadres: full-time functionaries of the Communist Party or the government; anyone exercising leadership in an ordinary political or working situation.

Caesar, Gaius Julius: the Roman military commander, writer, and dictator who lived from 100 to 44 B.C.E.

Cathay: western European name given to northern China in the Middle Ages.

Catherine: saint and martyr of the Catholic church who was beheaded in the early Christian centuries.

Catiline: infamous conspirator who lived from about 108 to 62 B.C.E.; sought the overthrow of the Roman Republic, but the plot was exposed by the great orator Cicero (106–43 B.C.E.).

Chang Tsai: Chang Heng-ch'u who lived from 1020 to 1077; Neo-Confucian scholar whose outlook confirmed the ideological tendencies among generations of later scholars.

Charter of Paris: agreement reached in 1990 by the 35 participating nations of the Conference on Security and Cooperation in Europe (CSCE) declaring the commitment to develop further the peace and security of Europe and to cooperate on a wide range of economic issues and human rights.

Ch'eng Hao: also, Master Chieng; Neo-Confucian scholar who lived from 1032–1085; his philosophical idealism established a new trend in Sung China.

Ch'eng I (Ch'uan): brother of Ch'eng Hao; lived from 1033–1107; established the rationalistic wing of Neo-Confucianism.

Chiang Kai-shek: Chinese nationalist leader who lived from 1887 to 1975; he and his party, the Kuomintang, were defeated by the Chinese Communists in 1949; president of the Republic of China (Taiwan) from 1949 until his death.

Chieh: notorious ruler of the half-legendary Hsia dynasty who eventually lost his kingdom to T'ang of Shang in 1523 B.C.E.

Chios: Greek island in the eastern Mediterranean Sea.

Chou: reference to Wu, king of Chou, who succeeded to the imperial throne and established the Chou dynasty (1027–221 B.C.E.).

Christina, Grand Duchess: descendant of French kings; a powerful woman in late Renaissance Florence, she died in 1636; mother of the Grand Duke Cosimo II d'Medici (r. 1609–1621); niece of Catherine d'Medici, queen of France.

Chuang Tzu: Chinese mystical philosopher who lived from 399?–295 B.C.E.; his brand of Taoism moved beyond the original teachings of Lao Tzu and others.

Chu Hsi: brilliant and highly influential Neo-Confucian scholar who lived from 1130–1200; attempted to synthesize other contemporary Chinese religious outlooks within a Confucian context and to adopt what was profound in them; followed Mencius's belief in the original goodness of human nature.

Confucius: most influential of the ancient Chinese philosophers who lived from 551 to 479 B.C.E.; founder of the Confucian school; traditionally considered the editor of the Confucian Classics and the author of works such as the *Analects*; taught his disciples the importance of propriety and humaneness in the individual as well as in the state.

Connolly, James: Irish labor leader and military commander of the Irish forces during the rebellion of 1916 who lived from 1868 to 1916; founded the Irish Socialist Republican Party in 1896; executed by the British after the Easter Rebellion.

Constituent Assembly: another name for the French National Assembly (1789–1791); called such because it was preparing a written constitution.

Continental Congress: the First Continental Congress convened on 5 September 1774 and included 55 elected delegates from 12 American colonies; the Second Continental Congress gathered in May 1775, and after more than a year the delegates voted for independence.

Convention: name of the French government from 1793–1795 under the control of Robespierre and the Committee of Public Safety.

Crimean War: conflict fought between 1854 and 1856 that began when Russia and Ottoman Turkey went to war in 1853; came to involve many European nations, including Prussia and Great Britain.

Cromwell, Oliver: English statesman, parliamentarian, and prominent Puritan who lived from 1599 to 1658; Parliamentary general in the mid-seventeenth century English civil war; became Lord Protector of England in 1653 after the beheading of King Charles I, and ruled until his death.

David: king of Israel and Judah from ca. 1000 to 961 B.C.E.

Din-i-Ilahi: lit., "Divine Faith"; a syncretic monotheistic religion founded in 1581 by Emperor Akbar influenced especially by Sufi mysticism, which also incorporated Zoroastrian rituals; the new faith had little mass appeal and rapidly disintegrated after the king's death in 1605.

d'Medici: famous family of Renaissance Florence, Italy.

Doctrines, The: reference to the teachings in the ascribed works of Confucius, which according to tradition included the *Analects*, "The Great Learning," "The Doctrine of the Mean," and *The Spring and Autumn Annals*.

Dominican: religious order of Friars Preachers, called the Dominicans, founded in the early thirteenth century by Saint Dominic (1170–1234).

Don Philip: son of King Charles V who lived from 1527–1598 and who ruled Spain from 1556 until his death.

Dostoevsky, Feodor: Russian novelist, philosopher, and mystic who lived from 1821 to 1881.

Dowager Empress: the title of the arch-conservative T'zu-hsi who died in 1908; representative of the old order in China, she perhaps poisoned her son Emperor T'ung-chih in 1874 and installed her nephew on the throne; responsible for suppressing the Hundred Days' Reform and supported the Boxer Rebellion of 1898–1900.

Edo: capital of the Tokugawa shoguns from 1603 to 1867; modern Tokyo.

Emancipation Proclamation: President Lincoln's preliminary proclamation to abolish the institution of slavery was issued on 22 September 1862, and was followed by a final call for freedom for Blacks on 1 January 1863; serves as the basis for the Thirteenth Amendment to the U.S. Constitution, adopted in 1865.

Eros: lit., "love" or "desire"; Freud construes the term as the will to live, relating it to the libido.

Espanola: island discovered by Columbus in 1492; modern Haiti and the Dominican Republic.

Esprit des Lois, L': significant masterwork of the French philosopher Baron de Montesquieu (1689–1755) first published in Geneva in 1748; treats the rational basis for the existence of laws in society.

417

feudalism: sociopolitical system that operated in early medieval Europe and medieval Japan that embodies the element of reciprocal rights and obligations between lord and vassal.

Feuerbach, Ludwig: influential German philosopher, theologian, and moralist who lived from 1804 to 1872; a student of Hegel, he became one of the founders of modern materialism; his works inspired Marx and Engels, Sartre, and other modern philosophers.

Five Year Economic Plans: a series of continuous economic plans initiated by Nehru's government in April 1951, the first of which called for a modest 11 percent growth in national income by 1956 and an overall increase in the value of annual production of goods and services.

for-itself: "Being-for-itself," construed as consciousness conceived as a lack of Being, which is understood by Sartre as all-embracing and objective rather than individual and subjective and distinct from Existence; Being includes both "for-itself" and "in-itself."

Four Virtues: humanity, righteousness, propriety, and wisdom.

Francis of Assisi: saint of the Catholic church born around 1181 and died in 1226; founder of the order of Friars Minor, or Franciscans, and noted for his humility and charity.

Gambetta, Leon: French statesman and politician who lived from 1832 to 1882.

Gandhi, Indira: daughter of Nehru, the widow of Feroze Gandhi (d. 1960), who was no relation to the Mahatma, lived from 1917 to 1984; served three terms as prime minister of India from 1966 to her assassination in 1984 by her own Sikh bodyguards.

Gandhi, Rajiv: son of Indira Gandhi who lived from 1944 to 1991; named his mother's successor as prime minister in 1984; he was assassinated in 1991.

garaad: Afro-Muslim word meaning "chief."

General Relativity: Einstein's theory of the universe set forth in his Special Theory of Relativity (1905) and General Theory of Relativity (1915); postulates that time and space are not absolutes but are affected by mass and velocity and are relative to the person perceiving them.

Genghis Khan: great Mongol leader and conqueror who lived from about 1167 to 1227.

Gladstone, William: leader of the British Liberal Party who lived from 1809 to 1898; served as prime minister of Great Britain four terms, the last in 1892.

glasnost: Russian word meaning "openness."

Gokhale, Gopal Krishna: Indian public servant who lived from 1866 to 1915; took particular interest in reforming the Indian state under British rule and in the problems of Indian emigrants to South Africa.

Gromyko, Andrei: Russian diplomat who lived from 1909 to 1989.

Guizot, François: French statesman and historian who lived from 1787 to 1874; supporter of constitutional monarchy who served as premier of France in 1847–1848; forced into retirement because of his failure to control the Revolution of 1848.

hajj: Arabic term meaning pilgrimage to Mecca, the fifth of the "Five Pillars" of Islam.

Hayes, Rutherford B.: one-term Republican president of the United States who lived from 1822 to 1893; contested result of 1876 election, which was settled by a special election commission in favor of Hayes; succeeded to office in 1877.

Hegel, Georg: highly influential German idealist philosopher who lived from 1770 to 1831.

Helsinki Final Act: although not a formal treaty, an agreement reached in 1975 by 35 Western nations that ratified the de facto European territorial boundaries set up after World War II and established "Helsinki watch committees" for the surveillance of human rights.

Herodotus: Greek historian who lived from about 484 to after 430 B.C.E.; known as the "father of history" and author of a history of the Persian-Greek wars.

Homer: the name attached to the author of the Greek classics *Iliad* and *Odyssey*, the first great works in Greek literature that assumed their final form in the mid-eighth century B.C.E.

Hsiang Yu: a military leader and contender for the throne after the fall of the Ch'in dynasty in the late third century B.C.E.

Hsiao Ching: reference to "The Book of Filial Piety" which deals with an important concept of Confucianism.

Huang Ch'ao: a rebel leader who revolted against the T'ang dynasty in 875.

Hundred Days' Reform: abortive political movement of 1898; spurred on by China's defeat in the Sino-Japanese war in 1895; reformers sought to improve economic conditions and to establish representative government in China.

I and Ch'i: Po-I and Su-Ch'i were princes of the Shang dynasty (1523–1027 B.C.E.), one of whom was to ascend the imperial throne, but refused and deferred to his brother; the succession problem led to the establishment of the Chou dynasty (1027–221 B.C.E.).

Ikko Sect: Japanese sect of the Amida Buddha established in the thirteenth century; known also as the "True Pure Land" sect; see Shinran.

in-itself: "Being-in-itself," or nonconscious Being that extends beyond what knowledge of it people may possess.

Indian National Congress: representative institution organized in 1885 that became the organizational vehicle for India's first great nationalist movement; during and after World War II worked toward the independence of India.

innatism: theory of knowledge that postulates all morally right judgments or all science consists of a governing reality or objects that transcend sensory experience.

Izanagi: primal Japanese male deity who according to the *Nihongi* was one of two gods who helped create the first generation of gods and the world.

Izanami: primal Japanese female deity who according to the *Nihongi* was one of two gods who helped create the first generation of gods and the world.

Jacobin: the Society of Friends of the Constitution, called the Jacobin Club for short; bourgeois political group influential in events of the French Revolution from 1789 to 1795; the Directory, the legitimate French government, closed the Club and executed its foremost member, Robespierre, in 1795.

jati: basic social unit among the Hindu caste system; also the clergy or ascetics among the Jains.

Jinnah, Mohammed Ali: prominent Muslim statesman and politician in India who lived from 1876 to 1948; president of the All India Muslim League and the first governor general of Pakistan.

John Paul II: first Polish pope to head the Catholic church; he began his pontificate in 1978.

Johnson, Samuel: English writer and literary critic known as Dr. Johnson who lived from 1709 to 1784; founded his Literary Club in the 1760s.

Julius II: pope of the Catholic church from 1503 to 1513; patron of the arts and artists, including Michelangelo who designed the pope's tomb.

Ka'ba: lit., "cube"; a gray-black stone structure in Mecca construed by Muslims as the Holy of Holies and, hence, the focus of prayer orientation and Hajj pilgrimage.

Keats, John: English Romantic poet and essayist who lived from 1795 to 1821; his poetry is remarkable for its vivid imagery and sensuality; one of his best known poems is "Ode On a Grecian Urn."

Khayyam, Omar: Persian Sufi poet born about 1015 and who died about 1125; author of the *Rubaiyat*.

khedive: title of the Turkish viceroys of Egypt meaning "great ruler."

Kierkegaard, Søren Aabye: Danish philosopher and religious thinker who lived from 1813 to 1855; considered the first important existentialist philosopher.

Kojiki: ancient Japanese chronicle, *Records of Ancient Matters*, compiled in the early eighth century under Chinese influence; substantiates the divine origins of the Japanese rulers and their empire.

Krishna: Hindu god; the eighth avatar, or incarnation, of Vishnu; the ideal warrior-king; one of the most popular deities among contemporary Hindus.

Kuan Chung: adviser to Duke Huan of Ch'i during China's Spring and Autumn period (722–481 B.C.E.); responsible for the kingdom of Ch'i becoming a powerful state and the duke first among Chinese princes.

Kuan Ning: Kuan Ning and Hua Hsin of the Three Kingdoms period (222–280) were reading together, sitting on one mat. Hua neglected his reading so Kuan cut the mat on which they sat and continued to study on his separate seat.

Kublai Khan: Mongol emperor of China who lived from 1215 to 1294; established the Yüan dynasty (1279–1368) through continued conquests and bureaucratization.

419

Kuomintang: official ruling party of the modern Republic of China (Taiwan); founded by Sun Yat-sen in 1905 and eventually headed by Chiang Kai-shek, who was forced into exile by Chinese Communists in the late 1940s.

kustars: Russian peasants engaged in a cottage industry.

la ilaha illa 'Llah: Koranic slogan meaning "the decision is God's alone" (Sura 6:57).

Lafayette: French general and statesman who fought in the American Revolution who lived from 1757 to 1834.

laissez-faire: attitude of noninterference reflected in economic policies that allow owners and manufacturers to set conditions of labor and competition with little or no governmental hindrance.

Lamarck, Jean Baptiste Pierre Antonine: French naturalist and man of letters who lived from 1744 to 1829.

Las Casas, Bartholomew: bishop of Chiapas, Central America who defended the natives of Mesoamerica in the debate of Valladolid, Spain, from 1550 to 1555.

Leibnitz, Gottfried Wilhelm: German rationalist philosopher and mathematician who lived from 1646 to 1716; in his *Systematic Theology*, written in 1686 and published in 1819, he attempted a reconciliation of Protestant and Catholic faiths

Leo X: Giovanni d'Medici, who reigned as pope of the Catholic church from 1513 to 1521, during which time Martin Luther and others had begun the Protestant Reformation in western Europe.

Levellers: seventeenth-century English dissident group comprised of lower class farmer-tenants who strove to establish a more democratic government in England and to initiate social reforms.

Li Ch'uang: Li Tzu-ch'eng, rebel leader who took the capital of Peking and forced the last Ming emperor to commit suicide; Li was then defeated by the Manchus.

Liao Ngo Ode: reference to the *Hsiao Ching*, the *Book of Filial Piety*, an important Confucian text.

Lycurgus: legendary Spartan lawgiver, flourished in the late ninth century B.C.E.

Lyell, Sir Charles: Scottish geologist who lived from 1797 to 1875; his *Principles of Geology* published between 1830 and 1833 earned him the name of "the father of modern geology."

Macaulay, Catherine: prolific British writer and historian known as "the female Thucydides" who lived from 1731 to 1791.

MacBride, John: Irish revolutionary who lived from 1865 to 1916; the estranged husband of Maud Gonne, a woman who held Yeats's affections for years; after the Easter Rebellion, he was tried by court martial and shot.

MacDonagh, Thomas: Irish writer who lived from 1878 to 1916; close associate of Patrick Pearse, and deeply committed to Ireland's cultural heritage; executed by the British after the Easter Uprising of 1916.

Mahomet II (Mehmed): learned poet and able administrator of the Ottoman Empire who reigned as sultan from 1444 to 1446, 1451 to 1481; his efforts resulted in the collapse of Constantinople in 1453.

Matsudaira Sadanobu: influential Japanese statesman who lived from 1758 to 1829; shogunal premier for Tenari Tokugawa (1773–1841), one of the last Tokugawa rulers of Japan; ably administered the government until his retirement in 1801.

Mean: Confucian notion of "the Golden Mean," maintaining the middle way, doing nothing in excess; similar in nature to the Buddhist "Middle Way" and the Christian "Golden Rule."

Meiji: name adopted by the boy-emperor Mutsuhito (1852–1912) who reigned from 1867 to 1912 when the Tokugawa Shogunate fell in 1868; Meiji Era of Reform lasted for about a generation, during which time Japan was partially westernized.

Mencius: Meng tzu (372?–289 B.C.E.), scholar who wrote the *Book of Mencius*; champion of the orthodox school of Confucianism; held firm to the belief in the original goodness of human nature.

Metternich, Prince Clemond von: conservative politician of Austria and influential European diplomat who played a major role in the Congress of Vienna of 1814–15; he lived from 1773 to 1859.

Mitterrand, François: born in 1916, he was elected president of France in 1981; a moderate socialist, he headed the revitalized French Socialist Party in the 1980s.

Morley, John Viscount: English statesman and author who lived from 1838 to 1923.

Mythra: old Persian god of light and regeneration; popular among Roman soldiers in Late Antiquity, Mythraism was a significant mystery cult that once rivaled Christianity.

National Assembly: government that came into existence on 17 June 1789 by revolutionary declaration of the Third Estate of France.

Naoroji, Dadabhai: first Indian member of the British House of Commons who lived from 1825 to 1917; known as "the grand old man of Congress," he was leader of the moderate faction of the Indian National Congress.

Nazarene: Christian.

Neoclassical: Western literary and artistic movement with roots in the mid-seventeenth century that revived classical forms and styles.

Neo-Confucianism: Chinese philosophical movement especially prominent during the Sung (960–1279) and Ming (1368–1644) periods; major topics of debate are the nature and principle of humanity and things.

Newton, Sir Isaac: influential astronomer, physicist, and philosopher who lived from 1642 to 1727; publication of his *Mathematical Principles of Natural Philosophy* in 1687 brought his own and other scientists' discoveries to fruition and thereby created a view of the universe that stood for nearly two hundred years.

Newtonianism: see Newton, Sir Isaac.

Nietzsche, Friedrich (Nietzschean): influential German philosopher who lived from 1844 to 1900; maintained a low opinion of human beings, and from a background of evolutionary thinking he developed the concept of a superman, a noble being who should lead and dominate the masses.

Nihongi: ancient Japanese chronicle, *Chronicles of Japan*, compiled in the early eighth century under Chinese influence; traces the origins of Japan to the mythic age of the gods.

Numa Pompilius: one of the early seventh-century B.C.E. priest-kings of Rome who is said to have organized the religious life of the community by establishing regular cults and the priesthood.

Oglethorpe, James Edward: English general and founder of the colony of Georgia in North America who lived from 1696 to 1785.

Omura Domain: the area around Nagasaki, Japan.

Opium War: the first Anglo-Chinese war broke out in 1839 as the Chinese attempted to enforce prohibitions against opium trafficking by the British; the Chinese capitulated in 1842 and accepted the Treaty of Nanking.

Oriente: eastern district of Cuba from which Fidel Castro came.

padshah: Turkish word meaning "emperor."

Pai Ch'i: famous general of Ch'in during the Warring States period, who occupied more than seventy cities for King Chao-hsiang Wang of Ch'in.

P'an-Ku: cosmic man in ancient Chinese cosmogony; myth relates that he appeared when the world was still in chaos, and over the next 18 thousand years he grew 10 feet a day as yin and yang organized the universe; P'an-Ku enriched the scene by his own self-distribution.

Paris Commune: revolutionary municipal council lasting from March to May 1871; the result of fierce republican patriotism, the commune was set up to counter the National Assembly in Versailles, a government installed with Germany's approval after the Franco-Prussian War of 1871.

Paul: the Christian apostle from Tarsus; non-Palestinian Jew born about the same time as Jesus of Nazareth and died around 67 C.E.; called the "second founder of Christianity" and author of many letters in the New Testament canon.

Paul III: Alessandro Farnese, who lived from 1468 to 1549; pope of the Catholic church from 1534 to 1549 who encouraged the Catholic Reformation movement especially by convening the Council of Trent in 1545.

Pearse, Patrick: Irish poet and founder of St. Edna's School, Dublin, who lived from 1840 to 1916; elected president of the Provisional Government during the Easter Uprising; he was tried by a British court martial and shot in 1916.

perestroika: Russian word meaning "restructuring" with specific reference to the economy.

physiocrats: a group of eighteenth-century economic philosophers who concerned themselves with fiscal and tax reform and attempted to develop means by which to increase the national wealth of France.

Plato: lived from 428 to 348 B.C.E.; a pupil of Socrates, major Greek philosopher and author of many classic works, including the *Republic*.

pogrom: an organized attack or massacre of Jews.

positivism: philosophical attitude originating with the French thinker Auguste Comte (1789–1857) that came to mean an insistence on verifiable facts, the avoidance of fanciful thinking, and the rigorous questioning of all assumptions.

proletariat (proletarian): according to Marxist doctrine, the class of modern wage-laborers who, having no means of production of their own, are reduced to selling their labor in order to live.

Propertius: Roman poet of the Augustan Age known for his erotic elegies who lived from about 50 to 15 B.C.E.

Ptolemy: Greek astronomer from Alexandria whose best-known work is the *Geographia*, or *Geography*; he lived from 87 to 150 C.E.

Puranas: Hindu popular epics, stories, or poems about sectarian gods and sages; a part of the smriti, or non-Vedic canon that includes the *Mahabharata*.

Pushkin, Alexander: great Russian poet who lived from 1799 to 1837.

Pythagoras: sixth century B.C.E. philosopher who believed in the transmigration of souls and that "number" was the essence of being.

quibla: direction of Muslim prayer worship; originally Muhammad had selected Jerusalem as the quibla, but sometime during his exile in Medina (ca 622–630), the Prophet changed its orientation toward Mecca and the Ka'ba.

Ravallac: man who assassinated King Henry IV of France in 1610.

Reds and Whites: reference to the Bolshevik and Menshevik factions respectively in the Russian Social-Democratic Party; opponents in the Russian civil war in the 1920s.

Rig Veda: collection of over one thousand Sanskrit hymns, poems, and rituals held sacred by Hindus.

Robespierre, Maximilien: one of the Jacobin leaders of the French Revolution who lived from 1758 to 1794; headed the Committee of Public Safety during "The Terror" (1793–1794).

Romains, Jules: French novelist and playwright who lived from 1885 to 1972.

Rump Parliament: term applied to the English House of Commons which sat in 1649 after Colonel Pride excluded 143 members; the so-called Long Parliament of 1641 became extremely short of members—only 78 remained after the purge, of whom 20 refused to take their seats.

Sabi(an): west Eurasian people from Sheba.

Saint-Germain, Treaty of: one of five treaties—this one with Austria—signed by the Allies and Central Powers in 1919 at the end of World War I.

samurai: lit., "one who serves"; traditional warrior class in feudal Japan.

Sankaracharya: Shankara (fl. 750); influential Hindu philosopher and exponent of the doctrine of pure monism (*advaita*), a nondualistic perspective that postulates the Ultimate Reality as one and undifferentiated; hence, Brahman alone is real, the world is illusion and false.

Santangel, Raphael Sanchez de: treasurer to King Ferninand V of Castile (1452–1516) and Queen Isabella of Castile and Leon (1451–1504).

Second Coming: reference to the Christian tradition of the return of Jesus Christ at the Apocalypse, for which see the gospel of Matthew 24:31–46.

shah-rah: royal or imperial road.

shah-wuwar: royal horseman.

Shelley, Percy Bysshe: English Romantic poet who lived from 1792 to 1822; husband of Mary Wollstonecraft Shelley (1797–1851), who herself wrote the Gothic novel *Frankenstein*.

Shi'a, Shi'ite: the sect of Islam that rejects the legitimacy of the first three caliphs, or successors to the Prophet Muhammad; the Muslim political/religious party of 'Ali, son-in-law of Muhammad and hence legitimate caliph, with roots in the 650s.

Shinran: lived from 1173 to 1262; founder of the Japanese "True Pure Land" sect of the Amida Buddha. The Amida, the Buddha of Infinite Light, is one of five Buddhas of meditation whose origins may be traced to India around the second century C.E.; his cult passed from Nepal and Tibet and, thence, into China and Japan; worship of this personification of mercy, wisdom, love, and compassion ensures the devotee's salvation.

Shinto: lit., "Way of the higher spirits and gods"; Chinese name for the native religion of Japan although not a system of doctrines, but rather a reverence for extraordinary realities in the Japanese experience.

Shiva: major Hindu god; rigorous asceticism generates his power as destroyer/creator.

shogun: lit., "Barbarian Subduing Generalissimo"; head of the military government of Japan from 1192 to 1867.

Siura Carbak: a general name for the Indian religious sect of Jains.

Six Robbers: the six senses that avoid perception or give wrong perception.

Southern barbarians: derogatory term used by the Japanese referring to western Europeans.

Spiritus Mundi: Yeats's poetic description of "a general storehouse of images which have ceased to be a property of any personality or spirit."

Stanton, Elizabeth Cady: highly influential advocate of American women's rights who lived from 1815 to 1902.

START Treaty: Strategic Arms Reduction Talks; agreement reached between the United States and the Soviet Union in 1985 that would allow the removal of land-based intermediate-range missiles in Europe.

Stendhal: French novelist who lived from 1783 to 1842.

Sublime Porte: building in Istanbul in which the grand vizier and other officials of the Ottoman Empire resided; symbolic of the empire itself.

Sufi: lit., "woolen-clad ones"; devotees of Islam's mystical sects with origins in eighth-century Persia.

Sun Goddess: Amaterasu, the female Shinto deity who, according to ancient Japanese myths, produced the line of emperors along with Susanoo.

Sunni: the Muslim sect of the orthodox majority; one who believes that leadership of the Islamic community could be bestowed on any true, able believer, not just a descendant of Muhammad.

Susanoo: Japanese male storm god who was particularly unruly; according to Shinto tradition, he helped produce the line of emperors along with Amaterasu.

Tagore, Rabindranath: influential Indian poet and essayist who lived from 1861 to 1914.

Tamerlane: also Timur; known among Christians and Muslims alike as the "Scourge of God," this descendant of Genghis Khan ruled a vast empire in central and southwest Eurasia; planned an attack on China prior to his death in 1405.

T'ang: according to Confucian tradition, T'ang founded the Shang dynasty in the late sixteenth century B.C.E. and asserted that the Hsia emperor whom he replaced had lost the "mandate of Heaven."

Tantra(s): lit., "extension"; commentaries on Buddhist or Hindu sacred texts that are directed toward magic and the personification of concepts.

Tao: lit., "the Way"; ancient Chinese conception of the eternal way of the universe immanent in all things.

Tauhid: a non-Koranic word, initially appearing in the Hadith, decreeing the absolute transcendence of Allah; connotes the act of unification of the one God and the proclamation of his unicity, or the affirmation that the unique God is one in himself, and one in his nature as God.

Thales: according to ancient Greek tradition, the "first" philosopher who flourished around 600 B.C.E.

Themistocles: Athenian statesman and general who lived from about 528 to 462 B.C.E.; helped lead the Greeks against the Persian invasion of 480 B.C.E.

Thoreau, Henry David: American essayist and naturalist who lived from 1817 to 1862.

Twenty-sixth of July Movement: anti-Batista organization led by Fidel Castro and Frank País; name derived from Castro's attack on the Moncada army barracks in 1953.

Tzu-Kung: pupil of Confucius who lived from 520–450? B.C.E., noted for his eloquence; obtained a diplomatic post in the kingdom of Wei and served with great distinction.

ulama: lit., "the learned"; Islamic protectors of tradition and theology who can work for or against established governing authorities.

Ultatlan: the capital city and chief temple center of the Quiché kingdom of Guatemala.

Vedanta: lit., "the end of the Vedas"; sacred Hindu commentaries on Vedic hymns such as the Upanishads.

Vedas (-ic): ancient brahminic ritual poems and hymns that are a part of the *shruti*, "that which is heard."

Versailles, Treaty of: one of five treaties signed in Paris by the Allied Powers in June 1919 that effectively ended World War I; Versailles involved Germany and the Allies.

Vishnu: major Hindu deity proclaimed the "preserver"; among his ten official avatars are Rama and Krishna.

Wallace, Alfred: English naturalist and philosopher who lived from 1823 to 1913.

Wang Yang-ming: Neo-Confucian scholar who lived from 1473 to 1529; he taught that the reason or governing principle of things is not found in nature but rather within the mind or human consciousness.

Way: the path to personal and societal happiness and harmony; each of China's philosophies offers its own version of the "Way."

Wen: Wen Wang of the ancient Chinese Chou dynasty; he surrendered the territory of what is today Honan province.

White Lotus: secret Chinese dissident society and anti-imperial association founded in the Southern Sung period (1127–1279) that was strongly Buddhist in orientation and whose devotees refused to pay imperial taxes or contribute corvee labor; major uprising of the sect occurred in 1798, which seriously threatened the stability of the Manchu dynasty.

Wu: according to Confucian tradition, Wu founded the Chou dynasty in the late eleventh century B.C.E. and asserted that the Shang emperor whom he replaced had lost the "mandate of Heaven."

Xavier, Francis: Spanish saint of the Catholic church who lived from 1506 to 1552; Jesuit priest and great pioneer missionary to east Eurasia.

yang: ancient Chinese concept for active, warm, dry, masculine principle in nature; the complement of yin.

Yang Chen: a scholar-official of the Later Han dynasty (25–221 C.E.) noted for uprightness.

Yellow Turbans: Chinese dissident movement prompted by the agrarian crisis of the 180s C.E.; led by Taoist patriarch Chang Chiao of the Taiping, "great peace" sect; helped to precipitate the collapse of the Han dynasty in the early third century C.E.

Yen-tzu: noted disciple of Confucius who flourished around 500 B.C.E.; he was content with simple living.

yin: ancient Chinese concept for passive, cool, moist, feminine principle in nature; complement of yang.

Yu: legendary founder of the Hsia dynasty in the twenty-third century B.C.E.

Zemski Sobor: occasional gathering of the various estates of the Russian realm called by Muscovite czars to consider important matters; essentially abandoned by Peter the Great (1682–1725).

Zionism: secular and/or religious movement whose followers are dedicated to the establishment of a Jewish national homeland or to maintaining the modern state of Israel.

Zoroaster: founder of an ancient religious tradition native to Iran, with origins in the early to mid-first millennium B.C.E.; teachings elaborate an ethical code and postulate an essential dualistic world which serves as the battleground for the forces of light and darkness, good and evil.

Zoroastrian: follower of the religion founded by Zoroaster.